ENQUIRE WITHIN

UPON

EVERYTHING

"Whether you wish to model a flower in wax; to study the rules of etiquette; to serve a relish for breakfast or supper; to supply a delicious entrée for the dinner table; to plan a dinner for a large party or a small one; to cure a headache; to make a will; to get married; to bury a relative; whatever you may wish to do, make, or to enjoy, provided your desire has relation to the necessities of domestic life, I shall be happy to assist you, and therefore hope you will not fail to 'Enquire Within.'"—*Editor*.

ENQUIRERS ARE REFERRED TO THE INDEX

TWO HUNDRED AND SEVENTY-SEVENTH THOUSAND

LONDON
HOULSTON AND WRIGHT
65, PATERNOSTER ROW
MDCCCLXV.

WORKS OF THE SAME SERIES.

London: J. & W. Rider, Printers, 14, Bartholomew Close.

ADVERTISEMENT TO THE TWENTY-SEVENTH EDITION.

"Enquire Within" is deeply indebted for past favours, and anxious to obtain the cordial and warm recommendation of its friends in all parts of the world: Cheapness and varied usefulness are its characteristics, and in little more than seven years

TWO HUNDRED AND SEVENTY-SEVEN THOUSAND

Copies have been issued.

The New Edition has been brought out with the intention of its being still more worthy of success. No really useful part has been omitted. The Classification has been improved, in accordance with many friendly suggestions, and Additions have been made, both modern and interesting.

Banting and Diet, the favourite game of Croquêt, Decalcomanie and Diaphanie, &c., have been added. Enquirers on the laws of Landlord and Tenant, Husband and Wife, Debtor and Creditor, are supplied with latest information. Diseases and their Remedies, and Medicines, their Uses and Doses, have received special attention. In addition to a very carefully arranged Index, a new Summary of Contents has been supplied, and no labour or expense has been spared, with the hope that every Reader may receive complete and satisfactory replies from

ENQUIRE WITHIN UPON EVERYTHING.

Twenty-four Volumes are now published as cheap companions of this favourite Work, which are enumerated as under. The entire Series contains upwards of SEVEN THOUSAND pages of closely printed matter. They are entirely original in Plan, executed with the most conscientious care,—and embrace the very essence of demonstrative Truth and inductive Reasoning. The Indices have been prepared with great labour, and alone occupy above 500 pages. A vast Fund of valuable Information, embracing every Subject of Interest or Utility, is thus attainable, and at a merely nominal Cost.

These Works are in such general demand, that the Sale has already reached

ONE MILLION OF HALF-CROWN VOLUMES.

The attention of all parties interested in the dissemination of sound theoretical Instruction and practical Knowledge is particularly directed to this Series of Popular and Valuable Books.

1—3. "DAILY WANTS, THE DICTIONARY OF," a Cyclopædia embracing nearly 1,200 pages of sound Information upon all matters of Practical and Domestic Utility. The sale of nearly 100,000 copies of this Work affords the best evidence of its intrinsic value.

4—7. "USEFUL KNOWLEDGE, THE DICTIONARY OF," a Book of Reference upon History, Geography, Science, Statistics, &c. A Companion Work to the "Dictionary of Daily Wants."

8 & 9. "MEDICAL AND SURGICAL KNOWLEDGE, THE DICTIONARY OF," a complete Practical Guide on Health and Disease, for Families, Emigrants, and Colonists.

10. "THE PRACTICAL HOUSEWIFE AND FAMILY MEDICAL GUIDE," a Series of Instructive Papers on Cookery, Food, Treatment of the Sick, &c., &c.

11. "THE CORNER CUPBOARD," containing Domestic Information, numerous Needlework Designs, and Instructions for the Aquarium, Skeleton Plants, &c.

12. "THE INTERVIEW," a Companion to "ENQUIRE WITHIN," containing additional Information upon Domestic Matters.

13. "THE FAMILY SAVE-ALL," a System of Secondary Cookery, with Invaluable Hints for Economy in the use of every Article of Household Consumption.

14. "NOTICES TO CORRESPONDENTS," a Work full of curious Matters of Fact; a collection of important Information on all subjects, from real Answers to Correspondents of various Magazines and Newspapers.

15 & 16. "LIFE DOUBLED BY THE ECONOMY OF TIME," and "HOW A PENNY BECAME A THOUSAND POUNDS." The first of these Works teaches the Value of Moments, and shows how Life may be abridged and fall short of its true aim and happiness, by a careless indifference to trifles of Time. The second Work pursues a similar argument with reference to Money, which is the representative of all things of material Value.

17. "THE REASON WHY, HOUSEWIFE'S DOMESTIC SCIENCE," affording to the Manager of Domestic Affairs intelligible Reasons for the various duties she has to superintend or to perform.

18. "THE REASON WHY, GENERAL SCIENCE," a Collection of many Hundreds of Reasons for things which, though generally received, are imperfectly understood.

19. "THE REASON WHY, NATURAL HISTORY," giving REASONS for very numerous interesting Facts in connection with the Habits and Instincts of the various Orders of the Animal Kingdom.

20. "THE REASON WHY, GARDENING AND FARMING," giving some Thousands of Reasons for various Facts and Phenomena in reference to the Cultivation and Tillage of the Soil.

21. "THE REASON WHY, HISTORICAL," designed to simplify the study of English History, and to arouse a disposition to trace the connection between the Cause and the Event.

22. "THE REASON WHY, BIBLICAL AND SACRED HISTORY," a Family Guide to Scripture Readings, and a Hand-book for Biblical Students.

23. "THE REASON WHY, DENOMINATIONAL," giving the Origin, History, and Tenets of the various Christian Sects, with the Reasons assigned *by themselves* for their specialities of Faith and forms of Worship.

24. "THE REASON WHY, PHYSICAL GEOGRAPHY AND GEOLOGY," containing upwards of 1,200 Reasons, explanatory of the Physical Phenomena of the Earth, its Geological History, and the Geographical distribution of Plants, Animals, and the Human Families.

LONDON, *April*, 1865.

PREFACE BY THE EDITOR.

If there be any among my Readers who, having turned over the pages of "ENQUIRE WITHIN," have hastily pronounced them to be confused and ill-arranged, let them at once refer to THE INDEX,* and for ever hold their peace.

The INDEX is, to the vast congregation of useful hints and receipts that fill the boundary of this volume, like the DIRECTORY to the great aggregation of houses and people in London.

No one, being a stranger to London, would run about asking for "MR. SMITH." But, remembering the Christian name and the profession of the individual wanted, would turn to the DIRECTORY, and trace him out.

Like a house, every paragraph in "ENQUIRE WITHIN" has its number,—and the INDEX is the DIRECTORY which will explain what Facts, Hints, and Instructions *inhabit* that number.

For, if it be not a misnomer, I am prompted to say that "ENQUIRE WITHIN" is *peopled* with thousands of ladies and gentlemen, who have approved of the plan of the work, and contributed something to its store of useful information. There they are, waiting to be questioned, and ready to reply. Only a short time ago, the facts and information now assuming the conventional forms of printing types, were active thoughts in the minds of many persons. Their fingers traced those thoughts upon the page, for the benefit of whomsoever might need information. We must not separate the thought from the mind which gave it birth; we must not look upon these writings as we should upon the traces left by the snail upon the green leaf, having neither form nor meaning. Behind each page some one lives to answer for the correctness of the information imparted, just as certainly as where, in the window of a dwelling, you see a paper

* The Index will be found at page 357.

directing you to "ENQUIRE WITHIN," some one is there to answer you.

Old Dr. KITCHINER lives at No. 45; Mrs. HITCHING lives at 202; Mrs. CHILD lives at 1805; Mr. BANTING at 1663; Dr. STENHOUSE at 1670; Dr. ERASMUS WILSON at 1594; Dr. SOUTH-WOOD SMITH at 1638; Dr. BLAIR at 1957; M. SOYER at 1064; Dr. BABINGTON at 2163; Dr. CLARKE at 2140; a DOCTOR lives at 451; a GARDENER at 224; a SCHOOLMASTER at 168; a DANCING MASTER at 124; an ARTIST at 2296; a NATURALIST at 2085; a MODELLER at 2102; a COOK at 972; a PHILANTHROPIST at 1287; a LAWYER at 1359; a SURGEON at 767; a CHESS PLAYER at 57; a CHEMIST at 632; a BREWER at 2044; and so on.

Well! there they live—always at home—knock at their doors —ENQUIRE WITHIN, NO FEES TO PAY!!

We have taken so much care in selecting our information, and have been aided by so many kind friends in the production of our Volume, that we cannot turn to any page without at once being reminded of the GENEROUS FRIEND WHO ABIDES THERE.

To some extent, though in a far less degree, we have been indebted to the authors of the following useful books. In the first place we must express our chief obligations to "Dr. KITCHINER's COOK's ORACLE;" to "THE COOK," in "*Houlston and Wright's Industrial Library;*" "THE SHOPKEEPER's GUIDE," "THE WIFE's OWN COOKERY," "HOME TRUTHS FOR HOME PEACE," "THE PRACTICAL HOUSEWIFE," and to several of the Volumes of the "REASON WHY" SERIES.

LONDON, *April*, 18CF.

CONTENTS.

ON THE PUBLICATION OF THE

TWO HUNDRED AND SIXTIETH THOUSAND

OF

"ENQUIRE WITHIN."

BY THE EDITOR.

ONLY a few short years have sped
  Since I this work of love begun;
By thousands sought, by millions read,
  All their approving smiles I've won.
Now, while reflecting on the past,
  My day of life seems closing in,
Let me, while powers of reason last,
          " Enquire Within."

Oh, ye—who gentle are and fair—
  Who to these modest pages turn,
To raise a smile, to soothe a care,
  Or some moot point of duty learn,—
Forget not this: that whilst you live,
  Your hearts may yield to pride or sin;
Take, then, the warning here I give,—
          " Enquire Within."

Would you acquire the greatest peace—
  The sweetest joy—this world can give?
Bid hatred, pride, and envy cease,
  And learn a Christian's life to live;
Each eve, before your eyelids close,
  And slumbers of the night begin,
That your own heart may find repose,
          " Enquire Within."

TABLE,

SHOWING THE CONTENTS OF THE SEPARATE NUMBERS OF "ENQUIRE WITHIN."

☞ By the aid of the above Table, persons having the numbers of "ENQUIRE WITHIN" unbound can easily refer to the contents. Those who are desirous of special information upon the subjects treated of in the numbers can at all times obtain them separately, price THREEPENCE, post free.

ENQUIRE WITHIN

UPON

EVERYTHING.

1. Choice of Articles of Food. —Nothing is more important in the affairs of housekeeping than the choice of wholesome food. We have been amused by a conundrum which is as follows:— "A man went to market and bought *two* fish. When he reached home he found they were the same as when he had bought them; yet there were *three!* How was this?" The answer is—"He bought two mackarel, and one *smelt!*" Those who envy him his bargain need not care about the following rules; but to others they will be valuable :—

2. MACKAREL must be perfectly fresh, or it is a very indifferent fish; it will neither bear carriage, nor being kept many hours out of the water. The firmness of the flesh, and the clearness of the eyes, must be the criterion of fresh mackarel, as they are of all other fish.

3. TURBOT, and all flat white fish, are rigid and firm when fresh; the under side should be of a rich cream colour. When out of season, or too long kept, this becomes a bluish white, and the flesh soft and flaccid. A clear bright eye in fish is also a mark of being fresh and good.

4. COD is known to be fresh by the rigidity of the muscles (or flesh); the redness of the gills, and clearness of the eyes. Crimping much improves this fish.

5. SALMON.—The flavour and excellence of this fish depends upon its freshness, and the shortness of time since it was caught; for no method can completely preserve the delicate flavour it has when just taken out of the water. A great deal of what is brought to London has been packed in ice, and comes from the Scotch and Irish rivers, and, though perfectly fresh, is not quite equal to Thames salmon.

6. HERRINGS should be eaten when very fresh; and, like mackarel, will not remain good many hours after they are caught. But they are very excellent, especially for breakfast relishes, either salted, split, dried, and peppered, or pickled.

7. FRESH-WATER FISH. — The remarks as to firmness and clear fresh eyes apply to this variety of fish, of which there are carp, tench, pike, perch, &c.

8. LOBSTERS, recently caught, have always some remains of muscular action in the claws, which may be excited by pressing the eyes with the finger; when this cannot be produced, the lobster must have been too long kept. When boiled, the tail preserves its elasticity if fresh, but loses it as soon as it becomes stale. The heaviest lobsters are the best; when light they are watery and poor. Hen lobsters may generally be known by the spawn, or by the breadth of the "flap."

9. CRAB AND CRAYFISH must be chosen by observations similar to those given above in the choice of lobsters. Crabs have an agreeable smell when fresh.

B

10. PRAWNS AND SHRIMPS, when fresh, are firm and crisp.

11. OYSTERS.—If fresh, the shell is firmly closed; when the shells of oysters are open, they are dead, and unfit for food. The small-shelled oysters, the Byfleet, Colchester, and Milford, are the finest in flavour. Larger kinds, called rock oysters, are generally considered only fit for stewing and sauces, though some persons prefer them.

12. BEEF.—The grain of ox beef, when good, is loose, the meat red, and the fat inclining to yellow. Cow beef, on the contrary, has a closer grain, a whiter fat, but meat scarcely as red as that of ox beef. Inferior beef, which is meat obtained from ill-fed animals, or from those which had become too old for food, may be known by a hard, skinny fat, a dark red lean, and, in old animals, a line of horny texture running through the meat of the ribs. When meat pressed by the finger rises up quickly, it may be considered as that of an animal which was in its prime; when the dent made by pressure returns slowly, or remains visible, the animal had probably passed its prime, and the meat consequently must be of inferior quality.

13. VEAL should be delicately white, though it is often juicy and well-fla-voured when rather dark in colour. Butchers, it is said, bleed calves pur-posely before killing them, with a view to make the flesh white, but this also makes it dry and flavourless. On ex-amining the loin, if the fat enveloping the kidney be white and firm-looking, the meat will probably be prime and recently killed. Veal will not keep so long as an older meat, especially in hot or damp weather: when going, the fat becomes soft and moist, the meat flabby and spotted, and somewhat porous like sponge. Large, overgrown veal is in-ferior to small, delicate, yet fat veal. The fillet of a cow-calf is known by the udder attached to it, and by the soft-ness of the skin; it is preferable to the veal of a bull-calf.

14. MUTTON.—The meat should be firm and close in grain, and red in colour, the fat white and firm. Mutton is in its prime when the sheep is about five years old, though it is often killed much younger. If too young, the flesh feels tender when pinched; if too old, on being pinched it wrinkles up, and so remains. In young mutton, the fat readily separates; in old, it is held together by strings of skin. In sheep diseased of the rot, the flesh is very pale-coloured, the fat inclining to yel-low; the meat appears loose from the bone, and, if squeezed, drops of water ooze out from the grains; after cooking, the meat drops clean away from the bones. Wether mutton is preferred to that of the ewe; it may be known by the lump of fat on the inside of the thigh.

15. LAMB.—This meat will not keep long after it is killed. The large vein in the neck is bluish in colour when the fore quarter is fresh, green when be-coming stale. In the hind quarter, if not recently killed, the fat of the kidney will have a slight smell, and the knuckle will have lost its firmness.

16. PORK.—When good, the rind is thin, smooth, and cool to the touch; when changing, from being too long killed, it becomes flaccid and clammy. Enlarged glands, called kernels, in the fat, are marks of an ill-fed or diseased pig.

17. BACON should have a thin rind, and the fat should be firm, and tinged red by the curing; the flesh should be of a clear red, without intermixture of yellow, and it should firmly adhere to the bone. To judge the state of a ham, plunge a knife into it to the bone; on drawing it back, if particles of meat adhere to it, or if the smell is disagree-able, the curing has not been effectual, and the ham is not good; it should, in such a state, be immediately cooked. In buying a ham, a short thick one is to be preferred to one long and thin. Of English hams, Yorkshire, West-moreland, and Hampshire are most esteemed; of foreign, the Westphalian.

18. VENISON.—When good, the fat

is clear, bright, and of considerable thickness. To know when it is necessary to cook it, a knife must be plunged into the haunch; and from the smell the cook must determine on dressing or keeping it.

19. TURKEY.—In choosing poultry, the age of the bird is the chief point to be attended to. An old turkey has rough and reddish legs; a young one smooth and black. Fresh killed, the eyes are full and clear, and the feet moist. When it has been kept too long, the parts about the vent have a greenish appearance.

20. COMMON DOMESTIC FOWLS, when young, have the legs and combs smooth; when old they are rough, and on the breast long hairs are found instead of feathers. Fowls and chickens should be plump on the breast, fat on the back, and white-legged.

21. GEESE.—The bills and feet are red when old, yellow when young. Fresh killed, the feet are pliable, stiff when too long kept. Geese are called green while they are only two or three months old.

22. DUCKS. — Choose them with supple feet and hard plump breasts. Tame ducks have yellow feet, wild ones red.

23. PIGEONS are very indifferent food when they are too long kept. Suppleness of the feet shows them to be young; the state of the flesh is flaccid when they are getting bad from keeping. Tame pigeons are larger than the wild.

24. HARES AND RABBITS, when old, have the haunches thick, the ears dry and tough, and the claws blunt and ragged. A young hare has claws smooth and sharp, ears that easily tear, and a narrow cleft in the lip. A leveret is distinguished from a hare by a knob or small bone near the foot.

25. PARTRIDGES, when young, have yellowish legs and dark-coloured bills. Old partridges are very indifferent eating.

26. WOODCOCKS AND SNIPES, when old, have the feet thick and hard; when these are soft and tender, they are both

young and fresh killed. When their bills become moist, and their throats muddy, they have been too long killed. (See FOOD IN SEASON.)

Names and Situations of the Various Joints.

27. Meats.—In different parts of the kingdom the method of cutting up carcases varies. That which we describe below is the most general, and is known as the English method.

i. BEEF—*Fore Quarter.* — Fore rib (five ribs); middle rib (four ribs); chuck (three ribs). Shoulder piece (top of fore leg); brisket (lower or belly part of the ribs); clod (fore shoulder blade); neck; shin (below the shoulder); cheek. *Hind quarter.*—Sirloin; rump; aitchbone—these are the three divisions of the upper part of the quarter; buttock and mouse-buttock, which divide the thigh; veiny piece, joining the buttock; thick flank and thin flank (belly pieces) and leg. The sirloin and rump of both sides form a baron. *Beef is in season all the year; best in the winter.*

ii. MUTTON.—Shoulder; breast (the belly); over which are the loin (chump, or tail end); loin (best end); and neck (best end); neck (scrag end). A chine is two necks; a saddle two loins; then there are the leg and head. *Mutton is the best in winter, spring, and autumn.*

iii. LAMB is cut into fore quarter and hind quarter; a saddle, or loin; neck, breast, leg, and shoulder. *Grass lamb is in season from Easter to Michaelmas; house lamb from Christmas to Lady-day.*

iv. PORK is cut into leg, hand, or shoulder; hind-loin; fore-loin; belly-part; spare-rib (or neck); and head. *Pork is in season nearly all the year.*

v. VEAL is cut into neck (scrag end); neck (best end); loin (best end); loin (chump, or tail end); fillet (upper part of hind leg); hind knuckle, which joins the fillet; knuckle of fore leg; blade (bone of shoulder); breast (best end); breast (brisket end), and hand. *Veal is always in season, but dear in the winter and spring.*

vi. VENISON is cut into haunch (or back); neck; shoulder; and breast. *Doe venison is best in January, October, November, and December, and buck venison in June, July, August, and September.*

vii. SCOTTISH MODE OF DIVISION.— According to the English method the carcase of beef is disposed of more economically than upon the Scotch plan. The English plan affords better steaks, and better joints for roasting; but the Scotch plan gives a greater variety of pieces for boiling. The names of pieces in the Scotch plan, not found in the English, are the hough, or hind leg; the nineholes, or English buttock; the large and small runner, taken from the rib and chuck pieces of the English plan; the shoulder-lyer, the English shoulder, but cut differently; the spare-rib or fore-sye, the sticking piece, &c. The Scotch also cut mutton differently.

viii. OX-TAIL is much esteemed for purposes of soup; so also is the CHEEK. The TONGUE is highly esteemed.

ix. CALVES' HEADS are very useful for various dishes; so also are their KNUCKLES, FEET, HEART, &c.

28. Relative Economy of the Joints.

i. THE ROUND is, in large families, one of the most profitable parts: it is usually boiled, and, like most of the boiling parts of beef, is generally sold in London at a penny per pound less than roasting joints.

ii. THE BRISKET is also a penny a pound less in price than the roasting parts. It is not so economical a part as the round, having more bone to be weighed with it, and more fat. Where there are children, very fat joints are not desirable, being often disagreeable to them, and sometimes prejudicial, especially if they have a dislike to fat. This joint also requires more cooking than many others; that is to say, it requires a double allowance of time to be given for boiling it; it will, when served, be hard and scarcely digestible if no more time be allowed to boil it

than that which is sufficient for other joints and meats. When stewed it is excellent; and when cooked fresh (*i.e.*, unsalted), an excellent stock for soup may be extracted from it, and yet the meat will serve as well for dinner.

iii. THE EDGEBONE, OR AITCHBONE, is not considered to be a very economical joint, the bone being large in proportion to the meat; but the greater part of it, at least, is as good as that of any prime part. It sells at a penny a pound less than roasting joints.

iv. THE RUMP is the part of which the London butcher makes great profit, by selling it in the form of steaks. In the country, as there is not an equal demand for steaks, the whole of it may be purchased as a joint, and at the price of other prime parts. It may be turned to good account in producing many excellent dishes. If salted, it is simply boiled; if used unsalted, it is generally stewed.

v. THE VEINY PIECE is sold at a low price per pound; but, if hung for a day or two, it is very good and very profitable. Where there are a number of servants and children to have an early dinner, this part of beef will be found desirable.

vi. THE LEG AND SHIN afford excellent stock for soup; and, if not reduced too much, the meat taken from the bones may be served as a stew with vegetables; or it may be seasoned, pounded with butter, and potted; or, chopped very fine, and seasoned with herbs, and bound together by egg and bread crumbs, it may be fried in balls, or in the form of large eggs, and served with a gravy made with a few spoonfuls of the soup.

vii. OX CHEEK makes excellent soup. The meat, when taken from the bones, may be served as a stew.

viii. THE SIRLOIN AND THE RIBS are the roasting parts of beef, and these bear in all places the highest price. The most profitable of these two joints at a family table is the ribs. The bones, if removed from the beef before it is roasted, will assist in forming the basis of a soup. When boned, the meat of the ribs is often rolled up, tied with strings, and roasted; and this is the best way of using it, as it enables the carver to distribute equally the upper part of the meat with the fatter and more skinny parts, at the lower end of the bones.

29. Indications of Wholesome Mushrooms.—Whenever a fungus is pleasant in flavour and odour, it may be considered wholesome; if, on the contrary, it have an offensive smell, a bitter, astringent, or styptic taste, or even if it leave an unpleasant flavour in the mouth, it should not be considered fit for food. The colour, figure, and texture of these vegetables do not afford any characters on which we can safely rely; yet it may be remarked that in colour the pure yellow, gold colour, bluish pale, dark or lustre brown, wine red, or the violet, belong to many that are eatable; whilst the pale or sulphur yellow, bright or blood-red, and the greenish, belong to few but the poisonous. The safe kinds have most frequently a compact, brittle texture; the flesh is white; they grow more readily in open places, such as dry pastures and waste lands, than in places humid or shaded by wood. In general, those should be suspected which grow in caverns and subterranean passages, on animal matter undergoing putrefaction, as well as those whose flesh is soft or watery.

30. To Distinguish Mushrooms from Poisonous Fungi.
i. Sprinkle a little salt on the spongy part or gills of the sample to be tried. If they turn yellow, they are poisonous, —if black, they are wholesome. Allow the salt to act before you decide on the question.
ii. False mushrooms have a warty cap, or else fragments of membrane, adhering to the upper surface, are heavy, and emerge from a vulva or bag; they grow in tufts or clusters in woods, on the stumps of trees, &c., whereas the true mushrooms grow in pastures.

iii. False mushrooms have an astringent, styptic, and disagreeable taste.
iv. When cut they turn blue.
v. They are moist on the surface, and generally,
vi. Of a rose or orange colour.
vii. The gills of the true mushroom are of a pinky red, changing to a liver colour.
viii. The flesh is white.
ix. The stem is white, solid, and cylindrical.

31. Food in Season.
There is an old maxim, "A place for everything, and everything in its place." To which we beg to add another, "A season for everything, and everything in season."

32. JANUARY.
[Those Fish, Poultry, &c., distinguished by *Italics* are to be had in the highest perfection.]
i. FISH.—Barbel, brill, carp, cod, crabs, cray-fish, dabbs, *dace*, eels, flounders, *haddocks*, herrings, lampreys, ling, lobsters, mussels, oysters, perch, pike, plaice, prawns, salmon-trout, shrimps, skate, smelt, soles, sprats, sturgeon, *tench*, thornback, turbot, *whiting*.
ii. MEAT.—Beef, house-lamb, mutton, pork, veal, and doe venison.
iii. POULTRY AND GAME.—Capons, chickens, ducks, wild-ducks, fowls, geese, grouse, *hares*, larks, moor-game, partridges, pheasants, pigeons (tame), pullets, *rabbits*, snipes, turkeys (hen), widgeons, woodcocks.
iv. VEGETABLES.—Beet, brocoli (white and purple), brussels sprouts, cabbage, cardoons, carrots, celery, chervil, cole-wort, cresses, endive, garlic, herbs (dry), kale (Scotch), leeks, lettuces, mint, mustard, onions, parsley, parsnips, potatoes, rape, rosemary, sage, salsify, savoy, scorzonera, shalots, skirrets, sorrel, spinach (winter), tarragon, thyme, turnips.
v. FORCED VEGETABLES.—Asparagus, cucumbers, Jerusalem artichokes, and mushrooms.
vi. FRUIT.—Almonds. Apples: French

pippin, golden pippin, golden russet, Kentish pippin, nonpareil, winter pearmain. Pears: Bergamot d'Hollande, Bon Chrétien, Charmontel, Colmar, winter beurré. Grapes: English and foreign. Chestnuts, medlars, nuts, oranges, walnuts.

83. February.

i. Fish.—Barbel, brill, carp, cockles, cod, crabs, cray-fish, dabbs, dace, eels, flounders, haddocks, herrings, lampreys, ling, lobsters, mussels, oysters, perch, pike, plaice, prawns, salmon, shrimps, skate, smelts, soles, sturgeon, tench, thornback, turbot, whiting.

ii. Meat.—Beef, house-lamb, mutton, pork, veal.

iii. Poultry and Game.—Capons, chickens, ducklings, fowl (wild), green geese, hares, partridges, pheasants, pigeons (tame and wild), pullets with egg, rabbits (tame), snipes, turkeys, turkey poults, woodcocks.

iv. Vegetables.—Beet, brocoli (white and purple), burnet, cabbage, cardoons, carrots, celery, chervil, colewort, cresses, endive, garlic, dry herbs, leeks, lettuces, mint, mustard, mushrooms, onions, parsnips, parsley, potatoes, radish, rape, rosemary, sage, salsify, savoy, scorzonera, shalots, skirrets, sorrel, spinach, sprouts, tarragon, thyme, turnips, winter savoury.

v. Forced Vegetables.—Asparagus, cucumbers, Jerusalem artichokes.

vi. Fruit.—Apples: French pippin, golden pippin, golden russet, Holland pippin, Kentish pippin, nonpareil, Wheeler's russet, winter pearmain. Chestnuts, oranges. Pears: Bergamot, de Pasque, winter Bon Chrétien, winter Russelet.

84. March.

i. Fish.—Brill, carp, cockles, cod, conger-eels, crabs, dabbs, dory, eels, flounders, ling, lobsters, mackarel, mullets, mussels, oysters, perch, pike, plaice, prawns, salmon, salmon-trout, shrimps, skate, smelts, soles, sturgeon, turbot, tench, and whiting.

ii. Meat.—Beef, house-lamb, mutton, pork, veal.

iii. Poultry and Game.—Capons, chickens, ducklings, fowls, green geese, grouse, leverets, moor-game, pigeons, rabbits, snipes, turkeys, woodcocks.

iv. Vegetables.—Artichokes (Jerusalem), beet, brocoli (white and purple), brussels sprouts, cabbage, cardoons, carrots, celery, chervil, colewort, cresses, endive, garlic, herbs (dry), kale (sea and Scotch), lettuces, mint, mushrooms, mustard, onions, parsley, parsnips, potatoes, rape, rosemary, sage, savoy, shalots, sorrel, spinach, tarragon, thyme, turnips, turnip-tops.

v. Forced Vegetables. — Asparagus, beans, cucumbers, and rhubarb.

vi. Fruit. —Apples: French pippins, golden russet, Holland pippin, John apple, Kentish pippin, nonpareil, Norfolk beaufin, Wheeler's russet. Chestnuts, oranges. Pears: Bergamot, Bugi, Charmontel, St. Martial, winter Bon Chrétien. Strawberries (forced).

85. April.

i. Fish.—Brill, carp, chub, cockles, cod, conger-eels, *crabs*, dabbs, dory, eels, flounders, halibut, herrings, ling, *lobsters*, mackarel, mullets, mussels, oysters, perch, pike, *prawns*, plaice, *salmon*, shrimps, *skate*, smelts, soles, sturgeon, *tench*, trout, turbot, whitings.

ii. Meat.—Beef, grass-lamb, house-lamb, mutton, pork, veal.

iii. Poultry and Game.—Chickens, ducklings, fowls, green geese, leverets, pigeons, pullets, rabbits, turkey poults, wood-pigeons.

iv. Vegetables. — Asparagus, brocoli, chervil, colewort, cucumbers, endive, fennel, herbs of all sorts, lettuce, onions, parsley, parsnips, peas, purslane, radishes, sea-kale, sorrel, spinach, small salad, tarragon, turnip-radishes, turnip-tops, and rhubarb.

v. Fruit. — Apples: Golden russet, John apple, nonpareil, Wheeler's russet. Nuts, oranges. Pears: Bergamot, Bon Chrétien, Bugi, Carmelite, francreal, St. Martial. A few strawberries, walnuts. Forced: Apricots, cherries, strawberries.

36. MAY.

i. FISH.—Brill, carp, chub, cod, conger-eels, *crabs*, cray-fish, dabbs, dace, dory, eels, flounders, gurnets, haddock, halibut, herring, ling, *lobsters*, mackarel, mullet, perch, pike, plaice, *prawns, salmon*, shrimps, *skate*, smelts, soles, sturgeon, tench, trout, turbots, whitings.

ii. MEAT.—Beef, grass-lamb, house-lamb, mutton, pork, veal.

iii. POULTRY AND GAME.—Chickens, ducklings, fowls, green geese, leverets, pigeons, pullets, rabbits, wood-pigeons.

iv. VEGETABLES. — Angelica, artichokes, asparagus, balm, kidney-beans, cabbage, carrots, cauliflowers, chervil, cucumbers, fennel, herbs of all sorts, lettuce, mint, onions, parsley, peas, new potatoes, purslane, radishes, rhubarb, salad of all sorts, sea-kale, sorrel, spinach, thyme, turnips.

v. FRUIT. — Apples : John apple, golden russet, winter russet. May-duke cherries ; currants; gooseberries ; melons. Pears : L'amozette, winter green-scarlet strawberries. Forced : Apricots, nutmeg peaches, strawberries.

37. JUNE.

i. FISH. — Carp, cod, conger-eels, *crabs*, cray-fish, dabbs, dace, dory, eels, flounders, gurnets, haddocks, herrings, ling, *lobsters*, mackarel, mullet, perch, pike, plaice, *prawns, salmon, salmon-trout, skate*, smelts, soles, sturgeon, tench, trout, turbot, whitebait, whitings.

ii. MEAT.—Beef, *grass-lamb*, house-lamb, mutton, pork, veal, buck venison.

iii. POULTRY AND GAME.—Chickens, ducklings, fowls, green geese, leverets, pigeons, plovers, pullets, rabbits, turkey poults, wheat-ears, wood-pigeons.

iv. VEGETABLES. — Angelica, artichoke, asparagus, beans (French, kidney, and Windsor), white beet, cabbage, carrots, cauliflowers, chervil, cucumbers, endive, herbs of all sorts, leeks, lettuce, onions, parsley, peas, potatoes, purslane, radishes, salad of all sorts, spinach, turnips, vegetable marrow.

v. FOR DRYING.—Burnet, mint, tarragon, orange-thyme.

vi. FOR PICKLING.—Garlic.

vii. FRUIT.—Apples : John apple, stone pippin, golden russet. Apricots. Cherries : Duke, bigaroon, black-heart. Currants ; gooseberries; melons. Pears : Winter green. Strawberries. Forced : Grapes, nectarines, peaches, pines.

38. JULY.

i. FISH.—Barbel, brill, carp, cod, conger-eels, *crabs*, cray-fish, dabbs, *dace*, dory, eels, flounders, gurnets, haddocks, herrings, ling, *lobsters, mackarel*, mullet, perch, pike, plaice, *prawns*, salmon, skate, soles, tench, thornback, trout.

ii. MEAT.—Beef, *grass-lamb*, mutton, veal, buck venison.

iii. POULTRY AND GAME.—*Chickens*, ducks, fowls, *green geese*, leverets, pigeons, plovers, rabbits, turkey poults, wheat-ears, *wild pigeons*, wild rabbits.

iv. VEGETABLES.—Artichokes, asparagus, balm, beans (French, kidney, scarlet, and Windsor), carrots, cauliflowers, celery, chervil, cucumbers, endive, finochia, herbs of all sorts, lettuces, mint, mushrooms, peas, potatoes, purslane, radishes, rocombole, salads of all sorts, salsify, scorzonera, sorrel, spinach, turnips.

v. FOR DRYING.—Knotted marjoram, mushrooms, winter savoury.

vi. FOR PICKLING.—French beans, red cabbage, cauliflowers, garlic, gherkins, nasturtiums, onions.

vii. FRUIT.—Apples: Codlin, jennetting, Margaret, summer pearmain, summer pippin. Apricots, cherries, currants, *damsons*, gooseberries, melons, nectarines, peaches. Pears: Catherine, greenchisel, jargonelle, musque. Oranges, pineapples, plums, raspberries, strawberries.

39. AUGUST.

i. FISH.—Barbel, brill, carp, cod, conger-eels, crabs, cray-fish, dabbs, *dace*, eels, flounders, gurnets, haddocks, herrings, lobsters, *mackarel*, mullet, oysters, *perch, pike*, plaice, *prawns*, salmon, skate, soles, tench, thornback, *turbot*, whitings.

ii. MEAT.—Beef, grass-lamb, mutton, veal, buck venison.

iii. POULTRY AND GAME.—Chickens,

ducks, fowls, *green geese, grouse* (from 12th), leverets, moor-game, pigeons, plovers, rabbits, turkeys, turkey poults, wheat-ears, wild ducks, wild pigeons, wild rabbits.

iv. VEGETABLES.—Artichokes, beans (French, kidney, scarlet, and Windsor), white beet, carrots, cauliflowers, celery, cucumbers, endive, finochia, pot-herbs of all sorts, leeks, lettuces, mushrooms, onions, peas, potatoes, purslane, radishes, salad of all sorts, salsify, scorzonera, shalots, spinach, turnips.

v. FOR DRYING.—Basil, sage, thyme.

vi. FOR PICKLING. — Red cabbage, capsicums, chilies, tomatos, walnuts.

vii. FRUIT.—Apples: Codlin, summer pearmain, summer pippin. Cherries, currants, damsons, figs, filberts, gooseberries, grapes, melons, mulberries, nectarines, peaches. Pears: Jargonelle, summer Bon Chrétien, Windsor. Plums: Greengages, Orleans. Raspberries, Alpine strawberries.

40. SEPTEMBER.

i. FISH.—Barbel, brill, carp, cockles, cod, conger-eels, crab, *dace*, eels, flounders, gurnets, haddocks, hake, herrings, lobsters, mullet, mussels, *oysters, perch, pike*, plaice, prawns, shrimps, soles, tench, thornback, turbot, whitings.

ii. MEAT.—Beef, mutton, pork, veal, buck venison.

iii. POULTRY AND GAME.—Chickens, ducks, fowls, green geese, *grouse, hares,* larks, leverets, *moor-game, partridges,* pigeons, plovers, rabbits, *teal,* turkey, turkey poults, wheat-ears, *wild ducks,* wild pigeons, wild rabbits.

iv. VEGETABLES.—Artichokes, Jerusalem artichokes, beans (French and scarlet), cabbages, carrots, cauliflowers, celery, cucumbers, endive, finochia, herbs of all sorts, leeks, lettuces, mushrooms, onions, parsnips, peas, potatoes, radishes, salad of all sorts, shalots, turnips.

v. FRUIT.—Apples: White Caville, pearmain, golden rennet. Cherries (Morella), damsons, figs, filberts. Grapes: Muscadine, Frontignac, red and black Hamburgh, Malmsey. Hazel nuts, med-

lars, peaches. Pears: Bergamot, brown beurré. Pineapples, plums, quinces, strawberries, walnuts.

41. OCTOBER.

i. FISH.—Barbel, brill, turbot, carp, cockles, cod, conger-eels, crabs, *dace, dory,* eels, gudgeon, haddocks, *hake,* halibut, herrings, lobsters, mussels, oysters, perch, *pike,* prawns, salmon-trout, shrimps, smelts, soles, tench, thornback, turbot, whitings.

ii. MEAT.—Beef, mutton, pork, veal, doe venison.

iii. POULTRY AND GAME.—Chickens, dotterel, ducks, fowls, green geese, grouse, hares, larks, moor-game, partridges, *pheasants,* pigeons, rabbits, snipes, teal, turkey, wheat-ears, widgeon, wild ducks, wild pigeons, wild rabbits, woodcocks.

iv. VEGETABLES.—Artichokes, Jerusalem artichokes, brocoli, cabbages, cauliflowers, celery, coleworts, endive, herbs of all sorts, leeks, onions, parsnips, peas, potatoes, radishes, rocombole, salad, savoys, scorzonera, skirrets, shalots, spinach (winter), tomatos, truffles, turnips.

v. FRUIT.—Apples: Pearmain, golden pippin, golden rennet, royal russet. Black and white bullace, damsons, late figs, almonds, filberts, hazel nuts, grapes, medlars. Peaches: Old Newington, October. Pears: Bergamot, beurré, Charmontel, Bon Chrétien, cresau, swan's-egg. Quinces, services, walnuts.

42. NOVEMBER.

i. FISH.—Barbel, brill, turbot, carp, cockles, cod, crabs, *dace, dory,* eels, gudgeons, gurnets, haddocks, *hake,* halibut, herrings, ling, lobsters, mussels, oysters, perch, *pike,* plaice, prawns, salmon, shrimps, skate, smelts, soles, sprats, tench, thornback, turbot, whitings.

ii. MEAT.—Beef, house-lamb, mutton, pork, veal, doe venison.

iii. POULTRY AND GAME.—Chickens, dotterel, ducks, fowls, *geese, grouse, hares,* larks, moor-game, partridges, pheasants, pigeons, rabbits, *snipes, teal,* turkey, wheat-ears, widgeon, wild ducks, *woodcocks.*

iv. VEGETABLES. — Jerusalem artichokes, chard beets, borecole, brocoli, cabbages, cardoons, carrots, celery, chervil, coleworts, endive, herbs of all sorts, leeks, lettuces, onions, parsnips, potatoes, salad, savoys, scorzonera, skirrets, shalots, spinach, tomatos, turnips.

v. FRUIT.—Almonds. Apples: Holland pippin, golden pippin, Kentish pippin, nonpareil, winter pearmain, Wheeler's russets. Bullace, chestnuts, hazel nuts, grapes, medlars. Pears: Bergamot, Bezy de Charmontelle, Colmar, cressau, Spanish Bon Chrétien. Services, walnuts.

43. DECEMBER.

i. FISH.—Barbel, brill, turbot, carp, cockles, *cod*, crabs, dab, *dory*, eels, gudgeon, gurnets, haddocks, hake, halibut, herrings, *ling*, lobsters, mackarel, mussels, oysters, perch, pike, plaice, ruffe, salmon, shrimps, *skate*, smelts, soles, sprats, sturgeon, *tench*, whitings.

ii. MEAT.—Beef, house-lamb, mutton, pork, veal, doe venison.

iii. POULTRY AND GAME.—Capons, chickens, dotterel, ducks, fowls, geese, grouse, guinea-fowl, hares, larks, moorgame, partridges, pea-fowl, pheasants, pigeons, rabbits, snipes, teal, turkey, wheat-ears, widgeon, wild ducks, woodcocks.

iv. VEGETABLES. — Jerusalem artichokes, beets, borecole, white and purple brocoli, cabbages, cardoons, carrots, celery, endive, herbs of all sorts, leeks, lettuces, onions, parsnips, potatoes, salad, savoys, scorzonera, skirrets, shalots, spinach, truffles, turnips, *forced* asparagus.

v. FRUIT.—Almonds. Apples: Golden pippin, nonpareil, winter pearmain, golden russet. Chestnuts, hazel nuts, a few grapes, medlars, oranges. Pears: Bergamot, beurré d'hiver, Colmar, Holland. St. Germain's walnuts.

44. Drying Herbs.—Fresh herbs are preferable to dried ones, but as they cannot always be obtained, it is most important to dry herbs at the proper seasons :—*Basil* is in a fit state for drying about the middle of August. *Burret* in June, July, and August. *Chervil* in May, June, and July. *Elder Flowers* in May, June, and July. *Fennel* in May, June, and July. *Knotted Marjoram* during July. *Lemon Thyme,* end of July and through August. *Mint,* end of June and July. *Orange Flowers,* May, June, and July. *Orange Thyme* (a delicious herb), June and July. *Parsley,* May, June, and July. *Sage,* August and September. *Summer Savoury,* end of July and August. *Tarragon,* June, July, and August. *Thyme,* end of July and August. *Winter Savoury,* end of July and August.

These herbs always at hand will be a great aid to the cook. Herbs should be gathered on a dry day ; they should be immediately well cleansed, and dried by the heat of a stove or Dutch oven. The leaves should then be picked off, pounded and sifted, put into stoppered bottles labelled, and put away for use.

45. Dr. Kitchiner's Rules for Marketing.—The best rule for marketing is to pay ready money for everything, *and to deal with the most respectable tradesmen* in your neighbourhood. If you leave it to their integrity to supply you with a good article at the fair market price, you will be supplied with better provisions, and at as reasonable a rate as those *bargain-hunters* who trot " *around, around, around about* " a market till they are trapped to buy some *unchewable* old poultry, *tough* tup-mutton, *stringy* cow-beef, or *stale* fish, at a very little less than the price of prime and proper food. With *savings* like these they toddle home in triumph, cackling all the way, like a goose that has got ankle-deep into good luck. All the skill of the most accomplished cook will avail nothing unless she is furnished with prime provisions. The best way to procure these is to deal with shops of established character : you may appear to pay, perhaps, ten *per cent.* more than you would were you to deal with those who pretend to sell cheap, but you would be much more than in that proportion better served. Every trade has its tricks and deceptions; those who follow them can deceive you if they please, and they are too apt to do so if you provoke the exercise of their over-reaching talent. Challenge them to a game at "*Catch who can*," by entirely relying on your own judgment, and you will soon find nothing but very long experience can make you equal to the combat of marketing to the utmost advantage. If you think a tradesman has imposed upon you, never use a second word, if the first will not do, nor drop the least hint of an imposition; the only method to induce him to make an abatement is the hope of future favours; pay the demand, and deal with the gentleman no more; but do not let him see that you are displeased, or as soon as you are out of sight your reputation will suffer as much as your pocket has. Before you go to market, look over your larder, and consider well what things are wanting—especially on a Saturday. No well-regulated family can suffer a disorderly caterer to be jumping in and out to make purchases on a Sunday morning. You will be enabled to manage much better if you will make out a bill of fare for the week on the Saturday before; for example, for a family of half a dozen—

Sunday—Roast beef and pudding.
Monday—Fowl, what was left of pudding fried, or warmed in the Dutch oven.
Tuesday—Calf's head, apple pie.
Wednesday—Leg of mutton.
Thursday—Ditto broiled or hashed, and pancakes.
Friday—Fish, pudding.
Saturday—Fish, or eggs and bacon.

It is an excellent plan to have certain things on certain days. When your butcher or poulterer knows what you will want, he has a better chance of doing his best for you; and never think of ordering beef for roasting except for Sunday. When you order meat, poultry, or fish, tell the tradesman when you intend to dress it: he will then have it in his power to serve you with provision that will do him credit, which the finest meat, &c., in the world will never do, unless it has been kept a proper time to be ripe and tender.—*Kitchiner's Cook's Oracle.*

46. The Family Circle.—Under this title, a series of friendly parties have been instituted by a group of acquaintances in London. The following form of invitation, and the rules of the Family Circle, will be found interesting, probably useful:—

Will you do me the favour of meeting here, as a guest, on —— next, at seven precisely, a few friends who have kindly joined in an attempt to commence occasional pleasant and social parties, of which the spirit and intent will be better understood by the perusal of the few annexed remarks and rules from
Yours sincerely,   ——

"They manage it better in France," is a remark to be often applied with reference to social life in England, and the writer fancies that the prevalence here of a few bad customs, easily changed, causes the disadvantageous difference between ourselves and our more courteous and agreeable neighbours.

i. Worldly appearance; the phantom leading many to suppose that wealth is the standard of worth—in the minds of friends, a notion equally degrading to both parties.
ii. Overdress; causing unnecessary expense and waste of time.
iii. Expensive entertainments, as regards refreshments.
iv. Late hours.

The following brief rules are suggested, in a hope to show the way to a more constant, easy, and friendly intercourse amongst friends, the writer feeling convinced that society is equally beneficial and requisite—in fact, that mankind in seclusion, like the sword in the scabbard, often loses polish, and gradually rusts.

RULE I. That meetings be held in rotation at each member's house, for the enjoyment of conversation; music, grave and gay;

dancing, gay only ; and card-playing at limited stakes.

RULE II. That such meetings commence at seven and end about or after twelve, and that members and guests be requested to remember that punctuality has been called the politeness of kings.

RULE III. That as gentlemen are allowed for the whole season to appear, like the raven, in one suit, ladies are to have the like privilege ; and that no lady be allowed to quiz or notice the habits of another lady ; and that demi-toilette in dress be considered the better taste in the family circle; not that the writer wishes to raise or lower the proper standard of ladies' dress, which ought to be neither too high nor too low, but at a happy medium.

RULE IV. That any lady infringing the last rule be liable to reproof by the oldest lady present at the meeting, if the oldest lady, like the oldest inhabitant, can be discovered.

RULE V. That every member or guest be requested to bring with them their own vocal, instrumental, or dance music, and take it away with them, if possible, to avoid loss and confusion.

RULE VI. That no member or guest, able to sing, play, or dance, refuse, unless excused by medical certificate ; and that no cold or sore throat be allowed to last more than a week.

RULE VII. That as every member or guest known to be able to sing, play, or dance, is bound to do so if requested, the performer (especially if timid) is to be kindly criticised and encouraged; it being a fact well known, that the greatest masters of an art are always the most lenient critics, from their deep knowledge of the feeling, intelligence, and perseverance required to at all approach perfection.

RULE VIII. That gentlemen present do pay every attention to ladies, especially visitors ; but such attention is to be general, and not particular—for instance, no gentleman is to dance more than three times with one lady during the evening, except in the case of lovers, privileged to do odd things during their temporary lunacy, and also married couples, who are expected to dance together at least once during the evening, and oftener if they please.

RULE IX. That to avoid unnecessary expense, the refreshments be limited to cold meat, sandwiches, bread, cheese, butter, vegetables, fruits, tea, coffee, negus, punch, malt liquors, &c., &c.

RULE X. That all personal or face to face laudatory speeches (commonly called toasts, or, as may be, roasts) be for the future forbidden, without permission or inquiry, for reasons following :—That as the family circle includes bachelors and spinsters, and he, she, or they may be secretly engaged, it will be therefore cruel to excite hopes that may be disappointed ; and that as some well-informed Benedict of long experience may after supper advise the bachelor to find the way to woman's heart—*vice versa*, some deep-feeling wife or widow, by " pity moven," may, perhaps, after supper advise the spinster the other way, which, in public, is an impropriety manifestly to be avoided.

RULE XI. (*suggested by a lady*). That any lady, after supper, may (if she please) ask any gentleman apparently diffident, or requiring encouragement, to dance with her, and that no gentleman can of course, refuse so kind a request.

RULE XII. That no gentleman be expected to escort any lady home on foot beyond a distance of three miles, unless the gentleman be positive and the lady agreeable.

RULE THE LAST. That as the foregoing remarks and rules are intended, in perfect good faith and spirit, to be considered general and not personal, no umbrage is to be taken, and the reader is to bear in mind the common and homely saying,—

" Always at trifles scorn to take offence,
  It shows great pride and very little sense."

P.S.—To save trouble to both parties, this invitation be deemed accepted, without the necessity to reply, unless refused within twenty-four hours.

47. Evening Pastime.

Among the innocent recreations of the fireside, there are few more commendable and practicable than those afforded by what are severally termed Anagrams, Charades, Conundrums, Enigmas, Puzzles, Rebuses, Riddles, Transpositions, &c. Of these there are such a variety, that they are suited to every capacity ; and they present this additional attraction, that ingenuity may be exercised in the *invention* of them, as well as in their solution. Many persons who have become noted for their literary compositions may date the origin of their success to the time when they attempted the composition of a trifling enigma or charade.

48. ANAGRAMS are formed by the transposition of the letters of words or sentences, or names of persons, so as to produce a word, sentence, or verse, of pertinent or of widely different meaning. They are very difficult to discover, but are exceedingly striking when good. The following are some of the most remarkable :—

Transposed	*forms—*
Astronomers	No more stars.
Catalogues	Got as a clue.
Elegant	Neat leg.
Impatient	Tim in a pet.
Immediately	I met my Delia.
Masquerade	Queen as mad.
Matrimony	Into my arm.
Melodrama	Made moral.
Midshipman	Mind his map.
Old England	Golden land.
Parishioners	I hire parsons.
Parliament	Partial men.
Penitentiary	Nay I repent.
Presbyterians	Best in prayer.
Radical Reform	Rare mad frolic.
Revolution	To love ruin.
Sir Robert Peel	Terrible poser.
Sweetheart	There we sat.
Telegraphs	Great helps.

49. CONUNDRUMS.—These are simple catches, in which the sense is playfully cheated, and are generally founded upon words capable of double meaning. The following are examples :—

Where did Charles the First's executioner dine, and what did he take?

He took a chop at the King's Head.

When is a plant to be dreaded more than a mad dog?

When it's madder.

What is majesty stripped of its externals?

It is *a jest.* [The *m* and the *y*, externals, are taken away.]

Why is hot bread like a caterpillar?

Because it's the grub that makes the butter fly.

Why did the accession of Victoria throw a greater damp over England than the death of King William?

Because the King was missed (mist) *while the Queen was reigning* (raining).

Why should a gouty man make his will?

To have his legatees (leg at ease).

Why are bankrupts more to be pitied than idiots?

Because bankrupts are broken, while idiots are only cracked.

Why is the treadmill like a true convert?

Because it's turning is the result of conviction.

When may a nobleman's property be said to be all feathers?

When his estates are all entails (hen-tails).

50. THE CHARADE is a poetical or other composition founded upon a word, each syllable of which constitutes a *noun*, and the whole of which word constitutes another noun of a somewhat different meaning from those supplied by its separate syllables. Words which fully answer these conditions are the best for the purposes of charades; though many other words are employed. In writing, the first syllable is termed "*My first,*" the second syllable, "*My second,*" and the complete word, "*My whole.*" The following is an example of a Poetical Charade :—

The breath of the morning is sweet;
    The earth is bespangled with flowers;
And buds in a countless array
    Have ope'd at the touch of the showers.
The birds, whose glad voices are ever
    A music delightful to hear,
Seem to welcome the joy of the morning,
    As the hour of the bridal draws near.
What is that which now steals on *my first,*
    Like a sound from the dreamland of love,
And seems wand'ring the valleys among,
    That they may the nuptials approve?
'Tis a sound which *my second* explains,
    And it comes from a sacred abode,
And it merrily trills as the villagers throng
    To greet the fair bride on her road.
How meek is her dress, how befitting a bride
    So beautiful, spotless, and pure!
When she weareth *my second,* oh, long may it be
    Ere her heart shall a sorrow endure.
See the glittering gem that shines forth from her hair—
    'Tis *my whole,* which a good father gave;
'Twas worn by her mother with honour before—
    But she sleepeth in peace in her grave.

'Twas her earnest request, as she bade them
  adieu,
That when her dear daughter the altar drew
  near,
She should wear the same gem that her mother
  had worn
When she as a bride full of promise stood
  there.

51. THE ANSWER is *Ear-ring.* The
bells *ring,* the sound steals upon the
ear, and the bride wears an *ear-ring.*
Charades may be sentimental or hu-
morous, in poetry or prose; they may
also be *acted,* in which manner they
afford considerable amusement.

52. ACTED CHARADES.—A drawing
room with folded doors is the best for
the purpose. Various household appliances are employed to fit up something
like a stage, and to supply the fitting
scenes. Characters dressed in costumes
made up of handkerchiefs, coats, shawls,
table-covers, &c., come on and perform
an extempore play, founded upon the
parts of a word, and its *whole,* as
indicated above. For instance, the
events explained in the poem above
might be *acted*—glasses might be rung
for bells—something might be said in
the course of the dialogues about the
sound of the bells being delightful to
the *ear;* there might be a dance of the
villagers, in which a *ring* might be
formed; a wedding might be performed;
and so on. Though for *acting* Charades
there are many better words, because
Ear-ring could with difficulty be *represented* without at once betraying
the meaning. There is a little work
entitled " Family Pastime," and
another work, " Philosophy and Mirth
united by Pen and Pencil," also " Merry
Evenings for Merry People; or, Drawing
Room Charades," * which supply a large
number of these Charades. But the
following is the only complete list of
words ever published upon which
Charades may be founded :—

* " Family Pastime," One Shilling.
  " Philosophy and Mirth," One Shilling.
  " Merry Evenings for Merry People; or,
Drawing Room Charades," One Shilling.
  All published by Houlston and Wright, 65,
Paternoster Row, London.

53. Words which may be converted into **Acting** or **Written**
Charades :—

Aid-less	But-ton	Fire-man
Air-pump	Cab-in	Fire-pan
Ale-house	Can-did	Fire-ship
Ann-ounce	Can-ton	Fire-work
Arch-angel	Care-ful	Fir-kin
Arm-let	Car-pet	Fish-hook
Art-less	Car-rot	Flag-rant
Ass-ail	Cart-ridge	Flip-pant
Ba-boon	Chair-man	Flood-gate
Back-bite	Chamber-maid	Fond—ling
Back-slide	Cheer-ful	Foot-ball
Bag-gage	Cheer-less	Foot-man
Bag-pipe	Christ-mas	Foot-pad
Bag-dad	Church-yard	Foot-step
Bail-able	Clans-men	Foot-stool
Bale-ful	Clerk-ship	For-age
Band-age	Cob-web	For-bear
Band-box	Cock-pit	For-bid
Bane-ful	Cod-ling	Fox-glove
Bar-bed	Coin-age	Free-hold
Bar-gain	Con-fined	Free-stone
Bar-rack	Con-firm	Fret-work
Bar-row	Con-form	Friend-ship
Bat-ten	Con-tent	Frost-bite
Beard-less	Con-test	Fur-long
Bid-den	Con-tract	Gain-say
Bird-lime	Con-verse	Gang-way
Birth-right	Cork-screw	Glow-worm
Black-guard	Count-less	Glut-ton
Blame-less	Court-ship	God-father
Block-head	Crab-bed	God-mother
Boat-man	Cross-bow	God-daughter
Boot-jack	Cur-tail	God-son
Book-worm	Cut-throat	God-like
Bound-less	Dark-some	God-child
Bow-ling	Day-break	Gold-finch
Brace-let	Death-watch	Gold-smith
Brain-less	Dog-ma	Goose-berry
Break-fast	Don-key	Grand-father
Breath-less	Drink-able	Grate-ful
Brick-bat	Drug-get	Grave-stone
Brick-dust	Duck-ling	Green-finch
Bride-groom	Ear-ring	Grey-hound
Bride-cake	Earth-quake	Grim-ace
Brim-stone	Ear-wig	Grind-stone
Broad-cloth	False-hood	Ground-plot
Broad-side	Fan-atic	Ground-sel
Broad-sword	Fare-well	Guard-ship
Brow-beat	Far-thing	Gun-powder
Bug-bear	Fear-less	Had-dock
Bull-dog	Fee-ling	Hail-stone
Bump-kin	Field-fare	Hail-storm
Buoy-ant	Fire-lock	Half-penny

Ham-let
Ham-mock
Hand-cuff
Hang-man
Hap-pen
Hard-ship
Harts-horn
Head-land
Head-less
Head-long
Head-stone
Head-strong
Hear-say
Heart-less
Heart-sick
Heart-string
Hedge-hog
Heir-less
Heir-loom
Hell-hound
Hell-kite
Hence-forth
Hen-roost
Herb-age
Herds-man
Her-self
Hid-den
High-land
High-way
Hind-most
Hoar-frost
Hob-goblin
Hogs-head
Home-bred
Honey-bag
Honey-comb
Honey-moon
Honey-suckle
Hood-wink
Horse-back
Horse-shoe
Host-age
Hot-bed
Hot-house
Hot-spur
Hounds-ditch
Hour-glass
House-hold
House-maid
House-wife
Hum-drum
Hump-back
Hurri-cane
Ill-nature
Ill-usage
In-action
In-born

In-crease
In-justice
Ink-ling
In-land
In-mate
In-no-cent
In-sane
In-spirit
In-tent
Inter-meddle
Inter-sect
Inter-view
In-valid
In-vent
In-vest
In-ward
Ire-ful
Iron-mould
I-sing-lass
Jaco-bite
Joy-ful
Joy-less
Justice-ship
Key-stone
Kid-nap
King-craft
King-fisher
Kins-man
Kit-ten
Knight-hood
Know-ledge
Lace-man
Lady-bird
Lady-ship
Lamp-black
Land-lady
Land-lord
Land-mark
Land-scape
Land-tax
Lap-dog
Lap-pet
Laud-able
Law-giver
Law-suit
Lay-man
Leap-frog
Leap-year
Lee-ward
Life-guard
Like-wise
Live-long
Load-stone
Log-book
Log-wood
Loop-hole
Lord-ship

Love-sick
Low-land
Luck-less
Luke-warm
Ma-caw
Mad-cap
Mad-house
Mad-man
Mag-pie
Main-mast
Main-sail
Main-spring
Mam-moth
Man-age
Man-date
Marks-man
Mar-row
Mass-acre
Match-less
May-game
Meat-man
Mis-chance
Mis-chief
Mis-count
Mis-deed
Mis-judge
Mis-quote
Moon-light
Moon-beam
Muf-fin
Name-sake
Nan-keen
Nap-kin
Neck-lace
Neck-cloth
Nest-ling
News-paper
Nick-name
Night-cap
Night-gown
Night-mare
Night watch
Nine-fold
Noon-tide
North-star
North-ward
Not-able
Not-ice
No-where
Nut-gall
Nut-meg
Oak-apple
Oat-cake
Oat-meal
Off-end
Oil-man
O-men

On-set
O-pen
O-pinion
Over-act
Over-awe
Over-bear
Over-board
Over-boil
Over-burden
Over-cast
Over-charge
Over-cloud
Over-come
Over-court
Over-do
Over-due
Over-eye
Over-feed
Over-flow
Over-grown
Over-head
Over-hear
Over-heard
Over-joy
Over-lade
Over-lay
Over-leap
Over-load
Over-look
Over-mast
Over-match
Over-right
Over-pass
Over-pay
Over-peer
Over-plus
Over-poise
Over-power
Over-press
Over-rack
Over-rate
Over-reach
Over-ripen
Over-rule
Over-roast
Over-run
Over-see
Over-seer
Over-set
Over-shade
Over-shadow
Over-shoe
Over-shoot
Over-sight
Over-size
Over-sleep
Over-spread

Over-stock
Over-strain
Over-sway
Over-swell
Over-take
Over-throw
Over-took
Over-value
Over-work
Our-selves
Out-act
Out-bid
Out-brave
Out-brazen
Out-cast
Out-cry
Out-do
Out-grow
Out-law
Out-line
Out-live
Out-march
Out-rage
Out-ride
Out-run
Out-sail
Out-sell
Out-shine
Out-side
Out-sleep
Out-sit
Out-spread
Out-stare
Out-stretch
Out-talk
Out-vie
Out-ward
Out-weigh
Out-wit
Out-work
Out-worn
Ox-gall
Ox-lip
Pack-age
Pack-cloth
Pad-dock
Pad-lock
Pain-ful
Pain-less
Pal-ace
Pal-ate
Pal-let
Pan-cake
Pan-tiles
Pa-pa
Pa-pal
Par-able

Pa-rent
Pa-ring
Par-snip
Par-son
Par-took
Part-ridge
Pass-able
Pass-over
Pas-time
Patch-work
Pa-tent
Path-way
Pat-ten
Peace-able
Pea-cock
Pear-led
Peer-age
Peer-less
Pen-knife
Pen-man
Pen-man-ship
Penny-worth
Per-jury
Pert-in-a-city
Pick-lock
Pick-pocket
Pie-bald
Pike-staff
Pill-age
Pin-cushion
Pine-apple
Pip-kin
Pitch-fork
Pit-men
Plain-tiff
Play-fellow
Play-game
Play-house
Play-wright
Plough-man
Plough-share
Pole-cat
Pol-lute
Pop-gun
Pop-in-jay
Port-able
Port-hole
Post-age
Post-chaise
Post-date
Post-house
Post-man
Post-office
Pot-ash
Pot-hook
Pound-age
Prim-rose

Prior-ship	Seam-less	Slip-board	Stream-let	Thread-bare	Wal-nut
Prop-a-gate	Seam-stress	Slip-shod	Strip-ling	Three-fold	Wan-ton
Punch-bowl	Sea-nymph	Slip-slop	Summer-house	Three-score	Ward-robe
Quad-rant	Sea-piece	Slope-wise	Sum-mary	Thresh-old	Ward-ship
Quench-less	Sea-port	Slow-worm	Summer-set	Through-out	Ward-mote
Quick-lime	Sea-sick	Snip-snap	Sun-beam	Thunder-struck	Ware-house
Quick-sand	Sea-son	Snip-pet	Sun-burnt	Thunder-bolt	War-fare
Quick-set	Sea-ward	Snow-ball	Sun-day	Till-age	War-like
Quick-silver	Second-hand	Snow-drop	Sun-dry	Tin-gent	War-rant
Rain-bow	Seed-cake	Snuff-box	Sun-flower	Tip-pet	Wash-ball
Ram-pant	Seed-ling	Sod-den	Sun-less	Tip-staff	Waste-ful
Ran-sack	Seed-pearl	Sol-ace	Sup-plant	Tire-some	Watch-ful
Rap-a-city	Seeds-man	So-lo	Sup-pliant	Title-page	Watch-man
Rasp-berry	Seed-time	Sol-vent	Sup-port	Toad-stool	Watch-word
Rattle-snake	Sex-tile	Some-body	Sup-port-able	Toil-some	Water-course
Rare-mouse	Sex-ton	Some-time	Sup-position	Tom-boy	Water-fall
Red-breast	Shame-less	Some-how	Sup-press	Tooth-ache	Water-fowl
Red-den	Sham-rock	Some-what	Swans-down	Top-knot	Water-man
Rid-dance	Shape-less	Some-where	Sweep-stake	Top-most	Water-mark
Ring-leader	Sharp-set	Song-stress	Sweet-bread	Top-sail,	Water-mill
Ring-let	Sheep-cot	Son-net	Sweet-briar	Touch-stone	Water-work
Ring-tail	Sheep-shearing	Southern-wood	Sweet-heart	Touch-wood	Way-lay
Ring-worm	Sheep-walk	Span-king	Sweet-william	Towns-man	Way-ward
Rolling-pin	Sheet-anchor	Spare-rib	Sweet-willow	Toy-shop	Weather-cock
Room-age	Shell-fish	Spar-row	Swine-herd	Track-less	Weather-glass
Rose-water	Shift-less	Speak-able	Sword-man	Trap-door	Weather-wise
Rot-ten	Ship-board	Speech-less	Tar-get	Tre-foil	Web-bed
Round-about	Ship-wreck	Spite-ful	Tar-tar	Trip-thong	Web-foot
Round-house	Shirt-less	Sports-man	Taw-dry	Trip-let	Wed-lock
Run-a-gate	Shoe-maker	Spot-less	Tax-able	Trod-den	Week-day
Rush-light	Shoe-string	Spring-halt	Tea-cup	Turn-pike	Wel-come
Safe-guard	Shop-board	Spruce-beer	Teem-ful	Turn-spit	Wel-fare
Sal-low	Shop-keeper	Stair-case	Teem-less	Turn-stile	Well-born
Sand-stone	Shop-man	Star-board	Tell-tale	Tutor-age	Well-bred
Sat-in	Shore-less	Star-gazer	Ten-able	Twelfth-tide	Wheel-wright
Sat-ire	Short-hand	Star-less	Ten-a-city	Twelfth-night	Where-at
Sauce-box	Short-lived	Star-light	Ten-ant	Two-fold	Where-by
Sauce-pan	Short-sighted	Star-like	Ten-dance	Two-pence	Whet-stone
Saw-dust	Shot-free	Star-ling	Ten-don	Vain-glory	Whip-cord
Saw-pit	Shoulder-belt	States-man	Ten-dril	Van-guard	Whip-hand
Scare-crow	Shrove-tide	Stead-fast	Ten-or	Vault-age	Whirl-pool
Scarf-skin	Side-board	Steel-yard	Thank-ful	Up-hill	Whirl-wind
Scar-let	Side-long	Steer-age	Thank-less	Up-hold	White-wash
School-fellow	Side-saddle	Step-dame	Them-selves	Up-braid	Whit-low
School-master	Side-ways	Step-daughter	Thence-forth	Up-land	Whit-sun-tide
School-mistress	Sight-less	Step-father	There-after	Up-right	Who-ever
Soot-free	Silk-weaver	Step-mother	There-at	Up-roar	Whole-sale
Screech-owl	Silk-worm	Steward-ship	There-by	Up-shot	Whole-some
Scul-lion	Silver-smith	Stiff-neck	There-fore	Up-ride	Wil-low
Sea-born	Sin-less	Still-born	There-from	Up-start	Wild-fire
Sea-calf	Six-fold	Stock-jobber	There-in	Up-ward	Wind-lass
Sea-coal	Skim-milk	Stone-fruit	There-on	Use-less	Wind-mill
Sea-faring	Skip-jack	Store-fruit	There-to	Wag-on	Wind-pipe
Sea-girt	Sky-lark	Store-house	There-with	Wag-tail	Win-now
Sea-gull	Sky-light	Stow-age	Thick-set	Wain-scot	Wise-acre
Sea-maid	Slap-dash	Strata-gem	Thought-ful	Waist-coat	Wit-less
Sea-man	Sleeve-less	Straw-berry	Thought-less	Wake-ful	Wolf-dog

Wood-cock	Work-house	Wrath-less
Wood-land	Work-man	Wrist-band
Wood-man	Work-shop	Writ-ten
Wood-note	Worm-wood	Year-ling
Wood-nymph	Wrath-ful	Youth-ful

54. ENIGMAS are compositions of a different character, based upon *ideas*, rather than upon words, and frequently constructed so as to mislead, and to surprise when the solution is made known. Enigmas may be founded upon simple catches, like Conundrums, in which form they are usually called RIDDLES, such as—

> "Though you set me on foot,
>   I shall be on my head."

The answer is, *A nail in a shoe.* The celebrated Enigma on the letter H, by Lord Byron, is an admirable specimen of what may be rendered in the form of an Enigma.

55. REBUSES are a class of Enigma generally formed by the first, sometimes the first and last, letters of words, or of transpositions of letters, or additions to words. Dr. Johnson, however, represents Rebus to be a word represented by a picture. And putting the Doctor's definition and our own explanation together, the reader may glean a good conception of the nature of the Rebus. Example :—

> The father of the Grecian Jove ;
>   A little boy who's blind ;
> The foremost land in all the world ;
>   The mother of mankind ;
> A poet whose love-sonnets are
>   Still very much admired ;—
> The *initial* letters will declare
>   A blessing to the tired.

Answer — *Saturn ; Love ; England ; Eve ; Plutarch. The initials form sleep.*

The excellent little work mentioned at page 21, entitled "Philosophy and Mirth united by Pen and Pencil," has this novelty, that many of the Enigmas are accompanied by enigmatical pictures, so that the eye is puzzled as well as the ear.

56. PUZZLES vary much. One of the simplest that we know is this :—

Take away half of *thirteen* and let *eight* remain.

Write XIII on a slate, or on a piece of paper—rub out the lower half of the figures, and VIII will remain.

57. Laws of Chess.—The rules given below are based upon the code published in "Walker's Art of Chess Play." The word *piece* frequently includes the *pawn*.

i. If the board or pieces be improperly placed, or are deficient in number (except in the case of odds), the game must be recommenced, if the error is discovered before the fourth move on each side (the eighth move of the game). If not discovered before this stage, the game must proceed.

ii. If a player give odds, and yet omit to remove the odds from the board at the commencement, he may recommence the game, and remove the odds given, provided he discover his error before playing his fourth move. But if he has made his fourth move, the game must be played out ; and should the player who agreed to give the odds win the game, it shall nevertheless be considered drawn.

iii. When parties play even, they draw lots for the first move of the first game. The first move is afterwards taken alternately throughout the sitting, except when a game is drawn, when he who had the first move in that game still claims it, a drawn game being of no account. He who gains the move has also the choice of colour. Each player uses the same colour throughout the sitting. When a match is made for a given number of games, the move passes alternately throughout the match. A player giving odds has the choice of men, and takes the move in every game, unless agreed to the contrary.

iv. A player who gives the odds of a piece, may give it each game from the king's or queen's side, at his option. If he gives the odds of a pawn, he must give the king's bishop's pawn, unless otherwise stipulated. The player who receives the odds of a certain number of moves at the commencement, must not with those moves cross from his own half of the board.

v. If a player, in his turn to play, touch one of his men, he must move that piece, if it can legally move, unless, when he first touches it, he says aloud, "*J'adoube*." No penalty is attached to touching a piece, unless it is your turn to move.

vi. If the player touch his king, with the intention of moving him, and then find that he cannot do so without placing the king in check, no penalty can be inflicted on his replacing his king and moving elsewhere. [Otherwise ?] If the player should touch a man which cannot be moved without placing his king in check, he must move his king instead.

vii. If a player about to move touch one of his adversary's men, without saying "*J'adoube*" when he first touches it, he must take that piece, if it can be lawfully taken. Should it not be taken, he must, as a penalty, move his king; but should the king be unable to play without going into check, no penalty can be enforced. It is not allowed to castle upon a compulsory move of the king.

viii. While you hold your piece you may move it anywhere allowed by the rules; but when you quit your hold the move is completed, and must be abided by.

ix. If you inadvertently move one of your adversary's pieces instead of your own, he may compel you to take the piece you have touched, should it be *en prise;* or to replace it and move your king, or to leave it on the square to which you have moved it, and forego any other move at that time. Should you capture one of the adverse pieces with another, instead of one of your own, the capture holds good, if your opponent so decides.

x. If the player takes a piece through a false move, his adversary may compel him to take such piece with one that can lawfully take it; or to move the piece that has been touched,

if such move does not expose the king to check; or he may be directed to move his king.

xi. If you take one of your own men, instead of one of your adversary's, you may be compelled to move one of the two pieces touched, at the option of your opponent. Mr. Walker thinks that the penalty should be to lose the man you have improperly taken off.

xii. An opponent has the option of punishing a false move, by claiming the false move as your move, by compelling you to move the piece touched, as you may think fit, or to replace the piece and move your king.

xiii. The king must never be exposed to check by any penalty enforced.

xiv. If you move twice running, you may be compelled to abide by both moves, or to retract the second.

xv. Unlimited time is allowed for the moves [unless otherwise agreed]. If one player insists upon the postponement of the termination of a game, against the will of his opponent, the game is forfeited by him who will not play on.

xvi. When a pawn is moved two squares, it is liable to be taken, *en passant*, by a pawn, but not by a piece.

xvii. If you touch both king and rook, intending to castle, you must move one of the two pieces, at the option of your adversary; or he may compel you to complete the castling. You cannot take a piece and castle at the same time; nor does the rook check as it passes to its new position; but it may check on its position after castling.

xviii. False castling is liable to the same penalties as a false move.

xix. When a player gives the odds of a rook, he does not relinquish the right of castling on the side from which the rook has been taken, all other conditions being lawful, as if the rook were in its place.

xx. When you give check you must say so aloud. If check is not called on either side, but subsequently discovered, you must endeavour to recall all the moves back to the period when the check first occurred.

xxi. You are not compelled to cry check when you attack the queen.

xxii. If you cry check, and afterwards alter your determination, you are not compelled to abide by the intention, provided you have not touched the piece.

xxiii. When a pawn reaches the opposite side of the board it may be replaced by any piece, at the option of the owner, and irrespective of the pieces already owned by him.

xxiv. Stall mate is a drawn game.

xxv. Drawn games count for nothing; and he who moved first in the drawn game moves first in the following.

xxvi. If you declare to win a game, or position, and only draw it, you are accounted the loser.

xxvii. When you have either of the following advantages of force, you are compelled to give check-mate in fifty moves, or the game is considered drawn.

King and queen against king.
King and rook against king.
King and two bishops against king.
King, bishop, and knight, against king.
King and queen against king and rook.
King and rook against king and minor piece.
King and pawn against king.
King and two pawns against king and pawn.

xxviii. If you move after your adversary has made a false move, or committed other irregularity, you cannot claim the penalties.

xxix. Spectators are forbidden to make remarks.

xxx. Disputes to be referred to a third party.

58. Rules of the Game of Draughts.—The nine laws for regulating the game of draughts are as follows:—

i. Each player takes the first move alternately, whether the last game be won or drawn.

ii. Any action which prevents the adversary from having a full view of the men is not allowed.

iii. The player who touches a man must play him.

iv. In case of standing the huff, which means omitting to take a man when an opportunity for so doing occurred, the other party may either take the man, or insist upon his man, which has been so omitted by his adversary, being taken.

v. If either party, when it is his turn to move, hesitate above three minutes, the other may call upon him to play; and if, after that, he delay above five minutes longer, then he loses the game.

vi. In the losing game, the player can insist upon his adversary taking all the men, in case opportunities should present themselves for their being so taken.

vii. To prevent unnecessary delay, if one colour have no pieces, but two kings on the board, and the other no piece, but one king, the latter can call upon the former to win the game in twenty moves; if he does not finish it within that number of moves, the game to be relinquished as drawn.

viii. If there are three kings to two on the board, the subsequent moves are not to exceed forty.

59. Whist.—(Upon the principles of Hoyle's games.) — Great silence and attention must be observed by the players. Four persons cut for partners; the two highest are against the two lowest. The partners sit opposite to each other, and the person who cuts the lowest card is entitled to the deal. The ace is the lowest in cutting.

i. SHUFFLING.—Each person has a right to shuffle the cards before the deal; but it is usual for the elder hand only, and the dealer after.

ii. CUTTING.—The pack is then cut by the right hand adversary; and the dealer distributes the cards, one by one, to each of the players, beginning with the person who sits on his left hand, until he comes to the last card, which he turns up, being the trump, and leaves on the table till the first trick is played.

iii. FIRST PLAY.—The person on the left hand side of the dealer is called the elder, and plays first; whoever wins the trick becomes elder hand, and plays again; and so on, till all the cards are played out.

iv. MISTAKES.—No intimations, or signs of any kind, during the play of the cards, are permitted between the partners. The mistake of one party is the game of the adversary, except in a revoke, when the partners may inquire if he has any of the suit in his hand.

v. COLLECTING TRICKS.—The tricks belonging to each party should be turned and collected by the respective partners of whoever wins the first trick in every hand. All above six tricks reckon towards the game.

vi. HONOURS.—The ace, king, queen, and knave of trumps are called honours; and when either of the partners have three separately, or between them, they count two points towards the game; and in case they have four honours, they count four points.

vii. GAME.—The *game consists of ten points.*

60. TERMS USED IN WHIST. —*Finessing*, is the attempt to gain an advantage; thus:— If you have the best and third best card of the suit led, you put on the third best, and run the risk of your adversary having the second best; if he has it not, which is two to one against him, you are then certain of gaining a trick.

Forcing, is playing the suit of which your partner or adversary has not any, and which he must trump, in order to win.

Long Trump, means the having one or more trumps in your hand when all the rest are out.

Loose Card, means a card in hand of no value, and the most proper to throw away.

Points.—Ten make the game; as many as are gained by tricks or honours, so many points are set up to the score of the game.

Quart, is four successive cards in any suit.

Quart Major, is a sequence of ace, king, queen, and knave.

Quint, is five successive cards in any suit.

Quint Major, is a sequence of ace, king, queen, knave, and ten.

See-saw, is when each partner turns a suit, and when they play those suits to each other for that purpose.

Score, is the number of points set up. The following is the most approved method of scoring:—

1	2	3	4	5	6	7	8	9
				0	0	00	000	0
0	00	000	0000	00	000	0	0	0
								0

Slam, is when either party win every trick.

Tenace, is possessing the first and third best cards, and being the last player; you consequently catch the adversary when that suit is played: as, for instance, in case you have ace and queen of any suit, and your adversary leads that suit, you must win two tricks, by having the best and third best of the suit played, and being the last player.

Tierce, is three successive cards in any suit.

Tierce Major, is a sequence of ace, king, and queen.

61. RULES FOR PLAYING WHIST. —i. Lead from your strong suit, and be cautious how you change suits; and keep a commanding card to bring it in again.

ii. Lead through the strong suit and up to the weak; but not in trumps, unless very strong in them.

iii. Lead the highest of a sequence; but if you have a quart or cinque to a king, lead the lowest.

iv. Lead through an honour, particularly if the game is much against you.

v. Lead your best trump, if the adversaries be eight, and you have no honour; but not if you have four trumps, unless you have a sequence.

vi. Lead a trump if you have four or five, or a strong hand; but not if weak.

vii. Having ace, king, and two or three small cards, lead ace and king if weak in trumps, but a small one if strong in them.

viii. If you have the last trump, with some winning cards, and one losing card only, lead the losing card.

ix. Return your partner's lead, not the adversaries'; and if you have only three originally, play the best; but you need not return it immediately, when you win with a king, queen, or knave, and have only small ones, or when you hold a good sequence, have a strong suit, or have five trumps.

x. Do not lead from ace queen, or ace knave.

xi. Do not lead an ace, unless you have a king.

xii. Do not lead a thirteenth card, unless trumps be out.

xiii. Do not trump a thirteenth card, unless you be last player, or want the lead.

xiv. Keep a small card to return your partner's lead.

xv. Be cautious in trumping a card when strong in trumps, particularly if you have a strong suit.

xvi. Having only a few small trumps, make them when you can.

xvii. If your partner refuses to trump a suit, of which he knows you have not the best, lead your best trump.

xviii. When you hold all the remaining trumps, play one, and then try to put the lead in your partner's hand.

xix. Remember how many of each suit are out, and what is the best card left in each hand.

xx. Never force your partner if you are weak in trumps, unless you have a renounce, or want the odd trick.

xxi. When playing for the odd trick, be cautious of trumping out, especially if your partner be likely to trump a suit; and make all the tricks you can early, and avoid finessing.

xxii. If you take a trick, and have a sequence, win it with the lowest.

62. LAWS OF WHIST.—DEALING.—i. If a card be turned up in dealing, the adverse party may call a new deal, unless they have been the cause; then the dealer has the option.

ii. If a card be faced in the deal, the dealer must deal again, unless it be the last deal.

iii. If any one play with twelve cards, and the rest have thirteen, the deal to stand good, and the player to be punished for each revoke; but if any have fourteen cards, the deal is lost.

iv. The dealer to leave the trump card on the table till his turn to play; after which none may ask what card was turned up, only what is trumps.

v. No person may take up the cards while dealing; if the dealer in that case should miss the deal, to deal again, unless his partner's fault; and if a card be turned up in dealing, no new deal, unless the partner's fault.

vi. If the dealer put the trump card on the rest, with face downwards, he is to lose the deal.

63. PLAYING OUT OF TURN.—vii. If any person play out of his turn, the adversary may call the card played at any time, if he do not make him revoke; or if either of the adverse party be to lead, may desire his partner to name the suit, which must be played.

viii. If a person supposes he has won the trick, and leads again before his partner has played, the adversary may oblige his partner to win it, if he can.

ix. If a person lead, and his partner play before his turn, the adversary's partner may do the same.

x. If the ace, or any other card of a suit, be led, and any person play out of turn, whether his partner have any of the suit led or not, he is neither to trump it nor win it, provided he do not revoke.

64. REVOKING.—xi. If a revoke happen to be made, the adversary may add three to their score, or take three tricks from them, or take down three from their score; and, if up, must remain at nine.

xii. If any person revoke, and, before the cards be turned, discover it, the adversary may cause the highest or lowest of the suit led, or call the card then played at any time, if it do not cause a revoke.

xiii. No revoke to be claimed till the trick be turned and quitted, or the party who revoked, or his partner, have played again.

xiv. If any person claim a revoke, the adverse party are not to mix their cards, upon forfeiting the revoke.

xv. No revoke can be claimed after the cards are cut for a new deal.

CALLING HONOURS.—xvi. If any person call, except at the point of eight, the adverse party may consult, and have a new deal.

xvii. After the trump card is turned up, no person may remind his partner to call, on penalty of losing one point.

xviii. If the trump card be turned up, no honours can be set up unless before claimed; and scoring honours, not having them, to be scored against them.

xix. If any person call at eight, and be answered, and the opposite parties have thrown down their cards, and it appear they have not their honours, they may consult, and have a new deal or not.

xx. If any person answer without an honour, the adversaries may consult, and stand the deal or not.

xxi. If any person call at eight, after he has played, the adversaries may call a new deal.

65. SEPARATING AND SHOWING THE CARDS.—xxii. If any person separate a card from the rest, the adverse party may call it if he name it; but if he call a wrong card, he or his partner are liable, for once, to have the highest or lowest card called in any suit led during that deal.

xxiii. If any person throw his cards on the table, supposing the game lost, he may not take them up, and the adversaries may call them, provided he do not revoke.

xxiv. If any person be sure of winning every trick in his hand, he may show his cards, but is liable to have them called.

OMITTING TO PLAY TO A TRICK.— xxv. If any person omit to play to a trick, and it appear he has one card more than the rest, it shall be at the option of the adversary to have a new deal.

RESPECTING WHO PLAYED A PARTICULAR CARD.—xxvi. Each person ought to lay his card before him; and if either of the adversaries mix their cards with his, his partner may demand each person to lay his card before him, but not to inquire who played any particular card.

These laws are agreed to by the best judges.

66. MAXIMS FOR WHIST.— LEADER.—i. Begin with the suit of which you have most in number; for, when the trumps are out, you will probably make several tricks by it.

ii. If you hold equal numbers in different suits, begin with the strongest, because it is the least liable to injure your partner.

iii. Sequences are always eligible leads, as supporting your partner without injuring your own hand.

iv. Lead from a king or queen, rather than from an ace; for, since the adversaries will lead from those suits which you do not, your ace will do them most harm.

v. Lead from a king rather than a queen, and from a queen rather than from a knave; for the stronger the suit, the less is your partner endangered.

vi. Lead not from ace queen, or ace knave, till necessary; for, if that suit be led by the adversaries, you have a good chance of making two tricks in it.

vii. In all sequences to a queen, knave, or ten, begin with the highest, because it will frequently distress your left-hand adversary.

viii. Having ace, king, and knave,

lead the king; for, if strong in trumps, you may wait the return of this suit, and finesse the knave.

ix. Having ace, queen, and one small card, lead the small one; for, by this lead, your partner has a chance to make the knave.

x. Having ace, king, and two or three small cards, play ace and king if weak, but a small card if strong in trumps: you may give your partner the chance of making the first trick.

xi. Having king, queen, and one small card, play the small one; for your partner has an equal chance to win, and you need not fear to make king or queen.

xii. Having king, queen, and two or three small cards, lead a small card if strong, and the king if weak in trumps; for strength in trumps entitles you to play a backward game, and give your partner a chance of winning the first trick; but if weak in trumps, lead the king or queen, to secure a trick in that suit.

xiii. Having an ace, with four small cards, and no other good suit, play a small card if strong in trumps, and the ace if weak; for strength in trumps may enable you to make one or two of the small cards, although your partner cannot support the lead.

xiv. Having king, knave, and ten, lead the ten; for, if your partner hold the ace, you have a good chance to make three tricks, whether he pass the ten or not.

xv. Having king, queen, and ten, lead the king; for, if it fail, by putting on the ten, upon the return of that suit from your partner, you have a chance of making two tricks.

xvi. Having queen, knave, and nine, lead the queen; for, upon the return of that suit from your partner, by putting on the nine, you will, probably, make the knave.

67. SECOND HAND.—i. Having ace, king, and small ones, play a small card if strong in trumps, but the king if weak in them; for, otherwise, your ace or king might be trumped in the latter

case, and no hazards should be run with few trumps but in critical cases.

ii. Having ace, queen, and small cards, play a small one, for, upon the return of that suit, you will, probably, make two tricks.

iii. Having ace, knave, and small cards, play a small one, for, upon the return of the suit, you will, perhaps, make two tricks.

iv. Having ace, ten, or nine, with small cards, play a small one, for, by this method, you have a chance of making two tricks in the suit.

v. Having king, queen, ten, and small cards, play the queen; for, by playing the ten upon the return of the suit, you will, probably, make two tricks in it.

vi. Having king, queen, and small cards, play a small card if strong in trumps, but the queen if weak in them; for strength in trumps warrants playing a backward game, and it is always advantageous to keep back your adversaries' suit.

vii. If you hold a sequence to your highest card in the suit, play the lowest of it, for, by this means, your partner will be informed of your strength.

viii. Having queen, knave, and small ones, play the knave, because you will, probably, secure a trick.

ix. Having queen, ten, and small ones, play a small one, for your partner has an equal chance to win.

x. Having either ace, king, queen, or knave, with small cards, play a small one, for your partner has an equal chance to win the trick.

xi. Having either ace, king, queen, or knave, with one small card only, play the small one, for, otherwise, your adversary will finesse upon you.

xii. If a queen be led, and you hold the king, put that on, for if your partner hold the ace, you do no harm; and, if the king be taken, the adversaries have played two honours to one.

xiii. If a king be led, and you hold ace, knave, and small ones, play the ace, for it cannot do the adversary a greater injury.

68. THIRD HAND.—i. Having ace and king, play the ace and return the king, because you should not keep the command of your partner's strong suit.

ii. Having ace and queen, play the ace, and return the queen; for, although it may prove better in some cases to put on the queen, yet, in general, your partner is best supported by this method.

iii. Having ace and knave, play the ace and return the knave, in order to strengthen your partner's hand.

iv. Having king and knave, play the king; and, if it win, return the knave, for the reason in No. iii.

v. Always play the best when your partner plays a small card, as it best supports your partner.

vi. If you hold the ace and one small card only, and your partner lead the king, put on the ace, and return the small one; for, otherwise, your ace will be an obstruction to his suit.

vii. If you hold the king and one small card only, and your partner lead the ace, if the trumps be out, play the king; for, by putting on the king, there will be no obstruction to the suit.

69. FOURTH HAND.—i. If a king be led, and you hold ace, knave, and a small card, play the small one; for, supposing the queen to follow, you probably make both ace and knave.

ii. When the third hand is weak in his partner's lead, you may often return that suit to great advantage; but this rule must not be applied to trumps, unless you are very strong indeed.

70. CASES IN WHICH YOU SHOULD RETURN YOUR PARTNER'S LEAD IMMEDIATELY.—i. When you win with the ace and can return an honour, for that will greatly strengthen his hand.

ii. When he leads a trump, in which case return the best remaining in your hand (unless you held four originally), except the lead be through an honour.

iii. When your partner has trumped out; for then it is evident he wants to make his great suit.

iv. When you have no good card in any other suit; for then you entirely depend on your partner.

71. CASES IN WHICH YOU SHOULD NOT RETURN YOUR PARTNER'S LEAD IMMEDIATELY.—i. If you win with the king, queen, or knave, and have only small cards left; for the return of a small card will more distress than strengthen your partner.

ii. If you hold a good sequence; for then you may shew a strong suit, and not injure his hand.

iii. If you have a strong suit; because leading from a strong suit directs your partner, and cannot injure him.

iv. If you have a good hand; for, in this case, you ought to consult your own hand.

v. If you hold five trumps; for then you are warranted to play trumps, if you think it right.

72. LEADING TRUMPS.—i. Lead trumps from a strong hand, but never from a weak one, by which means you will secure your good cards from being trumped.

ii. Trump not out with a bad hand, although you hold five small trumps; for, since your cards are bad, it is only trumping for the adversaries' good ones.

iii. Having ace, king, knave, and three small trumps, play ace and king; for the probability of the queen's falling is in your favour.

iv. Having ace, king, knave, and one or two small trumps, play the king, and wait the return from your partner to put on the knave, in order to win the queen; but, if you particularly wish the trumps out, play two rounds, and then your strong suit.

v. Having ace, king, and two or three small trumps, lead a small one; this is to let your partner win the first trick; but if you have good reason for getting out the trumps, play three rounds, or play ace and king, and then proceed with your strong suit.

vi. If your adversaries be eight, and you do not hold an honour, throw off your best trump, for, if your partner has not two honours, you have lost the game; and if he holds two honours, it is most advantageous to lead a trump.

vii. Having ace, queen, knave, and small trumps, play the knave; for, by this means, the king only can make against you.

viii. Having ace, queen, ten, and one or two small trumps, lead a small one, for it will give your partner a chance to win the trick, and keep the command in your own hand.

ix. Having king, queen, ten, and small trumps, lead the king; for, if the king be lost, upon the return of trumps you may finesse the ten.

x. Having king, knave, ten, and small ones, lead the knave, because it will prevent the adversaries from making a small trump.

xi. Having queen, knave, nine, and small trumps, lead the queen; for, if your partner hold the ace, you have a good chance of making the whole suit.

xii. Having queen, knave, and two or three small trumps, lead the queen, for the reason in No. xi.

xiii. Having knave, ten, eight, and small trumps, lead the knave; for, on the return of trumps, you probably may finesse the eight to advantage.

xiv. Having knave, ten, and three small trumps, lead the knave, because it will most distress your adversaries, unless two honours are held on your right hand; the odds against which are about three to one.

xv. Having only small trumps, play the highest; by which you will support your partner all you can.

xvi. Having a sequence, begin with the highest; by this means, your partner is best instructed how to play his hand, and cannot possibly be injured.

xvii. If any honour be turned up on your left, and the game much against you, lead a trump the first opportunity; for, your game being desperately bad, this method is the most likely to retrieve it.

xviii. In all other cases it is dangerous leading through an honour, unless you be strong in trumps, or have a good hand; because all the advantage of trumping through an honour lies in your partner's finessing.

xix. Supposing it hereafter proper to lead trumps, when an honour is turned up on your left, you, holding only one honour, with a small trump, play the honour, and next the small one; because it will greatly strengthen your partner's hand, and cannot hurt your own.

xx. If an honour be turned up on the left, and you hold a sequence, lead the highest of it, because it will prevent the last hand from injuring your partner.

xxi. If a queen be turned up on the left, and you hold ace, king, and a small one, lead the small trump, because you will have a chance of getting the queen.

xxii. If a queen be turned up on the left, and you hold a knave, with small ones, lead the knave; for the knave cannot be of service, as the queen is on your left.

xxiii. If an honour be turned up by your partner, and you are strong in trumps, lead a small one; but if weak in them, lead the best you have; by this play the weakest hand will support the strongest.

xxiv. If an ace be turned up on the right, you holding king, queen, and knave, lead the knave: a secure lead.

xxv. If an ace be turned up on the right, and you hold king, queen, and ten, lead the king, and upon the return of trumps play the ten; for, by this means, you show a great strength to your partner, and will, probably, make two tricks in them.

xxvi. If a king be turned up on the right, and you hold queen, knave, and nine, lead knave, and, upon the return of trumps, play the nine, because it may prevent the ten from making.

xxvii. If a king be turned up on your right, and you hold knave, ten, and nine, lead the nine, and, upon the return of trumps, play the ten; because this method will best disclose your strength in trumps.

xxviii. If a queen be turned up on

the right, and you hold ace, king, and knave, lead the king, and, upon the return of trumps, play the knave, because you are then certain to make the knave.

xxix. If a queen be turned up on the right, and you hold ace, king, and small ones, lead the king; and, upon the return of trumps, you may finesse, unless the queen falls, for, otherwise, the queen will make a trick.

xxx. If a knave be turned up on the right, and you hold king, queen, and ten, lead the queen, and, upon the return of trumps, play the ten; for, by this means, you will make the ten.

xxxi. If a knave be turned up on the right, and you hold king, queen, and small ones, lead the king; and, if that come home, play a small one, for it is probable your partner holds the ace.

xxxii. If a knave be turned up on the right, and you hold king and ten or queen and ten, with two small cards, lead a small one; and, upon the return of trumps, play the ten, for it is five to four that your partner holds one honour.

73. WHEN YOU TURN UP AN HONOUR IN WHIST.—i. If you turn up an ace, and hold only one small trump with it, if either adversary lead the king, put on the ace.

ii. But, if you turn up an ace, and hold two or three small trumps with it, and either adversary lead the king, put on a small one; for, if you play the ace, you give up the command in trumps.

iii. If you turn up the king, and hold only one small trump with it, and your right-hand adversary lead a trump, play the king.

iv. If you turn up a king, and hold two or three small trumps with it, if your right-hand adversary lead a trump, play a small one.

v. If you turn up a queen or knave, and hold, besides, only small trumps, if your right-hand adversary lead a trump, put on a small one.

vi. If you hold a sequence to the honour turned up, play it last.

74. PLAYING FOR THE ODD TRICK.

—i. Be cautious of trumping out, notwithstanding you have a good hand.

ii. Never trump out, if your partner appears likely to trump a suit.

iii. If you are moderately strong in trumps, force your partner, for by this you probably make a trick.

iv. Make your tricks early, and be cautious of finessing.

v. If you hold a single card of any suit, and only two or three small trumps, lead the single card.

75. CALCULATIONS OF WHIST. — i. It is about five to four that your partner holds one card out of any two.

ii. It is about five to two that he holds one card out of three.

iii. It is about four to one that he holds one card out of any four.

iv. It is two to one that he does not hold a certain card.

v. It is about three to one that he does not hold two cards out of any three.

vi. It is about three to two that he does not hold two cards out of any four.

76. Cribbage.—The game of Cribbage differs from all other games by its immense variety of chances. It is reckoned useful to young people in the science of calculation. It is played with the whole pack of cards, generally by two persons, and sometimes by four. There are also five different modes of playing—that is, with five, six, or eight cards; but the games are principally those with five and six cards. The rules vary a little in different companies, but the following are those most generally observed :—

77. TERMS USED IN CRIBBAGE.— i. *Crib.*—The crib is composed of the cards thrown away by each party, and the dealer is entitled to score whatever points are made by them.

ii. *Pairs* are two similar cards, as two aces or two kings. Whether in hand or playing they reckon for two points.

iii. *Pairs-Royal* are three similar cards, and reckon for six points, whether in hand or playing.

iv. *Double Pairs-Royal* are four similar

cards, and reckon for twelve points, whether in hand or playing. The points gained by pairs, pairs-royal, and double pairs-royal, in playing, are thus effected: — Your adversary having played a seven and you another, constitutes a pair, and entitles you to score two points; your antagonist then playing a third seven, makes a pair-royal, and he marks six; and your playing a fourth is a double pair-royal, and entitles you to twelve points.

v. *Fifteens.*—Every fifteen reckons for two points, whether in hand or playing. In hand they are formed either by two cards, such as a five and any tenth card, a six and a nine, a seven and an eight, or by three cards, as a two, a five, and an eight, &c. And in playing thus, if such cards are played as make together fifteen, the two points are to be scored towards the game.

vi. *Sequences* are three or four more successive cards, and reckon for an equal number of points, either in hand or play. In playing a sequence, it is of no consequence which card is thrown down first; as thus :—your adversary playing an ace, you a five, he a three, you a two, then he a four, he counts five for the sequence.

vii. *Flush.*—When the cards are all of one suit, they reckon for as many points as there are cards. For a flush in the crib, the card turned up must be of the same suit as those put out in the crib.

viii. *Noddy.*—The knave of the suit turned up reckons for one point; if a knave be turned up, the dealer is to mark two; but it cannot be reckoned again; and when played it does not score anything.

ix. *End Hole.*—The point scored by the last player, if he makes under thirty-one; if he makes thirty-one exactly, he is to mark two. To obtain either of these is considered a great advantage.

x. *Last.*—Three points taken at the commencement of the game of five-card cribbage by the non-dealer.

78. RULES OF CRIBBAGE. — i. The adverse parties cut the cards to determine who shall be dealer; the lowest card has it. The ace is the lowest.

ii. In dealing, the dealer may discover his own cards, but not those of his adversary—who may mark two, and call a fresh deal.

iii. Should too many cards be dealt to either, the non-dealer may score two, and demand another deal, if the error be detected previous to taking up the cards; if he do not wish a new deal, the extra cards must be drawn away. When any player has more than the proper number of cards in hand, the opponent may score four, and call a new deal.

iv. If any player meddle with the pack after dealing, till the period of cutting it for the turn-up card, then his opponent may score two points.

v. If any player take more than he is entitled to, the other party should not only put him back as many points as are overscored, but likewise take the same extra number for his own game.

vi. Should either party even meddle with his own pegs unnecessarily, the opponent may score two points; and if any one take out his front peg, he must place the same back behind the other. If any be misplaced by accident, a by-stander may replace the same, according to the best of his judgment; but he should never otherwise interfere.

vii. If any player neglect to set up what he is entitled to, the adversary is allowed to take the points so omitted.

viii. Each player may place his own cards, when done with, upon the pack.

ix. In five-card cribbage, the cards are to be dealt one by one; but when played with six cards, then it is customary to give three, and if with eight cards, four at a time.

x. The non-dealer, at the commencement of the game, in five-card cribbage, scores three points, called *three for last ;* but in six and eight-card cribbage this is not to be done.

xi. In what is called the Bath game, they reckon flushes upon the board; that is, when three cards of the same suit are played successively, the party playing the third scores three points; if the adversary play a fourth of the same suit, then he is to score four, and so on for four, five, six, or as long as the same suit continues to be played in uninterrupted succession, and that the whole number of pips do not reckon thirty-one.

79. FIVE - CARD CRIBBAGE. — It is unnecessary to describe cribbage-boards; the sixty-one points or holes marked thereon make the game. We have before said that the party cutting the lowest card deals; after which, each player is first to lay out two of the five cards for the crib, which always belongs to the dealer; next, the adversary is to cut the remainder of the pack, and the dealer to turn up and lay upon the crib the uppermost card, for which, if a knave, he is to mark two points. The card turned up is to be reckoned by both parties, whether in showing their hands or crib. After laying out and cutting as above mentioned, the eldest hand is to play a card, which the other should endeavour to pair, or find one, the pips of which, reckoned with the first, will make fifteen; then the non-dealer must play another card, and try to make a pair, pair-royal, sequence, flush (where allowed of), or fifteen, provided the cards already played have not exceeded that number; and so on alternately, until the pips on the cards played make thirty-one, or the nearest possible number under that.

80. COUNTING FOR GAME.—When the party, whose turn it may be to play, cannot produce a card that will make thirty-one, or come under that number, he is then to say "Go" to his antagonist, who, thereupon, will be entitled to score one, or must play any card or cards he may have that will make thirty-one, or under; and if he can make exactly thirty-one, he is to take two points; if not, one: the last player has often opportunity this way to make pairs or sequences. Such cards as remain after this are not to be played; but each party having, during the play, scored his points gained, in the manner before directed, must proceed, the non-dealer first to count and take for his hand, then the dealer for his hand, and also for his crib, reckoning the cards every way they can possibly be varied, and always including the turned-up card. Points.

For every fifteen 2
Pair, or two of a sort . . . 2
Pair-royal, or three of a sort . 6
Double pair-royal, or four ditto 12
Knave of the turned-up suit . 1
Sequences and flushes, whatever number.

81. MAXIMS FOR LAYING OUT THE CRIB CARDS.—It is always requisite, in laying out cards for the crib, that every player should consider not only his own hand, but also to whom the crib belongs, as well as the state of the game; for what might be proper in one situation would be highly imprudent in another. When any player possesses a pair-royal, it is generally advisable to lay out the other cards for crib, unless it belongs to the adversary, and they consist of two fives, a deuce and a trois, five and six, seven and eight, five and any other tenth card, or that the game be almost finished. A player, when he does not thereby materially injure his hand, should for his own crib lay out close cards, in hope of making a sequence; or two of a suit, in expectation of a flush; or any that of themselves amount to fifteen, or such as reckoned with others will make that number, except when the antagonist be nearly up, and it may be expedient to keep such cards as probably may prevent him from gaining at play. The opposite method should be pursued in respect to the adversary's crib, which each person should endeavour to baulk, by laying out those cards that are not likely to prove to advantage, unless at such a stage of the game when it may be of consequence to keep in hand cards likely to tell in play, or when the non-dealer would be either out by his hand, or has reason for judging the crib of little moment. A king is the best card to baulk a crib, as none can form a sequence beyond it, except in some companies, where king, queen, ace, are allowed as a sequence; and either a king or queen, with an ace, six, seven, eight, or nine, are good ones to put out. Low cards are generally the most likely to gain at play; the flushes and sequences, particularly if the latter be also flushes, constitute the most eligible hands, as thereby the player will often be enabled either to assist his own crib, or baulk that of the opponent, to whom a knave should never be given, if with propriety it can be retained.

82. THREE OR FOUR-HAND CRIBBAGE differs only from the preceding, as the parties put out but one card each to the crib, and when thirty-one, or the nearest approximating number has been made, then the next eldest hand leads, and the players go on again in rotation, with any remaining cards, till all are played out, before they proceed to show. For three-hand cribbage triangular boards are used.

83. THREE-HAND CRIBBAGE is sometimes played, wherein one person sits out, not each game, but each deal, in rotation. In this the first dealer generally wins. The chances in this game are often so great, that even between skilful gamesters it is possible, at five-card cribbage, when the adversary is fifty-six, for a lucky player, who had not previously made a single hole, to be more than up in two deals, his opponent getting no farther than sixty in that time; and in four-hand cribbage a case may occur, wherein none of the parties hold a single point in hand, and yet the dealer and his friend, with the assistance of a knave turned up, may make sixty-one by play in one deal, while the adversaries only get twenty-four; and although this may not happen for many years, yet similar games may now and then be met with.

84. SIX-CARD CRIBBAGE varies from that played with five, as the players (always only two) commence on an equality, without scoring any points for the last, retain four cards in hand, and all the cards are to be played out, as in three and four-hand cribbage, with five cards. At this game it is of advantage to the last player to keep as close as possible, in hopes of coming in for fifteen, a sequence, or pair, besides the end hole, or thirty-one. The first dealer is reckoned to have some trifling advantage, and each player may, on the average, expect to make twenty-five points in every two deals. The first non-dealer is considered to have the preference, when he gains ten or more the first hand, the dealer not making more than his average number.

85. THE GREATEST POSSIBLE NUMBER that can be gained by the show of any hand or crib, either in five or six-card cribbage, is twenty-nine; it is composed of three fives and a knave, with a fourth five, of the same suit as the knave, turned up; this very seldom happens; but twenty-four is an uncommon number, and may be formed of four threes and a nine, or two fours, one five, and two sixes; and some other combinations that experience will point out.

86. EIGHT-CARD CRIBBAGE is sometimes played, but very seldom.

87. HACKNEY COACH CRIBBAGE.— Some ingenious people in London invented a game of chance which they styled playing at cribbage by hackney coaches; that is, two persons placed themselves at a window in some crowded thoroughfare, one would take all the coaches from the right, the other from the left; the figures on the doors of the carriages were reckoned as cards in show, and every person that happened to sit, stand, or hold at the back of any of them, was called a noddy, and scored one.

88. ODDS OF THE GAME OF CRIBBAGE.—The average number estimated to be held from the cards in hand is rather more than four, and under five; to be gained in play, two for the dealer, and one for the adversary, making in all an average of six throughout the game; the probability of the crib is five; so that each player ought to make sixteen in two deals: by which it will appear the dealer has somewhat the advantage, supposing the cards to run equal, and the players well matched. By attending to this calculation, any person may judge whether he be at home or not, and thereby play his game accordingly; either making a grand push when he is behind and holds good cards, or endeavouring to baulk his adversary when his hand proves indifferent.

89. All-Fours is usually played by two persons; not unfrequently by four. Its name is derived from the four chances, called *high, low, Jack, game,* each making a point. A complete pack of cards must be provided, six of which are to be dealt to each party, three at a time; and the next card, the thirteenth, is to be turned up for the trump by the dealer, who, if it prove a knave, is to score one point. The party who cuts the highest card is to deal first. The cards rank in the same manner as at whist, for whoever scores the first ten points wins.

90. LAWS OF ALL-FOURS.—i. A new deal can be demanded, if in dealing the dealer discovers any of the adversary's cards; if, to either party, too many cards have been dealt: in the latter case, it is optional with the parties, provided it be done before a card has been played, but not after, to draw from the opposing hand the extra card.

ii. If the dealer expose any of his own cards, the deal is to stand good.

iii. No person can beg more than once in each hand, except by mutual agreement.

iv. Each party must trump or follow suit if they can, on penalty of the adversary scoring one point.

v. If either player score wrong, it must be taken down, and the adversary shall either score four points or one, as may have previously been agreed.

vi. When a trump is played, it is allowable to ask your adversary if it be either high or low.

vii. One card may count all-fours; for example, the eldest hand holds the knave and stands his game, the dealer has neither trump, ten, ace, nor court-card; it will follow that the knave will be both high, low, Jack, and game, as explained by—

91. TERMS USED IN ALL-FOURS.—i. *High.*—The highest trump out, the holder to score one point.

ii. *Low.*—The lowest trump out, the original holder to score one point, even if it be taken by the adversary.

iii. *Jack.*—The knave of trumps, the holder to score one, unless it be won by the adversary, in that case the winner is to score the point.

iv. *Game.*—The greatest number that, in the tricks gained, can be shown by either party, reckoning—

Four for an ace.	*One* for a knave.
Three for a king.	*Ten* for a ten.
Two for a queen	

The other cards do not count: thus it may happen that a deal may be played without having any to reckon for game.

v. *Begging* is when the eldest hand, disliking his cards, uses his privilege, and says, " *I beg;*" in which case the dealer must either suffer his adversary to score one point, saying, " *Take one,*" or give each three cards more from the pack, and then turn up the next card, the seventh, for trumps; if, however, the trump turned up be of the same suit as the first, the dealer must go on, giving each three cards more, and turning up the seventh, until a change of suit for trumps shall take place.

92. MAXIMS FOR ALL-FOURS. — i. Always make your knave as soon as you can.

ii. Strive to secure your tens: this is to be done by playing any small cards, by which you may throw the lead into your adversary's hand.

iii. Win your adversary's best cards when you can, either by trumping or with superior cards.

iv. If, being eldest hand, you hold either ace, king, or queen of trumps, without the knave or ten, play them immediately, as, by this means, you have a chance to win the knave or ten.

93. Domino. — DESCRIPTION OF THE GAME.—This game is played by two or four persons, with twenty-eight pieces of oblong ivory, plain at the back, but on the face divided by a black line in the middle, and indented with spots, from one to a double-six, which pieces are a double-blank, ace-blank, double-ace, deuce-blank, deuce-ace, double-deuce, trois-blank, trois-ace, trois-deuce, double-trois, four-blank, four-ace, four-deuce, four trois, double-four, five-blank, five-ace, five-deuce, five-trois, five-four, double-five, six-blank, six-ace, six-deuce, six-trois, six-four, six-five, and double-six. Sometimes a double set is played with, of which double-twelve is the highest.

94. METHOD OF PLAYING DOMINOES.—At the commencement of the game the dominoes are well mixed together, with their faces upon the table. Each person draws one, and if four play, those who choose the two highest are partners against those who take the two lowest; drawing the latter also serves to determine who is to lay down the first piece, which is reckoned a great advantage. Afterwards each player takes seven pieces at random. The eldest hand having laid down one, the next must pair him at either end of the piece he may choose, according to the number of pips, or the blank in the compartment of the piece; but whenever any one cannot match the part, either of the domino last put down, or of that unpaired at the other end of the row, then he says "*Go;*" and the next is at liberty to play. Thus they play alternately, either until one party has played all his pieces, and thereby won the game, or till the game be *blocked*; that is, when neither party can play, by matching the pieces where unpaired at either end; then that party wins who has the smallest number of pips on the pieces remaining in their possession. It is to the advantage of every player to dispossess himself as early as possible of the heavy pieces,

such as a double-six, five, four, &c. Sometimes, when two persons play, they take each only seven pieces, and agree to *play* or *draw, i. e.,* when one cannot come in, or pair the pieces upon the board at the end unmatched, he then is to draw from the fourteen pieces in stock till he find one to suit.

95. LOO. — DESCRIPTION OF THE GAME.—Loo, or lue, is subdivided into limited and unlimited loo; it is a game the complete knowledge of which can easily be acquired, and is played two ways, both with five and three cards, though most commonly with five dealt from a whole pack, either first three and then two, or by one at a time. Several persons may play together, but the greatest number can be admitted when with three cards only.

96. METHOD OF PLAYING LOO.—After five cards have been given to each player another is turned up for trump; the knave of clubs generally, or sometimes the knave of the trump suit, as agreed upon, is the highest card, and is styled pam; the ace of trumps is next in value, and the rest in succession, as at whist. Each player has the liberty of changing for others, from the pack, all or any of the five cards dealt, or of throwing up the hand, in order to escape being looed. Those who play their cards, either with or without changing, and do not gain a trick, are looed; as is likewise the case with all who have stood the game, when a flush or flushes occur; and each, excepting any player holding pam, of an inferior flush, is required to deposit a stake, to be given to the person who sweeps the board, or divided among the winners at the ensuing deal, according to the tricks which may then be made. For instance, if every one at dealing stakes half-a-crown, the tricks are entitled to sixpence apiece, and whoever is looed must put down half-a-crown, exclusive of the deal: sometimes it is settled that each person looed shall pay a sum equal to what happens to be on the table at the time. Five cards of a suit, or four with pam, compose a flush, which sweeps the board, and yields only to a superior flush, or the elder hand. When the ace of trumps is led, it is usual to say, "*Pam, be civil;*" the holder of which last-mentioned card is then expected to let the ace pass. When loo is played with three cards, they are dealt by one at a time, pam is omitted, and the cards are not exchanged, nor permitted to be thrown up.

97. Put. — The game of put is played with an entire pack of cards, generally by two, but sometimes by four persons. At this game the cards have a different value from all others. The best card in the pack is a *trois*, or three; the next a *deuce*, or two; then come in rotation, as at other games, the ace, king, queen, knave, ten, &c. The dealer distributes three cards to each player, by one at a time; whoever cuts the lowest card has the deal, and five points make the game, except when both parties say, "*I put*"—for then the score is at an end, and the contest is determined in favour of that party who may win two tricks out of three. When it happens that each player has won a trick, and the third is a tie—that is, covered by a card of equal value—the whole goes for nothing, and the game must begin anew.

98. Two - Handed Put. — The eldest hand should play a card; and whether the adversary pass it, win it, or tie it, you have a right to say, "*I put*," or place your cards on the pack. If you accept the first and your opponent decline the challenge, you score one : if you prefer the latter, your adversary gains a point; but if, before he play, your opponent says, "*I put*," and you do not choose to see him, he is entitled to add one to his score. It is sometimes good play to say, "*I put*," before you play a card: this depends on the nature of your hand.

99. Four - Handed Put. — Each party has a partner, and when three cards are dealt to each, one of the players gives his partner his best card, and throws the other two away: the dealer is at liberty to do the same to his part-

ner, and *vice versa*. The two persons who have received their partners' cards play the game, previously discarding their worst card for the one they have received from their partners. The game then proceeds as at two-handed put.

100. Laws of Put.—i. When the dealer accidentally discovers any of his adversary's cards, the adversary may demand a new deal.

ii. When the dealer discovers any of his own cards in dealing, he must abide by the deal.

iii. When a faced card is discovered during the deal, the cards must be reshuffled, and dealt again.

iv. If the dealer give his adversary more cards than are necessary, the adversary may call a fresh deal, or suffer the dealer to draw the extra cards from his hand.

v. If the dealer give himself more cards than are his due, the adversary may add a point to his game, and call a fresh deal if he pleases, or draw the extra cards from the dealer's hand.

vi. No bystander must interfere, under penalty of paying the stakes.

vii. Either party saying, "*I put*"— that is, "I play,"—cannot retract, but must abide the event of the game, or pay the stakes.

101. Speculation is a noisy round game, at which several may play, using a complete pack of cards, bearing the same import as at whist, with fish or counters, on which such a value is fixed as the company may agree. The highest trump in each deal wins the pool; and whenever it happens that not one is dealt, then the company pool again, and the event is decided by the succeeding *coup*. After determining the deal, &c., the dealer pools six fish, and every other player four; then three cards are given to each, by one at a time, and another turned up for trump. The cards are not to be looked at, except in this manner: The eldest hand shows the uppermost card, which, if a trump, the company may speculate on, or bid for—the highest bidder buying and paying for it, provided the price offered be approved of by the seller. After this is settled, if the first card does not prove a trump, then the next eldest is to show the uppermost card, and so on—the company speculating as they please, till all are discovered, when the possessor of the highest trump, whether by purchase or otherwise, gains the pool. To play at speculation well, a recollection only is requisite of what superior cards of that particular suit have appeared in the preceding deals, and calculating the probability of the trump offered proving the highest in the deal then undetermined.

102. Connexions.—Three or four persons may play at this game. If the former number, ten cards each are to be given; but if the latter, only eight are dealt, and bear the same import as at whist, except that diamonds are always trumps. The connexions are formed as follows :—

i. By the two black aces.

ii. The ace of spades and king of hearts.

iii. The ace of clubs and king of hearts.

FOR THE FIRST CONNEXION, 2s. are drawn from the pool; for the second, 1s.; for the third, and by the winner of the majority in tricks, 6d. each is taken. These sums are supposing gold staked: when only silver is pooled, then pence are drawn. A trump played in any round where there is a connexion wins the trick, otherwise it is gained by the player of the first card of connexions; and, after a connexion, any following player may trump without incurring a revoke; and also, whatever suit may be led, the person holding a card of connexion is at liberty to play the same; but the others must, if possible, follow suit, unless one of them can answer the connexion, which should be done in preference. No money can be drawn till the hands are finished; then the possessors of the connexions are to take first, according to precedence, and those having the majority of tricks take last.

103. Matrimony.—The game of matrimony is played with an entire pack of cards, by any number of persons from five to fourteen. It consists of five chances, usually marked on a board, or sheet of paper, as follows :—

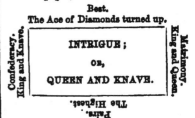

This game is generally played with counters, and the dealer puts what he pleases on each or any chance, the other players depositing each the same quantity, except one—that is, when the dealer stakes twelve, the rest of the company lay down eleven each. After this, two cards are dealt round to every one, beginning on the left; then to each person one other card, which is turned up, and he who so happens to get the ace of diamonds sweeps all. If it be not turned up, then each player shows his hand; and any of them having matrimony, intrigue, &c., takes the counters on that point; and when two or more people happen to have a similar combination, the oldest hand has the preference; and, should any chance not be gained, it stands over to the next deal. —*Observe :* The ace of diamonds turned up takes the whole pool, but when in hand ranks only as any other ace; and if not turned up, nor any ace in hand, then the king, or next superior card, wins the chance styled best.

104. Pope Joan.—Pope, a game somewhat similar to that of matrimony, is played by a number of people, who generally use a board painted for this purpose, which may be purchased at most turners' or toy shops. The eight of diamonds must first be taken from the pack, and after settling the deal, shuffling, &c., the dealer dresses the board, by putting fish, counters, or other stakes, one each to ace, king, queen, knave, and game; two to matrimony, two to intrigue, and six to the nine of diamonds, styled Pope. This dressing is, in some companies, at the individual expense of the dealer, though, in others, the players contribute two stakes apiece towards the same. The cards are next to be dealt round equally to every player, one turned up for trump, and about six or eight left in the stock to form stops; as, for example, if the ten of spades be turned up, the nine consequently becomes a stop; the four kings, and the seven of diamonds, are always fixed stops, and the dealer is the only person permitted, in the course of the game, to refer occasionally to the stock for information what other cards are stops in their respective deals. If either ace, king, queen, or knave happen to be the turned-up trump, the dealer may take whatever is deposited on that head; but when pope be turned up, the dealer is entitled both to that and the game, besides a stake for every card dealt to each player. Unless the game be determined by pope being turned up, the eldest hand must begin by playing out as many cards as possible; first the stops, then pope, if he have it, and afterwards the lowest card of his longest suit, particularly an ace, for that never can be led through; the other players are to follow, when they can, in sequence of the same suit, till a stop occurs, and the party having the stop thereby becomes eldest hand, and is to lead accordingly; and so on, until some person parts with all his cards, by which he wins the pool (game), and becomes entitled besides to a stake for every card not played by the others, except from any one holding pope, which excuses him from paying; but if pope has been played, then the party having held it is not excused. King and queen form what is denominated matrimony; queen and knave make intrigue, when in the same hand; but neither these, nor ace, king, queen, knave, or pope, entitle the holder to the stakes deposited thereon, unless played out; and no claim can be allowed after the board be dressed for the suc-

ceeding deal; but in all such cases the stakes are to remain for future determination. This game only requires a little attention to recollect what stops have been made in the course of the play; as, for instance, if a player begin by laying down the eight of clubs, then the seven in another hand forms a stop, whenever that suit be led from any lower card; or the holder, when eldest, may safely lay it down, in order to clear his hand.

105. Cassino.—The game of cassino is played with an entire pack of cards, generally by four persons, but sometimes by three, and often by two.

106. TERMS USED IN CASSINO.— i. *Great Cassino*, the ten of diamonds, which reckons for two points.

ii. *Little Cassino*, the two of spades, which reckons for one point.

iii. *The Cards* is when you have a greater share than your adversary, and reckons for three points.

iv. *The Spades* is when you have the majority of that suit, and reckons for one point.

v. *The Aces:* each of which reckons for one point.

vi. *Lurched* is when your adversary has won the game before you have gained six points.

In some deals at this game it may so happen that neither party win anything, as the points are not set up according to the tricks, &c., obtained, but the smaller number is constantly subtracted from the larger, both in cards and points; and if they both prove equal, the game commences again, and the deal goes on in rotation. When three persons play at this game, the two lowest add their points together, and subtract from the highest; but when their two numbers together either amount to or exceed the highest, then neither party scores.

107. LAWS OF CASSINO.—i. The deal and partners are determined by cutting, as at whist, and the dealer gives four cards, by one at a time, to every player, and either regularly as he deals, or by one, two, three, or four at a time, lays four more, face upwards, upon the board, and, after the first cards are played, four others are to be dealt to each person, until the pack be concluded; but it is only in the first deal that any cards are to be turned up.

ii. The deal is not lost when a card is faced by the dealer, unless in the first round, before any of the four cards are turned up upon the table; but if a card happen to be faced in the pack, before any of the said four be turned up, then the deal must be begun again.

iii. Any person playing with less than four cards must abide by the loss; and should a card be found under the table, the player whose number is deficient is to take the same.

iv. Each person plays one card at a time, with which he may not only take at once every card of the same denomination upon the table, but likewise all that will combine therewith; as, for instance, a ten takes not only every ten, but also nine and ace, eight and deuce, seven and three, six and four, or two fives; and if he clear the board before the conclusion of the game, he is to score a point; and whenever any player cannot pair or combine, then he is to put down a card.

v. The tricks are not to be counted before all the cards are played; nor may any trick but that last won be looked at, as every mistake must be challenged immediately.

vi. After all the pack is dealt out, the player who obtains the last trick sweeps all the cards then remaining unmatched upon the table.

108. Vingt-un.—DESCRIPTION OF THE GAME.—The game of *Vingt-un,* or twenty-one, may be played by two or more persons; and, as the deal is advantageous, and often continues long with the same person, it is usual to determine it at the commencement by turning up the first ace, or any other mode that may be agreed upon.

109. METHOD OF PLAYING VINGT-UN.—The cards must all be dealt out in succession, unless a natural Vingt-un occur, and in the meantime the pone,

or youngest hand, should collect those that have been played, and shuffle them together, ready for the dealer, against the period when he shall have distributed the whole pack. The dealer is first to give two cards, by one at a time, to each player, including himself; then to ask every person in rotation, beginning with the eldest hand on the left, whether he stands or chooses another card, which, if required, must be given from off the top of the pack, and afterwards another, or more, if desired, till the points of the additional card or cards, added to those dealt, exceed or make twenty-one exactly, or such a number less than twenty-one as may be judged proper to stand upon. But when the points exceed twenty-one, then the cards of that individual player are to be thrown up directly, and the stakes to be paid to the dealer, who also is, in turn, entitled to draw additional cards; and, on taking a Vingt-un, is to receive double stakes from all who stand the game, except such other players, likewise having twenty-one, between whom it is thereby a drawn game; and when any adversary has a Vingt-un, and the dealer not, then the opponent so having twenty-one, wins double stakes from him. In other cases, except a natural Vingt-un happen, the dealer pays single stakes to all whose numbers under twenty-one are higher than his own, and receives from those who have lower numbers; but nothing is paid or received by such players as have similar numbers to the dealer; and when the dealer draws more than twenty-one, he is to pay to all who have not thrown up.

110. NATURAL VINGT-UN.—Twenty-one, whensoever dealt in the first instance, is styled a *Natural Vingt-un,* it should be declared immediately, and entitles the possessor to the deal, besides double stakes from all the players, unless there shall be more than one natural Vingt-un; in which case, the younger hand or hands having the same, are excused from paying to the eldest, who takes the deal of course.

Observe : An ace may be reckoned either as eleven or one; every court-card is counted as ten, and the rest of the pack according to their points.

111. THE ODDS OF NATURAL VINGT-UN merely depend upon the average number of cards likely to come under or exceed twenty-one : for example, if those in hand make fourteen exactly, it is seven to six that the one next drawn does not make the number of points above twenty-one; but if the points be fifteen, it is seven to six against that hand: yet it would not, therefore, always be prudent to stand at fifteen, for as the ace may be calculated both ways, it is rather above an even bet that the adversary's two first cards amount to more than fourteen. A natural Vingt-un may be expected once in seven coups when two, and twice in seven when four people play, and so on, according to the number of players.

112. Quadrille. — The game of *Quadrille* is played by four persons, and the number of cards required is forty; the four tens, nines, and eights being discarded from the pack. The deal is made by distributing the cards to each player, three at a time for two rounds, and four at a time for one round; commencing with the right-hand player, who is eldest hand. The trump is made by the person who plays, with or without calling, by naming spades, clubs, diamonds, or hearts, and the suit so named becomes trumps.

113. THE TWO FOLLOWING TABLES will show *the rank and order of the cards, when trumps or when not so.*

114. (i.) WHEN TRUMPS :—

Clubs and Spades.	*Hearts and Diamonds.*
Spadille, the ace of spades.	Spadille, the ace of spades.
Manille, the deuce of spades or of clubs.	Manille, the seven of hearts or of diamonds.
Basto, the ace of clubs.	Basto, the ace of clubs.
	Punto, the ace of hearts or of diamonds.

Clubs and Spades.		*Hearts and Diamonds.*	
King.	Six.	King.	Three.
Queen.	Five.	Queen.	Four.
Knave.	Four.	Knave.	Five.
Seven.	Three.	Deuce.	Six.
11 in all.		12 in all.	

115. (ii.) WHEN NOT TRUMPS:—

Clubs and Spades.		*Hearts and Diamonds.*	
King.	Five.	King.	Three.
Queen.	Four.	Queen.	Four.
Knave.	Three.	Knave.	Five.
Seven.	Deuce.	Ace.	Six.
Six.		Deuce.	Seven.
9 in all.		10 in all.	

116. FROM THESE TABLES IT WILL BE OBSERVED that spadille and basto are always trumps; and that the red suits have one trump more than the black,—the former twelve, and the latter only eleven.

117. A TRUMP CALLED MANILLE, between spadille and basto, is in black the deuce, and in red the seven; they are the second cards when trumps, and the last in their respective suits when not trumps. Example: the deuce of spades being second trump when they are trumps, and the lowest card when clubs, hearts, or diamonds are trumps, and so of the rest.

118. PUNTO IS THE ACE OF HEARTS or diamonds, which is above the king, and the fourth trump, when either of those suits are trumps; but is below the knave, and ace of diamonds and hearts when they are not trumps. The two of hearts or diamonds is always superior to the three; the three to the four; the four to the five; and the five to the six : the six is only superior to the seven when it is not trumps, for when the seven is manille, it is the second trump.

119. THERE ARE THREE MATADORES, viz., spadille, manille, and basto; whose privilege is, when the player has no other trumps but them, and trumps are led, he is not obliged to play them, but may play what card he thinks proper, provided, however, that the trump led is of an inferior value; but if spadille should be led, he that has manille or basto only is compelled to lead it, which is the case with basto in respect to manille, the superior matadore always forcing the inferior.

120. TERMS USED IN QUADRILLE. —i. *To ask leave* is to ask leave to play with a partner, by calling a king.

ii. *Basto* is the ace of clubs, and always the third best trump.

iii. *Bast* is a penalty incurred by not winning when you stand your game, or by renouncing ; in which cases you pay as many counters as are down.

iv. *Cheville* is being between the eldest hand and the dealer.

v. *Codille* is when those who defend the pool make more tricks than those who defend the game, which is called winning the codille.

vi. *Consolation* is a claim to the game, always paid by those who lose, whether by codille or demise.

vii. *Devole* is when he who stands the game makes no trick.

viii. *Double* is to play for double stakes, with regard to the game, the consolation, the sans prendre, the matadores, and the devole.

ix. *Force.*—The ombre is said to be forced when a strong trump is played for the adversary to over-trump. He is, like-wise, said to be forced when he asks leave, and one of the other players obliges him to play sans prendre ; or pass, by offering to play sans prendre.

x. *Forced spadille* is, when all have passed, he who has spadille is obliged to play it.

xi. *Forced sans prendre* is when, hav-ing asked leave, one of the players offers to play alone, in which case you are obliged to play alone or pass.

xii. *Friend* is the player who has the king called.

xiii. *Impasse.*—To make the impasse is when, being in cheville, the knave of a suit is played, of which the player has the king.

xiv. *Manille* is, in black, the deuce of spades or clubs ; in red, the seven of hearts or diamonds, and is always the second best trump.

xv. *Mark* means the fish put down by the dealer.

xvi. *Mille* is a mark of ivory which is sometimes used, and stands for ten fish.

xvii. *Matadores*, or matts, are spadille, manille, and basto, which are always the three best trumps. False matadores are any sequence of trumps, following the matadores regularly.

xviii. *Ombre* is the name given to him who stands the game, by calling or play-ing sans appeler, or sans prendre.

xix. *Party* is the duration of the game, according to the number of tours agreed to be played.

xx. *Pass* is the term used when you have not either a hand to play alone, or with calling a king.

xxi. *Ponto,* or *Punto,* is the ace of diamonds, when diamonds are trumps ; or hearts, when they are trumps, and is then the fourth trump.

xxii. *Pool.*—The pool consists of the fishes which are staked for the deals, or the counters put down by the players, or the basts which go to the game. To defend the pool is to be against him who stands the game.

xxiii. *Prise* is the number of fish or counters given to each player at the commencement of the game.

xxiv. *Régle* is the order to be observed at the game.

xxv. *Remise* is when they who stand the game do not make more tricks than they who defend the pool, and then they lose by remise.

xxvi. *Renounce* is not to play in the suit led when you have it ; likewise, when, not having any of the suit led, you win with a card that is the only one you have of that suit in which you play.

xxvii. *Reprise* is synonymous with party.

xxviii. *Report* is synonymous with reprise and party.

xxix. *Roi rendu* is the king surren-dered when called and given to the ombre, for which he pays a fish ; in which case, the person to whom the game is given up must win the game alone.

xxx. *Spadille* is the ace of spades, which is always the best trump.

xxxi. *Sans appeler* is playing without calling a king.

xxxii. *Sans prendre* is erroneously used for sans appeler, meaning the same.

xxxiii. *Tenace* is to wait with two trumps that must make when he who has two others is obliged to lead, such as the two black aces against manille or punto.

xxxiv. *Tours* are the counters, which they who win put down, to mark the number of coups played.

xxxv. *Vole* is to get all the tricks, either with a friend or alone, sans prendre, or declared at the first of the deal.

121. Laws of Quadrille. — i. The cards are to be dealt by fours and threes, and in no other manner. The dealer is at liberty to begin by four or three. If in dealing there is a faced card, there must be a new deal, unless it is the last card.

ii. If there are too many or too few cards, it is also a new deal.

iii. No penalty is inflicted for dealing wrong, but the dealer must deal again.

iv. He who has asked leave is obliged to play.

v. No one should play out of his turn: if, however, he does, he is not basted for it, but the card played may be called at any time in that deal, provided it does not cause a revoke; or either of the adversaries may demand the partner of him who played out of his turn, or his own partner, to play any suit he thinks fit.

vi. No matadore can be forced but by a superior matt; but the superior forces the inferior, when led by the first player.

vii. Whoever names any suit for trumps must abide by it, even though it should happen to be his worst suit.

viii. If you play with eleven cards you are basted.

ix. If you play sans prendre or have matadores, you are to demand them before the next dealer has finished his deal, otherwise you lose the benefit.

x. If any one name his trump without asking leave, he must play alone,

unless the youngest hand and the rest have passed.

xi. If any person play out of his turn, the card may be called at any time, or the adversary may call a suit.

xii. If the person who won the sixth trick play the seventh card, he must play the vole.

xiii. If you have four kings, you may call a queen to one of your kings, or call one of your kings; but you must not call the queen of trumps.

xiv. If a card be separated from the rest, and it is seen, it must be played if the adverse party has seen it, unless the person who separated it play sans prendre.

xv. If the king called, or his mated queen, play out of turn, no vole can be played.

xvi. No one is to be basted for a renounce unless the trick be turned and quitted; and if any person renounce and it is discovered, if the player should happen to be basted by such renounce, all the parties are to take up their cards and play them over again.

xvii. Forced spadille is not obliged to make three tricks.

xviii. The person who undertakes to play the vole has the preference of playing before him who offers to play sans prendre.

xix. The player is entitled to know who is his king called, before he declares for the vole.

xx. When six tricks are won, the person who won the sixth must say, "I play (or, do not play) the vole;" or "I ask;" and no more.

xxi. He who has passed once has no right to play after, unless he has spadille; and he who asks must play, unless somebody else play sans prendre.

xxii. If the players show their cards before they have won six tricks, they may be called.

xxiii. Whoever has asked leave cannot play sans prendre, unless he be forced.

xxiv. Any person may look at the tricks when he is to lead.

xxv. Whoever, playing for a vole,

loses it, has a right to stakes, sans prendre, and matadores.

xxvi. Forced spadille cannot play for the vole.

xxvii. If any person discover his game he cannot play the vole.

xxviii. No one is to declare how many trumps are out.

xxix. He who plays and does not win three tricks, is basted alone, unless forced spadille.

xxx. If there are two cards of a sort, it is a void deal, if discovered before the deal is played out.

122. RULES FOR LEARNERS.—i. When you are the ombre, and your friend leads from a matt, play your best trump, and then lead the next best the first opportunity.

ii. If you possess all the trumps continue to lead them, except you hold certain other winning cards.

iii. If all the other matts are not revealed by the time you have six tricks, do not run a risk in playing for the vole.

iv. When you are the friend called, and hold only a matt, lead it; but if it be guarded by a small trump, lead that. But when the ombre is last player, lead the best trump you possess.

v. Punto in red, or king of trumps in black, are good cards to lead when you are best; and should either of them succeed, then play a small trump.

vi. If the ombre lead to discover his friend, and you have king, queen, and knave, put on the knave.

vii. Preserve the suit called, whether friend or foe.

viii. When playing against a lone hand, never lead a king unless you have the queen; nor change the suit: and prevent, if possible, the ombre from being last player.

ix. You are to call your strongest suits, except you have a queen guarded; and if elder hand, you have a better chance than middle hand.

x. A good player may play a weaker game, either elder or younger, than middle hand.

123. Quinze. — DESCRIPTION OF THE GAME.—Quinze is of French origin,

and is so called from fifteen being the number to count out. It is usually played by two persons only, and is much admired for its simplicity and fairness, as it depends entirely upon chance, is soon decided, and does not require that attention which most other games do. It is, therefore, particularly calculated for those who love to sport upon an equal chance.

METHOD OF PLAYING.—The cards must be shuffled by the two players, and when they have cut for deal (which falls to the lot of him who cuts the lowest), the dealer has the liberty at this, as well as all other games, to shuffle them again. When this is done, the adversary cuts them; after which, the dealer gives one card to his opponent, and one to himself. Should the dealer's adversary not approve of his card, he is entitled to have as many cards given to him, one after the other, as will make fifteen, or come nearest to that number; which are usually given from the top of the pack: for example—if he should have a deuce, and draw a five, which amounts to seven, he must continue going on, in expectation of coming nearer to fifteen. If he draw an eight, which will make just fifteen, he, as being eldest hand, is sure of winning the game. But if he overdraw himself, and make more than fifteen, he loses, unless the dealer should happen to do the same; which circumstance constitutes a drawn game; and the stakes are consequently doubled. In this manner they persevere, until one of them has won the game, by standing and being nearest to fifteen. At the end of each game the cards are packed and shuffled, and the players again cut for deal. The advantage is invariably on the side of the elder hand.

124. Quadrilles. — THE FIRST SET. *First Figure, Le Pantalon.—*Right and left. Balances to partners; turn partners. Ladies chain. Half promenade; half right and left. (Four times.)—*Second Figure, L' Eté.—*Leading lady and opposite gentleman advance and retire; chassez to right and left:

cross over to each other's places; chassez to right and left. Balancez and turn partners. (Four times.) *Or Double L'Été.*—Both couples advance and retire at the same time; cross over : advance and retire again; cross to places. Balancez and turn partners. (Four times.) *Third Figure, La Poule.*—Leading lady and opposite gentleman cross over, giving right hands; recross, giving left hands, and fall in a line. Set four in a line; half promenade. Advance two, and retire (twice). Advance four, and retire; half right and left. (Four times.) *Fourth Figure, Trenise.*—The first couple advance and retire twice, the lady remaining on the opposite side; the two ladies go round the first gentleman, who advances up the centre; balancez and turn hands. (Four times.) *Fifth Figure, La Pastorale.* — The leading couple advance twice, leaving the lady opposite the second time. The three advance and retire twice. The leading gentleman advance and set. Hands four half round; half right and left.* (Four times.) *Sixth Figure, Galop Finale.*—Top and bottom couples galopade quite round each other. Advance and retire; four advance again, and change the gentlemen. Ladies' chain. Advance and retire four, and regain your partners in your places. The fourth time all galopade for an unlimited period. (Four times.) *Or,* All galopade or promenade, eight bars. Advance four *en galop oblique,* and retire, then half promenade, eight bars. Advance four, retire, and return to places with the half promenade, eight bars. Ladies' chain, eight bars. Repeated by the side couples, then by the top and bottom, and lastly by the side couples, finishing with grand promenade.

125. LANCERS.—i. *La Rose.*—First gentleman and opposite lady advance and set—turn with both hands, retiring to places—return, leading outside—set and turn at corners. ii. *La Lodoiska.* —First couple advance twice, leaving the lady in the centre — set in the

<hr>

* This or the Trenise must be omitted.

centre — turn to places—all advance in two lines—all turn partners. iii. *La Dorset.*—First lady advance and stop, then the opposite gentleman—both retire, turning round—ladies' hands across half round, and turn the opposite gentlemen with left hands—repeat back to places, and turn partners with left hands. iv. *L'Étoile.* — First couple set to couple at right—set to couple at left—change places with partners, and set, and pirouette to places—right and left with opposite couple. v. *Les Lanciers.* —The grand chain. The first couple advance and turn facing the top; then the couple at right advance behind the top couple; then the couple at left, and the opposite couple, do the same, forming two lines. All change places with partners and back again. The ladies turn in a line on the right, the gentlemen in a line on the left. Each couple meet up the centre. Set in two lines, the ladies in one line, the gentlemen in the other. Turn partners to places. Finish with the grand chain.

126. THE CALEDONIANS. — *First Figure.*—The first and opposite couples hands across round the centre and back to places — set and turn partners. Ladies' chain. Half promenade—half right and left. Repeated by the side couples. *Second Figure.*— The first gentleman advance and retire twice. All set at corners, each lady passing into the next lady's place on the right. Promenade by all. Repeated by the other couples. *Third Figure.*—The first lady and opposite gentleman advance and retire, bending to each other. First lady and opposite gentleman pass round each other to places. First couple cross over, having hold of hands, while the opposite couple cross on the outside of them—the same reversed. All set at corners, turn, and resume partners. All advance and retire twice, in a circle with hands joined—turn partners. *Fourth Figure.*— The first lady and opposite gentleman advance and stop; then their partners advance; turn partners to places. The four ladies move to right, each taking the next lady's place, and stop—the four gentlemen move to left, each taking the next gentleman's place, and stop—the ladies repeat the same to the right —then the gentlemen to the left. All join hands and promenade round to places, and turn partners. Repeated by the other couples. *Fifth Figure.*—The first couple promenade or waltz round inside the figure. The four ladies advance, join hands round, and retire— then the gentlemen perform the same —all set and turn partners. Chain figure of eight half round, and set. All promenade to places and turn partners. All change sides, join right hands at corners, and set—back again to places. Finish with grand promenade. — These three are the most admired of the quadrilles: the First Set invariably takes precedence of every other dance.

127. SPANISH DANCE.— Danced in a circle or a line by sixteen or twenty couples. The couples stand as for a Country Dance, except that the first gentleman must stand on the ladies' side, and the first lady on the gentlemen's side. First gentleman and second lady balancez to each other, while first lady and second gentleman do the same, and change places. First gentleman and partner balancez, while second gentleman and partner do the same, and change places. First gentleman and second lady balancez, while first lady and second gentleman do the same, and change places. First gentleman and second lady balancez to partners, and change places with them. All four join hands in the centre, and then change places, in the same order as the foregoing figure, four times. All four poussette, leaving the second lady and gentleman at the top, the same as in a Country Dance. The first lady and gentleman then go through the same figure with the third lady and gentleman, and so proceed to the end of the dance. This figure is sometimes danced in eight bars time, which not only hurries and inconveniences the dancers, but also ill accords with the music.

128. WALTZ COTILLON.—Places the same as quadrille. First couple waltz round inside; first and second ladies advance twice and cross over, turning twice; first and second gentlemen do the same; third and fourth couples the same; first and second couples waltz to places, third and fourth do the same; all waltz to partners, and turn half round with both hands, meeting the next lady; perform this figure until in your places; form two side lines, all advance twice and cross over, turning twice; the same, returning; all waltz round; the whole repeated four times.

129. LA GALOPADE is an extremely graceful and spirited dance, in a continual chassez. An unlimited number may join; it is danced in couples, as waltzing.

130. THE GALOPADE QUADRILLES.— 1st, Galopade. 2nd, Right and left, sides the same. 3rd, Set and turn hands all eight. 4th, Galopade. 5th, Ladies' chain, sides the same. 6th, Set and turn partners all eight. 7th Galopade. 8th, Tirois, sides the same. 9th, Set and turn partners all eight. 10th, Galopade. 11th, Top lady and bottom gentleman advance and retire, the other six do the same. 12th, Set and turn partners all eight. 13th, Galopade. 14th, Four ladies advance and retire, gentlemen the same. 15th, Double ladies' chain. 16th, Set and turn partners all eight. 17th, Galopade, 18th, Poussette, sides the same. 19th, Set and turn. 20th, Galopade waltz.

131. THE MAZURKA.—This dance is of Polish origin—first introduced into England by the Duke of Devonshire, on his return from Russia. It consists of twelve movements; and. the first eight bars are played (as in quadrilles) before the first movement commences.

132. THE REDOWA WALTZ is composed of three parts, distinct from each other. 1st, The pursuit. 2nd, The waltz called Redowa. 3rd, The waltz à Deux Temps, executed to a peculiar measure, and which, by a change of the rhythm, assumes a new character. The middle of the floor must be reserved for the dancers who execute the promenade, called the pursuit, while those who dance the waltz turn in a circle about the room. The position of the gentleman is the same as for the waltz. The gentleman sets out with the left foot, and the lady with the right. In the pursuit the position is different, the gentleman and his partner face, and take each other by the hand. They advance or fall back at pleasure, and balance in advance and backwards. To advance, the step of the pursuit is made by a glissade forward, without springing, *coupé* with the hind foot, and *jeté* on it. You recommence with the other foot, and so on throughout. The retiring step is made by a sliding step of the foot backwards, without spring, *jeté* with the front foot, and *coupé* with the one behind. It is necessary to advance well upon the sliding step, and to spring lightly in the two others, *sur place*, balancing equally in the *pas de poursuite*, which is executed alternately by the left in advance, and the right backwards. The lady should follow all the movements of her partner, falling back when he advances, and advancing when he falls back. Bring the shoulders a little forward at each sliding step, for they should always follow the movement of the leg as it advances or retreats; but this should not be too marked. When the gentleman is about to waltz, he should take the lady's waist, as in the ordinary waltz. The step of the Redowa, in turning, may be thus described. For the gentleman—*jeté* of the left foot, passing before the lady. *Glissade* of the right foot behind to the fourth position aside—the left foot is brought to the third position behind— then the *pas de basque* is executed by the right foot, bringing it forward, and you recommence with the left. The *pas de basque* should be made in three very equal beats, as in the Mazurka. The lady performs the same steps as the gentleman, beginning by the *pas de basque* with the right foot. To waltz à deux temps to the measure of the Redowa, we should make each step upon each beat of the bar, and find our-

selves at every two bars, the gentleman with his left foot forwards, and the lady with her right, that is to say, we should make one whole and one half step to every bar. The music is rather slower than for the ordinary waltz.

133. VALSE CELLARIUS.—The gentleman takes the lady's left hand with his right, moving one bar to the left by *glissade*, and two hops on his left foot, while the lady does the same to the right, on her right foot; at the second bar they repeat the same with the other foot — this is repeated for sixteen bars; they then waltz sixteen bars, *glissade* and two hops, taking care to occupy the time of two bars to get quite round. The gentleman now takes both hands of the lady, and makes the grand square —moving three bars to his left—at the fourth bar making two beats while turning the angle; his right foot is now moved forward to the other angle three bars—at the fourth, beat again while turning the angle; the same repeated for sixteen bars—the lady having her right foot forward when the gentleman has his left foot forward; the waltz is again repeated; afterwhich several other steps are introduced, but which must needs be seen to be understood.

134. CIRCULAR WALTZ.—The dancers form a circle, then promenade during the introduction—all waltz sixteen bars—set, holding partner's right hand, and turn—waltz thirty-two bars —rest, and turn partners slowly—face partner and chassez to the right and left —pirouette lady twice with the right hand, all waltz sixteen bars—set and turn—all form a circle, still retaining the lady by the right hand, and move round to the left, sixteen bars—waltz for finale.

135. POLKA WALTZES.—The couples take hold of hands as in the usual waltz. *First Waltz.* The gentleman hops the left foot well forward, then back; and *glissades* half round. He then hops the right foot forward and back, and *glissades* the other half round. The lady performs the same steps, beginning with the right foot. *Second.* The gentleman, hopping, strikes the left heel three times against the right heel, and then jumps half round on the left foot; he then strikes the right heel three times against the left, and jumps on the right foot, completing the circle. The lady does the same steps with reverse feet. *Third.* The gentleman raises up the left foot, steps it lightly on the ground forward, then strikes the right heel smartly twice, and *glissades* half round. The same is then done with the other foot. The lady begins with the right foot.

136. VALSE A DEUX TEMPS.—This waltz contains, like the common waltz, three times, but differently divided. The first time consists of a gliding step; the second a chassez, including two times in one. A chassez is performed by bringing one leg near the other, then moving it forward, backward, right, left, and round. The gentleman begins by sliding to the left with his left foot, then performing a chassez towards the left with his right foot without turning at all during the first two times. He then slides backwards with his right leg, turning half round; after which he puts his left leg behind, to perform a chassez forward, turning then half round for the second time. The lady waltzes in the same manner, except that the first time she slides to the right with the right foot, and also performs the chassez on the right, and continues the same as the gentleman, except that she slides backwards with her right foot when the gentleman slides with his left foot to the left; and when the gentleman slides with his right foot backwards, she slides with the left foot to the left. To perform this waltz gracefully, care must be taken to avoid jumping, but merely to slide, and keep the knees slightly bent.

137. CIRCASSIAN CIRCLE.—The company is arranged in couples round the room—the ladies being placed on the right of the gentlemen,—after which, the first and second couples lead off the dance. *Figure.* Right and left, set and turn partners—ladies chain, walts.—At the conclusion, the first couple with fourth, and the second with the third couple, recommence the figure,—and so on until they go completely round the circle, when the dance is concluded.

138. POLKA.—In the polka there are but two principal steps, all others belong to fancy dances, and much mischief and inconvenience is likely to arise from their improper introduction into the ball-room. *First step.* The gentleman raises the left foot slightly behind the right, the right foot is then jumped upon, and the left brought forward with a glissade. The lady commences with the right, jumps on the left, and glissades with the right. The gentleman during his step has hold of the lady's left hand with his right. *Second step.* The gentleman lightly hops the left foot forward on the heel, then hops on the toe, bringing the left foot slightly behind the right. He then glissades with the left foot forward; the same is then done, commencing with the right foot. The lady dances the same step, only beginning with the right foot.—There are a variety of other steps of a fancy character, but they can only be understood with the aid of a master, and even when well studied, must be introduced with care. The polka should be danced with grace and elegance, eschewing all *outré* and ungainly steps and gestures, taking care that the leg is not lifted too high, and that the dance is not commenced in too abrupt a manner. Any number of couples may stand up, and it is the privilege of the gentleman to form what figure he pleases, and vary it as often as his fancy and taste may dictate. *First Figure.* Four or eight bars are devoted to setting forwards and backwards, turning from and towards your partner, making a slight hop at the commencement of each set, and holding your partner's left hand; you then perform the same step (forwards) all round the room. *Second Figure.* The gentleman faces his partner, and does the same step backwards all round the room, the lady following with the opposite foot, and doing the step forwards. *Third figure.* The same as the second figure, only reversed, the lady stepping backwards, and the gentleman forwards, always going the same way round the room. *Fourth figure.* The same step as figures two and three, but turning as in a waltz.

139. THE GORLITZA is similar to the polka, the figures being waltzed through.

140. THE SCHOTTISCHE.—The gentleman holds the lady precisely as in the polka. Beginning with the left foot, he slides it forward, then brings up the right foot to the place of the left, slides the left foot forward, and springs or hops on this foot. This movement is repeated to the right. He begins with the right foot, slides it forward, brings up the left foot to the place of the right foot, slides the right foot forward again, and hops upon it. The gentleman springs twice on the left foot, turning half round; twice on the right foot; twice *encore* on the left foot, turning half round; and again twice on the right foot, turning half round. Beginning again, he proceeds as before. The lady begins with the right foot, and her step is the same in principle as the gentleman's. Vary, by a *reverse turn;* or by going in a straight line round the room. Double, if you like, each part, by giving four bars to the first part, and four bars to the second part. The *time* may be stated as precisely the same as in the Polka; but let it not be forgotten that *La Schottische* ought to be danced *much slower.*

141. COUNTRY DANCES.—*Sir Roger de Coverley.*—First lady and bottom gentleman advance to centre, salute, and retire; first gentleman and bottom lady, same. First lady and bottom gentleman advance to centre, turn, and retire; first gentleman and bottom lady the same. Ladies promenade, turning off to the right down the room, and back to places, while gentlemen do the same, turning to the left; top couple remain at bottom; repeat to the end of dance.

142. LA POLKA COUNTRY DANCES.

—All form two lines, ladies on the right, gentlemen on the left. *Figure.* Top lady and second gentleman heel and toe (polkå step) across to each other's place—second lady and top gentleman the same. Top lady and second gentleman retire back to places—second lady and top gentleman the same. Two couples polka step down the middle and back again—two first couples polka waltz. First couple repeat with the third couple, then with fourth, and so on to the end of dance.

143. THE HIGHLAND REEL.—This dance is performed by the company arranged in parties of three, along the room in the following manner: a lady between two gentlemen, in double rows. All advance and retire—each lady then performs the reel with the gentleman on her right hand, and retires with the opposite gentleman to places — hands three round and back again—all six advance and retire—then lead through to the next trio, and continue the figure to the end of the room. Adopt the Highland step, and music of three-part tune.

144. TERMS USED TO DESCRIBE THE MOVEMENTS OF DANCES.

Balances.—Set to partners.

Chaine Anglaise.—The top and bottom couples right and left.

Chaine Anglaise double.—The right and left double.

Chaine des Dames.—The ladies' chain.

Chaine des Dames double.—The ladies' chain double, which is performed by all the ladies commencing at the same time.

Chassez.—Move to the right and left.

Chassez croisez.—Gentlemen change places with partners, and back again.

Demie Chaine Anglaise.—The four opposite persons half right and left.

Demie Promenade. —All eight half promenade.

Dos-à-dos.—The two opposite persons pass round each other.

Demi Moulinet.—The ladies all advance to the centre, giving hands, and return to places.

La Grande Chaine.—All eight chasses quite round, giving alternately right and left hands to partners, beginning with the right.

Le Grand Rond.—All join hands and advance and retire twice.

Pas d'Allemande. — The gentlemen turn the partners under their arms.

Traverses.—The two opposite persons change places.

Vis-à-vis.—The opposite partner.

145. Scandal—Live it down.

Should envious tongues some malice frame,
To soil and tarnish your good name,
    Live it down !

Grow not dishearten'd; 'tis the lot
Of all men, whether good or not :
    Live it down !

Rail not in answer, but be calm;
For silence yields a rapid balm:
    Live it down !

Go not among your friends and say,
Evil hath fallen on my way :
    Live it down !

Far better thus yourself alone
To suffer, than with friends bemoan
The trouble that is all your own :
    Live it down !

What though men *evil* call your *good ?*
So CHRIST himself, misunderstood,
Was nail'd unto a cross of wood !
And now shall you, for lesser pain,
Your inmost soul for ever stain,
By rendering evil back again?
    Live it down !

146. Errors in Speaking. — There are several kinds of errors in speaking. The most objectionable of them are those in which words are employed that are unsuitable to convey the meaning intended. Thus, a person wishing to express his intention of going to a given place, says, "I *propose* going," when, in fact, he *purposes* going. An amusing illustration of this class of error was overheard by ourselves. A venerable matron was speaking of her son, who, she said, was quite stage-struck. "In fact," remarked the old lady, "he is going to a *premature* per-formance this evening!" Considering that most *amateur* performances are *premature*, we hesitate to say that this word was misapplied; though, evidently, the maternal intention was to convey quite another meaning.

147. Other Errors Arise from the substitution of sounds similar to the words which should be employed; that is, spurious words instead of genuine ones. Thus, some people say "*renumerative*," when they mean "*remunerative*." A nurse, recommending her mistress to have one of the newly-invented carriages for her child, advised her to purchase a *preamputator !*

148. Other Errors are Occasioned by imperfect knowledge of the English grammar. Thus, many people say, "Between you and I," instead of "Between you and *me.*" By the misuse of the adjective : "What *beautiful* butter !" What a *nice* landscape !" They should say, "What a *beautiful landscape !*" "What *nice butter !*" And by numerous other departures from the rules of grammar, which will be pointed out hereafter.

149. By the Mispronunciation of Words. Many persons say *pronounciation* instead of *pronunciation ;* others say pro-nun'-she-a-shun, instead of pro-nun-ce-a-shun.

150. By the Misdivision of Words and syllables. This defect makes the words *an ambassador* sound like *a nam-bassador,* or *an adder* like *a nadder.*

151. By Imperfect Enunciation, as when a person says *hebben* for *heaven, ebber* for *ever, jocholate* for *chocolate,* &c.

152. By the Use of Provincialisms, or words retained from various dialects, of which we give the following examples :—

153. Cambridgeshire, Cheshire, Suffolk, &c.—Foyne, twoyne, for *fine, twine ;* ineet for *night ;* ä-mon for *man ;* poo for *pull.*

154. Cumberland, Scotland, &c. —Ouil, bluid, for *cool, blood ;* spwort, scworn, whoam, for *sport, scorn, home ;* a-theere for *there ;* ë-reed, seeven, for *red, seven;* bleedin' for *bleeding;* hawf for *half;* saumon for *salmon.*

155. DEVONSHIRE, CORNWALL, &c. —F-vind for *find;* fet for *fetch;* wid for *with;* zee for *see;* tudder for *the other;* drash, droo, for *thrash,* and *through;* gewse for *goose;* Toosday for *Tuesday.*

156. ESSEX, LONDON, &c.—V-wiew for *view;* vent for *went;* vite for *white;* ven for *when;* vot for *what.*

157. HEREFORD, &c.—Clom for *olimb;* hove for *heave;* puck for *pick;* rep for *reap;* sled for *sledge.*

158. LEICESTERSHIRE, LINCOLN-SHIRE, LANCASHIRE, &c.—Housen for *houses;* a-loyne for *lane;* mon for *man;* thik for *this;* brig for *bridge;* thack, pick, for *thatch, pitch.*

159. YORKSHIRE, &c.—Foyt for *foot;* foight for *fight;* o-noite, foil, coil, hoil, for *note, foal, coal, hole;* loyne for *lane;* o-nooin, gooise, fooil, tooil, for *noon, goose, fool, tool;* spwort, scworn, whoam, for *sport, scorn, home;* g-yet for *gate.*

160. THE FOLLOWING EXAMPLES of provincial dialects will be found very amusing :—

161. THE CORNWALL SCHOOLBOY. —An ould man found, one day, a young gentleman's portmantle, as he were a going to es dennar; he took'd et en and gived et to es wife, and said, " Mally, here's a roul of lither, look, see, I sup-poase some poor ould shoemaker or other have los'en; tak'en, and put'en a top of the teaster of tha bed; he'll be glad to hab'en agin sum day, I dear say." The ould man, Jan, that was es neame, went to es work as before. Mally than opened the portmantle, and found en et three hunderd pounds. Soon after thes, the ould man not being very well, Mally said, " Jan, I've saaved away a little money, by the bye, and as thee caan't read or write, thee shu'st go to scool" (he were then nigh threescore and ten). He went but a very short time, and comed hoam one day and said, "Mally, I waint go to scool no more, 'caase the childer do be laffen at me; they can tell their letters, and I

caan't tell my A, B, C, and I wud rayther go to work agen." " Do as thee wool," ses Mally. Jan had not been out many days, afore the young gentle, man came by that lost the portmantle, and said, " Well, my ould man, did'ee see or hear tell o' sich a thing as a port-mantle ?" " Portmantle, sar, was't that un, sumthing like thickey ?" (pointing to one behind es saddle). I vound one the t'other day zackly like that." " Where es et ?" " Come along, I carr'd'en and gov'en to my ould 'ooman, Mally; thee sha't av'en, nevr vear.— Mally, where es that roul of lither I broft en tould thee to put en a top of the teaster of the bed, *afore I go'd to scool ?*" " Drat thee emperance," said the young gentleman; "thee art be-wattled; *that were afore I were born."* So he druv'd off, and left all the three hunderd pounds with Jan and Mally.

162. THE MIDDLESEX THIMBLE-RIGGER.—Now, then, my jolly sports, men, I've got more money than the parson of the parish. Those as don't play can't vin, and those as are here harn't there ! I'd hold any on you, from a tanner to a sovereign, or ten, as you don't tell which thimble the pea is under." "It's there, sir." "I barr tellings." "I'll go it again." "Vat you don't see don't look at, and vat you do see don't tell. I'll hould you a soveren, sir, you don't tell me vitch thimble the pea is under." "Lay him, sir (in a whisper), it's under the middle 'un. I'll go you halves." "Lay him another; that's right." "I'm blow'd, but we've lost; who'd a thought it ?" Smack goes the flat's hat over his eyes; exit the confederates, with a loud laugh.

163. THE HARNET AND THE BITTLE, —WILTSHIRE.

A harnet set in a hollur tree,—
A proper spiteful twoad was he;
And a merrily sung, while he did set
His stinge as shearp as a bagganet;
 "Oh, who so vine and bowld as I ?
 I vears not bee, nor waspe, nor vly ! '

A bittle up thuck tree did clim,
And scornfully did look at him.

Zays he, "Zur harnet, who giv' thee
A right to zet in thuck there tree ?
  Vor ael you zengs zo nation vine,
  I tell 'e 'tis a house o' mine.''

The harnet's conscience velt a twinge,
But grawin' bowld wi' his long stinge,
Zays he, " Possession s the best laaw ;
Zo here th' sha'n't put a claaw !
  Be off, and leave the tree to me,
  The mixen's good enough for thee !''

Just then a yuckel passin' by,
Was axed by them the cause to try :
. "Ha ! ha ! I zee how tis ! " says he,
"They'll make a vamous munch vor me !"
  His bill was shearp, his stomach lear,
  Zo up he snapped the caddlin' pair!

MORAL.

All you as be to laaw inclined, .
This leetle stowry bear in mind ;
Vor if to laaw you aims to gwo,
You'll vind thy'll allus zar'e zo :
You'll meet the vate o' these here two,
They'll take your cwoat and carcase too !

164. MEASTER GODDIN used to zay as how children costed a sight o' money to breng um' up, and 'twas all very well whilst um was leetle, and zucked th' mother, but when um begind to zuck the vather, 'twas nation akkerd !

165. YORKSHIRE.—Men an' women is like so monny cards, played wi' be two opponants, Time an' Eternity : Time gets a gam' noo an' then, and hez t'pleasure o' keepin' his cards for a bit, bud Eternity's be far t'better hand, an' proves, day be day, an' hoor be hoor, 'at he's winnin incalcalably fast.—"Hoo sweet, hoo varry sweet is life !" as t' flee said when he wur stuck i' treacle !

166. Persons bred in these localities, and in Ireland and Scotland, retain more or less of their provincialisms ; and, therefore, when they move into other districts, they become conspicuous for the peculiarities of their speaking. In many cases they appear vulgar and uneducated, when they are not so. It is, therefore, very desirable for all persons to approach the recognized standard of correctness as nearly as possible.

167. To CORRECT THESE ERRORS by a systematic course of study would involve a closer application than our readers generally could afford, and would require much more space than we can devote to the subject. We will therefore give numerous Rules and Hints, in a concise and simple form, which will be of great assistance to inquirers. These Rules and Hints will be founded upon the authority of scholars, the usages of the bar, the pulpit, and the senate, and the authority of societies formed for the purpose of collecting and diffusing knowledge pertaining to the language of this country.

168. Rules and Hints for Correct Speaking.—1. *Who* and *whom* are used in relation to persons, and *which* in relation to things. But it was once common to say, "the man *which*." This should now be avoided. It is now usual to say, " Our Father *who* art in heaven," instead of " *which* art in heaven."

2. *Whose* is, however, sometimes applied to things as well as to persons. We may therefore say, "The country *whose* inhabitants are free." [Grammarians differ in opinion upon this subject, but general usage justifies the rule.]

3. *Thou* is employed in solemn discourse, and *you* in common language. *Ye* (plural) is also used in serious addresses, and *you* in familiar language.

4. The uses of the word *It* are various, and very perplexing to the uneducated. It is not only used to imply persons, but things, and even ideas, and therefore, in speaking or writing, its assistance is constantly required. The perplexity respecting this word arises from the fact that in using it in the construction of a long sentence, sufficient care is not taken to insure that when *it* is employed it really points out or refers to the object intended. For instance, "It was raining when John set out in his cart to go to the market, and he was delayed so long that it was over before he arrived." Now what is to be understood by this sentence ? Was the rain over ? or the market ? Either or both might be inferred from the con-

struction of the sentence, which, therefore, should be written thus :—" It was
raining when John set out in his cart
to go to the market, and he was delayed
so long that the market was over before he arrived."

5. *Rule.*—After writing a sentence
always look through it, and see that
wherever the word *It* is employed, it
refers to or carries the mind back to the
object which it is intended to point out.

6. The general distinction between
This and *That* is, *this* denotes an object
present or near, in time or place, *that*
something which is absent.

7. *These* refers, in the same manner,
to present objects, while *those* refers to
things that are remote.

8. *Who* changes, under certain conditions, into *whose* and *whom*. But *that*
and *which* always remain the same.

9. *That* may be applied to nouns or
subjects of all sorts; as, the *girl that*
went to school, the *dog that* bit me, the
ship that went to London, the *opinion
that* he entertains.

10. The misuse of these pronouns
gives rise to more errors in speaking
and writing than any other cause.

11. When you wish to distinguish
between two or more persons, say,
" *Which* is the happy man ?"—not
who—" *Which* of those ladies do you
admire ?"

12. Instead of " *Who* do you think
him to be ?"—Say, "*Whom* do you think
him to be ?"

13. *Whom* should I see ?

14. To *whom* do you speak ?

15. *Who* said so ?

16. *Who* gave it to you ?

17. Of *whom* did you procure them ?

18. *Who* was *he* ?"

19. *Who* do men say that *I* am ?

20. *Whom* do they represent *me* to
be ? *

21. In many instances in which *who*

* Persons who wish to become well acquainted with the principles of *English Grammar* by an easy process, are recommended to
procure "The Useful Grammar," price 3d.,
published by Houlston and Wright.

is used as an interrogative, it does not
become *whom;* as " *Who* do you speak
to ?" " *Who* do you expect ?" " *Who*
is she married to ?" " *Who* is this reserved for ?" " *Who* was it made by ?"
Such sentences are found in the writings
of our best authors, and it would be
presumptuous to consider them as un-
grammatical. If the word *whom* should
be preferred, then it would be best to
say, " For *whom* is this reserved ?" &c.

22. Instead of "After *which* hour,"
say "After *that* hour."

23. *Self* should never be added to
his, their, mine, or *thine.*

24. *Each* is used to denote every
individual of a number.

25. *Every* denotes all the individuals
of a number.

26. *Either* and *or* denote an alternative : "I will take *either* road, at
your pleasure;" "I will take this *or*
that."

27. *Neither* means *not either;* and
nor means *not the other.*

28. *Either* is sometimes used for
each—"Two thieves were crucified, on
either side one."

29. " Let *each* esteem others as good
as themselves," should be, "Let *each*
esteem others as good as *himself.*"

30. "There are bodies *each* of which
are so small," should be, "each of
which *is* so small."

31. Do not use double superlatives,
such as *most straightest, most highest,
most finest.*

32. The term *worser* has gone out of
use; but *lesser* is still retained.

33. The use of such words as *chiefest,
extremest,* &c., has become obsolete,
because they do not give any superior
force to the meanings of the primary
words, *chief, extreme,* &c.

34. Such expressions as *more impossible, more indispensable, more universal, more uncontrollable, more unlimited,* &c., are objectionable, as they
really enfeeble the meaning which it is
the object of the speaker or writer to
strengthen. For instance, *impossible*
gains no strength by rendering it *more*
impossible. This class of error is com-

mon with persons who say, "A *great large* house," A *great big* animal," "A *little small* foot," "A *tiny little* hand."

35. *Here, there,* and *where,* originally denoting place, may now, by common consent, be used to denote other meanings; such as, "*There* I agree with you, "*Where* we differ," "We find pain *where* we expected pleasure," "*Here* you mistake me."

36. *Hence, whence,* and *thence,* denoting departure, &c., may be used without the word *from.* The idea of *from* is included in the word *whence* —therefore it is unnecessary to say, "*From whence.*"

37. *Hither, thither,* and *whither,* denoting to a place, have generally been superseded by *here, there,* and *where.* But there is no good reason why they should not be employed. If, however, they are used, it is unnecessary to add the word *to,* because that is implied— "*Whither* are you going?" "*Where* are you going?" Each of these sentences is complete. To say, "Where are you going *to?*" is redundant.

38. Two *negatives* destroy each other, and produce an affirmative. "*Nor* did he *not* observe them," conveys the idea that he *did* observe them.

39. But negative assertions are allowable. "His manners are not unpolite," which implies that his manners are, in some degree, marked by politeness.

40. Instead of "I *had* rather walk," say "I would rather walk."

41. Instead of "I *had better* go," say "It were better that I should go."

42. Instead of "I doubt not *but* I shall be able to go," say "I doubt not that I shall be able to go."

43. Instead of "Let you and *I,*" say "Let you and me."

44. Instead of "I am not so tall as *him,*" say "I am not so tall as he."

45. When asked "Who is there?" do not answer "*Me,*" but "I."

46. Instead of "For you and *I,*" say "For you and me."

47. Instead of "*Says I,*" say "I said."

48. Instead of "You are taller than *me,*" say "You are taller than I."

49. Instead of "I *ain't,*" or "I *arn't,*" say "I am not."

50. Instead of "Whether I be present or *no,*" say "Whether I be present or not."

51. For "Not that I know *on,*" say "Not that I know."

52. Instead of "*Was* I to do so," say "Were I to do so."

53. Instead of "I would do the same if I *was him,*" say "I would do the same if I were he."

54. Instead of "I *had as lief* go myself," say "I would as soon go myself," or "I would rather."

55. It is better to say "Bred and born," than "Born and bred."

56. It is better to say "Six weeks ago," than "Six weeks back."

57. It is better to say "Since which time," than "Since when."

58. It is better to say "I repeated it," than "I said so over again."

59. It is better to say "A physician," or "A surgeon" (according to his degree), than "A medical man."

60. Instead of "He was too young to *have* suffered much," say "He was too young to suffer much."

61. Instead of "*Less* friends," say "Fewer friends." Less refers to quantity.

62. Instead of "A *quantity* of people," say "A number of people."

63. Instead of "*He and they* we know," say "Him and them."

64. Instead of "*As* far as I can see," say "So far as I can see."

65. Instead of "If I am *not mistaken,*" say "If I mistake not."

66. Instead of "You are *mistaken,*" say "You mistake."

67. Instead of "What *beautiful* tea!" say "What good tea!"

68. Instead of "What a *nice* prospect!" say "What a *beautiful* prospect!"

69. Instead of "A *new pair* of gloves," say "A pair of new gloves."

70. Instead of saying "*He* belongs to the *house,*" say "The house belongs to him."

71. Instead of saying "*Not no* such thing," say "Not any such thing."

72. Instead of "I hope you'll think nothing *on* it," say "I hope you'll think nothing of it."

73. Instead of "Restore it *back* to me," say "Restore it to me."

74. Instead of "I suspect the *veracity* of his story," say "I doubt the truth of his story."

75. Instead of "I seldom *or ever* see him," say "I seldom see him."

76. Instead of "*Rather warmish*," or "A *little* warmish," say "Rather warm."

77. Instead of "I expected *to have* found him," say "I expected to find him."

78. Instead of "*Shay*," say "Chaise."

79. Instead of "He is a very *rising* person," say "He is rising rapidly."

80. Instead of "Who *learns* you music?" say "Who teaches you music?"

81. Instead of "I *never* sing *whenever* I can help it," say "I never sing when I can help it."

82. Instead of "Before I do that I must *first* ask leave," say "Before I do that I must ask leave."

83. Instead of "To *get over* the difficulty," say "To overcome the difficulty."

84. The phrase "*get over*" is in many cases misapplied, as, to "get over a person," to "get over a week," to "get over an opposition."

85. Instead of saying "The *observation* of the rule," say "The observance of the rule."

86. Instead of "A man *of* eighty years of age," say "A man eighty years old."

87. Instead of "Here *lays* his honoured head," say "Here lies his honoured head."

88. Instead of "He died from *negligence*," say "He died through neglect," or "in consequence of neglect."

89. Instead of "Apples are plenty," say "Apples are plentiful."

90. Instead of "The *latter end* of the year," say "The end, or the close of the year."

91. Instead of "The *then* government," say "The government of that age, or century, or year, or time."

92. Instead of "For *ought* I know," say "For aught I know."

93. Instead of "A *couple* of chairs," say "Two chairs."

94. Instead of "*Two couples*," say "Four persons."

95. But you may say "A married couple," or, "A married pair," or, "A couple of fowls," &c., in any case where one of each sex is to be understood.

96. Instead of "They are *united together* in the bonds of matrimony," say "They are united in matrimony," or, "They are married."

97. Instead of "We travel *slow*," say "We travel slowly."

98. Instead of "He plunged *down* into the river," say "He plunged into the river."

99. Instead of "He jumped *from off* of the scaffolding," say "He jumped off from the scaffolding."

100. Instead of "He came the last *of all*," say "He came the last."

101. Instead of "*universal*," with reference to things that have any limit, say "general;" "generally approved," instead of "universally approved;" "generally beloved," instead of "universally beloved."

102. Instead of "They ruined *one another*," say "They ruined each other."

103. Instead of "If *in case* I succeed," say "If I succeed."

104. Instead of "A *large enough* room," say "A room large enough."

105. Instead of "This villa *to let*," say "This villa to be let."

106. Instead of "I am slight in comparison *to* you," say "I am slight in comparison with you."

107. Instead of "I went *for* to see him," say "I went to see him."

108. Instead of "The cake is all *eat up*," say "The cake is all eaten."

109. Instead of "It is bad *at the best*," say "It is very bad."

110. Instead of "Handsome is *as* handsome does," say "Handsome is who handsome does."

111. Instead of "As I *take* it," say "As I see," or, "As I understand it."

112. Instead of "The book fell *on* the floor," say "The book fell to the floor."

113. Instead of "His opinions are *approved of* by all," say "His opinions are approved by all."

114. Instead of "I will add *one more* argument," say "I will add one argument more," or "another argument."

115. Instead of "Captain Reilly was killed *by* a bullet," say "Captain Reilly was killed with a bullet."

116. Instead of "A sad curse is war," say "War is a sad curse."

117. Instead of "He stands *six foot* high," say "He measures six feet," or, "His height is six feet."

118. Instead of "I go *every now and then*," say "I go often, or frequently."

119. Instead of "Who finds him in clothes," say "Who provides him with clothes."

120. Say "The first two," and "the last two," instead of "the *two first*," "the two last;" leave out all expletives, such as "of all," "first of all," "last of all," "best of all," &c., &c.

121. Instead of "His health was *drank with enthusiasm*," say "His health was drunk enthusiastically."

122. Instead of "*Except* I am prevented," say "Unless I am prevented."

123. Instead of "In its *primary sense*," say "In its primitive sense."

124. Instead of "It grieves me to *see* you," say "I am grieved to see you."

125. Instead of "Give me *them* papers," say "Give me those papers."

126. Instead of "*Those* papers I hold in my hand," say "These papers I hold in my hand."

127. Instead of "I could scarcely imagine but *what*," say "I could scarcely imagine but that."

128. Instead of "He was a man *notorious* for his benevolence," say "He was noted for his benevolence."

129. Instead of "She was a woman *celebrated* for her crimes," say "She was notorious on account of her crimes."

130. Instead of "What may your name be?" say "What is your name?"

131. Instead of "Bills are requested not to be stuck here," say "Bill-stickers are requested not to stick bills here."

132. Instead of "By *smoking it often* becomes habitual," say "By smoking often it becomes habitual."

133. Instead of "I lifted it *up*," say "I lifted it."

134. Instead of "It is *equally of the same* value," say "It is of the same value," or "equal value."

135. Instead of "I knew it *previous* to your telling me," say "I knew it previously to your telling me."

136. Instead of "You *was* out when I called," say "You were out when I called."

137. Instead of "I thought I should *have won* this game," say "I thought I should win this game."

138. Instead of "*This* much is certain," say "Thus much is certain," or, "So much is certain."

139. Instead of "He went away *as it may be* yesterday week," say "He went away yesterday week."

140. Instead of "He came *the Saturday as it may be before the Monday*," specify the Monday on which he came.

141. Instead of "Put your watch *in* your pocket," say "Put your watch into your pocket."

142. Instead of "He has *got* riches," say "He has riches."

143. Instead of "Will you *set* down?" say "Will you sit down?"

144. Instead of "The hen is *setting*," say "The hen is sitting."

145. Instead of "It is raining very *hard*," say "It is raining very fast."

146. Instead of "No, *thankee*," say "No, thank you."

147. Instead of "I cannot do it without *farther* means," say "I cannot do it without further means."

148. Instead of "No sooner *but*," or "No other *but*," say "than."

149. Instead of "*Nobody else* but her," say "Nobody but her."

150. Instead of "He fell *down* from

the balloon," say "He fell from the balloon."

151. Instead of "He rose *up* from the ground," say "He rose from the ground."

152. Instead of "*These* kind of oranges *are* not good," say "This kind of oranges is not good."

153. Instead of "Somehow or *another*," say "Somehow or other."

154. Instead of "*Undeniable* references required," say "Unexceptionable references required."

155. Instead of "I cannot *rise* sufficient funds," say "I cannot raise sufficient funds."

156. Instead of "I cannot *raise* so early in the morning," say "I cannot rise so early in the morning."

157. Instead of "*Well*, I don't know," say "I don't know."

158. Instead of "*Will* I give you some more tea?" say "Shall I give you some more tea?"

159. Instead of "Oh dear, what *will* I do," say Oh dear, what shall I do."

160. Instead of "I think *indifferent* of it," say "I think indifferently of it."

161. Instead of "I will send it *conformable* to your orders," say "I will send it conformably to your orders."

162. Instead of "Give me a *few* broth," say "Give me some broth."

163. Instead of "*Her* said it was hers," say "She said it was hers."

164. Instead of "To be *given away gratis*," say "To be given away."

165. Instead of "Will you enter in?" say "Will you enter?"

166. Instead of "*This* three days or more," say "These three days or more."

167. Instead of "He is a bad *grammarian*," say "He is not a grammarian."

168. Instead of "We *accuse him for*," say "We accuse him of."

169. Instead of "We *acquit* him *from*," say "We acquit him of."

170. Instead of "I am averse *from* that," say "I am averse to that."

171. Instead of "I confide *on* you," say "I confide in you."

172. Instead of "I differ *with* you," say "I differ from you."

173. Instead of "As soon *as ever*," say "As soon as."

174. Instead of "The *very best*," or "The *very worst*," say "The best, or the worst."

175. Instead of "A *winter's morning*," say "A winter morning, or, "A wintry morning."

176. Instead of "Fine morning, *this* morning," say "This is a fine morning."

177. Instead of "How *do* you do?" say "How are you?"

178. Instead of "Not so well as I could wish," say "Not quite well."

179. Avoid such phrases as "No great shakes," "Nothing to boast of," "Down in my boots," "Suffering from the blues." All such sentences indicate vulgarity.

180. Instead of "No one *cannot* prevail upon him," say "No one can prevail upon him."

181. Instead of "No one *hasn't* called," say "No one has called."

182. Avoid such phrases as "If I was you," or even, "If I were you." Better say "I advise you how to act."

183. Instead of "You have a *right* to pay me," say "It is right that you should pay me."

184. Instead of "I am going *on* a tour," say "I am about to take a tour," or "going."

185. Instead of "I am going *over* the bridge," say "I am going *across* the bridge."

186. Instead of "He is coming here," say "He is coming hither."

187. Instead of "He lives opposite the square," say "He lives opposite to the square."

188. Instead of "He *belongs* to the Reform Club," say "He is a member of the Reform Club."

189. Avoid such phrases as "I am up to you," "I'll be down upon you," "Cut," or "Mizzle."

190. Instead of "I *should just* think I could," say "I think I can."

191. Instead of "There has been a *good deal*," say "There has been much."

192. Instead of "*Following up* a principle, say "Guided by a principle."

193. Instead of "Your *obedient, humble servant*," say "Your obedient," or, "Your humble servant."

194. Instead of saying "The effort you are making *for* meeting the bill," say "The effort you are making to meet the bill."

195. Instead of saying "It *shall* be submitted to investigation and inquiry," say "It shall be submitted to investigation," or "to inquiry."

196. Dispense with the phrase "*Conceal from themselves the fact ;*" it suggests a gross anomaly.

197. Never say "*Pure and unadulterated,*" because the phrase embodies a repetition.

198. Instead of saying "Adequate for," say "Adequate to."

199. Instead of saying "A *surplus over and above,* say "A surplus."

200. Instead of saying "A *lasting and permanent* peace," say "A permanent peace."

201. Instead of saying "I left you *behind* at London," say "I left you behind me at London."

202. Instead of saying "*Has been* followed by immediate dismissal," say "Was followed by immediate dismissal."

203. Instead of saying "Charlotte was met *with* Thomas," say "Charlotte was met by Thomas." But if Charlotte and Thomas were walking together, "Charlotte and Thomas were met by," &c.

204. Instead of "It is strange that no author should *never* have written," say "It is strange that no author should ever have written."

205. Instead of "I won't never write, say "I will never write."

206. To say "Do *not* give him *no more* of your money," is equivalent to saying "Give him some of your money." Say "Do not give him *any* of your money."

207. Instead of saying "They are not what nature *designed* them," say "They are not what nature designed them to be."

208. Instead of "By this *means,*" say "By these means."

209. Instead of saying "A beautiful *seat and gardens,*" say "A beautiful seat and its gardens."

210. Instead of "All that was *wanting,*" say "All that was wanted."

211. Instead of saying "I had not the pleasure of hearing his sentiments when I wrote that letter," say "I had not the pleasure of having heard," &c.

212. Instead of "The quality of the apples *were* good," say "The quality of the apples was good."

213. Instead of "The want of learning, courage, and energy *are* more visible," say "is more visible."

214. Instead of "We are conversant *about* it," say "We are conversant with it."

215. Instead of "We called *at* William," say "We called on William."

216. Instead of "We die *for* want," say "We die of want."

217. Instead of "He died *by* fever," say "He died of fever."

218. Instead of "I *enjoy* bad health," say "My health is not good."

219. Instead of "*Either* of the three," say "Any one of the three."

220. Instead of "Better *nor* that," say "Better than that."

221. Instead of "We often think *on* you," say "We often think of you."

222. Instead of "Though he came, I did not see him," say "Though he came, yet I did not see him."

223. Instead of "Mine is *so* good as yours," say "Mine is as good as yours."

224. Instead of "He was remarkable handsome," say "He was remarkably handsome."

225. Instead of "Smoke ascends *up* the chimney," say "Smoke ascends the chimney."

226. Instead of "You will *some* day be convinced," say "You will one day be convinced."

227. Instead of saying "Because I don't chose to," say "Because I would rather not."

228. Instead of *"Because* why?" say "Why?"

229. Instead of "That *there* boy," say "That boy."

230. Instead of "Direct your letter to me," say "Address your letter to me."

231. Instead of "The horse is not *much worth*," say "The horse is not worth much."

232. Instead of "The *subject-matter* of debate, say "The subject of debate."

233. Instead of saying "When he *was* come back," say "When he had come back."

234. Instead of saying "His health has been *shook*," say "His health has been shaken."

235. Instead of "It was *spoke* in my presence," say "It was spoken in my presence."

236. Instead of "*Very* right," or "*Very* wrong," say "Right," or "Wrong."

237. Instead of "The *mortgager* paid him the money," say "The mortgagee paid him the money." The mortgagee lends; the mortgager borrows.

238. Instead of "This town is not *as* large as we thought," say "This town is not so large as we thought."

239. Instead of "I *took you to be* another person," say "I mistook you for another person."

240. Instead of "On *either* side of the river," say "On each side of the river."

241. Instead of "*There's* fifty," say "There are fifty."

242. Instead of "The *best* of the two," say "The better of the two."

243. Instead of "My clothes have *become too small* for me," say "I have grown too stout for my clothes."

244. Instead of "Is Lord Palmerston *in?*" say "Is Lord Palmerston within?"

245. Instead of "Two *spoonsful* of physic," say "Two spoonfuls of physic."

246. Instead of "He *must* not do it," say "He needs not do it."

247. Instead of "She said, says she," say "She said."

248. Avoid such phrases as "I said, says I," "Thinks I to myself, thinks I," &c.

249. Instead of "I don't think so," say "I think not."

250. Instead of "He was in *eminent* danger," say "He was in *imminent* danger."

251. Instead of "The weather is *hot*," say "The weather is very warm."

252. Instead of "I *sweat*," say "I perspire."

253. Instead of "I *only* want two shillings," say "I want only two shillings."

254. Instead of "Whatsomever," say "Whatever," or "Whatsoever."

255. Avoid such exclamations as "God bless me!" "God deliver me!" "By God!" "By Gor'!" "My Lor'!" "Upon my soul!" &c.

256. "THOU SHALT NOT TAKE THE NAME OF THE LORD THY GOD IN VAIN."

169. Pronunciation.—Accent is a particular stress or force of the voice upon certain syllables or words. This mark ' in printing denotes the syllable upon which the stress or force of the voice should be placed.

170. A WORD MAY HAVE MORE THAN ONE ACCENT. Take as an instance aspiration. In uttering this word we give a marked emphasis of the voice upon the first and third syllables, and therefore those syllables are said to be accented. The first of these accents is less distinguishable than the second, upon which we dwell longer, therefore the second accent is called the primary, or chief accent of the word.

171. WHEN THE FULL ACCENT FALLS ON A VOWEL, that vowel should have a long sound, as in *vo'cal ;* but when it falls on a consonant, the preceding vowel has a short sound, as in *hab'it.*

172. To OBTAIN A GOOD KNOWLEDGE OF PRONUNCIATION, it is advisable for the reader to listen to the examples given by good speakers, and by educated persons. We learn the pronunciation of words, to a great extent, by *imitation*, just as birds acquire the notes of other birds which may be near them.

173. BUT IT WILL BE VERY IMPORTANT to bear in mind that there are many words having a double meaning or application, and that the difference of meaning is indicated by the difference of the accent. Among these words, *nouns* are distinguished from *verbs* by this means: *nouns* are mostly accented on the first syllable, and *verbs* on the last.

174. NOUN SIGNIFIES NAME; *nouns* are the names of persons and things, as well as of things not material and palpable, but of which we have a conception and knowledge, such as *courage, firmness, goodness, strength;* and *verbs* express *actions, movements,* &c. If the word used signifies that anything has been done, or is being done, or is, or is to be done, then that word is a *verb*.

175. THUS, WHEN WE SAY that anything is "an in'sult," that word is a *noun*, and is accented on the first syllable; but when we say he did it "to insult' another person," the word insult' implies *acting*, and becomes a *verb*, and should be accented on the last syllable. The effect is, that, in speaking, you should employ a different pronunciation in the use of the same word, when uttering such sentences as these:—"What an in'sult!" "Do you mean to insult' me?" In the first instance you would lay the stress of voice upon the *in'*, and in the latter case upon the *sult'*.

176. WE WILL NOW GIVE A LIST of nearly all the words that are liable to this variation:—

Ab'ject	To abject'
Ab'sent	To absent'
Ab'stract	To abstract'
Ac'cent	To accent'
Af'fix	To affix'
As'sign	To assign'
At'tribute	To attribute'
Aug'ment	To augment'
Bom'bard	To bombard'
Col'league	To colleague'
Col'lect	To collect'
Com'pact	To compact'
Com'plot	To complot'
Com'pound	To compound'
Com'press	To compress'
Con'cert	To concert'
Con'crete	To concrete'
Con'duct	To conduct'
Con'fect	To confect'
Con'fine	To confine'
Con'flict	To conflict'
Con'serve	To conserve'
Con'sort	To consort'
Con'test	To contest'
Con'text	To context'
Con'tract	To contract'
Con'trast	To contrast'
Con'verse	To converse'
Con'vert	To convert'
Con'vict	To convict'
Con'voy	To convoy'
Des'cant	To descant'
Des'ert	To desert'
De'tail	To detail'
Di'gest	To digest'
Dis'cord	To discord'
Dis'count	To discount'
Es'cort	To escort'
Es'say	To essay'
Ex'ile	To exile'
Ex'port	To export'
Ex'tract	To extract'
Fer'ment	To ferment'
Fore'taste	To foretaste'
Fre'quent	To frequent'
Im'part	To impart'
Im'port	To import'
Im'press	To impress'
In'cense	To incense'
In'crease	To increase'
In'lay	To inlay'
In'sult	To insult'
Ob'ject	To object'
Per'fume	To perfume'
Per'mit	To permit'
Pre'fix	To prefix'
Pre'mise	To premise'
Pre'sage	To presage'
Pres'ent	To present'
Prod'uce	To produce'
Proj'ect	To project'
Prot'est	To protest'
Reb'el	To rebel'
Rec'ord	To record'
Ref'use	To refuse'
Re'tail	To retail'

Sub'ject	To subject'
Sur'vey	To survey'
Tor'ment	To torment'
Tra'ject	To traject'
Trans'fer	To transfer'
Trans'port	/ To transport'

177. CEMENT' IS AN EXCEPTION to the above rule, and should always be accented on the last syllable. So also the word Consols'.

178. HINTS TO "COCKNEY" SPEAK-ERS.—The most objectionable error of the Cockney, that of substituting the *v* for the *w*, and *vice versa*, is, we believe, pretty generally abandoned. Such sentences as "Are you going to Vest Vickham?" "This is werry good weal," &c., were too intolerable to be retained. Moreover, there has been a very able schoolmaster at work during the past thirteen years. This schoolmaster is no other than the loquacious Mr. *Punch,* from whose works we quote a few admirable exercises:—

i. LOW COCKNEY.—"Seen that party lately?" "What! the party with the wooden leg, as come with—" "No, no—not that party. The party, you know, as—" "Oh! ah! I know the party you mean, now." "Well, a party told me as he can't agree with that other party, and he says that if another party can't be found to make it all square, he shall look out for a party as will.—(*And so on for half an hour.*)

ii. POLICE.—"Lor, Soosan, how's a feller to eat meat such weather as this? Now, a bit o' pickled salmon and cowcumber, or a lobster salid, *might* do."

iii. COCKNEY YACHTSMAN.—(Example of affectation.) Scene : the Regatta Ball. —"I say, Tom, what's that little craft with the black velvet flying at the fore, close under the lee scuppers of the man-of-war?" "Why, from her fore-and-aft rig, and the cut of her mainsail, I should say she's down from the port of London; but I'll signal the commodore to come and introduce us!"

iv. OMNIBUS DRIVER.—*Old acquaintance.* "'Ave a drop, Bill?" *Driver.* "Why, yer see, Jim, this 'ere young hoss has only bin in 'arness once afore,

and he's such a beggar to bolt, ten to one if I leave 'im he'll be a-runnin' hoff, and a smashin' into suthun. Howsoever — here —(*handing reins to a timid passenger*)—lay hold, sir, I'LL CHANCE IT !"

v. COSTERMONGER (*to extremely genteel person*).—"I say, guv'ner, give us a hist with this 'ere bilin' o' greens!" (A large hamper of market stuff.)

vi. GENTEEL COCKNEY (*by the seaside*). — *Blanche.* "How grand, how solemn, dear Frederick, this is! I really think the ocean is more beautiful under this aspect than under any other !"— *Frederick.* "H'm—ah! Per-waps. By the way, Blanche, there's a fella shwimping. S'pose we ask him if he can get us some pwawns for breakfast to-mowaw mawning ?"

vii. STUCK-UP COCKNEY. — (*Small Swell enters a tailor's shop.*) "A— Brown, A— want some more coats!" *Snip.* "Yes, sir. Thank you, sir. How many would you please to want?" *Small Swell.* "A— let me see; A—ll have eight. A— no, I'll have nine ; and look here! A—shall want some trousers." *Snip.* "Yes, sir, thank you, sir. How many would you like?" *Small Swell.* "A— I don't know exactly. S'pose we say twenty-four pairs; and look here! Show me some patterns that won't be worn by any snobs !"

viii. COCKNEY FLUNKEY.—(*Country Footman meekly enquires of London Footman*)—"Pray, sir, what do you think of our town? A nice place, ain't it ?" *London Footman (condescendingly).* "Vell, Joseph, I likes your town well enough. It's clean : your streets are hairy ; and you've lots of rewins. But I don't like your champagne, it's all gewsberry !"

ix. COCKNEY CABBY (*politely*).— "Beg pardon, sir ; please don't smoke in the keb, sir ; ladies do complain o' the 'bacca uncommon. Better let me smoke it for yer outside, sir!"

x. MILITARY COCKNEY.—*Lieutenant Blazer (of the Plungers).* — "Gwood gwacious! Here's a howible go! The

Infantwy's going to gwow a moustache!" *Cornet Huffey (whose face is whiskerless).* "Yaw don't mean that! Wall! there's only one alternative for us. WE must shave!"

xi. JUVENILE LOW COCKNEY.—"Jack! Whereabouts is 'Amstid-am?" *Jack.* Well, I can't say exackerley, but I know it's somewhere near 'Ampstid-'eath!"

xii. COCKNEY DOMESTIC. — *Servant girl.* "Well, mam—Heverythink considered, I'm afraid you won't suit me. I've always bin brought up genteel: and I couldn't go nowheres where there ain't no footman kep'."

xiii. ANOTHER.—*Lady.* "Wish to leave! why I thought, Thompson, you were very comfortable with me!" *Thompson (who is extremely refined).* "Ho yes, mum! I don't find no fault with you, mum—nor yet with master—but the truth *his*, mum—the *hother* servants is so 'orrid vulgar and hignorant, and speaks so hungrammatical, that I reely cannot live in the same 'ouse with 'em—and I should like to go this day month, if so be has it won't illconvenience you!"

xiv. COCKNEY WAITER.—"'Am, sir? Yessir? Don't take anything with your 'am, do you, sir?" *Gentleman.* "Yes, I do; I take the letter H!"

xv. COCKNEY HAIRDRESSER.—"They say, sir, the cholera is in the Hair, sir!" *Gent (very uneasy).* "Indeed! Ahem! Then I hope you're very particular about the brushes you use." *Hairdresser.* "Oh, I see you don't hunderstand me, sir; I don't mean the 'air of the 'ed, but the *hair hof* the *hatmosphere*!"

xvi. COCKNEY SWEEP (*seated upon a donkey*).—"Fitch us out another penn'orth o' strawberry hice, with a dollop o' lemon water in it."

xvii. FEMININE COCKNEY (*by the seaside*).—"Oh, Harriet, dear, put on your hat and let us thee the stheamboat come in. The thea is tho rough!—and the people will be *tho* abthurdly thick!"

179. LONDONERS who desire to correct the defects of their utterance cannot do better than to exercise themselves frequently upon those words respecting which they have been in error.

180. HINTS FOR THE CORRECTION OF THE IRISH BROGUE.—According to the directions given by Mr. B. H. Smart, an Irishman wishing to throw off the brogue of his mother country should avoid hurling out his words with a superfluous quantity of breath. It is not *broadher* and *widher* that he should say, but the *d*, and every other consonant, should be neatly delivered by the tongue, with as little riot, clattering, or breathing as possible. Next let him drop the roughness or rolling of the *r* in all places but the beginning of syllables; he must not say *stor-rum* and *far-rum*, but let the word be heard in one smooth syllable. He should exercise himself until he can convert *plaze* into *please*, *plinty* into *plenty*, *Jasus* into *Jesus*, and so on. He should modulate his sentences, so as to avoid directing his accent all in one manner—from the acute to the grave. Keeping his ear on the watch for good examples, and exercising himself frequently upon them, he may become master of a greatly improved utterance.

181. HINTS FOR CORRECTING THE SCOTCH BROGUE.—The same authority remarks that as an Irishman uses the closing accent of the voice too much, so a Scotchman has the contrary habit, and is continually drawling his tones from the grave to the acute, with an effect which, to southern ears, is suspensive in character. The smooth guttural *r* is as little heard in Scotland as in Ireland, the trilled *r* taking its place. The substitution of the former instead of the latter must be a matter of practice. The peculiar sound of the *u*, which in the north so often borders on the French *u*, must be compared with the several sounds of the letter as they are heard in the south; and the long quality which a Scotchman is apt to give to the vowels that ought to be essentially short, must be clipped. In fact, aural observation and lingual exercise are the only sure means to the end; so that a Scotchman going to a

well for a bucket of water, and finding a countryman bathing therein, would not exclaim, " Hey, Colin, dinna ye ken the watter's for drink, and nae for bathin' ?"

182. Of Provincial Brogues it is scarcely necessary to say much, as the foregoing advice applies to them. One militiaman exclaimed to another, " Jim, you bain't in step." "Bain't I ?" exclaimed the other; " well, change yourn !" Whoever desires knowledge must strive for it. It must not be dispensed with after the fashion of Tummus and Jim, who held the following dialogue upon a vital question :—*Tummus.* " I zay, Jim, be you a purtectionist ?" *Jim.* " E'as I be." *Tummus.* " Wall, I zay, Jim, what *be* purtection ?" *Jim.* " Loa'r, Tummus, doan't 'ee knaw ?" *Tummus.* " Naw, I doan't." *Jim.* " Wall, I doan't knaw as I can tell 'ee, Tummus, *vur I doan't ezakerly knaw mysel' !*"

183. Rules of Pronunciation.

i. C before *a*, *o*, and *u*, and in some other situations, is a close articulation, like *k*. Before *e*, *i*, and *y*, *c* is precisely equivalent to *s* in *same*, *this*; as in *cedar, civil, cypress, capacity.*

ii. E final indicates that the preceding vowel is long; as in hate, mete, sire, robe, lyre, abate, recede, invite, remote, intrude.

iii. E final indicates that *c* preceding has the sound of *s*; as in *lace, lance*; and that *g* preceding has the sound of *j*, as in *charge, page, challenge.*

iv. E final, in proper English words, never forms a syllable, and in the most-used words, in the terminating unaccented syllable it is silent. Thus, *motive, genuine, examine, juvenile, reptile, granite*, are pronounced *motiv, genuin, examin, juvenil, reptil, granit.*

v. E final, in a few words of foreign origin, forms a syllable; as *syncope, simile.*

vi. E final is silent after *l* in the following terminations,—*ble, cle, dle, fle, gle, kle, ple, tle, zle*; as in *able, manacle, cradle, ruffle, mangle, wrinkle, supple,* *rattle, puzzle*, which are pronounced *a'bl, man'acl, cra'dl, ruf'fl, man'gl, wrin'kl, sup'pl, puz'zl.*

vii. E is usually silent in the termination *en*; as in *token, broken*; pronounced *tokn, brokn.*

viii. OUS, in the termination of adjectives and their derivatives, is pronounced *us*; as in *gracious, pious, pompously.*

ix. CE, CI, TI, before a vowel, have the sound of *sh*; as in *cetaceous, gracious, motion, partial, ingratiate*; pronounced *cetashus, grashus, moshon, parshal, ingrashiate.*

x. TI, after a consonant, have the sound of *ch*; as in *Christian, bastion*; pronounced *Chrischan, baschan.*

xi. SI, after an accented vowel, are pronounced like *zh*; as in *Ephesian, confusion*; pronounced *Ephezhan, confushan.*

xii. When CI or TI precede similar combinations, as in pronun*ci*ation, nego*ti*ation, they may be pronounced *ce* instead of *she*, to prevent a repetition of the latter syllable; as *pronunceashon* instead of *pronunsheashon.*

xiii. GH, both in the middle and at the end of words, are silent; as in *caught, bought, fright, nigh, sigh*; pronounced *caut, baut, frite, ni, si.* In the following exceptions, however, *gh* are pronounced as *f* :— *cough, chough, clough, enough, laugh, rough, slough, tough, trough.*

xiv. When WH begin a word, the aspirate *h* precedes *w* in prónunciation; as in *what, whiff, whale*; pronounced *hwat, hwiff, hwale, w* having precisely the sound of *oo*, French *ou.* In the following words *w* is silent :—*who, whom, whose, whoop, whole.*

xv. H after *r* has no sound or use; as in *rheum, rhyme*; pronounced *reum, ryme.*

xvi. H should be sounded in the middle of words; as in fore*h*ead, ab*h*or, be*h*old, ex*h*aust, in*h*abit, un*h*orse.

xvii. H should always be sounded except in the following words :—heir, herb, honest, honour, hospital, hostler, hour, humour, and humble, and all their derivatives,—such as humorously, derived from humour.

xviii. K and G are silent before *n*; as *know, gnaw*; pronounced *no, naw.*

xix. W before *r* is silent; as in *wring, wreath*; pronounced *ring, reath.*

xx. B after *m* is silent; as in *dumb, numb*; pronounced *dum, num.*

xxi. L before *k* is silent; as in *balk, walk, talk*; pronounced *bauk, wauk, tauk.*

xxii. PH have the sound of *f*; as in *philosophy*; pronounced *filosophy.*

xxiii. NG has two sounds; one as in *singer*, the other as in *fin-ger.*

xxiv. N after *m*, and closing a syllable, is silent; as in *hymn, condemn.*

xxv. P before *s* and *t* is mute; as in *psalm, pseudo, ptarmigan*; pronounced *sâm, sudo, tarmigan.*

xxvi. R has two sounds, one strong and vibrating, as at the beginning of words and syllables, such as *robber, reckon, error*; the other as at the terminations of words, or when it is succeeded by a consonant, as *farmer, morn.*

xxvii. Before the letter R there is a slight sound of *e* between the vowel and the consonant. Thus, *bare, parent, apparent, mere, mire, more, pure, pyre*, are pronounced nearly *baer, paerent, appaerent, me-er, mier, moer, puer, pyer.* This pronunciation proceeds from the peculiar articulation *r*, and it occasions a slight change of the sound of *a*, which can only be learned by the ear.

xxviii. There are other rules of pronunciation affecting the combinations of vowels, &c.; but as they are more difficult to describe, and as they do not relate to errors which are commonly prevalent, we shall content ourselves with giving examples of them in the following list of words.

184. Words with their Pronunciations.

Again, a-*gen*, not as spelled.

Alien, ale-*yen*, not a-*lye-n.*

Antipodes, an-*tip*-o-dees.

Apostle, without the *t.*

Arch, *artch* in compounds of our own language, as in archbishop, archduke; but *ark* in words derived from the Greek, as archaic, ar-*ka*-ik; archæology, ar-ke-*ol*-o-gy; archangel, ark-*ain*-gel; archetype, *ar*-ke-type; archiepiscopal, ar-ke-*e-pis*-co pal; archipelago, ar-ke-*pel*-a-go; archives, *ar*-kivs, &c.

Asia, asha.

Asparagus, not asparagrass.

Awkward, awk-*wurd*, not awk-*urd.*

Bade, bad.

Because, be-*caws*, not be-*cos.*

Been, bin.

Beloved, as a verb, be-*luvd*; as an adjective, be-*luv*-ed. Blessed, cursed, &c., are subject to the same rule.

Beneath, with the *th* in breath, not with the *th* in breathe.

Biog'raphy, as spelled, not beography.

Buoy, bwoy, not boy.

By and my, in conversation, b'e, m'e. When emphatic, and in poetic reading, by and my.

Canal', as spelled, not ca-*nel.*

Caprice, capreece.

Catch, as spelled, not ketch,

Chaos, ka-oss.

Charlatan, sharlatan.

Chasm, kasm.

Chasten, chasn.

Chivalry, shivalry.

Chemistry, *kim*-is-trey.

Choir, kwire.

Clerk, klerk.

Combat, *kum*-bat.

Conduit, *kun*-dit.

Corps, core; plural, cores.

Covetous, *cuv*-e-tus, not cur-e-chus.

Courteous, *curt*-yus.

Courtesy (politeness), *cur*-te-sey.

Courtesy (a lowering of the body), *curt*-sey.

Oresses, as spelled, not *cresses.*

Cu'riosity, cu-re-*os*-e-ty, not curosity.

Cushion, *coosh*-un, not coosh-*in.*

Daunt, dânt, not dawnt.

Design and desist have the sound of *s*, not of *z.*

Desire should have the sound of *z.*

Despatch, de-*spatch*, not *dis*-patch.

Dew, due, not doo.

Diamond, as spelled, not *di*-mond.

Diploma, de-*plo*-ma, not dip-lo-ma.

Diplomacy, de-*plo*-ma-cy, not *dip*-lo-ma-cy.

Direct, de-*reckt*, not *di*-rect.

Divers (several), *di*-vers; but diverse (different), di-*verse.*

Dome, as spelled, not doom.

Drought, drowt, not drawt.

Duke, as spelled, not dook.

Dynasty, *dyn*-as-te, not *dy*-nas-ty.

Edict, *e*-dickt, not *ed*-ickt.

E'en and e'er, een and air.

Egotism, *eg*-o-tism, not *e*-go-tism.

Either, *e*-ther, not *i*-ther.

Engine, *en*-jin, not *in*-jin.

Ensign, *en*-sign ; ensigncy, *en*-sin-cey.

Epistle, without the *t*.

Epitome, e-*pit*-o-me.

Epoch, *ep*-ock, not *e*-pock.

Equinox, *eq*-kwe-nox, not *e*-qui-nox.

Europe, *U*-rope, not *U*-rup. Euro-*pe*-an, not Eu-ro-pean.

Every, *ev*-er-ey, not *ev*-ry.

Executor, egz-*ec*-utor, not with the sound of *s*.

Extraordinary, ex-*tror*-de-nar-ey, not ex-tra-ordinary, nor extrornarey.

February, as spelled, not Febuary.

Finance, fe-*nance*, not *fi*nance.

Foundling, as spelled, not *fond*-ling.

Garden, *gar*-dn, not gar-den, nor gard-ing.

Gauntlet, *gant*-let, not gannt-let.

Geography, as spelled, not *jography*, nor ge-hography.

Geometry, as spelled, not *jom*-etry.

Haunt, hant, not hawnt.

Height, hite, not highth.

Heinous, *hay*-nus, not *hee*-nus.

Highland, *hi*-land, not *hee*-land.

Horizon, ho-*ri*-zn, not *hor*-i-zon.

Housewife, *hus*-wif.

Hymeneal, hy-men-*e*-al, not hy-menal.

Instead, in-*sted*, not instid.

Isolate, *is*-o-late, not *i*-so-late, nor *is*-olate.

Jalap, *jal*-ap, not jolup.

January, as spelled, not January nor Janeway.

Leave, as spelled, not leaf.

Legend, *led*-gend, not *le*-gend.

Lieutenant, lev-*ten*-ant, not leu-*ten*-ant.

Many, *men*-ney, not man-ny.

Marchioness, *mar*-shun-ess, not as spelled.

Massacre, *mas*-sa-cur, not mas-sa-cre.

Mattress, as spelled, not *mat*-trass.

Matron, *ma*-trun, not mat-ron.

Medicine, *med*-e-cin, not *med*-cin.

Minute (sixty seconds), *min*-it.

Minute (small), mi-*nute*.

Miscellany, *mis*-cellany, not mis-*cel*-lany.

Mischievous, *mis*-chiv-us, not mis-*cheev*-us.

Ne'er, for never, nare.

Neighbourhood, *nay*-bur-hood, not *nay*-bur-wood.

Nephew, *nev*-u, not *nef*-u.

New, nū, not noo.

Notable (worthy of notice), *no*-ta-bl.

Notable (thrifty), *not*-a-bl.

Oblige, as spelled, not obleege.

Oblique, ob-*leek*, not o-*blike*.

Odorous, o-dur-us, not *od*-ur-us.

Of, ov, except when compounded with there, here, and where, which should be pronounced here-*of*, there-*of*, and where-*of*.

Off, of, not awf.

Organisation, or-gan-e-*za*-shun, not or-ga-ni-za-shun.

Ostrich, *os*-tritch, not *os*-tridge.

Pageant, *pad*-jent, not *pa*-jant.

Parent, *par*-ent, not par-ent.

Partisan, par-te-*zan*, not par-te-*san*, nor par-ti-zan.

Patent, *pat*-ent, not *pa*-tent.

Physiognomy, not physionnomy.

Pincers, *pin*-cers, not pinch-ers.

Plaintiff, as spelled, not plan-tiff.

Pour, pore, not so as to rhyme with our.

Precedent (an example), *press*-e-dent ; pre-*ce*-dent is the pronunciation of the adjective.

Prologue, *prol*-og, not *pro*-loge.

Quadrille, ka-*dril*, not quod-ril.

Quay, key, not as spelled.

Radish, as spelled, not red-ish.

Raillery, *ral*-ler-ey, not as spelled.

Rather, not raather.

Resort, rezort.

Resound, rezound.

Respite, *res*-pit, not as spelled.

Rout (a party ; and to rout) should be pronounced rowt. Route (a road), root.

Saunter, *san*-ter, not sawnter.

Sausage, *saw*-sage, not sos-sidge, nor sas-sage.

Schedule, *shed*-ule, not shed-dle.

Seamstress, sem-stress.

Sewer, soor, not shore, nor shure.

Shire, sheer, not as spelled.

Sbone, shōn, not shun, nor as spelled.

Soldier, *sole*-jer.

Solecism, *sol*-e-cism, not *so*-le-cism.

Soot, as spelled, not sut.

Sovereign, *sov*-er-in, not suv-er-in.

Specious, *spe*-shus, not *spesh*-us.

Stomacher, *stum*-a-cher.

Stone (weight), as spelled, not stun.

Synod, *syn*-ud, not *sy*-nod.

Tenure, *ten*-ure, not *te*-nure.

Tenet, *ten*-et, not *te*-net.

Than, as spelled, not thun.

Tremor, *trem*-ur, not *tre*-mor.

Twelfth, should have the th sounded.

Umbrel la, as spelled, not um-ber-el-la.

Vase, vāze, not vawse.

Was, wos, not wuz.

Weary, *weer*-ey, not wary.

Were, wer, not ware.

Wont, wunt, not as spelled.

Wrath, rawth, not rath: as an adjective it is spelled wroth, and pronounced with the vowel sound shorter, as wrăth'-ful, &c.

Yacht, yot, not yat.

Yeast, as spelled, not yĕst.

Zenith, zen-ith, not ze-nith.

Zodiac, zo-de-ak.

Zoology should have both o's sounded, as zo-ol-o-gy, not zoo-lo-gy.

PRONOUNCE—

—ace, not iss, as furnace, not furniss.

—age, not idge, as cabbage, courage, postage, village.

—ain, ane, not in, as certain, certane, not certin.

—ate, not it, as moderate, not moderit.

—ct, not c, as aspect, not aspec; subject, not subjec.

—ed, not id, or ud, as wicked, not wickid, or wickud.

—el, not l, model, not modl; novel, not novl.

—en, not n, as sudden, not suddn.—Burden, burthen, garden, lengthen, seven, strengthen, often, and a few others, have the e silent.

—ence, not unce, as influence, not influ-unce.

—es, not is, as pleases, not pleasis.

—ile should be pronounced il, as fertil, not fertile, in all words except chamomile (cam), exile, gentile, infantile, reconcile, and senile, which should be pronounced ile.

—in, not n, as Latin, not Latn.

—nd, not n, as husband, not husban; thousand, not thousan.

—ness, not niss, as carefulness, not carefulniss.

—ng, not n, as singing, not singin; speaking, not speakin.

—ngth, not nth, as strength, not strenth.

—son, the o should be silent; as in treason, trea-sn, not trea-son.

—tal, not tle, as capital, not capitle; metal, not mettle; mortal, not mortle; periodical, not periodicle.

—xt, not x, as next, not nex.

185. Punctuation.—Punctuation teaches the method of placing *Points*, in written or printed matter, in such a manner as to indicate the pauses which would be made by the author if he were communicating his thoughts orally instead of by written signs.

186. WRITING AND PRINTING are substitutes for oral communication; and correct punctuation is essential to convey the meaning intended, and to give due force to such passages as the author may wish to impress upon the mind of the person to whom they are being communicated.

187. THE POINTS are as follow :—

The Comma ,
The Semicolon ;
The Colon :
The Period, or Full Point .
The Apostrophe '
The Hyphen, or Conjoiner -
The Note of Interrogation ?
The Note of Exclamation !
The Parenthesis ( )
The Asterisk, or Star *

As these are all the points required in simple epistolary composition, we will confine our explanations to the rules which should govern the use of them.

188. THE OTHER POINTS, however, are the paragraph ¶; the section §; the dagger †; the double dagger ‡; the rule —; the parallel ‖; the bracket [ ]; and some others. These, however, are quite unnecessary, except for elaborate works, in which they are chiefly used for notes or marginal references.

189. THE COMMA , denotes the shortest pause; the semicolon ; a little longer pause than the comma; the colon : a little longer pause than the semicolon; the period, or full-point . the longest pause.

190. THE RELATIVE DURATION of these pauses is described as—

	While you count
Comma	One
Semicolon	Two.
Colon	Three.
Period	Four.

This, however, is not an infallible rule, because the duration of the pauses should be regulated by the degree of rapidity with which the matter is being read. In slow reading, the duration of the pauses should be increased.

191. THE OTHER POINTS are rather indications of expression, and of meaning and connection, than of pauses, and therefore we will notice them separately.

192. THE MISPLACING of even so

slight a point, or pause, as the comma, will often alter the meaning of a sentence. The contract made for lighting the town of Liverpool, during the year 1819, was thrown void by the misplacing of a comma in the advertisements, thus:—"The lamps at present are about 4050, and have in general two spouts each, composed of not less than twenty threads of cotton." The contractor would have proceeded to furnish each lamp with the said twenty threads; but this being but half the usual quantity, the commissioners discovered that the difference arose from the comma following instead of preceding the word *each*. The parties agreed to annul the contract, and a new one was ordered.

193. THE FOLLOWING SENTENCE shows how difficult it is to read without the aid of the points used as pauses:—

Death waits not for storm nor sunshine within a dwelling in one of the upper streets respectable in appearance and furnished with such conveniences as distinguish the habitations of those who rank among the higher classes of society a man of middle age lay on his last bed momently awaiting the final summons all that the most skilful medical attendance all that love warm as the glow that fires an angel's bosom could do had been done by day and night for many long weeks had ministering spirits such as a devoted wife and loving children are done all within their power to ward off the blow but there he lay his raven hair smoothed off from his noble brow his dark eyes lighted with unnatural brightness and contrasting strongly with the pallid hue which marked him as an expectant of the dread messenger.

194. THE SAME SENTENCE, properly pointed, and with capital letters placed after full-points, according to the adopted rule, may be easily read and understood:—

Death waits not for storm nor sunshine. Within a dwelling in one of the upper streets, respectable in appearance, and furnished with such conveniences as distinguish the habitations of those who rank among the higher classes of society, a man of middle age lay on his last bed, momently awaiting the final summons. All that the most skilful medical attendance—all that love, warm as the glow

that fires an angel's bosom, could do, had been done; by day and night, for many long weeks, had ministering spirits, such as a devoted wife and loving children are done all within their power to ward off the blow. But there he lay, his raven hair smoothed off from his noble brow, his dark eyes lighted with unnatural brightness, and contrasting strongly with the pallid hue which marked him as an expectant of the dread messenger.

195. THE APOSTROPHE ' is used to indicate the combining of two words in one,—as John's book, instead of John, his book; or to show the omission of parts of words, as Glo'ster, for Gloucester—tho' for though. These abbreviations should be avoided as much as possible. Cobbett says the apostrophe "ought to be called the mark of *laziness* and vulgarity." The first use, however, of which we gave an example, is a necessary and proper one.

196. THE HYPHEN, or conjoiner - is used to unite words which, though they are separate and distinct, have so close a connection as almost to become one word, as water-rat, wind-mill, &c. It is also used in writing and printing, at the end of a line, to show where a word is divided and continued in the next line. Look down the ends of the lines in this column, and you will notice the hyphen in several places.

197. THE NOTE OF INTERROGATION ? indicates that the sentence to which it is put asks a question; as, "What is the meaning of that assertion? What am I to do?"

198. THE NOTE OF EXCLAMATION or of admiration ! indicates surprise, pleasure, or sorrow; as, "Oh! Ah! Goodness! Beautiful! I am astonished! Woe is me!"

Sometimes, when an expression of strong surprise or pleasure is intended, two notes of this character are employed, thus ! !

199. THE PARENTHESIS ( ) is used to prevent confusion by the introduction to a sentence of a passage not necessary to the sense thereof. "I am going to meet Mr. Smith (though I am no admirer of him) on Wednesday next."

It is better, however, as a rule, not to employ parenthetical sentences.

200. THE ASTERISK, OR STAR * may be employed to refer from the text to a note of explanation at the foot of a column, or at the end of a letter. *⁎* Three stars are sometimes used to call particular attention to a paragraph.

201. Hints upon Spelling. — The following rules will be found of great assistance in writing, because they relate to a class of words about the spelling of which doubt and hesitation are frequently felt:—

i. All words of one syllable ending in *l*, with a single vowel before it, have double *l* at the close: as, *mill, sell.*

ii. All words of one syllable ending in *l*, with a double vowel before it, have one *l* only at the close: as, *mail, sail.*

iii. Words of one syllable ending in *l*, when compounded, retain but one *l* each: as, *fulfil, skilful.*

iv. Words of more than one syllable ending in *l* have one *l* only at the close: as, *delightful, faithful;* except *befall, downfall, recall, unwell,* &c.

v. All derivatives from words ending in *l* have one *l* only: as, *equality,* from *equal; fulness,* from *full;* except they end in *er* or *ly*: as, *mill, miller; full, fully.*

vi. All participles in *ing* from verbs ending in *e* lose the *e* final: as, *have, having; amuse, amusing;* unless they come from verbs ending in double *e*, and then they retain both: as, *see, seeing; agree, agreeing.*

vii. All adverbs in *ly* and nouns in *ment* retain the *e* final of the primitives: as, *brave, bravely; refine, refinement;* except *acknowledgment, judgment,* &c.

viii. All derivatives from words ending in *er* retain the *e* before the *r*: as, *refer, reference;* except *hindrance,* from *hinder; remembrance* from *remember; disastrous* from *disaster; monstrous* from *monster; wondrous* from *wonder; cumbrous* from *cumber,* &c.

ix. Compound words, if both end not in *l*, retain their primitive parts entire: as, *millstone, changeable, raceless;* except *always, also, deplorable, although, almost, admirable,* &c.

x. All one-syllables ending in a consonant, with a single vowel before it, double that consonant in derivatives: as, *sin, sinner; ship, shipping; big, bigger; glad, gladder,* &c.

xi. One-syllables ending in a consonant, with a double vowel before it, do not double the consonant in derivatives: as, *sleep, sleepy; troop, trooper.*

xii. All words of more than one syllable ending in a single consonant, preceded by a single vowel, and accented on the last syllable, double that consonant in derivatives: as, *commit, committee; compel, compelled; appal, appalling; distil, distiller.*

xiii. Nouns of one syllable ending in *y*, preceded by a consonant, change *y* into *ies* in the plural; and verbs ending in *y*, preceded by a consonant, change *y* into *ies* in the third person singular of the present tense, and into *ied* in the past tense and past participle: as, *fly, flies; I apply, he applies; we reply, we replied,* or *have replied.* If the *y* be preceded by a vowel, this rule is not applicable: as, *key, keys; I play, he plays;* we have *enjoyed* ourselves.

xiv. Compound words whose primitives end in *y* change *y* into *i*: as, *beauty, beautiful; lovely, loveliness.*

202. H OR NO H? THAT IS THE QUESTION. — Few things point so directly to the want of *cultivation* as the misuse of the letter H by persons in conversation. We hesitate to assert that this common defect in speaking indicates the absence of *education*—for, to our surprise, we have heard even educated persons frequently commit this common and vulgar error. Now, for the purpose of assisting those who desire to improve their mode of speaking, we intend to tell a little story about our next door neighbour, Mrs. Alexander Hitching,—or, as she frequently styled herself, with an air of conscious dignity, MRS. HALEXANDER 'ITCHING. Her husband was a post-captain of some distinction, seldom at home, and therefore Mrs. A. H. (or, as she rendered it, Mrs. *H. I.*) felt it incumbent upon herself to represent her own dignity, and the dignity of her husband also. Well, this Mrs. Hitching was a next-door neighbour of ours—a most agreeable lady in many respects, middle aged, good looking, uncommonly fond of talking, of active, almost of fussy habits, very good tempered and good natured, but with a most unpleasant habit of misusing the letter H to such a degree that our sensitive nerves have often been shocked when in her society. But we must beg the reader, if Mrs. H. should be an acquaintance of his, not to breathe a word of our having written this account of her—or there would be no limit to her "*h*indignation." And, as her family is very numerous, it will be necessary to keep the matter as quiet as can be, for it will scarcely be possible to mention the subject anywhere, without "'orrifying" some of her relations, and instigating them to make Mrs. H. become our "*h*enemy," instead of remaining, as we wish her to do, our intimate friend.

One morning, Mrs. H. called upon me, and asked me to take a walk, saying that it was her *h*object to look out for an 'ouse, as her lease had nearly terminated; and as she had often heard her dear 'Itching say that he would like to settle in the neighbourhood of 'Ampstead 'Eath, she should like me to assist her by my judgment in the choice of a residence.

"I shall be most happy to accompany you," I said.

"I knew you would," said she: "and I am sure a *h*our or two in your society will give me pleasure. It's so long since we've 'ad a gossip. Besides which, I want a change of *h*air."

I glanced at her peruke, and for a moment laboured under the idea that she intended to call at her hairdresser's; but I soon recollected.

"I suppose we had better take the *h*omnibus," she remarked, "and we can get out at the foot of the 'ill."

I assented, and in a few minutes we were in the street, in the line of the omnibus, and one of those vehicles soon appearing—

"Will you 'ail it?" inquired she.

So I hailed it at once, and we got in. Now Mrs. H. was so fond of talking that the presence of strangers never restrained her—a fact which I have often had occasion to regret. She was no sooner within the omnibus than she began remarking upon the *h*inconvenience of such vehicles, because of their smallness, and the *h*insolence of many of the conductors. She thought that the proprietors ought only to 'ire men upon whose civility they could depend. Then she launched out into larger topics—said she thought that the *H*emperor of *H*austria—(here I endeavoured to interrupt her by asking whether she had any idea of the part of Hampstead she would like; but she would complete her remarks by saying)—must be as appy as the days are long, now that the *H*empress had presented him with a *h*are to the throne! (Some of the passengers smiled, and, turning round, looked out of the windows.)

I much wished for our arrival at the spot where we should alight, for she commenced a story about an 'andsome young nephew of hers, who was a distinguished *h*officer of the *h*army. This was suggested to her, no doubt, by the presence in the omnibus of a fine-looking young fellow, with a moustache. She said that at present her nephew was stationed in *H*ireland; but he expected soon to be *h*ordered to the Crimea.

The gentleman with the moustache seemed much amused, and smilingly asked her whether her nephew was at all *h*ambitious? I saw that he (the gentleman with the moustache) was jesting, and I would have given anything to have been released from the unpleasant predicament I was in. But what was my annoyance when Mrs. H. proceeded to say to this youth, whose face was radiant with humour, that it was the 'ight of her nephew's *h*ambition to serve his country in the *h*our of need;

and then she proceeded to ask her fellow-traveller his opinion of the *h*upshot of the war—remarking that she 'oped it would soon be *h*over!

At this moment I felt so nervous that I pulled out my handkerchief, and endeavoured to create a diversion by making a loud nasal noise, and remarking that I thought the wind very cold, when an accident happened which took us all by surprise: one of the large wheels of the omnibus dropped off, and all the passengers were jostled down into a corner; but, fortunately, without serious injury. Mrs. H., however, happening to be under three or four persons, raised a loud cry for "'elp! 'elp!" She was speedily got out, when she assured us that she was not 'urt; but she was in such a state of *h*agitation that she wished to be taken to a chemist's shop, to get some *H*aromatic vinegar, or some *H*oe de Cologne! The chemist was exceedingly polite to her, for which she said she could never express her *h*obligations—an assertion which seemed to me to be literally true. It was some time before she resumed her accustomed freedom of conversation; but as we ascended the hill she explained to me that she should like to take the house as tenant from 'ear to 'ear!—but she thought landlords would *h*object to such an agreement, as when they got a good tenant they liked to 'old 'im as long as they could. She expressed an opinion that 'Ampstead must be very 'ealthy, because it was so 'igh *h*up.

We soon reached the summit of the hill, and turned through a lane which led towards the Heath, and in which villas and cottages were smiling on each side. "Now, there's a *h*elegant little place!" she exclaimed, "just suited to my *h*ideas — about *h*eight rooms, and a *h*oriel *h*over the *h*entrance." But it was not to let—so we passed on.

Presently, she saw something likely to suit her, and as there was a bill in the window, "To be Let—Enquire Within," she gave a loud rat-a-tat-tat at the door.

The servant opened it.

"I see this 'ouse is to let."

"Yes, ma'am it is; will you walk in?"

"'Ow many rooms are there?"

"Eleven, ma'am; but if you will step in, mistress will speak to you."

A very graceful lady made her appearance at the parlour door, and invited us to step in. I felt exceedingly nervous, for I at once perceived that the lady of the house spoke with that accuracy and taste which is one of the best indications of refinement.

"The house *is* to let—and a very pleasant residence we have found it."

"'Ave you *h*occupied it long?"

"Our family has resided here for more than nine years."

"Then, I suppose, your lease 'as run *h*out!"

"No! we have it for five years longer: but my brother, who is a clergyman, has been appointed to a living in Yorkshire, and for his sake, and for the pleasure of his society, we desire to remove."

"Well—there's nothing like keeping families together for the sake of 'appiness. Now, there's my poor dear 'Itching"—[here she paused, as if somewhat affected, and some young ladies who were in the room drew their heads together, and appeared to consult about their needlework; but I saw, by dimples upon their cheeks, which they could not conceal, that they were smiling], "'e's 'itherto been *h*at 'ome so seldom, that I've 'ardly *h*ever known what 'appiness *h*is."

I somewhat abruptly broke in upon the conversation, by suggesting that she had better look through the house, and enquire the conditions of tenancy. We consequently went through the various rooms, and in every one of them she had "an *h*objection to this," or "a 'atred for that," or would give "an 'int which might be useful" to the lady when she removed. The young ladies were heard tittering very much as we walked across the staircases, for it generally happened on these occasions that Mrs. H. broke out, in a loud voice, with her imperfect elocution. I felt so much annoyed, that I determined to cure Mrs. H. of her defective speaking.

In the evening, after returning home, we were sitting by the fire, and felt comfortable and chatty, when I proposed to Mrs. Hitching the following enigma, the author of which, Henry Mayhew, Esq., had favoured me with a copy of it:—

The Vide Vorld you may search, and my
    fellow not find;
I dwells in a Wacuum, deficient in Vind;
In the Wissage I'm seen—in the Woice I am
    heard,
And yet I'm invisible, gives went to no Vurd.
I'm not much of a Vag, for I'm vanting in
    Vit;
But distinguished in Werse for the Wollums
    I've writ.
I'm the head of all Willains, yet far from the
    Vurst—
I'm the foremost in Wice, though in Wirtue
    the first.
I'm not used to Veapons, and ne'er goes to
    Vor;
Though in Walour invincible—in Wictory
    sure ;
The first of all Wiands and Wictuals is mine—
Rich in Wen'son and Weal, but deficient in
    Vine.
To Wanity given, I in Welwets abound;
But in Voman, in Vife, and in Vidow ain't
    found;
Yet conspicuous in Wirgins, and I'll tell you,
    between us,
To persons of taste I'm a bit of a Wenus ;
Yet none take me for Veal—or for Voe in its
    stead,
For I ranks not among the sveet Voo'd, Vun,
    and Ved!

Before the recital of the enigma was half completed, Mrs. Hitching laughed heartily—she saw, of course, the meaning of it—that it was a play upon the Cockney error of using the V instead of the W, and the latter instead of the V. Several times, as I proceeded, she exclaimed "Hexcellent! hexcellent!" and when I had finished, she remarked that it was very "Aingenious," and enough to "hopen the heyes" of the Cockneys

to their stupid and vulgar manner of speaking.

A more difficult and delicate task lay before me. I told her that as she was so much pleased with the first enigma, I would submit another by the same author. I felt very nervous, but determined to proceed :—

I dwells in the Herth, and I breathes in the
    Hair ;
If you searches the Hocean, you'll find that
    I'm there.
The first of all Hangels, in Holympus am Hi,
Yet I'm banished from 'Eaven, expelled from
    on 'Igh.
But though on this Horb I am destined to
    grovel,
I'm ne'er seen in an 'Ouse, in an 'Ut, nor an
    'Ovel ;
Not an 'Oss nor an 'Unter e'er bears me, alas !
But often I'm found on the top of a Hass.
I resides in a Hattic, and loves not to roam,
And yet I'm invariably absent from 'Ome.
Though 'ushed in the 'Urricane, of the Hatmo-
    sphere part,
I enters no 'Ed, I creeps into no 'Art.
Only look, and you'll see in the Heye I
    appear,
Only hark, and you'll 'ear me just breathe
    in the Hear ;
Though in sex not an 'E, I am (strange para-
    dox !)
Not a bit of an 'Effer, but partly a Hox.
Of Heternity Hi'm the beginning! And,
    mark,
Though I goes not with Noar, I am first in
    the Hark.
I'm never in 'Ealth — have with Fysic no
    power;
I dies in a Month, but comes back in a Hour !

I noticed during the progress of this enigma, in reciting which I ventured to emphasise the misplaced h's as much as possible, that occasional blushes and smiles passed over Mrs. Hitching's face. After it was finished, there was a pause of some minutes. At last she said, "Very good, very clever." She carefully avoided using any word in which the h, hard or soft, was required. I saw she was timid, and I then determined to complete the task I had begun by repeating the following enigma by Byron, upon the same letter :—

'Twas whispered in heaven, 'twas muttered
in hell,
And echo caught faintly the sound as it fell:
On the confines of earth 'twas permitted to
rest,
And the depths of the ocean its presence con-
fessed.
'Twill be found in the sphere when 'tis riven
asunder,
Be seen in the lightning, and heard in the
thunder.
'Twas allotted to man with his earliest breath,
Attends at his birth, and awaits him in death;
It presides o'er his happiness, honour, and
health,
Is the prop of his house, and the end of his
wealth.
Without it the soldier and seaman may roam,
But woe to the wretch who expels it from
home.
In the whispers of conscience its voice will be
found,
Nor e'en in the whirlwind of passion be
drowned.
'Twill not soften the heart, and though deaf
to the ear,
'Twill make it acutely and instantly hear.
But in shade let it rest, like a delicate flower—
Oh, breathe on it softly—it dies in an hour.

She was much pleased, but seemed
thoughtful, and once or twice in conversation checked herself, and corrected
her pronunciation of words that were
difficult to her.

A few days afterwards, I called upon
her, and upon being introduced to the
parlour to wait for her appearance, I saw
lying upon her table the following

**MEMORANDUM ON THE USE OF THE
LETTER H.**

Pronounce—Herb,	'Erb.
" Heir,	'Eir.
" Honesty.	'Onesty.
" Honour,	'Onour.
" Hospital,	'Ospital.
" Hostler.	'Ostler.
" Hour,	'Our.
" Humour,	'Umour.
" Humble,	'Umble.
" Humility,	'Umility.

*In all other cases the H is to be sounded when
it begins a word.*

Mem.—Be careful to sound the *H* slightly
in such words as where, when, what, why—
don't say were, wen, wat, wy.

I am happy to say that it is now a
pleasure to hear Mrs. Hitching's conversation. I only hope that others may
improve as she has done.

203. Conversation.—There are
many talkers, but few who know how
to converse agreeably. Speak distinctly, neither too rapidly nor too
slowly. Accommodate the pitch of
your voice to the hearing of the person
with whom you are conversing. Never
speak with your mouth full. Tell your
jokes, and laugh afterwards. Dispense
with superfluous words — such as,
"Well, I should think."

204. THE WOMAN who wishes her
conversation to be agreeable will avoid
conceit or affectation, and laughter
which is not natural and spontaneous.
Her language will be easy and un-
studied, marked by a graceful carelessness, which, at the same time, never
oversteps the limits of propriety. Her
lips will readily yield to a pleasant
smile; she will not love to hear herself talk; her tones will bear the impress of sincerity, and her eyes kindle
with animation as she speaks. The
art of pleasing is, in truth, the very
soul of good breeding; for the precise
object of the latter is to render us
agreeable to all with whom we asso-
ciate—to make us, at the same time,
esteemed and loved.

205. WE NEED SCARCELY ADVERT
to the rudeness of interrupting any one
who is speaking, or to the impropriety
of pushing, to its full extent, a discussion which has become unpleasant.

206. SOME MEN HAVE A MANIA for
Greek and Latin quotations: this is
peculiarly to be avoided. It is like
pulling up the stones from a tomb
wherewith to kill the living. Nothing
is more wearisome than pedantry.

207. IF YOU FEEL YOUR INTEL-
LECTUAL SUPERIORITY to any one with
whom you are conversing, do not seek to
bear him down: it would be an inglo-
rious triumph, and a breach of good manners. Beware, too, of speaking lightly of
subjects which bear a sacred character.

208. WITLINGS OCCASIONALLY GAIN A REPUTATION in society; but nothing is more insipid and in worse taste than their conceited harangues and self-sufficient air.

209. IT IS A COMMON IDEA that the art of writing and the art of conversation are one; this is a great mistake. A man of genius may be a very dull talker.

210. THE TWO GRAND MODES of making your conversation interesting, are to enliven it by recitals calculated to affect and impress your hearers, and to intersperse it with anecdotes and smart things. Rivasol was a master in the latter mode.

211. Composition.—If you would write to any purpose, you must be perfectly free from without, in the first place, and yet more free from within. Give yourself the natural rein; think on no pattern, no patron, no paper, no press, no public: think on nothing, but follow your own impulses. Give yourself as you are, what you are, and how you see it. Every man sees with his own eyes, or does not see at all. This is incontrovertibly true. Bring out what you have. If you have nothing, be an honest beggar rather than a respectable thief. Great care and attention should be devoted to epistolary correspondence, as nothing exhibits want of taste and judgment so much as a slovenly letter. Since the establishment of the penny postage it is recognized as a rule that all letters should be prepaid; indeed, many persons make a point of never taking in an unpaid letter. The following hints may be worthy of attention:—

212. ALWAYS PUT A STAMP on your envelope, at the top of the right-hand corner.

213. LET THE DIRECTION be written very plain; this will save the postman trouble, and facilitate business by preventing mistakes.

214. AT THE HEAD OF YOUR LETTER, in the right-hand corner, put your address in full; with the day of the month underneath; do not omit this, though you may be writing to your most intimate friend three or four times a day.

215. WHAT YOU HAVE TO SAY IN YOUR LETTER, say as plainly as possible, as if you were speaking: this is the best rule. Do not revert three or four times to one circumstance, but finish as you go on.

216. LET YOUR SIGNATURE be written as plainly as possible (many mistakes will be avoided, especially in writing to strangers), and without any flourishes, as these do not add in any way to the harmony of your letter. We have seen signatures that have been almost impossible to decipher, being a mere mass of strokes, without any form to indicate letters. This is done chiefly by the ignorant, and would lead one to suppose that they were ashamed of signing what they had written.

217. DO NOT CROSS YOUR LETTERS: surely paper is cheap enough now to admit of your using an extra half-sheet, in case of necessity. (This practice is chiefly prevalent amongst young ladies.)

218. IF YOU WRITE TO A STRANGER for information, or on your own business, be sure to send a stamped envelope with your address plainly written; this will not fail to procure you an answer.

219. IF YOU ARE NOT A GOOD WRITER it is advisable to use the best ink, paper, and pens; as, though they may not alter the character of your handwriting, yet they will assist to make your writing look better.

220. THE PAPER on which you write should be clean, and neatly folded.

221. THERE SHOULD NOT BE STAINS on the envelope; if otherwise, it is only an indication of your own slovenliness.

222. CARE must be taken in giving titled persons, to whom you write, their proper designations.

223. To those who Write for the Press. — It would be a great favour to editors and printers, should those who write for the press observe the following rules. They are reasonable, and correspondents will regard them as such :— i. Write with black ink, on white paper, wide ruled. ii. Make the pages small, one-fourth that of a foolscap sheet. iii. Leave the second page of each leaf blank. iv. Give to the written page an ample margin *all round.* v. Number the pages in the order of their succession. vi. Write in a plain, bold hand, with less respect to beauty. vii. Use no abbreviations which are not to appear in print. viii. Punctuate the manuscript as it should be printed. ix. For italics underscore one line, for small capitals, two; capitals, three. x. Never interline without the caret to show its place. xi. Take special pains with every letter in proper names. xii. Review every word, to be sure that none is illegible. xiii. Put directions to the printer at the head of the first page. xiv. Never write a private letter to the editor on the printer's copy, but always on a separate sheet.

224. Gardening Operations for the Year.

225. JANUARY. — FLOWER OF THE MONTH.—Christmas Rose.

226. GARDENING OPERATIONS.—Indoor preparations for future operations must be made, as in this month there are only five hours a day available for outdoor work, unless the season be unusually mild. Mat over tulip-beds, begin to force roses. Pot over seakale and plant dried roots of border flowers in mild weather. Take strawberries in pots into the greenhouse. Prune and plant gooseberry, currant, fruit, and deciduous trees and shrubs. Cucumbers and melons to be sown in the hot-bed. Apply manures.

227. FEBRUARY.—FLOWERS OF THE MONTH.—Snowdrop and Violet.

228. GARDENING OPERATIONS. — Transplant pinks, carnations, sweet williams, candituft, campanulas, &c., sweet and garden peas and lettuces, for succession of crops, covering the ground with straw, &c. Sow also savoys, leeks, and cabbages. Prune and nail walnut trees, and towards the end of the month plant stocks for next year's grafting,

also cuttings of poplar, elder, willow-trees, for ornamental shrubbery. Sow fruit and forest tree seeds.

229. MARCH. — FLOWER OF THE MONTH.—Primrose.

230. GARDENING OPERATIONS. — " Spring flowers " to be sown. Border flowers to be planted out. Tender annuals to be potted out under glasses. Mushroom beds to be made. Sow artichokes, Windsor beans, and cauliflowers for autumn : lettuces and peas for succession of crops, onions, parsley, radishes, savoys, asparagus, red and white cabbages, and beets ; turnips, early brocoli, parsnips, and carrots. Plant slips and parted roots of perennial herbs. Graft trees and protect early blossoms. Force rose-tree cuttings under glasses.

231. APRIL. — FLOWER OF THE MONTH.—Cowslip.

232. GARDENING OPERATIONS. — Sow for succession peas, beans, and carrots ; parsnips, celery, and seakale. Sow " spring flowers." Plant evergreens, dahlias, chrysanthemums, and the like, also potatoes, slips of thyme, parted roots, lettuces, cauliflowers, cabbages, onions. Lay down turf, remove caterpillars. Sow and graft camelias, and propagate and graft fruit and rose trees by all the various means in use. Sow cucumbers and vegetable marrows for planting out. *This is the most important month in the year for gardeners.*

233. MAY. — FLOWER OF THE MONTH.—Hawthorn.

234. GARDENING OPERATIONS. — Plant out your seedling flowers as they are ready, and sow again for succession larkspur, mignonette, and other spring flowers. Pot out tender annuals. Remove auriculas to a N.E. aspect. Take up bulbous roots as the leaves decay. Sow kidney beans, brocoli for spring use, cape for autumn, cauliflowers for December ; Indian corn, cress, onions to plant out as bulbs next year, radishes, aromatic herbs, turnips, cabbages, savoys, lettuces, &c. Plant celery, lettuces, and annuals ; thin spring crops ; stick peas, &c. Earth up potatoes, &c. Moisten mushroom beds.

235. JUNE. — FLOWERS OF THE MONTH.—Water-lily and Honeysuckle.

236. GARDENING OPERATIONS. — Sow giant stocks to flower next spring. Slip myrtles to strike, and lay pinks, carnations, roses, and evergreens. Plant annuals in borders, and auriculas in shady places. Sow kidney beans, pumpkins, cucumbers for pickling, and (late in the month) endive and lettuces. Plant out cucumbers, marrows, leeks, celery, brocoli, cauliflowers, savoys, and seedlings, and plants propagated by slips. Earth up potatoes, &c. Cut herbs for drying when in flower.

237. JULY. — FLOWERS OF THE MONTH.—Rose and Carnation.

238. GARDENING OPERATIONS. — Part auricula and polyanthus roots. Take up summer bulbs as they go out of flower, and plant saffron crocus and autumn bulbs. Gather seeds. Clip evergreen borders and hedges, strike myrtle slips under glasses. Net fruit trees. Finish budding by the end of the month. Head down espaliers. Sow early dwarf cabbages to plant out in October for spring; also endive, onions, kidney beans for late crop, and turnips. Plant celery, endive, lettuces, cabbages, leeks, strawberries, and cauliflowers. Stick peas. Tie up salads. Earth celery. Take up onions, &c., for drying.

239. AUGUST.—FLOWERS OF THE MONTH.—Harebell and Mallow.

240. GARDENING OPERATIONS. — Sow flowers to bloom indoors in winter, and pot all young stocks raised in the greenhouse. Sow early red cabbages, cauliflowers for spring and summer use, cos and cabbage lettuce for winter crop. Plant out winter crops. Dry herbs and mushroom spawn. Plant out strawberry roots, and net currant trees, to preserve the fruit through the winter.

241. SEPTEMBER.—FLOWERS OF THE MONTH.—Clematis, or Traveller's Joy, Arbutus, and Meadow Saffron.

242. GARDENING OPERATIONS. — Plant crocuses, scaly bulbs, and evergreen shrubs. Propagate by layers and cuttings of all herbaceous plants, currant, gooseberry, and other fruit trees.

Plant out seedling pinks. Sow onions for spring plantation, carrots, spinach, and Spanish radishes in warm spots. Earth up celery. House potatoes and edible bulbs. Gather pickling cucumbers. Make tulip and mushroom beds.

243. OCTOBER.—FLOWERS OF THE MONTH.—China-aster, Holly, and Ivy.

244. GARDENING OPERATIONS. — Sow rose-tree seeds and fruit stones, also larkspurs and the hardier annuals to stand the winter, also hyacinths and smooth bulbs in pots and glasses. Plant young trees, cuttings of jasmine, honeysuckle, and evergreens. Sow mignonette for pots in winter. Plant cabbages, &c., for spring. Cut down asparagus, separate roots of daisies, irises, &c. Trench, drain, and manure.

245. NOVEMBER.—FLOWERS OF THE MONTH.—Laurestine and Wych Hazel.

246. GARDENING OPERATIONS. — Sow sweet peas for an early crop. Take up dahlia roots. Complete beds for asparagus and artichokes. Plant dried roots of border flowers, daisies, &c. Take potted mignonette indoors. Set strawberries. Sow peas, leeks, beans, and radishes. Plant rhubarb in rows. Prune hardy trees, and plant stocks of fruit trees. Store carrots, &c. Shelter from frost where it may be required. Plant shrubs for forcing. Continue to trench and manure vacant ground.

247. DECEMBER.—FLOWERS OF THE MONTH.—Cyclamen and Winter Aconite. (Holly berries are now available for floral decoration.)

248. GARDENING OPERATIONS. — Continue in open weather to prepare vacant ground for spring, and to protect plants from frost. Cover bulbous roots with matting. Dress flower borders. Prepare forcing ground for cucumbers, and force asparagus and seakale. Plant gooseberry, currant, apple, and pear trees. Roll grass-plats if the season be mild and not too wet. Prepare poles, stakes, pea-sticks, &c., for spring.

249. KITCHEN GARDEN. — This is one of the most important parts of general domestic economy, whenever the situation of a house will permit a family to avail themselves of its assistance in aid of butcher's bills. It is, indeed, much to be regretted that small plots of ground, in the immediate vicinity of the metropolis more especially, are too often frittered away into shrubberies and baby gardens, when they might more usefully be employed in raising vegetables for the family, during the week-day residence in town, than wasting their sweetness on the smoky air in all the pride of lilac, hollyhock, and bachelor's buttons, to be merely smelled to by the whole immigrating household on the day of rest. With a little care and attention, a kitchen garden, though small, might be rendered not only useful, but, in fact, as ornamental as a modern grass carpet; and the same expense incurred to make the ground a labyrinth of sweets, might suffice to render it agreeable to the palate as well as to the olfactory nerves, and that even without offending the most delicate optics. It is only in accordance with our plan to give the hint, and to record such novel points as may facilitate the proposed arrangement. It is one objection to the adoption of a kitchen garden in front of the dwelling, or in sight of the family apartments, that its very nature makes it rather an eyesore than otherwise at all seasons. This, however, is an objection that may be readily got over by a little attention to neatness and good order, whilst the plants themselves, if judiciously attended to, and the borders sown or planted with ranunculus, polyanthus, mignonette, &c., in succession, will really be ornamental; but then, in cutting the plants for use, the business must be done neatly—all useless leaves cleared from the ground, the roots no longer wanted taken up, and the ravages of insects must be guarded against by sedulous extirpation. It will also be found a great improvement, where space will admit of it, to surround the beds with neat espaliers, with fruit trees, or even gooseberry and currant bushes, trained along them, instead of these being suffered to grow in a state of ragged wildness.

250. Artificial Mushroom Beds.

—Mushrooms may be grown in pots, boxes, or hampers. Each box may be three feet long, one and a half broad, and seven inches in depth. Let each box be half filled with horse-dung from the stables (the fresher the better, and if wet, to be dried for three or four days before it is put into the boxes); the dung is to be well beat down in the box. After the second or third day, if any heat has arisen amongst the dung, break each spawn brick into three parts as equally as possible, then lay the pieces about four inches apart upon the surface of the dung in the box; here they are to lie for six days, when it will probably be found that the side of the spawn next to the dung has begun to run in the dung below; then add one and a half inch more of fresh dung on the top of the spawn in the box, and beat it down as formerly. In the course of a fortnight, when you find that the spawn has run through the dung, the box will be ready to receive the mould on the top; this mould must be two and a half inches deep, well beat down, and the surface made quite even. In the space of five or six weeks the mushrooms will begin to come up; if then the mould seems dry, give a gentle watering with lukewarm water. The box will continue to produce from six weeks to two months, if duly attended to by giving a little water when dry, for they need neither *light* nor *free air*. If cut as button mushrooms each box will yield from twenty-four to forty-eight pints, according to the season and other circumstances. They may be kept in dry dark cellars, or any other places where the frost will not reach them. And by preparing in succession of boxes, mushrooms may be had all the year through.—They may be grown without the dung, and be of a finer flavour. Take a little straw, and lay it carefully in the bottom of the mushroom-box, about an inch thick, or rather more. Then take some of the spawn bricks and break them down—each brick into about ten pieces, and lay the fragments on the straw, as close to each other as they will lie. Cover them up with mould three and a half inches deep, and well pressed down. When the surface appears dry, give a little tepid water, as directed for the last way of raising them; but this method needs about double the quantity of water that the former does, owing to having no moisture in the bottom, while the other has the dung. The mushrooms will begin to start in a month or five weeks, sometimes sooner, sometimes later, according to the heat of the place where the boxes are situated. The spawn bricks may be obtained from seedsmen, or be collected from meadows.

251. Dwarf Plants. — Take a cutting of the plant you wish to dwarf —say a myrtle, for instance—and having set it in a pot, wait until you are satisfied that it has taken root; then take a cutting from it, and place it in a miniature flower pot, taking care to fill it more than three parts with fine sand, the remainder with mould. Put it under a glass on the chimney-piece, or in any warm place, and give it very small quantities of water.

252. To clear Rose Trees from Blight. — Take sulphur and tobacco dust in equal quantities, and strew it over the trees of a morning when the dew is on them. The insects will disappear in a few days. The trees should then be syringed with a decoction of elder leaves.

253. To prevent Mildew on all sorts of Trees.—The best preventive against mildew is to keep the plant subject to it occasionally syringed with a decoction of elder leaves, which will prevent the fungus growing on them.

254. Toads are among the best friends the gardener has; for they live almost exclusively on the most destructive kinds of vermin. Unsightly, therefore, though they may be, they should on all accounts be encouraged; they should never be touched nor molested in any way; on the contrary, places of shelter should be made for them, to which they may retire from the burning heat of the sun. If you have none in your garden, it will be quite worth your while to search for them in your walks, and bring them home, taking care to handle them tenderly, for although they have neither the will nor the power to injure you, a very little rough treatment will injure them; no cucumber or melon frame should be without one or two.—*Glenny's Gardening for Children.*

255. Slugs and Snails are great enemies to every kind of garden plant, whether flower or vegetable; they wander in the night to feed, and return at daylight to their haunts: the shortest and surest direction is, "Rise early, catch them, and kill them." If you are an early riser, you may cut them off from their day retreats, or you may lay cabbage leaves about the ground, especially on the beds which they frequent. Every morning examine these leaves, and you will find a great many taking refuge beneath: if they plague you very much, search for their retreat, which you can find by their slimy track, and hunt there for them day by day; lime and salt are very annoying to snails and slugs; a pinch of salt kills them, and they will not touch fresh lime; it is a common practice to sprinkle lime over young crops, and along the edges of beds, about rows of peas and beans, lettuces and other vegetables; but when it has been on the ground some days, or has been moistened by rain, it loses its strength.

256. Trap for Snails.—Snails are particularly fond of bran; if a little is spread on the ground, and covered over with a few cabbage-leaves or tiles, they will congregate under them in great numbers, and by examining them every morning, and destroying them, their numbers will be materially decreased.

257. Grubs on orchard trees, and gooseberry and currant bushes, will sometimes be sufficiently numerous to spoil a crop; but if a bonfire be made with dry sticks and weeds on the windward side of the orchard, so that the smoke may blow among the trees, you will destroy thousands; for the grubs have such an objection to smoke, that very little of it makes them roll themselves up and fall off: they must be swept up afterwards.

258. Caterpillars and Aphides.—A garden syringe or engine, with a cap on the pipe full of very minute holes, will wash away these disagreeable visitors very quickly. You must bring the pipe close to the plant, and pump hard, so as to have considerable force on, and the plant, however badly infested, will soon be cleared, without receiving any injury. Every time that you use the syringe or garden engine, you must immediately rake the earth under the trees, and kill the insects you have dislodged, or many will recover and climb up the stems of the plants.

259. Butterflies and Moths, however pretty, are the worst enemies one can have in a garden; a single insect of this kind may deposit eggs enough to overrun a tree with caterpillars, therefore they should be destroyed at any cost of trouble. The only moth that you must spare is the common black and red one; the grubs of this feed exclusively on groundsel, and are therefore a valuable ally of the gardener.

260. Wasps destroy a good deal of fruit, but every pair of wasps killed in spring saves the trouble and annoyance of a swarm in autumn; it is necessary, however, to be very careful in any attempt upon a wasp, for its sting is painful and lasting. In case of being stung, get the blue-bag from the laundry, and rub it well into the wound as soon as possible. Later in the season, it is customary to hang vessels of beer, or water and sugar, in the fruit-trees, to entice them to drown themselves.

261. To protect Dahlias from Earwigs.—Dip a piece of wool or cotton in oil, and slightly tie it round the stalk, about a foot from the earth. The stakes which you will put into the ground to support your plants must also be surrounded by the oiled cotton or wool, or the insects will climb up them to the blossoms and tender tops of the stems.

262. To free Plants from Leaf-Lice.—M. Braun, of Vienna, gives the following as a cheap and easy mode of effecting it:—Mix one ounce of flowers of sulphur with one bushel of sawdust; scatter this over the plants infected with these insects, and they will soon be freed, though a second application may possibly be necessary.

263. A Moral.

I HAD a little spot of ground,
  Where blade nor blossom grew,
Though the bright sunshine all around
  Life-giving radiance threw.
I mourned to see a spot so bare
  Of leaves of healthful green,
And thought of bowers, and blossoms fair,
  I frequently had seen.

Some seeds of various kinds lay by—
  I knew not what they were—
But, rudely turning o'er the soil,
  I strewed them thickly there;
And day by day I watched them spring
  From out the fertile earth,
And hoped for many a lovely thing
  Of beauty and of worth.

But as I marked their leaves unfold
  As weeds before my view,
And saw how stubbornly and bold
  The thorns and nettles grew—
I sighed to think that I had done,
  Unwittingly, a thing
That, where a beauteous bower should thrive,
  But worthless weeds did bring.

And thus I mused: the things we do,
  With little heed or ken,
May prove of worthless growth, and strew
  With thorns the paths of men;
For little deeds, like little seeds,
  May flowers prove, or noxious weeds!

264. Taking a House.—Before taking a house, be careful to calculate that the rent is not too high in proportion to your means; for remember that the rent is a claim that must be paid with but little delay, and that the landlord has greater power over your property than any other creditor.

265. HAVING DETERMINED THE AMOUNT OF RENT which you can afford to pay, be careful to select the best house which can be obtained for that sum. And in making that selection let the following matters be carefully considered:

266. FIRST—CAREFULLY REGARD THE HEALTHFULNESS OF THE SITUATION. Avoid the neighbourhood of graveyards, and of factories giving forth unhealthy vapours; avoid low and damp districts, the course of canals, and localities of reservoirs of water, gas works, &c.; make inquiries as to the drainage of the neighbourhood, and inspect the drainage and water supply of the premises. A house standing on an incline is likely to be better drained than one standing upon the summit of a hill, or on a level below a hill. Endeavour to obtain a position where the direct sunlight falls upon the house, for this is absolutely essential to health; and give preference to a house the openings of which are sheltered from the north and east winds.

267. SECOND—CONSIDER THE DISTANCE OF THE HOUSE from your place of occupation: and also its relation to provision markets, and shops in the neighbourhood.

268. HAVING CONSIDERED THESE MATERIAL AND LEADING FEATURES, examine the house in detail, carefully looking into its state of repair; notice the windows that are broken; whether the chimneys smoke; whether they have been recently swept; whether the paper on the walls is damaged, especially in the lower parts, and the corners, by the skirtings; whether the locks, bolts, handles of doors, and window-fastenings are in proper condition; make a list of the fixtures; ascertain whether all rent and taxes have been paid by the previous tenant, and whether the person from whom you take the house is the original landlord, or his agent or tenant. And do not commit yourself by the signing of any agreement until you are satisfied upon all these points, *and see that all has been done which the landlord had undertaken.*

269. If you are about to Furnish a House, do not spend all your money, be it much or little. Do not let the beauty of this thing, and the cheapness of that, tempt you to buy unnecessary articles. Dr. Franklin's maxim was a wise one—"Nothing is cheap that we do not want." Buy merely enough to get along with at first. It is only by experience that you can tell what will be the wants of your family. If you spend all your money, you will find you have purchased many things you do not want, and have no means left to get many things which you do want. If you have enough, and more than enough, to get everything suitable to your situation, do not think you must spend it all, merely because you happen to have it. Begin humbly. As riches increase, it is easy and pleasant to increase in comforts; but it is always painful and inconvenient to decrease. After all, these things are viewed in their proper light by the truly judicious and respectable. Neatness, tastefulness, and good sense may be shown in the management of a small household, and the arrangement of a little furniture, as well as upon a larger scale; and these qualities are always praised, and always treated with respect and attention. The consideration which many purchase by living beyond their income, and, of course, living upon others, is not worth the trouble it costs. The glare there is about this false and wicked parade is deceptive; it does not, in fact, procure a man valuable friends, or extensive influence.

270. Carpets.—In buying carpets, as in everything else, those of the best quality are cheapest in the end. As it is extremely desirable that they should look as clean as possible, avoid buying carpet that has any white in it. Even a very small portion of white interspersed through the pattern will in a short time give a dirty appearance to the whole; and certainly no carpet can be worse for use than one with a white ground.

271. A CARPET IN WHICH ALL THE

D 2

COLOURS ARE LIGHT never has a clean, bright effect, from the want of dark tints to contrast and set off the light ones.

272. FOR A SIMILAR REASON, carpets whose colours are all of what artists call middle tint (neither dark nor light), cannot fail to look dull and dingy, even when quite new.

273. THE CAPRICES OF FASHION at times bring these ill-coloured carpets into vogue; but in apartments where elegance is desirable, they always have a bad effect.

274. FOR A CARPET TO BE REALLY BEAUTIFUL and in good taste, there should be, as in a picture, a judicious disposal of light and shadow, with a gradation of very bright and of very dark tints; some almost white, and others almost or quite black.

275. THE MOST TRULY CHASTE, rich, and elegant carpets are those where the pattern is formed by one colour only, but arranged in every variety of shade. For instance, we have seen a Brussels carpet entirely red; the pattern formed by shades or tints varying from the deepest crimson (almost a black), to the palest pink (almost a white). Also one of green only, shaded from the darkest bottle-green, in some parts of the figure, to the lightest pea-green in others. Another, in which there was no colour but brown, in all its various gradations, some of the shades being nearly black, others of a light buff. All these carpets had much the look of rich cut velvet.

276. THE CURTAINS, SOFAS, &c., must be of corresponding colours, that the effect of the whole may be noble and elegant.

277. CARPETS of many gaudy colours are much less in demand than formerly. Two colours only, with the dark and light shades of each, will make a very handsome carpet.

278. A VERY LIGHT BLUE GROUND, with the figure of shaded crimson or purple, looks extremely well; so does a salmon colour or buff ground, with a deep green figure; or a light yellow ground, with a shaded blue figure.

279. IF YOU CANNOT OBTAIN A HEARTH-RUG that exactly corresponds with the carpet, get one entirely different; for a decided contrast looks better than a bad match.

280. WE HAVE SEEN VERY HANDSOME HEARTH-RUGS with a rich, black velvet-looking ground, and the figure of shaded blue, or of various tints of yellow and orange.

281. No CARPET decidedly light-coloured throughout looks effective on the floor, or continues long clean.

282. In Choosing Paper for a Room, avoid that which has a variety of colours, or a large showy figure, as no furniture can appear to advantage with such. Large figured papering makes a small room look smaller.

283. The best Covering for a Kitchen Floor is a thick unfigured oil-cloth, of one colour.

284. Family Tool Chests.—Much inconvenience and considerable expense might be saved, if it were the general custom to keep in every house certain tools for the purpose of performing at home what are called small jobs, instead of being always obliged to send for a mechanic and pay him for executing little things that, in most cases, could be sufficiently well done by a man or boy belonging to the family, if the proper instruments were at hand.

285. THE COST OF THESE ARTICLES is very trifling, and the advantages of having them always in the house are far beyond the expense.

286. FOR INSTANCE, there should be an axe, a hatchet, a saw (a large wood-saw also, with a buck or stand, if wood is burned), a claw-hammer, a mallet, two gimlets of different sizes, two screw-drivers, a chisel, a small plane, one or two jack-knives, a pair of large scissors or shears, and a carpet fork or stretcher.

287. ALSO AN ASSORTMENT OF NAILS of various sizes, from large spikes down to small tacks, not forgetting brass-headed nails, some larger and some smaller.

288. Screws, likewise, will be found very convenient, and hooks on which to hang things.

289. The Nails and screws should be kept in a wooden box, made with divisions to separate the various sorts, for it is very troublesome to have them mixed.

290. And let care be taken to keep up the supply, lest it should run out unexpectedly, and the deficiency cause delay and inconvenience at a time when their use is wanted.

291. It is well to have somewhere, in the lower part of the house, a deep light closet, appropriated entirely to tools, and things of equal utility, for executing promptly such little repairs as convenience may require, without the delay or expense of procuring an artisan. This closet should have at least one large shelf, and that about three feet from the floor.

292. Beneath this Shelf may be a deep drawer, divided into two compartments. This drawer may contain cakes of glue, pieces of chalk, and balls of twine of different size and quality.

293. There may be Shelves at the sides of the closet for glue-pots, paste-pots and brushes, pots for black, white, green, and red paint, cans of painting oil, paint-brushes, &c.

294. Against the Wall, above the large shelf, let the tools be suspended, or laid across nails or hooks of proper size to support them.

295. This is much better than keeping them in a box, where they may be injured by rubbing against each other, and the hand may be hurt in feeling among them to find the thing that is wanted.

296. But when hung up against the back wall of the closet, of course each tool can be seen at a glance.

297. We have been shown an excellent and simple contrivance for designating the exact places allotted to all these articles in a very complete tool closet.

298. On the Closet Wall, directly under the large nails that support the tools, is drawn with a small brush dipped in black paint or ink, an outline representation of the tool or instrument belonging to that particular place.

299. For instance, under each Saw is sketched the outline of that saw, under each gimlet a sketch of that gimlet, under the screw-drivers are slight drawings of screw-drivers.

300. So that when bringing back any Tool that has been taken away for use, the exact spot to which it belongs can be found in a moment; and all confusion in putting them up and finding them again is thus prevented.

301. Wrapping Paper may be piled on the floor under the large shelf. It can be bought very low by the ream, at the large paper warehouses; and every house should keep a supply of it in several varieties. For instance, coarse brown paper for common purposes, that denominated ironmonger's paper, which is strong, thick, and in large sheets, is useful for packing heavy articles; and equally so for keeping silks, ribbons, blondes, &c., as it preserves their colours.

302. Printed Papers are unfit for wrapping anything, as the printing ink rubs off on the articles enclosed in them, and also soils the gloves of the person that carries the parcel.

303. When Shopping, if the person at the counter proceeds to wrap up your purchase in a newspaper (a thing rarely attempted in a genteel shop), refuse to take it in such a cover. It is the business of every respectable shopkeeper to provide proper paper for this purpose, and printed paper is not proper.

304. Waste Newspapers had best be used for lighting fires and singeing poultry.

305. Waste Paper that has been written on, cut into slips, and creased and folded, makes very good allumettes or lamp-lighters. These matters may appear of trifling importance, but order and regularity are necessary to happiness.

306. Beds for the Poor.—

Beech-tree leaves are recommended for filling the beds of poor persons. They should be gathered on a dry day in the autumn, and perfectly dried. It is said that they smell grateful, and will not harbour vermin. They are also very springy.

307. To Preserve Tables.—A piece of oil-cloth (about twenty inches long) is a useful appendage to a common sitting-room. Kept in the closet, it can be available at any time to place jars upon, &c., &c., which are likely to soil your table during the process of dispensing their contents: a wing and duster are harmonious accompaniments to the oil-cloth.

308. Gilt Frames may be protected from flies and dust by oiled tarlatan pinned over them. Tarlatan, already prepared, may be purchased at the upholsterer's. If it cannot be procured, it is easily made by brushing boiled oil over cheap tarlatan. It is an excellent material for keeping dust from books, vases, wool work, and every description of household ornament.

309. Damp Walls.—The following method is recommended to prevent the effect of damp walls on paper in rooms:—Line the damp part of the wall with sheet lead, rolled very thin, and fastened up with small copper nails. It may be immediately covered with paper. The lead is not to be thicker than that which lines tea-chests.

310. Bedrooms should not be scoured in the winter time, as colds and sickness may be produced thereby. Dry scouring, upon the French plan, which consists of scrubbing the floors with dry brushes, may be resorted to, and will be found more effective than can at first be imagined. If a bedroom is wet scoured, a dry day should be chosen—the windows should be opened, the linen removed, and a fire should be lit when the operation is finished.

311. To get rid of a bad Smell in a Room newly painted.—Place a vessel full of lighted charcoal in the middle of the room, and throw on it two or three handfuls of juniper berries, shut the windows, the chimney, and the door close; twenty-four hours afterwards, the room may be opened, when it will be found that the sickly, unwholesome smell will be entirely gone. The smoke of the juniper berry possesses this advantage, that should anything be left in the room, such as tapestry, &c., none of it will be spoiled.

312. Paint.—To get rid of the smell of oil paint plunge a handful of hay into a pailful of water, and let it stand in the room newly painted.

313. If a Larder, by its Position, will not admit of opposite windows, then a current of air must be admitted by means of a flue from the outside.

314. For Keeping a Door open, place a brick covered neatly with a piece of carpeting against the door.

315. To Ascertain whether a Bed be Aired.—Introduce a glass goblet between the sheets for a minute or two, just when the warming-pan is taken out; if the bed be dry, there will only be a slight cloudy appearance on the glass, but if not, the damp of the bed will assume the more formidable appearance of drops, the warning of danger.

316. To prevent the Smoking of a Lamp.—Soak the wick in strong vinegar, and dry it well before you use it; it will then burn clear and bright, and give much satisfaction for the trifling trouble in preparing it.

317. Water of every kind, except rain water, will speedily cover the inside of a tea-kettle with an unpleasant crust; this may easily be guarded against by placing a clean oyster-shell in the tea-kettle, which will always keep it in good order, by attracting the particles of earth or of stone.

318. To Soften Hard Water, or purify river water, simply boil it, and then leave it exposed to the atmosphere.

319. Cabbage Water should be thrown away immediately it is done with, and the vessel rinsed with clean water, or it will cause unpleasant smells.

320. A little Charcoal mixed with clear water thrown into a sink will disinfect and deodorize it.

321. Where a Chimney Smokes only when a fire is first lighted, it may be guarded against by allowing the fire to kindle gradually.

322. Ground Glass.—The frosted appearance of ground glass may be very nearly imitated by gently dabbing the glass over with a piece of glazier's putty, stuck on the ends of the fingers. When applied with a light and even touch, the resemblance is considerable.

323. Family Clocks ought only to be oiled with the very purest oil, purified by a quart of lime water to a gallon of oil, in which it has been well shaken, and suffered to stand for three or four days, when it may be drawn off.

324. Neat Mode of Soldering.—Cut out a piece of tinfoil the size of the surfaces to be soldered. Then dip a feather in a solution of sal ammoniac, and wet over the surfaces of the metal, then place them in their proper position with the tinfoil between. Put it so arranged on a piece of iron hot enough to melt the foil. When cold the surfaces will be found firmly soldered together.

325. Maps and Charts.—Maps, charts, or engravings may be effectually varnished by brushing a very delicate coating of gutta percha solution over their surface. It is perfectly transparent, and is said to improve the appearance of pictures. By coating both sides of important documents they can be kept waterproof and preserved perfectly.

326. Furniture made in the winter, and brought from a cold warehouse into a warm apartment, is very liable to crack.

327. Paper Fire-Screens should be coated with transparent varnish, otherwise they will soon become soiled and discoloured.

328. Pastils for Burning.—Cascarilla bark, eight drachms; gum benzoin, four drachms; yellow sanders, two drachms; styrax, two drachms; olibanum, two drachms; charcoal, six ounces; nitre, one drachm and a half; mucilage of tragacanth, sufficient quantity. Reduce the substances to a powder, and form into a paste with the mucilage, and divide into small cones; then put them into an oven until quite dry.

329. Easy Method of Breaking Glass to any required Figure.—Make a small notch by means of a file on the edge of a piece of glass, then make the end of a tobacco-pipe, or of a rod of iron of the same size, red hot in the fire, apply the hot iron to the notch, and draw it slowly along the surface of the glass in any direction you please; a crack will follow the direction of the iron.

330. Bottling and Fining.—Corks should be sound, clean, and sweet. Beer and porter should be allowed to stand in the bottles a day or two before being corked. If for speedy use, wiring is not necessary. Laying the bottles on their sides will assist the ripening for use. Those that are to be kept should be wired, and put to stand upright in sawdust. Wines should be bottled in spring. If not fine enough, draw off a jugful and dissolve isinglass in it, in the proportion of half an ounce to ten gallons, and then pour back through the bung-hole. Let it stand a few weeks longer. Tap the cask above the lees. When the isinglass is put into the cask, stir it round with a stick, taking great care not to touch the lees at the bottom. For white wine only, mix with the isinglass a quarter of a pint of milk to each gallon of wine, some whites of eggs, beaten with some of the wine. One white of an egg to four gallons makes a good fining.

331. To Sweeten Casks.—Mix half a pint of vitriol with a quart of water, pour it into the barrel, and roll it about; next day add one pound of chalk, and roll again. Bung down for three or four days, then rinse well with hot water.

332. Oil Paintings hung over the mantel-piece are liable to wrinkle with the heat.

333. To Loosen Glass Stoppers of Bottles.—With a feather rub a drop or two of salad oil round the stopper, close to the mouth of the bottle or decanter, which must then be placed before the fire, at the distance of about eighteen inches; the heat will cause the oil to insinuate itself between the stopper and the neck. When the bottle or decanter has grown warm, gently strike the stopper on one side, and then on the other, with any light wooden instrument; then try it with the hand: if it will not yet move, place it again before the fire, adding another drop of oil. After a while strike again as before; and, by persevering in this process, however tightly it may be fastened in, you will at length succeed in loosening it. This is decidedly the best plan.

334. Lamp Wicks.—Old cotton stockings may be made into lamp wicks, and will answer very well.

335. The Best Lamp Oil is that which is clear and nearly colourless, like water.

336. China Teapots are the safest, and, in many respects, the most pleasant. Wedgwood ware is very apt, after a time, to acquire a disagreeable taste.

337. Care of Linen. — When linen is well dried and laid by for use, nothing more is necessary than to secure it from damp and insects; the latter may be agreeably performed by a judicious mixture of aromatic shrubs and flowers, cut up and sewed in silken bags, to be interspersed among the drawers and shelves. These ingredients may consist of lavender, thyme, roses, cedar shavings, powdered sassafras, cassia lignea, &c., into which a few drops of otto of roses, or other strong-scented perfume, may be thrown. In all cases it will be found more consistent with economy to examine and repair all washable articles, more especially linen, that may stand in need of it, previous to sending them to the laundry. It will also be prudent to have every article carefully numbered, and so arranged, after wash-ing, as to have their regular turn and term in domestic use.

338. Mending.—When you make a new article always save the pieces until "mending day," which may come sooner than expected. It will be well even to buy a little extra quantity for repairs. Read over repeatedly the "Domestic Hints" at page 239. These numerous paragraphs contain most valuable suggestions, that will be constantly useful if well remembered. They should be read frequently that their full value may be secured. Let your domestics also read them, for nothing more conduces to good housekeeping than for the servant to understand the "system" which her mistress approves of.

339. Cleansing of Furniture.—The cleaning of furniture forms an important part of domestic economy, not only in regard to neatness, but also in point of expense.

340. The Readiest Mode indeed consists in good manual rubbing, or the essence of elbows, as it is whimsically termed; but our finest cabinet work requires something more, where brilliancy of polish is of importance.

341. The Italian Cabinet-Work in this respect excels that of any other country. The workmen first saturate the surface with olive oil, and then apply a solution of gum arabic in boiling alcohol. This mode of varnishing is equally brilliant, if not superior, to that employed by the French in their most elaborate works.

342. But Another Mode may be substituted, which has less the appearance of a hard varnish, and may always be applied so as to restore the pristine beauty of the furniture by a little manual labour. Heat a gallon of water, in which dissolve one pound and a half of potash: add a pound of virgin wax, boiling the whole for half an hour, then suffer it to cool, when the wax will float on the surface. Put the wax into a mortar, and triturate it with a marble pestle, adding soft water to it until it forms a soft paste, which, laid neatly on furniture, or even on paintings, and carefully rubbed when dry with a woollen rag, gives a polish of great brilliancy, without the harshness of the drier varnishes.

343. MARBLE CHIMNEY-PIECES may also be rubbed with it, after cleaning with diluted muriatic acid, or warm soap and vinegar; but the iron or brass work connected with them requires other processes.

344. POLISHED IRON WORK may be preserved from rust by a mixture not very expensive, consisting of copal varnish intimately mixed with as much olive oil as will give it a degree of greasiness, adding thereto nearly as much spirit of turpentine as of varnish.

345. CAST IRON WORK is best preserved by the common method of rubbing with black lead.

346. IF RUST HAS MADE ITS APPEARANCE on grates or fire-irons, apply a mixture of tripoli, with half its quantity of sulphur, intimately mingled on a marble slab, and laid on with a piece of soft leather. Or emery and oil may be applied with excellent effect; not laid on in the usual slovenly way, but with a spongy piece of the fig-tree fully saturated with the mixture. This will not only clean but polish, and render the use of whiting unnecessary.

347. BRASS ORNAMENTS, when not gilt or lackered, may be cleaned the same way, and a fine colour given to them, by two simple processes.

348. The FIRST is to beat sal ammoniac into a fine powder, then to moisten it with soft water, rubbing it on the ornaments, which must be heated over charcoal, and rubbed dry with bran and whiting.

349. The SECOND is to wash the brass work with roche alum boiled in strong ley, in proportion of an ounce to a pint; when dry, it must be rubbed with fine tripoli. Either of these processes will give to brass the brilliancy of gold.

350. Carpets.—If the corner of a carpet becomes loose and prevents the door opening, or trips every one up that enters the room, nail it down at once.

A dog's-eared carpet marks the sloven as well as the dog's-eared book. An English gentleman, travelling some years ago in Ireland, took a hammer and tacks with him, because he found dog's-eared carpets at all the inns where he rested. At one of these inns he tacked down the carpet, which, as usual, was loose near the door, and soon afterwards rang for his dinner. While the carpet was loose the door could not be opened without a hard push; so when the waiter came up, he just unlatched the door, and then going back a couple of yards, he rushed against it, as his habit was, with a sudden spring, to force it open. But the wrinkles of the carpet were no longer there to stop it, and not meeting with the expected resistance, the unfortunate waiter fell full length into the room. It had never entered his head that so much trouble might be saved by means of a hammer and half a dozen tacks, until his fall taught him that makeshift is a very unprofitable kind of shift. There are a good many houses in England where a similar practical lesson might be of service.

351. Cleaning Carpets.—Take a pail of cold water, and add to it three gills of ox-gall. Rub it into the carpet with a soft brush. It will raise a lather, which must be washed off with clear cold water. Rub dry with a clean cloth. In nailing down a carpet after the floor has been washed, be certain that the floor is quite dry, or the nails will rust and injure the carpet. Fuller's earth is used for cleaning carpets, and weak solutions of alum or soda are used for reviving the colours. The crumb of a hot wheaten loaf rubbed over a carpet has been found effective.

352. Beat a Carpet on the wrong side first; and then more gently on the right side. Beware of using sticks with sharp points, which may tear the carpet.

353. Sweeping Carpets.—Persons who are accustomed to use tea-leaves for sweeping their carpets, and find that they leave stains, will do well to employ fresh cut grass instead. It is better than tea-leaves for preventing dust, and gives the carpets a very bright, fresh look.

354. A Half-worn Carpet may be made to last longer by ripping it apart, and transposing the breadths.

355. A Stair Carpet should never be swept down with a long broom, but always with a short-handled brush, and a dust-pan held closely under each step of the stairs.

356. Oil-Cloth should never be scrubbed with a brush, but, after being first swept, it should be cleansed by washing with a large soft cloth and lukewarm or cold water. On no account use soap or hot water, as either will bring off the paint.

357. Straw Matting may be cleaned with a large coarse cloth dipped in salt and water, and then wiped dry: the salt prevents the matting from turning yellow.

358. Method of Cleaning Paper-Hangings.—Cut into eight half quarters a quartern loaf, two days old; it must neither be newer nor staler. With one of these pieces, after having blown off all the dust from the paper to be cleaned, by the means of a good pair of bellows, begin at the top of the room, holding the crust in the hand, and wiping lightly downward with the crumb, about half a yard at each stroke, till the upper part of the hangings is completely cleaned all round. Then go round again, with the like sweeping stroke downwards, always commencing each successive course a little higher than the upper stroke had extended, till the bottom be finished. This operation, if carefully performed, will frequently make very old paper look almost equal to new. Great caution must be used not by any means to rub the paper hard, nor to attempt cleaning it the cross or horizontal way. The dirty part of the bread, too, must be each time cut away, and the pieces renewed as soon as it may become necessary.

359. Rosewood Furniture should be rubbed gently every day with a clean soft cloth to keep it in order.

360. Ottomans and Sofas, whether covered with cloth, damask, or chintz, will look much the better for being cleaned occasionally with bran and flannel.

361. Dining Tables may be polished by rubbing them for some time with a soft cloth and a little cold-drawn linseed oil.

362. A Mahogany Frame should be first well dusted, and then cleaned with a flannel dipped in sweet oil.

363. To Clean Cane-bottom Chairs.—Turn up the chair bottom, &c., and with hot water and a sponge wash the canework well, so that it may become completely soaked. Should it be very dirty you must add soap. Let it dry in the open air, if possible, or in a place where there is a thorough draught, and it will become as tight and firm as when new, provided it has not been broken.

364. Alabaster.—For cleaning it there is nothing better than soap and water. Stains may be removed by washing with soap and water, then whitewashing the stained part, letting it stand some hours, then washing off the whitewash, and rubbing the stained part.

365. To Clean Marble.—Take two parts of common soda, one part of pumice stone, and one part of finely powdered chalk; sift it through a fine sieve, and mix it with water; then rub it well all over the marble, and the stains will be removed; then wash the marble over with soap and water, and it will be as clean as it was at first.

366. Glass should be washed in cold water, which gives it a brighter and clearer look than when cleansed with warm water.

367. Glass Vessels, and other utensils, may be purified and cleaned by rinsing them out with powdered charcoal.

368. Bottles.—There is no easier method of cleaning glass bottles than putting into them fine coals, and well shaking, either with water or not, hot or cold, according to the substance that fouls the bottle. Charcoal left in a bottle or jar for a little time will take away disagreeable smells.

369. Cleaning Japanned Waiters, Urns, &c.—Rub on with a sponge a little white soap and some lukewarm water, and wash the waiter or urn quite clean. Never use hot water, as it will cause the japan to scale off. Having wiped it dry, sprinkle a little flour over it; let it rest a while, and then rub it with a soft dry cloth, and finish with a silk handkerchief. If there are white heat marks on the waiters, they will be difficult to remove; but you may try rubbing them with a flannel dipped in sweet oil, and afterwards in spirits of wine. Waiters and other articles of *papier maché* should be washed with a sponge and cold water, without soap, dredged with flour while damp, and after a while wiped off, and then polished with a silk handkerchief.

370. Papier Mache articles should be washed with a sponge and cold water, without soap, dredged with flour while damp, and polished with a flannel.

371. Brunswick Black for Varnishing Grates.—Melt four pounds of common asphaltum, and add two pints of linseed oil, and one gallon of oil of turpentine. This is usually put up in stoneware bottles for sale, and is used with a paint brush. If too thick, more turpentine may be added. Cost: asphalte, 1s. per pound; linseed, 6d. per pint; turpentine, 8d. per pint.

372. Blacking for Stoves may be made with half a pound of black lead finely powdered, and (to make it stick) mix with it the whites of three eggs well beaten; then dilute it with sour beer or porter till it becomes as thin as shoe-blacking; after stirring it, set it over hot coals to simmer for twenty minutes; when cold it may be kept for use.

373. To Clean Knives and Forks.—Wash the blades in warm (but not hot) water, and afterwards rub them lightly over with powdered rotten-stone wet to a paste with a little cold water, then polish them with a clean cloth.

374. Where Painted Wainscot or other woodwork requires cleaning, fuller's earth will be found cheap and useful; and on wood not painted it forms an excellent substitute for soap.

375. Boards, to Scour.—Lime, one part; sand, three parts; soft soap, two parts. Lay a little on the boards with the scrubbing brush, and rub thoroughly. Rinse with clean water, and rub dry. This will keep the boards of a good colour, and will also keep away vermin.

376. Charcoal.—All sorts of glass vessels and other utensils may be purified from long retained smells of every kind, in the easiest and most perfect manner, by rinsing them out well with charcoal powder, after the grosser impurities have been scoured off with sand and potash. Rubbing the teeth and washing out the mouth with fine charcoal powder, will render the teeth beautifully white, and the breath perfectly sweet, where an offensive breath has been owing to a scorbutic disposition of the gums. Putrid water is immediately deprived of its bad smell by charcoal. When meat, fish, &c., from intense heat, or long keeping, are likely to pass into a state of corruption, a simple and pure mode of keeping them sound and healthful is by putting a few pieces of charcoal, each about the size of an egg, into the pot or saucepan wherein the fish or flesh is to be boiled. Among others, an experiment of this kind was tried upon a turbot, which appeared to be too far gone to be eatable; the cook, as advised, put three or four pieces of charcoal, each the size of an egg, under the strainer, in the fish kettle; after boiling the proper time, the turbot came to the table sweet and firm.

377. To Take out Stains from Mahogany Furniture.—Stains and spots may be taken out of mahogany furniture with a little aquafortis or oxalic acid and water, rubbing the part by means of a cork, till the colour is restored; observing afterwards to wash the wood well with water, and to dry and polish as usual.

378. To take Ink-Stains out of Mahogany.—Put a few drops of spirits of nitre in a teaspoonful of water, touch the spot with a feather dipped in the mixture, and on the ink disappearing, rub it over immediately with a rag wetted in cold water, or there will be a white mark, which will not be easily effaced.

379. To remove Ink-Stains from Silver.—The tops and other portions of silver inkstands frequently become deeply discoloured with ink, which is difficult to remove by ordinary means. It may, however, be completely eradicated by making a little chloride of lime into a paste with water, and rubbing it upon the stains. Chloride of lime has been misnamed "The general bleacher," but it is a foul enemy to all metallic surfaces.

380. To take Ink-Stains out of a Coloured Table-Cover.—Dissolve a teaspoonful of oxalic acid in a teacup of hot water; rub the stained part well with the solution.

381. To take Ink out of Boards.—Strong muriatic acid, or spirits of salts, applied with a piece of cloth; afterwards well washed with water.

382. Oil Grease may be removed from a hearth by covering it immediately with thick hot ashes, or with burning coals.

383. Marble may be Cleaned by mixing up a quantity of the strongest soap-lees with quicklime, to the consistence of milk, and laying it on the marble for twenty-four hours; clean it afterwards with soap and water.

384. Silver and Plated Ware should be washed with a sponge and warm soapsuds every day after using, and wiped dry with a clean soft towel.

385. Bronzed Chandeliers, Lamps, &c., should be merely dusted with a feather-brush, or with a soft cloth, as washing them will take off the bronzing.

386. To clean Brass Ornaments.—Wash the brasswork with roche alum boiled to a strong ley, in the proportion of an ounce to a pint. When dry, it must be rubbed with fine tripoli.

387. For Cleaning Brasses belonging to mahogany furniture, either powdered whiting or scraped rotten-stone, mixed with sweet oil and rubbed on with a buckskin, is good.

388. Brasses, Britannia Metal, Tins, Coppers, &c., are cleaned with a mixture of rotten-stone, soft soap, and oil of turpentine, mixed to the consistency of stiff putty. The stone should be powdered very fine and sifted; and a quantity of the mixture may be made sufficient to last for a long while. The articles should first be washed with hot water, to remove grease; then a little of the above mixture, mixed with water, should be rubbed over the metal; then rub off briskly with dry, clean rag or leather, and a beautiful polish will be obtained.

389. To preserve Steel Goods from Rust.—After bright grates have been thoroughly cleaned, they should be dusted over with unslacked lime, and thus left until wanted. The coils of piano wires, thus sprinkled, will keep from rust for many years. Table-knives which are not in constant use ought to be put in a case in which sifted quicklime is placed, about eight inches deep. They should be plunged to the top of the blades, but the lime should not touch the handles.

390. Iron and Steel Goods from Rust.—Dissolve half an ounce of camphor in one pound of hog's lard; take off the scum: mix as much black lead as will give the mixture an iron colour. Iron and steel goods, rubbed over with this mixture, and left with it on twenty-four hours, and then dried with a linen cloth, will keep clean for months. Valuable articles of cutlery should be wrapped in ZINC FOIL, or be kept in boxes lined with zinc. This is at once an easy and most effective method.

391. Iron Wipers.— Old soft towels, or pieces of old sheets or table-cloths, make excellent iron wipers.

392. To Clean Looking-Glasses.— First wash the glass all over with lukewarm soapsuds and a sponge. When dry, rub it bright with a buckskin and a little prepared chalk finely powdered.

393. To Clean Mirrors, &c.— If they should be hung so high that they cannot be conveniently reached, have a pair of steps to stand upon; but mind that they stand steady. Then take a piece of soft sponge, well washed, and cleaned from everything gritty, just dip it into water and squeeze it out again, and then dip it into some spirit of wine. Rub it over the glass; dust it over with some powder blue or whiting sifted through muslin; rub it lightly and quickly off again with a cloth; then take a clean cloth, and rub it well again, and finish by rubbing it with a silk handkerchief. If the glass be very large, clean one-half at a time, as otherwise the spirit of wine will dry before it can be rubbed off. If the frames are not varnished, the greatest care is necessary to keep them quite dry, so as not to touch them with the sponge, as this will discolour or take off the gilding. To clean the frames, take a little raw cotton in the state of wool, and rub the frames with it; this will take off all the dust and dirt without injuring the gilding. If the frames are well varnished, rub them with spirit of wine, which will take out all spots, and give them a fine polish. Varnished doors may be done in the same manner. Never use any cloth to *frames* or *drawings*, or unvarnished oil paintings, when cleaning and dusting them.

394. China and Glass-Ware.—The best material for cleansing either porcelain or glass-ware, is fuller's earth: but it must be beaten into a fine powder, and carefully cleared from all rough or hard particles, which might endanger the polish of the brilliant surface.

395. In CLEANING porcelain, it must also be observed that some species require more care and attention than others, as every person must have observed that china-ware in common use frequently loses some of its colours.

396. THE RED, especially of vermillion, is the first to go, because that colour, together with some others, is laid on by the Chinese after burning.

397. THE MODERN CHINESE PORCELAIN is not, indeed, so susceptible of this rubbing or wearing off, as vegetable reds are now used by them instead of the mineral colour.

398. MUCH OF THE RED now used in China is actually produced by the *anotto* extracted from the cuttings of scarlet cloth, which have long formed an article of exportation to Canton.

399. IT OUGHT to be taken for granted that all china or glass-ware is well tempered: yet a little careful attention may not be misplaced, even on that point; for though ornamental china or glass-ware is not exposed to the action of hot water in common domestic use, yet it may be injudiciously immersed therein for the purpose of cleaning; and as articles intended solely for ornament are not so highly annealed as others, it will be proper never to apply water beyond a tepid temperature.

400. AN INGENIOUS and simple mode of annealing glass has been some time in use by chemists. It consists in immersing the vessel in cold water, gradually heated to the boiling point, and suffered to remain till cold, when it will be fit for use. Should the glass be exposed to a higher temperature than that of boiling water, it will be necessary to immerse it in oil.

401. To take Marking-Ink out of Linen.—Use a saturated solution of cyanuret of potassium applied with a camel-hair brush. After the marking ink disappears, the linen should be well washed in cold water.

402. To take Stains of Wine out of Linen.—Hold the articles in milk while it is boiling on the fire, and the stains will soon disappear.

403. Fruit Stains in Linen.— To remove them, rub the part on each side with yellow soap, then tie up a piece of pearlash in the cloth, &c., and soak well in hot water, or boil: afterwards expose the stained part to the sun and air until removed.

404. Mildewed Linen may be restored by soaping the spots while wet, covering them with fine chalk scraped to powder, and rubbing it well in.

405. To keep Moths, Beetles, &c., from Clothes.—Put a piece of camphor in a linen bag, or some aromatic herbs, in the drawers, among linen or woollen clothes, and neither moth nor worm will come near them.

406. Clothes Closets that have become infested with moths should be well rubbed with a strong decoction of tobacco, and repeatedly sprinkled with spirits of camphor.

407. Iron Stains may be removed from marble by wetting the spots with oil of vitriol, or with lemon-juice, or with oxalic acid diluted in spirit of wine, and, after a quarter of an hour, rubbing them dry with a soft linen cloth.

408. To remove Stains from Floors. — For removing spots of grease from boards, take equal parts of fuller's earth and pearlash, a quarter of a pound of each, and boil in a quart of soft water; and, while hot, lay it on the greased parts, allowing it to remain on them for ten or twelve hours; after which it may be scoured off with sand and water. A floor much spotted with grease should be completely washed over with this mixture the day before it is scoured. Fuller's earth and ox-gall, boiled together, form a very powerful cleansing mixture for floors or carpets. Stains of ink are removed by strong vinegar; or salts of lemon will remove them.

409. Scouring Drops for removing Grease.—There are several preparations of this name; one of the best is made as follows :—Camphine, or spirit of turpentine, three ounces; essence of lemon, one ounce; mix. Cost: camphine, 8d. per pint; essence of lemon, 8d. per ounce. Scouring drops are usually put up in small half-ounce phials for sale; these may be obtained at from 9d. to 1s. per dozen.

410. To take Grease out of Velvet or Cloth. — Procure some turpentine and pour it over the part that is greasy; rub it till quite dry with a piece of clean flannel; if the grease be not quite removed, repeat the application, and when done, brush the part well, and hang up the garment in the open air to take away the smell.

411. Medicine Stains may be removed from silver spoons by rubbing them with a rag dipped in sulphuric acid, and washing it off with soapsuds.

412. To Extract Grease Spots from Books or Paper. — Gently warm the greased or spotted part of the book or paper, and then press upon it pieces of blotting-paper, one after another, so as to absorb as much of the grease as possible. Have ready some fine clear essential oil of turpentine heated almost to a boiling state, warm the greased leaf a little, and then, with a soft clean brush, apply the heated turpentine to both sides of the spotted part. By repeating this application, the grease will be extracted. Lastly, with another brush dipped in rectified spirit of wine, go over the place, and the grease will no longer appear, neither will the paper be discoloured.

413. Stains and Marks from Books.—A solution of oxalic acid, citric acid, or tartaric acid, is attended with the least risk, and may be applied upon the paper and prints without fear of damage. These acids, taking out writing ink, and not touching the printing, can be used for restoring books where the margins have been written upon, without injuring the text.

414. To take Writing Ink out of Paper.—Solution of muriate of tin, two drachms; water, four drachms. To be applied with a camel-hair brush.

After the writing has disappeared, the paper should be passed through water, and dried.

415. A Hint on Household Management.—Have you ever observed what a dislike servants have to anything cheap? They hate saving their master's money. I tried this experiment with great success the other day. Finding we consumed a vast deal of soap, I sat down in my thinking chair, and took the soap question into consideration, and I found reason to suspect we were using a very expensive article, where a much cheaper one would serve the purpose better. I ordered half a dozen pounds of both sorts, but took the precaution of changing the papers on which the prices were marked before giving them into the hands of Betty. "Well, Betty, which soap do you find washes best?" "Oh, please sir, the dearest, in the blue paper; it makes a lather as well again as the other." "Well, Betty, you shall always have it then;" and thus the unsuspecting Betty saved me some pounds a year, and washed the clothes better.—*Rev. Sidney Smith.*

416. Domestic Rules. — Mrs. Hamilton, in her "Cottagers of Glenburnie," gives three simple rules for the regulation of domestic affairs, which deserve to be remembered, and which would, if carried into practice, be the means of saving time, labour, and patience, and of making every house a "well-ordered" one. They are as follows:—i. Do everything in its proper time. ii. Keep everything to its proper use. iii. Put everything in its proper place.

417. An ever-Dirty Hearth, and a grate always choked with cinders and ashes, are infallible evidences of bad housekeeping.

418. Economy. — If you have a strip of land, do not throw away soapsuds. Both ashes and soapsuds are good manure for bushes and young plants.

419. WOOLLEN CLOTHES should be washed in very hot suds, and not rinsed. Lukewarm water shrinks them.

420. Do NOT let coffee and tea stand in tin.

421. SCALD your wooden-ware often, and keep your tin-ware dry.

422. PRESERVE the backs of old letters to write upon.

423. IF YOU HAVE CHILDREN who are learning to write, buy coarse white paper by the quantity, and keep it locked up, ready to be made into writing-books. This does not cost half so much as it does to buy them at the stationer's.

424. SEE THAT NOTHING IS THROWN AWAY which might have served to nourish your own family or a poorer one.

425. AS FAR AS POSSIBLE, have pieces of bread eaten up before they become hard; spread those that are not eaten, and let them dry, to be pounded for puddings, or soaked for brewis.

426. BREWIS is made of crusts and dry pieces of bread, soaked a good while in hot milk, mashed up, and eaten with salt. Above all, do not let crusts accumulate in such quantities that they cannot be used. With proper care, there is no need of losing a particle of bread.

427. ALL THE MENDING in the house should be done once a week if possible.

428. NEVER PUT OUT SEWING. If it be not possible to do it in your own family, hire some one into the house, and work with them.

429. A WARMING-PAN full of coals, or a shovel of coals, held over varnished furniture, will take out white spots. Care should be taken not to hold the clothes near enough to scorch : and the place should be rubbed with a flannel while warm.

430. SAL-VOLATILE or hartshorn will restore colours taken out by acid. It may be dropped upon any garment without doing harm.

431. NEW IRON should be very gradually heated at first. After it has become inured to the heat, it is not so likely to crack.

432. CLEAN A BRASS KETTLE, before using it for cooking, with salt and vinegar. — The oftener carpets are shaken the longer they wear; the dirt that collects under them grinds out the threads.

433. LINEN RAGS should be carefully saved, for they are extremely useful in sickness. If they have become dirty and worn by cleaning silver, &c., wash them and scrape them into lint.

434. IF YOU ARE TROUBLED TO GET SOFT WATER FOR WASHING, fill a tub or barrel half full of wood ashes, and fill it up with water, so that you may have ley whenever you want it. A gallon of strong ley, put into a great kettle of hard water, will make it as soft as rain water. Some people use pearlash, or potash; but this costs something, and is very apt to injure the texture of the cloth.

435. Do NOT LET KNIVES be dropped into hot dish-water. It is a good plan to have a large tin pot to wash them in, just high enough to wash the blades *without wetting* the handles.

436. IT IS BETTER to accomplish perfectly a very small amount of work, than to half do ten times as much.

437. CHARCOAL POWDER will be found a very good thing to give knives a first-rate polish.

438. A BONNET AND TRIMMINGS may be worn a much longer time, if the dust be brushed well off after walking.

439. MUCH KNOWLEDGE may be obtained by the good housewife observing how things are managed in well-regulated families.

440. APPLES intended for dumplings should not have the core taken out of them, as the pips impart a delicious flavour to the dumpling.

441. A RICE PUDDING is most excellent without either eggs or sugar, if baked gently: it keeps better without eggs.

442. "WILFUL WASTE MAKES WOFUL WANT."—Do not cook a fresh joint whilst any of the last remains uneaten —hash it up, and with gravy and a little management, eke out another day's dinner.

443. THE SHANKS OF MUTTON make a good stock for nearly any kind of gravy, and they are very cheap—a dozen may be had for a penny, enough to make a quart of delicious soup.

444. THICK CURTAINS, closely drawn around the bed, are very injurious, because they not only confine the effluvia thrown off from our bodies whilst in bed, but interrupt the current of pure air.

445. REGULARITY in the payment of accounts is essential to housekeeping. All tradesmen's bills should be paid weekly, for then any errors can be detected whilst the transactions are fresh in the memory.

446. ALLOWING CHILDREN TO TALK incessantly is a mistake. We do not mean to say that they should be restricted from talking in proper seasons, but they should be taught to know when it is proper for them to cease.

447. Blacking for Leather Seats, &c.—Beat well the yolks of two eggs and the white of one; mix a tablespoonful of gin and a teaspoonful of sugar, thicken it with ivory black, add it to the eggs, and use as common blacking; the seats or cushions being left a day or two to harden. This is good for dress boots and shoes.

448. Black Reviver for Black Cloth.—Bruised galls, one pound; logwood, two pounds; green vitriol, half a pound; water, five quarts. Boil for two hours, and strain. Used to restore the colour of black cloth. Cost: galls, 1s. 4d. per pound; logwood, 2d. per pound; green vitriol, 1d. per pound.

449. A Green Paint for Garden Stands, &c., may be obtained by mixing a quantity of mineral green and white lead, ground in turpentine, with a small portion of turpentine varnish, for the first coat; for the second, put as much varnish in the colour as will produce a good gloss.

450. Hints for Home Comfort.

i. Eat slowly and you will not over-eat.

ii. Keeping the feet warm will prevent headaches.

iii. Late at breakfast — hurried for dinner—cross at tea.

iv. A short needle makes the most expedition in plain sewing.

v. Between husband and wife little attentions beget much love.

vi. Always lay your table neatly, whether you have company or not.

vii. Put your balls or reels of cotton into little bags, leaving the ends out.

viii. Whatever you may choose to give away, always be sure to *keep your temper*.

ix. Dirty windows speak to the passer-by of the negligence of the inmates.

x. In cold weather a leg of mutton improves by being hung three, four, or five weeks.

xi. When meat is hanging, change its position frequently, to equally distribute the juices.

xii. There is much more injury done by admitting visitors to invalids than is generally supposed.

xiii. Matches, out of the reach of children, should be kept in every bed-room. They are cheap enough.

xiv. Apple and suet dumplings are lighter when boiled in a net than a cloth. Scum the pot well.

xv. When chamber towels get thin in the middle, cut them in two, sew the selvages together, and hem the sides.

xvi. When you are particular in wishing to have precisely what you want from a butcher's, go and purchase it yourself.

xvii. One flannel petticoat will wear nearly as long as two, if turned behind part before, when the front begins to wear thin.

xviii. People in general are not aware how very essential to the health of the inmates is the free admission of light into their houses.

xix. When you dry salt for the table, do not place it in the salt-cells until it is cold, otherwise it will harden into a lump.

xx. Never put away plate, knives and forks, &c., uncleaned, or great inconve-

nience will arise when the articles are wanted.

xxi. Feather beds should be opened every third year, the ticking well dusted, soaped, and waxed, the feathers dressed and returned.

xxii. Persons of defective sight, when threading a needle, should hold it over something white, by which the sight will be assisted.

xxiii. In mending sheets and shirts, put the pieces sufficiently large, or in the first washing the thin parts give way, and the work is all undone.

xxiv. Reading by candle-light, place the candle behind you, that the rays may pass over your shoulder on to the book. This will relieve the eyes.

xxv. A wire fire-guard, for each fire-place in a house, costs little, and greatly diminishes the risk to life and property. Fix them before going to bed.

xxvi. In winter, get the work forward by daylight, to prevent running about at night with candles. Thus you escape grease spots, and risks of fire.

xxvii. Be at much pains to keep your children's feet dry and warm. Don't bury their bodies in heavy flannels and wools, and leave their knees and legs naked.

xxviii. Apples and pears, cut into quarters and stripped of the rind, baked with a little water and sugar, and eaten with boiled rice, are capital food for children.

xxix. A leather strap, with a buckle to fasten, is much more commodious than a cord for a box in general use for short distances; cording and uncording is a tedious job.

xxx. After washing, overlook linen, and stitch on buttons, hooks and eyes, &c.; for this purpose keep a "housewife's friend," full of miscellaneous threads, cottons, buttons, hooks, &c.

xxxi. For ventilation open your windows both at top and bottom. The fresh air rushes in one way, while the foul makes its exit the other. This is letting in your friend and expelling your enemy.

xxxii. There is not any real economy in

purchasing cheap calico for gentlemen's night-shirts. Cheap calico soon wears into holes, and becomes discoloured in washing.

xxxiii. Sitting to sew by candle-light at a table with a dark cloth on it is injurious to the eyesight. When no other remedy presents itself, put a sheet of white paper before you.

xxxiv. Persons very commonly complain of indigestion: how can it be wondered at, when they seem, by their habit of swallowing their food wholesale, to forget for what purpose they are provided with teeth?

xxxv. Never allow your servants to put wiped knives on your table, for, generally speaking, you may see that they have been wiped with a dirty cloth. If a knife is brightly cleaned, they are compelled to use a clean cloth.

xxxvi. There is not anything gained in economy by having very young and inexperienced servants at low wages; they break, waste, and destroy more than an equivalent for higher wages, setting aside comfort and respectability.

xxxvii. No article in dress tarnishes so readily as black crape trimmings, and few things injure it more than damp; therefore, to preserve its beauty on bonnets, a lady in nice mourning should in her evening walks, at all seasons of the year, take as her companion an old parasol to shade her crape.

451. Domestic Pharmacopœia.

In compiling this part of our hints, we have endeavoured to supply that kind of information which is so often wanted in the time of need, and cannot be obtained when a medical man or a druggist is not near. The doses are all fixed for adults, unless otherwise ordered. The various remedies are arranged in sections, according to their uses, as being more easy for reference.

452. Collyria, or Eye Washes.

453. ALUM. — Dissolve half a drachm of alum in eight ounces of water. Use, as an astringent. When the strength of the alum is doubled, and only half the quantity of water used, it acts as a discutient, but not as an eye-water.

454. COMMON.—Add half an ounce of diluted acetic acid to three ounces of decoction of poppy heads. Use, as an anodyne wash.

455. COMPOUND ALUM.—Dissolve alum and white vitriol, of each one drachm, in one pint of water, and filter through paper. Use, as an astringent wash.

456. ZINC AND LEAD.—Dissolve white vitriol and acetate of lead, of each seven grains, in four ounces of elder-flower water; add one drachm of laudanum (tincture of opium), and the same quantity of spirit of camphor; then strain. Use, as a detergent wash.

457. ACETATE OF ZINC.—Dissolve half a drachm of white vitriol in five ounces of water. Dissolve two scruples of acetate of lead in five ounces of water. Mix these solutions, then set aside for a short time, and afterwards filter. Use, as an astringent; this forms a most valuable collyrium.

458. SULPHATE OF ZINC.—Dissolve twenty grains of white vitriol in a pint of water or rose water. Use, for weak eyes.

459. ZINC AND CAMPHOR.—Dissolve a scruple of white vitriol in ten ounces of water, then add one drachm of spirit of camphor, and strain. Use, as a stimulant.

460. COMPOUND ZINC. — Dissolve fifteen grains of white vitriol in eight ounces of camphor water (*Mistura camphora*), and the same quantity of decoction of poppy heads. Use, as an anodyne and detergent; useful for weak eyes.

461. Confections and Electuaries.

462. CONFECTIONS are used as vehicles for the administration of more active medicines, and *Electuaries* are made for the purpose of rendering some remedies palatable. Both should be kept in closely covered jars.

463. ALMOND CONFECTION. — Re-

move the outer coat from an ounce of sweet almonds, and beat them well in a mortar with one drachm of powdered gum arabic, and half an ounce of white sugar.   *Use*, to make a demulcent mixture, known as "almond emulsion."

464. ALUM CONFECTION.—Mix two scruples of powdered alum with four scruples of treacle. *Dose*, half a drachm. *Use*, as an astringent in sore throat and relaxed uvula, and ulcerations of the mouth.

465. ORANGE CONFECTION.—Take one ounce of the freshly rasped rind of orange, and mix it with three ounces of white sugar, and beat together till perfectly incorporated. *Dose*, from one drachm to one ounce. *Use*, as a gentle stomachic and tonic, and for giving tonic powders in.

466. BLACK PEPPER CONFECTION. —Take of black pepper and elecampane root, each one ounce; fennel seeds, three ounces; honey and sugar, of each two ounces. Rub the dry ingredients to a fine powder, and when the confection is wanted, add the honey, and mix well. *Dose*, from one to two drachms. *Use*, in hæmorrhoids, or piles.

467. COWHAGE.—Mix as much of the fine hairs or spiculæ of cowhage into treacle as it will take up. *Dose*, a teaspoonful every morning and evening. *Use*, as an anthelmintic.

468. SENNA CONFECTION.—Take of senna, powdered, four ounces; figs, half a pound, cassia pulp, tamarind pulp, and the pulp of prunes, each four ounces; coriander seeds, powdered, two ounces; liquorice root, one ounce and a half; sugar, one pound and a quarter; water, one pint and a half. Rub the senna with the coriander, and separate, by sifting, five ounces of the mixture. Boil the water, with the figs and liquorice added, until it is reduced to one half; then press out and strain the liquor. Evaporate the strained liquor in a jar by boiling until twelve fluid ounces remain; then add the sugar, and make a syrup. Now mix the pulps with the syrup, add the sifted powder, and mix well. *Use*, purgative.

469. CASTOR OIL AND SENNA CONFECTION.—Take one drachm of powdered gum arabic, and two ounces of confection of senna, and mix, by gradually rubbing together in a mortar, with half an ounce of castor oil. *Dose*, from half an ounce to an ounce. *Use*, purgative.

470. SULPHUR AND SENNA CONFECTION.—Take of sulphur and sulphate of potash, each half an ounce; of confection of senna, two ounces; and oil of aniseed, twenty minims; mix well. *Dose*, from one to two drachms. *Use*, purgative.

471. CREAM OF TARTAR CONFECTION.—Take one ounce of cream of tartar, one drachm of jalap, and half a drachm of powdered ginger; mix into a thick paste with treacle. *Dose*, two drachms. *Use*, purgative.

472. ANTISPASMODIC ELECTUARY. — Take six drachms of powdered valerian and orange leaves, mixed and made into an electuary, with a sufficient quantity of syrup of wormwood. *Dose*, from one to two drachms, to be taken two or three times a day.

473. Decoctions.—These should only be made as they are wanted; pipkins or tin saucepans should be used for the purpose; and no decoction should be boiled longer than ten minutes.

474. CHIMAPHILA.—Take one ounce of pyrola (chimaphila, or winter-green), and boil it in a pint and a half of water until it is only one pint; then strain. *Dose*, from one to two ounces, four times a day. *Use*, in dropsies, as a diuretic.

475. LOGWOOD.—Boil one ounce and a half of bruised logwood in two pints of water until it comes to one pint; then add one drachm of bruised cassia, and strain. *Dose*, from one to two ounces. *Use*, as an astringent.

476. DANDELION.—Take two ounces of the freshly-sliced root, and boil in two pints of water until it comes to one pint; then add one ounce of compound tincture of horseradish. *Dose*, from two to four ounces. *Use*, in a sluggish state of the liver.

477. Embrocations and Liniments.—These remedies are used externally as local stimulants, to relieve deep-seated inflammations when other means cannot be employed, as they are more easily applied locally.

478. ANODYNE AND DISCUTIENT.—Take two drachms of scraped white soap, half a drachm of extract of henbane, and dissolve them by a gentle heat in six ounces of olive oil. *Use,* about half an ounce to be well rubbed into the part twice a day, for glandular enlargements which are painful and stubborn.

479. STRONG AMMONIATED.—Add one ounce of strong liquid ammonia (*Liquoris ammoniæ fortius*) to two ounces of olive oil; shake them well together until they are properly mixed. *Use,* employed as a stimulant in rheumatic pains, paralytic numbnesses, chronic glandular enlargements, lumbago, sciatica, &c. This embrocation must be used with care, and only employed in very obstinate cases.

480. COMPOUND AMMONIATED.—Add six drachms of oil of turpentine to the strong ammoniated liniment above. *Use,* for the diseases mentioned under the head of strong ammoniated liniment, and chronic affections of the knee and ankle joints.

481. LIME AND OIL.—Take equal parts of common linseed oil and lime water (*Liquor calcis*), and shake well. *Use,* applied to burns, scalds, sun peelings, &c.

482. CAMPHORATED.—Take half an ounce of camphor and dissolve it in two ounces of olive oil. *Use,* as a stimulant, soothing application, in stubborn breasts, glandular enlargements, dropsy of the belly, and rheumatic pains.

483. SOAP LINIMENT WITH SPANISH FLIES.—Take three ounces and a half of soap liniment, and half an ounce of tincture of Spanish flies; mix and shake well. *Use,* as a stimulant to chronic bruises, sprains, rheumatic pains, and indolent swellings.

484. TURPENTINE.—Take two ounces and a half of resin cerate (*Ceratum resinæ*), and melt it by standing the vessel in hot water; then add one ounce and a half of oil of turpentine, and mix.

Use, as a stimulant application to ulcers, burns, scalds, &c.

485. ENEMAS.—These are a peculiar kind of medicines, administered by injecting them into the rectum or outlet of the body. The intention is either to empty the bowels, kill worms, protect the lining membrane of the intestines from injury, restrain copious discharges, allay spasms in the bowels, or to nourish the body. These clysters, or glysters, are administered by means of bladders and pipes, or a proper apparatus.

486. LAXATIVE.—Take two ounces of Epsom salts, and dissolve in three quarters of a pint of gruel, or thin broth, with an ounce of olive oil. *Use,* as all enemas are used.

487. NUTRITIVE.—Take twelve ounces of strong beef tea, and thicken with hartshorn shavings or arrowroot.

488. TURPENTINE.—Take half an ounce of oil of turpentine, the yolk of one egg, and half a pint of gruel. Mix the turpentine and egg, and then add the gruel. *Use,* as an anthelmintic.

489. COMMON.—Dissolve one ounce of salt in twelve ounces of gruel.

490. CASTOR OIL.—Mix two ounces of castor oil with one drachm of starch, then rub them together, and add fourteen ounces of thin gruel. *Use,* purgative.

491. OPIUM.—Rub three grains of opium with two ounces of starch, then add two ounces of warm water. *Use,* as an anodyne, in colic, spasms, &c.

492. OIL.—Mix four ounces of olive oil with half an ounce of mucilage and half a pint of warm water. *Use,* as a demulcent.

493. ASSAFŒTIDA.—Mix one drachm of the tincture of assafœtida in a pint of barley water. *Use,* as an anthelmintic, or in convulsions from teething.

494. GARGLES.—These are remedies used to stimulate chronic sore throats, or a relaxed state of the swallow, or uvula.

495. ACIDULATED.—Mix one part of white vinegar with three parts of honey of roses, and twenty-four of barley water. *Use,* in chronic inflammations of the throat, malignant sore throat, &c.

496. ASTRINGENT. — Take two drachms of roses and mix with eight ounces of boiling water, infuse for one hour, strain, and add one drachm of alum and one ounce of honey of roses. *Use*, in severe sore throat, relaxed uvula, &c.

497. FOR SALIVATION.—Mix from one to four drachms of bruised gall-nuts with a pint of boiling water, and infuse for two hours, then strain and sweeten.

498. TONIC AND STIMULANT.—Mix six ounces of decoction of bark with two ounces of tincture of myrrh, and half a drachm of diluted sulphuric acid. *Use*, in scorbutic affections.

499. ALUM.—Dissolve one drachm of alum in fifteen ounces of water, then add half an ounce of treacle and one drachm of diluted sulphuric acid. *Use*, astringent.

500. MYRRH.—Add six drachms of tincture of myrrh to seven ounces of infusion of linseed, and then add one drachm of diluted sulphuric acid. *Use*, as a detergent.

501. FOR SLIGHT INFLAMMATION OF THE THROAT.—Add one drachm of sulphuric ether to half an ounce of syrup of marsh-mallows, and six ounces of barley water. This may be used frequently.

502. Lotions.—Lotions are usually applied to the parts required by means of a piece of linen rag or piline, wetted with them, or by wetting the bandage itself.

503. EMOLLIENT.—Use decoction of marsh-mallow or linseed.

504. ELDER FLOWERS.—Add two drachms and a half of elder flowers to one quart of boiling water, infuse for one hour, and strain. *Use*, as a discutient.

505. SEDATIVE. — Dissolve one drachm of extract of henbane in twenty-four drachms of water.

506. OPIUM. — Mix two drachms of bruised opium with half a pint of boiling water, allow it to grow cold, and use for painful ulcers, bruises, &c.

507. STIMULANT. — Dissolve one drachm of caustic potash in one pint of water, and then gradually pour it upon twenty-four grains of camphor and one drachm of sugar, previously bruised together in a mortar. *Used* as in fungoid and flabby ulcers.

508. ORDINARY.—Mix one drachm of salt with eight ounces of water. *Used* for foul ulcers and flabby wounds.

509. COLD EVAPORATING. — Add two drachms of Goulard's extract (*Liquor plumbi diacetatis*), and the same quantity of sulphuric ether (*Ether sulphurious*), to a pint of cold water. *Use*, as a lotion for contusions, sprains, inflamed parts, &c.

510. HYDROCHLORATE OF AMMONIA. —Dissolve two drachms of sal ammoniac (*Ammoniæ hydrochloras*) in six ounces of water, then add an ounce of distilled vinegar and the same quantity of rectified spirit. *Use*, as a refrigerant.

511. YELLOW LOTION.—Dissolve one grain of corrosive sublimate (*Hydrargyri chloridum*, A VIOLENT POISON) in an ounce of lime water, taking care to bruise the crystals of the salt in order to assist its solution. *Use*, as a detergent.

512. BLACK WASH. — Add half a drachm of calomel to four ounces of lime water, or eight grains to an ounce of lime water ; shake well. *Use*, as a detergent.

513. ACETATE OF LEAD WITH OPIUM. —Take twenty grains of acetate of lead, and a drachm of powdered opium, mix, and add an ounce of vinegar and four ounces of warm water, set aside for an hour, then filter. *Use*, as an astringent.

514. CREOSOTE.—Add a drachm of creosote to a pint of water, and mix by shaking. *Use*, as an application in *tinea capitis*, or other cutaneous diseases.

515. GALLS.— Boil one drachm of bruised galls in twelve ounces of water until only half a pint remains, then strain, and add one ounce of laudanum. *Use*, as an astringent and sedative·

516. Ointments and Cerates.
—These remedies are used as topical applications to parts, generally ulcers, and are usually spread upon linen or other materials.

517. CAMPHORATED.—Mix half an ounce of camphor with one ounce of lard, having, of course, previously powdered the camphor, by adding a few drops of spirit of wine. *Use,* as a discutient and stimulant in indolent tumours.

518. CHALK.—Mix as much prepared chalk as you can into some lard, so as to form a thick ointment. *Use,* as an application to burns and scalds.

519. FOR ITCH.—Mix four drachms of sublimed sulphur, two ounces of lard, and half a drachm of diluted sulphuric acid together. This is to be rubbed into the body.

520. FOR SCROFULOUS ULCERATIONS.—Mix one drachm of ioduret of zinc and one ounce of lard together. *Use,* twice a day to the ulcerations.

521. CATECHU.—Mix one ounce of powdered catechu, two drachms and a half of powdered alum, one ounce of powdered white rosin, and two ounces and a half of olive oil, together. *Use,* to apply to flabby and indolent ulcerat ons.

522. TARTAR EMETIC.—Mix twenty grains of tartar emetic and ten grains of white sugar with one drachm and a half of lard. *Use,* as a counter-irritant in white swellings, &c.

523. Pills.

524. STRONG PURGATIVE.—Take of powdered aloes, scammony, and gamboge each fifteen grains, mix, and add sufficient Venice turpentine to make into a mass, then divide into twelve pills. *Dose,* one or two occasionally.

525. MILDER PURGATIVE. — Take four grains of powdered scammony and the same quantity of compound extract of colocynth, and two grains of calomel; mix well, and add two drops of oil of cloves, or thin gum-water, to enable the ingredients to combine properly, and divide into two pills. *Dose,* one or two when necessary.

526. COMMON PURGATIVE.—Take of powdered jalap and compound extract of colocynth each four grains, of calomel two grains, mix as usual, and divide into two pills. *Dose,* one or two occasionally.

527. TONIC. — Mix twenty-four grains of extract of gentian and the same of purified green vitriol (*sulphate of iron*) together, and divide into twelve pills. *Dose,* one or two when necessary. *Use,* in debility.

528. COUGH.—Mix one drachm of compound powder of ipecacuanha with one scruple of gum ammoniacum and one of dried squill bulb in powder. Make into a mass with mucilage, and divide into twenty pills. *Dose*—one, three times a day.

529. ASTRINGENT. — Mix sixteen grains of acetate of lead (*sugar of lead*) with four grains of opium, and make into a mass with extract of dandelion, so as to make eight pills. *Dose,* from one to two. *Use,* as an astringent in obstinate diarrhœa, dysentery, and spitting of blood.

530. Mixtures.

531. FEVER, SIMPLE.—Add three ounces of spirit of mindererus (*Liquor ammoniæ acetatis*), three drachms of spirits of sweet nitre, four drachms of antimonial wine, and a drachm of syrup of saffron, to four ounces of water, or medicated water, such as cinnamon, aniseed, &c. *Dose* for an adult, one or two tablespoonfuls every three hours. *Use,* as a diaphoretic.

532. AROMATIC.—Mix two drachms of aromatic confection with two drachms of compound tincture of cardamoms, and eight ounces of peppermint water. *Dose,* from one ounce to one and a half. *Use,* in flatulent colic and spasms of the bowels.

533. CATHARTIC. — Dissolve two ounces of Epsom salts in six ounces of compound infusion of senna, then add two ounces of peppermint water. *Dose,* from one and a half to two ounces. *Use,* as a warm and active cathartic.

534. DIURETIC.—Dissolve in three

ounces of camphor mixture, one drachm of powdered nitre; add five ounces of the decoction of broom, with six drachms of sweet spirits of nitre, and three drachms of tincture of squills; mix. *Dose,* one teaspoonful every two hours, or two tablespoonfuls every three hours. *Use,* excellent in dropsies.

535. COUGH.—Dissolve three grains of tartar emetic and fifteen grains of opium in one pint of boiling water, then add four ounces of treacle, two ounces of vinegar, and one pint more of boiling water. *Dose,* from two teaspoonfuls to two tablespoonfuls, according to circumstances, every three hours, or three times a day. *Use,* in common catarrh, bronchitis, and irritable cough.

536. COUGH (FOR CHILDREN).—Mix three drachms of ipecacuanha wine with half an ounce of oxymel of squills, the same quantity of syrup of tolu, one ounce of mucilage, and two ounces of water. *Dose,* one teaspoonful for children under one year, two teaspoonfuls from one to five years, and a tablespoonful from five years, every time the cough is troublesome.

537. ANTI-SPASMODIC.—Dissolve fifty grains of camphor in two drachms of chloroform, and then add two drachms of compound tincture of lavender, six drachms of mucilage of gum arabic, eight ounces of aniseed, cinnamon, or some other aromatic water, and two ounces of distilled water; mix well. *Dose,* one tablespoonful every half hour if necessary. *Use,* in cholera in the cold stage, when cramps are severe, or exhaustion very great; and as a general anti-spasmodic in doses of one dessert spoonful when the spasms are severe.

538. TONIC AND STIMULANT.—Dissolve one drachm of extract of bark, and half a drachm of powdered gum arabic, in six ounces of water, and then add one ounce of syrup of marsh-mallow, and the same quantity of syrup of tolu. *Dose,* one tablespoonful every three hours. *Use,* after fevers and catarrhs.

539. STOMACHIC.—Take twenty grains of powdered rhubarb, and rub it

down in three ounces and a half of peppermint water, then add sal volatile and compound tincture of gentian, each one drachm and a half; mix. *Dose,* from one to one ounce and a half. *Use,* as a tonic, stimulant, and stomachic.

540. Drinks.

541. TAMARIND.—Boil two ounces of the pulp of tamarinds in two pints of milk, then strain. *Use,* as a refrigerant drink.

542. TAMARIND.—Boil two ounces of the pulp in two pints of warm water, and allow it to get cold, then strain. *Use,* refrigerant.

543. Powders.

544. COMPOUND SODA.—Mix twenty-four grains of calomel, thirty-six grains of sesqui-carbonate of soda, and one drachm of compound chalk powder, together. Divide into twelve powders. One of the powders to be given for a dose when required. *Use,* as a mild purgative for children during teething.

545. TONIC.—Mix one drachm of powdered rhubarb with the same quantity of dried carbonate of soda, then add two drachms of powdered calumba root. *Dose,* from ten to twenty grains as a tonic after fevers, in all cases of debility, and dyspepsia attended with acidity.

546. RHUBARB AND MAGNESIA.—Mix one drachm of powdered rhubarb with two drachms of carbonate of magnesia, and half a drachm of ginger. *Dose,* from fifteen grains to one drachm. *Use,* as a purgative for children.

547. SULPHUR AND POTASH.—Mix one drachm of sulphur with four scruples of bicarbonate of potash, and two scruples of nitre. *Dose,* from half a drachm to one drachm. *Use,* as a purgative, diuretic, and refrigerant.

548. ANTI-DIARRHŒAL.—Mix one grain of powdered ipecacuanha, and one grain of powdered opium, with the same quantity of camphor. *Dose,* one of these powders to be given in jam, treacle, &c., once or twice a day; but to adults only.

549. ANTI-SPASMODIC. —Mix four grains of subnitrate of bismuth, forty-eight grains of carbonate of magnesia, and the same quantity of white sugar, and then divide in four equal parts. *Dose*, one-fourth part. *Use*, in obstinate pain in the stomach with cramps, unattended by inflammation.

550. ANTI-PERTUSSAL, OR AGAINST HOOPING-COUGH.—Mix one drachm of powdered belladonna root, and two ounces of white sugar, together. *Dose*, six grains morning and evening for children under one year; nine grains for those under two and three years of age; fifteen grains for those between five and ten; and thirty grains for adults. *Caution*, this should be prepared by a chemist, as the belladonna is a poison, and occasional doses of castor oil should be given while it is being taken.

551. PURGATIVE (COMMON).—Mix ten grains of calomel, with one drachm of powdered jalap, and twenty grains of sugar. *Dose*, one-half of the whole for adults.

552. SUDORIFIC. —Mix six grains of compound antimonial powder, two grains of ipecacuanha, and two grains of sugar, together. *Dose*, as mixed, to be taken at bed-time. *Use*, in catarrh and fever.

553. Miscellaneous.

554. ETHEREAL TINCTURE OF MALE FERN.—Digest one ounce male fern buds in eight ounces of sulphuric ether, then strain. *Dose*, thirty drops early in the morning. *Use*, to kill tapeworm.

555. EMULSION, LAXATIVE. —Rub down an ounce of castor oil in two drachms of mucilage of gum arabic, add three ounces of dill water, and a drachm of tincture of jalap, gradually. *Dose*, as prepared, the whole to be taken while fasting in the morning.

556. EMULSION, PURGATIVE.—Rub down six grains of scammony with six drachms of white sugar in a mortar, and gradually add four ounces of almond emulsion, and two drops of oil of cloves. *Dose*, as prepared, early in the morning.

557. TO PREVENT PITTING AFTER SMALL-POX.—Spread a sheet of thin leather with the ointment of ammoniacum with mercury, and cut out a place for the mouth, eyes, and nostrils. This forms what is called a mask, and, after anointing the eyelids with a little blue ointment (*Unguentum hydrargyri*), it should be applied to the face, and allowed to remain for three days for the distinct kind, and four days for the running variety. *Period to apply it :—Before* the spots fill with matter, although it will answer sometimes even after they have become pustulous. It may be applied to any part in the same way.

558. ANOTHER METHOD, and one more reliable, is that of touching every pustule, or poc, on the face or bosom with a camel-hair pencil dipped in a weak solution of lunar caustic (*nitrate of silver*), made in the proportion of two grains of nitrate of silver to one ounce of distilled water. The time for application is about the seventh day, while each pustule is filled with a limpid fluid, or before suppuration takes place, the lotion arresting that action, and by preventing the formation of matter, saving the skin from being pitted; a result that follows from the conversion of the adipose tissue into pus.

559. A THIRD METHOD of effecting the same purpose is by passing a fine needle through each poc, when fully distended with lymph; the escape of the fluid averting, as in the other mode, the suppuration which would otherwise ensue.

560. MUCILAGE OF GUM ARABIC.—Rub one ounce of gum arabic in a mortar, with four ounces of warm water. *Use*, for coughs, &c.

561. MUCILAGE OF STARCH.—Rub one drachm of starch with a little water, and gradually add five ounces of water, then boil until it forms a mucilage. *Use*, for enemas, topical applications, and demulcents.

562. Diseases.

For the proper Remedies and their Doses see "Prescriptions."

563. It should be clearly understood, that in all cases of disease, the advice of a skilful physician is of the first importance. It is not, therefore, intended by the following information to supersede the important and necessary practice of the medical man; but rather, by exhibiting the treatment required, to show in what degree his aid is imperative. In cases, however, where the disorder may be simple and transient, or in which remote residence, or other circumstances, may deny the privilege of medical attendance, the following particulars will be found of the utmost value. Moreover, the hints given upon what should be AVOIDED will be of great service to the patient, since the *physiological* is no less important than the *medical* treatment of disease.

564. APOPLEXY.—Immediate and large bleeding from the arm, cupping at the back of the neck, leeches to the temples, aperients Nos. 1 and 7, one or two drops of croton oil rubbed or dropped on the tongue. Avoid excesses, intemperance, animal food.

565. BILE, BILIOUS, OR LIVER COMPLAINTS.—Abstinence from malt liquors, cool homœopathic cocoa for drink, no tea or coffee, few vegetables, no broths or soups; lean juicy meat not overcooked for dinner, with occasionally stale bread and a slice of toasted bacon for breakfast. Nos. 59 and 60.

566. CHICKEN POX.—Mild aperients, No. 4, succeeded by No. 7, and No. 8, if much fever accompany the eruption.

567. CHILBLAINS. — Warm, dry woollen clothing to exposed parts in cold weather, as a preventive. In the first stage, frictions with No. 63, used cold. When ulcers form they should be poulticed with bread and water for a day or two, and then dressed with calamine cerate. Or chilblains in every stage, whether of simple inflammation or open ulcer, may always be successfully treated by the extract of lead (*Liquor plumbi acetatis*), used pure or applied on lint twice a day.

568. COMMON CONTINUED FEVER.—Aperients in the commencement, No. 1, followed by No. 7, then diaphoretics, No. 8, and afterwards tonics, No. 16, in the stage of weakness. Avoid all excesses.

569. COMMON COUGH.—The linctus, No. 57 or No. 58, abstinence from malt liquor, and protection from cold damp air. Avoid cold, damp, and draughts.

570. CONSTIPATION.—The observance of a regular period of evacuating the bowels, which is most proper in the morning after breakfast. The use of mild aperients, No. 62, brown bread instead of white. There should be an entire change in the dietary for a few days while taking opening medicine.

571. CONSUMPTION. — The disease may be complicated with various morbid conditions of the lungs and heart, which require appropriate treatment. To allay the cough, No. 57 is an admirable remedy. Avoid cold, damp, excitement, and over exertion.

572. CONVULSIONS (CHILDREN).—If during teething, free lancing of the gums, the warm bath, cold applications to the head, leeches to the temples, an emetic, and a laxative clyster, No. 24.

573. CROUP.—Leeches to the throat, with hot fomentations as long as the attack lasts; the emetic, No. 19, afterwards the aperient, No. 5. Avoid cold and damp.

574. DROPSY.—Evacuate the water by means of No. 11, and by rubbing camphorated oil into the body night and morning.

575. EPILEPSY.—If accompanied or produced by fulness of the vessels of the head, leeches to the temples, blisters, and No. 1 and No. 7. If from debility or confirmed epilepsy, the mixture, No. 22. Avoid drinking and excitement.

576. ERUPTIONS ON THE FACE.—The powder, No. 34, internally, sponging the face with the lotion, No. 35. Avoid excesses in diet.

577. ERYSIPELAS.—Aperients, if the patient be strong, No. 1, followed by No. 7, then tonics, No. 31 ; No. 31 from the commencement in weak subjects.

578. FAINTNESS.—Effusion of cold water on the face, stimulants to the nostrils, pure air, and the recumbent position ; afterwards, avoidance of the exciting cause. Avoid excitement.

579. FROST - BITE AND FROZEN LIMBS. — No heating or stimulating liquors must be given. Rub the parts affected with ice, cold, or snow water, and lay the patient on a cold bed.

580. GOUT.—The aperients No. 1, followed by No. 28, bathing the parts with gin-and-water; for drink, weak tea or coffee. Warmth by flannels. Abstain from wines, spirits, and animal food.

581. GRAVEL.—No. 5, followed by No. 7, the free use of magnesia as an aperient. The pill No. 26. Abstain from fermented drinks, hard water. Another form of gravel must be treated by mineral acids, given three times a day.

582. HOOPING COUGH. — Hooping cough may be complicated with congestion or inflammation of the lungs, or convulsions, and then becomes a serious disease. If uncomplicated, No. 58.

583. HYSTERICS.—The fit may be prevented by the administration of thirty drops of laudanum, and as many of ether. When it has taken place open the windows, loosen the tight parts of the dress, sprinkle cold water on the face, &c. A glass of wine or cold water when the patient can swallow. Avoid excitement and tight lacing.

584. INDIGESTION.—The pills No. 2, with the mixture No. 22, at the same time abstinence from veal, pork, mackarel, salmon, pastry, and beer; for drink, homœopathic cocoa, a glass of cold spring water the first thing every morning. Avoid excesses.

585. INFLAMMATION OF THE BLADDER.—Bleeding, aperients No. 5 and No. 7, the warm bath, afterwards opium: the pill No. 12, three times a day till relieved. Avoid fermented liquors, &c.

586. INFLAMMATION OF THE

BOWELS.—Leeches, blisters, fomentations, hot baths, iced drinks, the pills No. 33; move the bowels with clysters, if necessary, No. 24. Avoid cold, indigestible food, &c.

587. INFLAMMATION OF THE BRAIN.—Application of cold to the head, bleeding from the temples or back of the neck by leeches or cupping; aperients No. 1, followed by No. 7; mercury to salivation, No. 18. Avoid excitement, study, intemperance.

588. INFLAMMATION OF THE KIDNEYS.—Bleeding from the arm, leeches over the seat of pain, aperients No. 5, followed by No. 64, the warm bath. Avoid violent exercise, rich living.

589. INFLAMMATION OF THE LIVER.—Leeches over the right side, the seat of pain, blisters, aperients No. 1, followed by No. 7, afterwards the pills No. 23, till the gums are slightly tender. Avoid cold, damp, intemperance, and anxiety.

590. INFLAMMATION OF THE LUNGS.—Bleeding from the arm or over the painful part of the chest by leeches, succeeded by a blister; the demulcent mixture, No. 17, to allay the cough, with the powders No. 18. Avoid cold, damp, and draughts.

591. INFLAMMATION OF THE STOMACH.—Leeches to the pit of the stomach, followed by fomentations, cold iced water for drink, bowels to be evacuated by clysters; abstinence from all food except cold gruel, milk and water, or tea. Avoid excesses, and condiments.

592. INFLAMMATORY SORE THROAT.—Leeches and blisters externally, aperients No. 1, followed by No. 7, gargle to clear the throat, No. 20. Avoid cold, damp, and draughts.

593. INFLAMED EYES.—The bowels to be regulated by No. 5, a small blister behind the ear or on the nape of the neck—the eye to be bathed with No. 39.

594. INFLUENZA. — No. 4 as an aperient and diaphoretic. No. 17 to allay fever and cough. No. 31 as a tonic, when weakness only remains.

Avoid cold and damp, use clothing suited to the changes of temperature.

595. INTERMITTENT FEVER, OR AGUE.— Take No. 16 during the intermission of the paroxysm of the fever; keeping the bowels free with a wineglass of No. 7. Avoid bad air, stagnant pools, &c.

596. ITCH.—The ointment of No. 32, or lotion No. 33.

597. JAUNDICE.—The pills No. 1, afterwards the mixture No. 7, drinking freely of dandelion tea.

598. LOOSENESS OF THE BOWELS (ENGLISH CHOLERA).—One pill No. 23, repeated if necessary; afterwards the mixture No. 25. Avoid unripe fruits, acid drinks, ginger beer; wrap flannel around the abdomen.

599. MEASLES.—A well-ventilated room, aperients No. 4, with No. 17 to allay the cough and fever.

600. MENSTRUATION (EXCESSIVE).—No. 47 during the attack, with rest in the recumbent position; in the intervals, No. 46.

601. MENSTRUATION (SCANTY).—In strong patients, cupping the loins, exercise in the open air, 47, the feet in warm water before the expected period, the pills No. 45; in weak subjects, No. 46. Gentle and regular exercise. Avoid hot rooms, and too much sleep.

602. MENSTRUATION (PAINFUL).—No. 48 during the attack; in the intervals, No. 45 twice a week, with No. 46. Avoid cold, mental excitement, &c.

603. MUMPS.—Fomentation with a decoction of camomiles and poppy heads; No. 4 as an aperient, and No. 9 during the stage of fever. Avoid cold, and attend to the regularity of the bowels.

604. NERVOUSNESS.—Cheerful society, early rising, exercise in the open air, particularly on horseback, and No. 15. Avoid excitement, study, and late meals.

605. PALPITATION OF THE HEART.—The pills No. 2, with the mixture No. 15.

606. PILES.—The paste No. 38, at the same time a regulated diet. When the piles are external, or can be reached, one or two applications of the extract of . . . with an occasional dose of . . . electuary, will generally succeed in curing them.

607. QUINSEY.—A blister applied all round the throat: an emetic, No. 19, commonly succeeds in breaking the abscess; afterwards the gargle No. 20. Avoid cold and damp.

608. RHEUMATISM.—Bathe the affected parts with No. 27, and take internally No. 28, with No. 29 at bedtime, to ease pain, &c. Avoid damp and cold, wear flannel.

609. RICKETS.—The powder No. 37, a dry, pure atmosphere, a nourishing diet.

610. RINGWORM.—The lotion No. 36, with the occasional use of the powder No. 5. Fresh air and cleanliness.

611. SCARLET FEVER.—Well ventilated room, sponging the body when hot with cold or tepid vinegar, or spirit and water; aperients, No. 4; diaphoretics, No. 8. If dropsy succeed the disappearance of the eruption, frequent purging with No. 5, succeeded by No. 7.

612. SCROFULA.—Pure air, light but warm clothing, diet of fresh animal food; bowels to be regulated by No. 6 and No. 30, taken regularly for a considerable time.

613. SCURVY. — Fresh animal and vegetable food, and the free use of ripe fruits and lemon juice. Avoid cold and damp.

614. SMALL-POX. — A well-ventilated apartment, mild aperients; if fever be present, No. 7, succeeded by diaphoretics No. 8, and tonics No. 16 in the stage of debility, or decline of the eruption.

615. ST. VITUS'S DANCE. — The occasional use, in the commencement, of No. 5, followed by No. 7, afterwards No. 61.

616. THRUSH.—One of the powders No. 6 every other night; in the intervals a dessertspoonful of the mixture No. 22

three times a day; white spots to be dressed with the honey of borax.

617. TIC DOLOREUX.—Regulate the bowels with No. 3, and take in the intervals of pain No. 31. Avoid cold, damp, and mental anxiety.

618. TOOTHACHE. — Continue the use of No. 3 for a few alternate days. Apply liquor ammonia to reduce the pain, and when that is accomplished, fill the decayed spots with silver succedaneum without delay, or the pain will return. A drop of creosote, or a few drops of chloroform on cotton, applied to the tooth, or a few grains of camphor placed in the decayed opening, or camphor moistened with turpentine, will often afford instant relief.

619. TYPHUS FEVER. — Sponging the body with cold or tepid water, a well-ventilated apartment, cold applications to the head and temples. Aperients No. 4, with refrigerants No. 9; tonics No. 16 in the stage of debility.

620. WATER ON THE BRAIN. — Local bleeding by means of leeches, blisters, aperients No. 5, and mercurial medicines No. 18.

621. WHITES.—The mixture No. 43, with the injection No. 44. Clothing light but warm, moderate exercise in the open air, country residence.

622. WORMS IN THE INTESTINES.— The aperient No. 5 followed by No. 7, afterwards the free use of lime water and milk in equal parts, a pint daily. Avoid unwholesome food.

623. Prescriptions.

To be used in the Cases enumerated under the head " Diseases."

624. The following prescriptions, originally derived from various prescribers' Pharmacopœias, embody the favourite remedies employed by the most eminent physicians:—

1. Take of powdered aloes, nine grains; extract of colocynth, compound, eighteen grains; calomel, nine grains; tartrate of antimony, two grains; mucilage, sufficient to make a mass, which is to be divided into six pills; two to be taken every twenty-four

hours, till they act thoroughly on the bowels: in cases of inflammation, apoplexy, &c.

2. Powdered rhubarb, Socotrine aloes, and gum mastiche, each one scruple: make into twelve pills: one before and one after dinner.

3. Compound extract of colocynth, extract of jalap, and Castile soap, of each one scruple; make into twelve pills.

4. James's powder, five grains; calomel, three grains: in fevers, for adults. For children, the following:—Powdered camphor, one scruple; calomel and powdered scammony, of each nine grains; James's powder, six grains; mix, and divide into six powders. Half of one powder twice a day for an infant a year old; a whole powder for two years; and for four years, the same three times a day.

5. James's powder, six grains; powdered jalap, ten grains; mix, and divide into three or four powders, according to the child's age: in one powder if for an adult.

6. Powdered rhubarb, four grains; mercury and chalk, three grains; ginger in powder, one grain: an alterative aperient for children.

7. Dried sulphate of magnesia, six drachms; sulphate of soda, three drachms; infusion of senna, seven ounces; tincture of jalap, and compound tincture of cardamoms, each half an ounce: in acute diseases generally; take two tablespoonfuls every four hours till it operates freely.

8. Nitrate of potass, one drachm and a half; spirits of nitric ether, half an ounce; camphor mixture, and the spirit of mindererus, each four ounces: in fevers, &c.; two tablespoonfuls three times a day, and for children a dessertspoonful every four hours.

9. Spirit of nitric ether, three drachms; dilute nitric acid, two drachms; syrup, three drachms; camphor mixture, seven ounces: in fevers, &c., with debility; dose as last.

10. Spirit of mindererus and camphor mixture, of each three ounces and a half;

wine of antimony, one drachm and a half; wine of ipecacuanha, one drachm and a half; syrup of tolu, half an ounce: dose as last.

11. Decoction of broom, half a pint; cream of tartar, one ounce; tincture of squills, two drachms: in dropsies; a third part three times a day.

12. Pills of soap and opium, five grains for a dose, as directed.

13. Compound powder of ipecacuanha, seven to twelve grains for a dose, as directed.

14. Battley's solution of opium, from ten to forty drops; camphor mixture, an ounce and a half: in a draught at bedtime.

15. Ammoniated tincture of valerian, six drachms; camphor mixture, seven ounces: a fourth part three times a day; in spasmodic and hysterical disorders.

16. Disulphate of quina, half a drachm; dilute sulphuric acid, twenty drops; compound infusion of roses, eight ounces: two tablespoonfuls every four hours, in intermittent and other fevers, during the absence of the paroxysm.

17. Almond mixture, seven ounces and a half; wine of antimony and ipecacuanha, of each one drachm and a half: a tablespoonful every four hours; in cough with fever, &c.

18. Calomel, one grain; powdered white sugar, two grains; to make a powder to be placed on the tongue every two or three hours. Should the calomel act on the bowels, powdered kino is to be substituted for the sugar.

19. Antimony and ipecacuanha wines, of each an ounce; a teaspoonful every ten minutes till it vomits: but for an adult a large tablespoonful to be taken.

20. Compound infusion of roses, seven ounces; tincture of myrrh, one ounce.

21. Decoction of bark, six ounces; aromatic confection, one drachm; tincture of opium, five drops.

22. Infusion of orange peel, seven ounces; tincture of hops, half an ounce; and a drachm of carbonate of soda: two tablespoonfuls twice a day. Or, infusion of valerian, seven ounces;

carbonate of ammonia, two scruples; compound tincture of bark, six drachms; spirits of ether, two drachms: one tablespoonful every twenty-four hours.

23. Blue pill, four grains; opium, half a grain: to be taken three times a day.

24. FOR A CLYSTER.—A pint and a half of gruel or fat broth, a tablespoonful of castor oil, one of common salt, and a lump of butter; mix, to be injected slowly. A third of this quantity enough for an infant.

25. Chalk mixture, seven ounces; aromatic and opiate confection, of each one drachm; tincture of catechu, six drachms: two tablespoonfuls every two hours.

26. Carbonate of soda, powdered rhubarb, and Castile soap, each one drachm; make thirty-six pills; three twice a day.

27. LOTION. — Common salt, one ounce; distilled water, seven ounces; spirits of wine, one ounce: mix.

28. Dried sulphate of magnesia, six drachms; heavy carbonate of magnesia, two drachms; wine of colchicum, two drachms; water, eight ounces: take two tablespoonfuls every four hours.

29. Compound powder of ipecacuanha, ten grains; powdered guaiacum, four grains: in a powder at bedtime.

30. Brandish's solution of potash; thirty drops twice a day in a wineglass of beer.

31. Disulphate of quina, half a drachm; dilute sulphuric acid, ten drops; compound infusion of roses, eight ounces: two tablespoonfuls every four hours, and as a tonic in the stage of weakness succeeding fever.

32. Flowers of sulphur, two ounces; hog's lard, four ounces; white hellebore powder, half an ounce; oil of lavender, sixty drops.

33. Hydriodate of potass, two drachms; distilled water, eight ounces.

34. Flowers of sulphur, half a drachm; carbonate of soda, a scruple; tartarized antimony, one-eighth of a grain: one powder, night and morning, in eruptions of the skin or face.

35. Milk of bitter almonds, seven ounces; bichloride of mercury, four grains; spirits of rosemary, one ounce: bathe the eruption with this lotion three times a day.

36. Sulphate of zinc, two scruples; sugar of lead, fifteen grains; distilled water, six ounces: the parts to be washed with the lotion two or three times a day.

37. Carbonate of iron, six grains; powdered rhubarb, four grains: one powder night and morning.

38. Elecampane powder, two ounces; sweet fennel-seed powder, three ounces; black pepper powder, one ounce; purified honey, and brown sugar, of each two ounces: the size of a nutmeg, two or three times a day.

39. Sulphate of zinc, twelve grains; wine of opium, one drachm; rose water, six ounces.

40. Common salt, one ounce; water, four ounces; spirits of wine and vinegar, each two ounces: the parts to be bathed or rubbed with this lotion frequently.

41. Spirit of wine and distilled vinegar, each one ounce; rose water, six ounces: the parts to be kept constantly damp with the lotion.

42. Linseed oil and lime water, equal quantities; anoint the injured parts frequently with a feather.

43. Sulphate of magnesia, six drachms; sulphate of iron, ten grains; diluted sulphuric acid, forty drops; tincture of cardamoms (compound), half an ounce; water, seven ounces: a fourth part night and morning.

44. Decoction of oak bark, a pint; dried alum, half an ounce: for an injection, a syringeful to be used night and morning.

45. Compound gamboge pill, and a pill of assafœtida and aloes, of each half a drachm: make twelve pills; two twice or three times a week.

46. Griffiths' mixture — one tablespoonful three times a day.

47. Ergot of rye, five grains; in a powder, to be taken every four hours.

48. Powdered opium, half a grain; camphor, two grains: in a pill; to be taken every three or four hours whilst in pain.

49. Balsam of copaiba, half an ounce; powdered cubebs, half an ounce; solution of potass, three drachms; powdered acacia, two drachms; laudanum, twenty drops; cinnamon water, seven ounces; one tablespoonful three times a day.

50. Tartarized antimony, two grains; sulphate of magnesia, six drachms; nitrate of potass, one drachm; compound tincture of cardamoms, half an ounce; water, eight ounces.

51. Lime water, two ounces; calomel, one scruple: make a lotion, to be applied by means of soft lint.

52. Blue pill, five grains; powdered opium, half a grain: two pills at night and one in the morning.

53. Biniodide of mercury, two grains; hydriodate of potass, one drachm; extract of sarsaparilla, one ounce; water, eight ounces: one tablespoonful three times a day.

54. Sulphate of zinc, twenty-four grains, in a wineglass of water; to be given for an emetic, and repeated if necessary.

55. Dill water, one and a half ounces; volatile tincture of valerian, twenty drops; tincture of castor, one drachm; spirits of sulphuric ether, twenty drops: make a draught, to be taken three times a day.

56. Syrup of poppies, oxymel of squills, of each one ounce; solution of potass, two drachms: a teaspoonful frequently.

57. Syrup of balsam of tolu, two ounces; the muriate of morphia, two grains; muriatic acid, twenty drops: a teaspoonful twice a day.

58. Salts of tartar, two scruples; twenty grains of powdered cochineal; ¼ lb. of honey; water, half a pint: boil, and give a tablespoonful three times a day.

59. Calomel, ten grains; Castile soap, extract of jalap, extract of colocynth, of each one scruple; oil of juniper, five drops: make into fifteen pills; one three times a day.

60. Infusion of orange peel, eight

ounces; carbonate of soda, one drachm; and compound tincture of cardamoms, half an ounce: take a tablespoonful three times a day, succeeding the pills.

61. Carbonate of iron, three ounces; syrup of ginger, sufficient to make an electuary: a teaspoonful three times a day.

62. Take of Castile soap, compound extract of colocynth, compound rhubarb pill, and the extract of jalap, of each one scruple; oil of carraway, ten drops: make into twenty pills, and take one after dinner every day whilst necessary.

63. Spirit of rosemary, five parts; spirit of wine, or spirit of turpentine, one part.

64. Take of thick mucilage, one ounce; castor oil, twelve drachms; make into an emulsion: add mint water, four ounces; spirit of nitre, three drachms; laudanum, one drachm; mixture of squills, one drachm; and syrup, seven drachms: mix; two tablespoonfuls every six hours.

625. Medicines (Aperient).— In the spring time of the year, the judicious use of aperient medicines is much to be commended.

626. SPRING APERIENTS. — For children, an excellent medicine is—i. Brimstone and treacle, prepared by mixing an ounce and a half of sulphur, and half an ounce of cream of tartar, with eight ounces of treacle; and, according to the age of the child, giving from a small teaspoonful to a dessertspoonful, early in the morning, two or three times a week. As this sometimes produces sickness, the following may be used:— ii. Take of powdered Rochelle salts one drachm and a half, powdered jalap and powdered rhubarb each fifteen grains, ginger two grains; mix. Dose for a child above five years, one *small* teaspoonful; above ten years, a *large* teaspoonful; above fifteen, half the whole, or two teaspoonfuls; and for a person above twenty, three teaspoonfuls, or the whole, as may be required by the habit of the person. This medicine may be dissolved in warm water, mint, or common tea. The powder can be

kept for use in a wide-mouthed bottle, and be in readiness for any emergency. The druggist may be directed to treble or quadruple the quantities, as convenient.

627. APERIENT PILLS.—To some adults all liquid medicines produce such nausea that pills are the only form in which aperients can be exhibited; the following is a useful formula: —iii. Take of compound rhubarb pill a drachm and one scruple, of powdered ipecacuanha ten grains, and of extract of hyoscyamus one scruple; mix, and beat into a mass, and divide into twenty-four pills: take one or two, or if of a very costive habit, *three* at bedtime.— iv. For persons requiring a more powerful aperient, the same formula, with twenty grains of compound extract of colocynth, will form a good purgative pill. The mass receiving this addition must be divided into thirty, instead of twenty-four pills.

628. BLACK DRAUGHT. — v. The common aperient medicine known as black draught is made in the following manner:— Take of senna leaves six drachms, bruised ginger half a drachm, sliced liquorice root four drachms, Epsom salts two and a half ounces, boiling water half an imperial pint. Keep this standing on the hob or near the fire for three hours, then strain, and after allowing it to grow cool, add of sal volatile one drachm and a half, of tincture of senna, and of tincture of cardamoms, each half an ounce. (This mixture will keep a long time in a cool place.) Dose, a wineglassful for an adult; and two tablespoonfuls for young persons about fifteen years of age. It is not a suitable medicine for children.

629. TONIC APERIENT.—vi. Take of Epsom salts one ounce, diluted sulphuric acid one drachm, infusion of quassia chips half an *imperial* pint, compound tincture of rhubarb two drachms. Half a wineglassful for a dose twice a day.

630. INFANTS' APERIENT. — vii. Take of rhubarb five grains, magnesia three grains, white sugar a scruple, grey powder five grains; mix. Dose, for an infant from twelve to eighteen months of age, from one-third to one-half of the whole.—viii. A useful laxative for children is composed of calomel five grains, and sugar a scruple, made into five powders; half of one of these for a child from birth to one year, and a whole one from that age to three years.

631. FLOUR OF BRIMSTONE is a mild aperient in doses of about a quarter of an ounce; it is best taken in milk. Flour of brimstone, which is also called sublimed sulphur, is generally put up in ounce packets at 1d.; its wholesale price is 4d. per pound.

632. Medicines.—PREPARATIONS OF THEM.— The following directions are of the utmost value in connection with the DOMESTIC PHARMACOPŒIA, DISEASES, PRESCRIPTIONS, and POISONS. *They will be found most important to emigrants, attendants upon the sick, and persons who reside out of the reach of medical aid, sailors, &c., &c. They contain instructions not only for the compounding of medicines, but most useful hints and cautions upon the application of leeches, blisters, poultices, &c.*

633. ARTICLES REQUIRED FOR MIXING MEDICINES.—Three glass measures, one to measure ounces, another to measure drachms, and a measure for minims, drops, or small doses. *A pestle and mortar,* both of glass and Wedgwoodware, a glass funnel, and glass stirring rods. *A spatula,* or flexible knife, for spreading ointments, making pills, &c. *A set of scales and weights. A small slab of marble,* slate, or porcelain, for making pills upon, mixing ointments, &c.

634. MEDICINE WEIGHTS AND MEASURES. — *Weights.* — When you open your box containing the scales and weights, you will observe that there are several square pieces of brass, of different sizes and thicknesses, and stamped with a variety of characters. These are the weights, which we will now explain.

635. MEDICINES ARE MADE up by troy weight, although drugs are bought by avoirdupois weight, and of course you know that there are only twelve ounces to the pound troy, which is marked ℔.; then each ounce, which contains eight drachms, is marked ℥i.; each drachm, containing three scruples, is marked ℨi.; and each scruple of twenty grains is marked ℈i. The grain weights are marked by little circles, each circle signifying a grain. Each of the grain weights, in addition to the circles denoting their several weights, bears also the stamp of a crown. Care must be taken not to mistake this for one of the numerals. Besides these weights you will find others marked ℈ss, which means half a scruple; ℨss, meaning half a drachm; and ℥ss, meaning half an ounce. When there are ounces, drachms, or scruples, the number of them is shown by Roman figures, thus :—i. ii. iii. iv. v., &c., and prescriptions are written in this style.

636. MEASURES.—Liquid medicines are measured by the following table :—

60 minims	are contained in	1 fluid drachm.
8 fluid drachms.		1 fluid ounce.
16 fluid ounces...		1 pint.
8 pints		1 gallon.

And the signs which distinguish each are as follows :—c. means a gallon; o, a pint; f℥, a fluid ounce; fℨ, a fluid drachm; and ℳ, a minim, or drop. Formerly drops used to be ordered, but as the size of a drop must necessarily vary, minims are always directed to be employed now for any particular medicine, although for such medicines as oil of cloves, essence of ginger, &c., drops are frequently ordered.

637. IN ORDER THAT WE MAY MEASURE MEDICINES ACCURATELY, there are graduated glass vessels for measuring ounces, drachms, and minims.

638. WHEN PROPER MEASURES ARE NOT AT HAND, it is necessary to adopt some other method of determining the quantities required, and therefore we have drawn up the following table for that purpose :—

A tumbler.........		10 ounces.
A teacup	usually contains about	6 ,,
A wineglass		2 ,,
A tablespoon		4 drachms.
A dessertspoon .		2 ,,
A teaspoon		1 ,,

These quantities refer to ordinary sized spoons and vessels. Some cups hold half as much more, and some table-spoons contain six drachms. Many persons keep a medicine-glass, which is graduated so as to show the number of spoonfuls it contains.

639. Process of Making Medicines.—To POWDER SUBSTANCES.—Place the substance in the mortar, and strike it *gently* with direct perpendicular blows of the pestle, until it separates into several pieces, then remove all but a small portion, which bruise gently at first, and rub the pestle round and round the mortar, observing that the circles described by the pestle should gradually decrease in diameter, and then increase again, because by this means every part of the powder is subjected to the process of pulverization. In powdering substances, making emulsions, and whenever using a mortar, the pestle should always travel *from the right to the left.*

640. SOME SUBSTANCES require to be prepared in a particular manner before they can be powdered, or to be assisted by adding some other body. For example, camphor powders more easily when a few drops of spirits of wine are added to it; mace, nutmegs, and such oily aromatic substances are better for the addition of a little white sugar; resins and gum-resins should be powdered in a cold place, and if they are intended to be dissolved, a little fine well-washed white sand mixed with them assists the process of powdering. Tough roots, like gentian and calumba, should be cut into thin slices; and fibrous roots, like ginger, cut slanting, otherwise the powder will be full of small fibres. Vegetable matters require to be dried before they are powdered, such as peppermint, loosestrife, senna, &c.

641. BE CAREFUL NOT TO POUND TOO HARD in a glass, porcelain, or Wedge-wood-ware mortar; they are intended only for substances that pulverize easily, and for the purpose of mixing or incorporating medicines. Never use acids in a marble mortar, and be sure that you do not powder galls or any other astringent substances in any but a brass mortar.

642. SIFTING is frequently required for powdered substances, and this is usually done by employing a fine sieve, or tying the powder up in a piece of muslin, and striking it against the left hand over a piece of paper.

643. FILTERING is frequently required for the purpose of obtaining clear fluids, such as infusions, eye-washes, and other medicines; and it is, therefore, highly important to know how to perform this simple operation. We must first of all make the filter-paper; this is done by taking a square sheet of white blotting paper, and doubling it over, so as to form an angular cup. We next procure a piece of wire, and twist it into a form to place the funnel in, to prevent it passing too far into the neck of the bottle. Open out the filter-paper very carefully, and having placed it in the funnel, moisten it with a little water. Then place the wire in the space between the funnel and the bottle, and pour the liquid gently down the side of the paper, otherwise the fluid is apt to burst the paper.

644. MACERATION is another process that is frequently required to be performed in making up medicines, and consists simply in immersing the medicines in *cold water* or spirits for a certain time.

645. DIGESTION resembles maceration, except that the process is assisted by a gentle heat. The ingredients are placed in a flask, such as salad oil is sold in, which should be fitted with a plug of tow or wood, and have a piece of wire twisted round the neck. The flask is held by means of the wire over the flame of a spirit lamp, or else placed in some sand warmed in an old iron saucepan over the fire, care being taken not to place more of the flask below the sand than the portion occupied by the ingredients.

646. INFUSION is one of the most frequent operations required in making up medicines, its object being to extract the aromatic and volatile principles of substances, that would be lost by decoction or digestion; and to extract the soluble from the insoluble parts of bodies. Infusions may be made with cold water, in which case they are weaker, but more pleasant. The general method employed consists in slicing, bruising, or rasping the ingredients first, then placing them in a common jug (which should be as globular as possible), and pouring boiling water over them; cover the jug with a cloth folded six or eight times, but if there be a lid to the jug so much the better; when the infusion has stood the time directed, hold a piece of *very coarse* linen over the spout, and pour the liquid through it into another jug.

647. DECOCTION, or boiling, is employed to extract the mucilaginous or gummy parts of substances, their bitter, astringent, or other qualities, and is nothing more than boiling the ingredients in a saucepan with the lid slightly raised. Be sure never to use an iron saucepan for astringent decoctions, such as oak-bark, galls, &c., as they will turn the saucepan black, and spoil the decoction. The enamelled saucepans are very useful for decoctions, but an excellent plan is to put the ingredients into a jar and boil the jar, thus preparing it by a water bath, as it is technically termed; or by using a common pipkin, which answers still better. No decoction should be allowed to boil for more than ten minutes.

648. EXTRACTS are made by evaporating the liquors obtained by infusion or decoction, but these can be bought much cheaper and better of chemists and druggists, and so can tinctures, confections, cerates and plasters, and syrups; but as every one is not always in the neighbourhood of druggists, we shall give recipes for those most generally useful, and the method of making them.

649. Precautions to be observed in Giving Medicines.—SEX.—Medicines for females should not be so strong as those for males, therefore it is advisable to reduce the doses about one-third.

650. TEMPERAMENT.—Persons of a phlegmatic temperament bear stimulants and purgatives better than those of a sanguine temperament, therefore the latter require smaller doses.

651. HABITS.—Purgatives never act so well upon persons accustomed to take them as upon those who are not, therefore it is better to change the form of purgative from pill to potion, powder to draught, or aromatic to saline. Purgatives should never be given when there is an irritable state of the bowels.

652. STIMULANTS AND NARCOTICS never act so quickly upon persons accustomed to use spirits freely as upon those who live abstemiously.

653. CLIMATE.—The action of medicines is modified by climate and seasons. In summer, certain medicines act more powerfully than in winter, and the same person cannot bear the dose in July that he could in December.

654. GENERAL HEALTH.—Persons whose general health is good, bear stronger doses than the debilitated and those who have suffered for a long time.

655. IDIOSYNCRASY. — Walker's Dictionary will inform you that "idiosyncrasy" means a peculiar temperament or disposition not common to people generally. For example, some persons cannot take calomel in the smallest dose without being salivated, or rhubarb without having convulsions; others cannot take squills, opium, senna, &c., and this peculiarity is called the patient's idiosyncrasy, therefore it is wrong to *insist* upon their taking these medicines.

656. FORMS BEST SUITED FOR ADMINISTRATION.—Fluids act quicker than solids, and powders sooner than pills.

657. BEST METHOD OF PREVENTING THE NAUSEOUS TASTE OF MEDICINES.—Castor oil may be taken in milk, coffee, or spirit, such as brandy; but the best method of covering the nauseous flavour is to put a tablespoonful of strained orange juice in a wine glass, pour the castor oil into the centre of the juice, and then squeeze a few drops of lemon juice upon the top of the oil. Cod liver oil may be taken, like castor oil, in orange juice. Peppermint water almost neutralizes the nauseous taste of Epsom salts; a strong solution of extract of liquorice, that of aloes; milk, that of cinchona bark; and cloves of senna.

658. AN EXCELLENT WAY TO PREVENT THE TASTE OF MEDICINES is to have the medicine in a glass, as usual, and a tumbler of water by the side of it; take the medicine, and retain it in the mouth, which should be kept closed, and if you then commence drinking the water, the taste of the medicine is washed away. Even the bitterness of quinine and aloes may be prevented by this means. If the nostrils are firmly compressed by the thumb and finger of the left hand, while taking a nauseous draught, and so retained till the mouth has been washed out with water, the disagreeable taste of the medicine will be quite unperceived.

659. GIVING MEDICINES TO PERSONS.—Medicines should be given in such a manner that the effect of the first dose shall not have ceased when the next dose is given, therefore the intervals between the doses should be regulated accordingly.

660. DOSES OF MEDICINE FOR DIFFERENT AGES.—It must be plain to every one that children do not require such powerful medicine as adults or old people, and therefore it is desirable to have some fixed method of determining or regulating the administration of doses of medicine. Now we will suppose that the dose for a full-grown person is one drachm, then the following proportions will be suitable for the various ages given; keeping in view other circumstances, such as sex, temperament, habits, climate, state of *general health*, and idiosyncrasy.

Age.	Proportion.	Proportionate Dose.
7 weeks	one-fifteenth	or grains 4
7 months	one-twelfth	or grains 5
Under 2 years	one-eighth	or grains 7½
,, 3 ,,	one-sixth	or grains 10
,, 4 ,,	one-fourth	or grains 15
,, 7 ,,	one-third	or scruple 1
,, 14 ,,	one-half	or drachm ½
,, 20 ,,	two-fifths	or scruples 2
above 21 ,,	the full dose	or drachm 1
,, 65 ,,	The inverse	gradation

661. Drugs, with their Properties and Doses.—We have arranged the various drugs according to their properties, and have given the doses of each; but in compiling this we have necessarily omitted many from each class, because they cannot be employed except by a medical man. The *doses* are meant for adults.

662. MEDICINES HAVE BEEN DIVIDED into four grand classes—1. General stimulants; 2. Local stimulants; 3. Chemical remedies; 4. Mechanical remedies.

663. General Stimulants.—General stimulants are subdivided into two classes, diffusible and permanent stimulants: the first comprising narcotics and anti-spasmodics, and the second tonics and astringents.

664. Narcotics are medicines which stupify and diminish the activity of the nervous system. Given in small doses, they generally act as stimulants, but an increased dose produces a sedative effect. Under this head we include alcohol, camphor, ether, the hop, and opium.

665. ALCOHOL, or rectified spirit, is a very powerful stimulant, and is never used as a remedy without being diluted to the degree called proof spirit; and even then it is seldom used internally. It is *used externally* in restraining bleeding, when there is not any vessel of importance wounded. It is also used as a lotion to burns, and is applied by dipping a piece of lint into the spirit, and laying it over the part. Freely diluted (one part to eighteen) with water, it forms a useful eye-wash in the last stage of ophthalmia. *Used internally,* it acts as a very useful stimulant when diluted and taken moderately, increasing the general excitement, and giving energy to the muscular fibres; hence it becomes very useful in certain cases of debility, especially in habits disposed to create acidity; and in the low stage of typhus fevers. *Dose.*—It is impossible to fix anything like a dose for this remedy, as much will depend upon the individual; but diluted with water and sweetened with sugar, from half an ounce to two ounces may be given three or four times a day. In cases of extreme debility, however, much will depend upon the disease. *Caution.*—Remember that alcohol is an irritant *poison,* and that the indulgence in its use daily originates dyspepsia, or indigestion, and many other serious complaints. Of all kinds of spirits the best as a tonic and stomachic is *brandy.*

666. CAMPHOR is not a very steady stimulant, as its effect is transitory; but in large doses it acts as a narcotic, abating pain and inducing sleep. In moderate doses it operates as a diaphoretic, diuretic, and anti-spasmodic, increasing the heat of the body, allaying irritation and spasm. It is *used externally* as a liniment when dissolved in oil, alcohol, or acetic acid, being employed to allay rheumatic pains; and it is also useful as an embrocation in sprains, bruises, chilblains, and, when combined with opium, it has been advantageously employed in flatulent colic, and severe diarrhœa, being rubbed over the bowels. *When reduced to a fine powder,* by the addition of a little spirit of wine and friction, it is very useful as a local stimulant to indolent ulcers, especially when they discharge a foul kind of matter; a pinch is taken between the finger and thumb, and sprinkled into the ulcer, which is then dressed as usual. *When dissolved in oil of turpentine,* and a few drops are

placed in a hollow tooth and covered with jeweller's wool, or scraped lint, it gives almost instant relief to toothache. *Used internally,* it is apt to excite nausea, and even vomiting, especially when given in the solid form. *As a stimulant* it is of great service in all low fevers, malignant measles, malignant sore throat, and confluent small-pox; and when combined with opium and bark, it is extremely useful in checking the progress of malignant ulcers, and gangrene. *As a narcotic* it is very useful, because it allays pain and irritation, without increasing the pulse very much. *When powdered and sprinkled* upon the surface of a blister, it prevents the cantharides acting in a peculiar and painful manner upon the bladder. *Combined with senna,* it increases its purgative properties; and it is also used to correct the nausea produced by squills, and the irritating effects of drastic purgatives and mezereon. *Dose,* from four grains to half a scruple, repeated at short intervals when used in small doses, and long intervals when employed in large doses. *Doses of the various preparations.*—Camphor mixture, from half an ounce to three ounces; compound tincture of camphor (*paregoric elixir*), from fifteen minims to two drachms. *Caution.*—When given in an overdose it acts as a poison, producing vomiting, giddiness, delirium, convulsions, and sometimes death. Opium is the best antidote for camphor, whether in excess or taken as a poison. *Mode of exhibition.*—It may be rubbed up with almond emulsion, or mucilage, or the yolk of eggs, and by this means suspended in water, or combined with chloroform as a mixture, in which form it is a valuable stimulant in cholera and other diseases. (*See* MIXTURES.)

667. ETHER is a diffusible stimulant, narcotic and anti-spasmodic. *Sulphuric Ether* is *used externally* both as a stimulant and a refrigerant. In the former case its evaporation is prevented by covering a rag moistened with it with oiled silk, in order to relieve headache; and in the latter case it is allowed to

evaporate, and thus produce coldness: hence it is applied over scalded surfaces by means of rags dipped in it. *As a local application*, it has been found to afford almost instant relief in earache, when combined with almond oil, and dropped into the ear. *Internally*, it is used as a stimulant and narcotic in low fevers and cases of great exhaustion. *Dose*, from fifteen minims to half a drachm, repeated at short intervals, as its effects soon pass off. It is usually given in a little camphor julep, or water.

668. NITRIC ETHER is a refrigerant, diuretic, and anti-spasmodic, and is well known as "*sweet spirit of nitre.*" *Used externally*, its evaporation relieves headache, and it is sometimes applied to burns. *Internally*, it is used to relieve nausea, flatulence, and thirst in fevers; also as a diuretic. *Dose*, from ten minims to one drachm.

669. COMPOUND SPIRIT OF SULPHURIC ETHER is a very useful stimulant, narcotic, and anti-spasmodic. *Used internally* in cases of great exhaustion, attended with irritability. *Dose*, from half a drachm to two drachms, in camphor julep. When combined with laudanum, it prevents the nauseating effects of the opium, and acts more beneficially as a narcotic.

670. THE HOP is a narcotic, tonic, and diuretic; it reduces the frequency of the pulse, and does not affect the head, like most anodynes. *Used externally*, it acts as an anodyne and discutient, and is useful as a fomentation for painful tumours, rheumatic pains in the joints, and severe contusions. A pillow stuffed with hops acts as a narcotic. When the powder is mixed with lard, it acts as an anodyne dressing in painful ulcers. *Dose*, of the *extract*, from five grains to one scruple; of the *tincture*, from half a drachm to two drachms; of the *powder*, from three grains to one scruple; of the *infusion*, half an ounce to one and a half ounce.

671. OPIUM is a stimulant, narcotic, and anodyne. *Used externally* it acts almost as well as when taken into the stomach, and without affecting the head or causing nausea. Applied to irritable ulcers in the form of tincture, it promotes their cure, and allays pain. Cloths dipped in a strong solution, and applied over painful bruises, tumours, or inflamed joints, allay pain. A small piece of solid opium stuffed into a hollow tooth relieves toothache. A weak solution of opium forms a valuable collyrium in ophthalmia. Two drops of the wine of opium dropped into the eye, acts as an excellent stimulant in bloodshot eye; or after long-continued inflammation, it is useful in strengthening the eye. Applied as a liniment, in combination with ammonia and oil, or with camphorated spirit, it relieves muscular pain. When combined with oil of turpentine, it is useful as a liniment in spasmodic colic. *Used internally*, it acts as a very powerful stimulant; then as a sedative, and finally as an anodyne and narcotic, allaying pain in the most extraordinary manner, by acting directly upon the nervous system. In acute rheumatism it is a most excellent medicine when combined with calomel and tartrate of antimony; but its exhibition requires the judicious care of a medical man. *Doses of the various preparations.* — *Confection of opium*, from five grains to half a drachm; *extract of opium*, from one to five grains' (this is a valuable form, as it does not produce so much after derangement of the nervous system as solid opium); *pills of soap and opium*, from five to ten grains; *compound ipecacuanha powder* ("Dover's Powder"), from ten to fifteen grains; *compound kino powder*, from five to fifteen grains; *wine of opium*, from ten minims to one drachm. *Caution.*— Opium is a powerful *poison* when taken in too large a quantity (*See* POISONS), and therefore should be used with extreme caution. It is on this account that we have omitted some of its preparations. The best antidote for opium is camphor.

672. Anti-Spasmodics are medicines which possess the power of overcoming the spasms of the muscles, or

allaying any severe pain which is not attended by inflammation. The class includes a great many, but the most safe and serviceable are ammonia, assafœtida, galbanum, valerian, bark, ether, camphor, opium, and chloroform; with the minerals, oxide of zinc and calomel.

673. AMMONIA, OR "VOLATILE SALT," is an anti-spasmodic, antacid, stimulant, and diaphoretic. *Used externally*, combined with oil, it forms a cheap and useful liniment, but it should be dissolved in *proof* spirit before the oil is added. One part of this salt, and three parts of extract of belladonna, mixed and spread upon leather, makes an excellent plaster for relieving rheumatic pains. As a local stimulant it is well known, as regards its effects in hysterics, faintness, and lassitude, when applied to the nose, as common smelling salts. It is *used internally* as an adjunct to infusion of gentian in dyspepsia or indigestion, and in moderate doses in gout. *Dose*, from five to fifteen grains. *Caution.*—Overdoses act as a narcotic and irritant poison.

674. BICARBONATE OF AMMONIA, USED INTERNALLY the same as the "volatile salt." *Dose*, from six to twelve grains. It is frequently combined with Epsom salts.

675. SOLUTION OF SESQUICARBONATE OF AMMONIA, used the same as the "volatile salt." *Dose*, from half a drachm to one drachm, combined with some milky fluid, like almond emulsion.

676. ASSAFŒTIDA is an anti-spasmodic, expectorant, excitant, and anthelmintic. *Used internally*, it is extremely useful in dyspepsia, flatulent colic, hysteria, and nervous diseases; and where there are no inflammatory symptoms, it is an excellent remedy in hooping cough and asthma. *Used locally* as an enema, it is useful in flatulent colic, and convulsions that come on through teething. *Doses of various preparations.* —*Solid gum*, from five to ten grains as pills; *mixture*, from half an ounce to one ounce; *tincture*, from fifteen minims to one drachm; *ammoniated tincture*,

from twenty minims to one drachm. *Caution.*—Never give it when inflammation exists.

677. GALBANUM is stimulant, antispasmodic, expectorant, and deobstruent. *Used externally*, it assists in dispelling indolent tumours when spread upon leather as a plaster, and is useful in weakness of the legs from rickets, being applied as a plaster to the loins. *Employed internally*, it is useful in chronic or old-standing rheumatism and hysteria. *Doses of preparations.*—Of the *gum*, from ten to fifteen grains as pills; *tincture*, from fifteen minims to one drachm. It may be made into an emulsion with mucilage and water.

678. VALERIAN is a powerful antispasmodic, tonic, and excitant, acting chiefly on the nervous centres. *Used internally*, it is employed in hysteria, nervous languors, and spasmodic complaints generally. It is useful in low fevers. *Doses of various preparations.* —*Powder*, from ten grains to half a drachm, three or four times a day; *tincture*, from two to four drachms; *ammoniated tincture*, from one to two drachms; *infusion*, from two to three ounces, or more.

679. BARK, or, as it is commonly called, "Peruvian Bark," is an antispasmodic, tonic, astringent, and stomachic. *Used externally*, it is an excellent detergent for foul ulcers, and those that heal slowly. *Used internally*, it is particularly valuable in intermittent fever or ague, malignant measles, dysentery, diarrhœa, intermittent rheumatism, St. Vitus' dance, indigestion, nervous affections, malignant sore throat, and erysipelas; its use being indicated in all cases of debility. *Doses of its preparations.*—*Powder*, from five grains to two drachms, mixed in wine, water, milk, syrup, or solution of liquorice; *infusion*, from one to three ounces; *decoction*, from one to three ounces; *tincture* and *compound tincture*, each from one to three drachms. *Caution.*—If it causes oppression at the stomach, combine it with an aromatic; if it causes vomiting, give it in wine or soda water;

if it purges, give opium; and if it constipates, give rhubarb.

680. ETHER (SULPHURIC) is given internally as an anti-spasmodic in difficult breathing and spasmodic asthma; also in hysteria, cramp of the stomach, hiccough, locked jaw, and cholera. It is useful in checking sea-sickness. *Dose*, from twenty minims to one drachm. *Caution.*—An overdose produces apoplectic symptoms.

681. CAMPHOR is given internally as an anti-spasmodic in hysteria, cramp in the stomach, flatulent colic, and St. Vitus' dance. *Dose*, from two to twenty grains.

682. OPIUM is employed internally in spasmodic affections, such as cholera, spasmodic asthma, hooping cough, flatulent colic, and St. Vitus' dance. *Dose*, from one-sixth of a grain to two grains of the solid opium, according to the disease.

683. OXIDE OF ZINC is an anti-spasmodic, astringent, and tonic. *Used externally*, as an ointment, it forms an excellent astringent in affections of the eyelids, arising from relaxation; or as a powder, it is an excellent detergent for unhealthy ulcers. *Used internally*, it has proved efficacious in St. Vitus' dance, and some other spasmodic affections. *Dose*, from one to six grains, twice a day.

684. CALOMEL is an anti-spasmodic, alterative deobstruent, purgative, and errhine. *Used internally*, combined with opium, it acts as an anti-spasmodic in locked jaw, cholera, and many other spasmodic affections. As an alterative and deobstruent, it has been found useful in leprosy and itch, when combined with antimonials and guaiacum, and in enlargement of the liver and glandular affections. It acts beneficially in dropsies, by producing watery motions. In typhus it is of great benefit when combined with antimonials; and it may be given as a purgative in almost any disease, provided there is not any inflammation of the bowels, irritability of the system, or great debility. *Dose*, as a deobstruent and alterative, from one to five grains, daily; as a cathartic, from five to fifteen grains; to produce ptyalism, or salivation, from one to two grains, in a pill, with a quarter of a grain of opium, night and morning. *Caution.*—When taking calomel, exposure to cold or dampness should be guarded against, as such an imprudence would bring out an eruption of the skin, attended with fever. When this does occur, leave off the calomel, and give bark, wine, and purgatives; take a warm bath twice a day, and powder the surface of the body with powdered starch.

685. TONICS are given to improve the tone of the system, and restore the natural energies and general strength of the body. They consist of bark, quassia, gentian, camomile, wormwood, and angostura bark.

686. QUASSIA is a simple tonic, and can be used with safety by any one, as it does not increase the animal heat, or quicken the circulation. *Used internally*, in the form of infusion, it has been found of great benefit in indigestion and nervous irritability, and is useful after bilious fevers and diarrhœa. *Dose of the infusion*, from one and a half to two ounces, three times a day.

687. GENTIAN is an excellent tonic and stomachic; but when given in large doses, it acts as an aperient. It is *used internally* in all cases of general debility, and when combined with bark, is used in intermittent fevers. It has also been employed in indigestion, and it is sometimes used, combined with volatile salt, in that disease; but at other times alone, in the form of infusion. After diarrhœa, it proves a useful tonic. *Used externally*, its infusion is sometimes applied to foul ulcers. *Dose*, of the *infusion*, one and a half to two ounces; of the *tincture*, one to four drachms; of the *extract*, from ten to thirty grains.

688. CAMOMILE.—The flowers of the camomile are tonic, slightly anodyne, anti-spasmodic, and emetic. They are *used externally* as fomentations, in colic, faceache, and tumours, and to unhealthy ulcers. They are *used internally* in the form of infusion, with carbonate of soda, ginger, and other stomachic remedies, in dyspepsia, flatulent colic, debility following dysentery and gout. Warm infusion of the flowers acts as an emetic; and the powdered flowers are sometimes combined with opium or kino, and given in intermittent fevers. *Dose*, of the *powdered* flowers, from ten grains to one drachm, twice or thrice a day; of the *infusion*, from one to two ounces, as a tonic, three times a day: and from six ounces to one pint, as an emetic; of the *extract*, from five to twenty grains.

689. WORMWOOD is a tonic and anthelmintic. It is *used externally* as a discutient and antiseptic. It is *used internally* in long-standing cases of dyspepsia, in the form of infusion, with or without aromatics. It has also been used in intermittents. *Dose*, of the *infusion*, from one to two ounces, three times a day; of the *powder*, from one to two scruples.

690. ANGOSTURA BARK, or Cusparia, is a tonic and stimulant. It expels flatulence, increases the appetite, and produces a grateful warmth in the stomach. It is *used internally* in intermittent fevers, dyspepsia, hysteria, and all cases of debility, where a stimulating tonic is desirable, particularly after bilious diarrhœa. *Dose*, of the *powder*, from ten to fifteen grains, combined with cinnamon powder, magnesia, or rhubarb; of the *extract*, from three to ten grains; of the *infusion*, from one to two ounces. *Caution.*—It should never be given in inflammatory diseases or hectic fever.

691. Astringents are medicines given for the purpose of diminishing excessive discharges, and to act indirectly as tonics. This class includes catechu, kino, oak bark, logwood, rose leaves, chalk, and white vitriol.

692. CATECHU is a most valuable astringent. It is *used externally*, when powdered, to promote the contraction of flabby ulcers. As a local astringent it is useful in relaxed uvula, a small piece being dissolved in the mouth;

small, spotty ulcerations of the mouth and throat, and bleeding gums, and for these two affections it is used in the form of infusion to wash the parts. It is *given internally* in diarrhœa, dysentery. and hemorrhage from the bowels. *Dose*, of the *infusion*, from one to three ounces; of the *tincture*, from one to four drachms; of the *powder*, from ten to thirty grains. *Caution.*—It must not be given with soda or any alkali; nor metallic salts, albumen, or gelatine, as its property is destroyed by this combination.

693. KINO is a powerful astringent. It is *used externally* to ulcers, to give tone to them when flabby, and discharging foul and thin matter. It is *used internally* in the same diseases as catechu. *Dose*, of the *powder*, from ten to fifteen grains; of the *tincture*, from one to two drachms; of the *compound powder*, from ten to twenty grains; of the *infusion*, from a half to one and a half ounce. *Caution.*—Kino is used in combination with calomel, when salivation is intended, to prevent, by its astringency, the action of the calomel on the bowels, and thereby insure its affecting the constitution.—(See CATECHU.)

694. OAK BARK is an astringent and tonic. It is *used externally*, in the form of decoction, to restrain bleeding from lacerated surfaces. As a local astringent, it is used in the form of decoction, as a gargle in sore throat and relaxed uvula. It is *used internally* in the same diseases as catechu, and when combined with aromatics and bitters, in intermittent fevers. *Dose* of the *powder*, from fifteen to thirty grains; of the *decoction*, from two to eight drachms.

695. LOGWOOD is not a very satisfactory astringent. It is *used internally* in diarrhœa, the last stage of dysentery, and a lax state of the intestines. *Dose*, of the *extract*, from ten grains to one drachm; of the *decoction*, from one to three ounces, three or four times a day.

696. ROSE LEAVES are astringent and tonic. They are *used internally* in spitting of blood, hemorrhage from the stomach, intestines, &c., as a gargle for sore throat, and for the night sweats of consumption. The infusion is frequently used as a tonic with diluted sulphuric acid (oil of vitriol), after low fevers, or in combination with Epsom salts and sulphuric acid in certain states of the bowels. *Dose* of *infusion*, from two to four ounces.

697. CHALK, when prepared by washing, becomes an astringent as well as antacid. It is *used internally* in diarrhœa, in the form of mixture, and *externally* as an application to burns, scalds, and excoriations. *Dose* of the *mixture*, from one to two ounces.

698. WHITE VITRIOL, or Sulphate of Zinc, is an astringent, tonic, and emetic. It is *used externally* as a collyrium for ophthalmia (*See* DOMESTIC PHARMACOPŒIA), and as a detergent for scrofulous ulcers, in the proportion of three grains of the salt to one ounce of water. It is *used internally* in indigestion, and many other diseases; *but it should not be given unless ordered by a medical man, as it is a poison.*

699. Local Stimulants.—Local stimulants comprise emetics, cathartics, diuretics, diaphoretics, expectorants, sialogogues, errhines, and epispastics.

700. Emetics are medicines given for the purpose of causing vomiting, as in cases of poisoning. They consist of ipecacuanha, camomile, antimony, copper, zinc, and several others.

701. IPECACUANHA is an emetic, diaphoretic, and expectorant. It is *used internally* to excite vomiting, in doses of from ten to twenty grains of the powder, or one to one and a half ounce of the infusion, every half hour until vomiting takes place. To make it act well and easily, the patient should drink half pints of warm water after each dose of the infusion. As a diaphoretic, it should be given in doses of three grains, mixed with some soft substance, such as crumbs of bread, and repeated every four hours. *Dose* of the *wine*, from twenty minims to one drachm as a diaphoretic, and from one drachm to one and a half ounce as an emetic.

Caution.—Do not give more than the doses named above, because, although a safe emetic, yet it is an acrid narcotic poison.

702. MUSTARD is too well known to require describing. It is an emetic, diuretic, stimulant, and rubefacient. It is *used externally* as a poultice (which is made of the powder, bread crumbs, and water; or of one part of mustard to two of flour: vinegar is not necessary), in all cases where a stimulant is required, such as sore throats, rheumatic pains in the joints, cholera, cramps in the extremities, diarrhœa, and many other diseases. When applied it should not be left on too long, as it is apt to cause ulceration of the part. From ten to thirty minutes is quite long enough. When *used internally* as an emetic, a large teaspoonful mixed with a tumbler of warm water generally operates quickly and safely, frequently when other emetics have failed. In dropsy it is sometimes given in the form of whey, which is made by boiling half an ounce of the bruised seeds in a pint of milk, and straining off the curd. From three to four ounces of this is to be taken for a dose three times a day.

703. Cathartics are divided into laxatives and purgatives. The former comprise manna, tamarinds, castor oil, sulphur, and magnesia; the latter, senna, rhubarb, jalap, colocynth, buckthorn, aloes, cream of tartar, scammony, calomel, Epsom salts, Glauber's salts, sulphate of potash, and Venice turpentine.

704. MANNA is a very gentle laxative, and therefore used for children and delicate persons. *Dose* for *children*, from one to two drachms; and for *adults*, from one to two ounces, combined with rhubarb and cinnamon water.

705. TAMARINDS are generally laxative and refrigerant. As it is agreeable, this medicine will generally be eaten by children when they will not take other medicines. *Dose*, from half to one ounce. As a refrigerant beverage in fevers it is extremely grateful.

706. CASTOR OIL is a most valuable medicine, as it generally operates quickly and mildly. It is *used externally*, combined with citron ointment, as a topical application in common leprosy. It is *used internally* as an ordinary purgative for infants, as a laxative for adults, and in diarrhœa and dysentery. In colic it is very useful and safe; and also after delivery. *Dose* for *infants*, from forty drops to two drachms; for *adults*, from half to one and a half ounce.

707. SULPHUR.—Sublimed sulphur is laxative and diaphoretic. It is *used externally* in skin diseases, especially itch, both in the form of ointment and as a vapour bath. It is *used internally* in hemorrhoids, combined with magnesia, as a laxative for children, and as a diaphoretic in rheumatism. *Dose*, from one scruple to two drachms, mixed in milk or with treacle. When combined with an equal proportion of cream of tartar, it acts as a purgative.

708. MAGNESIA.—*Calcined magnesia* possesses the same properties as the carbonate. *Dose*, from ten to thirty grains, in milk or water. *Carbonate of magnesia* is an antacid and laxative, and is very useful for children when teething, and for heartburn in adults. *Dose*, from a half to two drachms, in water or milk.

709. SENNA is a purgative, but is apt to gripe when given alone; therefore it is combined with some aromatic, such as cloves or ginger, and the infusion should be made with *cold* instead of hot water. It usually acts in about four hours, but its action should be assisted by drinking warm fluids. *Dose*, of the *confection*, commonly called "*lenitive electuary*," from one to three or four drachms at bedtime; of the *infusion*, from one to two ounces; of the *tincture*, from one to two drachms; of the *syrup* (used for children), from one drachm to one ounce. *Caution.*—Do not give senna, in any form except confection, in hemorrhoids, and never in irritability of the intestines.

710. RHUBARB is a purgative, astringent, and stomachic. It is *used externally* in the form of powder to ulcers, to promote a healthy action. It is given *internally* in diarrhœa, dys-

pepsia, and a debilitated state of the bowels. Combined with a mild preparation of calomel (*cum cretâ*), it forms an excellent purgative for children. *Dose*, of the *infusion*, from one to two ounces; of the *powder*, from one scruple to half a drachm as a purgative, and from six to ten grains as a stomachic; of the *tincture* and *compound tincture*, from one to four drachms; of the *compound pill*, from ten to twenty grains.

711. JALAP is a powerful cathartic and hydrogogue, and is therefore apt to gripe. *Dose*, of the *powder*, from ten to thirty grains, combined with a drop or two of aromatic oil; of the *compound powder*, from fifteen to forty grains; of the *tincture*, from one to three drachms; of the *extract*, from ten to twenty grains. The watery extract is better than the alcoholic.

712. COLOCYNTH is a powerful drastic cathartic, and should never be given alone, unless ordered by a medical man, as its action is too violent for some constitutions. *Dose*, of the *extract*, from five to fifteen grains; of the *compound extract*, from five to fifteen grains; of the *compound colocynth pill*, the best of all its preparations, from ten to twenty grains.

713. BUCKTHORN is a brisk purgative for children in the form of syrup. *Dose* of the *syrup*, from one to six drachms.

714. ALOES is a purgative and cathartic in large, and tonic in smaller doses. *Dose*, of *powder*, from two to ten grains, combined with soap, bitter extracts, or other purgative medicines, and given in the form of pills; of the *compound pill*, from five to twenty grains; of the *pill of aloes* and *myrrh*, from five to twenty grains; of the *tincture*, from four drachms to one ounce; of the *compound tincture*, from one to four drachms; of the *extract*, from six to ten grains; of the *compound decoction*, from four drachms to two ounces.

715. CREAM OF TARTAR is a purgative and refrigerant. It is *used inter-*

nally in dropsy, especially of the belly, in doses of from one scruple to one drachm. As a refrigerant drink it is dissolved in hot water, and sweetened with sugar, and is used in febrile diseases, care being taken not to allow it to rest too much upon the bowels. *Dose*, as a *purgative*, from two to four drachms; as a *hydrogogue*, from four to six drachms, mixed with honey or treacle. *Caution.*—Its use should be followed by tonics, especially gentian and angostura.

716. SCAMMONY is a drastic purgative, generally acting quickly and powerfully; sometimes producing nausea, and even vomiting, and being very apt to gripe. It is *used internally*, to produce watery evacuations in dropsy, to remove intestinal worms, and correct the slimy motions of children. *Dose*, of the *powder*, from five to sixteen grains, given in liquorice water, treacle, or honey; of the *confection*, from twenty to thirty grains. *Caution.*—Do not give it in an irritable or inflamed state of the bowels.

717. EPSOM SALTS is a purgative and diuretic. It generally operates quickly, and therefore is extremely useful in acute diseases. It is found to be beneficial in dyspepsia when combined with infusion of gentian and a little ginger. It forms an excellent enema with olive oil. *Dose*, from a half to two ounces, dissolved in warm tea or water. Infusion of roses partially covers its taste and assists its action. It is a noted fact with regard to Epsom salts, that the *larger* the amount of water in which they are taken, the *smaller* the dose of salts required: thus, half an ounce properly dissolved may be made a strong dose. The action and efficacy of Epsom salts may be very greatly increased by the addition of one grain of tartar emetic with a dose of salts.

718. GLAUBER'S SALT is a very good purgative. *Dose*, from a half to two ounces, dissolved in warm water.

719. SULPHATE OF POTASH is a cathartic and deobstruent. It is *used internally*, combined with aloes or rhubarb, in obstructions of the bowels, and is an excellent saline purgative in dyspepsia and jaundice. *Dose* of the *powdered salt*, from ten grains to one drachm.

720. VENICE TURPENTINE is cathartic, diuretic, stimulant, and anthelmintic. It is *used externally* as a rubefacient, and is given *internally* in flatulent colic, in tapeworm, rheumatism, and other diseases. *Dose*, as a *diuretic*, from ten grains to one drachm; as a *cathartic*, from ten to twelve drachms; as an *anthelmintic*, from one to two ounces every eight hours, till the worm be ejected.

721. Diuretics are medicines which promote an increased secretion of urine. They consist of nitre, acetate of potassa, squills, juniper, and oil of turpentine, and many others, vegetable and mineral.

722. NITRE is a diuretic and refrigerant. It is *used externally* as a detergent when dissolved in water, and as a lotion to inflamed and painful rheumatic joints. It is given *internally* in doses of from ten grains to half a drachm, or even one drachm; in spitting blood it is given in one drachm doses with great benefit. As a topical application it is beneficial in sore throat, a few grains being allowed to dissolve in the mouth.

723. ACETATE OF POTASSA is diuretic and cathartic. It is given *internally* in dropsy with great benefit, in doses of from one scruple to one drachm, every three or four hours, to act as a diuretic in combination with infusion of quassia. *Dose*, as a *cathartic*, from two to three drachms.

724. SQUILLS is diuretic and expectorant when given in small doses; and emetic and purgative when given in large doses. It is *used internally* in dropsies, in combination with calomel and opium; in asthma, with ammoniacum; in catarrh, in the form of oxymel. *Dose*, of the *dried bulb powdered*, from one to two grains every six hours; of the *compound pill*, from ten to fifteen grains; of the *tincture*, from ten minims to half a drachm; of the oxymel, from a half to two drachms; of the vinegar, from twenty minims to two drachms.

725. JUNIPER is diuretic and stomachic. It is given *internally* in dropsies. *Dose*, of the *infusion*, from two to three ounces every four hours; of the *oil*, from one to five minims.

726. OIL OF TURPENTINE is a diuretic, anthelmintic, and rubefacient. It is *used externally* in flatulent colic, sprinkled over flannels dipped in hot water and wrung out dry. It is *used internally* in the same diseases as Venice turpentine. *Dose*, from five minims to two drachms.

727. Diaphoretics are medicines given to increase the secretion from the skin by sweating. They comprise acetate of ammonia, calomel, antimony, opium, camphor, and sarsaparilla.

728. SOLUTION OF ACETATE OF AMMONIA is a most useful diaphoretic. It is *used externally* as a discutient, as a lotion to inflamed milk-breasts, as an eye-wash, and a lotion in scald head. It is given *internally* to promote perspiration in febrile diseases, which it does most effectually, especially when combined with camphor mixture. This is the article so frequently met with in prescriptions, and called spirits of mindererus (*liquor ammonia acetatis*). *Dose*, from a half to one and a half ounce every three or four hours.

729. ANTIMONY.—*Tartar emetic* is diaphoretic, emetic, expectorant, alterative, and rubefacient. It is *used externally* as an irritant in white swellings and deep-seated inflammations, in the form of an ointment. It is given *internally* in pleurisy, bilious fevers, and many other diseases; but its exhibition requires the skill of a medical man, to watch its effects. *Dose*, from one-sixth of a grain to four grains. *Caution.*—It is a *poison*, and therefore requires great care in its administration.

730. ANTIMONIAL POWDER is a diaphoretic, emetic, and alterative. It is given *internally*, in febrile diseases, to produce determination to the skin; in rheumatism, when combined with opium or calomel, it is of great benefit. *Dose*, from three grains to ten grains every four hours, taking plenty of warm fluids between each dose.

731. SARSAPARILLA is diaphoretic, alterative, diuretic, and tonic. It is given *internally* in cutaneous diseases, old-standing rheumatism, scrofula, and debility. *Dose*, of the *decoction*, from four to eight ounces; of the *compound decoction*, from four to eight ounces; of the *extract*, from five grains to one drachm.

732. Expectorants are medicines given to promote the secretion from the windpipe, &c. They consist of antimony, ipecacuanha, squills, ammoniacum, and tolu.

733. AMMONIACUM is an expectorant, antispasmodic, diuretic, and deobstruent. It is *used externally* as a discutient, and is given *internally*, with great benefit, in asthma, hysteria, and chronic catarrh. *Dose*, from ten to twenty grains.

734. TOLU is an excellent expectorant, when there are no inflammatory symptoms. It is given *internally* in asthma and chronic catarrh. *Dose*, of the *balsam*, from five to thirty grains, combined with mucilage and suspended in water; of the *tincture*, from a half to one drachm; of the *syrup*, from a half to four drachms.

735. Sialogogues are given to increase the flow of saliva or spittle. They consist of ginger and calomel, pelletory of Spain, tobacco, the acids, and some others.

736. GINGER is a sialogogue, carminative, and stimulant. It is *used internally* in flatulent colic, dyspepsia, and to prevent the griping of medicines. When chewed, it acts as a sialogogue, and is therefore useful in relaxed uvula. *Dose*, from ten to twenty grains of the *powder;* of the *tincture*, from ten minims to one drachm.

737. Epispastics and **Rubefacients** are those remedies which are applied to blister and cause redness of the surface. They consist of cantharides, ammonia, Burgundy pitch, and mustard.

738. CANTHARIDES, or Spanish flies,

when used internally, are diuretic and stimulant; and epispastic and rubefacient when applied externally. *Mode of application.*—A portion of the blistering plaster is spread with the thumb upon brown paper, linen, or leather, to the size required; its surface then *slightly* moistened with olive oil and sprinkled with camphor, and the plaster applied by a *light* bandage: or it is spread on adhesive plaster, and attached to the skin by the adhesive margin of the plaster. *Caution.*—If a blister is to be applied to the head, shave it at least ten hours before it is put on; and it is better to place a thin piece of gauze, wetted with vinegar, between the skin and the blister. If a distressing feeling be experienced about the bladder, give warm and copious draughts of linseed tea, milk, or decoction of quince seeds, and apply warm fomentations of milk and water to the blistered surface. The *period required* for a *blister* to remain on varies from eight to ten hours for adults, and from twenty minutes to two hours for children: as soon as it is removed, if the blister is not raised, apply a "spongio-piline" poultice, and it will then rise properly. When it is required to act as a rubefacient, the blister should remain on from one to three hours for adults, and from fifteen to forty minutes for children. *To dress a blister.*—Cut the bag of cuticle containing the serum at the lowest part, by snipping it with the scissors, so as to form an opening like this—V; and then apply a piece of calico, spread with spermaceti or some other dressing. Such is the ordinary method; but a much better and more expeditious plan, and one that prevents all pain and inconvenience in the healing, is, after cutting the blister as directed above, to immediately cover it with a warm bread and water poultice for about an hour and a half, and on the removal of the poultice to dust the raw surface with violet powder; apply a handkerchief to retain the powder, and lastly dust the part every two hours. It will be healed in twelve hours. *Caution.*—Never at-

tempt to take cantharides internally, except under the advice of a medical man, as it is a poison, and requires extreme caution in its use.

739. BURGUNDY PITCH is warmed and spread upon linen or leather, and applied over the chest in cases of catarrh, difficult breathing, and hooping cough; over the loins in debility or lumbago; and over any part that it is desirable to excite a mild degree of inflammation in.

740. Chemical Remedies.—The chemical remedies comprise refrigerants, antacids, antalkalies, and escharotics.

741. Refrigerants are medicines given for the purpose of suppressing an unnatural heat of the body. They are Seville oranges, lemons, tamarinds, nitre, and cream of tartar.

742. SEVILLE ORANGES and sweet oranges are formed into a refrigerant beverage, which is extremely grateful in febrile diseases. The *rind* is an agreeable mild tonic, carminative, and stomachic. *Dose*, of the *tincture*, from one to four drachms; of the *infusion*, from one to two ounces.

743. LEMONS are used to form a refrigerant beverage, which is given to quench thirst in febrile and inflammatory diseases. Lemon *juice* is given with carbonate of potash (half an ounce of the juice to twenty grains of the salt), and taken while effervescing, allays vomiting; a tablespoonful, taken occasionally, allays hysterical palpitations of the heart. It is useful in scurvy caused by eating too much salt food, but requires to be taken with sugar. The *rind* forms a nice mild tonic and stomachic in certain forms of dyspepsia. *Dose* of the *infusion* (made the same as orange peel), from one to two ounces.

744. Antacids are given to correct acidity in the system. They are soda, ammonia, chalk, and magnesia.

745. SODA, CARBONATE OF, and *Sesquicarbonate of Soda*, are antacids and deobstruents. They are *used internally* in acidity of the stomach and dyspepsia.

124

TO-DAY, LAYS PLANS FOR MANY YEARS TO COME ;

Dose of both preparations, from ten grains to half a drachm.

746. Antalkalies are given to neutralize an alkaline state of the system. They are citric acid, lemon juice, and tartaric acid.

747. CITRIC ACID is used to check profuse sweating, and as a substitute for lemon juice when it cannot be procured. *Dose*, from ten to thirty grains.

748. TARTARIC ACID, when largely diluted, forms an excellent refrigerant beverage and antalkali. It enters into the composition of extemporaneous soda and Seidlitz waters. *Dose*, from ten to thirty grains.

749. Escharotics are remedies used to destroy the vitality of a part. They comprise lunar caustic, bluestone, and solution of chloride of zinc.

750. BLUESTONE, or Sulphate of Copper, is used in a solution of from four to fifteen grains to the ounce of water, and applied to foul and indolent ulcers, by means of rag dipped in it; and is rubbed in substance on fungous growths, warts, &c., to destroy them. *Caution.*—It is a poison.

751. LUNAR CAUSTIC, or *Nitrate of Silver*, is an excellent remedy in erysipelas when applied in solution (one drachm of the salt to one ounce of water), which should be brushed all over the inflamed part, and for an inch beyond it. This blackens the skin, but it soon peels off. To destroy warts, proud flesh, and unhealthy edges of ulcers, &c., it is invaluable; and as an application to bed sores, pencilled over with a solution of the same strength, and in the same manner as for erysipelas. *Caution.*—It is a poison.

752. SOLUTION *of Chloride of Zinc*, more commonly known as Sir William Burnett's "Disinfecting Fluid," is a valuable escharotic in destroying the parts of poisoned wounds, such as the bite of a mad dog. It is also very useful in restoring the hair after the scalp has been attacked with ringworm; but its use requires extreme caution, as it is a powerful escharotic. In itch, diluted (one part to thirty-two) with water, it appears to answer very well. *Caution.*—It is a most powerful poison.

753. Mechanical Remedies.—The mechanical remedies comprise anthelmintics, demulcents, diluents, and emollients.

754. Anthelmintics are medicines given for the purpose of expelling or destroying worms. They are cowhage, scammony, male fern root, calomel, gamboge, tin, and turpentine.

755. COWHAGE is used to expel the round worm, which it does by wounding it with the fine prickles. *Dose* of the *confection*, for a child three or four years old, a teaspoonful early, for three mornings, followed by a dose of castor oil. (*See* DOMESTIC PHARMACOPŒIA, p. 96.) The mechanical anthelmintics are strictly confined to those agents which kill the worm in the body by piercing its cuticle with the sharp darts or spiculæ of the cowhage hairs, or the fine metallic points of the powdered tin (*pulvis stanni*). When these drops are employed, they should be given in honey or treacle for ten or fifteen days, and an aperient powder every fourth morning, to expel the killed worms.

756. MALE FERN ROOT is a powerful anthelmintic, and an astringent. It is used to kill tapeworm. *Dose*, three drachms of the powdered root mixed in a teacupful of water, to be taken in the morning while in bed, and followed by a brisk purgative two hours afterwards; or thirty drops of the ethereal tincture, to be taken early in the morning. (*See* DOMESTIC PHARMACOPŒIA, p. 96.)

757. GAMBOGE is a powerful drastic and anthelmintic. It is *used internally* in dropsies, and for the expulsion of tapeworm; but its use requires caution, as it is an irritant poison. *Dose*, from two to six grains, in the form of pills, combined with colocynth, soap, rhubarb, or bread-crumbs.

758. Demulcents are used to diminish irritation, and soften parts by protecting them with a viscid matter. They are tragacanth, linseed, marshmallow, mallow, liquorice, arrowroot, isinglass, suet, wax, and almonds.

759. TRAGACANTH is used to allay tickling cough, and lubricate abraded parts. It is usually given in the form of mucilage. *Dose*, from ten grains to one drachm, or more.

760. LINSEED is emollient and demulcent. It is *used externally*, when reduced to powder, as a poultice; and the oil, combined with lime water, is applied to burns and scalds. It is *used internally* as an infusion in diarrhœa, dysentery, and irritation of the intestines after certain poisons, and in catarrh. *Dose* of the *infusion*, as much as the patient pleases.

761. MARSH-MALLOW is *used internally* in the same diseases as linseed. The leaves are *used externally* as a fomentation, and the boiled roots are bruised and applied as an emollient poultice. *Dose*, the same as linseed.

762. MALLOW is *used externally* as a fomentation and poultice in inflammation, and the infusion is *used internally* in dysentery, diseases of the kidneys, and the same diseases as marsh-mallow. It is also used as an enema. The *dose* is the same as for linseed and marsh-mallow.

763. LIQUORICE is an agreeable demulcent, and is given in the form of decoction in catarrh, and some forms of dyspepsia; and the extract is used in catarrh. *Dose*, of the *extract*, from ten grains to one drachm; of the *decoction*, from two to four ounces.

764. ARROWROOT, isinglass, almonds, suet, and wax, are too well known to require descriptions. (*See* DOMESTIC PHARMACOPŒIA, p. 98, for preparations.)

765. Diluents are chiefly watery compounds, such as weak tea, water, thin broth, gruel, weak infusions of balm, horehound, pennyroyal, ground ivy, mint, and sage.

766. Emollients consist of unctuous remedies, such as cerates and ointments, and any materials that combine heat with moisture,—poultices of bread, bran, linseed meal, carrots, and turnips. (*See* SPONGIO-PILINE, No. 780, p. 127.)

767. Domestic Surgery.—This will comprise such hints and advice as will enable any one to act on an emergency, or in ordinary trivial accidents requiring simple treatment: and also to distinguish between serious and simple accidents, and the best means to adopt in all cases that are likely to fall under a person's notice. These hints will be of the utmost value to heads of families, to emigrants, and to persons who are frequently called upon to attend the sick. We strongly recommend the Parent, Emigrant, and Nurse, *to read over these directions occasionally,—to regard it as a duty to do so at least three or four times a year*, so as to be prepared for emergencies whenever they may arise. When accidents occur, people are too excited to acquire immediately a knowledge of what they should do; and many lives have been lost for want of this knowledge. Study, therefore, at moderate intervals, the *Domestic Surgery, Treatment of Poisons, Rules for the Prevention of Accidents, How to Escape from Fires, the Domestic Pharmacopœia, &c.*, which will be found in various pages of *Enquire Within*. And let it be impressed upon your mind that THE INDEX will enable you to refer to *anything* you may require IN A MOMENT. Don't trouble to hunt through the pages; but when you wish to ENQUIRE WITHIN, remember that the INDEX is the knocker, by which the door of knowledge may be opened.

768. Dressings.—These are substances usually applied to parts for the purpose of soothing, promoting their reunion when divided, protecting them from external injuries, as a means of applying various medicines, to absorb discharges, protect the surrounding parts, and insure cleanliness.

769. CERTAIN INSTRUMENTS are required for the application of dressings in domestic surgery, viz., — scissors, a pair of tweezers or simple forceps, a knife, needles and thread, a razor, a lancet, a piece of lunar caustic in a quill, and a sponge.

770. THE MATERIALS REQUIRED for dressings consist of lint, scraped linen, carded cotton, tow, ointment spread on calico, adhesive plaster, compresses, pads, bandages, poultices, old rags of linen or calico, and water.

771. THE FOLLOWING RULES should be attended to in applying dressings :— i. Always prepare the new dressing before removing the old one. ii. Always have hot and cold water at hand, and a vessel to place the foul dressings in. iii. Have one or more persons at hand ready to assist, and tell each person what they are to do before you commence, it prevents confusion ; thus one is to wash out and hand the sponges, another to heat the adhesive plaster, or hand the bandages and dressings, and, if requisite, a third to support the limb, &c. iv. Always stand on the outside of a limb to dress it. v. Place the patient in as easy a position as possible, so as not to fatigue him. vi. Arrange the bed *after* changing the dressings ; but in some cases you will have to do so before the patient is placed on it. vii. Never be in a hurry when applying dressings, do it quietly. viii. When a patient requires moving from one bed to another, the best way is for one person to stand on each *side* of the patient, and each to place an arm behind his back, while he passes his arms over their necks, then let their other arms be passed under his thighs, and by holding each other's hands, the patient can be raised with ease, and removed to another bed. If the leg is injured, a third person should steady it ; and if the arm, the same precaution should be adopted. Sometimes a stout sheet is passed under the patient, and by several people holding the sides, the patient is lifted without any fatigue or much disturbance.

772. LINT MAY BE MADE in a hurry by nailing the corners of a piece of old linen to a board, and scraping its surface with a knife. It is used either alone or spread with ointment. Scraped lint is the fine filaments from ordinary lint, and is used to stimulate ulcers and absorb discharges ; it is what the French call *charpie*.

773. SCRAPED LINT IS MADE into various shapes for particular purposes.

For example, when it is screwed up into a conical or wedge-like shape, it is called a *tent*, and is used to dilate fistulous openings, so as to allow the matter to escape freely ; to plug wounds, so as to promote the formation of a clot of blood, and thus arrest bleeding. When it is rolled into little balls they are called *boulettes*, and are used for absorbing matter in cavities, or blood in wounds. Another useful form is made by rolling a mass of scraped lint into a long roll, and then tying it in the middle with a piece of thread ; the middle is then doubled and pushed into a deep-seated wound, so as to press upon the bleeding vessel, while the ends remain loose and assist in forming a clot ; or it is used in deep-seated ulcers to absorb the matter and keep the edges apart. This form is called the *bourdonnet*. Another form is called the *pelote*, which is merely a ball of scraped lint tied up in a piece of linen rag, commonly called a dabber. This is used in the treatment of protrusion of the navel in children.

774. CARDED COTTON is used as a dressing for superficial burns, and care should be taken to free it from specks, as flies are apt to lay their eggs there, and generate maggots.

775. TOW IS CHIEFLY EMPLOYED as a padding for splints, as a compress, and also as an outer dressing where there is much discharge from a surface.

776. OINTMENTS ARE SPREAD on calicoes, lint, or even thin layers of tow, by means of a knife ; they should not be spread too thick.

777. ADHESIVE PLASTER is cut into strips, ranging in width, according to the nature of the wound, &c., but the usual width is about three-quarters of an inch. Isinglass plaster is not so irritating as diachylon, and is more easily removed.

778. COMPRESSES ARE MADE of pieces of linen, calico, lint, or tow, doubled or cut into various shapes. They are used to confine dressings in their places, and to apply an equal pressure on parts. They should be free from darns, hems, and knots. Ordinary compresses are square, oblong, and triangular. The *pierced compress* is made by folding up a square piece of linen five or six times on itself, and then nicking the surface with scissors, so as to cut out small pieces. It is then opened out, and spread with ointment. It is applied to discharging surfaces, for the purpose of allowing the matter to pass freely through the holes, and is frequently covered with a thin layer of tow. Compresses are also made in the shape of a Maltese cross, and half a cross, sometimes split singly, and at other times doubly, or they are graduated by placing square pieces of folded cloth on one another, so arranged that they decrease in size each time. They are used for keeping up pressure upon certain parts.

779. PADS ARE MADE by sewing tow inside pieces of linen, or folding linen and sewing the pieces together. They are used to keep off pressure from parts, such as that caused by splints in fractures.

780. POULTICES ARE USUALLY MADE of linseed meal, oatmeal, or bread, either combined with water or other fluids; sometimes they are made of carrots, charcoal, potatoes, yeast, and linseed meal, mustard, &c., but the best and most economical kind of poultice is a fabric made of sponge and wool felted together, and backed by Indian rubber, It is called "Markwick's Patent Spongio-Piline." The method of using this poultice is as follows: — A piece of the material of the required form and size is cut off, and the edges are pared or bevelled off with a pair of scissors, so that the caoutchouc may come in contact with the surrounding skin, in order to prevent evaporation of the fluid used; for, as it only forms the vehicle, we can employ the various poultices generally used with much less expenditure of time and money, and increased cleanliness. For example,—a *vinegar* poultice is made by moistening the fabric with distilled vinegar; an *alum* poultice, by using a strong solution of alum; a *charcoal* poultice, by sprinkling powdered charcoal on the moistened

surface of the material; a *yeast* poultice, by using warmed yeast, and moistening the fabric with hot water, which is to be well squeezed out previous to the absorption of the yeast; a *beer* poultice, by employing warm porter-dregs or strong beer as the fluid; and a *carrot* poultice, by using the expressed and evaporated liquor of boiled carrots. The material costs about one farthing a square inch, and may be obtained of the chemist. As a fomentation it is most invaluable, and by moistening the material with compound camphor liniment or hartshorn, it acts the same as a mustard poultice. Full directions will, no doubt, be supplied to those who purchase the material, if inquired for.

781. Bandages. — Bandages are strips of calico, linen, flannel, muslin, elastic webbing, bunting, or some other substance, of various lengths, such as three, four, eight, ten, or twelve yards, and one, one and a half, two, two and a half, three, four, or six inches wide, free from hems or darns, soft and unglazed. They are better after they have been washed. Their uses are to retain dressings, apparatus, or parts of the body in their proper positions, support the soft parts, and maintain equal pressure.

782. BANDAGES ARE SIMPLE AND COMPOUND; the former are simple slips rolled up tightly like a roll of ribbon. There is also another simple kind, which is rolled from both ends—this is called a double-headed bandage. The compound bandages are formed of many pieces.

783. BANDAGES FOR THE HEAD should be two inches wide and five yards long; for the neck, two inches wide and three yards long; for the arm, two inches wide and seven yards long; for the leg, two inches and a half wide and seven yards long; for the thigh, three inches wide and eight yards long; and for the body, four or six inches wide and ten or twelve yards long.

784. To APPLY A SINGLE-HEADED BANDAGE, lay the *outside of the end* next to the part to be bandaged, and hold the roll between the little, ring, and middle fingers, and the palm of the left hand, using the thumb and forefinger of the same hand to guide it, and the right hand to keep it firm, and pass the bandage partly round the leg towards the left hand. It is sometimes necessary to reverse this order, and therefore it is well to be able to use both hands. Particular parts require a different method of applying bandages, and therefore we shall describe the most useful separately; and there are different ways of putting on the same bandage, which consist in the manner the folds or turns are made. For example, the *circular* bandage is formed by horizontal turns, each of which overlaps the one made before it; the *spiral* consists of spiral turns; the *oblique* follows a course oblique or slanting to the centre of the limb; and the *recurrent* folds back again to the part whence it started.

785. CIRCULAR BANDAGES are used for the *neck*, to retain dressings on any part of it, or for blisters, setons, &c.; for the *head*, to keep dressings on the forehead or any part contained within a circle passing round the head; for the *arm*, previous to bleeding; for the *leg*, above the knee; and for the *fingers*, &c.

786. To CONFINE THE ENDS OF BANDAGES some persons use pins, others slit the end for a short distance, and tie the two strips into a knot, and some use a strip of adhesive plaster. Always place the point of a pin in such a position that it cannot prick the patient, or the person dressing the limb, or be liable to draw out by using the limb; therefore, as a general rule, turn the head of the pin from the free end of the bandage, or towards the upper part of the limb. The best mode is to *sew* the bandage on. A few stitches will hold it more securely than pins can.

787. THE OBLIQUE BANDAGE is generally used for arms and legs, to retain dressings.

788. THE SPIRAL BANDAGE is generally applied to the trunk and extremities, but is apt to fall off even when very carefully applied; therefore we generally use another, called the recurrent, which folds back again.

789. THE RECURRENT BANDAGE is the best kind of bandage that we can employ for general purposes. The method of putting it on is as follows:— Apply the end of the bandage that is free, with the outside of it next the skin, and hold this end with the finger and thumb of the left hand, while some one supports the heel of the patient; then with the right hand pass the bandage over the piece you are holding, and keep it crossed thus, until you can place your right forefinger upon the spot where it crosses the other bandage, where it must be kept firm. Now hold the roll of the bandage in your left hand, with the palm turned upwards, and *taking care to keep that part of the bandage between your right forefinger, and the roll in your left hand, quite slack ;* turn your left hand over, and bring the bandage down upon the leg ; then pass the roll under the leg towards your right hand, and repeat this until the leg is bandaged up to the knee, taking care *not to drag* the bandage at any time during the process of bandaging. When you arrive at the knee, pass the bandage round the leg in circles just below the knee, and pin it as usual. Bandaging is very easy, and if you once see any one apply a bandage properly, and attend to these rules, there will not be any difficulty; but bear one thing in mind, without which you will never put on a bandage even decently ; and that is, *never to drag* or pull at a bandage, but make the turns while it is slack, and you have your right forefinger placed upon the point where it is to be folded down. When a limb is properly bandaged, the folds should run in a line corresponding to the shin-bone. *Use,* to retain dressings, and for varicose veins.

790. A BANDAGE FOR THE CHEST is always placed upon the patient in a sitting posture; and it may be put on in circles, or spirally. *Use,* in fractures of the ribs, to retain dressings, and after severe contusions.

791. A Bandage for the Belly is placed on the patient as directed in the last, carrying it spirally from above downwards. *Use*, to compress the belly after dropsy, or retain dressings.

792. The Hand is Bandaged by crossing the bandage over the back of the hand. *Use*, to retain dressings.

793. For the Head, a bandage may be circular, or spiral, or both ; in the latter case, commence by placing one circular turn just over the ears ; then bring down from left to right, and round the head again, so as to alternate a spiral with a circular turn. *Use*, to retain dressings on the head or over the eye ; but this form soon gets slack. The circular bandage is the best, crossing it over both eyes.

794. For the Foot.—Place the end just above the outer ankle, and make two circular turns, to prevent its slipping ; then bring it down from the inside of the foot over the instep towards the outer part ; pass it under the sole of the foot, and upwards and inwards over the instep towards the inner ankle, then round the ankle and repeat again. *Use*, to retain dressings to the instep, heel, or ankle.

795. For the Leg and Foot, commence and proceed as directed in the preceding paragraph; then continue it up the leg as ordered in the *Recurrent Bandage*.

796. As it sometimes happens that it is necessary to apply a bandage at once, and the materials are not at hand, it is desirable to know how to substitute something else *that any one may apply with ease*. This is found to be effected by handkerchiefs, and an experienced surgeon (Mr. Mayor) has paid great attention to this subject, and brought it to much perfection. It is to him, therefore, that we are indebted for most of these hints.

797. Any Ordinary Handkerchief will do ; but a square of linen folded into various shapes answers better. The shapes generally required are as follows :—The triangle, the long square, the cravat, and the cord.

798. The Triangular Handkerchief is made by folding it from corner to corner. *Use*, as a bandage for the head. *Application.*—Place the base round the head, and the short part hanging down behind, then tie the long ends over it.

799. The Long Square is made by folding the handkerchief into three parts, by doubling it once upon itself. *Use*, as a bandage to the ribs, belly, &c. If one handkerchief is not long enough, sew two together.

800. The Cravat is folded as usual with cravats. *Use*, as a bandage for the head, arms, legs, feet, neck, &c.

801. The Cord is used to compress vessels, when a knot is made in it, and placed over the vessel to be compressed. It is merely a handkerchief twisted in its long diameter.

802. Two or more Handkerchiefs must sometimes be applied, as in a broken collar-bone, or when it is necessary to keep dressings under the arm. The bandage is applied by knotting the two ends of one handkerchief together, and passing the left arm through it, then passing another handkerchief under the right arm, and tying it. By this means we can brace the shoulders well back, and the handkerchief will press firmly over the broken collar-bone: besides, this form of bandage does not readily slip or get slack, but it requires to be combined with the sling, in order to keep the arm steady.

803. For an Inflamed Breast that requires support, or dressings to be kept to it, tie two ends of the handkerchief round the neck, and bring the body of it over the breast, and pass it upwards and backwards under the arm of that side, and tie the ends around the neck.

804. An Excellent Sling is formed by placing one handkerchief around the neck, and knotting the two ends over the breast bone, then placing the other in triangle under the arm, to be supported with the base near to the hand; tie the ends over the handkerchief, and pin the top to the other part, after passing it around the elbow.

805. Apparatus.—When a person receives a severe contusion of the leg or foot, or breaks his leg, or has painful ulcers over the leg, or is unable from some cause to bear the pressure of the bedclothes, it is advisable to know how to keep them from hurting the leg. This may be done by bending up a fire-guard, or placing a chair, resting upon the edge of its back and front of the seat, over the leg, or putting a box on each side of it, and placing a plank over them; but the best way is to make a *cradle*, as it is called. This is done by getting three pieces of wood, and three pieces of iron wire, and passing the wire or hoop through the wood. This can be placed to any height, and is very useful in all cases where pressure cannot be borne. Wooden hoops cut in halves answer better than the wire.

806. WHEN A PERSON BREAKS HIS LEG, and *splints* cannot be had directly, get bunches of straw or twigs, roll them up in handkerchiefs, and placing one on each side of the leg or arm, bind another handkerchief firmly around them; or make a long bag about three inches in diameter, or even more, of coarse linen duck, or carpet, and stuff this full of bran, sawdust, or sand, sew up the end, and use this the same as the twigs. It forms an excellent extemporaneous splint. Another good plan is to get a hat-box made of chip, and cut it into suitable lengths; or for want of all these, some bones out of a pair of stays, and run them through a stout piece of rug, protecting the leg with a fold of rug, linen, &c. A still better splint or set of splints can be extemporized by cutting a sheet of thick pasteboard into proper sized slips, then passing each piece through a basin of hot water to soften it. It is then applied to the fractured limb like an ordinary splint, when it hardens as it dries, taking the exact shape of the part to which it is applied.

807. WHEN DRY WARMTH IS REQUIRED to be applied to any part of the body, fry a flour pancake and lay it over the part; or warm some sand and place in the patient's socks, and lay it to the part; salt does as well, and may be put into a paper bag; or warm water put into ginger-beer bottles or stone jars, and rolled up in flannel.

808. Minor Operations. — BLEEDING is sometimes necessary at once in certain accidents, such as concussion, and therefore it is well to know how to do this. First of all, bind up the arm above the elbow with a piece of bandage or a handkerchief pretty firmly, then place your finger over one of the veins at the bend of the arm, and feel if there is any pulsation; if there is, try another vein, and if it does not pulsate or beat, choose that one. Now rub the arm from the wrist towards the elbow, place the left thumb upon the vein, and hold the lancet as you would a pen, and nearly at right angles to the vein, taking care to prevent its going in too far, by keeping the thumb near to the point, and resting the hand upon the little finger. Now place the point of the lancet on the vein, push it suddenly inwards, depress the elbow, and raise the hand upwards and outwards, so as to *cut obliquely across* the vein. When sufficient blood is drawn off, which is known by feeling the pulse at the wrist, and near the thumb, bandage the arm. If the pulse feel like a piece of cord, more blood should be taken away, but if it is soft, and can be easily pressed, the bleeding should be stopped. When you bandage the arm, place a piece of lint over the opening made by the lancet, and pass a bandage lightly but firmly around the arm, so as to cross it over the bend of the elbow, in the form of a figure 8.

809. DRY CUPPING is performed by throwing a piece of paper dipped into spirit of wine, and ignited, into a wine-glass, and placing it over the part, such as the neck, temples, &c. It thus draws the flesh into the glass, and causes a determination of blood to the part, which is useful in headache, and many other complaints. This is an excellent method of extracting the poison from wounds made by adders, mad dogs, fish, &c.

810. ORDINARY CUPPING is performed the same as dry cupping, with this exception, that the part is scarified or scratched with a lancet, so as to cause the blood to flow; or by the application of a scarificator, which makes by one action from seven to twenty-one light superficial cuts. Then the glass is placed over it again with the lighted paper in it, and when sufficient blood has been taken away, then the parts are sponged, and a piece of sticking plaster applied over them.

811. Leeches and their Application.—The leech used for medical purposes is called the *hirudo medicinalis*, to distinguish it from other varieties, such as the horse-leech and the Lisbon leech. It varies from two to four inches in length, and is of a blackish brown colour, marked on the back with six yellow spots, and edged with a yellow line on each side. Formerly leeches were supplied by Lincolnshire, Yorkshire, and other fenny countries, but latterly most of the leeches are procured from France, where they are now becoming scarce.

812. WHEN LEECHES ARE APPLIED to a part, it should be thoroughly freed from down or hair by shaving, and all liniments, &c., carefully and effectually cleaned away by washing. If the leech is hungry it will soon bite, but sometimes great difficulty is experienced in getting them to fasten. When this is the case, roll the leech into a little porter, or moisten the surface with a little blood, or milk, or sugar and water. Leeches may be applied by holding them over the part with a piece of linen cloth, or by means of an inverted glass, under which they must be placed.

813. WHEN APPLIED TO THE GUMS, care should be taken to use a leech glass, as they are apt to creep down the patient's throat: a large swan's quill will answer the purpose of a leech glass. When leeches are gorged they will drop off themselves; never *tear* them off from a person, but just dip the point of a moistened finger into some salt and touch them with it.

814. LEECHES ARE SUPPOSED TO ABSTRACT about two drachms of blood, or six leeches draw about an ounce; but this is independent of the bleeding after they have come off, and more blood generally flows then than during the time they are sucking. The total amount of blood drawn and subsequently lost by each leech-bite, is nearly half an ounce.

815. AFTER LEECHES COME AWAY, encourage the bleeding by flannels dipped in hot water and wrung out dry, and then apply a warm "spongio-piline" poultice. If the bleeding is not to be encouraged, cover the bites with a rag dipped in olive oil, or spread with spermaceti ointment, having previously sponged the parts clean.

816. WHEN BLEEDING CONTINUES from leech-bites, and it is desirable to stop it, apply pressure with the fingers over the part, or dip a rag in a strong solution of alum and lay over them, or use the tincture of sesquichloride of iron, or apply a leaf of matico to them, placing the under surface of the leaf next to the skin, or touch each bite with a finely-pointed piece of lunar caustic, or lay a piece of lint soaked in the extract of lead over the bites; and if all these tried in succession fail, pass a fine needle through a fold of the skin so as to include the bite, and twist a piece of thread round it. Be sure never to allow any one to go to sleep with leech-bites bleeding, without watching them carefully; and never apply too many to children; or place them where their bites can be compressed if necessary. In other words, *never apply leeches to children except over a bone.*

817. AFTER LEECHES HAVE BEEN USED they should be placed in water containing sixteen per cent. of salt, which facilitates the removal of the blood they contain; and they should afterwards be placed one by one in warm water, and the blood forced out by *gentle* pressure. The leeches should then be thrown into fresh water, which is to be renewed every twenty-four hours; and they may then be re-applied after an interval of eight or ten days: a second time they may be disgorged. The best plan, however, is to strip the leech by drawing the thumb and forefinger of the right hand along its body from the tail to the mouth, the leech being firmly held at the sucker extremity by the fingers of the left hand. By this means, with a few minutes' rest between each application, the same leech may be used four or five times in succession.

818. If a Leech be accidentally Swallowed, or by any means should get into the body, employ an emetic, or enema of salt and water.

819. Scarification is useful in severe contusions, and inflammation of parts. It is performed by scratching or slightly cutting through the skin with a lancet, holding the lancet as you would a pen when you are ruling lines on paper.

820. Terms used to express the Properties of Medicines.

821. Absorbents are medicines which destroy acidities in the stomach and bowels, such as magnesia, prepared chalk, &c.

822. Alteratives are medicines which restore health to the constitution, without producing any sensible effect, such as sarsaparilla, sulphur, &c.

823. Analeptics are medicines that restore the strength which has been lost by sickness, such as gentian, bark, &c.

824. Anodynes are medicines which relieve pain, and they are divided into three kinds, *sedatives, hypnotics,* and *narcotics* (see these terms); camphor is anodyne as well as narcotic.

825. Antacids are medicines which destroy acidity, such as lime, magnesia, soda, &c.

826. Antalkalies are medicines given to neutralize alkalies in the system, such as citric, nitric, or sulphuric acids, &c.

827. Anthelmintics are medicines used to expel and destroy worms from the stomach and intestines, such as turpentine, cowhage, male fern, &c.

828. Antibilious are medicines which are useful in bilious affections, such as calomel, &c.

829. Antirheumatics are medicines used for the cure of rheumatism, such as colchicum, iodide of potash, &c.

830. Antiscorbutics are medicines against scurvy, such as citric acid, &c.

831. Antiseptics are substances used to correct putrefaction, such as bark, camphor, charcoal, vinegar, and creosote.

832. Antispasmodics are medicines which possess the power of overcoming spasms of the muscles, or allaying severe pain from any cause unconnected with inflammation, such as valerian, ammonia, opium, and camphor.

833. Aperients are medicines which move the bowels gently, such as rhubarb, manna, and grey powder.

834. Aromatics are cordial, spicy, and agreeably-flavoured medicines, such as cardamoms, cinnamon, &c.

835. Astringents are medicines which contract the fibres of the body, diminish excessive discharges, and act indirectly as tonics, such as oak bark, galls, &c.

836. Attenuants are medicines which are supposed to thin the blood, such as ammoniated iron, &c.

837. Balsamics are medicines of a soothing kind, such as tolu, Peruvian balsam, &c.

838. Carminatives are medicines which allay pain in the stomach and bowels, and expel flatulence, such as aniseed water, &c.

839. Cathartics are strong purgative medicines, such as jalap, &c.

840. Cordials are exhilarating and warming medicines, such as aromatic confection, &c.

841. Corroborants are medicines and food which increase the strength, such as iron, gentian, meat, and wine.

842. Demulcents correct acrimony, diminish irritation, and soften parts by covering their surfaces with a mild and viscid matter, such as linseed tea, gum, mucilage, honey, and marsh-mallow.

843. DEOBSTRUENTS are medicines which remove obstructions, such as iodide of potash, &c.

844. DETERGENTS clean the surfaces over which they pass, such as soap, &c.

845. DIAPHORETICS produce perspiration, such as tartrate of antimony, James's powder, and camphor.

846. DIGESTIVES are remedies applied to ulcers or wounds, to promote the formation of matter, such as resin ointments, warm poultices, &c.

847. DISCUTIENTS possess the power of repelling or resolving tumours, such as galbanum, mercury, and iodine.

848. DIURETICS act upon the kidneys and bladder, and increase the flow of urine, such as nitre, squills, cantharides, camphor, antimony, and juniper.

849. DRASTICS are violent purgatives, such as gamboge, &c.

850. EMETICS produce vomiting, or the discharge of the contents of the stomach, such as mustard and hot water, tartar emetic, ipecacuanha, sulphate of zinc, and sulphate of copper.

851. EMOLLIENTS are remedies used externally to soften the parts they are applied to, such as spermaceti, palm oil, &c.

852. EPISPASTICS are medicines which blister or cause effusion of serum under the cuticle, such as Spanish flies, Burgundy pitch, rosin, and galbanum.

853. ERRHINES are medicines which produce sneezing, such as tobacco, &c.

854. ESCHAROTICS are medicines which corrode or destroy the vitality of the part to which they are applied, such as lunar caustic, &c.

855. EXPECTORANTS are medicines which increase expectoration, or the discharge from the bronchial tubes, such as ipecacuanha, squills, opium, ammoniacum.

856. FEBRIFUGES are remedies used in fevers, such as all the antimonials, bark, quinine, mineral acids, arsenic.

857. HYDRAGOGUES are medicines which have the effect of removing the fluid of dropsy, by producing watery evacuations, such as gamboge, calomel, &c.

858. HYPNOTICS are medicines that relieve pain by procuring sleep, such as hops, henbane, morphia, poppy.

859. LAXATIVES are medicines which cause the bowels to act rather more than natural, such as manna, &c.

860. NARCOTICS are medicines which cause sleep or stupor, and allay pain, such as opium, &c.

861. NUTRIENTS are remedies that nourish the body, such as sugar, sago, &c.

862. PAREGORICS are medicines which actually assuage pain, such as compound tincture of camphor, henbane, hops, opium.

863. PROPHYLACTICS are remedies employed to prevent the attack of any particular disease, such as quinine, &c.

864. PURGATIVES are medicines that promote the evacuation of the bowels, such as senna, aloes, jalap, salts.

865. REFRIGERANTS are medicines which suppress an unusual heat of the body, such as wood sorrel, tamarind, &c.

866. RUBEFACIENTS are medicaments which cause redness of the skin, such as mustard, &c.

867. SEDATIVES are medicines which depress the nervous energy, and destroy sensation, so as to compose, such as foxglove. (*See* PAREGORICS.)

868. SIALOGOGUES are medicines which promote the flow of saliva or spittle, such as salt, calomel, &c.

869. SOPORIFICS are medicines which induce sleep, such as hops, &c.

870. STIMULANTS are remedies which increase the action of the heart and arteries, or the energy of the part to which they are applied, such as food, wine, spirits, ether, sassafras, which is an internal stimulant, and savine, which is an external one.

871. STOMACHICS restore the tone of the stomach, such as gentian, &c.

872. STYPTICS are medicines which constrict the surface of a part, and prevent the effusion of blood, such as kino, Friar's balsam, extract of lead, and ice.

873. SUDORIFICS promote profuse perspiration or sweating, such as ipecacuanha, antimony, James's powder, ammonia.

874. TONICS give general strength to the constitution, restore the natural energies, and improve the tone of the system, such as all the vegetable bitters, most of the minerals, also some kinds of food, wine, and beer.

875. VESICANTS are medicines which blister, such as strong liquid ammonia, &c.

876. Special Rules for the Prevention of Cholera.

i. We urge the necessity, in all cases of cholera, of an instant recourse to medical aid, and also under every form and variety of indisposition : for all disorders are found to merge in the dominant disease.

ii. LET IMMEDIATE RELIEF be sought under disorder of the bowels especially, however slight. The invasion of cholera may thus be readily prevented.

iii. LET EVERY IMPURITY, animal and vegetable, be quickly removed to a distance from the habitation, such as slaughter-houses, pig-sties, cesspools, necessaries, and all other domestic nuisances.

iv. LET ALL UNCOVERED DRAINS be carefully and frequently cleansed.

v. LET THE GROUNDS in and around the habitation be drained, so as effectually to carry off moisture of every kind.

vi. LET ALL PARTITIONS be removed from within and without habitations, which unnecessarily impede ventilation.

vii. LET EVERY ROOM be daily thrown open for the admission of fresh air ; this should be done about noon, when the atmosphere is most likely to be dry.

viii. LET DRY SCRUBBING be used in domestic cleansing in place of water cleansing.

ix. LET EXCESSIVE FATIGUE, and exposure to damp and cold, especially during the night, be avoided.

x. LET THE USE of cold drinks and acid liquors, especially under fatigue, be avoided, or when the body is heated.

xi. LET THE USE of cold acid fruits and vegetables be avoided.

xii. LET EXCESS in the use of ardent and fermented liquors and tobacco be avoided.

xiii. LET A POOR DIET, and the use of impure water in cooking, or for drinking, be avoided.

xiv. LET THE WEARING of wet and insufficient clothes be avoided.

xv. LET A FLANNEL or woollen belt be worn round the belly.

xvi. LET PERSONAL CLEANLINESS be carefully observed.

xvii. LET EVERY CAUSE tending to depress the moral and physical energies be carefully avoided. Let exposure to extremes of heat and cold be avoided.

xviii. LET CROWDING of persons within houses and apartments be avoided.

xix. LET SLEEPING in low or damp rooms be avoided.

xx. LET FIRES be kept up during the night in sleeping or adjoining apartments, the night being the period of most danger from attack, especially under exposure to cold or damp.

xxi. LET ALL BEDDING and clothing be daily exposed during winter and spring to the fire, and in summer to the heat of the sun.

xxii. LET THE DEAD be buried in places remote from the habitations of the living. By the timely adoption of simple means such as these, cholera, or other epidemic, will be made to lose its venom.

877. Rules for the Preservation of Health.

878. PURE ATMOSPHERIC AIR is composed of nitrogen, oxygen, and a *very* small proportion of carbonic acid gas. Air once breathed has lost the chief part of its oxygen, and acquired a proportionate increase of carbonic acid gas. *Therefore,* health requires that we breathe the same air once only.

879. THE SOLID PART OF OUR BODIES is continually wasting, and requires to be repaired by fresh substances.

Therefore, food, which is to repair the loss, should be taken with due regard to the exercise and waste of the body.

880. THE FLUID PART OF OUR BODIES also wastes constantly; there is but one fluid in animals, which is water. *Therefore*, water only is necessary, and no artifice can produce a better drink.

881. THE FLUID OF OUR BODIES is to the solid in proportion as nine to one. *Therefore*, a like proportion should prevail in the total amount of food taken.

882. LIGHT EXERCISES AN IMPORTANT INFLUENCE upon the growth and vigour of animals and plants. *Therefore*, our dwellings should freely admit the solar rays.

883. DECOMPOSING ANIMAL AND VEGETABLE SUBSTANCES yield various noxious gases, which enter the lungs and corrupt the blood. *Therefore*, all impurities should be kept away from our abodes, and every precaution be observed to secure a pure atmosphere.

884. WARMTH IS ESSENTIAL to all the bodily functions. *Therefore*, an equal bodily temperature should be maintained by exercise, by clothing, or by fire.

885. EXERCISE WARMS, INVIGORATES, and purifies the body; clothing preserves the warmth the body generates; fire imparts warmth externally. *Therefore*, to obtain and preserve warmth, exercise and clothing are preferable to fire.

886. FIRE CONSUMES THE OXYGEN of the air, and produces noxious gases. *Therefore*, the air is less pure in the presence of candles, gas, or coal fire, than otherwise, and the deterioration should be repaired by increased ventilation.

887. THE SKIN IS A HIGHLY-ORGANIZED MEMBRANE, full of minute pores, cells, bloodvessels, and nerves; it imbibes moisture or throws it off, according to the state of the atmosphere and the temperature of the body. It also "breathes," as do the lungs (though less actively). All the internal organs sympathize with the skin. *Therefore*, it should be repeatedly cleansed.

888. LATE HOURS AND ANXIOUS PURSUITS exhaust the nervous system, and produce disease and premature death. *Therefore*, the hours of labour and study should be short.

889. MENTAL AND BODILY EXERCISE are equally essential to the general health and happiness. *Therefore*, labour and study should succeed each other.

890. MAN WILL LIVE MOST HEALTHILY upon simple solids and fluids, of which a sufficient but temperate quantity should be taken. *Therefore*, over indulgence in strong drinks, tobacco, snuff, opium, and all mere indulgences, should be avoided.

891. SUDDEN ALTERNATIONS OF HEAT AND COLD are dangerous (especially to the young and the aged). *Therefore*, clothing, in quantity and quality, should be adapted to the alternations of night and day, and of the seasons. *And therefore, also*, drinking cold water when the body is hot, and hot tea and soups when cold, are productive of many evils.

892. MODERATION IN EATING and drinking, short hours of labour and study, regularity in exercise, recreation, and rest, cleanliness, equanimity of temper and equality of temperature,—these are the great essentials to that which surpasses all wealth, *health of mind and body*.

893. Mischief Makers.

OH, could there in this world be found
Some little spot of happy ground,
Where village pleasures might go round,
   Without the village tattling!
How doubly blest that place would be,
Where all might dwell in liberty,
Free from the bitter misery
   Of gossips' endless prattling.

If such a spot were really known,
Dame Peace might claim it as her own,
And in it she might fix her throne,
   For ever and for ever :
There, like a queen, might reign and live,
While every one would soon forgive
The little slights they might receive,
   And be offended never.

'Tis mischief-makers that remove
Far from our hearts the warmth of love,
And lead us all to disapprove
   What gives another pleasure.

They seem to take one's part—but when
They've heard our cares, unkindly then
They soon retail them all again,
    Mixed with their poisonous measure.

And then they've such a cunning way
Of telling ill-meant tales : they say,
" Don't mention what I've said, I pray,
    I would not tell another ;"—
Straight to your neighbour's house they go,
Narrating everything they know ;
And break the peace of high and low,
    Wife, husband, friend, and brother.

Oh, that the mischief-making crew
Were all reduced to one or two,
And they were painted red or blue,
    That every one might know them :
Then would our villagers forget
To rage and quarrel, fume and fret,
Or fall into an angry pet,
    With things so much below them.

For 'tis a sad, degrading part,
To make another's bosom smart,
And plant a dagger in the heart
    We ought to love and cherish.
Then let us evermore be found
In quietness with all around,
While friendship, joy, and peace abound,
    And angry feelings perish !

894. Signs of the Weather.

895. Dew.—If the dew lies plentifully on the grass after a fair day, it is a
sign of another fair day. If not, and there
is no wind, rain must follow. A red
evening portends fine weather ; but if it
spread too far upwards from the horizon in the evening, and especially
morning, it foretells wind or rain, or
both. When the sky, in rainy weather,
is tinged with sea green, the rain will
increase ; if with deep blue, it will be
showery.

896. Clouds.—Previous to much
rain falling, the clouds grow bigger, and
increase very fast, especially before
thunder. When the clouds are formed
like fleeces, but dense in the middle and
bright towards the edges, with the sky
bright, they are signs of a frost, with hail,
snow, or rain. If clouds form high in air,
in thin white trains like locks of wool,
they portend wind, and probably rain.
When a general cloudiness covers the
sky, and small black fragments of clouds
fly underneath, they are a sure sign of
rain, and probably it will be lasting.
Two currents of clouds always portend
rain, and, in summer, thunder.

897. Heavenly Bodies.—A hazi-
ness in the air, which fades the sun's
light, and makes the orb appear whitish,
or ill-defined—or at night, if the moon
and stars grow dim, and a ring encircles
the former, rain will follow. If the sun's
rays appear like Moses' horns—if white
at setting, or shorn of his rays, or if he
goes down into a bank of clouds in the
horizon, bad weather is to be expected.
If the moon looks pale and dim, we expect rain ; if red, wind; and if of her
natural colour, with a clear sky, fair
weather. If the moon is rainy throughout, it will clear at the change, and,
perhaps, the rain return a few days
after. If fair throughout, and rain at
the change, the fair weather will probably return on the fourth or fifth day.

898. Weather Precautions.—
If the weather appears doubtful, always
take the precaution of having an umbrella when you go out, particularly in
going to church ; you thereby avoid incurring one of three disagreeables ; in
the first place, the chance of getting
wet—or encroaching under a friend's
umbrella—or being under the necessity
of borrowing one, consequently involving the trouble of returning it, and
possibly (as is the case nine times out
of ten) inconveniencing your friend
by neglecting to do so. Those who
disdain the use of umbrellas generally
appear with shabby hats, tumbled
bonnet ribbons, wrinkled silk dresses,
&c., &c., the consequence of frequent
exposure to unexpected showers, to say
nothing of colds taken, no one can tell
how.

899. Leech Barometer.—Take
an eight-ounce phial, and put in it three
gills of water, and place in it a healthy
leech, changing the water in summer
once a week, and in winter once in a
fortnight, and it will most accurately
prognosticate the weather. If the
weather is to be fine, the leech lies
motionless at the bottom of the glass,

and coiled together in a spiral form ; if rain may be expected, it will creep up to the top of its lodgings, and remain there till the weather is settled ; if we are to have wind, it will move through its habitation with amazing swiftness, and seldom goes to rest till it begins to blow hard ; if a remarkable storm of thunder and rain is to succeed, it will lodge for some days before almost continually out of the water, and discover great uneasiness in violent throes and convulsive-like motions ; in frost as in clear summer-like weather it lies constantly at the bottom ; and in snow as in rainy weather it pitches its dwelling in the very mouth of the phial. The top should be covered over with a piece of muslin.

900. The Chemical Barometer.
—Take a long narrow bottle, such as an old-fashioned Eau-de-Cologne bottle, and put into it two and a half drachms of camphor, and eleven drachms of spirit of wine ; when the camphor is dissolved, which it will readily do by slight agitation, add the following mixture :—Take water, nine drachms ; nitrate of potash (saltpetre), thirty-eight grains ; and muriate of ammonia (sal ammoniac), thirty-eight grains. Dissolve these salts in the water prior to mixing with the camphorated spirit ; then shake the whole well together. Cork the bottle well, and wax the top, but afterwards make a very small aperture in the cork with a red-hot needle. The bottle may then be hung up, or placed in any stationary position. By observing the different appearances which the materials assume, as the weather changes, it becomes an excellent prognosticator of a coming storm or of a sunny sky.

901. Significations of Names.
Aaron, *Hebrew*, a mountain.
Abel, *Hebrew*, vanity.
Abraham, *Hebrew*, the father of many.
Adam, *Hebrew*, red earth.
Adolphus, *Saxon*, happiness and help.
Albert, *Saxon*, all bright.
Alexander, *Greek*, a helper of men.
Alfred, *Saxon*, all peace.
Ambrose, *Greek*, immortal.

Amos, *Hebrew*, a burden.
Andrew, *Greek*, courageous.
Anthony, *Latin*, flourishing.
Archibald, *German*, a bold observer.
Arnold, *German*, a maintainer of honour.
Arthur, *British*, a strong man.
Augustus, Augustin, } *Latin*, venerable, grand.
Baldwin, *German*, a bold winner.
Bardulph, *German*, a famous helper.
Barnaby, *Hebrew*, a prophet's son.
Bartholomew, *Hebrew*, the son of him who made the waters to rise.
Beaumont, *French*, a pretty mount.
Bede, *Saxon*, prayer.
Benjamin, *Hebrew*, the son of a right hand.
Bennet, *Latin*, blessed.
Bernard, *German*, bear's heart.
Bertram, *German*, fair, illustrious.
Boniface, *Latin*, a well-doer.
Brian, *French*, having a thundering voice.
Cadwallader, *British*, valiant in war.
Cæsar, *Latin*, adorned with hair.
Caleb, *Hebrew*, a dog.
Cecil, *Latin*, dim-sighted.
Charles, *German*, noble-spirited.
Christopher, *Greek*, bearing Christ.
Clement, *Latin*, mild-tempered.
Conrad, *German*, able counsel.
Constantine, *Latin*, resolute.
Crispin, *Latin*, having curled locks.
Cuthbert, *Saxon*, known famously.
Daniel, *Hebrew*, God is judge.
David, *Hebrew*, well-beloved.
Denis, *Greek*, belonging to the god of wine.
Dunstan, *Saxon*, most high.
Edgar, *Saxon*, happy honour.
Edmund, *Saxon*, happy peace.
Edward, *Saxon*, happy keeper.
Edwin, *Saxon*, happy conqueror.
Egbert, *Saxon*, ever bright.
Elijah, *Hebrew*, God the Lord.
Elisha, *Hebrew*, the salvation of God.
Ephraim, *Hebrew*, fruitful.
Erasmus, *Greek*, lovely, worthy to be loved.
Ernest, *Greek*, earnest, serious.
Evan, or Ivon, *British*, the same as John.
Everard, *German*, well reported.
Eugene, *Greek*, nobly descended.
Eustace, *Greek*, standing firm.
Ezekiel, *Hebrew*, the strength of God.
Felix, *Latin*, happy.
Ferdinand, *German*, pure peace.
Francis, *German*, free.
Frederic, *German*, rich peace.
Gabriel, *Hebrew*, the strength of God.
Geoffrey, *German*, joyful.

F

George, *Greek*, a husbandman.
Gerard, *Saxon*, all towardliness.
Gideon, *Hebrew*, a breaker.
Gilbert, *Saxon*, bright as gold.
Giles, *Greek*, a little goat.
Godard, *German*, a godly disposition.
Godfrey, *German*, God's peace.
Godwin, *German*, victorious in God.
Griffith, *British*, having great faith.
Guy, *French*, the mistletoe shrub.
Hannibal, *Punic*, a gracious lord.
Harold, *Saxon*, a champion.
Hector, *Greek*, a stout defender.
Henry, *German*, a rich lord.
Herbert, *German*, a bright lord.
Hercules, *Greek*, the glory of Hera, or Juno.
Hezekiah, *Hebrew*, cleaving to the Lord.
Horatio, *Italian*, worthy to be beheld.
Howel, *British*, sound or whole.
Hubert, *German*, a bright colour.
Hugh, *Dutch*, high, lofty.
Humphrey, *German*, domestic peace.
Ingram, *German*, of angelic purity.
Isaac, *Hebrew*, laughter.
Jacob, *Hebrew*, a supplanter.
James, or Jacques, beguiling.
Joab, *Hebrew*, fatherhood.
Job, *Hebrew*, sorrowing.
Joel, *Hebrew*, acquiescing.
John, *Hebrew*, the grace of the Lord.
Jonah, *Hebrew*, a dove.
Jonathan, *Hebrew*, the gift of the Lord.
Joscelin, *German*, just.
Joseph, *Hebrew*, addition.
Josias, *Hebrew*, the fire of the Lord.
Joshua, *Hebrew*, a Saviour.
Lambert, *Saxon*, a fair lamb.
Lancelot, *Spanish*, a little lance.
Laurence, *Latin*, crowned with laurels.
Lazarus, *Hebrew*, destitute of help.
Leonard, *German*, like a lion.
Leopold, *German*, defending the people.
Lewis, *French*, the defender of the people.
Lionel, *Latin*, a little lion.
Llewellin, *British*, like a lion.
Lucius, *Latin*, shining.
Luke, *Greek*, a wood or grove.
Mark, *Latin*, a hammer.
Martin, *Latin*, martial.
Matthew, *Hebrew*, a gift or present.
Maurice, *Latin*, sprung of a Moor.
Meredith, *British*, the roaring of the sea.
Michael, *Hebrew*, who is like God?
Morgan, *British*, a marmer.
Moses, *Hebrew*, drawn out.
Nathaniel, *Hebrew*, the gift of God.
Neal, *French*, somewhat black.

Nicolas, *Greek*, victorious over the people.
Noel, *French*, belonging to one's nativity.
Norman, *French*, one born in Normandy.
Obadiah, *Hebrew*, the servant of the Lord.
Oliver, *Latin*, an olive.
Orlando, *Italian*, counsel for the land.
Osmund, *Saxon*, house peace.
Oswald, *Saxon*, ruler of a house.
Owen, *British*, well descended.
Patrick, *Latin*, a nobleman.
Paul, *Latin*, small, little.
Percival, *French*, a place in France.
Peregrine, *Latin*, outlandish.
Peter, *Greek*, a rock or stone.
Philip, *Greek*, a lover of horses.
Phineas, *Hebrew*, of bold countenance.
Ralph, contracted from Radolph, or
Randal, or Ranulph, *Saxon*, pure help.
Raymund, *German*, quiet peace.
Reuben, *Hebrew*, the son of vision.
Reynold, *German*, a lover of purity.
Richard, *Saxon*, powerful.
Robert, *German*, famous in counsel.
Roger, *German*, strong counsel.
Rowland, *German*, counsel for the land.
Rufus, *Latin*, reddish.
Solomon, *Hebrew*, peaceable.
Samson, *Hebrew*, a little son.
Samuel, *Hebrew*, heard by God.
Saul, *Hebrew*, desired.
Sebastian, *Greek*, to be reverenced.
Simeon, *Hebrew*, hearing.
Simon, *Hebrew*, obedient.
Stephen, *Greek*, a crown or garland.
Swithin, *Saxon*, very high.
Theobald, *Saxon*, bold over the people.
Theodore, *Greek*, the gift of God.
Theodosius, *Greek*, given of God.
Theophilus, *Greek*, a lover of God.
Thomas, *Hebrew*, a twin.
Timothy, *Greek*, a fearer of God.
Toby, or Tobias, *Hebrew*, the goodness of the
    Lord.
Valentine, *Latin*, powerful.
Vincent, *Latin*, conquering.
Vivian, *Latin*, living.
Walter, *German*, a conqueror.
Walwin, *German*, a conqueror.
William, *German*, defending many.
Zaccheus, *Syriac*, innocent.
Zachary, *Hebrew*, remembering the Lord.
Zebedee, *Syriac*, having an inheritance.
Zedekiah, *Hebrew*, the justice of the Lord.

Adeline, *German*, a princess.
Agatha, *Greek*, good.
Agnes, *German*, chaste.

Alethea, *Greek*, the truth.
Althea, *Greek*, hunting.
Alice, Alisia, *German*, noble.
Amy, Amelia, *French*, a beloved.
Anna, Anne, or Hannah, *Hebrew*, gracious.
Arabella, *Latin*, a fair altar.
Aureola, *Latin*, like gold.
Barbara, *Latin*, foreign or strange.
Beatrice, *Latin*, making happy.
Benedicta, *Latin*, blessed.
Bernice, *Greek*, bringing victory.
Bertha, *Greek*, bright or famous.
Blanche, *French*, fair.
Bona, *Latin*, good.
Bridget, *Irish*, shining bright.
Cassandra, *Greek*, a reformer of men.
Catharine, *Greek*, pure or clean.
Charity, *Greek*, love, bounty.
Charlotte, *French*, all noble.
Caroline, *feminine of Carolus, the Latin of Charles*, noble-spirited.
Chloe, *Greek*, a green herb.
Christiana, *Greek*, belonging to Christ.
Cecilia, *Latin*, from Cecil.
Cicely, *a corruption of Cecilia*.
Clara, *Latin*, clear or bright.
Constance, *Latin*, constant.
Deborah, *Hebrew*, a bee.
Diana, *Greek*, Jupiter's daughter.
Doreas, *Greek*, a wild roe.
Dorothy, *Greek*, the gift of God.
Edith, *Saxon*, happiness.
Eleanor, *Saxon*, all fruitful.
Eliza, Elizabeth, *Hebrew*, the oath of God.
Emily, *corrupted from Amelia*.
Emma, *German*, a nurse.
Esther, Heather, *Hebrew*, secret.
Eve, *Hebrew*, causing life.
Eunice, *Greek*, fair victory.
Eudoia, *Greek*, prospering in the way.
Frances, *German*, free.
Gertrude, *German*, all truth.
Grace, *Latin*, favour.
Hagar, *Hebrew*, a stranger.
Helena, *Greek*, alluring.
Jane, *softened from Joan ; or,*
Janne, *the feminine of John*.
Janet, Jeannette, little Jane.
Joyce, *French*, pleasant.
Isabella, *Spanish*, fair Eliza.
Judith, *Hebrew*, praising.
Julia, Juliana, *feminine of Julius*.
Letitia, *Latin*, joy of gladness.
Lois, *Greek*, better.
Lucretia, *Latin*, a chaste Roman lady.
Lucy, *Latin, feminine of Lucius*.
Lydia, *Greek*, descended from Lud.

Mabel, *Latin*, lovely.
Magdalene, Maudlin, *Syriac*, magnificent.
Margaret, *German*, a pearl.
Martha, *Hebrew*, bitterness.
Mary, *Hebrew*, bitter.
Maud, Matilda, *Greek*, a lady of honour.
Mercy, *English*, compassion.
Mildred, *Saxon*, speaking mild.
Nest, *British, the same as Agnes*.
Nicola, *Greek, feminine of Nicolas*.
Olympia, *Greek*, heavenly.
Orabilis, *Latin*, to be entreated.
Parnell, or Petronilla, little Peter.
Patience, *Latin*, bearing patiently.
Paulina, *Latin, feminine of Paulinus*.
Penelope, *Greek*, a turkey.
Persis, *Greek*, destroying.
Philadelphia, *Greek*, brotherly love.
Philippa, *Greek, feminine of Philip*.
Phœbe, *Greek*, the light of life.
Phyllis, *Greek*, a green bough.
Priscilla, *Latin*, somewhat old.
Prudence, *Latin*, discretion.
Pysche, *Greek*, the soul.
Rachel, *Hebrew*, a lamb.
Rebecca, *Hebrew*, fat or plump.
Rhode, *Greek*, a rose.
Rosamund, *Saxon*, rose of peace.
Rosa, *Latin*, a rose.
Rosabella, *Italian*, a fair rose.
Rosecleer, *English*, a fair rose.
Ruth, *Hebrew*, trembling.
Sabina, *Latin*, sprung from the Sabines.
Salome, *Hebrew*, perfect.
Sapphira, *Greek*, like a sapphire stone.
Sarah, *Hebrew*, a princess.
Sibylla, *Greek*, the counsel of God.
Sophia, *Greek*, wisdom.
Sophronia, *Greek*, of a sound mind.
Susan, Susanna, *Hebrew*, a lily.
Tabitha, *Syriac*, a roe.
Temperance, *Latin*, moderation.
Theodosia, *Greek*, given by God.
Tryphosa, *Greek*, delicious.
Tryphena, *Greek*, delicate.
Vida, *Erse, feminine of David*.
Ursula, *Latin*, a female bear.
Walburg, *Saxon*, gracious.
Winifred, *Saxon*, winning peace
Zenobia, *Greek*, the life of Jupiter.

902. Hints on the Barometer.

903. *Why does a Barometer indicate the Pressure of the Atmosphere?* Because it consists of a tube containing quicksilver, closed at one end, and open at the other, so that the pressure of air upon the open end balances the weight of the column of mercury (quicksilver); and when the pressure of the air upon the open surface of the mercury increases or decreases, the mercury rises or falls in response thereto.

904. *Why is a Barometer called also a " Weather Glass"* ? Because changes in the weather are generally preceded by alterations in the atmospheric pressure. But we cannot perceive those changes as they gradually occur; the alteration in the height of the column of mercury, therefore, enables us to know that atmospheric changes are taking place, and by observation we are enabled to determine certain rules by which the state of the weather may be foretold with considerable probability.

905. *Why does the Hand of the Weather Dial change its Position when the Column of Mercury rises or falls ?* Because a weight which floats upon the open surface of the mercury is attached to a string, having a nearly equal weight at the other extremity; the string is laid over a revolving pivot, to which the hand is fixed, and the friction of the string turns the hand as the mercury rises or falls.

906. *Why does Tapping the Face of the Barometer sometimes cause the Hand to Move?* Because the weight on the surface of the mercury frequently leans against the side of the tube, and does not move freely. And, also, the mercury clings to the sides of the tube by capillary attraction; therefore, tapping on the face of the barometer sets the weight free, and overcomes the attraction which impedes the rise or fall of the mercury.

907. *Why does the Fall of the Barometer denote the Approach of Rain?* Because it shows that as the air cannot support the full weight of the column of mercury, the atmosphere must be thin with watery vapours.

908. *Why does the Rise of the Barometer denote the Approach of Fine Weather ?* Because the external air, becoming dense, and free from highly elastic vapours, presses with increased force upon the mercury upon which the weight floats; that weight, therefore, sinks in the short tube as the mercury rises in the long one, and in sinking, turns the hand to Change, Fair, &c.

909. *When does the Barometer stand highest ?* When there is a duration of frost, or when north-easterly winds prevail.

910. *Why does the Barometer stand highest at these Times ?* Because the atmosphere is exceedingly dry and dense, and fully balances the weight of the column of mercury.

911. *When does the Barometer stand lowest ?* When a thaw follows a long frost, or when south-west winds prevail.

912. *Why does the Barometer stand lowest at these Times ?* Because much moisture exists in the air, by which it is rendered less dense and heavy.*

913. Cheap Fuel.—One bushel of small coal or sawdust, or both mixed together, two bushels of sand, one bushel and a half of clay: Let these be mixed together with common water, like ordinary mortar; the more they are stirred and mixed together the better; then make them into balls, or with a small mould make them in the shape of bricks, pile them in a dry place, and when they are hard and sufficiently dry, they may be used. A fire cannot be lighted with them, but when the fire is quite lighted, put them on behind with a coal or two in front, and they will be found to keep up a stronger fire than any fuel of the common kind.

914. Economy of Fuel.—There is no part of domestic economy which everybody professes to understand better than the management of a fire, and yet there is no branch in the household arrangement where there is a greater

---

* From "The Reason Why — General Science, containing 1,400 Reasons for things generally believed but imperfectly understood. London: Houlston and Wright, 2s. 6d.

proportional and unnecessary waste than arises from ignorance and mismanagement in this article.

915. It is an Old Adage that we must stir no man's fire until we have known him seven years; but we might find it equally prudent if we were careful as to the stirring of our own.

916. Anybody, indeed, can take up a Poker and toss the coals about: but that is not stirring a fire!

917. In short, the Use of a Poker applies solely to two particular points —the opening of a dying fire, so as to admit the free passage of the air into it, and sometimes, but not always, through it; or else approximating the remains of a half-burned fire, so as to concentrate the heat, whilst the parts still ignited are opened to the atmosphere.

918. The Same Observation may apply to the use of a pair of bellows, the mere blowing of which at random, nine times out of ten, will fail; the force of the current of air sometimes blowing out the fire, as it is called—that is, carrying off the caloric too rapidly,—and at others, directing the warmed current from the unignited fuel, instead of into it.

919. To prove this, let any person sit down with a pair of bellows to a fire only partially ignited, or partially extinguished; let him blow, at first, not into the burning part, but into the dead coals close to it, so that the air may partly extend to the burning coal.

920. After a few Blasts let the bellows blow into the burning fuel, but directing the stream partly towards the dead coal; when it will be found that the ignition will extend much more rapidly than under the common method of blowing furiously into the flame at random.

921. If the Consumer, instead of ordering a large supply of coals at once, will at first content himself with a sample, he may with very little trouble ascertain who will deal fairly with him; and, if he wisely pays ready money, he will be independent of his coal merchant; a situation which few families, even in genteel life, can boast of.

922. Indeed we cannot too often repeat the truth, that to deal for ready money only, in all the departments of domestic arrangement, is the truest economy.

923. Ready Money will always command the best and cheapest of every article of consumption, if expended with judgment: and the dealer, who intends to act fairly, will always prefer it.

924. Trust not him who seems more anxious to give credit than to receive cash.

925. The former hopes to secure custom by having a hold upon you in his books; and continues always to make up for his advance, either by an advanced price, or an inferior article; whilst the latter knows that your custom can only be secured by fair dealing.

926. There is, likewise, Another Consideration, as far as economy is concerned, which is not only to buy with ready money, but to buy at proper seasons; for there is with every article a cheap season and a dear one; and with none more than coals: insomuch that the master of a family who fills his coal cellar in the middle of the summer, rather than the beginning of the winter, will find it filled at less expense than it would otherwise cost him: and will be enabled to see December's snows falling without feeling his enjoyment of his fireside lessened by the consideration that the cheerful blaze is supplied at twice the rate that it need have done, if he had exercised more foresight.

927. We must now call to the recollection of our readers, that chimneys often smoke, and that coals are often wasted, by throwing too much fuel at once upon a fire.

928. To prove this Observation, it is only necessary to remove the superfluous coal from the top of the grate, when the smoking instantly ceases: as to the waste, that evidently proceeds from the frequent intemperate and injudicious use of the poker, which not only throws a great portion of the small coals among the cinders, but often extinguishes the fire it was intended to foster.

929. Whenever Oil is used for the purpose of artificial light, it should be kept free from all exposure to atmospheric air; as it is apt to absorb considerable quantities of oxygen. If oil is very coarse or tenacious, a very small quantity of oil of turpentine may be added.

930. Candles improve by keeping a few months. If wax candles become discoloured or soiled, they may be restored by rubbing them over with a clean flannel slightly dipped in spirits of wine.

931. In Lighting Candles, always hold the match to the side of the wick, and not over the top.

932. Night Lights.—Field's and Child's night lights are generally known and are easily obtainable. But under circumstances where they cannot be procured, the waste of candles may be thus applied. Make a *fine* cotton, and wax it with white wax. Then cut into the requisite lengths. Melt the grease and pour into pill boxes, previously either fixing the cotton in the centre, or dropping it in just before the grease sets. If a little white wax be melted with the grease, all the better. In this manner, the ends and drippings of candles may be used up. When set to burn, place in a saucer, with sufficient water to rise to the extent of the 16th of an inch around the base of the night light.

933. Revolving Ovens.—These ovens, which may probably be obtained through ironmongers and hardwaremen in the country by order, when suspended in front of any common fire by means of a bottle-jack or a common worsted string, will bake bread, cakes, pies, &c., in a much more equal and perfect manner than either a side oven or an American oven, without depriving the room of the heat and comfort of the fire. We have tested these facts, and can pronounce the revolving oven

to be a household treasure. By an ordinary fire, in any room in the house, it will bake a four-pound loaf in an hour and twenty minutes. It also bakes pastry remarkably well, and all the care it requires is merely to give it a look now and then to see that it keeps turning. In one family the saving has been found to be 3s. 6d. per week—a large proportion of the earnings of many poor families. The cost of the oven is 8s. 6d. We have no doubt that in many families the saving through grinding their own wheat, and baking their own bread by the means we have pointed out, will be as much as 10s. per week; and in large establishments, schools, &c., considerably more.

934. Yeast.—Boil, say on Monday morning, two ounces of the best hops in four quarts of water for half an hour; strain it, and let the liquor cool to new-milk warmth; then put in a small handful of salt and half a pound of sugar; beat up one pound of the best flour with some of the liquor, and then mix well all together. On Wednesday add three pounds of potatoes, boiled, and then mashed, to stand till Thursday; then strain it and put it into bottles, and it is ready for use. *It must be stirred frequently while it is making, and kept near the fire.* Before using, shake the bottle up well. It will keep in a cool place for two months, and is best at the latter part of the time. The beauty of this yeast is that it ferments spontaneously, not requiring the aid of other yeast; and if care be taken to let it ferment well in the earthen bowl in which it is made, you may cork it up tight when bottled. The quantity above given will fill four seltzer-water bottles. The writer of the above receipt has used this yeast for many months, and never had lighter bread than it affords, and never knew it to fail.

935. Yeast.—The following yeast has undergone the test of thirty-six years:—For a stone of flour (but a greater quantity does not require so much in proportion),—into two quarts of water put a nip (a quarter of an ounce) of hops, two potatoes sliced, a table-spoonful of malt or sugar (this may be omitted, but the yeast is better with it); boil for twenty minutes, strain through a sieve, let the liquor stand till new-milk warm, then add the quickening; let it stand in a large jar or jug till sufficiently risen; first put into an earthen bottle containing a pint or two quarts, according to the size of the baking, part of the yeast for a future quickening; let it stand uncorked an hour or two, and put into a cool place till wanted for a fresh making. For a first quickening a little German yeast will do. Any plain cook or housewife will readily make the yeast and use it. Put the remainder of it to half or more of the flour, and two quarts of warm water; stir well, let it stand to rise, knead up with the rest of the flour, put it into or upon tins, let it stand to rise, bake, and you will have good bread.

936. Domestic Yeast.—Ladies who are in the habit (and a most laudable and comfortable habit it is) of making domestic bread, cake, &c., are informed that they can easily manufacture their own yeast by attending to the following directions:—Boil one pound of good flour, a quarter of a pound of brown sugar, and a little salt, in two gallons of water, for one hour. When milk-warm, bottle it, and cork it close. It will be fit for use in twenty-four hours. One pint of this yeast will make eighteen pounds of bread.

937. Pure and Cheap Bread.— A friend informs us that for more than twelve months he has ground his own flour by a small hand-mill, which produces seventeen pounds of good meal bread for twenty pounds of wheat (quite good enough for any one to eat), and that since himself and family have used this bread they have never had occasion for medical advice. They also use the same meal for puddings, &c. The price of a mill is £4 10s. There are mills which grind and dress the wheat at one operation. To grind twenty pounds of wheat would take a boy or a servant about forty or fifty minutes. Such mills

may be obtained at any ironmonger's. The saving in the cost of bread amounts to nearly one-third, which would soon cover the cost of the mill, and effect a most important saving, besides promoting health, by avoiding the evil effects of adulterated flour.

938. Home-made Bread.—To one quartern of flour (three pounds and a half), add a dessertspoonful of salt, and mix them well; mix about two tablespoonfuls of good fresh yeast with half a pint of water a little warm, but not hot; make a hole with your hand in the middle of the flour, but not quite touching the bottom of the pan; pour the water and yeast into this hole, and stir it with a spoon till you have made a thin batter; sprinkle this over with flour, cover the pan over with a dry cloth, and let it stand in a warm room for an hour; not near the fire, except in cold weather, and then not too close; then add a pint of water a little warm, and knead the whole well together, till the dough comes clean through the hand (some flour will require a little more water; but in this, experience must be your guide); let it stand again for about a quarter of an hour, and then bake at pleasure.

939. Indian Corn Flour and Wheaten Bread.—The peculiarity of this bread consists in its being composed in part of Indian corn flour, which will be seen by the following analysis by the late Professor Johnston, to be much richer in gluten and fatty matter than the flour of wheat, to which circumstance it owes its highly nutritive character:—

	English Fine Wheaten Flour.	Indian Corn Flour.
Water	16	14
Gluten	10	12
Fat	2	8
Starch, &c..	72	66
	100	100

Take of Indian corn flour half a stone (7 lb.), pour upon it four quarts of boiling water, stirring it all the time; let it stand till about new-milk warm, then mix it with a stone of fine wheaten flour, to which a quarter of a pound of salt has been previously added. Make a depression on the surface of this mixture, and pour into it two quarts of yeast, which should be thickened to the consistence of cream with some of the flour; let it stand all night; on the following morning the whole should be well kneaded, and allowed to stand for three hours; then divide it into loaves, which are better baked in tins, in which they should stand for half an hour, then bake. Thirty-two pounds of wholesome, nutritive, and very agreeable bread will be the result. It is of importance that the flour of Indian corn should be procured, as Indian corn meal is that which is commonly met with at the shops, and the coarseness of the husk in the meal might to some persons be prejudicial.

940. To make Bread with German Yeast.—To one quartern of flour add a dessertspoonful of salt as before; dissolve one ounce of dried German yeast in about three tablespoonfuls of cold water, add to this one pint and a half of water a little warm, and pour the whole into the flour; knead it well immediately, and let it stand as before directed for one hour: then bake at pleasure. It will not hurt if you make up a peck of flour at once, and bake three or four loaves in succession, provided you do not keep the dough too warm. German yeast may be obtained at almost any corn-chandler's in the metropolis and suburbs. In winter it will keep good for a week in a dry place, and in summer it should be kept in cold water, and the water changed every day. Wheat meal requires a little more yeast than fine flour, or a longer time to stand in the dough for rising. For domestic baking, in the absence of a large oven, Ball's Portable Revolving Ovens can be used, in front of any fire; they bake equally, perfectly, and produce five pounds of bread from three pounds and a half of flour, without the addition of potatoes or rice. With one of these ovens and a good side oven you may make a double use of your fire, by baking at the side and in front at the same time; and where there is no side oven, or only a bad one, these ovens are invaluable. You may bake five pounds and a half of bread, or eight pounds of meat, in one hour and a half, without depriving the room of the heat or comfort of the fire: and two ovens may be used at the same time in front of an ordinary fire, side by side.

941. Unfermented Bread.—Three pounds wheat meal; half an ounce, avoirdupois, muriatic acid; half an ounce, avoirdupois, carbonate soda; water enough to make it of a proper consistence. For white flour, four pounds of flour; half an ounce, avoirdupois, muriatic acid; half an ounce, avoirdupois, carbonate soda; water, about a quart. The way of making is as follows:—First mix the soda and flour well together by rubbing in a pan; then pour the acid into the water, and mix well by stirring. Mix all together to the required consistence, and bake in a hot oven immediately. The gain from this method of baking is as follows:—four pounds of wheat meal made seven pounds nine ounces of excellent light bread; and four pounds of seconds flour made six pounds of excellent light bread. It keeps moist longer than bread made with yeast, and is far more sweet and digestible. This is especially recommended to persons who suffer from indigestion, who will find the brown bread invaluable.

942. Bread (Cheap and Excellent Kind).—Simmer slowly, over a gentle fire, a pound of rice in three quarts of water, till the rice has become perfectly soft, and the water is either evaporated or imbibed by the rice: let it become cool, but not cold, and mix it completely with four pounds of flour; add to it some salt, and about four tablespoonfuls of yeast. Knead it very thoroughly, for on this depends whether or not your good materials produce a superior article. Next let it rise well before the fire, make it up into loaves with a little of the flour—which, for that purpose, you must reserve from your four pounds—and bake it rather long. This is an exceedingly good and cheap bread.

943. Economical and Nourishing Bread.—Suffer the miller to remove from the flour only the coarse flake bran. Of this bran, boil five or six pounds in four and a half gallons of water; when the goodness is extracted from the bran,—during which time the liquor will waste half or three quarters of a gallon,—strain it and let it cool. When it has cooled down to the temperature of new milk, mix it with fifty-six pounds of flour, and as much salt and yeast as would be used for other bread; knead it exceedingly well; let it rise before the fire, and bake it in small loaves: small loaves are preferable to large ones, because they take the heat more equally. There are two advantages in making bread with bran water instead of plain water; the one being that there is considerable nourishment in bran, which is thus extracted and added to the bread; the other, that flour imbibes much more of bran water than it does of plain water; so much more, as to give in the bread produced almost a fifth in weight more than the quantity of flour made up with plain water would have done. These are important considerations to the poor. Fifty-six pounds of flour, made with plain water, would produce sixty-nine and a half pounds of bread; made with bran water, it will produce eighty-three and a half pounds.

944. A great increase on Homemade Bread, even equal to one-fifth, may be produced by using bran water for kneading the dough. The proportion is three pounds of bran for every twenty-eight pounds of flour, to be boiled for an hour, and then strained through a hair sieve.

945. Rye and Wheat Flour, in equal quantities, make an excellent and economical bread.

946. Potatoes in Bread.—Place in a large dish fifteen pounds of flour near the fire to warm; take five pounds of good potatoes, those of a mealy kind being preferable, peel and boil them as if for the table, mash them fine, and then mix with them as much cold water as will allow all except small lumps to pass through a coarse sieve into the flour, which will now be ready to receive them; add yeast, &c., and mix for bread in the usual way. This plan has been followed for some years, finding that bread made according to it is much superior to that made of flour only, and on this ground alone we recommend its adoption; but in addition to that, taking the high price of flour, and moderately low price of potatoes, here is a saving of over twenty per cent., which is surely an object worth attending to by those of limited means.

947. Use of Lime Water in making Bread.—It has lately been found that water saturated with lime produces in bread the same whiteness, softness, and capacity of retaining moisture, as results from the use of alum; while the former removes all acidity from the dough, and supplies an ingredient needed in the structure of the bones, but which is deficient in the *cerealia*. The best proportion to use is, five pounds of water saturated with lime, to every nineteen pounds of flour. No change is required in the process of baking. The lime most effectually coagulates the gluten, and the bread weighs well; bakers must therefore approve of its introduction, which is not injurious to the system, like alum, &c. A large quantity of this kind of bread is now made in Munich, and is highly esteemed.

948. Rice Bread.—Take one pound and a half of rice, and boil it gently over a slow fire in three quarts of water about five hours, stirring it, and afterwards beating it up into a smooth paste. Mix this, while warm, into two gallons or four pounds of flour, adding at the same time the usual quantity of yeast. Allow the dough to work a certain time near the fire, after which divide it into loaves, and it will be found, when baked, to produce twenty-eight or thirty pounds of excellent white bread.

949. Apple Bread.—A very light, pleasant bread is made in France by a mixture of apples and flour, in the proportion of one of the former to two of the latter. The usual quantity of yeast is employed, as in making common bread, and is beaten with flour and warm pulp of the apples after they have boiled, and the dough is then considered as set; it is then put in a proper vessel, and allowed to rise for eight or twelve hours, and then baked in long loaves. Very little water is requisite: none, generally, if the apples are very fresh.

950. Pulled Bread.—Take from the oven an ordinary loaf when it is about *half baked*, and with the fingers, while the bread is yet hot, dexterously pull the half-set dough into pieces of irregular shape, about the size of an egg. Don't attempt to smooth or flatten them —the rougher their shapes the better. Set upon tins, place in a very slow oven, and bake to a rich brown. This forms a deliciously crisp crust for cheese. If you do not bake at home, your baker will prepare it for you, if ordered. Pulled bread may be made in the revolving ovens. It is very nice with wine instead of biscuits.

951. French Bread and Rolls. —Take a pint and a half of milk; make it quite warm; half a pint of small-beer yeast; add sufficient flour to make it as thick as batter; put it into a pan; cover it over, and keep it warm: when it has risen as high as it will, add a quarter of a pint of warm water, and half an ounce of salt,—mix them well together,—rub into a little flour two ounces of butter; then make your dough, not quite so stiff as for your bread; let it stand for three quarters of an hour, and it will be ready to make into rolls, &c.:—let them stand till they have risen, and bake them in a quick oven.

952. Rolls.—Mix the salt with the flour. Make a deep hole in the middle. Stir the warm water into the yeast, and pour it into the hole in the flour. Stir it with a spoon just enough to make a thin batter, and sprinkle some flour over the top. Cover the pan, and set it in a warm place for several hours. When it is light, add half a pint more of lukewarm water, and make it, with a little more flour, into a dough. Knead it very well for ten minutes. Then divide it into small pieces, and knead each separately. Make them into round cakes or rolls. Cover them, and set them to rise about an hour and a half. Bake them, and, when done, let them remain in the oven, without the lid, for about ten minutes.

953. Sally Lunn Tea Cakes. —Take one pint of milk quite warm, a quarter of a pint of thick small-beer yeast; put them into a pan with flour sufficient to make it as thick as batter, —cover it over, and let it stand till it has risen as high as it will, *i. e.*, about two hours: add two ounces of lump sugar, dissolved in a quarter of a pint of warm milk, a quarter of a pound of butter rubbed into the flour very fine,—then make the dough the same as for French rolls, &c.; let it stand half an hour: then make up the cakes, and put them on tins:—when they have stood to rise, bake them in a quick oven. Care should be taken never to mix the yeast with water or milk too hot or too cold, as either extreme will destroy the fermentation. In summer it should be lukewarm,—in winter a little warmer, —and in very cold weather, warmer still. When it has first risen, if you are not prepared, it will not harm' if it stand an hour.

954. Baking, Boiling, Broiling, Frying, Roasting, Stewing, and Spoiling. — A DIALOGUE between the DUTCH OVEN, the SAUCE-PAN, the SPIT, the GRIDIRON, and the FRYING-PAN, with reflections thereupon, in which all housekeepers and cooks are invited to take an interest.

955. We were once standing by our scullery, when all of a sudden we heard a tremendous clash and jingle— the Saucepan had tumbled into the

Frying-pan; the Frying-pan had shot its handle through the ribs of the Gridiron; the Gridiron had bestowed a terrible thump upon the hollow head of the Dutch Oven; and the Spit had dealt a very skilful stroke, which shook the sides of all the combatants, and made them ring out the noises by which we were startled. Musing upon this incident, we fancied that we overheard the following dialogue :—

956. Frying-pan.— Hollo, Saucepan! what are you doing here, with your dropsical corporation? Quite time that you were superannuated; you are a mere meat-spoiler. You adulterate the juices of the best joint, and give to the stomach of our master little else than watery compounds to digest.

957. Saucepan.—Well! I like your conceit! You—who harden the fibre of flesh so much, that there is no telling whether a steak came from a bullock, a horse, or a bear!—who can't fry a slice of potato, or a miserable smelt, but you must be flooded with oil or fat, to keep your spiteful nature from burning or biting the morsel our master should enjoy. Not only that—you open your mouth so wide, that the soot of the chimney drops in, and frequently spoils our master's dinner; or you throw the fat over your sides, and set the chimney in a blaze!

958. Spit.—Go on! go on! six one, and half-a-dozen the other!

959. Dutch Oven.—Well, Mr. Spit, you needn't try to foment the quarrel. You require more attention than any of us; for if you are not continually watched, and helped by that useful little attendant of yours they call a Jack, your lazy, lanky figure would stand still, and you would expose the most delicious joint to the ravages of the fire. In fact, you need not only a Jack to keep you going, but a cook to constantly baste the joint confided to your care, without which our master would have but a dry bone to pick. Not only so, but you thrust your spear-like length through the best meat, and make an unsightly gash in a joint which otherwise might be an ornament to the table.

960. Spit.—What, Dutch Oven, is that you? venerable old sobersides, with a hood like a monk! Why, you are a mere dummy—as you are placed so you remain; there you stand in one place, gaping wide and catching the coals as they fall; if you were not well watched, you would burn the one half, and sodden the other, of whatever you were required to prepare. Bad luck to *your* impertinence!

961. Gridiron. — Peace! peace! We all have our merits and our demerits.—At this remark of the Gridiron, there was a general shout of laughter.

962. Saucepan.—Well, I declare! I never thought that I should have *my* merits classed with those of the miserable skeleton called a Gridiron. That is a joke! A thing with six ribs and a tail to compare with so useful a member of the *cuisine* community as myself! Why you, Gridiron, waste one half of the goodness of the meat in the fire, and the other half you send to the table tainted with smoke, and burnt to cinders!—A loud rattle of approbation went round, as the poor Gridiron fell under this torrent of derision from the Saucepan.

963. Coming away from the scene of confusion, I ordered the scullerymaid to go instantly and place each of the utensils that lay in disorder upon the ground, into its proper place, charging her to cleanse each carefully, until it should be required for use.

964. Returning to my library, I thought it would form no mean occupation were I to spend a few hours in reflection upon the relative claims of the disputants. I did so, and the following is the result :—

965. The Gridiron.—The Gridiron, though the simplest of cooking instruments, is by no means to be despised. The Gridiron, and indeed all cooking utensils, should be kept scrupulously clean; and when it is used, the bars should be allowed to get warm before the meat is placed upon it, otherwise the parts crossed by the bars will be insufficiently dressed. The fire should be sharp, clear, and free from smoke. The heat soon forms a film upon the surface of the meat, by which the juices are retained. Chops and steaks should not be too thick nor too thin. From a half to three quarters of an inch is the proper thickness. Avoid thrusting the fork into the meat, by which you release the juice. There is a description of gridiron in which the bars are grooved to catch the juice of the meat; but a much better invention is the upright gridiron, which is attached to the front of the grate, and has a pan at the bottom to catch the gravy. Kidneys, rashers, &c., dressed in this manner will be found delicious. There are some, however, who think that the dressing of meat *over* the fire secures a flavour which cannot otherwise be obtained. Remember that the Gridiron is devoted to the cooking of small dishes, or snacks, for breakfast, supper, and luncheon, and is therefore a most useful servant, ready at a moment's notice. Remember, also, that every moment which is lost, after the Gridiron has delivered up his charge, is a delay to the prejudice of the Gridiron. From the Gridiron to the table without loss of time should be the rule.

966. THE FRYING-PAN is less a favourite, in our estimation, than the Gridiron; but not to be despised, nevertheless. He is a noisy and a greasy servant, requiring much watchfulness. Like the Gridiron, the Frying-pan requires a clear but not a large fire, and the pan should be allowed to get thoroughly hot, and be well covered with fat, before meat is put into it. The excellence of frying very much depends upon the sweetness of the oil, butter, lard, or fat that may be employed. The Frying-pan is very useful in the warming of cold vegetables and other kinds of food, and in this respect may be considered a real friend of economy. All know the relish afforded by a pan-

cake—a treat which the Gridiron would be unable to afford us,—to say nothing of eggs and bacon, and various kinds of fish, to which both the Saucepan and the Gridiron are quite unsuited, because they require that which is the essence of frying, *boiling and browning in fat.*

967. THE SPIT is a very noble and very useful implement of cookery; as ancient, we presume, as he is straightforward at his work. Perhaps the process of roasting stands only second in the rank of excellence in cookery. The process is perfectly sound in its chemical effects upon the food, while the joint is kept so immediately under the eye of the cook, that it must be the fault of that functionary if it does not go to the table in the highest state of perfection. The process of roasting may be commenced very slowly, by the meat being kept a good distance from the fire, and gradually brought forward, until it is thoroughly soaked within and browned without. The Spit has this advantage over the Oven, and especially over the common oven, that the meat retains its own flavour, not having to encounter the evaporation from fifty different dishes, and that the steam from its own substance passes entirely away, leaving the essence of the meat in its primest condition.

968. THE DUTCH OVEN, though not so royal an instrument as the Spit, is, nevertheless, of great utility for small dishes of various kinds, which the Spit would spoil by the magnitude of its operations, or the Oven destroy by the severity of its heat. It combines, in fact, the advantages of roasting and baking, and may be adopted for compound dishes, and for warming cold scraps: it is easily heated, and causes no material expenditure of fuel.

969. THE SAUCEPAN. — When we come to speak of the Saucepan, we have to consider the claims of a very large, ancient, and useful family; and perhaps, looking at the generic orders of the Saucepan, all other cooking implements must yield to its claims. There are large saucepans, which we dignify with the name of Boilers, and small saucepans, which come under the denomination of Stewpans. There are few kinds of meat or fish which it will not receive, and dispose of in a satisfactory manner; and few vegetables for which it is not adapted. The Saucepan, rightly used, is a very economical servant, allowing nothing to be lost; that which escapes from the meat while in its charge forms broth, or may be made the basis of soups. Fat rises upon the surface of the water, and may be skimmed off; while in various stews it combines, in an eminent degree, what we may term the *fragrance* of cookery, and the *piquancy* of taste. The French are perfect masters of the use of the Stewpan. And we shall find that, as all cookery is but an aid to digestion, the operations of the Stewpan resemble the action of the stomach very closely. The stomach is a close sac, in which solids and fluids are mixed together, macerated in the gastric juice, and dissolved by the aid of heat and motion, occasioned by the continual contractions and relaxations of the coats of the stomach during the action of digestion. This is more closely resembled by the process of stewing than by any other of our culinary methods.

970. In this rapid review of the claims of various cooking utensils, we think that we have done justice to each. They all have their respective advantages; besides which, they contribute to the VARIETY presented by our tables, without which the routine of eating would be very monotonous and unsatisfactory.

971. There is one process to which we must yet allude—the process of SPOILING. Many cooks know how to *produce* a good dish, but too many of them know how to spoil it. They leave fifty things to be done just at the critical moment when the chief dish should be watched with an eye of keenness, and attended by a hand thoroughly expert. Having spent three hours in making a joint hot and rich, they forget that a

quarter of an hour, after it is taken from the fire, may impair or spoil all their labours. The serving up of a dinner may be likened to the assault upon Sebastopol. Looking upon the joint as the Malakoff, and the surrounding dishes as the redans, the bastions, and the forts, they should all be seized simultaneously, and made the prize of the commander-in-chief and his staff around the dinner-table. Such a victory will always do the cook the highest honour, and entitle him to the gratitude of the household.

972. Various Processes of Cooking.

i. "In the hands of an expert cook," says Majendie, "alimentary substances are made almost entirely to change their nature, their form, consistence, odour, savour, colour, chemical composition, &c.; everything is so modified, that it is often impossible for the most exquisite sense of taste to recognize the substance which makes up the basis of certain dishes. The greatest utility of the kitchen consists in making the food agreeable to the senses, and rendering it easy of digestion."

ii. To some extent the claims of either process of cooking depend upon the taste of the individual. Some persons may esteem the peculiar flavour of fried meats, while others will prefer broils or stews. It is important, however, to understand the theory of each method of cooking; so that whichever may be adopted, may be done well. Bad cooking, though by a good method, is far inferior to good cooking by a bad method.

973. Roasting. — BEEF. — The

noble sirloin of about fifteen pounds (if much thicker the outside will be done too much before the inner side is sufficiently roasted), will require to be before the fire about three and a half or four hours. Take care to spit it evenly, that it may not be heavier on one side than the other; put a little clean dripping into the dripping pan (tie a sheet of paper over it to preserve the fat), baste it well as soon as it is put down, and every quarter of an hour all the time it is roasting, till the last half-hour; then take off the paper and make some gravy for it, stir the fire and make it clear; to brown and froth it, sprinkle a little salt over it, baste it with butter, and dredge it with flour; let it go a few minutes longer, till the froth rises, take it up, put it on the dish, &c. Garnish it with hillocks of horseradish, scraped as fine as possible with a very sharp knife.

974. A YORKSHIRE PUDDING is an excellent accompaniment.

975. RIBS OF BEEF. — The three first ribs, of fifteen or twenty pounds, will take three hours, or three and a half; the fourth and fifth ribs will take as long, managed in the same way as the sirloin. Paper the fat and the thin part, or it will be done too much, before the thick part is done enough.

976. RIBS OF BEEF BONED AND ROLLED.—When you have kept two or three ribs of beef till quite tender, take out the bones, and skewer it as round as possible (like a fillet of veal): before they roll it, some cooks egg it, and sprinkle it with veal stuffing. As the meat is in a solid mass, it will require more time at the fire than in the preceding receipt: a piece of ten or twelve pounds weight will not be well and thoroughly roasted in less than four and a half or five hours. For the first half-hour it should not be less than twelve inches from the fire, that it may get gradually warm to the centre; the last half-hour before it is finished, sprinkle a little salt over it, and if you so wish, froth it, flour it, &c.

977. MUTTON.—As beef requires a large sound fire, mutton must have a brisk and sharp one: if you wish to have mutton tender it should be hung as long as it will keep, and then good eight-tooth, i. e., four years old mutton, is as good eating as venison.

978. THE LEG, HAUNCH, AND SADDLE, will be the better for being hung up in a cool airy place for four or five days at least; in temperate weather,

a week; in cold weather, ten days. A leg of eight pounds will take about two hours; let it be well basted.

979. A CHINE OR SADDLE—i. e., the two loins, of ten or eleven pounds—two hours and a half. It is the business of the butcher to take off the skin and skewer it on again, to defend the meat from extreme heat, and preserve its succulence. If this is neglected, tie a sheet of paper over it; baste the strings you tie it on with directly, or they will burn. About a quarter of an hour before you think it will be done, take off the skin or paper, that it may get a pale brown colour, and then baste it, and flour it lightly to froth it.

980. A SHOULDER, of seven pounds, an hour and a half. Put the spit in close to the shank-bone, and run it along the blade-bone.

981. A LOIN OF MUTTON, from an hour and a half to an hour and three quarters. The most elegant way of carving this is to cut it lengthwise, as you do a saddle. A neck, about the same time as a loin. It must be carefully jointed, or it is very difficult to carve.

982. THE NECK AND BREAST are, in small families, commonly roasted together. The cook will then crack the bones across the middle before they are put down to roast. If this is not done carefully, they are very troublesome to carve. A breast, an hour and a quarter.

983. A HAUNCH—i. e., the leg and part of the loin of mutton. Send up two sauce-boats with it; one of rich-drawn mutton gravy, made without spice or herbs, and the other of sweet sauce. It generally weighs about fifteen pounds, and requires about three hours and a half to roast it.

984. MUTTON (Venison fashion).— Take a neck of good four or five-year-old Southdown wether mutton, cut long in the bones; let it hang, in temperate weather, at least a week. Two days before you dress it, take allspice and black pepper, ground and pounded fine, a quarter of an ounce each, rub them together, and then rub your mutton well with this mixture twice a day.

When you dress it, wash off the spice with warm water, and roast it in paste.

985. VEAL requires particular care to roast it a nice brown. Let the fire be the same as for beef; a sound large fire for a large joint, and a brisker for a smaller: put it at some distance from the fire to soak thoroughly, and then draw it nearer to finish it brown. When first laid down it is to be basted; baste it again occasionally. When the veal is on the dish, pour over it half a pint of melted butter: if you have a little brown gravy by you, add that to the butter. With those joints which are not stuffed, send up forcemeat in balls, or rolled into sausages, as garnish to the dish, or fried pork sausages: bacon and greens are always expected with veal.

986. Fillet of Veal, of from twelve to sixteen pounds, will require from four to five hours at a good fire; make some stuffing or forcemeat, and put it under the flap, that there may be some left to eat cold, or to season a hash: brown it, and pour good melted butter over it. Garnish with thin slices of lemon, and cakes or balls of stuffing, or duck stuffing, or fried pork sausages, curry sauce, bacon and greens, &c.

987. A LOIN is the best part of the calf, and will take about three hours roasting. Paper the kidney fat, and the back: some cooks send it up on a toast, which is eaten with the kidney and the fat of this part, which is more delicate than any marrow, &c. If there is more of it than you think will be eaten with the veal, before you roast it cut it out, it will make an excellent suet pudding: take care to have your fire long enough to brown the ends.

988. A SHOULDER OF VEAL, from three hours to three hours and a half: stuff it with the forcemeat ordered for the fillet of veal, in the under side.

989. NECK, best end, will take two hours. The scrag part is best made into a pie or broth. Breast, from an hour and a half to two hours. Let the caul remain till it is almost done, then take it off, to brown it; baste, flour, and froth it.

990. VEAL SWEETBREAD.—Trim a fine sweetbread—it cannot be too fresh; parboil it for five minutes, and throw it into a basin of cold water; roast it plain, or beat up the yolk of an egg, and prepare some fine bread-crumbs. When the sweetbread is cold, dry it thoroughly in a cloth, run a lark spit or a skewer through it, and tie it on the ordinary spit; egg it with a paste brush, powder it well with bread-crumbs, and roast it. For sauce, fried bread-crumbs round it, and melted butter with a little mushroom ketchup and lemon juice, or serve on buttered toast, garnished with egg sauce, or with gravy.

991. LAMB is a delicate, and commonly considered tender meat; but those who talk of tender lamb, while they are thinking of the age of the animal, forget that even a chicken must be kept a proper time after it has been killed, or it will be tough picking. Woeful experience has warned us to beware of accepting an invitation to dinner on Easter Sunday; and unless commanded by a thorough-bred gourmand, our incisors, molars, and principal viscera, have protested against the imprudence of encountering young, tough stringy mutton under the misnomer of grass-lamb. To the usual accompaniments of roasted meat, green mint sauce or a salad is commonly added: and some cooks, about five minutes before it is done, sprinkle it with a little minced parsley.

992. GRASS-LAMB is in season from Easter to Michaelmas.

993. HOUSE-LAMB from Christmas to Lady-day.

994. WHEN GREEN MINT cannot be got, mint vinegar is an acceptable substitute for it.

995. HIND-QUARTER of eight pounds will take from an hour and three quarters to two hours; baste and froth it.

996. FORE-QUARTER of ten pounds, about two hours.

997. IT IS A PRETTY GENERAL CUSTOM, when you take off the shoulder from the ribs, to squeeze a Seville orange over them, and sprinkle them with a little pepper and salt.

998. LEG of five pounds, from an hour to an hour and a half.

999. SHOULDER, with a quick fire, an hour.

1000. RIBS, about an hour to an hour and a quarter; joint it nicely; crack the ribs across, and bend them up to make it easy to carve.

1001. LOIN, an hour and a quarter. Neck, an hour. Breast, three quarters of an hour.

1002. Poultry, Game, &c.

	H. M.
A small capon, fowl, or chicken, requires	0 20
A large fowl	0 45
A capon, full size	0 35
A goose	1 0
Wild ducks, and grouse	0 15
Pheasants, and Turkey poults	0 20
A moderate sized turkey, stuffed	1 15
Partridges	0 25
Quail	0 10
A hare, or rabbit . . . . about	1 0
Leg of pork, ¼ hour for each pound, and above that allowance	0 20
A chine of pork	0 20
A neck of mutton	1 30
A haunch of venison . . about	3 30

1003. ROASTING, BY CAUSING THE CONTRACTION of the cellular substance which contains the fat, expels more fat than boiling. The free escape of watery particles in the form of vapour, so necessary to produce flavour, must be regulated by frequent basting with the fat which has exuded from the meat, combined with a little salt and water—otherwise the meat would burn, and become hard and tasteless. A brisk fire at first will, by charring the outside, prevent the heat from penetrating, and therefore should only be employed when the meat is half roasted.

1004. THE LOSS BY ROASTING varies, according to Professor Donovan, from 14⅜ths to nearly double that rate per cent. The average loss on roasting butcher's meat is 22 per cent.; and on domestic poultry is 20¼.

1005. THE LOSS PER CENT. ON ROASTING BEEF, viz., on sirloins and ribs together, is 19½th; on mutton, viz., legs and shoulders together, 24⅜ths; on fore-quarters of lamb, 22½rd; on ducks, 27¼th; on turkeys, 20¼; on geese, 19¼; on chickens, 14⅜ths. So that it will be seen by comparison with the per-centage given of the loss by boiling, that roasting is not so economical; especially when we take into account that the loss of weight by boiling is not actual loss of economic materials, for we then possess the principal ingredients for soups; whereas, after roasting, the fat only remains. The average loss in boiling and roasting together is 18 per cent. according to Donovan, and 28 per cent. according to Wallace—a difference that may be accounted for by supposing a difference in the fatness of the meat, duration and degree of heat, &c., employed.

1006. Boiling.—This most simple of culinary processes is not often performed in perfection; it does not require quite so much nicety and attendance as roasting; to skim your pot well, and keep it really boiling (the slower the better) all the while—to know how long is required for doing the joint, &c., and to take it up at the critical moment when it is done enough—comprehends almost the whole art and mystery. This, however, demands a patient and perpetual vigilance, of which few persons are, unhappily, capable. The cook must take especial care that the water really boils all the while she is cooking, or she will be deceived in the time; and make up a sufficient fire (a frugal cook will manage with much less fire for boiling than she uses for roasting) at first, to last all the time, without much mending or stirring, and thereby save much trouble. When the pot is coming to a boil, there will always, from the cleanest meat and clearest water, rise a scum to the top of it; proceeding partly from the foulness of the meat, and partly from the water: this must be carefully taken off, as soon as it rises. On this depends the good appearance of all boiled things — an essential matter. When you have scummed well, put in some cold water, which will throw up the rest of the scum. The oftener it is scummed, and the clearer the surface of the water is kept, the cleaner will be the meat. If let alone, it soon boils down and sticks to the meat, which, instead of looking delicately white and nice, will have that coarse appearance we have too often to complain of, and the butcher and poulterer will be blamed for the carelessness of the cook, in not scumming her pot with due diligence. Many put in milk, to make what they boil look white, but this does more harm than good: others wrap it up in a cloth; but these are needless precautions; if the scum be attentively removed, meat will have a much more delicate colour and finer flavour that it has when muffled up. This may give rather more trouble—but those who wish to excel in their art must only consider how the processes of it can be most perfectly performed: a cook who has a proper pride and pleasure in her business will make this her maxim and rule on all occasions. Put your meat into cold water, in the proportion of about a quart of water to a pound of meat; it should be covered with water during the whole of the process of boiling, but not drowned in it; the less water, provided the meat be covered with it, the more savoury will be the meat, and the better will be the broth in every respect. The water should be heated gradually, according to the thickness, &c., of the article boiled; for instance, a leg of mutton of ten pounds weight should be placed over a moderate fire, which will gradually make the water hot, without causing it to boil for about forty minutes; if the water boils much sooner, the meat will be hardened, and shrink up as if it was scorched—by keeping the water a certain time heating without boiling, its fibres are dilated, and it yields a quantity of scum, which must be taken off as soon as it rises, for the reasons already mentioned. "If a vessel containing water be placed over a steady fire, the water will grow continually hotter, till it reaches the limit

of boiling; after which, the regular accessions of heat are wholly spent in converting it into steam: the water remains at the same pitch of temperature, however fiercely it boils. The only difference is, that with a strong fire it sooner comes to boil, and more quickly boils away, and is converted into steam." Such are the opinions stated by Buchanan in his "Economy of Fuel." There was placed a thermometer in water in that state which cooks call gentle simmering—the heat was 212°, i.e., the same degree as the strongest boiling. Two mutton chops were covered with cold water, and one boiled fiercely, and the other simmered gently, for three-quarters of an hour; the flavour of the chop which was simmered was decidedly superior to that which was boiled; the liquor which boiled fast was in like proportion more savoury, and, when cold, had much more fat on its surface; this explains why quick boiling renders meat hard, &c.—because its juices are extracted in a greater degree.

1007. RECKON THE TIME from the meat first coming to a boil. The old rule, of fifteen minutes to a pound of meat, we think rather too little; the slower it boils, the tenderer, the plumper, and whiter it will be. For those who choose their food thoroughly cooked (which all will who have any regard for their stomachs), twenty minutes to a pound will not be found too much for gentle simmering by the side of the fire; allowing more or less time, according to the thickness of the joint and the coldness of the weather; always remembering, the slower it boils the better. Without some practice it is difficult to teach any art; and cooks seem to suppose they must be right, if they put meat into a pot, and set it over the fire for a certain time—making no allowance, whether it simmers without a bubble, or boils at a gallop.

1008. FRESH KILLED MEAT will take much longer time boiling than that which has been kept till it is what the butchers call ripe, and longer in cold than in warm weather; if it be frozen, it must be thawed before boiling as before roasting; if it be fresh killed, it will be tough and hard, if you stew it ever so long, and ever so gently. In cold weather, the night before you dress it, bring it into a place of which the temperature is not less than forty-five degrees of Fahrenheit's thermometer. The size of the boiling-pots should be adapted to what they are to contain; the larger the saucepan the more room it takes upon the fire; and a larger quantity of water requires a proportionate increase of fire to boil it. In small families, we recommend block tin saucepans, &c., as lightest and safest: if proper care is taken of them, and they are well dried after they are cleansed, they are by far the cheapest; the purchase of a new tin saucepan being little more than the expense of tinning a copper one. Take care that the covers of your boiling-pots fit close, not only to prevent unnecessary evaporation of the water, but that the smoke may not insinuate itself under the edge of the lid, and give the meat a bad taste.

1009. THE FOLLOWING TABLE will be useful as an average of the time required to boil the various articles:—

	H.	M.
A ham, 20 lbs. weight, requires .	6	30
A tongue (if dry), after soaking .	4	0
A tongue out of pickle. . . 2¼ to	3	0
A neck of mutton	1	30
A chicken	0	20
A large fowl	0	45
A capon.	0	35
A pigeon	0	15

1010. IF YOU LET MEAT OR POULTRY REMAIN IN THE WATER after it is done enough, it will become sodden and lose its flavour.

1011. BEEF AND MUTTON a little underdone (especially very large joints, which will make the better hash or broil) is preferred by some people. Lamb, pork, and veal are uneatable if not thoroughly boiled,—but do not overdo them. A trivet, or fish-drainer, put on the bottom of the boiling-pot, raising the contents about an inch and a half from the bottom, will prevent that side of the meat which comes next the bottom being done too much, and the lower part will be as delicately done as the upper; and this will enable you to take out the meat without inserting a fork, &c., into it. If you have not a trivet, use four skewers, or a soup-plate laid the wrong side upwards.

1012. TAKE CARE OF THE LIQUOR you have boiled poultry or meat in; in five minutes you may make it into soup.

1013. THE GOOD HOUSEWIFE never boils a joint without converting the broth into some sort of soup.

1014. IF THE LIQUOR BE TOO SALT, use only half the quantity, and the rest water; wash salted meat well with cold water before you put it into the boiler.

1015. BOILING EXTRACTS A PORTION OF THE JUICE of meat, which mixes with the water, and also dissolves some of its solids; the more fusible parts of the fat melt out, combine with the water, and form soup or broth. The meat loses its red colour, becomes more savoury in taste and smell, and more firm and digestible. If the process is continued *too long*, the meat becomes indigestible, less succulent, and tough.

1016. THE LOSS BY BOILING varies, according to Professor Donovan, from 6¼ to 16 per cent. The average loss on boiling butcher's meat, pork, hams, and bacon, is 12; and on domestic poultry, is 14¾.

1017. THE LOSS PER CENT. on boiling salt beef is 15; on legs of mutton, 10; hams, 12¼; salt pork, 13½; knuckles of veal, 8½; bacon, 6½; turkeys, 16; chickens, 13½.

1018. Economy of Fat. — In most families many members are not fond of fat—servants seldom like it: consequently there is frequently much wasted; to avoid which, take off bits of suet fat from beefsteaks, &c., previous to cooking; they can be used for puddings. With good management there need be no waste in any shape or form.

1019. Broiling requires a brisk, rapid heat, which, by producing a greater degree of change in the affinities of the raw meat than roasting, generates a higher flavour, so that broiled meat is more savoury than roast. The surface becoming charred, a dark-coloured crust is formed, which retards the evaporation of the juices; and, therefore, if properly done, broiled may be as tender and juicy as roasted meat.

1020. Baking does not admit of the evaporation of the vapours so rapidly as by the processes of broiling and roasting; the fat is also retained more, and becomes converted, by the agency of the heat, into an empyreumatic oil, so as to render the meat less fitted for delicate stomachs, and more difficult to digest. The meat is, in fact, partly boiled in its own confined water, and partly roasted by the dry, hot air of the oven. The loss by baking has not been estimated; and, as the time required to cook many articles must vary with their size, nature, &c., we have considered it better to leave that until giving the receipts for them.

1021. Frying is of all methods the most objectionable, from the foods being less digestible when thus prepared, as the fat employed undergoes chemical changes. Olive oil in this respect is preferable to lard or butter. The crackling noise which accompanies the process of frying meat in a pan is occasioned by the explosions of steam formed in fat, the temperature of which is much above 212 degrees. If the meat is very juicy it will not fry well, because it becomes sodden before the water is evaporated; and it will not brown, because the temperature is too low to scorch it. To fry fish well the fat should be boiling hot (600 degrees), and the fish *well dried* in a cloth; otherwise, owing to the generation of steam, the temperature will fall so low that it will be boiled in its own steam, and not be browned. Meat, or indeed any article, should be frequently turned and agitated during frying, to promote the evaporation of the watery particles. To make fried things look well, they should be done over *twice* with egg and stale bread-crumbs.

1022. Bastings.—i. Fresh butter; ii. clarified suet; iii. minced sweet herbs, butter, and claret, especially for mutton and lamb; iv. water and salt; v. cream and melted butter, especially for a flayed pig; vi. yolks of eggs, grated biscuit, and juice of oranges.

1023. Dredgings.—i. Flour mixed with grated bread; ii. sweet herbs dried and powdered, and mixed with grated bread; iii. lemon-peel dried and pounded, or orange-peel, mixed with flour; iv. sugar finely powdered, and mixed with pounded cinnamon, and flour or grated bread; v. fennel seeds, corianders, cinnamon, and sugar, finely beaten, and mixed with grated bread or flour; vi. for young pigs, grated bread or flour, mixed with beaten nutmeg, ginger, pepper, sugar, and yolks of eggs; vii. sugar, bread, and salt mixed.

1024. The Housewife who is anxious to dress no more meat than will suffice for the meal, should know that beef loses about one pound in four in boiling, but in roasting, loses in the proportion of one pound five ounces, and in baking about two ounces less, or one pound three ounces; mutton loses in boiling about fourteen ounces in four pounds; in roasting, one pound six ounces.

1025. Cooks should be cautioned against the use of charcoal in any quantity, except where there is a free current of air; for charcoal is highly prejudicial in a state of ignition, although it may be rendered even actively beneficial when boiled, as a small quantity of it, if boiled with meat on the turn, will effectually cure the unpleasant taint.

1026. Preparation of Vegetables.—There is nothing in which the difference between an elegant and an ordinary table is more seen, than in the dressing of vegetables, more especially of greens; they may be equally as fine at first, at one place as at another, but their look and taste are afterwards very different, entirely from the careless way in which they have been cooked. They are in greatest perfection when in greatest plenty, *i. e.*, when in full season. By season, we do not mean those early days, when luxury in the buyers, and avarice in the sellers about London, force the various vegetables, but the time of the year in which, by nature and common culture; and the mere operation of the sun and climate, they are most plenteous and in perfection.

1027. POTATOES and peas are seldom worth eating before Midsummer.

1028. UNRIPE VEGETABLES are as insipid and unwholesome as unripe fruits.

1029. AS TO THE QUALITY OF VEGETABLES, the middle size are preferred to the largest or the smallest; they are more tender, juicy, and full of flavour, just before they are quite full-grown: freshness is their chief value and excellence, and I should as soon think of roasting an animal alive, as of boiling vegetables after they are dead. The eye easily discovers if they have been kept too long; they soon lose their beauty in all respects.

1030. ROOTS, GREENS, SALADS, &c., and the various productions of the garden, when first gathered, are plump and firm, and have a fragrant freshness no art can give them again; though it will refresh them a little to put them into cold spring water for some time before they are dressed.

1031. To Boil Vegetables.— Soft water will preserve the colour best of such as are green; if you have only hard water, put to it a teaspoonful of carbonate of potash.

1032. TAKE CARE TO WASH AND CLEANSE THEM thoroughly from dust, dirt, and insects,—this requires great attention. Pick off all the outside leaves, trim the vegetables nicely, and if they are not quite fresh-gathered and have become flaccid, it is absolutely necessary to restore their crispness before cooking them, or they will be tough and unpleasant; lay them in a pan of clean water, with a handful of salt in it, for an hour before you dress them. Most

vegetables being more or less succulent, their full proportion of fluids is necessary for their retaining that state of crispness and plumpness which they have when growing.

1033. ON BEING CUT OR GATHERED, the exhalation from their surface continues, while from the open vessels of the cut surface there is often great exudation or evaporation, and thus their natural moisture is diminished; the tender leaves become flaccid, and the thicker masses or roots lose their plumpness. This is not only less pleasant to the eye, but is a serious injury to the nutritious powers of the vegetable; for in this flaccid and shrivelled state its fibres are less easily divided in chewing, and the water which exists in the form of their respective natural juices, is less directly nutritious.

1034. THE FIRST CARE IN THE PRESERVATION OF SUCCULENT VEGETABLES, therefore, is to prevent them from losing their natural moisture. They should always be boiled in a saucepan by themselves, and have plenty of water: if meat is boiled with them in the same pot, they will spoil the look and taste of each other.

1035. To HAVE VEGETABLES DELICATELY CLEAN, put on your pot, make it boil, put a little salt in, and skim it perfectly clean before you put in the greens, &c., which should not be put in till the water boils briskly; the quicker they boil the greener they will be.

1036. WHEN THE VEGETABLES SINK, they are generally done enough, if the water has been kept constantly boiling. Take them up immediately, or they will lose their colour and goodness. Drain the water from them thoroughly before you send them to table. This branch of cookery requires the most vigilant attention.

1037. IF VEGETABLES are a minute or two too long over the fire, they lose all their beauty and flavour.

1038. IF NOT THOROUGHLY BOILED TENDER, they are tremendously indigestible, and much more troublesome during their residence in the stomach than underdone meats.

1039. TAKE CARE YOUR VEGETABLES ARE FRESH.—To preserve or give colour in cookery many good dishes are spoiled; but the rational epicure, who makes nourishment the main end of eating, will be content to sacrifice the shadow to enjoy the substance. As the fishmonger often suffers for the sins of the cook, so the cook often gets undeservedly blamed · instead of the greengrocer.

1040. TO CLEANSE VEGETABLES OF INSECTS.—Make a strong brine of one pound and a half of salt to one gallon of water; into this, place the vegetables with the stalk ends uppermost, for two or three hours: this will destroy all the insects which cluster in the leaves, and they will fall out and sink to the bottom of the water.

1041. Potatoes. — We are all potato eaters (for ourselves, we esteem potatoes beyond any other vegetable), yet few persons know how to cook them. Shall we be bold enough to commence our hints by presuming to inform our "grandmothers" how

1042. TO BOIL POTATOES. — Put them into a saucepan with scarcely sufficient water to cover them. Directly the skins begin to break, lift them from the fire, and as rapidly as possible pour off *every drop* of the water. Then place a coarse (we need not say clean) towel over them, and return them to the fire again until they are thoroughly done, and quite dry. A little salt, to flavour, should be added to the water before boiling.

1043. POTATOES FRIED WITH FISH. —Take cold fish and cold potatoes. Pick all the bones from the former, and mash the fish and the potatoes together; form into rolls, and fry with lard until the outsides are brown and crisp. For this purpose, the drier kinds of fish, such as cod, hake, &c., are preferable; turbot, soles, eels, &c., are not so good. This is an economical and excellent relish.

1044. POTATOES MASHED WITH ONIONS.—Prepare some boiled onions, by putting them through a sieve, and mix them with potatoes. Regulate the portions according to taste.

1045. POTATO CHEESECAKES.—One pound of mashed potatoes, quarter of a pound of currants, quarter of a pound of sugar and butter, and four eggs, to be well mixed together; bake them in patty-pans, having first lined them with puff paste.

1046. POTATO COLCANON. — Boil potatoes and greens and spinach, separately; mash the potatoes; squeeze the greens dry; chop them quite fine, and mix them with the potatoes with a little butter, pepper, and salt. Put into a mould, buttering it well first: let it stand in a hot oven for ten minutes.

1047. POTATOES ROASTED UNDER MEAT.—Half boil large potatoes; drain the water; put them into an earthen dish, or small tin pan, under meat roasting before the fire; baste them with the dripping. Turn them to brown on all sides; send up in a separate dish.

1048. POTATO BALLS RAGOUT.— Add to a pound of potatoes a quarter of a pound of grated ham, or some sweet herbs, or chopped parsley, an onion or shalot, salt, pepper, and a little grated nutmeg, and other spice, with the yolk of a couple of eggs; then dress as *Potatoes Escalloped*.

1049. POTATO SNOW. — Pick out the whitest potatoes, put them on in cold water; when they begin to crack, strain, and put them in a clean stewpan before the fire till they are quite dry, and fall to pieces; rub them through a wire sieve upon the dish they are to be sent up on, and do not disturb them afterwards.

1050. POTATOES FRIED WHOLE.— When nearly boiled enough, put them into a stewpan with a bit of butter, or some clean beef dripping; shake them about often, to prevent burning, till they are brown and crisp; drain them from the fat. It will be an improvement if they are floured and dipped into the yolk of an egg, and then rolled in finely· sifted bread-crumbs. .

1051. POTATOES FRIED IN SLICES.
—Peel large potatoes, slice them about
a quarter of an inch thick, or cut them
into shavings, as you would peel a
lemon; dry them well in a clean cloth,
and fry them in lard or dripping. Take
care that the fat and frying-pan are
quite clean; put it on a quick fire, and
as soon as the lard boils, and is still, put
in the slices of potato, and keep moving
them until they are crisp; take them
up, and lay them to drain on a sieve.
Send to table with a little salt sprinkled
over them.

1052. POTATOES ESCALLOPED.—
Mash potatoes in the usual way; then
butter some nice clean scollop-shells,
patty-pans, or tea cups or saucers; put
in your potatoes; make them smooth at
the top; cross a knife over them; strew a
few fine bread-crumbs on them; sprinkle
them with a paste-brush with a few drops
of melted butter, and set them in a Dutch
oven. When nicely browned on the top,
take them carefully out of the shells,
and brown on the other side. Cold potatoes may be warmed up this way.

1053. POTATO SCONES.—Mash boiled
potatoes till they are quite smooth, adding a little salt; then knead out the flour,
or barley-meal, to the thickness required;
toast on the girdle, pricking them with
a fork to prevent them blistering. When
eaten with fresh or salt butter they are
equal to crumpets—even superior, and
very nutritious.

1054. POTATO PIE.—Peel and slice
your potatoes very thinly into a pie-
dish; between each layer of potatoes
put a little chopped onion, and sprinkle
a little pepper and salt; put in a little
water, and cut about two ounces of
fresh butter into bits, and lay them
on the top; cover it close with paste.
The yolks of four eggs may be added;
and when baked, a tablespoonful of good
mushroom ketchup poured in through
a funnel. Another method is to put
between the layers small bits of mutton, beef, or pork. In Cornwall, turnips are added. This constitutes (on
the Cornish method) a cheap and satisfactory dish for families.

1055. COLD POTATOES.—There are
few articles in families more subject to
waste, whether in paring, boiling, or
being actually wasted, than potatoes; and there are few cooks who do
not boil twice as many potatoes every
day as are wanted, and fewer still who
do not throw the residue away as being
totally unfit in any shape for the next
day's meal; yet if they would take the
trouble to beat up the despised cold
potatoes with an equal quantity of flour,
they would find them produce a much
lighter dumpling or pudding than they
can make with flour alone; and by the
aid of a few spoonfuls of good gravy,
they will provide a cheap and agreeable
appendage to the dinner table.

**1056. MASHED POTATOES AND
SPINACH OR CABBAGE.**—Moisten cold
mashed potatoes with a little white
sauce: take cold cabbage or spinach,
and chop it very finely. Moisten with
a brown gravy. Fill a tin mould
with layers of potatoes and cabbage;
cover the top, and put it into a stewpan of boiling water. Let it remain
long enough to warm the vegetables;
then turn the vegetables out and serve
them. Prepare by boiling the vegetables separately, and put them into
the mould in layers, to be turned out
when wanted. It forms a very pretty
dish for an entrée.

**1057. Cold Carrots and Tur-
nips.**—These may be added to soups, if
they have not been mixed with gravies:
or if warmed up separately, and put into
moulds in layers, they may be turned
out, and served the same as the potatoes and cabbage described above.

1058. French Beans.—Cut away
the stalk end, and strip off the strings,
then cut them into shreds. If not quite
fresh, have a basin of spring water,
with a little salt dissolved in it, and as
the beans are cleaned and stringed
throw them in: put them on the fire in
boiling water, with some salt in it; after
they have boiled fifteen or twenty
minutes, take one out and taste it; as
soon as they are tender take them up,
throw them into a cullender or sieve to

drain. Send up the beans whole when they are very young. When they are very large they look pretty cut into lozenges.

1059. Boiled Turnip Radishes. — Boil in plenty of salted water, and in about twenty-five minutes they will be tender; drain well, and send them to table with melted butter. Common radishes, when young, tied in bunches, boiled for twenty minutes, and served on a toast, are excellent.

1060. Asparagus (often miscalled "*asparagrass*"). — Scrape the stalks till they are clean; throw them into a pan of cold water, tie them up in bundles of about a quarter of a hundred each; cut off the stalks at the bottom to a uniform length, leaving enough to serve as a handle for the green part; put them into a stewpan of boiling water, with a handful of salt in it. Let it boil, and skim it. When they are tender at the stalk, which will be in from twenty to thirty minutes, they are done enough. Watch the exact time of their becoming tender; take them up that instant. While the asparagus is boiling, toast a round of a quartern loaf, about half an inch thick; brown it delicately on both sides; dip it lightly in the liquor the asparagus was boiled in, and lay it in the middle of a dish; melt some butter, but do not put it over them. Serve butter in a butter-boat.

1061. Artichokes. — Soak them in cold water, wash them well; put them into plenty of boiling water, with a handful of salt, and let them boil gently for an hour and a half or two hours; trim them and drain on a sieve; send up melted butter with them, which some put into small cups, one for each guest.

1062. Stewed Water-Cress. — The following receipt may be new, and will be found an agreeable and wholesome dish :—Lay the cress in strong salt and water, to clear it from insects. Pick and wash nicely, and stew it in water for about ten minutes; drain and chop, season with pepper and salt, add a little butter, and return it to the stewpan until well heated. Add a little vinegar previously to serving; put around it sippets of toast or fried bread. The above, made thin, as a substitute for parsley and butter, will be found an excellent sauce for a boiled fowl. There should be more of the cress considerably than of the parsley, as the flavour is much milder.

1063. Stewed Mushrooms. — Cut off the ends of the stalks, and pare neatly some middle-sized or button mushrooms, and put them into a basin of water with the juice of a lemon as they are done. When all are prepared, take them from the water with the hands to avoid the sediment, and put them into a stewpan with a little fresh butter, white pepper, salt, and a little lemon juice; cover the pan close, and let them stew gently for twenty minutes or half an hour; then thicken the butter with a spoonful of flour, and add gradually sufficient cream, or cream and milk, to make the same about the thickness of good cream. Season the sauce to palate, adding a little pounded mace or grated nutmeg. Let the whole stew gently until the mushrooms are tender. Remove every particle of butter which may be floating on the top before serving.

1064. Camp Cookery. — The following seven receipts were forwarded to us during the time of the Crimean War, from the Barrack Hospital at Scutari, by our late personal friend, Alexis Soyer. We may add, that we enjoyed the intimate acquaintance of M. Soyer during the period he was chief cook of the Reform Club, and we are indebted to him for many useful suggestions contained in this volume.

1065. Stewed Salt Beef and Pork a la Omar Pasha.—Put into a canteen saucepan about two pounds of well soaked beef, cut in eight pieces; half a pound of salt pork, divided in two, and also soaked; half a pound of rice, or six tablespoonfuls; a quarter of a pound of onions, or four middle-sized ones, peeled and sliced; two ounces of brown sugar, or a large tablespoonful; a quarter of an ounce of pepper, and five pints of water; simmer gently for three hours, remove the fat from the top, and serve. M. Soyer says, "The first time I made the above was in Sir John Campbell's camp kitchen, situated on the top of his rocky cavern, facing Sebastopol, near Cathcart's Hill, and among the distinguished pupils I had upon the occasion were Colonel Wyndham, Sir John Campbell, and Dr. Hall, Inspector General of the army in the Crimea, and other officers. This dish was much approved at dinner, and is enough for six people, and it cannot fail to be excellent if the receipt be closely followed." The London salt meat will require only a four hours' soaking, having been but lightly pickled.

1066. MUTTON SOUP. — Put the rations of six into a pan (half a pound of mutton will make a pint of good family soup), — six pounds of mutton, cut in four or six pieces; three quarters of a pound of mixed vegetables, or three ounces of preserved, as compressed vegetables are daily given to the troops; three and a half teaspoonfuls of salt; one teaspoonful of sugar, and half a teaspoonful of pepper, if handy; five tablespoonfuls of barley or rice; eight pints of water; let it simmer gently for three hours and a half, remove the fat, and serve. Bread and biscuit may be added in small quantities.

1067. PLAIN PEA SOUP.—Put in a pan six pounds of pork, well soaked and cut into eight pieces; pour six quarts of water over; one pound of split peas; one teaspoonful of sugar; half a teaspoonful of pepper; four ounces of fresh vegetables, or two ounces of preserved, if handy; let it boil gently for two hours, or until the peas are tender. When the pork is rather fat, as is generally the case, wash it only; a quarter of a pound of broken biscuit may be used for the soup. Salt beef, when rather fat and soaked, may be used for pea soup.

1068. FRENCH BEEF SOUP, OR POT AU FEU (CAMP FASHION).—Put into the kettle six pounds of beef, cut into two or three pieces, bone included; one pound of mixed green vegetables, or half a pound of preserved, in cakes; four teaspoonfuls of salt: if handy, one teaspoonful of pepper, one of sugar, and three cloves; and eight pints of water. Let it boil gently three hours; remove some of the fat, and serve. The addition of a pound and a half of bread, cut into slices, or one pound of broken biscuits, well soaked, will make a very nutritious soup. Skimming is not required.

1069. HOW TO STEW FRESH BEEF, PORK, MUTTON, AND VEAL. — Cut or chop two pounds of fresh beef into ten or twelve pieces; put these into a saucepan with one and a half teaspoonful of salt, one teaspoonful of sugar, half a teaspoonful of pepper, two middle-sized onions sliced, half a pint of water. Set on the fire for ten minutes until forming a thick gravy. Add a good tablespoonful of flour, stir on the fire a few minutes; add a quart and a half of water; let the whole simmer until the meat is tender. Beef will take from two hours and a half to three hours; mutton and pork, about two hours; veal, one hour and a quarter to one hour and a half; onions, sugar, and pepper, if not to be had, must be omitted; it will even then make a good dish; half a pound of sliced potatoes, or two ounces of preserved potatoes; ration vegetables may be added, also a small dumpling.

1070. PLAIN BOILED BEEF. — For six rations, put in a canteen saucepan six pounds of well soaked beef, cut in two, with three quarts of cold water; simmer gently three hours, and serve. About a pound of either carrots, turnips, parsnips, greens, or cabbage, as well as dumplings, may be boiled with it.

1071. COSSACK'S PLUM PUDDING.— Put into a basin one pound of flour, three quarters of a pound of raisins (stoned, if time be allowed), three quarters of a pound of the fat of salt pork (well washed, cut into small squares, or chopped), two tablespoonfuls of sugar or treacle; and half a pint of water;

mix all together; put into a cloth tied lightly; boil for four hours, and serve. If time will not admit, boil only two hours, though four are preferable. How to spoil the above:—Add anything to it.

1072. Cooking Meat.

1073. Beef Minced.— Cut into small dice remains of cold beef: the gravy reserved from it on the first day of it being served should be put in the stewpan, with the addition of warm water, some mace, sliced shalot, salt, and black pepper. Let the whole simmer gently for an hour. A few minutes before it is served, take out the meat and dish it; add to the gravy some walnut ketchup, and a little lemon juice or walnut pickle. Boil up the gravy once more, and, when hot, pour it over the meat. Serve it with bread sippets.

1074. Beef (with Mashed Potatoes).—Mash some potatoes with hot milk, the yolk of an egg, some butter and salt. Slice the cold beef and lay it at the bottom of a pie-dish, adding to it some sliced shalot, pepper, salt, and a little beef gravy; cover the whole with a thick paste of potatoes, making the crust to rise in the centre above the edges of the dish. Score the potato crust with the point of a knife in squares of equal sizes. Put the dish before a fire in a Dutch oven, and brown it on all sides; by the time it is coloured, the meat and potatoes will be sufficiently done.

1075. Beef Bubble and Squeak.—Cut into pieces convenient for frying, cold roasted or boiled beef; pepper, salt, and fry them; when done, lay them on a hot drainer, and while the meat is draining from the fat used in frying them, have in readiness a cabbage already boiled in two waters; chop it small, and put it in the frying-pan with some butter, add a little pepper and keep stirring it, that all of it may be equally done. When taken from the fire, sprinkle over the cabbage a very little vinegar, only enough to give it a slightly acid taste. Place the cabbage in the centre of the dish, and arrange the slices of meat neatly around it.

1076. Beef or Mutton Lobscous.—Mince, not too finely, some cold roasted beef or mutton. Chop the bones, and put them in a saucepan with six potatoes peeled and sliced, one onion, also sliced, some pepper, and salt; of these make a gravy. When the potatoes are completely incorporated with the gravy, take out the bones and put in the meat; stew the whole together for an hour before it is to be served.

1077. Beef Rissoles. — Mince and season cold beef, and flavour it with mushroom or walnut ketchup. Make of beef dripping a very thin paste, roll it out in thin pieces, about four inches square; enclose in each piece some of the mince, in the same way as for puffs, cutting each neatly all round: fry them in dripping to a very light brown. The paste can scarcely be rolled out too thin.

1078. Veal Minced.—Cut veal from the fillet or shoulder into very small dice; put into veal or mutton broth with a little mace, white pepper, salt, some lemon peel grated, and a tablespoonful of mushroom ketchup or mushroom powder, rubbed smooth into the gravy. Take out some of the gravy when nearly done, and when cool enough thicken it with flour, cream, and a little butter; boil it up with the rest of the gravy, and pour it over the meat when done. Garnish with bread sippets. A little lemon juice added to the gravy improves its flavour.

1079. Veal dressed with White Sauce.—Boil milk or cream with a thickening of flour and butter; put into it thin slices of cold veal, and simmer it in the gravy till it is made hot without boiling. When nearly done, beat up the yolk of an egg, with a little anchovy and white sauce; pour it gently to the rest, stirring it all the time; simmer again the whole together, and serve it with sippets of bread and curled bacon alternately.

1080. Veal Rissoles.—Mince and pound veal extremely fine; grate into it some remains of cooked ham. Mix these well together with white sauce, flavoured with mushrooms: form this mixture into balls, and enclose each in pastry. Fry them in butter to a light brown. The same mince may be fried in balls without pastry, being first cemented together with egg and bread-crumbs.

1081. Mutton Hashed.—Cut cold mutton into thin slices, fat and lean together; make gravy with the bones whence the meat has been taken, boiling them long enough in water, with onion, pepper, and salt; strain the gravy, and warm, but do not boil, the mutton in it. Then take out some of the gravy to thicken it with flour and butter, and flavour it with mushroom ketchup. Pour in the thickening and boil it up, having previously taken out the meat, and placed it neatly on the dish in which it is to go to the table. Pour over it the boiling gravy, and add sippets of bread.

1082. Lamb.—Fry slices or chops of lamb in butter till they are slightly browned. Serve them on a *purée* of cucumbers, or on a dish of spinach; or dip the slices in bread-crumbs, chopped parsley, and yolk of an egg; some grated lemon and a little nutmeg may be added. Fry them, and pour a little nice gravy over them when served.

1083. Pork.—Slices of cold pork, fried and laid on apple sauce, form an excellent side or corner dish. Boiled pork may also be made into rissoles, minced very fine like sausage meat, and seasoned sufficiently, but not over much.

1084. Round of Salt Beef.—Skewer it tight and round, and tie a fillet of broad tape about it. Put it into plenty of cold water, and carefully remove the scum; let it boil till all the scum is removed, and then put the boiler on one side of the fire, to continue simmering slowly till it is done. Half a round may be boiled for a small family. When you take it up, wash the scum off with a paste-brush—garnish with carrots and turnips.

1085. Aitchbone of Beef.—Ma-

nage in the same way as the round. The soft, marrow-like fat which lies on the back is best when hot, and the hard fat of the upper corner is best cold.

1086. Stewed Brisket of Beef.—Stew in sufficient water to cover the meat; when tender, take out the bones, and skim off the fat; add to the gravy, when strained, a glass of wine, and a little spice tied up in a muslin bag. (This can be omitted if preferred.) Have ready either mushrooms, truffles, or vegetables boiled, and cut into shapes. Lay them on and around the beef; reduce part of the gravy to glaze, lay it on the top, and pour the remainder into the dish.

1087. Beef Brisket may be baked, the bones being removed, and the holes filled with oysters, fat bacon, parsley, or all three in separate holes; these stuffings being chopped and seasoned to taste. Dredge it well with flour, pour upon it half a pint of broth, bake for three hours, skim off the fat, strain the gravy over the meat, and garnish with cut pickles.

1088. Pork, Spare-rib.—Joint it nicely before roasting, and crack the ribs across as lamb. Take care not to have the fire too fierce. The joint should be basted with very little butter and flour, and may be sprinkled with fine dried sage. It takes from two to three hours. Apple sauce, mashed potatoes, and greens, are the proper accompaniments, also good mustard, fresh made.

1089. Lamb Stove or Lamb Stew.—Take a lamb's head and lights, open the jaws of the head, and wash them thoroughly; put them in a pot with some beef stock, made with three quarts of water, and two pounds of shin of beef, strained; boil very slowly for an hour; wash and string two or three good handfuls of spinach; put it in twenty minutes before serving; add a little parsley, and one or two onions, a short time before it comes off the fire; season with pepper and salt, and serve all together in a tureen.

1090. Roast Beef Bones furnish a very relishing luncheon or supper, prepared with poached or fried eggs and mashed potatoes as accompaniments. Divide the bones, leaving good pickings of meat on each; score them in squares, pour a little melted butter over, and sprinkle with pepper and salt; put them on a dish; set in a Dutch oven for half or three quarters of an hour, according to the thickness of the meat; keep turning till they are quite hot and brown: or broil them on the gridiron. Brown but do not burn them. Serve with grill sauce.

1091. Marrow Bones.—Saw the bones evenly, so that they will stand steadily; put a piece of paste into the ends; set them upright in a saucepan, and boil till they are done enough,—a beef marrow bone will require from an hour and a half to two hours; serve fresh-toasted bread with them.

1092. Beef (Rump) Steak and Onion Sauce.—Peel and slice two large onions, put them into a quart stewpan, with two tablespoonfuls of water; cover the pan close, and set on a slow fire till the water has boiled away, and the onions have become a little browned; then add half a pint of good broth, and boil the onions till they are tender; strain the broth, and chop very fine; season with mushroom ketchup, pepper, and salt; put in the onions then, and let them boil gently for five minutes, pour into the dish, and lay over it a broiled rump steak. If instead of broth you use good beef gravy, it will be delicious.

1093. Beef Alamode and Veal ditto.—Take about eleven pounds of the mouse buttock,—or clod of beef,— or blade bone,—or the sticking-piece, or the like weight of the breast of veal ;— cut it into pieces of three or four ounces each ; put in three or four ounces of beef dripping, and mince a couple of large onions, and lay them into a large deep stewpan. As soon as it is quite hot, flour the meat, put it into the stewpan, continue stirring with a wooden spoon: when it has been on about ten minutes, dredge with flour, and keep doing so

till you have stirred in as much as you think will thicken it; then add by degrees about a gallon of boiling water; keep stirring it together; skim it when it boils, and then put in one drachm of ground black pepper, two of allspice, and two bay-leaves; set the pan by the side of the fire, or at a distance over it, and let it stew very slowly for about three hours: when you find the meat sufficiently tender, put it into a tureen, and it is ready for table.

1094. Ox-Cheek Stewed.—Prepare the day before it is to be eaten; clean the cheek and put it into soft water, just warm; let it lie for three or four hours, then put it into cold water, to soak all night; next day wipe it clean, put it into a stewpan, and just cover it with water; skim it well when it is coming to a boil, then put two whole onions, stick two or three cloves into each, three turnips quartered, a couple of carrots sliced, two bay-leaves, and twenty-four corns of allspice, a head of celery, and a bundle of sweet herbs, pepper, and salt; add cayenne and garlic, in such proportions as the palate that requires them may desire. Let it stew gently till perfectly tender, about three hours; then take out the cheek, divide into pieces fit to help at table; skim, and strain the gravy; melt an ounce and a half of butter in a stewpan; stir into it as much flour as it will take up; mix with it by degrees a pint and a half of the gravy; add a tablespoonful of mushroom or walnut ketchup, or port wine, and boil a short time. Serve up in a soup or ragout dish, or make it into barley broth. This is a very economical, nourishing, and savoury meal.

1095. Hashed Mutton or Beef.—Slice the meat small, trim off the brown edges, and stew down the trimmings with the bones, well broken, an onion, a bunch of thyme and parsley, a carrot cut into slices, a few pepper-corns, cloves, salt, and a pint and a half of water or stock. When this is reduced to little more than three quarters of a pint, strain it, clear it from the fat, thicken it with a large dessert-spoonful of flour or arrowroot, add salt and pepper, boil the whole for a few minutes, then lay in the meat and heat it well. Boiled potatoes are sometimes sliced hot into the hash.

1096. Irish Stew. — Take two pounds of potatoes; peel and slice them; cut rather more than two pounds of mutton chops, either from the loin or neck; part of the fat should be taken off; beef, two pounds, six large onions sliced, a slice of ham, or lean bacon, a spoonful of pepper, and two of salt. This stew may be done in a stewpan over the fire, or in a baker's oven, or in a close-covered earthen pot. First put a layer of potatoes, then a layer of meat and onions, sprinkle the seasoning, then a layer of potatoes, and again the meat and onions and seasoning; the top layer should be potatoes, and the vessel should be quite full. Then put in half a pint of good gravy, and a spoonful of mushroom ketchup. Let the whole stew for an hour and a half; be very careful it does not burn.

1097. First-Watch Stew. — Cut pieces of salt beef and pork into dice, put them into a stewpan with six whole peppercorns, two blades of mace, a few cloves, a teaspoonful of celery-seeds, and a faggot of dried sweet herbs; cover with water, and stew gently for an hour, then add fragments of carrots, turnips, parsley, or any other vegetables at hand, with two sliced onions, and some vinegar to flavour; thicken with flour or rice, remove the herbs, and pour into the dish with toasted bread, or freshly baked biscuit, broken small, and serve hot. When they can be procured, a few potatoes improve it very much.

1098. Ragout of Cold Veal. — Either a neck, loin, or fillet of veal will furnish this excellent ragout with a very little expense or trouble. Cut the veal into handsome cutlets; put a piece of butter, or clean dripping, into a frying-pan; as soon as it is hot, flour and fry the veal of a light brown; take it out, and if you have no gravy ready, put a pint of boiling water into the frying-pan, give it a boil-up for a minute, and strain it in a basin while you make some thickening in the following manner:—Put an ounce of butter into a stewpan; as soon as it melts, mix as much flour as will dry it up; stir it over the fire for a few minutes, and gradually add the gravy you made in the frying-pan; let them simmer together for ten minutes; season with pepper, salt, a little mace, and a wineglassful of mushroom ketchup or wine; strain it through a panis to the meat, and stew very gently till the meat is thoroughly warmed. If you have any ready-boiled bacon, cut it in slices, and put it to warm with the meat.

1099. Economical Dish.—Cut some rather fat ham or bacon into slices, and fry of a nice brown; lay them aside to keep warm; then mix equal quantities of potatoes and cabbage, bruised well together, and fry them in the fat left from the ham. Place the mixture at the bottom, and lay the slices of bacon on the top. Cauliflower, or brocoli, substituted for cabbage, is truly delicious; and, to any one possessing a garden, quite easily procured, as those newly blown will do. The dish must be well seasoned with pepper.

1100. Mock Goose (being a leg of pork skinned, roasted, and stuffed goose fashion).—Parboil the leg; take off the skin, and then put it down to roast; baste it with butter, and make a *savoury powder* of finely minced or dried and powdered sage, ground black pepper, salt, and some bread-crumbs, rubbed together through a cullender: add to this a little very finely minced onion; sprinkle it with this when it is almost roasted; put half a pint of made gravy into the dish, and goose stuffing under the knuckle skin; or garnish the dish with balls of it fried or boiled.

1101. Roast Goose. — When a goose is well picked, singed, and cleaned, make the stuffing, with about two ounces of onion (if you think the flavour of raw onions too strong, cut them in slices, and lay them in cold water for a couple of hours, add as much apple or potato as you have of onion), and half as much green sage, chop them very fine, adding four ounces, *i.e.*, about a large breakfast cupful, of stale bread-crumbs, a bit of butter about as big as a walnut, and a very little pepper and salt (to this some cooks add half the liver, parboiling it first), the yolk of an egg or two, and incorporating the whole well together, stuff the goose; do not quite fill it, but leave a little room for the stuffing to swell. Spit it, tie it on the spit at both ends, to prevent it swinging round, and to prevent the stuffing from coming out. From an hour and a half to an hour and three quarters will roast a fine full-grown goose. Send up gravy and apple sauce with it.

1102. Jugged Hare.—Wash it very nicely, cut it up in pieces proper to help at table, and put them into a jugging-pot, or into a stone jar, just sufficiently large to hold it well; put in some sweet herbs, a roll or two of rind of a lemon, and a fine large onion with five cloves stuck in it; and, if you wish to preserve the flavour of the hare, a quarter of a pint of water; if you are for a ragout, a quarter of a pint of claret or port wine, and the juice of a lemon. Tie the jar down closely with a bladder, so that no steam can escape; put a little hay in the bottom of the saucepan, in which place the jar; let the water boil for about three hours, according to the age and size of the hare (take care it is not over-done, which is the general fault in all made dishes), keeping it boiling all the time, and fill up the pot as it boils away. When quite tender, strain off the gravy from the fat, thicken it with flour, and give it a boil up; lay the hare in a soup dish, and pour the gravy over it. You may make a pudding the same as for roast hare, and boil it in a cloth, and when you dish up your hare, cut it in slices, or make forcemeat balls of it for garnish. For sauce, black currant jelly. A much easier and quicker

way is the following:—Prepare the hare as for jugging; put it into a stewpan with a few sweet herbs, half a dozen cloves, the same of all-spice and black pepper, two large onions, and a roll of lemon peel; cover it with water: when it boils, skim it clean, and let it simmer gently till tender (about two hours); then take it up with a slice, set it by a fire to keep hot while you thicken the gravy; take three ounces of butter and some flour, rub together, put in the gravy, stir it well, and let it boil about ten minutes; strain it through a sieve over the hare, and it is ready.

1103. Curried Beef, Madras Way.—Take about two ounces of butter, and place it in a saucepan, with two small onions cut up into slices, and let them fry until they are a light brown; then add a tablespoonful and a half of curry powder, and mix it up well. Now put in the beef, cut into pieces about an inch square; pour in from a quarter to a third of a pint of milk, and let it simmer for thirty minutes; then take it off, and place it in a dish, with a little lemon juice. Whilst cooking stir constantly, to prevent it burning. Send to table with a wall of mashed potatoes or boiled rice round it. It greatly improves any curry to add with the milk a quarter of a cocoa-nut, scraped very small, and squeezed through muslin with a little water; this softens the taste of the curry, and, indeed, no curry should be made without it.

1104. Ragout of Duck, or any kind of Poultry or Game.—Partly roast, then divide into joints, or pieces of a suitable size for helping at table. Set it on in a stewpan, with a pint and a half of broth, or, if you have no broth, water, with any little trimmings of meat to enrich it; a large onion stuck with cloves, a dozen berries each of allspice and black pepper, and the rind of half a lemon shaved thin. When it boils skim it very clean, and then let it simmer gently, with the lid close, for an hour and a half. Then strain off the liquor, and take out the limbs, which keep hot in a basin or deep dish. Rinse the stewpan, or use a clean one, in which put two ounces of butter, and as much flour or other thickening as will bring it to a stiff paste; add to it the gravy by degrees. Let it boil up, then add a glass of port wine, a little lemon juice, and a teaspoonful of salt; simmer a few minutes. Put the meat in a deep dish, strain the gravy over, and garnish with sippets of toasted bread. The flavour may be varied at pleasure by adding ketchup, curry powder, or any of the flavouring tinctures, or vinegar.

1105. To Dress Cold Turkey, Goose, Fowl, Duck, Pigeon, or Rabbit.—Cut them in quarters, beat up an egg or two (according to the quantity you dress) with a little grated nutmeg, and pepper and salt, some parsley minced fine, and a few crumbs of bread; mix these well together, and cover the fowl, &c., with this batter: broil them, or put them in a Dutch oven, or have ready some dripping hot in a pan, in which fry them a light brown colour; thicken a little gravy with some flour, put a large spoonful of ketchup to it, lay the fry in a dish, and pour the sauce round it; garnish with slices of lemon and toasted bread.

1106. Pulled Turkey, Fowl, or Chicken.—Skin a cold chicken, fowl, or turkey; take off the fillets from the breasts, and put them into a stewpan with the rest of the white meat and wings, side-bones, and merry-thought, with a pint of broth, a large blade of mace pounded, a shalot minced fine, the juice of half a lemon, and a roll of the peel, some salt, and a few grains of cayenne; thicken it with flour and butter, and let it simmer for two or three minutes, till the meat is warm. In the meantime score the legs and rump, powder them with pepper and salt, broil them nicely brown, and lay them on or round your pulled chicken. Three tablespoonfuls of good cream, or the yolks of as many eggs, will be a great improvement to it.

1107. Hashed Poultry, Game, or Rabbit.—Cut them into joints, put the trimmings into a stewpan with a quart of the broth they were boiled in, and a large onion cut in four; let it boil half an hour: strain it through a sieve; then put two tablespoonfuls of flour in a basin, and mix it well by degrees with the hot broth; set it on the fire to boil up, then strain it through a fine sieve: wash out the stewpan, lay the poultry in it, and pour the gravy or it (through a sieve); set it by the side of the fire to simmer very gently (it must not *boil*) for fifteen minutes; five minutes before you serve it up, cut the stuffing in slices, and put it in to warm, then take it out, and lay it round the edge of the dish, and put the poultry in the middle; carefully skim the fat off the gravy, then shake it round well in the stewpan, and pour it to the hash. You may garnish the dish with bread sippets lightly toasted.

1108. Ducks or Geese Hashed.—Cut an onion into small dice; put it into a stewpan with a bit of butter; fry it, but do not let it get any colour; put as much boiling water into the stewpan as will make sauce for the hash; thicken it with a little flour; cut up the duck, and put it into the sauce to warm; do not let it boil; season it with pepper and salt and ketchup. *The legs of geese, &c.*, broiled, and laid on a bed of apple sauce, are sent up for luncheon or supper.

1109. Grilled Fowl.—Take the remains of cold fowls, and skin them or not, at choice; pepper and salt them, and sprinkle over them a little lemon juice, and let them stand an hour; wipe them dry, dip them into clarified butter, and then into fine bread-crumbs, and broil gently over a clear fire. A little finely minced lean of ham or grated lemon peel, with a seasoning of cayenne, salt, and mace, mixed with the crumbs, will vary this dish agreeably. When fried instead of broiled, the fowls may be dipped into yolk of egg instead of butter.

1110. A Nice Way of serving up

a fowl that has been dressed.—Beat the whites of two eggs to a thick froth; add a small bit of butter, or some salad oil, flour, a little lukewarm water, and two tablespoonfuls of beer, beaten all together till it is of the consistency of very thick cream. Cut up the fowl into small pieces, strew over it some chopped parsley and shalot, pepper, salt, and a little vinegar, and let it lie till dinner-time; dip the fowl in the batter, and fry it in boiling lard, of a nice light brown. Veal that has been cooked may be dressed in the same way. The above is a genuine family receipt, long practised by a French servant.

1111. Any Kind of Curry.—Cut a good fowl up; skin it or not, as you please; fry it nicely brown: slice two or three onions, and fry them; put the fried fowl and onions into a stewpan with a tablespoonful of curry powder, and one clove of garlic; cover it with water or veal gravy: let it stew slowly for one hour, or till very tender; have ready, mixed in two or three spoonfuls of good cream, one teaspoonful of flour, two ounces of butter, juice of a lemon, some salt; after the cream is in, it must only have one boil up, not to stew. Any spice may be added if the curry powder is not highly seasoned. With chicken, rabbit, or fish, observe the same rule. Curry is made also with sweetbreads, breast of veal, veal cutlets, lamb, mutton or pork chops, lobster, turbot, soles, eels, oysters, &c. Any kind of white meat is fit for a curry.

1112. Curried Eggs.—Slice two onions and fry them in butter, add a tablespoonful of curry powder; let them stew in a pint of good broth till quite tender; mix a cup of cream, and thicken with arrowroot, or rice flour. Simmer a few minutes, then add six or eight hard-boiled eggs cut in slices; heat them thoroughly, but do not let them boil.

1113. Cold Meat Broiled, with Poached Eggs.—The inside of a sirloin of beef or a leg of mutton is the best for this dish. Cut the slices of equal thickness, and broil and brown them carefully and slightly over a clear smart fire, or in a Dutch oven; give those slices most fire that are least done; lay them in a dish before the fire to keep hot, while you poach the eggs and mash the potatoes. This makes a savoury luncheon or supper. The meat should be *underdone* the first time.

1114. Curried Oysters.—This receipt may be greatly modified, both in quantity and ingredients. Let a hundred of large oysters be opened into a basin without losing one drop of their liquor. Put a lump of fresh butter into a good-sized saucepan, and when it boils, add a large onion, cut into thin slices, and let it fry in the uncovered stewpan until it is of a rich brown: now add a bit more butter, and two or three tablespoonfuls of curry powder. When these ingredients are well mixed over the fire with a wooden spoon, add gradually either hot water, or broth from the stock-pot; cover the stewpan, and let the whole boil up. Meanwhile, have ready the meat of a cocoa-nut, grated or rasped fine, put this into the stewpan with an unripe apple, chopped. Let the whole simmer over the fire until the apple is dissolved, and the cocoa-nut very tender; then add a cupful of strong thickening made of flour and water, and sufficient salt, as a curry will not bear being salted at table. Let this boil up for five minutes. Have ready also a vegetable marrow, or part of one, cut into bits, and sufficiently boiled to require little or no further cooking. Put this in with a tomata or two:—either of these vegetables may be omitted. Now put into the stewpan the oysters with their liquor, and the milk of the cocoa-nut, if it be perfectly sweet; stir them well with the former ingredients; let the curry stew gently for a few minutes, then throw in the strained juice of half a lemon. Stir the curry from time to time with a wooden spoon, and as soon as the oysters are done enough, serve it up with a corresponding dish of rice on the opposite side of the table. The dish is considered at Madras the *ne plus ultra* of Indian cookery.

1115. Fried Oysters. — Large oysters are the best. Simmer for a minute or two in their own liquor; drain perfectly dry; dip in yolks of eggs, and then in bread-crumbs, seasoned with nutmeg, cayenne, and salt; fry them of a light brown. They are chiefly used as garnish for fish, or for rump steaks; but if intended to be eaten alone, make a little thick melted butter, moistened with the liquor of the oysters, and serve as sauce.

1116. Stewed Oysters. — The beard or fringe is generally taken off. When this is done, set on the beards with the liquor of the oysters, and a little white gravy, rich, but unseasoned; having boiled for a few minutes, strain off the beards, put in the oysters, and thicken the gravy with flour and butter (an ounce of butter to half a pint of stew), a little salt, pepper, and nutmeg, or mace, a spoonful of ketchup, and three of cream: some prefer a little essence of anchovy to ketchup, others the juice of a lemon, others a glass of white wine; the flavour may be varied according to taste. Simmer till the stew is thick, and the oysters warmed through, but avoid letting them boil. Lay toasted sippets at the bottom of the dish and round the edges.

1117. Bologna Sausages. — Take equal quantities of bacon, fat and lean, beef, veal, pork, and beef suet; chop them small, season with pepper, salt, &c., sweet herbs, and sage rubbed fine. Have a well-washed intestine, fill, and prick it; boil gently for an hour, and lay on straw to dry. They may be smoked the same as hams.

1118. Oxford Sausages. — To each pound of lean pork allow one pound of lean veal, one pound of fat, part pork and part veal. Chop and beat well with a lard-beater. Allow one pound of bread-crumbs, thyme, a little parsley; an ounce of sage leaves, chopped very small; two heads of leeks, or a little garlic, or shalot, chopped very fine; salt, pepper, and nutmeg.

To each pound allow one egg, the yolks and whites separately; beat both well, mix in the yolks, and as much of the whites as is necessary to moisten the bread, and make them.

1119. Worcester Sausages are made of beef, &c.; add allspice, and any other spices and herbs you may choose.

1120. Mutton Sausages.—The lean of the leg is the best. Add half as much of beef suet; that is, a pound of lean and half a pound of suet (this proportion is good for all sausages). Add oysters, anchovies chopped very fine, and flavour with seasoning. No herbs. These will require a little fat in the pan to fry.

1121. Veal Sausages are made exactly as Oxford sausages, except that you add ham fat, or fat bacon; and, instead of sage, use marjoram, thyme, and parsley.

1122. Preparing Sausage Skins.—Turn them inside out, and stretch them on a stick; wash and scrape them in several waters. When thoroughly cleansed, take them off the sticks, and soak in salt and water two or three hours before filling.

1123. Saveloys are made of salt pork, fat and lean, with bread-crumbs, pepper, and sage; they are always put in skins: boil half an hour slowly. These are eaten cold.

1124. Black Hog Pudding.—Catch the blood of a hog; to each quart of blood put a large teaspoonful of salt, and stir it without ceasing till it is cold. Simmer half a pint or a pint of Embden groats in a small quantity of water till tender; there must be no gruel. The best way of doing it is in a double saucepan, so that you need not put more water than will moisten them. Chop up (for one quart of blood) one pound of the inside fat of the hog, and a quarter of a pint of bread-crumbs, a tablespoonful of sage, chopped fine, a teaspoonful of thyme, three drachms each of allspice, salt, and pepper, and a teacupful of cream. When the blood is cold, strain it through a sieve, and add to it the fat, then the groats, and then the seasoning. When well mixed, put it into the skin of the largest guts, well cleansed; tie it in lengths of about nine inches, and boil gently for twenty minutes. Take them out and prick them when they have boiled a few minutes.

1125. Scotch Woodcock. — Three or four slices of bread; toast and butter well on both sides,—nine or ten anchovies washed, scraped, and chopped fine; put them between the slices of toast, — have ready the yolks of four eggs well beaten, and half a pint of cream — which set over the fire to thicken, but not boil,—then pour it over the toast, and serve it to table as hot as possible.

1126. Sweetbread. — Trim a fine sweetbread (it cannot be too *fresh*); parboil it for five minutes, and throw it into a basin of cold water. Then roast it plain—or beat up the yolk of an egg, and prepare some fine bread-crumbs; or when the sweetbread is cold, dry it thoroughly in a cloth; run a lark-spit or a skewer through it, and tie it on the ordinary spit; egg it with a paste-brush; powder it well with bread-crumbs, and roast it. For sauce, fried bread-crumbs, melted butter, with a little mushroom ketchup, and lemon juice, or serve on buttered toast, garnished with egg sauce, or with gravy. Instead of spitting the sweetbread, you may put it into a tin Dutch oven, or fry it.

1127. SWEETBREADS PLAIN.—Parboil and slice them as before, dry them in a clean cloth, flour them, and fry them a delicate brown; take care to drain the fat well, and garnish with slices of lemon, and sprigs of chervil or parsley, or crisp parsley. Serve with sauce, and slices of ham or bacon, or forcemeat balls.

1128. Kidneys.--Cut them through the long way, score them, sprinkle a little pepper and salt on them, and run a wire skewer through to keep them from curling on the gridiron, so that they may be evenly broiled. Broil over a clear fire, taking care not to prick them with the fork, turning them often till they are done; they will take about ten or twelve minutes, if the fire is brisk; or fry them in butter, and make gravy for them in the pan (after you have taken out the kidneys), by putting in a teaspoonful of flour; as soon as it looks brown, put in as much water as will make gravy; they will take five minutes more to fry than to broil.

1129. Devil.—The gizzard and rump, or legs, &c., of a dressed turkey, capon, or goose, or mutton or veal kidney, scored, peppered, salted, and broiled, sent up for a relish, being made very hot, has obtained the name of a "Devil."

1130. Bacon.—Dr. Kitchiner very justly says:—"The boiling of bacon is a very simple subject to comment upon; but our main object is to teach common cooks the art of dressing common food in the best manner. Cover a pound of nice streaked bacon with cold water, let it boil gently for three quarters of an hour; take it up, scrape the under side well, and cut off the rind: grate a crust of bread not only on the top, but all over it, as you would ham, put it before the fire for a few minutes, not too long, or it will dry and spoil it. Bacon is sometimes as salt as salt can make it, therefore before it is boiled it must be soaked in warm water for an hour or two, changing the water once; then pare off the rusty and smoked part, trim it nicely on the under side, and scrape the rind as clean as possible."

1131. Ham or Bacon Slices should not be more than one-eighth of an inch thick, and, for delicate persons, should be soaked in hot water for a quarter of an hour, and then well wiped and dried before broiling. If you wish to curl it, roll it up, and put a wooden skewer through it; then it may be dressed in a cheese-toaster or a Dutch oven.

1132. Relishing Rashers of Bacon.—If you have any *cold bacon*, you may make a very nice dish of it by

G

cutting it into slices about a quarter of an inch thick; grate some crust of bread, as directed for ham, and powder them well with it on both sides; lay the rashers in a cheese-toaster,—they will be browned on one side in about three minutes :—turn them and do the other. These are a delicious accompaniment to poached or fried eggs :—the bacon, having been boiled first, is tender and mellow.—They are an excellent garnish round veal cutlets, or sweetbreads, or calf's head hash, or green peas, or beans, &c.

1133. Anchovy Sandwiches, made with the above, will be found excellent.

1134. Anchovy Toast is made by spreading anchovy paste upon bread either toasted or fried.

1135. Scotch Porridge.—FOR FOUR PERSONS. — Boil three pints of water in a clean saucepan, add a teaspoonful of salt; mix very gradually, while the water is boiling, one pound of fine oatmeal, stirring constantly, while you put in the meal, with a round stick about eighteen inches long, called a "spirtle." Continue stirring for fifteen minutes; then pour into soup-plates, allow it to cool a little, and serve with sweet milk. Scotch porridge is one of the most nutritive diets that can be given, especially for young persons. It is sometimes boiled with milk instead of water, but the mixture is then rather rich for delicate stomachs.

1136. Scotch Brose. — This favourite Scotch dish is generally made with the liquor in which meat has been boiled. Put half a pint of oatmeal into a porringer with a little salt, if there be not enough in the broth,—of which add as much as will mix it to the consistence of hasty pudding or a little thicker,—lastly, take a little of the fat that swims on the broth and put it on the crowdie, and eat it in the same way as hasty pudding.

1137. Barley Broth (SCOTCH).— Dr. Kitchiner, from whose "Cook's Oracle" we take this receipt, after testing it, says:—"This is a most frugal, agreeable, and nutritive meal. It will neither lighten the purse nor lie heavy on the stomach. It will furnish you with a pleasant soup, AND MEAT for eight persons. Wash three quarters of a pound of Scotch barley in a little cold water; put it in a soup-pot with a shin or leg of beef, of about ten pounds weight, sawn into four pieces (tell the butcher to do this for you); cover it well with cold water; set it on the fire; when it boils, skim it very clean, and put in two onions, of about three ounces weight each; set it by the side of the fire to simmer very gently for about two hours; then skim all the fat clean off, and put in two heads of celery and a large turnip cut into small squares; season it with salt, and let it boil for an hour and a half longer, and it will be ready : take out the meat carefully with a slice (and cover it up, and set it by the fire to keep warm), and skim the broth well before you put it in the tureen. Put a quart of the soup into a basin, and about an ounce of flour into a stewpan, and pour the broth to it by degrees, stirring it well together; set it on the fire, and stir it till it boils, then let it boil up, and it is ready. Put the meat in a ragout dish, and strain the sauce through a sieve over the meat; you may put to it some capers, or minced gherkins, or walnuts, &c. If the beef has been stewed with proper care, in a very gentle manner, and taken up at 'the critical moment when it is just tender,' you will obtain an excellent savoury meal for eight people at the cost of five pence, i.e., only the cost of a glass of port wine." (At present prices, about ninepence per head.) The doctor omitted potatoes and bread from his calculation!

1138. Hotch-Potch (FOR SUMMER).—Make a stock from the neck or ribs of lamb or mutton, reserving some chops, which cook for a shorter time and serve in the tureen. Chop small, four turnips, four carrots, a few young onions, a little parsley, and one lettuce: boil for one hour. Twenty minutes before they are done, put in a cauliflower cut small, one quart of shelled peas, and a pint of young beans.

1139. Hotch-Potch (WINTER). —This can be made of beef or mutton, or, for those who are partial to Scotch cookery, a sheep's head and feet, one pound of old green peas, steeped all the night previously, one large turnip, three carrots, four leeks, a little parsley, all cut small, with the exception of one carrot, which should be grated; add a small bunch of sweet herbs, pepper, and salt. The peas take two hours and a half to cook; the other vegetables, two hours; the head, three hours; and the feet, four hours.

1140. Beef Broth may be made by adding vegetables to essence of beef —or you may wash a leg or shin of beef, crack the bone well (desire the butcher to do it for you), add any trimmings of meat, game, or poultry, heads, necks, gizzards, feet, &c.; cover them with cold water; stir it up well from the bottom, and the moment it begins to simmer, skim it carefully. Your broth must be perfectly clear and limpid; on this depends the goodness of the soups, sauces, and gravies of which it is the basis. Add some cold water to make the remaining scum rise, and skim it again. When the scum has done rising, and the surface of the broth is quite clear, put in one moderate sized carrot, a head of celery, two turnips, and two onions,—it should not have any taste of sweet herbs, spice, or garlic, &c.; either of these flavours can easily be added after, if desired,—cover it close, set it by the side of the fire, and let it simmer very gently (so as not to waste the broth) for four or five hours, or more, according to the weight of the meat. Strain it through a sieve into a clean and dry stone pan, and set it in the coldest place you have, if for after use.

1141. Beef Tea. — Beef extract, by adding water, forms the best beef tea or broth for invalids. (*See* BEEF EXTRACT, p. 173.)

1142. Clear Gravy Soup.—This may be made from shin of beef, which should not be large or coarse. The

meat will be found serviceable for the table. From ten pounds of the meat let the butcher cut off five or six from the thick fleshy part, and again divide the knuckle, that the whole may lie compactly in the vessel in which it is to be stewed. Pour in three quarts of cold water, and when it has been brought slowly to boil, and been well skimmed, throw in an ounce and a half of salt, half a large teaspoonful of peppercorns, eight cloves, two blades of mace, a faggot of savoury herbs, a couple of small carrots, and the heart of a root of celery; to these add a mild onion or not, at choice. When the whole has stewed very softly for four hours, probe the large bit of beef, and, if quite tender, lift it out for table; let the soup be simmered from two to three hours longer, and then strain it through a fine sieve, into a clean pan. When it is perfectly cold, clear off every particle of fat: heat a couple of quarts; stir in, when it boils, half an ounce of sugar, a small tablespoonful of good soy, and twice as much of Harvey's sauce, or, instead of this, of clear and fine mushroom ketchup. If carefully made, the soup will be perfectly transparent, and of good colour and flavour. A thick slice of ham will improve it, and a pound or so of the neck of beef, with an additional pint of water, will likewise enrich its quality. A small quantity of good broth may be made of the fragments of the whole, boiled down with a few fresh vegetables.

1143. Beef Glaze, or Portable Soup, is simply the essence of beef condensed by evaporation. It may be put into pots, like potted meats, or into skins, as sausages, and will keep for many months. If further dried in cakes or lozenges, by being laid on pans or dishes, and frequently turned, it will keep for years, and supply soup at any moment.

1144. Vermicelli Soup. — To three quarts of gravy soup, or stock, add six ounces of vermicelli. Simmer for half an hour; stir frequently.

1145. Vegetable Soup.—Peel

and cut into very small pieces three onions, three turnips, one carrot, and four potatoes, put them into a stewpan with a quarter of a pound of butter, the same of lean ham, and a bunch of parsley, pass them ten minutes over a sharp fire; then add a large spoonful of flour, mix well in, moisten with two quarts of broth, and a pint of boiling milk; boil up, keeping it stirred; season with a little salt and sugar, and run it through a hair sieve; put it into another stewpan, boil again, skim, and serve with fried bread in it.

1146. Asparagus Soup.—Two quarts of good beef or veal stock, four onions, two or three turnips, some sweet herbs, and the white parts of a hundred young asparagus,—if old, half that quantity,—and let them simmer till fit to be rubbed through a tammy; strain and season it; have ready the boiled green tops of the asparagus, and add them to the soup.

1147. Carrot Soup.—Scrape and wash half a dozen large carrots; peel off the red outside (which is the only part used for this soup); put it into a gallon stewpan, with one head of celery, and an onion cut into thin pieces; take two quarts of beef, veal, or mutton broth, or if you have any cold roast beef bones (or liquor in which mutton or beef has been boiled) you may make very good broth for this soup. When you have put the broth to the roots, cover the stewpan close, and set it on a slow stove for two hours and a half, when the carrots will be soft enough (some cooks put in a teacupful of bread-crumbs); boil for two or three minutes; rub it through a tammy or hair sieve, with a wooden spoon, and add as much broth as will make it a proper thickness, i.e., almost as thick as pea soup; put it into a clean stewpan, make it hot, season with the liquor in which meat has been boiled, add a good-sized fowl, with two or three leeks cut in pieces about an inch long, pepper, and salt; boil slowly about an hour, then put in as many more leeks, and give it three quarters of an hour longer.

This is very good made of good beef stock, and leeks put in at twice.

1148. Mince Meat.—Take seven pounds of currants well picked and cleaned; of finely chopped beef suet, the lean of a sirloin of beef minced raw, and finely chopped apples (Kentish or golden pippins), each three and a half pounds; citron, lemon peel, and orange peel cut small, each half a pound; fine moist sugar, two pounds; mixed spice, an ounce; the rind of four lemons and four Seville oranges; mix well, and put in a deep pan. Mix a bottle of brandy and white wine, the juice of the lemons and oranges that have been grated, together in a basin; pour half over and press down tight with the hand, then add the other half and cover closely. Some families make this one year so as to use the next.

1149. Minced Collops.—Two pounds of good rump steak, chopped very fine; six good-sized onions, also chopped small; put both into a stew-pan, with as much water or gravy as will cover the meat; stir it without ceasing till the water begins to boil; then set the stewpan aside, where the collops can simmer, not boil, for three quarters of an hour; just before serving, stir in a tablespoonful of flour, a little pepper and salt, and boil it up once. Serve with mashed potatoes round the dish. The above quantity will be enough for four persons.

1150. Forcemeat Balls. (For turtle, mock turtle, or made dishes.)— Pound some veal in a marble mortar, rub it through a sieve with as much of the udder as you have veal, or about a third of the quantity of butter: put some bread-crumbs into a stewpan, moisten them with milk, add a little chopped parsley and shalot, rub them well together in a mortar, till they form a smooth paste; put it through a sieve, and when cold, pound, and mix all together, with the yolks of three eggs boiled hard; season it with salt, pepper, and curry powder, or cayenne; add to it the yolks of two raw eggs, rub it well together, and make small balls: ten minutes before your soup is ready, put them in.

1151. Beef Extract (AS RECOMMENDED BY BARON LIEBIG).—Take a pound of good juicy beef from which all the skin and fat has been cut away, chop it up like sausage meat; mix it thoroughly with a pint of cold water, place it on the side of the stove to heat *very slowly*, and give an occasional stir. It may stand two or three hours before it is allowed to simmer, and will then require but fifteen minutes of gentle boiling. Salt should be added when the boiling commences, and this, for invalids in general, is the only seasoning required. When the extract is thus far prepared, it may be poured from the meat into a basin, and allowed to stand until any particles of fat on the surface can be skimmed off, and the sediment has subsided and left the soup quite clear, when it may be poured off gently, heated in a clean saucepan, and served. The scum should be well cleared as it accumulates.

1152. Potted Beef.—Take three or four pounds, or any smaller quantity, of lean beef, free from sinews, and rub it well with a mixture made of a handful of salt, one ounce of saltpetre, and one ounce of coarse sugar; let the meat lie in the salt for two days, turning and rubbing it twice a day. Put it into a stone jar with a little beef gravy, and cover it with a paste to keep it close. Bake it for several hours in a very slow oven, till the meat is tender; then pour off the gravy, which should be in a very small quantity, or the juice of the meat will be lost; pound the meat, when cold, in a marble mortar till it is reduced to a smooth paste, adding by degrees a little fresh butter melted. Season it as you proceed with pepper, allspice, nutmeg, pounded mace, and cloves, or such of these spices as are thought agreeable. Some flavour with anchovy, ham, shalots, mustard, wine, flavoured vinegar, ragout powder, curry powder, &c., according to taste. When it is thoroughly beaten and mingled together, press it closely into small shallow pots, nearly full, and fill them up with a layer a quarter of an inch thick of clarified butter, and tie them up with a bladder, or sheet of Indian rubber. They should be kept in a cool place.

1153. Strasburg Potted Meat.—Take a pound and a half of the rump of beef, cut into dice, and put it in an earthen jar, with a quarter of a pound of butter at the bottom; tie the jar close up with paper, and set over a pot to boil: when nearly done, add cloves, mace, allspice, nutmeg, salt, and cayenne pepper to taste; then boil till tender, and let it get cold. Pound the meat, with four anchovies washed and boned: add a quarter of a pound of oiled butter, work it well together with the gravy, warm a little, and add cochineal to colour. Then press into small pots, and pour melted mutton suet over the top of each.

1154. Brown Stock.—Put five pounds of shin of beef, three pounds of knuckle of veal, and some sheep's trotters or cow-heel into a closely-covered stewpan, to draw out the gravy, very gently, and allow it to become nearly brown. Then pour in sufficient boiling water to entirely cover the meat, and let it boil up, skimming it frequently; seasoning it with whole peppers, salt, and roots, herbs, and vegetables of any kind. That being done, let it boil gently five or six hours, pour the broth off from the meat, and let it stand during the night to cool. The following morning take off the scum and fat, and put it away in a stone jar for further use.

1155. Brown Stock may be made from all sorts of meat, bones, remnants of poultry, game, &c. The shin of beef makes an excellent stock.

1156. Brown Gravy.—Three onions sliced, and fried in butter to a nice brown; toast a large thin slice of bread a considerable time, until quite hard and of a deep brown. Take these, with any piece of meat, bone, &c., and some herbs, and set them on the fire, with water according to judgment, and stew down until a thick gravy is produced. Season, strain, and keep cool.

1157. Goose or Duck Stuffing. —Chop very fine about two ounces of onion, of *green* sage leaves about an ounce (both unboiled), four ounces of bread-crumbs, a bit of butter about as big as a walnut, &c., the yolk and white of an egg, and a little pepper and salt; some add to this a minced apple.

1158. Bacon is an extravagant article in housekeeping; there is often twice as much dressed as need be; when it is sent to table as an accompaniment to boiled poultry or veal, a pound and a half is plenty for a dozen people. A good German sausage is a very economical substitute for bacon; or fried pork sausage.

1159. The English, generally speaking, are very deficient in the practice of culinary economy; a French family would live well on what is often wasted in an English kitchen: the bones, dripping, pot-liquor, remains of fish, vegetables, &c., which are too often consigned to the grease-pot or the dust-heap, might, by a very trifling degree of management on the part of the cook, or mistress of a family, be converted into sources of daily support and comfort, at least to some poor pensioner or other, at an expense that even the miser could scarcely grudge.

1160. Calf's Head Pie.—Boil the head an hour and a half, or rather more. After dining from it, cut the remaining meat off in slices. Boil the bones in a little of the liquor for three hours; then strain it off, and let it remain till next day; then take off the fat. *To make the Pie.*—Boil two eggs for five minutes; let them get cold, then lay them in slices at the bottom of a pie-dish, and put alternate layers of meat and jelly, with pepper and chopped lemon also alternately, till the dish is full; cover with a crust and bake it. Next day turn the pie out upside down.

1161. Sea Pie. — Make a thick pudding crust, line a dish with it, or what is better, a cake-tin; put a layer of sliced onions, then a layer of salt beef

cut in slices, a layer of sliced potatoes, a layer of pork, and another of onions; strew pepper over all, cover with a crust, and tie down tightly with a cloth previously dipped in boiling water and floured. Boil for two hours, and serve hot in a dish.

1162. Rump-Steak Pie. — Cut three pounds of rump steak (that has been kept till tender) into pieces half as big as your hand, trim off all the skin, sinews, and every part which has not indisputable pretensions to be eaten, and beat them with a chopper. Chop very fine half a dozen shalots, and add to them half an ounce of pepper and salt mixed; strew some of the mixture at the bottom of the dish, then a layer of steak, then some more of the mixture, and so on till the dish is full; add half a gill of mushroom ketchup, and the same quantity of gravy, or red wine; cover it as in the preceding receipt, and bake it two hours. Large oysters, parboiled, bearded, and laid alternately with the steaks—their liquor reduced and substituted instead of the ketchup and wine, will be a variety.

1163. Raised Pies.—Put two pounds and a half of flour on the paste-board,—and set on the fire, in a sauce-pan, three quarters of a pint of water, and half a pound of good lard; when the water boils, make a hole in the middle of the flour, pour in the water and lard by degrees, gently incorporating the flour with a spoon, and when it is well mixed, knead it with your hands till it becomes stiff; dredge a little flour to prevent it sticking to the board, or you cannot make it look smooth: do not roll it with the rolling-pin, but with your hands, to about the thickness of a quart pot; cut it into six pieces, leaving a little for the covers; put one hand in the middle, and keep the other close on the outside till you have worked it either into an oval or a round shape: have your meat ready cut, and seasoned with pepper and salt: if pork, cut it in small slices—the griskin is the best for pasties: if you use mutton, cut it in very neat cutlets, and put them in the pies as you make them; roll out the covers with the rolling-pin just the size of the pie, wet it round the edge, put it on the pie, and press it together with your thumb and finger, and then cut it all round with a pair of scissors quite even, and pinch them inside and out, and bake them an hour and a half.

1164. Cold Partridge Pie.—Bone partridges—the number according to the size the pie is wanted, make some good force, and fill the partridges with it, put a whole raw truffle in each partridge (let the truffle be peeled); raise the pie, lay a few slices of veal in the bottom, and a thick layer of force; then the partridges, and four truffles to each partridge; then cover the partridges and truffles over with sheets of bacon, cover the pie in, and finish it. It will take four hours baking. Cut two pounds of lean ham (if eight partridges are in the pie) into very thin slices, put it in a stewpan along with the bones and giblets of the partridges, and any other loose giblets that are at hand, an old fowl, a faggot of thyme and parsley, a little mace, and about twenty-four shalots; add about a pint of stock. Set the stewpan on a stove to draw down for half an hour, then put three quarts of good stock; let it boil for two hours, then strain it off, and reduce the liquid to one pint; add sherry wine to it, and put aside till the pie is baked. When the pie has been out of the oven for half an hour, boil the residue strained from the bones, &c., of the partridges, and put it into the pie. Let it stand for twenty-four hours before it is eaten.—N.B. Do not take any of the fat from the pie, as that is what preserves it. A pie made in this manner will be eatable for three months after it is cut; in short, it cannot spoil in any reasonable time. All cold pies are made in this manner. Either poultry or game, when put into a raised crust, and intended not to be eaten until cold, should be boned, and the liquor that is to fill up the pie made from the bones, &c.

1165. Veal Pie.—Take some of the middle or scrag of a small neck; season it with pepper and salt, and put to it a few pieces of lean bacon or ham. If it be wanted of a high relish, add mace, cayenne, and nutmeg to the salt and pepper, and also forcemeat and egg balls, and if you choose add truffles, morels, mushrooms, sweetbreads cut into small bits, and cocks' combs blanched, if liked. Have a rich gravy to pour in after baking. It will be very good without any of the latter additions.

1166. Mutton Pie.—The following is a capital family dish:—Cut mutton into pieces about two inches square, and half an inch thick; mix pepper, pounded allspice, and salt together, dip the pieces in this; sprinkle stale bread-crumbs at the bottom of the dish; lay in the pieces, strewing the crumbs over each layer; put a piece of butter the size of a hen's egg at the top; add a wineglassful of water, and cover in, and bake in a moderate oven rather better than an hour. Take an onion, chopped fine; a faggot of herbs; half an anchovy; and add to it a little beef stock or gravy: simmer for a quarter of an hour; raise the crust at one end, and pour in the liquor—not the thick part. (*See* POTATO PIE, No. 1054.)

1167. Seven-Bell Pasty.—Shred a pound of suet fine, cut salt pork into dice, potatoes and onions small, rub a sprig of dried sage up fine; mix with some pepper, and place in the corner of a square piece of paste; turn over the other corner, pinch up the sides, and bake in a quick oven. If any bones, &c., remain from the meat, season with pepper and sage, place them with a gill of water in a pan, and bake with the pasty; when done, strain, and pour the gravy into the centre of the pasty.

1168. Apple Pie.—Pare, core, and quarter the apples; boil the cores and parings in sugar and water; strain off the liquor, adding more sugar; grate the rind of a lemon over the apples, and squeeze the juice into the syrup; mix half a dozen cloves with the fruit, put in a piece of butter the size of a walnut; cover with puff paste.

1169. Cup in a Pie-Dish.—The custom of placing an inverted cup in a fruit pie, the cook will inform us, is to retain the juice while the pie is baking in the oven, and prevent its boiling over; and she is the more convinced in her theory, because, when the pie is withdrawn from the oven, the cup will be found full of juice. When the cup is first put in the dish it is full of cold air, and when the pie is placed in the oven, this air will expand by the heat and fill the cup, and drive out all the juice and a portion of the present air it contains, in which state it will remain until removed from the oven, when the air in the cup will condense, and occupy a very small space, leaving the remainder to be filled with juice; but this does not take place till the danger of the juice boiling over is passed. If a small glass tumbler is inverted in the pie, its contents can be examined into while it is in the oven, and it will be found what has been advanced is correct.—*Gower's Scientific Phenomena of Domestic Life.*

1170. Excellent Paste for fruit or meat pies may be made with two-thirds of wheat flour, one-third of the flour of boiled potatoes, and some butter or dripping; the whole being brought to a proper consistence with warm water, and a small quantity of yeast added when lightness is desired. This will also make very pleasant cakes for breakfast, and may be made with or without spices, fruits, &c.

1171. Pastry for Tarts, &c.—Take of flour one pound; bicarbonate of soda, two drachms; muriatic acid, two drachms; butter, six ounces; water, enough to bring it to the consistence required.

1172. When much Pastry is made in a house, a quantity of fine flour should be kept on hand, in dry jars, and quite secured from the air, as it makes lighter pastry and bread when kept a short time, than when fresh ground.

1173. My Wife's Little Suppers.

1174. MEAT CAKES.—Take any cold meat, game, or poultry (if underdone, all the better), mince it fine, with a little fat bacon or ham, or an anchovy; season it with pepper and salt; mix well, and make it into small cakes three inches long, an inch and a half wide, and half an inch thick: fry these a light brown, and serve them with good gravy, or put into a mould, and boil or bake it. N.B.—Bread-crumbs, hard yolks of eggs, onions, sweet herbs, savoury spices, zest, or curry-powder, or any of the forcemeats.

1175. OYSTER PATTIES.—Roll out puff paste a quarter of an inch thick; cut it into squares with a knife, sheet eight or ten patty pans, put upon each a bit of bread the size of half a walnut; roll out another layer of paste of the same thickness, cut it as above, wet the edge of the bottom paste, and put on the top; pare them round to the pan, and notch them about a dozen times with the back of the knife, rub them lightly with yolk of egg, bake them in a hot oven about a quarter of an hour: when done, take a thin slice off the top, then with a small knife, or spoon, take out the bread and the inside paste, leaving the outside quite entire; then parboil two dozen of large oysters, strain them from their liquor, wash, beard, and cut them into four; put them into a stewpan with an ounce of butter rolled in flour, half a gill of good cream, a little grated lemon peel, the oyster liquor, free from sediment, reduced by boiling to one-half, some cayenne pepper, salt, and a teaspoonful of lemon juice; stir it over a fire five minutes, and fill the patties.

1176. LOBSTER PATTIES.—Prepare the patties as in the last receipt. Take a hen lobster already boiled; pick the meat from the tail and claws, and chop it fine; put it into a stewpan with a little of the inside spawn pounded in a mortar till quite smooth, an ounce of fresh butter, half a gill of cream, and half a gill of veal consommé, cayenne pepper, and salt, a teaspoonful of essence of anchovy, the same of lemon juice, and a tablespoonful of flour and water: stew it five minutes.

1177. EGG AND HAM PATTIES.—Cut a slice of bread two inches thick, from the most solid part of a stale quartern loaf; have ready a tin round cutter, two inches in diameter; cut out four or five pieces, then take a cutter two sizes smaller, press it nearly through the larger pieces, then remove with a small knife the bread from the inner circle: have ready a large stewpan full of boiling lard: fry them of a light brown colour, drain them dry with a clean cloth, and set them by till wanted; then take half a pound of lean ham, mince it small, add to it a gill of good brown sauce; stir it over the fire a few minutes, and put to it a small quantity of cayenne pepper and lemon juice: fill the shapes with the mixture, and lay a poached egg upon each.

1178. VEAL AND HAM PATTIES.—Chop about six ounces of ready-dressed lean veal, and three ounces of ham, very small; put it into a stewpan with an ounce of butter rolled in flour, half a gill of cream, half a gill of veal stock, a little grated nutmeg and lemon peel, some cayenne pepper and salt, a spoonful of essence of ham, and lemon juice, and stir it over the fire some time, taking care it does not burn.

1179. PUFF PASTE.—To a pound and a quarter of sifted flour, rub gently in with the hand half a pound of fresh butter; mix up with half a pint of spring water; knead it well, and set it by for a quarter of an hour; then roll it out thin, lay on it in small pieces three quarters of a pound more of butter, throw on it a little flour, double it up in folds, and roll it out thin three times, and set it by for about an hour *in a cold place.* Or, if a more substantial and savoury paste be desired, use the following:—

1180. PASTE FOR MEAT OR SAVOURY PIES.—Sift two pounds of fine flour to a pound and a half of good salt butter, break it into small pieces, and

wash it well in cold water; rub gently together the butter and flour, and mix it up with the yolks of three eggs, beat together with a spoon, and nearly a pint of spring water; roll it out, and double it in folds three times, and it is ready.

1181. CHICKEN AND HAM PATTIES.—Use the white meat from the breast of the chickens or fowls, and proceed as for veal and ham patties.

1182. PRIME BEEF SAUSAGES.—Take a pound of lean beef, and half a pound of suet, remove the skin, chop it fine as for mince collop, then beat it well with a roller, or in a marble mortar, till it is all well mixed and will stick together; season highly with zest, if you have it, and salt, or any mixed spices you please; make it into flat round cakes, about an inch thick, and shaped with a cup or saucer, and fry them a light brown. They should be served up on boiled rice, as for curry. If for company, you may do them with eggs and bread-crumbs; but they are quite as good without. Or they may be rolled in puff or pie paste, and baked.

1183. POTATO PUFFS.—Take cold roast meat, either beef, or mutton, or veal and ham, clear it from the gristle, cut it small, and season either with zest, or pepper and salt, and cut pickles; boil and mash some potatoes, and make them into a paste with one or two eggs; roll it out, with a dust of flour, cut it round with a saucer, put some of your seasoned meat on one half, and fold it over like a puff; pinch or nick it neatly round, and fry it a light brown. This is the most elegant method of preparing meat that has been dressed before.

1184. FRIED EGGS AND MINCED HAM OR BACON. — Choose some very fine bacon streaked with a good deal of lean; cut this into very thin slices, and afterwards into small square pieces; throw them into a stewpan and set it over a gentle fire, that they may lose some of their fat. When as much as will freely come is thus melted

from them, lay them on a warm dish.
Put into a stewpan a ladleful of melted
bacon or lard; set it on a stove; put in
about a dozen of the small pieces of
bacon, then incline the stewpan and
break in an egg. Manage this carefully,
and the egg will presently be done:
it will be very round, and the little
dice of bacon will stick to it all over,
so that it will make a very pretty appearance. Take care the yolks do not
harden. When the egg is thus done,
lay it carefully on a warm dish, and do
the others.

1185. FISH CAKE.—Take the meat
from the bones of any kind of cold fish,
which latter put with the head and fins
into a stewpan with a pint of water, a
little salt, pepper, an onion, and a faggot of sweet herbs, to stew for gravy.
Mince the meat, and mix it well with
crumbs of bread and cold potatoes,
equal parts, a little parsley and seasoning. Make into a cake, with the white
of an egg, or a little butter or milk;
egg it over, and cover with bread-
crumbs, then fry a light brown. Pour
the gravy over, and stew gently for
fifteen minutes, stirring it carefully
twice or thrice. Serve hot, and garnish
with slices of lemon, or parsley. These
cakes afford a capital relish from scraps
of cold fish. Housekeepers who would
know how to economize all kinds of
nutritious fragments, should refer to the
"Family Save-all," which supplies
a complete course of "Secondary
Cookery." *

1186. MARBLED GOOSE.—The following, though scarcely pertaining to
"My Wife's *Little* Suppers," is too delicious a relish to be overlooked. It is
suitable for larger supper parties, or as
a stock dish for families where visitors
are frequent. It is also excellent for
breakfasts, or for pic-nics:—Take a fine
mellow ox-tongue out of pickle, cut off
the root and horny part at the tip, wipe
dry, and boil till it is quite tender:
then peel it, cut a deep slit in its whole

* Published by Houlston and Wright.
Price 2s. 6d.

length, and lay a fair proportion of the
following mixture within it;—Mace
half an ounce, nutmeg half an ounce,
cloves half an ounce, salt two tablespoonfuls, and twelve Spanish olives.
The olives should be stoned, and all
the ingredients well pounded and
mixed together. Next take a barn-
door fowl and a good large goose, and
bone them. Lay the tongue inside the
fowl, rub the latter outside with the
seasoning, and having ready some
slices of ham divested of the rind, wrap
them tightly round the fowl; put
these inside the goose, with the remainder of the seasoning, sew it up, and
make all secure and of natural shape
with a piece of new linen and tape.
Put it in an earthern pan or jar just
large enough to hold it, with plenty of
clarified butter, and bake it for two
hours and a half in a slow oven; then
take it out, and when cold take out the
goose and set it in a sieve; take off the
butter and hard fat, which put by the
fire to melt, adding, if required, more
clarified butter. Wash and wipe out
the pan, put the bird again into it, and
take care that it is well covered with
the warm butter; then tie the jar down
with bladder and leather. It will keep
thus for a long time. When wanted
for the table, the jar should be placed
in a tub of hot water, so as to melt the
butter, the goose then can be taken out,
and sent to table cold.

1187. OYSTER PIE.—The following
directions may be safely relied upon.
Take a large dish, butter it, and spread
a rich paste over the sides and round
the edge, but not at the bottom. The
oysters should be fresh, and as large and
fine as possible. Drain off part of the
liquor from the oysters. Put them into
a pan, and season them with pepper,
salt, and spice. Stir them well with the
seasoning. Have ready the yolks of
eggs, chopped fine, and the grated bread.
Pour the oysters (with as much of their
liquor as you please) into the dish that
has the paste in it. Strew over them
the chopped egg and grated bread. Roll
out the lid of the pie, and put it on,

crimping the edges handsomely. Take a small sheet of paste, cut it into a square, and roll it up. Cut it with a sharp knife into the form of a double tulip. Make a slit in the centre of the upper crust, and stick the tulip in it. Cut out eight large leaves of paste, and lay them on the lid. Bake the pie in a quick oven.

1188. SALAD.—The mixing of salad is an art which it is easy to attain with care. The main point is to incorporate the several articles required for the salad, and to serve up at table as fresh as possible. The herbs should be "morning gathered," and they will be much refreshed by laying an hour or two in spring water. Careful picking, and washing, and drying in a cloth, in the kitchen, are also very important, and the due proportion of each herb requires attention. The sauce may be thus prepared :—Boil two eggs for ten or twelve minutes, and then put them in cold water for a few minutes, so that the yolks may become quite cold and hard. Rub them through a coarse sieve with a wooden spoon, and mix them with a tablespoonful of water or cream, and then add two tablespoonfuls of fine flask oil, or melted butter ; mix, and add by degrees a teaspoonful of salt, and the same quantity of mustard ; mix till smooth, when incorporate with the other ingredients about three tablespoonfuls of vinegar ; then pour this sauce down the side of the salad bowl, but do not stir up the salad till wanted to be eaten. Garnish the top of the salad with the white of the eggs, cut in slices ; or these may be arranged in such manner as to be ornamental on the table. Some persons may fancy they are able to prepare a salad without previous instruction, but, like everything else, a little knowledge in this case is not thrown away.

1189. Apple Puddings.—One pound of flour, six ounces of very finely minced beef suet ; roll thin, and fill with one pound and a quarter of boiling apples ; add the grated rind and strained juice of a small lemon, tie it in a cloth ; boil for one hour and twenty minutes, or longer. A small slice of fresh butter stirred into it when it is sweetened will be an acceptable addition ; grated nutmeg, or cinnamon in fine powder, may be substituted for lemon rind. For a richer pudding use half a pound of butter for the crust, and add to the apples a spoonful or two of orange or quince marmalade.

1190. Boston Apple Pudding.—Peel and core one dozen and a half of good apples ; cut them small ; put them into a stewpan with a little water, cinnamon, two cloves, and the peel of a lemon ; stew over a slow fire till soft ; sweeten with moist sugar, and pass it through a hair sieve ; add the yolks of four eggs and one white, a quarter of a pound of good butter, half a nutmeg, the peel of a lemon grated, and the juice of one lemon ; beat well together ; line the inside of a pie-dish with good puff paste ; put in the pudding, and bake half an hour.

1191. Bread Pudding.—Unfermented brown bread, two ounces ; milk, half a pint ; one egg ; sugar, quarter of an ounce. Cut the bread into slices, and pour the milk over it boiling hot ; let it stand till well soaked, and stir in the egg and sugar, well beaten, with a little grated nutmeg ; and bake or steam for one hour.

1192. Plum Pudding.—Take of flour, one pound ; bicarbonate of soda, two drachms ; muriatic acid, two drachms ; beef suet, eight ounces ; currants, eight ounces ; nutmeg and orange peel, grated fine, quarter of an ounce ; three eggs. To be boiled or steamed four hours.

1193. Cabinet Pudding.—Cut three or four muffins in two, pour over them boiling milk sufficient to cover them, cover them up until they are tender. Make a rich custard with eight eggs (only four whites), a pint of cream, a quarter of a pound of loaf sugar, an ounce of almonds, blanched and cut, lemon peel and nutmeg grated, and a glass of ratafia or brandy, and add to the soaked muffins. Butter a tin mould for boiling—for baking, a dish. Put a layer of dried cherries, greengages, apricots, or French plums; cover with the mixture, adding fruit and mixture alternately, until the mould or dish is quite full. Boil an hour, and serve with wine sauce. It should not float in the water, but stand in a stew-pan, and only water enough to reach half way up the mould. If for baking, it will not take so long. Lay a puff paste round the edges of the dish.

1194. Elegant Bread Pudding. —Take light white bread, and cut it in thin slices. Put into a pudding shape a layer of any sort of preserve, then a slice of bread, and repeat until the mould is almost full. Pour over all a pint of warm milk, in which four beaten eggs have been mixed; cover the mould with a piece of linen, place it in a saucepan with a little boiling water, let it boil twenty minutes, and serve with pudding sauce.

1195. Economical Family Pudding. —Bruise with a wooden spoon, through a cullender, six large or twelve middle-sized boiled potatoes; beat four eggs, mix with a pint of good milk, stir in the potatoes; sugar and seasoning to taste; butter the dish; bake half an hour. This receipt is simple and economical, as it is made of what is wasted in most families, viz., cold potatoes, which may be kept two or three days, till a sufficient quantity is collected. It is a weekly dish at our table. A teaspoonful of Scotch chip marmalade makes a delicious seasoning.

1196. Batter Pudding.—Take of flour, four ounces; bicarbonate of soda, two drachms; a little sugar, and one egg. Mix with milk to a thin batter, and bake in a well-buttered tin, in a brisk oven, half an hour. A few currants may be strewed in the bottom of the tin if preferred.

1197. Batter Pudding, Baked or Boiled.—Six ounces fine flour, a little salt, and three eggs; beat well with a little milk, added by degrees until it is the thickness of cream; put into a buttered dish; bake three quarters of an hour; or if boiled put it into a buttered and floured basin, tied over with a cloth; boil one hour and a half or more.

1198. Half-Pay Pudding.—An officer's wife is the contributor of the following:—Four ounces of each of the following ingredients, viz., suet, flour, currants, raisins, and bread-crumbs; two tablespoonfuls of treacle, half a pint of milk—all of which must be well mixed together, and boiled in a mould, for four hours. To be served up with wine or brandy sauce, if half-pay permit. From two to three hours we find sufficient; it is an excellent substitute for Christmas plum pudding, at the small expense of 6d. or 7d.

1199. Fig Pudding. — Three quarters of a pound of grated bread, half a pound of best figs, six ounces of suet, six ounces of moist sugar, a tea-cupful of milk, and a little nutmeg. The figs and suet must be chopped very fine. Mix the bread and suet first, then the figs, sugar, and nutmeg, one egg beaten well, and lastly the milk. Boil in a mould four hours. To be eaten with sweet sauce.

1200. Plain Suet Pudding.— Take of flour, one pound and a half; bicarbonate of soda, three drachms; muriatic acid, three drachms; beef suet, four ounces; powdered ginger, half a drachm; water or milk, one pint. Mix according to the directions given for the tea cake (No 1878), and boil or steam for two hours.

1201. Barley Pudding.—Take a quarter of a pound of Scotch or pearl barley. Wash, and simmer it in a small quantity of water; pour off the water, and add milk and flavourings as for rice puddings. Beat up with sugar and nutmeg, and mix the milk and barley in the same way. It may be more or less rich of eggs, and with or without the addition of butter, cream, or marrow. Put it into a buttered deep dish, leaving room for six or eight ounces of currants, and an ounce of candied peel, cut up fine, with a few apples cut in small pieces. An hour will bake it.

1202. Carrot Pudding.—Grate a raw red carrot; mix with double the weight of bread-crumbs, biscuit, or part of each: to a pound and a half put a pint of new milk or cream, or part of each, four or six ounces of clarified butter, three or four eggs well beaten, sugar to taste, a little nutmeg, and a glass of brandy; line or edge a dish with puff paste; pour in the mixture; put slices of candied lemon or orange peel on the top, and bake in a moderately hot oven.

1203. Potato Pudding.—Boil mealy potatoes in their skins, according to the rule laid down, skin and mash them with a little milk, pepper, and salt: this will make a good pudding to bake under roast meat. With the addition of a bit of butter, an egg, milk, pepper, and salt, it makes an excellent batter for a meat pudding baked. Grease a baking dish; put a layer of potatoes, then a layer of meat cut in bits, and seasoned with pepper, salt, a little allspice, either with or without chopped onions; a little gravy of roast meat is a great improvement: then put another layer of potatoes, then meat, and cover with potatoes. Put a buttered paper over the top, to prevent it from being burnt, and bake it an hour or an hour and a half.

1204. Almond Pudding and Sauce.—A large cupful of finely-minced beef suet, a teacupful of milk, four ounces of bread-crumbs, four ounces of well-cleaned currants, two ounces of almonds, half a pound of stoned raisins, three well-beaten eggs, and the whites of other two; sugar, nutmeg, and cinnamon, and a small glass of rum. Butter a shape, and place part of the raisins neatly in rows. Blanch the almonds; reserve the half of them to be placed in rows between the raisins just before serving. Mix all the remaining ingredients well together, put into the shape, and boil three hours. *The Sauce*—One teaspoonful of milk, and two yolks of eggs well

beaten, and some sugar; place on the fire and stir till it *just comes to the boil;* then let it cool. When lukewarm, stir into it a glass of sherry or currant wine, and serve in a sauce tureen. This sauce is a great improvement to the raisin pudding.

1205. Peas Pudding.—Dry a pint or quart of split peas thoroughly before the fire; then tie them up loosely in a cloth, put them into warm water, boil them a couple of hours, or more, until quite tender; take them up, beat them well in a dish with a little salt (some add the yolk of an egg), and a bit of butter. Make it quite smooth, tie it up again in a cloth, and boil it an hour longer. This is highly nourishing.

1206. Apple Dumplings.—Paste the same as for apple pudding, divide into as many pieces as dumplings are required; peel and core the apples; roll out your paste large enough; put in the apples; close the dumplings, tie them in cloths very tight. Boil them one hour; when you take them up, dip them quickly in cold water, and put them in a cup while you untie them; they will turn out without breaking.

1207. Rice Dumplings.—Pick and wash a pound of rice, and boil it gently in two quarts of water till it becomes dry—keeping the pot well covered, and not stirring it. Then take it off the fire, and spread it out to cool on the bottom of an inverted sieve, loosening the grains lightly with a fork, that all the moisture may evaporate. Pare a dozen pippins, or some large juicy apples, and scoop out the core; then fill up the cavity with marmalade, or with lemon and sugar. Cover every apple all over with a thick coating of the boiled rice. Tie up each in a separate cloth, and put them into a pot of cold water. They will require about an hour and a quarter after they begin to boil, perhaps longer.

1208. Boiled Custard.—Boil half a pint of new milk, with a piece of lemon peel, two peach leaves, half a stick of cassia, a few whole allspice, four or six ounces of white sugar.

Cream may be used instead of milk; beat the yolks and whites of four eggs, strain the milk through coarse muslin, or a hair sieve; then mix the eggs and milk very gradually together, and stir it well from the bottom, on the fire, till it thickens.

1209. Custard (Baked). — Boil in a pint of milk a few coriander seeds, a little cinnamon and lemon peel; sweeten with four ounces of loaf sugar, mix with it a pint of cold milk; beat eight eggs for ten minutes; add the other ingredients; pour it from one pan into another six or eight times, strain through a sieve; let it stand; skim the froth from the top, fill it in earthen cups, and bake immediately in a hot oven; give them a good colour; ten minutes will do them.

1210. French Batter. — Two ounces of butter cut into bits, pour on it less than a quarter of a pint of water boiling; when dissolved, add three quarters of a pint of water cold, so that it shall not be quite milk warm; mix by degrees smoothly with twelve ounces of fine dry flour and a small pinch of salt, if the batter be for fruit fritters, but with more if for meat or vegetables. Before used, stir into it the whites of two eggs beaten to solid froth; previously to this, add a little water if too thick. This is excellent for frying vegetables, and for fruit fritters.

1211. A Black Man's Recipe to Dress Rice. — Wash him well, much wash in cold water, the rice flour make him stick. Water boil all ready very fast. Throw him in, rice can't burn, water shake him too much. Boil quarter of an hour or little more; rub one rice in thumb and finger, if all rub away him quite done. Put rice in cullender, hot water run away; pour cup of cold water on him, put back rice in saucepan, keep him covered near the fire, then rice all ready. Eat him up!

1212. Yellow Rice. — Take one pound of rice, wash it clean, and put it into a saucepan which will hold three quarts; add to it half a pound of currants picked and washed, one quarter of an ounce of the best turmeric powder, previously dissolved in a cupful of water, and a stick of cinnamon; pour over them two quarts of cold water, place the saucepan uncovered on a moderate fire, and allow it to boil till the rice is dry, then stir in a quarter of a pound of sugar, and two ounces of butter: cover up, and place the pan near the fire for a few minutes, then mix it well and dish up. This is a favourite dish with the Japanese, and will be found excellent as a vegetable with roast meat, poultry, &c. It also forms a capital pudding, which may be improved by the addition of raisins, and a few blanched almonds.

1213. Boiled Rice for Curry. — Put the rice down in *cold* water, and let it come to a boil for a minute or so: strain it quite dry, and lay it on the hob in a stewpan without a cover to let the steam evaporate, then shake it into the dish while very hot. A squeeze of lemon juice after it boils will make it separate better. — The three last receipts were given to the editor of "Enquire Within" by a lady who had passed the greater part of her life in India, and who had them from native cooks.

1214. Lemon Rice. — Boil sufficient rice in milk, with white sugar to taste, till it is soft; put it into a pint basin or an earthenware blancmange mould, and leave it till cold. Peel a lemon very thick, cut the peel into shreds about half or three quarters of an inch in length, put them into a little water, boil them up, and throw the water away, lest it should be bitter, then pour about a teacupful of fresh water upon them; squeeze and strain the juice of the lemon, add it with white sugar to the water and shreds, and let it stew gently at the fire for two hours. (When cold it will be a syrup.) Having turned out the jellied rice into a cut-glass dish, or one of common delf, pour the syrup gradually over the rice, taking care the little shreds of the peel are equally distributed over the whole.

1215. Warming Cold Sweet Dishes.

1216. Rice Pudding.—Over the cold rice pudding pour a custard, and add a few lumps of jelly or preserved fruit. Remember to remove the baked coating of the pudding before the custard is poured over it.

1217. Apple Tart.—Cut into triangular pieces the remains of a cold apple tart: arrange the pieces around the sides of a glass or china bowl, and leave space in the centre for a custard to be poured in.

1218. Plum Pudding.—Cut into thin round slices cold plum pudding, and fry them in butter. Fry also Spanish fritters, and place them high in the centre of the dish, and the fried pudding all round the heaped-up fritters. Powder all with lump sugar, and serve them with wine sauce in a tureen.

1219. Fritters.—Make them of any of the batters directed for pancakes, by dropping a small quantity into the pan; or make the plainer sort, and dip pared apples, sliced and cored, into the batter, and fry them in plenty of hot lard. Currants, or sliced lemon as thin as paper, make an agreeable change. Fritters for company should be served on a folded napkin in the dish. Any sort of sweetmeat, or ripe fruit, may be made into fritters.

1220. Oyster Fritters.—Make a batter of flour, milk, and eggs; season a very little with nutmeg. Beard the oysters, and put as many as you think proper in each fritter.

1221. Potato Fritters.—Boil two large potatoes, bruise them fine, beat four yolks and three whites of eggs, and add to the above one large spoonful of cream, another of sweet wine, a squeeze of lemon, and a little nutmeg. Beat this batter well half an hour. It will be extremely light. Put a good quantity of fine lard into a stewpan, and drop a spoonful at a time of the batter into it. Fry them; and serve as a sauce, a glass of white wine, the juice of a lemon, one dessertspoonful of peach-leaf or almond water, and some white sugar, warmed together: not to be served in a dish.

1222. Apple Fritters.—Peel and core some fine pippins, and cut into slices. Soak them in wine, sugar, and nutmeg, for a few hours. Batter of four eggs to a tablespoonful of rose water, a tablespoonful of wine, and a tablespoonful of milk; thicken with enough flour, stirred in by degrees; mix two or three hours before wanted. Heat some butter in a frying-pan; dip each slice of apple separately in the batter, and fry brown; sift pounded sugar, and grate a nutmeg over them.

1223. Pancakes.—Make a light batter of eggs, flour, and milk; a little salt, nutmeg, and ginger may be added; fry in a small pan, in hot dripping or lard. Sugar and lemon should be served to eat with them. Or, when eggs are scarce, make the batter with small beer, ginger, and so forth; or water, with flour, and a very little milk, will serve, but not so well as eggs and all milk.

1224. Cream Pancakes.—Mix two eggs, well beaten, with a pint of cream, two ounces of sifted sugar, six of flour, a little nutmeg, cinnamon, and mace. Fry the pancakes thin, with a bit of butter.

1225. Rice Pancakes.—Boil half a pound of ground rice to a jelly in a pint of water or milk, and keep it well stirred from the bottom to prevent its being burnt; if too thick add a little more milk; take it off the fire; stir in six or eight ounces of butter, a pint of cream, six or eight eggs well beaten, a pinch of salt, sugar, and nutmeg, with as much flour as will make the batter thick enough. Fry them with lard or dripping.

1226. Scones.—Flour, two pounds; bicarbonate of soda, quarter of an ounce; salt, quarter of an ounce; sour buttermilk, one pint, more or less. Mix to the consistence of light dough, roll out about half an inch thick, and cut them out to any shape you please, and bake on a *girdle* over a clear fire about ten or fifteen minutes; turning them to brown on both sides—or they may be done on a hot plate, or ironing-stove. A girdle is a thin plate of cast iron about twelve or fourteen inches in diameter, with a handle attached, to hang it up by.—These scones are excellent for tea, and may be eaten either cold or hot, buttered, or with cheese.

1227. A Friar's Omelette.— Boil a dozen apples, as for sauce; stir in a quarter of a pound of butter, and the same of white sugar; when cold, add four eggs, well beaten; put it into a baking dish thickly strewed over with crumbs of bread, so as to stick to the bottom and sides; then put in the apple mixture; strew crumbs of bread over the top; when baked, turn it out and grate loaf sugar over it.

1228. Ordinary Omelette.— Take four eggs, beat the yolks and whites together with a tablespoonful of milk, a little salt and pepper; put two ounces of butter into a frying-pan to boil, and let it remain until it begins to brown; pour the batter into it, and let it remain quiet for a minute; turn up the edges of the omelette gently from the bottom of the pan with a fork; shake it, to keep it from burning at the bottom, and fry it till of a bright brown. It will not take more than five minutes frying.

1229. Miss Acton's Observations on Omelettes, Pancakes, Fritters, &c.--" There is no difficulty in making good omelettes, pancakes, or fritters; and, as they may be expeditiously prepared and served, they are often a very convenient resource when, on short notice, an addition is required to a dinner. The eggs for all of them should be well and lightly whisked; the lard for frying batter should be extremely pure in flavour, and quite hot when the fritters are dropped in; the batter itself should be smooth as cream, and it should be briskly beaten the instant before it is used. All fried pastes should be perfectly drained from the fat before they are served, and sent to table promptly when they are ready. Eggs may be dressed in a multiplicity of ways, but are seldom more relished in any form than in a well-made and expeditiously-served omelette. This may be plain, or seasoned with minced herbs and a very little shalot, when the last is liked, and is then called *Omelettes aux fines herbes;* or it may be mixed with minced ham or grated cheese: in any case, it should be light, thick, full-tasted, and *fried only on one side;* if turned in the pan, as it frequently is in England, it will at once be flattened and rendered tough. Should the slight rawness, which is sometimes found in the middle of the inside when the omelette is made in the French way, be objected to, a heated shovel, or a salamander, may be held over it for an instant, before it is folded on the dish. The pan for frying it should be quite small; for if it be composed of four or five eggs only, and then put into a large one, it will necessarily spread over it and be thin, which would render it more like a pancake than an omelette; the only partial remedy for this, when a pan of proper size cannot be had, is to raise the handle of it high, and to keep the opposite side close down to the fire, which will confine the eggs into a smaller space. No gravy should be poured into the dish with it, and, indeed, if properly made, it will require none. Lard is preferable to butter for frying batter, as it renders it lighter; but it must not be used for omelettes. Filled with preserves of any kind, it is called a sweet omelette."

1230. Baked Pears.— Take twelve large baking pears; pare and cut them into halves, leaving on the stem, about half an inch long; take out the core with the point of a knife, and place them close together in a block tin saucepan, the inside of which is quite bright, with the cover to fit quite close; put to them the rind of a lemon cut thin, with half its juice, a small stick of cinnamon, and twenty grains of allspice; cover them with spring water, and allow one pound of loaf sugar to a pint and a half of water: cover them up close, and bake them for six hours in a very slow oven;—they will be quite tender, and of a bright colour. Prepared cochineal is generally used for colouring the pears; but if the above is strictly attended to, it will be found to answer best.

1231. Apples served with Custard.—Pare and core apples; cut them in pieces; bake or stew them with as little water as possible; when they have become pulpy, sweeten and put them in a pie-dish, and, when cold, pour over them an unboiled custard, and put back into the oven till the custard is fixed. A Dutch oven will do. Equally good hot or cold.

1232. Apples in Syrup.—Pare and core some hard apples, and throw them into a basin of water; as they are done, clarify as much loaf sugar as will cover them; put the apples in along with the juice and rind of a lemon, and let them simmer till they are quite clear; care must be taken not to break them; place them on the dish they are to appear upon at table, and pour the syrup over. These are for immediate use.

1233. Apricots Stewed in Syrup.—Wipe the down from young apricots, and stew them as gently as possible in a syrup made of four ounces of sugar to half a pint of water, boiled the usual time.

1234. Mother Eve's Pudding.

If you would have a good pudding, observe
  what you're taught:
Take two pennyworth of eggs, when twelve for
  the groat;
And of the same fruit that Eve had once
  chosen,
Well pared and well chopped, at least half a
  dozen;
Six ounces of bread, (let your maid eat the
  crust,)
The crumbs must be grated as small as the
  dust;
Six ounces of currants from the stones you
  must sort,
Lest they break out your teeth, and spoil all
  your sport;
Five ounces of sugar won't make it too sweet;
Some salt and some nutmeg will make it complete;
Three hours let it boil, without hurry or flutter,
And then serve it up, without sugar or butter.

1235. Accidents.—*Always send for a surgeon immediately an accident occurs, but treat as directed until he arrives.*

1236. IN BOTH SCALDS AND BURNS, the following facts cannot be too firmly impressed on the mind of the reader, that in either of these accidents the *first, best,* and *often the only remedies required,* are sheets of wadding, fine wool or carded cotton, and in default of these, violet powder, flour, magnesia, or chalk. The object for which these several articles are employed is the same in each instance; namely, to exclude the air from the injured part; for if the air can be effectually shut out from the raw surface, and care is taken not to expose the tender part till the new cuticle is formed, the cure may be safely left to nature. The moment a person is called to a case of scald or burn, he should cover the part with a sheet or a portion of a sheet of wadding, taking care not to break any blister that may have formed, or stay to remove any burnt clothes that may adhere to the surface, but as quickly as possible envelop every part of the injury from all access of the air, laying one or two more pieces of wadding on the first, so as effectually to guard the burn or scald from the irritation of the atmosphere; and if the article used is wool or cotton, the same precaution, of adding more material where the surface is thinly covered, must be adopted; a light bandage finally securing all in their places. Any of the popular remedies recommended below may be employed when neither wool, cotton, nor wadding are to be procured, it being always remembered that that article which will best exclude the air from a burn or scald is the best, quickest, and least painful mode of treatment. And in this respect nothing has surpassed cotton loose or attached to paper as in wadding.

1237. IF THE SKIN IS MUCH INJURED in burns, spread some linen pretty thickly with chalk ointment, and lay over the part, and give the patient some brandy and water if much exhausted; then send for a medical man. If not much injured, and very painful, use the same ointment, or apply carded cotton dipped in lime water and linseed oil. If you please, you may lay cloths dipped. in ether over the parts, or cold lotions. Treat scalds in the same manner, or cover with scraped raw potato; but the chalk ointment is the best. In the absence of all these, cover the injured part with treacle, and dust over it plenty of flour.

1238. Body in Flames.—Lay the person down on the floor of the room, and throw the tablecloth, rug, or other large cloth over him, and roll him on the floor.

1239. Dirt in the Eye. — Place your forefinger upon the cheek-bone, having the patient before you; then draw up the finger, and you will probably be able to remove the dirt; but if this will not enable you to get at it, repeat this operation while you have a netting-needle or bodkin placed over the eyelid; this will turn it inside out, and enable you to remove the sand, or eyelash, &c., with the corner of a fine silk handkerchief. As soon as the substance is removed, bathe the eye with cold water, and exclude the light for a day. If the inflammation is severe, take a purgative, and use a refrigerant lotion.

1240. Lime in the Eye.—Syringe it well with warm vinegar and water (one ounce to eight ounces of water); take a purgative, and exclude light.

1241. Iron or Steel Spiculæ in the Eye.—These occur while turning iron or steel in a lathe, and are best remedied by doubling back the upper or lower eyelid, according to the situation of the substance, and with the flat edge of a silver probe, taking up the metallic particle, using a lotion made by dissolving six grains of sugar of lead, and the same of white vitriol, in six ounces of water, and bathing the eye three times a day till the inflammation subsides. Another plan is—Drop a solution of sulphate of copper (from one to three grains of the salt to one ounce of water) into the eye, or keep the eye open in a wineglassful of the solution. Take a purgative, bathe with cold lotion, and exclude light to keep down inflammation.

1242. Dislocated Thumb.—This is frequently produced by a fall. Make a clove hitch, by passing two loops of cord over the thumb, placing a piece of rag under the cord to prevent it cutting the thumb; then pull in the same line as the thumb. Afterwards apply a cold lotion.

1243. Cuts and Wounds.—Clean cut wounds, whether deep or superficial, and likely to heal by the first intention, should never be washed or cleaned, but at once evenly and smoothly closed by bringing both edges close together, and securing them in that position by adhesive plaster. Cut thin strips of sticking-plaster, and bring the parts together; or if large and deep, cut two broad pieces, so as to look like the teeth of a comb, and place one on each side of the wound, which must be cleaned previously. These pieces must be arranged so that they shall interlace one another; then, by laying hold of the pieces on the right side with one hand, and those on the other side with the other hand, and pulling them from one another, the edges of the wound are brought together without any difficulty.

1244. Ordinary Cuts are dressed by thin strips, applied by pressing down the plaster on one side of the wound, and keeping it there and pulling in the opposite direction; then suddenly depressing the hand when the edges of the wound are brought together.

1245. Contusions are best healed by laying a piece of folded lint, well wetted with the extract of lead, on the part, and, if there is much pain, placing a hot bran poultice over the dressing, repeating both, if necessary, every two hours. When the injuries are very severe, lay a cloth over the part, and suspend a basin over it filled with cold lotion. Put a piece of cotton into the basin, so that it shall allow the lotion to drop on the cloth, and thus keep it always wet.

1246. HÆMORRHAGE, when caused by an artery being divided or torn, may be known by the blood issuing out of the wound in leaps or jerks, and being of a bright scarlet colour. If a vein is injured, the blood is darker and flows continuously. To arrest the latter, apply pressure by means of a compress and bandage. To arrest arterial bleeding, get a piece of wood (part of a mop handle will do), and tie a piece of tape to one end of it; then tie a piece of tape loosely over the arm, and pass the other end of the wood under it; twist the stick round and round until the tape compresses the arm sufficiently to arrest the bleeding, and then confine the other end by tying the string round the arm. A compress made by enfolding a penny piece in several folds of lint or linen should, however, be first placed under the tape and over the artery. If the bleeding is very obstinate, and it occurs in the *arm*, place a cork underneath the string, on the inside of the fleshy part, where the artery may be felt beating by any one; if in the *leg*, place a cork in the direction of a line drawn from the inner part of the knee towards the outer part of the groin. It is an excellent thing to accustom yourself to find out the position of these arteries, or, indeed, any that are superficial, and to explain to every person in your house where they are, and how to stop bleeding. If a stick cannot be got, take a handkerchief, make a cord bandage of it, and tie a knot in the middle; the knot acts as a compress, and should be placed over the artery, while the two ends are to be tied around the thumb. Observe *always to place the ligature between the wound and the heart.* Putting your finger into a bleeding wound, and making pressure until a surgeon arrives, will generally stop violent bleeding.

1247. BLEEDING FROM THE NOSE, from whatever cause, may generally be stopped by putting a plug of lint into the nostrils; if this does not do, apply a cold lotion to the forehead;

raise the head, and place over it both arms, so that it will rest on the hands; dip the lint plug, *slightly moistened*, into some powdered gum arabic, and plug the nostrils again; or dip the plug into equal parts of powdered gum arabic and alum, and plug the nose. Or the plug may be dipped in Friar's balsam, or tincture of kino. Heat should be applied to the feet; and, in obstinate cases, the sudden shock of a cold key, or cold water poured down the spine, will often instantly stop the bleeding. If the bowels are confined, take a purgative.

1248. VIOLENT SHOCKS will sometimes stun a person, and he will remain unconscious. Untie strings, collars, &c.; loosen anything that is tight, and interferes with the breathing; raise the head; see if there is bleeding from any part; apply smelling-salts to the nose, and hot bottles to the feet.

1249. IN CONCUSSION, the surface of the body is cold and pale, and the pulse weak and small, the breathing slow and *gentle*, and the pupil of the eye generally contracted or small. You can get an answer by speaking loud, so as to arouse the patient. Give a little brandy and water, keep the place quiet, apply warmth, and do not raise the head too high. If you tickle the feet, the patient feels it.

1250. IN COMPRESSION OF THE BRAIN from any cause, such as apoplexy, or a piece of fractured bone pressing on it, there is loss of sensation. If you tickle the feet of the injured person he does not feel it. You cannot arouse him so as to get an answer. The pulse is slow and laboured; the breathing deep, laboured, and *snorting;* the pupil enlarged. Raise the head, loosen strings or tight things, and send for a surgeon. If one cannot be got at once, apply mustard poultices to the feet and thighs, leeches to the temples, and hot water to the feet.

1251. CHOKING.—When a person has a fish bone in the throat, insert the forefinger, press upon the root of the tongue, so as to induce vomiting; if this does not do, let him swallow a *large piece* of potato or soft bread; and if these fail, give a mustard emetic.

1252. FAINTING, HYSTERICS, &c.—Loosen the garments, bathe the temples with water or eau-de-Cologne; open the window, admit plenty of fresh air, dash cold water on the face, apply hot bricks to the feet, and avoid bustle and excessive sympathy.

1253. DROWNING.—Attend to the following *essential rules*:—i. Lose no time. ii. Handle the body gently. iii. Carry the body face downwards, with the head gently raised, and never hold it up by the feet. iv. Send for medical assistance immediately, and in the meantime act as follows:—v. Strip the body, rub it dry: then wrap it in hot blankets, and place it in a warm bed in a warm room. vi. Cleanse away the froth and mucus from the nose and mouth. vii. Apply warm bricks, bottles, bags of sand, &c., to the armpits, between the thighs, and to the soles of the feet. viii. Rub the surface of the body with the hands enclosed in warm dry worsted socks. ix. If possible, put the body into a warm bath. x. To restore breathing, put the pipe of a common bellows into one nostril, carefully closing the other, and the mouth; at the same time drawing downwards, and pushing gently backwards, the upper part of the windpipe, to allow a more free admission of air; blow the bellows gently, in order to inflate the lungs, till the breast be raised a little; then set the mouth and nostrils free, and press gently on the chest: repeat this until signs of life appear. The body should be covered the moment it is placed on the table, except the face, and all the rubbing carried on under the sheet or blanket. When they can be obtained, a number of tiles or bricks should be made tolerably hot in the fire, laid in a row on the table, covered with a blanket, and the body placed in such a manner on them, that their heat may enter the spine. When the patient revives, apply smelling-salts to the nose, give warm wine or brandy and water. *Cautions.*—i. Never rub the body with salt or spirits. ii. Never roll the body on casks. iii. Continue the remedies for twelve hours without ceasing.

1254. HANGING.—Loosen the cord, or whatever suspended the person; open the temporal artery or jugular vein, or bleed from the arm; employ electricity, if at hand, and proceed as for drowning, taking the additional precaution to apply eight or ten leeches to the temples.

1255. APPARENT DEATH FROM DRUNKENNESS. — Raise the head, loosen the clothes, maintain warmth of surface, and give a mustard emetic as soon as the person can swallow.

1256. APOPLEXY AND FITS GENERALLY.—Raise the head; loosen all tight clothes, strings, &c.; apply cold lotions to the head, which should be shaved; apply leeches to the temples, bleed, and send for a surgeon.

1257. SUFFOCATION FROM NOXIOUS GASES, &c.—Remove to the fresh air; dash cold vinegar and water in the face, neck, and breast; keep up the warmth of the body; if necessary, apply mustard poultices to the soles of the feet and spine, and try artificial respirations as in drowning, with electricity.

1258. LIGHTNING AND SUN STROKE.—Treat the same as apoplexy.

1259. Poisons, General Observations.

The abbreviations used are as follows:—
  E., effects or symptoms. T., treatment.
  A., antidotes or counter poisons.
  D. A., dangerous antidotes.

1260. A POISON IS A SUBSTANCE which is capable of altering or destroying some or all of the functions necessary to life. When a person is in good health, and is suddenly attacked, after having taken some food or drink, with violent pain, cramp in the stomach, feeling of sickness or nausea, vomiting, convulsive twitchings, and a sense of suffocation; or if he be seized, under the same circumstances, with giddiness, delirium, or unusual sleepiness, then poisoning may be supposed.

1261. POISONS HAVE BEEN DIVIDED

into four. classes:—i. Those causing local symptoms. ii. Those producing spasmodic symptoms. iii. Narcotic or sleepy symptoms; and iv. Paralytic symptoms. Poisons may be mineral, animal, or vegetable.

1262. i. ALWAYS SEND IMMEDIATELY FOR A MEDICAL MAN. ii. Save all fluids vomited, and articles of food, cups, glasses, &c., used by the patient before being taken ill, and lock them up. iii. Examine the cups to guide you in your treatment; that is, smell them, and look at them.

1263. As A RULE, GIVE EMETICS after poisons that cause sleepiness and raving;—chalk, milk, eggs, butter, and warm water, or oil, after poisons that cause vomiting and pain in the stomach and bowels, with purging; and when there is no inflammation about the throat, tickle it with a feather to excite vomiting.

1264. Arsenic. (*White arsenic; orpiment, or yellow arsenic; realgar, red arsenic; Scheele's green, or arsenite of copper; King's yellow; ague drops; and arsenical paste.*)—E. Little or no taste. Within an hour, heat and pain in the stomach, followed by vomiting of green, yellow, and bloody matter, burning, and violent thirst; purging, and twisting about the navel; pulse small, quick, and irregular, breathing laboured, voice hoarse, speaking painful; skin cold and clammy. Sometimes there are cramps and convulsions, followed by death.—T. Give plenty of warm water, *new milk* in large quantities, lime water, white of egg, mixed with gruel or honey, gruel, linseed tea; apply leeches to the bowels, foment, and give starch or gruel enemas. Scrape the iron rust off anything you can get at, mix it with plenty of water, and give in large draughts frequently, and give an emetic of mustard or ipecacuanha. The chief dependence, however, must be placed on the use of the stomach-pump. *Caution.*—Never give large draughts of fluid until those given before have been vomited, because the stomach will not contract properly if filled with fluid,

and the object is to get rid of the poison as speedily as possible.

1265. Copper. (*Blue vitriol, or bluestone; verdigris; verditer; verdigris crystals.*)—E. An acid, rough, disagreeable taste in the mouth; a dry, parched tongue, with sense of strangling in the throat; coppery eructations; frequent spitting; nausea; frequent desire and effort to vomit, or copious vomiting; severe darting pains in the stomach; griping; frequent purging; belly swollen and painful; skin hot, and violent burning thirst; breathing difficult; intense headache and giddiness, followed by cold sweats, cramps in the legs, convulsions, and death.—A. White of eggs mixed with water (twelve to one pint), to be given in wineglassfuls every two minutes; iron filings mixed with water, or very strong coffee, accompanied by small and repeated doses of castor oil.—D. A. Vinegar, bark, alkalies, gall nuts.—T. If there is much pain in the belly or stomach, apply leeches. Give large draughts of milk and water, to encourage vomiting.

1266. Mercury. (*Corrosive sublimate; calomel; red precipitate; vermilion; turbeth mineral; prussiate of mercury.*)—E. Acid metallic taste; tightness and burning in the throat; pain in the back part of the mouth, stomach, and bowels; anxiety of countenance; nausea; and vomiting of bloody and bilious fluids; profuse purging, and difficulty of making water; pulse small, hard, and quick; skin clammy, icy coldness of the hands and feet; and death in 24 or 36 hours. —A. White of eggs mixed with water, given as above; milk; flour and water, mixed pretty thick; linseed tea; and barley water.—T. Give large draughts of warm water, if you cannot get anything else; strong emetic of ipecacuanha, the stomach-pump, a dose of castor oil and laudanum. Foment the bowels with poppy-head fomentations, and apply leeches if the belly is very tender.

1267. Antimony. (*Tartar emetic; butter of; Kermes' mineral.*)—E. A rough metallic taste in the mouth, nausea, copious vomitings, sudden hiccough, purging, colicy pains, frequent and violent cramps, sense of choking, severe heartburn, pain at the pit of the stomach, difficult breathing, wildness of speech, cramps in the legs, and death.—A. Decoction or tincture of galls; strong tea; decoction or powder of Peruvian bark. —D. A. White vitriol, ipecacuanha, as emetics.—T. Give large draughts of water, or sugar and water, to promote vomiting; apply leeches to the throat and stomach, if painful; and give one grain of extract of opium dissolved in a wineglassful of sugar and water, as soon as the vomiting ceases, and repeat three times at intervals of a quarter of an hour; and finally, one grain, in a little castor oil emulsion, every six hours.

1268. Tin. (*Butter of tin; putty powder.*)—E. Colic and purging.—A. Milk.—T. Give warm or cold water to promote vomiting, or tickle the throat with a feather.

1269. Zinc. (*White vitriol; flowers of; chloride of.*)—E. An astringent taste, sensation of choking, nausea, vomiting, purging, pain and burning in the throat and stomach, difficult breathing, pallor and coldness of the surface, pinched face, cramps of the extremities, but, with the exception of the chloride, seldom death.—A. For the two first give copious draughts of milk, and white of eggs and water, mucilage, and olive oil; for the third, carbonate of soda, and warm water in frequent draughts, with the same as for the other compounds.—T. Relieve urgent symptoms by leeching and fomentations, and after the vomiting give castor oil. For the chloride, use frictions and warmth.

1270. Silver (*Lunar caustic; flowers of silver*); **Gold** (*Chloride of*); and **Bismuth** (*Nitrate; flowers of; pearl white*), are not frequently met with as poisons.—E. Burning pain in the throat, mouth, accompanied with the usual symptoms of corrosive poisons.—A. For silver, common salt and water; for gold and bismuth, no antidotes are known.—T. Give milk and mucilaginous fluids, and castor oil.

1271. Acids (*Hydrochloric,* or *spirit of salt; nitric,* or *aquafortis; sulphuric,* or *oil of vitriol*).—E. Acid burning taste, acute pain in the gullet and throat, vomiting of bloody fluid, which effervesces when chalk is added to it; hiccough, tenderness of the belly, cold sweats, pinched face, convulsions, and death. — A. Give *calcined* magnesia, chalk, soap and water. Administer frequent draughts of water to weaken the acid; the carbonate of soda, potass, or magnesia, to neutralize it; thick soapsuds, made with common soap; chalk, or in default of the alkalies and chalk, break down the plaster of the wall or ceiling, mix in water, and give the sufferer. Excite vomiting, and repeat the remedies till all the acid is neutralized.

1272. Chlorine (*gas*).—E. Violent coughing, tightness of the chest, debility, inability to stand. — A. The vapour of caustic ammonia to be inhaled, or ten drops of liquid ammonia to one ounce of water to be taken.—T. Dash cold water over the face, and relieve urgent symptoms.

1273. Lead (*Sugar of; red lead; wine sweetened by; and water impregnated with*). — E. Sugary astringent metallic taste, tightness of the throat, colicy pains, violent vomiting, hiccough, convulsions, and death.—A. Epsom or Glauber's salt; plaster of Paris; or phosphate of soda.—T. An emetic of sulphate of zinc (twenty-four grains to half a pint of water); leeches to belly; fomentations if necessary; and a castor oil mixture with laudanum.

1274. Phosphorus.—E. Intense burning and pain in the throat and stomach. — A. Magnesia and carbonate of soda. — T. Large draughts of cold water, and tickle the throat with a feather. *Caution.*—Do not give oil or milk.

1275. Lime.—E. Burning in the throat and stomach, cramps in the belly, hiccough, vomiting, and paralysis of limbs.—A. Vinegar or lemon juice.—T. Thin starch water to be drunk frequently.

1276. Alkalies. (*Caustic; potash; soda; ammonia.*)—E. Acrid, hot, disagreeable taste; burning in the throat, nausea, and vomiting bloody matter; profuse purging, pain in the stomach, colic, convulsions, and death.—A. Vinegar and vegetable acids.—T. Give linseed tea, milk, almond or olive oil, and excite vomiting.

1277. Baryta (*Carbonate, pure,* and *muriate*). (*See* LIME.)

1278. Nitre.—E. Heartburn, nausea, violent vomiting, purging, convulsions, difficult breathing, violent pain in the bowels, kidney, and bladder, with bloody urine.—T. Emetics, frequent draughts of barley water, with castor oil and laudanum.

1279. Narcotic Poisons. (*Bane berries; fools' parsley; deadly nightshade; water hemlock; thorn apple; opium; camphor, &c.*)—E. Giddiness, faintness, nausea, vomiting, stupor, delirium, and death.—T. Give emetics, large draughts of fluids, tickle the throat, apply smelling-salts to the nose, dash cold water over the face and chest, apply mustard poultices, and, above all, endeavour to rouse the patient by walking between two persons; and, if possible, by electricity; and give forty drops of sal-volatile in strong coffee every half-hour.

1280. Vegetable Irritating Poisons. (*Mezereon; monk's-hood; bitter apple; gamboge; white hellebore, &c.*)—E. Acrid, biting, bitter taste, choking sensation, dryness of the throat, retching, vomiting, purging, pains in the stomach and bowels, breathing difficult, and death.—T. Give emetics of camomile, mustard, or sulphate of zinc; large draughts of warm milk, or other bland fluids; foment and leech the belly if necessary, and give strong *infusion* of coffee.

1281. Oxalic Acid.—E. Vomiting and acute pain in the stomach, general debility, cramps, and death.—A. Chalk.—T. Give large draughts of lime water or magnesia.

1282. Spanish Flies.—E. Acrid taste, burning heat in the throat, stomach,

and belly, bloody vomitings, colic, purging, retention of urine, convulsions, death.—T. Large draughts of olive oil, thin gruel, milk, starch enemas, linseed tea, laudanum, and camphorated water.

1283. Poisonous Fish. (*Old-wife; sea-lobster; mussel; tunny; blower; rock-fish, &c.*)—E. Intense pain in the stomach after swallowing the fish, vomiting, purging, and sometimes cramps.—T. Give an emetic; excite vomiting by tickling the throat, and plenty of warm water. Follow emetics by active purgatives, particularly of castor oil and laudanum, or opium and calomel, and abate inflammation by the usual remedies.

1284. Bites of Reptiles. (*Viper; black viper; Indian serpents; rattle-snake.*)—E. Violent and quick inflammation of the part, extending towards the body, soon becoming livid; nausea, vomiting, convulsions, difficult breathing, mortification, cold sweats, and death.—T. Suppose that the wrist has been bitten: immediately tie a tape between the wound and the heart, scarify the parts with a penknife, razor, or lancet, and apply a cupping-glass over the bite, frequently removing it and bathing the wound with volatile alkali, or heat a poker and burn the wound well, or drop some of Sir Wm. Burnett's Disinfecting Fluid into the wound, or cauterize the bite freely with lunar caustic, but not till the part has been well sucked with the mouth, or frequently washed and cupped.   The strength is to be supported by brandy, ammonia, ether, and opium. Give plenty of warm drinks, and cover up in bed.

1285. Mad Animals, Bite of.—E. Hydrophobia, or a fear of fluids.—T. Tie a string tightly over the part, cut out the bite, and cauterize the wound with a red-hot poker, lunar caustic, or Sir Wm. Burnett's Disinfecting Fluid.   Then apply a piece of "spongio-piline," give a purgative, and plenty of warm drink. Whenever chloroform can be procured, sprinkle a few drops upon a handkerchief, and apply to the nose and mouth of the patient before cauterizing the wound. When the breathing appears difficult, cease the application of the chloroform. A physician, writing in the *Times*, strongly urges this course, and states that there is no danger, with ordinary care, in the application of the chloroform, while the cauterization may be more effectively performed.

1286. Insect Stings. (*Wasp, bee, gnat, hornet, gadfly, scorpion.*)—E. Swelling, nausea, and fever.—T. Press the barrel of a watch-key over the part, so as to expose the sting, which must be removed. Give fifteen drops of hartshorn or sal-volatile in half a wineglassful of camomile tea, and cover the part stung with a piece of lint soaked in extract of lead.

1287. Cautions for the Prevention of Accidents.—The following regulations should be engraved on the memory of all :—

i. As many sudden deaths come by water, particular caution is therefore necessary in its vicinity.

ii. Stand not near a tree, or any leaden spout, iron gate, or palisade, in times of lightning.

iii. Lay loaded guns in safe places, and never imitate firing a gun in jest.

iv. Never sleep near charcoal; if drowsy at any work where charcoal fires are used, take the fresh air.

v. Carefully rope trees before they are cut down, that when they fall they may do no injury.

vi. When benumbed with cold beware of sleeping out of doors; rub yourself, if you have it in your power, with snow, and do not hastily approach the fire.

vii. Beware of damps.

viii. Air vaults, by letting them remain open some time before you enter, or scattering powdered lime in them. Where a lighted candle will not burn, animal life cannot exist; it will be an excellent caution, therefore, before entering damp and confined places, to try this simple experiment.

ix. Never leave saddle or draught horses, while in use, by themselves; nor go immediately behind a led horse, as he is apt to kick.

x. Do not ride on footways.

xi. Be wary of children, whether they are up or in bed; and particularly when they are near the fire, an element with which they are very apt to amuse themselves.

xii. Leave nothing poisonous open or accessible; and never omit to write the word "POISON" in large letters upon it, wherever it may be placed.

xiii. In walking the streets keep out of the line of the cellars, and never look one way and walk another.

xiv. Never throw pieces of orange peel, or broken glass bottles, into the streets.

xv. Never meddle with gunpowder by candle-light.

xvi. In trimming a lamp with naphtha, never fill it. Leave space for the spirit to expand with warmth.

xvii. Never quit a room leaving the poker in the fire.

xviii. When the brass rod of the stair-carpet becomes loose, fasten it immediately.

xix. In opening effervescing drinks, such as soda water, hold the cork in your hand.

xx. Quit your house with care on a frosty morning.

xxi. Have your horses' shoes roughed directly there are indications of frost.

xxii. Keep lucifer matches in their cases, and never let them be strewed about.

1288. Accidents in Carriages. —It is safer, as a general rule, to keep your place than to jump out. Getting out of a gig over the back, provided you can hold on a little while, and run, is safer than springing from the side. But it is best to keep your place, and hold fast. In accidents people act not so much from reason as from excitement: but good rules, firmly impressed upon the mind, generally rise uppermost, even in the midst of fear.

1289. Life Belts.—An excellent and cheap life belt, for persons proceeding to sea, bathing in dangerous places, or learning to swim, may be thus made:—Take a yard and three quarters of strong jean, double, and divide it into nine compartments. Let there be a space of two inches after each third compartment. Fill the compartments with very fine cuttings of cork, which may be made by cutting up old corks, or (still better) purchased at the corkcutter's. Work eyelet holes at the bottom of each compartment, to let the water drain out. Attach a neck-band and waist-strings of stout boot-web, and sow them on strongly.

1290. ANOTHER.—Cut open an old boa, or victorine, and line it with fine cork-cuttings instead of wool. For ladies going to sea these are excellent, as they may be worn in stormy weather, without giving appearance of alarm in danger. They may be fastened to the body by ribands or tapes, of the colour of the fur. Gentlemen's waistcoats may be lined the same way.

1291. Charcoal Fumes.—The usual remedies for persons overcome with the fumes of charcoal in a close apartment are, to throw cold water on the head, and to bleed immediately; also apply mustard or hartshorn to the soles of the feet.

1292. Cautions in Visiting the Sick.—Do not visit the sick when you are fatigued, or when in a state of perspiration, or with the stomach empty—for in such conditions you are liable to take the infection. When the disease is very contagious, place yourself at the side of the patient which is nearest to the window. Do not enter the room the first thing in the morning, before it has been aired; and when you come away, take some food, change your clothing immediately, and expose the latter to the air for some days. Tobacco smoke is a preventive of malaria.

1293. Children and Cutlery.—Serious accidents having occurred to babies through their catching hold of the blades of sharp instruments, the following hint will be useful. If a child lay hold of a knife or razor, do not try to pull it away, or to force

open the hand; but, holding the child's hand that is empty, offer to its other hand anything nice or pretty, and it will immediately open the hand, and let the dangerous instrument fall.

1294. Directing Letters.—It may sound like being over particular, but we recommend persons to make a practice of fully addressing notes, &c., on all occasions; when, in case of their being dropped by careless messengers (which is not a rare occurrence), it is evident for whom they are intended, without undergoing the inspection of any other parties bearing a similar name.

1295. Prevention of Fires.—The following simple suggestions are worthy of observation:—Add one ounce of alum to the last water used to rinse children's dresses, and they will be rendered uninflammable, or so slightly combustible that they would take fire very slowly, if at all, and would not flame. This is a simple precaution, which may be adopted in families of children. Bed curtains, and linen in general, may also be treated in the same way. Since the occurrence of many lamentable deaths by fire, arising partly from the fashion of wearing crinoline, the tungstate of soda has been recommended for the purpose of rendering any article of female dress incombustible. A patent starch is also sold, with which the tungstate of soda is incorporated. The starch should be used whenever it can be procured; and any chemist will intimate to the purchaser the manner in which the tungstate of soda should be employed.

1296. Precautions in Case of Fire.—The following precautions should be impressed upon the memory of all our readers:—

1297. SHOULD a fire break out, send off to the nearest engine or police station.

1298. FILL BUCKETS WITH WATER, carry them as near the fire as possible, dip a mop into the water, and throw it in showers on the fire, until assistance arrives.

1299. If a Fire is violent, wet a blanket, and throw it on the part which is in flames.

1300. Should a Fire break out in the Kitchen Chimney, or any other, a blanket wetted should be nailed to the upper ends of the mantelpiece, so as to cover the opening entirely; the fire will then go out of itself: for this purpose two knobs should be permanently fixed in the upper ends of the mantelpiece, on which the blanket may be hitched.

1301. Should the bed or window curtains be on fire, lay hold of any woollen garment, and beat it on the flames until extinguished.

1302. Avoid leaving the Window or Door open in the room where the fire has broken out, as the current of air increases the force of the fire.

1303. Should the Staircase be burning, so as to cut off all communication, endeavour to escape by means of a trap-door in the roof, a ladder leading to which should always be at hand.

1304. Avoid Hurry and Confusion; no person except a fireman, friend, or neighbour, should be admitted.

1305. If a Lady's Dress takes Fire, she should endeavour to roll herself in a rug, carpet, or the first woollen garment she meets with.

1306. It is a Good Precaution to have always at hand a large piece of baize, to throw over a female whose dress is burning, or to be wetted and thrown over a fire that has recently broken out.

1307. A Solution of Pearlash in Water, thrown upon a fire, extinguishes it instantly. The proportion is a quarter of a pound, dissolved in some hot water, and then poured into a bucket of common water.

1308. It is Recommended to Householders to have two or three fire-buckets and a carriage-mop with a long handle near at hand; they will be found essentially useful in case of fire.

1309. All Householders, but particularly hotel, tavern, and inn-keepers, should exercise a wise precaution by directing that the last person up should perambulate the premises previous to going to rest, to ascertain that all fires are safe and lights extinguished.

1310. To Extinguish a Fire in a Chimney.—So many serious fires have been caused by chimneys catching fire, and not being quickly extinguished, that the following method of doing this should be made generally known. Throw some powdered brimstone on the fire in the grate, or ignite some on the hob, and then put a board or something in the front of the fireplace, to prevent the fumes descending into the room. The vapour of the brimstone, ascending the chimney, will then effectually extinguish the soot on fire.

1311. To Extinguish a Fire in the chimney, besides any water at hand, throw on it salt, or a handful of flour of sulphur, as soon as you can obtain it; keep all the doors and windows tightly shut, and hold before the fireplace a blanket, or some woollen article, to exclude the air.

1312. In Escaping from a Fire, creep or crawl along the room with your face close to the ground. Children should be early taught how to press out a spark when it happens to reach any part of their dress, and also that running into the air will cause it to blaze immediately.

1313. Reading in Bed at night should be avoided, as, besides the danger of an accident, it never fails to injure the eyes.

1314. To Heat a Bed at a moment's notice, throw a little salt into the warming-pan, and suffer it to burn for a minute previous to use.

1315. Flowers and shrubs should be excluded from a bed-chamber.

1316. Swimming.—Every person should endeavour to acquire the power of swimming. The fact that the exercise is a healthful accompaniment of bathing, and that lives may be saved by it, even when least expected, is a sufficient argument for the recommendation. The art of swimming is, in reality, very easy. The first consideration is not to attempt to learn to swim too hastily. That is to say, you must not expect to succeed in your efforts to swim, until you have become accustomed to the water, and have overcome your repugnance to the coldness and novelty of bathing. Every attempt will fail until you have acquired a certain confidence in the water, and then the difficulty will soon vanish.

1317. **Dr. Franklin's Advice to Swimmers.**—"The only obstacle to improvement in this necessary and life-preserving art is fear: and it is only by overcoming this timidity that you can expect to become a master of the following acquirements. It is very common for novices in the art of swimming to make use of corks or bladders to assist in keeping the body above water: some have utterly condemned the use of them: however, they may be of service for supporting the body while one is learning what is called the stroke, or that manner of drawing in and striking out the hands and feet that is necessary to produce progressive motion. But you will be no swimmer till you can place confidence in the power of the water to support you; I would, therefore, advise the acquiring that confidence in the first place; especially as I have known several who, by a little practice, necessary for that purpose, have insensibly acquired the stroke, taught, as it were, by nature. The practice I mean is this: choosing a place where the water deepens gradually, walk coolly into it till it is up to your breast; then turn round your face to the shore, and throw an egg into the water between you and the shore; it will sink to the bottom, and be easily seen there if the water be clear. It must lie in the water so deep that you cannot reach to take it up but by diving for it. To encourage yourself in order to do this, reflect that your progress will be from deep to shallow water, and that at any time you may, by bringing your legs under you, and standing on the bottom, raise your head far above the water; then plunge under it with your eyes open, which must be kept open on going under, as you cannot open the eyelids for the weight of water above you; throwing yourself toward the egg, and endeavouring by the action of your hands and feet against the water to get forward, till

within reach of it. In this attempt you will find that the water buoys you up against your inclination; that it is not so easy to sink as you imagine, and that you cannot, but by active force, get down to the egg. Thus you feel the power of water to support you, and learn to confide in that power, while your endeavours to overcome it, and reach the egg, teach you the manner of acting on the water with your feet and hands, which action is afterwards used in swimming to support your head higher above the water, or to go forward through it.

1318. "I would the more earnestly press you to the trial of this method, because I think I shall satisfy you that your body is lighter than water, and that you might float in it a long time with your mouth free for breathing, if you would put yourself into a proper posture, and would be still, and forbear struggling; yet, till you have obtained this experimental confidence in the water, I cannot depend upon your having the necessary presence of mind to recollect the posture, and the directions I gave you relating to it. The surprise may put all out of your mind.

1319. "THOUGH THE LEGS, ARMS, AND HEAD of a human body, being solid parts, are specifically somewhat heavier than fresh water, as the trunk, particularly the upper part, from its hollowness, is so much lighter than water, so the whole of the body, taken altogether, is too light to sink wholly under water, but some part will remain above until the lungs become filled with water, which happens from drawing water to them instead of air, when a person, in the fright, attempts breathing while the mouth and nostrils are under water.

1320. "THE LEGS AND ARMS ARE SPECIFICALLY LIGHTER than salt water, and will be supported by it, so that a human body cannot sink in salt water, though the lungs were filled as above, but from the greater specific gravity of the head. Therefore a person throwing himself on his back in salt water, and extending his arms, may easily lie so as to keep his mouth and nostrils free for breathing; and, by a slight motion of his hand, may prevent turning, if he should perceive any tendency to it.

1321. "IN FRESH WATER, IF A MAN THROW HIMSELF ON HIS BACK near the surface, he cannot long continue in that situation, but by proper action of his hands on the water; if he use no such action, the legs and lower part of the body will gradually sink till he come into an upright position, in which he will continue suspended, the hollow of his breast keeping the head uppermost.

1322. "BUT IF IN THIS ERECT POSITION the head be kept upright above the shoulders, as when we stand on the ground, the immersion will, by the weight of that part of the head that is out of the water, reach above the mouth and nostrils, perhaps a little above the eyes, so that a man cannot long remain suspended in water with his head in that position.

1323. "THE BODY CONTINUING SUSPENDED as before, and upright, if the head be leaned quite back, so that the face look upward, all the back part of the head being under water, and its weight consequently, in a great measure, supported by it, the face will remain above water quite free for breathing, will rise an inch higher every inspiration, and sink as much every expiration, but never so low as that the water may come over the mouth.

1324. "IF, THEREFORE, A PERSON UNACQUAINTED WITH SWIMMING, and falling accidentally into the water, could have presence of mind sufficient to avoid struggling and plunging, and to let the body take this natural position, he might continue long safe from drowning, till, perhaps, help should come; for, as to the clothes, their additional weight when immersed is very inconsiderable, the water supporting it; though, when he comes out of the water, he will find them very heavy indeed.

1325. "BUT I WOULD NOT ADVISE ANY ONE TO DEPEND ON HAVING THIS PRESENCE OF MIND on such an occasion, but learn fairly to swim, as I wish all men were taught to do in their youth; they would, on many occasions, be the safer for having that skill; and, on many more, the happier, as free from painful apprehensions of danger, to say nothing of the enjoyment in so delightful and wholesome an exercise. Soldiers particularly should, methinks, all be taught to swim; it might be of frequent use, either in surprising an enemy or saving themselves; and if I had now boys to educate, I should prefer those schools (other things being equal) where an opportunity was afforded for acquiring so advantageous an art, which, once learned, is never forgotten.

1326. "I KNOW BY EXPERIENCE, that it is a great comfort to a swimmer, who has a considerable distance to go, to turn himself sometimes on his back, and to vary, in other respects, the means of procuring a progressive motion.

1327. "WHEN HE IS SEIZED WITH THE

CRAMP in the leg, the method of driving it away is to give the parts affected a sudden, vigorous, and violent shock; which he may do in the air as he swims on his back.

1328. "DURING THE GREAT HEATS OF SUMMER, there is no danger in bathing, however warm we may be, in rivers which have been thoroughly warmed by the sun. But to throw one's self into cold spring water, when the body has been heated by exercise in the sun, is an imprudence which may prove fatal. I once knew an instance of four young men who, having worked at harvest in the heat of the day, with a view of refreshing themselves, plunged into a spring of cold water; two died upon the spot, a third next morning, and the fourth recovered with great difficulty. A copious draught of cold water, in similar circumstances, is frequently attended with the same effect in North America.

1329. "THE EXERCISE OF SWIMMING IS ONE OF THE MOST HEALTHY and agreeable in the world. After having swum for an hour or two in the evening one sleeps coolly the whole night, even during the most ardent heat of summer. Perhaps, the pores being cleansed, the insensible perspiration increases, and occasions this coolness. It is certain that much swimming is the means of stopping diarrhœa, and even of producing a constipation. With respect to those who do not know how to swim, or who are affected with diarrhœa at a season which does not permit them to use that exercise, a warm bath, by cleansing and purifying the skin, is found very salutary, and often effects a radical cure. I speak from my own experience, frequently repeated, and that of others, to whom I have recommended this.

1330. "WHEN I WAS A BOY, I amused myself one day with flying a paper kite; and approaching the banks of a lake, which was nearly a mile broad, I tied the string to a stake, and the kite ascended to a very considerable height above the pond, while I was swimming. In a little time, being desirous of amusing myself with my kite, and enjoying at the same time the pleasure of swimming, I returned, and loosening from the stake the string, with the little stick which was fastened to it, went again into the water, where I found that, lying on my back, and holding the stick in my hand, I was drawn along the surface of the water in a very agreeable manner. Having then engaged another boy to carry my clothes round the pond, to a place which I pointed out to him on the other side, I began to cross the pond with may kite, which carried me quite over without the least fatigue, and with the greatest pleasure imaginable. I was only obliged occasionally to halt a little in my course, and resist its progress, when it appeared that by following too quickly, I lowered the kite too much; by doing which occasionally I made it rise again. I have never since that time practised this singular mode of swimming, and I think it not impossible to cross, in this manner, from Dover to Calais."

1331. THOSE WHO PREFER THE AID OF BELTS will find it very easy and safe to make belts upon the plan explained; and by gradually reducing the floating power of the belts from day to day, they will gain confidence, and speedily acquire the art of swimming.

1332. Staining.—GENERAL OBSERVATIONS.—When *alabaster, marble,* and other *stones* are coloured, and the stain is required to be deep, it should be poured on boiling hot, and brushed equally over every part, if made with water; if with spirit, it should be applied cold, otherwise the evaporation, being too rapid, would leave the colouring matter on the surface, without any, or very little, being able to penetrate. In greyish or brownish stones, the stain will be wanting in brightness, because the natural colour combines with the stain; therefore, if the stone be a pure colour, the result will be a combination of the colour and stain. In staining *bone* or *ivory,* the colours will take better before than after polishing; and if any dark spots appear, they should be rubbed with chalk, and the article dyed again, to produce uniformity of shade. On removal from the boiling hot dye-bath, the bone should be immediately plunged into cold water, to prevent cracks from the heat. If *paper* or *parchment* is stained, a broad varnish brush should be employed, to lay the colouring on evenly. When the stains for *wood* are required to be very strong, it is better to soak and *not* brush them; therefore, if for inlaying or fine work, the wood should be previously split or sawn into proper thicknesses; and

when directed to be brushed several times over with the stains, it should be allowed to dry between each coating. When it is wished to render any of the stains more durable and beautiful, the work should be well rubbed with Dutch or common rushes after it is coloured, and then varnished with seed-lac varnish, or if a better appearance is desired, with three coats of the same, or shellac varnish. Common work only requires frequent rubbing with linseed oil and woollen rags. The remainder, with the exception of *glass,* will be treated of in this paper.

1333. ALABASTER, MARBLE, AND STONE, may be stained of a yellow, red, green, blue, purple, black, or any of the compound colours, by the stains used for wood.

1334. BONE AND IVORY. *Black.*— i. Lay the article for several hours in a strong solution of nitrate of silver, and expose to the light. ii. Boil the article for some time in a strained decoction of logwood, and then steep it in a solution of persulphate or acetate of iron. iii. Immerse frequently in ink, until of sufficient depth of colour.

1335. BONE AND IVORY. *Blue.*— i. Immerse for some time in a dilute solution of sulphate of indigo—partly saturated with potash—and it will be fully stained. ii. Steep in a strong solution of sulphate of copper.

1336. BONE AND IVORY. *Green.*— i. Dip blue-stained articles for a short time in nitro-hydrochlorate of tin, and then in a hot decoction of fustic. ii. Boil in a solution of verdigris in vinegar until the desired colour is obtained.

1337. BONE AND IVORY. *Red.*— i. Dip the articles first in the tin mordant used in dyeing, and then plunge into a hot decoction of Brazil wood — half a pound to a gallon of water—or cochineal. ii. Steep in red ink until sufficiently stained.

1338. BONE AND IVORY. *Scarlet.* — Use lac dye instead of the preceeding.

1339. BONE AND IVORY. *Violet.*—

Dip in the tin mordant, and then immerse in a decoction of logwood.

1340. Bone and Ivory. *Yellow.*—i. Impregnate with nitro-hydrochlorate of tin, and then digest with heat in a strained decoction of fustic. ii. Steep for twenty-four hours in a strong solution of the neutral chromate of potash, and then plunge for some time in a boiling solution of acetate of lead. iii. Boil the articles in a solution of alum—a pound to half a gallon—and then immerse for half an hour in the following mixture:—Take half a pound of turmeric, and a quarter of a pound of pearlash; boil in a gallon of water. When taken from this, the bone must be again dipped in the alum solution.

1341. Horn must be treated in the same manner as bone and ivory for the various colours given under that heading.

1342. Imitation of Tortoiseshell.—First steam and then press the horn into proper shapes, and afterwards lay the following mixture on with a small brush, in imitation of the mottle of tortoiseshell:—Take equal parts of quicklime and litharge, and mix with strong soap-lees; let this remain until it is thoroughly dry, brush off, and repeat two or three times, if necessary. Such parts as are required to be of a reddish brown should be covered with a mixture of whiting and the stain.

1343. Iron. *Black, for ships' guns, shots, &c.*—To one gallon of vinegar add a quarter of a pound of iron rust, let it stand for a week; then add a pound of dry lampblack, and three quarters of a pound of copperas: stir it up for a couple of days. Lay five or six coats on the gun, &c., with a sponge, allowing it to dry well between each. Polish with linseed oil and soft woollen rag, and it will look like ebony.

1344. Paper and Parchment. *Blue.*—i. Stain it green with the verdigris stain given in No. 1352, and brush over with a solution of pearlash—two ounces to the pint—till it becomes blue. ii. Use the blue stain for wood.

1345. Paper and Parchment.

Green and *Red.*—The same as for wood.

1346. Paper and Parchment. *Orange.*—Brush over with a tincture of turmeric, formed by infusing an ounce of the root in a pint of spirit of wine; let this dry, and give another coat of pearlash solution, made by dissolving two ounces of the salt in a quart of water.

1347. Paper and Parchment. *Purple.*—i. Brush over with the expressed juice of ripe privet berries. ii. The same as for wood.

1348. Paper and Parchment. *Yellow.*—i. Brush over with tincture of turmeric. ii. Add anatto or dragon's-blood to the tincture of turmeric, and brush over as usual.

1349. Wood. *Black.*—i. Drop a little sulphuric acid into a small quantity of water, brush over the wood and hold to the fire, it will be a fine black, and receive a good polish. ii. Take half a gallon of vinegar, an ounce of bruised nut galls, of logwood chips and copperas each half a pound—boil well; add half an ounce of the tincture of sesquichloride of iron, formerly called the muriated tincture, and brush on hot. iii. Use the stain given for ships' guns. iv. Take half a gallon of vinegar, half a pound of dry lampblack, and three pounds of iron rust, sifted. Mix, and let stand for a week. Lay three coats of this on hot, and then rub with linseed oil, and you will have a fine deep black. v. Add to the above stain an ounce of nut galls, half a pound of logwood chips, and a quarter of a pound of copperas; lay on three coats, oil well, and you will have a black stain that will stand any kind of weather, and one that is well suited for ships' combings, &c. vi. Take a pound of logwood chips, a quarter of a pound of Brazil wood, and boil for an hour and a half in a gallon of water. Brush the wood several times with this decoction while hot. Make a decoction of nut galls by simmering gently, for three or four days, a quarter of a pound of the galls in two quarts of water; give the wood three coats of this, and, while wet, lay on a solution of sulphate of iron (two ounces to a quart), and when dry, oil or varnish. vii. Give three coats with a solution of copper filings in aquafortis, and repeatedly brush over with the logwood decoction, until the greenness of the copper is destroyed. viii. Boil half a pound of logwood chips in two quarts of water, add an ounce of pearlash, and apply hot with a brush. Then take two quarts of the logwood decoction, and half an ounce of verdigris, and the same of copperas; strain, and throw in half a pound of iron rust. Brush the work well with this, and oil.

1350. WOOD. *Blue.* — i. Dissolve copper filings in aquafortis, brush the wood with it, and then go over the work with a hot solution of pearlash (two ounces to a pint of water), till it assumes a perfectly blue colour. ii. Boil a pound of indigo, two pounds of woad, and three ounces of alum, in a gallon of water; brush well over until thoroughly stained.

1351. IMITATION OF BOTANY BAY WOOD.—Boil half a pound of French berries (the unripe berries of the *rhamnus infectorius*) in two quarts of water till of a deep yellow, and while boiling hot give two or three coats to the work. If a deeper colour is desired, give a coat of logwood decoction over the yellow. When nearly dry, form the grain with No. viii. *black stain,* used hot; and when dry, dust and varnish.

1352. WOOD. *Green.*—Dissolve verdigris in vinegar, and brush over with the hot solution until of a proper colour.

1353. WOOD. *Mahogany Colour.*— *Dark.* i. Boil half a pound of madder and two ounces of logwood chips in a gallon of water, and brush well over while hot: when dry, go over the whole with pearlash solution, two drachms to the quart. ii. Put two ounces of dragon's-blood, bruised, into a quart of oil of turpentine; let the bottle stand in a warm place, shake frequently, and, when dissolved, steep the work in the mixture.

1354. WOOD. *Light Red Brown.*— i. Boil half a pound of madder and a quarter of a pound of fustic in a gallon of water; brush over the work when boiling hot, until properly stained. ii. The surface of the work being quite smooth, brush over with a weak solution of aquafortis, half an ounce to the pint, and then finish with the following:— Put four ounces and a half of dragon's blood and an ounce of soda, both well bruised, to three pints of spirits of wine; let it stand in a warm place, shake frequently, strain, and lay on with a soft brush, repeating until of a proper colour; polish with linseed oil or varnish.

1355. WOOD. *Purple.*—Brush the work several times with the logwood decoction used for No. vi. *black,* and when dry give a coat of pearlash solution—one drachm to a quart,—taking care to lay it on evenly.

1356. WOOD. *Red.*—i. Boil a pound of Brazil wood and an ounce of pearlash in a gallon of water, and while hot brush over the work until of a proper colour. Dissolve two ounces of alum in a quart of water, and brush the solution over the work before it dries. ii. Take a gallon of the above stain, add two more ounces of pearlash; use hot, and brush often with the alum solution. iii. Use a cold infusion of archil, and brush over with the pearlash solution used for No. 1353.

1357. IMITATION OF ROSEWOOD.— i. Boil half a pound of logwood in three pints of water till it is of a very dark red, add half an ounce of salt of tartar; stain the work with the liquor while boiling hot, giving three coats; then, with a painter's graining brush, form streaks with No. viii. *black stain;* let dry, and varnish. ii. Brush over with the logwood decoction used for No. vi. *black,* three or four times; put half a pound of iron filings into two quarts of vinegar; then with a graining brush, or cane bruised at the end, apply the iron filing solution in the form required, and polish with bees'-wax and turpentine when dry, or varnish.

1358. WOOD. *Yellow.* — i. Brush over with the tincture of turmeric. ii. Warm the work and brush over with weak aquafortis, then hold to the fire. Varnish or oil as usual.

1359. Employers and Employed.—It is customary with respect to domestic servants, that if the terms are not otherwise defined, the hiring is by the month, and may be put an end to by either party giving a month's warning; or, at the will of the employer, a month's wages.

1360. AN EMPLOYER MAY DISMISS A SERVANT upon paying wages for one month beyond the date of actual dismissal, the wages without service being deemed equivalent to the extra board and lodging with service.

1361. THERE ARE DISTINCTIONS WITH RESPECT TO CLERKS, and servants of a superior class. A month's warning or wages will not determine the engagements of servants of this class.

1362. THE TERMS UPON WHICH CLERKS and superior servants are employed being very various, it is desirable to have some specific agreement, or other proof of the conditions of service and wages.

1363. AGREEMENTS WITH MENIAL SERVANTS need not be stamped; but contracts of a higher and special character should be.

1364. THE TERMS OF AN AGREEMENT should be distinctly expressed, and be signed by both parties. And the conditions under which the agreement may be terminated by either party should be fully stated.

1365. EVERY AGREEMENT SHOULD BEAR EVIDENCE OF MUTUALITY of interest. If one party agrees to stay with another, and give gratuitous services, with the view of acquiring knowledge of a business, and the other party does not agree to employ and to *teach*, the agreement is void, as being without consideration.

1366. AN EMPLOYER MUST CONTRACT TO EMPLOY, as well as a servant to *serve*, otherwise the employer may put an end to the contract at his own pleasure. In such a case a servant may be dismissed without notice.

1367. AN AGREEMENT TO GIVE PERMANENT EMPLOYMENT, is received as extending only to a substantial and reasonable period of time, and that there shall be no immediate and peremptory dismissal, without cause.

1368. WHEN NO STIPULATION IS MADE at the time of the hiring, or in the agreement, that a servant shall be liable for breakages, injuries, from negligence, &c., the employer can only recover from the servant by due process of law.

1369. IT IS A PRUDENT STIPULATION that, if a servant quit his employ before the specified time, or without due notice, a certain amount of wages shall be forfeited; otherwise the employer can only recover by action for damages.

1370. IN THE CASE OF LIVERY SERVANTS, it should be agreed that, upon quitting service, they deliver up the liveries; otherwise disputes may arise that can only be determined by recourse to law.

1371. WHEN A MASTER TO WHOM AN APPRENTICE IS BOUND for a particular trade, changes that trade for another, the indenture binding the apprentice becomes null and void.

1372. IF A SERVANT, retained for a year, happen within the period of his service to fall sick, or to be hurt or lamed, or otherwise to become of infirm body by the act of God, while doing his master's business, the master cannot put such servant away, nor abate any part of his wages for such time.

1373. BUT THIS DOES NOT INTERFERE WITH THE RIGHT OF AN EMPLOYER to determine a contract for services in those cases where terms of discharge are specified in the contract of hiring. In such cases, inability to serve, through sickness or other infirmity, puts an end to right to wages, which are in consideration of such services.

1374. WHEN THE HIRING OF A SUPERIOR SERVANT is for a year, if the servant, prior to the expiration of the year, commits any act by which he may be lawfully discharged, he cannot claim wages for the part of the year which he may have served.

1375. BUT A MENIAL SERVANT MAY CLAIM up to the date of his dismissal, unless his discharge be for embezzlement or other felonious acts.

1376. UPON THE DEATH OF A SERVANT, his personal representative may claim arrears of wages due, unless the contract of employment specified and required the completion of any particular period.

1377. WHEN A MASTER BECOMES BANKRUPT, the court may order the payment of arrears of wages not exceeding three months, and not more than £30; but a servant or clerk is at liberty to prove upon the bankrupt's estate for any amount above that sum.

1378. RECEIPTS SHOULD BE TAKEN FOR WAGES PAID. Where servants have been under age, it has been held that moneys advanced for fineries and extravagances unbecoming to a servant did not constitute payment of wages, and the employer has been compelled to pay again.

1379. MONEYS PAID TO A MARRIED WOMAN, though for her own services, may be claimed again by her husband.

1380. A MASTER MAY BECOME LIABLE FOR MEDICAL ATTENDANCE upon his sick servant if he calls in his own medical man, and orders him to attend to the servant.

1381. WHEN A SERVANT IS DISCHARGED for any just cause, he cannot claim wages beyond the last pay-day under the contract of hiring.

1382. A GENERAL HIRING OF A CLERK or warehouseman is for a year, even though the wages be paid by the month, unless a month's warning or wages be specified in the contract of employment.

1383. WHERE A SERVANT RESERVES TO HIMSELF SPECIAL PRIVILEGES, such as particular portions of his time, the hiring becomes special, and cannot be governed by the terms of general engagements. So, also,

where a servant stipulates to be exempted from particular duties that usually belong to his situation.

1384. WHEN A SERVANT MAY REFUSE to perform any duty required from him, his right so to refuse will generally be determined by the usages prevailing among servants of a similar class.

1385. A SERVANT BEING SEDUCED FROM THE EMPLOYMENT of a master, the latter has a right of action against the seducer for losses sustained.

1386. IT IS AN ESTABLISHED MAXIM IN LAW, that whoever does an act by the hands of another shall be deemed to have done it himself. And hence, in many matters, masters are responsible for the acts of their servants. But if a servant does an unlawful act, not arising out of the discharge of his duties to his master, then the employer is not responsible.

1387. WHERE A SERVANT BUYS THINGS FOR AN EMPLOYER'S USE, the master is bound to see them paid for; and it is no release for the master to say that he gave the servant money to pay for them; nor that he contracted with the servant for the latter to supply them.

1388. AN ACTION WILL NOT LIE against an employer for giving an unfavourable character of a servant, even though it be in writing. Communications of this nature, in answer to inquiries, are considered privileged. But if it can be proved that an employer has given a *false* character from motives of *malice*, then an action for libel will lie against him; but the representations must be proved to be false as well as voluntary.

1389. Laws of Landlord and Tenant.

1390. LEASES.—A lease is a conveyance of premises or lands for a specified term of years, at a yearly rent, with definite conditions as to alterations, repairs, payment of rent, forfeiture, &c. Being an instrument of much importance, it should always be drawn by a

H

respectable attorney, who will see that all the conditions, in the interest of the lessee, are fulfilled.

1391. PRECAUTION. — In taking a lease, the tenant's solicitor should carefully examine the covenants, or if he take an underlease, he should ascertain the covenants of the original lease, otherwise, when too late, he may find himself so restricted in his occupation that the premises may be wholly useless for his purpose, or he may be involved in perpetual difficulties and annoyances; for instance, he may find himself restricted from making alterations convenient or necessary for his trade; he may find himself compelled to rebuild or pay rent in case of fire; he may find himself subject to forfeiture of his lease, or other penalty, if he should underlet or assign his interest, carry on some particular trade, &c.

1392. COVENANTS. — The covenants on the landlord's part are usually the granting of legal enjoyment of the premises to the lessee; the saving him harmless from all other claimants to title; and also for future assurance. On the tenant's part, they are usually to pay the rent and taxes; to keep the premises in suitable repair; and to deliver up possession when the term has expired.

1393. RENT AND TAXES. — The lessee covenants to pay the rent and all taxes, except the land and property taxes, which may be deducted from the rent.

1394. ASSIGNMENTS. — Unless there be a covenant against assignment, a lease may be assigned, that is, the whole interest of the lessee may be conveyed to another, or it may be underlet; if, therefore, it is intended that it should not, it is proper to insert a covenant to restrain the lessee from assigning or underletting. Tenants for terms of years may assign or underlet, but tenants at will cannot.

1395. REPAIRS. — A tenant who covenants to keep a house in repair is not answerable for its natural decay, but is bound to keep it wind and water tight, so that it does not decay for want of cover. A lessee who covenants to pay rent and keep the premises in repair, is liable to pay the rent although the premises may be burned down.

1396. NEGLECT OF REPAIRS BY LANDLORD. — If a landlord covenant to repair, and neglect to do so, the tenant may do it, and withhold so much of the rent. But it is advisable that notice thereof should be given by the tenant to the landlord, in the presence of a witness, prior to commencing the repairs.

1397. RIGHT OF LANDLORD TO ENTER PREMISES. — A landlord may enter upon the premises (having given previous notice), although not expressed in the lease), for the purpose of viewing the state of the property.

1398. TERMINATION OF LEASES. — A tenant must deliver up possession at the expiration of the term (the lease being sufficient notice), or he will continue liable to the rent as tenant by sufferance without any new contract; but if the landlord recognizes such tenancy by accepting a payment of rent after the lease has expired, such acceptance will constitute a tenancy: but previous to accepting rent, the landlord may bring his ejectment without notice; for, the lease having expired, the tenant is a trespasser. A lease covenanted to be void if the rent be not paid upon the day appointed, is good, unless the landlord make an entry.

1399. MARRIED WOMEN. — Married women (unless the power is expressly reserved them by marriage settlement) cannot grant leases; but husbands, seised in right of their wives, may grant leases for twenty-one years. If a wife is executrix, the husband and wife have the power of leasing, as in the ordinary case of husband and wife. Married women cannot (except by special custom) take leases; if husband and wife accept a lease, she may, after his death, accept or reject it, in the same manner as an infant may, and is not bound by the covenants, though she continues a tenant.

1400. COPYHOLDERS. — Copyholders

may not grant a lease for longer than one year, unless by custom, or permission of the lord; and the lease of a steward of a manor is not good, unless he is duly invested with a power for that purpose.

1401. NOTICES.—All notices, of whatever description, relating to tenancies, should be in writing, and the person serving the said notice should write on the back thereof a memorandum of the date on which it was served, and should keep a copy of the said notice, with a similar memorandum attached.

1402. YEARLY TENANCIES.—Houses are considered as let for the year, and the tenants are subject to the laws affecting annual tenancies, unless there be an agreement in writing to the contrary.

1403. *Agreement for taking a House on an Annual Tenancy.*—Memorandum of an undertaking, entered into this ——— day of ——— 186 , between R. A. of ——— and L. O. of ———, as follows.

The said R. A. doth hereby let unto the said L. O. a dwelling-house, situate in ———, in the parish of ———, for the term of one year certain, and so on from year to year, until half a year's notice to quit be given by or to either party, at the yearly rent of ——— pounds, payable quarterly; the tenancy to commence at ——— day next.

And the said R. A. doth undertake to pay the land-tax, the property-tax, and the sewer-rate, and to keep the said house in all necessary repairs, so long as the said L. O. shall continue therein. And the said L. O. doth undertake to take the said house of R. A. for the before-mentioned term and rent, and pay all taxes, except those on land, or property, and the sewer-rate, and the other conditions aforesaid.

Witness our hands, the day and year aforesaid.   R. A.
Witness, G. C.   L. O.

1404. PAYMENT OF TAXES BY LANDLORD.—If the landlord agree to pay all the rates and taxes, then a different wording of the agreement should take place, as thus;—

And the said R. A. doth undertake to pay all rates and taxes of whatever nature or kind, chargeable on the said house and premises, and to keep the said house in all necessary repairs, so long as the said L. O. shall continue therein.

1405. INDEMNITY FROM ARREARS.—If the landlord agree to secure the incoming tenant from all arrears (and the tenant should see to this) due on account of rent, rates, and taxes, the indemnification should be written on a separate paper, and in something like the following terms:—

1406. *Indemnification against Rents, Rates, and Taxes in Arrear.*—I, R. A., landlord of a certain house and premises now about to be taken and occupied by L. O., do hereby agree to indemnify the said L. O. from the payment of any rent, taxes, or rates in arrear, prior to the date of the day at which his said tenancy commences. As witness my hand this ——— day of ——— 186 ———

           R. A.
         Landlord of the above
Witness, G. C.   premises.

1407. *Agreement for taking a House for Three Years.*—Memorandum of an agreement made the ——— day of ——— 186 , between R. A., of ———, and L. O., of ———, as follows:—

The said R. A. doth let unto the said L. O. a house (and garden, if any), with appurtenances, situated in ———, in the parish of ———, for three years certain. The rent to commence from ——— day next, at and under the yearly rent of ———, payable quarterly, the first payment to be at ——— day next.

The said L. O. doth agree to take the said house (and garden) of the said R. A., for the term and rent payable in manner aforesaid; and that he will, at the expiration of the term, leave the house in as good repair as he found it, [wear and tear excepted]. Witness our hands.   R. A.
Witness, G. C.   L. O.

1408. Payment of Rent.—Rent is usually payable at the regular quarter-days, namely, Lady-day, or March 25th; Midsummer-day, or June 24th; Michaelmas-day, September 29th; and Christmas-day, December 25th. It is due at mid-day; but no proceedings for non-payment, where the tenant remains upon the premises, can be taken till the next day.

1409. Payment of Rent Imperative.—No consideration will waive the payment of the rent, should the landlord insist on demanding it. Even should the house be burnt, blown, or fall down, the tenant is still liable for rent; and the tenancy can only be voidable by the proper notice to quit, the same as if the house remained in the most perfect condition.

1410. Demanding Rent.—The landlord himself is the person most proper to demand rent; he may employ another person, but if he does, he must authorize him by letter, or by power of attorney; or the demand may be objected to.

1411. Receipt for Rent.—When an agent has been duly authorized, a receipt from him for any subsequent rent is a legal acquittance to the tenant, notwithstanding the landlord may have revoked the authority under which the agent acted, unless the landlord should have given the tenant notice thereof.

1412. Legal Tender.—A tender of rent should be in the current coin of the kingdom. But a tender of Bank of England notes is good, even in cases of distress.

1413. *Form of a Receipt for Rent.*—Received of Mr. R. A. the sum of ten pounds ten shillings, for a quarter's rent due at Lady-day last, for the house, No. ———— street. £10 10s.   [Stamp]   L. O.

1414. If the receipt be given by an agent, it should be signed,   G. C.,

Agent for L. O., landlord of the above premises.

1415. Care of Receipts for Rent.—Be careful of your last quarter's receipt for rent, for the production of that document bars all prior claim. Even when arrears have been due on former quarters, the receipt, if given for the last quarter, precludes the landlord from recovery thereof.

1416. Notice to Quit.—When either the landlord or tenant intends to terminate a tenancy, the way to proceed is by a notice to quit, which is drawn up in the two following ways:—

1417. *Form of a Notice to Quit from a Tenant to his Landlord.*—Sir,—I hereby give you notice, that on or before the ———— day of ———— next, I shall quit and deliver up possession of the house and premises I now hold of you, situate at ————, in the parish of ————, in the county of ————.

Dated the ———— day of ————, 186 .

Witness, G. C.,   L. O.

To Mr. R. A.

1418. *Notice from Landlord to his Tenant.*—Sir,—I hereby give you notice to quit the house and appurtenances, situate No. ————, which you now hold of me, on or before ———— next.

Dated ————, 186 .

(Signed)   R. A. (landlord).

To Mr. L. O.

1419. Notice to Quit.—An opinion is very generally entertained, however, that a quarter's warning to quit, where the house is of small rental, is sufficient notice; but where the rent is payable quarterly, or at longer intervals, this is a mistake, for unless a special agreement is made defining the time to be given as a warning, six months' notice to quit must be given, to expire on the same day of the year upon which the tenancy commenced. Where the rent is payable weekly or monthly, the notice to quit will be good if given for the week or month, provided care be taken that it expires upon the day of the week or month of the beginning of the tenancy.

1420. *Form of Notice from a Landlord to his Tenant to Quit or Pay an increased Rent.*—To Mr. R. A.—Sir,—I hereby give you notice to deliver up possession, and quit on or before ————, the [here state the house or apartment] and appurtenances which you now hold of me, in [insert the name of street, &c.], and in default of your compliance therewith, I do and will insist on your paying me for the same, the [annual or monthly] rent of ————, being an additional rental of ———— pounds per annum, [over and above the present annual rental] rent, for such time as you shall detain the key and keep possession over the said notice. Witness my hand, this ———— day of ———— 186 .

Witness, G. C.   L. O.

1421. Refusal to Give up Possession.—If a tenant holds over, after receiving a sufficient notice to quit, *in*

writing, he becomes liable to pay double the yearly value; if he holds over after having himself given even parole notice to quit, he is liable to pay double rent.

1422. Lodgings and Lodgers.

1423. PRECAUTIONS.—Before you take unfurnished apartments, satisfy yourself that the rent and taxes of the house are paid, for the goods of a lodger are liable to distress for arrears of these at any time while on the premises.

1424. BROKER ENTERING APARTMENTS.—A broker having obtained possession through the outer door, may break open any of the private doors of the lodgers, if necessary.

1425. RENTING FOR A SPECIFIC TERM.—If lodgings are taken for a certain and specified time, no notice to quit is necessary. If the lodger, however, continue after the expiration of the term, he becomes a regular lodger, unless there is an agreement to the contrary. If he owe rent, the housekeeper can detain his goods whilst on the premises, or distrain, as a landlord may distrain the goods of a tenant.

1426. LODGERS AND HOUSEHOLDERS BOUND BY THE SAME LAW.—No distinction exists between lodgers and other tenants as to the payment of their rent, or the turning them out of possession; they are also similarly circumstanced, with regard to distress for rent, as householders.

1427. WEEKLY TENANTS.—In case of weekly tenants, the rent should be paid weekly, for, if it is once let to run a quarter, and the landlord accept it as a quarter, the tenant cannot be forced to quit without a quarter's notice.

1428. YEARLY LODGERS.—Lodgings by the year should only be taken from a person who is either proprietor of the house, or holds possession for an unexpired term of years.

1429. Furnished Lodgings.

Furnished lodgings are usually let by the week, on payment of a fixed sum, part of which is considered as rent for the apartment, and part for the use of the furniture. In some instances an agreement is made for so much per week rent, and so much for the use of the furniture, and to place all moneys received to the account of the furniture, until that part of the demand shall be satisfied, as the landlord cannot distrain for the use of his furniture.

1430. LODGERS LEAVING APARTMENTS WITHOUT NOTICE.—Persons renting furnished apartments frequently absent themselves without apprising the householder, perhaps with the rent in arrear. If there is probable reason to believe that the lodger has left, on the second week of such absence the householder may send for a police constable, and in his presence enter the lodger's apartment, and take out the latter's property, and secure it until application is made for it. He may then enter upon the possession of the apartment; and if, after fourteen days' notice given by advertisement in the *London Gazette*, the lodger does not pay the arrears of rent, the householder may sell the property for the money due, reserving the surplus money, and such goods as it may not be necessary to sell (if any), and keeping them ready for delivery to the lodger when he shall demand them.

1431. VERBAL AGREEMENTS.—If a person make a verbal agreement to take lodgings at a future day, and decline to fulfil his agreement, the housekeeper has no remedy; but if he pay a deposit he partly executes an agreement, and the housekeeper has a remedy against him for not occupying the lodgings according to agreement.

1432. LANDLORD USING LODGER'S APARTMENTS.—If a landlord enter and use apartments while his tenant is in legal possession, without his consent, he forfeits his right to recover rent.

1433. LODGINGS TO IMMODEST WOMEN.—If lodgings are let to an immodest woman, to enable her to receive visitors of the male sex, the landlord cannot recover his rent. But if the landlord did not know the character of the woman when he let the lodgings, he may recover, but not if *after* he knew the fact he permitted her to remain as his tenant. If the woman, however, merely lodges there, and has her visitors elsewhere, her character will not affect his claim for rent.

1434. RENT RECOVERABLE.—If a lodger quit apartments without notice, the landlord can still recover his rent by action, although he has put up a bill in the window to let them.

1435. REMOVING GOODS.—Removing goods from furnished lodgings, with intent to steal, is a felony : unlawfully pledging is a misdemeanour.

1436. LIABILITY FOR RENT.—Where the lodger has removed, and there are no goods whereon to make a levy, the rent becomes a debt, and can only be recovered as such in the County Court of the district.

1437. *Agreement for Letting a Furnished House or Apartment.*—Memorandum of an agreement made and entered into this —— day of ——, 186 , between R. A., of ——, of the one part, and L. O., of ——, of the other part, as follows :—That the said R. A. agrees to let, and the said L. O. to take, all that messuage or tenement (with the garden and appurtenances thereto,) situate at, &c. [*or if an apartment be the subject of demise,* all the entire first floor, *particularly describing the other appurtenances*], together with all the furniture, fixtures, and other things mentioned and comprised in the schedule hereunder written, for the space of —— months, to be computed from the —— day of ——, at the rent of —— pounds per quarter, payable quarterly, the first quarterly payment to be made on the —— day of —— next ensuing the date hereof. And it is further agreed, by and between the said parties, that each party shall be at liberty to determine the said tenancy, on giving to the other a quarter's notice in writing. And the said L. O. agrees, that in the determination of the tenancy, he will deliver up the said dwelling-house (or the entire first floor, &c.), together with all the fixtures and furniture as aforesaid, in as good a condition as the same now are, reasonable wear and tear thereof excepted, and shall and will replace any of the crockery and china or other utensils that shall be broken or otherwise damaged. In witness, &c.— [*Here is to follow the Inventory, or List of Articles referred to above.*]

1438. Remedies to Recover Rent.—Distress is the most efficient remedy to recover rent, but care should be taken that it be done legally ; if the distress be illegal, the party aggrieved has a remedy by action for damages. Excessive distresses are illegal. The distrainer ought only to take sufficient to recover the rent due, and costs ; if, however, the articles sell for a greater sum than is sufficient to pay these, the remainder must be returned to the tenant, who can demand a bill of the sale, and recover the overplus, if any.

1439. DISTRESS, LEGAL AND ILLEGAL.—A distress can be made only for rent that is due, and cannot be made until the day after, nor unless it has been demanded by the landlord or his agent. The outer door must not be broken open for the purpose of distraining, neither can the distress be made between sun-setting and sun-rising, nor on Sunday, Good Friday, or Christmas-day, nor after the rent has been tendered to the landlord or his agent. A second distress can be made, if the value of the first is not enough to pay the rent and costs.

1440. SEIZURE OF GOODS REMOVED.—Goods conveyed off the premises to prevent a distress may be seized anywhere within thirty days after the removal, and if force is resorted to by the landlord, it must be in the presence of a constable ; but goods removed before the rent is actually due cannot be followed, but the rent can be recovered by action as a debt in the County Court. The general rule is, that nothing can be distrained which cannot be returned in the same condition as before the distress was made.

1441. BROKERS' AND APPRAISERS' DUTIES.—The distraining broker cannot be one of the appraisers, nor can he value the goods—such a proceeding would render the distress illegal, and the tenant could obtain damages. The persons chosen as appraisers must not be interested in the distress ; also, if the person distraining were chosen one of the appraisers, the distress would be illegal.

1442. BANKRUPTS' AND INSOLVENTS' RENT.—In cases of bankruptcy or insolvency, no more than one year's rent is obtainable by distress; if more be due, the landlord is only entitled to come in with the rest of the creditors for the further sum due.

1443. ILLEGAL CHARGES.—According to 57 Geo. III., cap. 65, no person distraining for rent shall take other charges than those in the above schedule; the party charging more can be sued for treble the amount unlawfully taken.

1444. AMOUNT OF RENT RECOVERABLE.—It is generally supposed that not more than four weeks' rent can be recovered from weekly tenants, four months' rent from monthly tenants, and four quarters' rent from quarterly or annual tenants; this, however, is not the case, for the alteration of the law, 7th and 8th Vic., cap. 96, secs. 18 and 67, operates only in cases of bankruptcy or insolvency, or where the goods are already distrained.

1445. EXPENSES :—

	£	s.	d.
Levying a distress	0	3	0
Man in possession, per day, if the rent due be under £20	0	2	6

Appraisement, 6d. in the pound on the value of the goods, if above £20.

Appraisement, 1s. in the pound on the value of the goods, if under £20.

Expenses of advertising, &c.

Catalogues, sale, and commission, 1s. in the pound on the produce of the sale.

1446. BROKERS' CHARGES.—Brokers must give copies of the charges in all cases.

1447. VALUATION AND SALE OF GOODS.—The goods, when valued, are usually bought by the appraiser at his own valuation, and a receipt at the bottom of the inventory, witnessed by the person who swore them, is a sufficient discharge.

1448. STAMPED AGREEMENTS. — Much uncertainty having existed as to the legal nature of the agreements on paper between landlords and tenants, the following communication to the proper authorities, and their reply, will be interesting to all concerned :—

1449. "To the Commissioners of Inland Revenue, Somerset House, London. — Middlesbro', Aug. 18th, 1855. — Sirs, — The seaport town of Middlesbro', in the county of York, contains about 14,000 inhabitants, and many dwelling-houses and shops are let from quarter to quarter, and from year to year, upon written memorandums of agreement, where the rents are under £20 a year; and as some difference of opinion exists respecting the proper stamp duties to be paid on such agreements, your opinion is requested, whether the common lease stamp for such an agreement will be sufficient, or what other stamps (if any) will such memorandums require ?— Your most obedient servant, WM. MYERS, Solicitor."

Answer.—" Inland Revenue Office, Somerset House, London, 27th August, 1855.—Sir, —The Board having had before them your letter of the 18th inst., I am directed, in reply, to state that the documents therein referred to will be chargeable with stamp duty as leases whether the tenancy be from quarter to quarter, or from year to year.—I am, sir, your obedient servant, THOMAS FINGLE. — W. Myers, Esq."

1450. STAMPED DOCUMENTS.—In all cases where the law requires a stamp, whether for an agreement or a receipt, do not omit it. As the stamp laws are liable to frequent alterations, it is best to refer to the tables in the recognized almanacs for the year, or to make inquiries at the Stamp offices.

1451. Debtor and Creditor.

1452. Bankruptcy. — The distinction formerly existing between insolvents and bankrupts is now abolished. All debtors, whether traders or not, are now subject to the laws of bankruptcy.

1453. ANY DEBTOR, NOT BEING A TRADER, who may go or remain abroad for the purpose of escaping his creditors, or shall, with a view of evading their just demands, make fraudulent conveyance or other transfer of his property, or any part thereof, may be adjudged a bankrupt.

1454. ANY DEBTOR, BEING A TRADER, lying in prison for debt for a period of fourteen days; or, not being a trader, for two calendar months, shall, by such imprisonment, be deemed to have committed an act of bankruptcy.

1455. ANY DEBTOR WHO SHALL FILE IN THE OFFICE OF THE CHIEF REGISTRAR, or with the registrar of a district court of bankruptcy, a declaration in writing that he is unable to meet his engagements, shall be deemed thereby to have committed an act of bankruptcy, provided a petition for adjudication in bankruptcy shall be filed by or against him, within two months from the time of such declaration.

1456. AN EXECUTION LEVIED UPON A DEBTOR'S GOODS, by seizure and sale thereof, for the satisfaction of any claim exceeding fifty pounds, constitutes an act of bankruptcy from the date of the seizure of such goods.

1457. IF WITHIN FOURTEEN DAYS OF THE SALE OF SUCH GOODS a petition for adjudication in bankruptcy against the debtor be presented, the proceeds of such sale shall be paid to the assignee in bankruptcy; the costs of the previous action and execution being first paid out of the proceeds of the sale.

1458. EVERY JUDGMENT CREDITOR who shall be entitled to sue or charge a debtor in execution, in respect of any debt amounting to fifty pounds, exclusive of costs, shall be entitled, at the end of one week from the signing of judgment, to sue out against the debtor, if a trader, or, not being a trader, at the end of one calendar month; and, whether he be in custody or not, to issue a judgment summons, requiring him to appear and be examined respecting his ability to satisfy the debt.

1459. WHEN THE SUMMONS IS DISOBEYED by the debtor, having been duly served, and when the creditor has obtained a peremptory order, fixing a day for payment, and the debtor does not, if a trader, within seven days, or a non-trader, within two calendar months, after service on him of the peremptory order, or within seven days after the day fixed by the peremptory order, pay the money or secure or compound for it to the satisfaction of the creditor, the creditor shall be entitled, at the end of the seven days, to issue against the debtor a judgment summons.

1460. THE DEBTOR, BEING THUS SUMMONED, may be examined on oath, and must produce such books and papers as may be demanded, touching his possession or power relating to property applicable to the satisfaction of the debt. And any debtor refusing to be thus sworn and examined may be committed by the court, as in the case of a bankrupt.

1461. AFTER THE SERVICE OF SUCH SUMMONS, whether the debtor may appear or not, there being no lawful impediment admitted by the court, the debtor may be adjudged a bankrupt, without the presentation of a petition or other proceeding. The debtor shall receive notice of such adjudication, and may appear to show cause against it. Otherwise, at the end of seven days, the adjudication shall be made absolute, and shall be published in the *Gazette*.

1462. EVERY PETITION FOR ADJUDICATION IN BANKRUPTCY must, except in cases specified, be filed and prosecuted within the district in which such debtor shall have resided, or carried on business, for the six months immediately preceding the time of filing such petition, or for the longest period during such six months. The excepted cases are those in which the court in London may order any such petition to be prosecuted in any district, with or without reference to the district in which the debtor may have resided or carried on business; or may transfer the further prosecution of any adjudication from the court of one district to the court of another.

1463. THE AMOUNT OF DEBT for which any creditor may petition for adjudication of bankruptcy against a debtor, whether a trader or not, shall be as follows:—The debt of a single creditor, or of two or more persons, being partners, shall amount to £50 or upwards. The debt of two creditors shall amount to £70 or upwards. The debt of three or more creditors shall amount to £100 or upwards.

1464. EVERY PERSON WHO HAS GIVEN CREDIT TO ANY DEBTOR, upon valuable consideration, for any sum payable at a certain time, which time shall not have arrived when such debtor committed an act of bankruptcy, may so petition or join in petitioning, whether he shall have any security for such sum or not.

1465. THE COURT MAY ORDER SATISFACTION TO BE MADE to a debtor by the petitioning creditor or creditors, if the adjudication shall be proved to have been wrongly or maliciously made.

1466. IF A DEBTOR, IMPRISONED FOR A DEBT, shall, through poverty, be unable to petition the court for an adjudication in bankruptcy against himself, he may petition *in formâ pauperis*, upon making an affidavit that he has not the means of paying the fees and expenses.

1467. IMMEDIATELY ON ADJUDICATION, the official assignee will take possession of the bankrupt's estate, and retain possession until the appointment of a creditors' assignee; but if the official assignee, or the court, upon the representation of any creditor, shall be of opinion that the keeping possession of the bankrupt's property is not requisite for the due protection of the creditors, such possession shall not be continued.

1468. AT THE FIRST MEETING OF CREDITORS, the majority of creditors in value may make an allowance to the bankrupt. At such meeting, or at any other, the bankrupt may submit a proposal to compound with or satisfy his creditors; and a majority in value of the creditors may resolve to supersede further proceedings in bankruptcy. In such case, the estate may be wound up as directed by the majority of creditors, and the bankrupt be entitled to apply for his discharge.

1469. AN ABSTRACT OF THE BANKRUPT'S STATEMENT OF ACCOUNTS shall be printed, and a copy be sent by post, within a week from the filing thereof, to each creditor who has proved.

1470. OFFICERS ON FULL PAY, HALF PAY, salary, or pension, beneficed clergymen, and others, may be allowed some portion of their emoluments; the whole being, in the first instance, paid to the assignees for the benefit of creditors.

1471. RENT AND LIABILITIES payable by instalments may be proved against the bankrupt's estate, proportionately up to the period of the bankruptcy, but not up to the stated periods of the payment of such rent or instalments, unless the bankruptcy occurred at a corresponding date.

1472. CLASSIFICATION BY CERTIFICATES IS ABOLISHED. — In cases where the discharge of a bankrupt shall be suspended, such discharge, when granted, shall state the period for which it was suspended, and the reasons for such suspension; and the same with regard to imprisonment.

1473. IF, AT THE APPLICATION FOR DISCHARGE, any creditor or creditors oppose, and charge the bankrupt with acts of misdemeanour, the court may, with the consent of the bankrupt, appoint a day for trying the bankrupt on the charge, and a jury may be appointed for such trial. But the court may order the bankrupt to be indicted and tried in one of the courts of criminal justice.

1474. IF THE COURT SHOULD BE OF OPINION that the bankrupt has carried on trade by fictitious capital; or that he could not have had, at the time when the debts were contracted, any probable expectation of being able to pay the same; or that, if a trader, he has, with intent to conceal the true state of his affairs, wilfully omitted to keep proper books of account; or, whether a trader or not, that his insolvency is attributable to rash and hazardous speculation, or unjustifiable extravagance in living; or that he has put any of his creditors to unnecessary expense by frivolous or vexatious defence to any action or suit to recover any debt due from him;—

P 2

1475. The Court may either Refuse an Order of Discharge; may suspend the same from taking effect for such time as the court may think fit; or may grant an order of discharge, subject to any conditions touching any salary, pay, emoluments, profits, wages, earnings, or income which may afterwards become due to the bankrupt, and touching after-acquired property of the bankrupt; or may sentence the bankrupt to be imprisoned for any period of time not exceeding one year from the date of such sentence.

1476. Arrangements with Creditors.—Bankruptcies may be superseded or annulled by arrangement with creditors. Every deed or instrument made and entered into between a debtor and his creditors, or a trustee on their behalf, shall be as valid and binding on all the creditors as if they were parties to and had duly executed the same, provided the following conditions be observed:—

1477. A Majority in Number, representing three-fourths in value, of the creditors of such debtor, whose debts shall respectively amount to £10 and upwards, shall, before or after the execution thereof by the debtor, in writing assent to or approve of such deed or instrument. If a trustee or trustees be appointed by such deed or instrument, such trustee or trustees shall execute the same. The execution of such deed or instrument by the debtor shall be attested by an attorney or solicitor.

1478. Breach of Promise of Marriage.—A verbal offer of marriage is sufficient whereon to ground an action for breach of promise of marriage. The conduct of the suitor, subsequent to the breaking off the engagement, would weigh with the jury in estimating damages. An action may be commenced although the gentleman is not married. The length of time which must elapse before action must be reasonable. A lapse of three years, or even half that time, without any attempt by the gentleman to renew the acquaintance, would lessen the damages very considerably—perhaps do away with all chance of success, unless the delay could be satisfactorily explained. The mode of proceeding is by an action at law. For this an attorney must be retained, who will manage the whole affair to its termination. The first proceeding (the writ, service thereof, &c.) costs from £2 to £5. The next proceeding—from a fortnight to a month after service of the writ—costs about £5 more. The whole costs, to the verdict of the jury, from £35 to £50, besides the expenses of the lady's witnesses. If the verdict be in her favour, the other side have to pay her costs, with the exception of about £10. If the verdict be against her, the same rule holds good, and she must pay her opponent's costs—probably from £60 to £70.

1479. Before Legal Proceedings are Commenced, a letter should be written to the gentleman, by the father or brother of the lady, requesting him to fulfil his engagement. A copy of this letter should be kept, and it had better be delivered by some person who can prove that he did so, and that the copy is correct: he should make a memorandum of any remarks or conversation.

1480. We give an Extract or two from the law authorities: they will, we have no doubt, be perused by our fair readers with great attention, and some satisfaction. "A man who was paying particular attentions to a young girl, was asked by the father of the latter, after one of his visits, what his intentions were, and he replied, 'I have pledged my honour to marry the girl in a month after Christmas;' and it was held that this declaration to the father, who had a right to make the inquiry, and to receive a true and correct answer, taken in connection with the visits to the house, and the conduct of the young people towards each other, was sufficient evidence of a promise of marriage."

1481. "The Common Law does not altogether discountenance long engagements to be married. If parties are young, and circumstances exist, showing that the period during which they had agreed to remain single was not unreasonably long, the contract is binding upon them; but if they are advanced in years, and the marriage is appointed to take place at a remote and unreasonably long period of time, the contract would be voidable, at the option of either of the parties, as being in restraint of matrimony. If no time is fixed and agreed upon for the performance of the contract, it is in contemplation of law *a contract to marry within a reasonable period after request.*

1482. "EITHER OF THE PARTIES, therefore, after the making of such a contract, may call upon the other to fulfil the engagement; and in case of a refusal, or a neglect so to do on the part of the latter within a reasonable time after the request made, the party so calling upon the other for a fulfilment of the engagement may treat the betrothment as at end, and bring an action for damages for a breach of the engagement. If both parties lie by for an unreasonable period, and neither renew the contract from time to time by their conduct or actions, nor call upon one another to carry it into execution, the engagement will be deemed to be abandoned by mutual consent, and the parties will be free to marry whom they please."

1483. "THE ROMAN LAW very properly considered the term of two years amply sufficient for the duration of a betrothment; and if a man who had engaged to marry a girl did not think fit to celebrate the nuptials within two years from the date of the engagement, the girl was released from the contract."

1484. Deed of Separation between a Man and his Wife. —This indenture, made the ——— day of ———, in the year of our Lord 1864, between Charles B—, of ———, of the first part, Anna R— B— (the wife of the said Charles B—) of the second part, and G— R— B— of the third part: Whereas the said Charles B— and Anna R—, his wife, have, for good reasons, determined to live separate and apart from each other, and on that consideration the said Charles B— hath consented to allow unto the said Anna R— B— a clear weekly payment or sum of *s.*, for her maintenance and support during her life, in manner hereinafter contained: And whereas the said G— R— B— hath agreed to become a party to these presents, and to enter into the covenant hereinafter contained on his part: Now this indenture witnesseth, that in pursuance of the said agreement, he, the said Charles B—, for himself, his heirs, executors, and administrators, doth covenant, promise, and agree, to and with the said G— R— B—, his executors, administrators, and assigns, in manner following, that is to say, that he, the said Charles B—, shall and will, from time to time, and at all times hereafter, permit and suffer the said Anna R— B— to live separate and apart from him, the said Charles B—, as if she was sole and unmarried, and in such place and places as to her from time to time shall seem meet; and that he, the said Charles B—, shall not nor will molest or disturb the said Anna R— B— in her person or manner of living, nor shall, at any time or times hereafter require, or by any means whatever, either by ecclesiastical censures, or by taking out citation, or other process, or by commencing or instituting any suit whatsoever, seek or endeavour to compel any restitution of conjugal rights, nor shall not nor will commence or prosecute proceedings of any description against the said Anna R— B— in any ecclesiastical court or elsewhere; nor shall nor will use any force, violence, or restraint to the person of the said Anna R— B—; nor shall nor will, at any time during the said separation, sue, or cause to be sued, any person or persons whomsoever for receiving, harbouring, lodging, protecting, or entertaining her, the said Anna R— B—, but that she, the said Anna

R— B—, may in all things live as if she were a *feme sole* and unmarried, without the restraint and coercion of the said Charles B—, or any person or persons by his means, consent, or procurement; and also that all the clothes, furniture, and other the personal estate and effects, of what nature or kind soever, now belonging, or at any time hereafter to belong to, or be in the actual possession of her, the said Anna R— B—; and all such sums of money and personal estate as she, the said Anna R— B—, or the said Charles B— in her right, shall or may at any time or times during the said separation acquire or be entitled to at law or in equity, by purchase, gift, will, intestacy, or otherwise, shall be the sole and separate property of the said Anna R— B—, to manage, order, sell, dispose of, and use the same in such manner, to all intents and purposes, as if she were a *feme sole* and unmarried: And further, that he, the said Charles B— his executors or administrators, or some or one of them, shall and will well and truly pay, or cause to be paid, unto the said G— R— B, his executors, administrators, or assigns, a clear weekly payment or sum of s. on Monday in each and every week during the life of the said Anna R— B—, but in trust for her, the said Anna R— B—, for her separate maintenance and support: And the said G— R— B— for himself, his heirs, executors, and administrators, doth hereby covenant and agree to and with the said Charles B—, his executors, administrators, and assigns, that she, the said Anna R—B—, shall not nor will not, at any time or times hereafter, in anywise molest or disturb him the said Charles B—, or apply for any restitution of conjugal rights, or for alimony, or for any further or other allowance or separate maintenance than the said weekly sum of s.; and that he, the said G— R— B—, his heirs, executors, or administrators, shall and will, from time to time, at all times hereafter, save, defend, and keep harmless and indemnify the said Charles B—, his heirs, executors, and administrators, and his and their lands and tenements, goods and chattels, of, from, and against all and all manner of action and actions, suit and suits, and all other proceedings whatsoever which shall or may at any time hereafter be brought, commenced, or prosecuted against him the said Charles B—, his heirs, executors, or administrators, or any of them, and also of, from, and against all and every sum and sums of money, costs, damages, and expenses which he, the said Charles B—, his executors, administrators, and assigns, shall or may be obliged to pay, or shall or may suffer, sustain, or be put unto, for, or by reason, or on account of any debt or debts which shall, at any time hereafter, during such separation as aforesaid, be contracted by the said Anna R— B—, or by reason, or means, or on account of any act, matter, cause, or thing whatsoever relating thereto. In witness whereof, the said parties to these presents have hereunto set their hands and seals, the day and year first above written.

1485. Divorce and other Matrimonial Causes.—The powers of the Ecclesiastical Court, so far as divorce is concerned, are abolished, and a new court, entitled the Court of Probate and Divorce, instituted.

1486. By Divorce *à mensâ et thoro* is meant a separation only; it does not sever the matrimonial tie, so as to permit the parties to contract another marriage. These are now called *judicial separations.*

1487. By Suits or Jacitation of Marriage is meant suits which are brought when a person maliciously and falsely asserts that he or she is already married to another, whereby a belief in their marriage is spread abroad, to the injury of the complaining party.

1488. By Absolute Divorce is meant a dissolution of the marriage, by which the parties are set absolutely free from all marital engagements, and capable of subsequent marriage. In these cases a *decree nisi* is first obtained, which is made absolute after the lapse of a certain time, unless the decree should be set aside by subsequent appeal.

1489. The Grounds of Divorce are very various, and in most cases fit only for confidential communication to a solicitor. In all cases a highly respectable professional adviser should be employed.

1490. A Sentence of Judicial Separation may be obtained either by the husband or the wife, on the ground of desertion without cause for two years or upwards. To constitute wilful desertion on the part of the husband, his absence must be against the will of his wife, and she must not have been a consenting party to it.

1491. Persons cannot be legally separated upon the mere disinclination of one or both to live together. The disinclination must be proved upon reasons that the law recognizes; and the court must see that those reasons actually exist.

1492. The Amount of Costs of a Judicial Separation or a divorce varies from £25 to £500 or more, according to the circumstances of the suit, and the litigation that may ensue. But a person being a pauper may obtain relief from the court by suing *in formâ pauperis*. Any such person must lay a case before counsel, and obtain an opinion from such counsel that he or she has reasonable grounds for appealing to the court for relief. The opinion of the counsel must then be laid before the judge ordinary, and leave be obtained to proceed with the suit.

1493. Magisterial Order for Protection of Wife's Property.—When a wife is able to prove that her husband has deserted her without cause and against her will, she may obtain from the Matrimonial Court, or from the judge ordinary, an order to protect her against his creditors, and against any person claiming under him, by way of purchase or otherwise, any property she may acquire by her own lawful industry, or may become possessed of after such desertion.

1494. The Order may in any case be obtained from the court, and when the wife lives in London, from a police magistrate; or where she lives in the country, from two magistrates sitting in petty sessions.

1495. The Order does not prevent the Husband returning to his Wife, but only prevents his taking her earnings while the desertion continues. While the husband and wife live together he is entitled (unless it be otherwise provided in the settlement) to all her earnings; and in general, if what she earns is paid to her without his authority, he can enforce a fresh payment to himself. When he has deserted her, this right will still continue, unless she either obtains a judicial separation or this protection order.

1496. The Order, when obtained, puts the wife in the same position with regard to ownership of property and the right to sue and be sued upon contracts (that is, all bargains and business transactions), as if she had obtained the decree of judicial separation, placing her, in fact, in the situation of a single woman.

1497. If, after this Order is made, the husband, or any creditor of his, or person claiming through him by purchase or otherwise, should seize or continue to hold any property of the wife, after notice of such order, the wife may bring an action against her husband or such other person, and may recover the property itself, and double its value in money.

1498. To Search for Wills.—If you wish to examine a will, your best course is to go to "The Wills Office," in Doctors' Commons, St. Paul's Churchyard; have on a slip of paper the name of the testator—this, on entering, give to a clerk whom you will see at a desk on the right. At the same time pay a shilling, and you will then be entitled to search all the heavy Index volumes for the testator's name. The name found, the clerk will hand over the will for perusal, and there is no difficulty whatever, *provided you* *know about the year of the testator's death.* The Indexes are all arranged and numbered according to their years. Not only the names of those who left wills are given, but also of those intestates to whose effects letters of administration have been granted. There is no charge beyond the shilling paid for entering. If you require a copy of the will, the clerk will calculate the expense, and you can have the copy in a few days. No questions whatever are asked —nor does the length of the will, or the time occupied in reading it, make any difference in the charge. Beyond the shilling paid on entering, there is no other demand whatever, unless for copying the whole, or a portion of the will. It may be as well to state that there are many wills which are not lodged in Doctors' Commons. Some are proved in the courts of the several bishops—Gloucester, York, Chester, for instance; and there they remain. The wills of all who resided in London or the neighbourhood, or who were possessed of money in the funds, are proved in Doctors' Commons; the wills of the wealthier classes are mostly proved there. In the country, and with small properties, the executors usually resort to the bishop of the diocese. Most of the wills, for instance, of shopkeepers, &c., who reside in Manchester, are proved in Chester. The same rules are observed in the country as in London, with regard to examination, &c. The fee—one shilling—is the same in all. Having ascertained that the deceased left a will, and that it has been proved, the next inquiry is, "*Where was it proved?*" The above explanation and remarks apply also to the administrations granted of the effects of those who died without wills.

1499. Making a Will. — The personal property of any person deceased, left undisposed of by deed or will, is divisible among his widow, should he leave one, and his next of kin, in the following order:—i. Children, grandchildren, great-grandchildren, &c. The next inheritors, in the absence of these, are,

—ii. Father;—if none, mother, and brothers and sisters, and their children (but not their grandchildren) ; iii. His grandfathers and grandmothers ;—if none, iv. His uncles and aunts ;—if none, v. His cousins, and great-nephews and nieces.

1500. If the Deceased leave a Widow, but no child or children, one half of his personal estate will fall to his widow, and the other half will be divisible among the next of kin. The father of an intestate without children is entitled to one half of his estate, if he leave a widow, and to the whole if he leave no widow. When the nearest of kin are the mother and the brothers and sisters, the personal estate is divisible in equal portions, one of which will belong to the mother, and one to each of the brothers and sisters ; and if there be children of a deceased brother or sister, an equal portion is divisible among each family of children.

1501. Wills, to be Valid, can only be made by persons at or above the age of twenty-one, and in a sound state of mind at the time of making the last will and testament; not attainted of treason; nor a felon; nor an outlaw. A female must be unmarried, unless the will is made by the consent of her husband, which consent must be expressed by some other deed or will, especially executed in her favour by her husband.

1502. No Will is Valid unless it is in Writing, signed at the foot or end thereof by the testator, or by some other person in his presence and by his direction. And such signature must be made or acknowledged by the testator, in the presence of two or more witnesses, all of whom must be present at the same time, and such witnesses must attest and subscribe the will in the presence and with the knowledge of the testator.

1503. A Will or Codicil once made cannot be altered or revoked, unless through a similar formal process to that under which it was made ; or by some other writing declaring an intention to revoke the same, and executed in the manner in which an original will is required to be executed; or by the burning, tearing, or otherwise destroying the same by the testator, or by some person in his presence and by his direction, with the intention of revoking the same.

1504. No Will or Codicil, or any part of either, that has once been revoked by any or all of these acts, can be revived again, unless it be executed in the manner that a fresh will or codicil is required to be.

1505. Alterations in Wills or Codicils require the signature of the testator and of two witnesses to be made upon the margin, or upon some other part of the will, opposite or near to the alteration.

1506. Every Will is revoked by the subsequent marriage of the testator or testatrix, except a will made in the exercise of a power of appointment, when the property appointed thereby would not, in default of appointment, pass to the heir, executor, or administrator, or next of kin of the testator or testatrix.

1507. There being no Stamp Duty, or tax, on a will itself, it should be written on plain parchment or paper. Nor is it necessary, though always advisable where means are sufficient, to employ a professional adviser to draw up and complete the execution of a will.

1508. If it be intended to give a Legacy to an illegitimate child, the testator must not class him with the lawful children, or designate him simply as the child of his reputed parent, whether father or mother, but must describe the child by name as the reputed child of —— or ——, so as to leave no doubt of identity.

1509. Wearing Apparel, Jewels, &c., belonging to a wife are considered in law her "paraphernalia;" and though liable for the husband's debts while living, cannot be willed away from her by her husband, unless he wills to her other things in lieu thereof, expressing such intention and desire in the will. The wife may then make her choice whether she will accept the substituted gift, or remain possessed of what the law declares her entitled to.

1510. Where Property is Considerable, and of different kinds,—or even where inconsiderable, if of different kinds, and to be disposed of to married or other persons, or for the benefit of children, for charities, or trusts of any description, it is absolutely necessary and proper that a qualified legal adviser should superintend the execution of the will.

1511. When a Person has Resolved upon Making a Will, he should select from among his friends persons of trust to become his executors, and should obtain their consent to act. And it is advisable that a duplicate copy of the will should be entrusted to the executor or executors. Or he should otherwise deposit a copy of his will, or the original will, in the office provided by the Probate Court for the safe custody of wills.

1512. The Following is a Simple Form of Will:—This is the last will and testament of J— B—, of No. 3, King's Road, Chelsea. I hereby give, devise, and bequeath to my wife Mary B—, her heirs, executors, and administrators, for her and their own use and benefit, absolutely and for ever, all my estate and effects, both real and personal, whatsoever and wheresoever, and of what nature and quality soever; and I hereby appoint her, the said Mary B—, sole executrix of this my will. In witness whereof I have hereunto set my hand this twentieth day of January, one thousand eight hundred and sixty-four. JOHN B—.

Signed by the said John B— in the presence of us, present at the same time, who, in his presence, and in the presence of each other, attest and subscribe our names as witnesses hereto.

JOHN WILLIAMS, 15, Oxford Street, Westminster.

HENRY JONES, 19, Regent Street, Westminster.

1513. Other Forms of Wills give particular legacies to adults, or to infants, with direction for application of interest during minority; to infants, to be paid at twenty-one without interest; specific legacies of government stock; general legacies of ditto; specific legacies of leasehold property or household property; immediate or deferred annuities; to daughters or sons for life, and after them their children; legacies with directions for the application of the money; bequests to wife, with conditions as to future marriage; define the powers of trustees, provide for and direct the payment of debts, &c. All these more complicated forms of wills require the superintendence of a professional adviser.

1514. Preserving Fruit.—The grand secret of preserving is to deprive the fruit of its water of vegetation in the shortest time possible; for which purpose the fruit ought to be gathered just at the point of proper maturity. An ingenious French writer considers fruit of all kinds as having four distinct periods of maturity—the maturity of vegetation, of honeyfication, of expectation, and of coction.

1515. The First Period he considers to be that when, having gone through the vegetable processes up to the ripening, it appears ready to drop spontaneously. This, however, is a period which arrives sooner in the warm climate of France than in the colder orchards of England; but its absolute presence may be ascertained by the general filling out of the rind, by the bloom, by the smell, and by the facility with which it may be plucked from the branch. But even in France, as generally practised in England, this period may be hastened, either by cutting circularly through the outer rind at the foot of the branch, so as to prevent the return of the sap, or by bending the branch to a horizontal position on an espalier, which answers the same purpose.

1516. The Second Period, or that of Honeyfication, consists in the ripeness and flavour which fruits of all kinds acquire if plucked a few days before arriving at their first maturity, and preserved under a proper degree of temperature. Apples may acquire or arrive at this second degree of maturity upon the tree, but it too often happens that the flavour of the fruit is thus lost, for fruit over ripe is always found to have parted with a portion of its flavour.

1517. The Third Stage, or of Expectation, as the theorist quaintly terms it, is that which is acquired by pulpy fruits, which, though sufficiently ripe to drop off the tree, are even then hard and sour. This is the case with several kinds both of apples and pears, not to mention other fruits, which always improve after keeping in the confectionery,—but with respect to the medlar and the quince, this maturity of expectation is absolutely necessary.

1518. The Fourth Degree of maturity, or of Coction, is completely artificial, and is nothing more nor less than the change produced upon fruit by the aid of culinary heat.

1519. Maturity of Vegetation.—We have already pointed out the first object necessary in the preservation of fruit, its maturity of vegetation, and we may apply the same principle to flowers or leaves which may be gathered for use.

1520. The Flowers ought to be gathered a day or two before the petals are ready to drop off spontaneously on the setting of the fruit; and the leaves must be plucked before the season has begun to rob them of their vegetable juices. The degree of heat necessary for the purpose of drying must next be considered, as it differs considerably with respect to different substances.

1521. Flowers or Aromatic Plants require the smallest increase of heat beyond the temperature of the season, provided that season be genial: something more for rinds or roots, and a greater heat for fruits; but this heat must not be carried to excess.

1522. Philosophic Confectioners may avail themselves of the thermometer; but practice forms the best guide in this case, and therefore we shall say, without speaking of degrees of Fahrenheit or Réaumur, that if the necessary heat for flowers is one, that for rinds and roots must be one and a quarter, that for fruits one and three quarters, or nearly double of what one may be above the freezing point.

1523. Hints about Making Preserves.—It is not generally known that boiling fruit a long time, and *skimming it well, without sugar*, and *without a cover* to the preserving-pan, is a very economical and excellent way—economical, because the bulk of the scum rises from the *fruit*, and not from the *sugar;* but the latter should be good. Boiling it without a *cover* allows the evaporation of all the watery particles therefrom, and renders the preserves firm and well flavoured. The proportions are, three quarters of a pound of sugar to a pound of fruit. Jam made in this way of currants, strawberries, raspberries, or gooseberries, is excellent. The sugar should be added after the skimming is completed.

1524. To make a Syrup.—Dissolve one pound of sugar in about a gill of water, boil for a few minutes, skimming it till quite clear. To every two pounds of sugar add the white of one egg well beaten. Boil very quickly, and skim carefully while boiling. In the season for "preserves" our readers may be glad of the above instructions, which have been adopted with great success.

1525. Covering for Preserves.—White paper cut to a suitable size, dipped in brandy, and put over the preserves when cold, and then a double paper tied over the top. All preserves should stand a night before they are covered. Instead of brandy, the white of eggs may be used to glaze the paper covering, and the paper may be pasted round the edge of the pot instead of tied—it will exclude the air better.

1526. To Bottle Fruits.—Burn a match in a bottle to exhaust all air, then place in the fruit to be preserved, quite dry, and without blemish; sprinkle sugar between each layer, put in the bung, and tie bladder over, setting the bottles, bung downwards, in a large stewpan of cold water, with hay between to prevent breaking. When the skin is just cracking, take them out. All preserves require exclusion from the air. Place a piece of paper dipped in sweet oil over the top of the fruit; prepare thin paper, immersed in gum-water, and while wet, press it over and around the top of the jar; as it dries, it will become quite firm and tight.

1527. Apples for keeping should be laid out on a *dry* floor for three weeks. They may then be packed away in layers, with dry straw between them. Each apple should be rubbed with a dry cloth as it is put away. They should be kept in a cool place, but should be sufficiently covered with straw to protect them from frost. They should be plucked on a dry day.

1528. Dried Apples are produced by taking fine apples of good quality, and placing them in a very slow oven for several hours. Take them out occasionally, rub and press them flat. Continue until they are done. If they look dry, rub over them a little clarified sugar.

1529. Preserved Rhubarb.—Peel one pound of the finest rhubarb, and cut it into pieces of two inches in length; add three quarters of a pound of white sugar, and the rind and juice of one lemon—the rind to be cut into narrow strips. Put all into a preserving kettle, and simmer gently until the rhubarb is quite soft; take it out carefully with a silver spoon, and put it into jars; then boil the syrup a sufficient time to make it keep well,—say one hour,—and pour it over the fruit. When cold, put a paper soaked in brandy over it, and tie the jars down with a bladder to exclude the air. This is a very good receipt, and should be taken advantage of in the spring.

1530. Dry Apricots.—Gather before ripe, scald in a jar put into boiling water, pare and stone them; put into a syrup of half their weight of sugar, in the proportion of half a pint of water to two pounds of sugar; scald, and then boil until they are clear. Stand for two days in the syrup, then put into a thin candy, and scald them in it. Keep two days longer in the candy, heating them each day, and then lay them on glasses to dry.

1531. Preserved Peaches.— Wipe and pick the fruit, and have ready a quarter of the weight of fine sugar in powder. Put the fruit into an ice-pot that shuts very close; throw the sugar over it, and then cover the fruit with brandy. Between the top and cover of the pot put a double piece of grey paper. Set the pot in a saucepan of water till the brandy is as hot as you can bear to put your finger into, but do not let it boil. Put the fruit into a jar, and pour on the brandy. Cover in same manner as preserves.

1532. Brandy Peaches.—Drop them into a weak boiling lye, until the skin can be wiped off. Make a thin syrup to cover them, boil until they are soft to the finger-nail; make a rich syrup, and add, after they come from the fire, and while hot, the same quantity of brandy as syrup. The fruit must be covered.

1533. Preserved Plums.—Cut your plums in half (they must not be quite ripe), and take out the stones. Weigh the plums, and allow a pound of loaf sugar to a pound of fruit. Crack the stones, take out the kernels, and break them in pieces. Boil the plums and kernels very slowly for about fifteen minutes, in as little water as possible. Then spread them on a large dish to cool, and strain the liquor. Next day add your syrup, and boil for fifteen minutes. Put into jars, pour the juice over when warm, and tie them up, when cold, with brandy paper. —Plums for common use are very good done in treacle. Put your plums into an earthen vessel that holds a gallon, having first slit each plum with a knife. To three quarts of plums put a pint of treacle. Cover them over, and set them on hot coals in the chimney corner. Let them stew for twelve hours or more, occasionally stirring,

and next day put them up in jars. Done in this manner, they will keep till the next spring.

1534. To Preserve Lemons, Whole, for Dessert. — Take six fine, fresh, well-shaped lemons, cut a hole just round the stalk, and with a marrow-spoon scoop out the pips, and press out the juice, but leave the pulp in the lemons. Put them into a bowl with two or three quarts of spring water, to steep out the bitterness. Leave them three days, changing the water each day; or only two days if you wish them to be very bitter. Strain the juice as soon as squeezed out, boil it with one pound of loaf sugar (setting the jar into which it was strained in a pan of boiling water fifteen or twenty minutes); tie it up, *quite hot*, with bladder, and set by till wanted. Taste the water the lemons are lying in at the end of the third day; if not bitter, lift the lemons out into a china-lined pan, pour the water through a strainer upon them, boil gently one or two hours; set by in the pan. Boil again next day, until so tender that the head of a large needle will easily pierce the rind. Put in one pound of loaf sugar, make it just boil, and leave to cool. Next day boil the syrup, and pour it on the lemons; add one pound of sugar, and hot water to supply what was boiled away. Lift out the lemons, and boil the syrup and pour on them again every day for a fortnight, then every three or four days, adding gradually three pounds of sugar. When the lemons look clear and bright, boil the syrup pretty hard, add the lemon juice which had been set by, just boil, skim: put the lemons into jars, pour the syrup upon them, and tie up the jars *instantly* with bladder.

1535. Preserved Ginger. — Scald the young roots till they become tender, peel them, and place in cold water, frequently changing the water: then put into a thin syrup, and, in a few days, put into jars, and pour a rich syrup over them.

1536. To Preserve Eggs.—It has been long known to housewives, that the great secret of preserving eggs fresh is to place the small end downwards, and keep it in that position—other requisites not being neglected, such as to have the eggs perfectly fresh when deposited for keeping, not allowing them to become wet, keeping them cool in warm weather, and avoiding freezing in winter. Take an inch board of convenient size, say a foot wide, and two and a half feet long, and bore it full of holes, each about an inch and a half in diameter; a board of this size may have five dozen holes bored in it, for as many eggs. Then nail strips of thin board two inches wide round the edges, to serve as a ledge. Boards such as this may now be made to constitute the shelves of a cupboard in a cool cellar. The only precaution necessary is to place the eggs as fast as they are laid in these holes, with the small end downwards, and they will keep for months perfectly fresh. The great advantage of this plan is the perfect ease with which the fresh eggs are packed away, and again obtained when wanted. A carpenter would make such a board for a trifling charge.

1537. ANOTHER METHOD OF PRESERVING EGGS.—The several modes recommended for preserving eggs any length of time are not always successful. The egg, to be preserved well, should be kept at a temperature so low that the air and fluids within its shell shall not be brought into a decomposing condition; and, at the same time, the air outside of its shell should be excluded, in order to prevent its action in any way upon the egg. The following mixture was patented several years ago by Mr. Jayne, of Sheffield. He alleged that by means of it he could keep eggs two years. A part of his composition is often made use of — perhaps the whole of it would be better. Put into a tub or vessel one bushel of quicklime, two pounds of salt, half a pound of cream of tartar, and mix the same together, with as much water as will reduce the composition, or mixture, to

that consistence that it will cause an egg put into it to swim with its top just above the liquid ; then place the eggs therein.

1538. Eggs may be Preserved by applying with a brush a solution of gum arabic to the shells, and afterwards packing them in dry charcoal dust.

1539. Bad Butter may be improved greatly by dissolving it in thoroughly hot water ; let it cool, then skim it off, and churn again, adding a little good salt and sugar. A small portion can be tried and approved before doing a larger quantity. The water should be merely hot enough to melt the butter, or it will become oily.

1540. Rancid Butter. — This may be restored by melting it in a water bath, with some coarsely powdered animal charcoal (which has been thoroughly sifted from dust), and strained through flannel.

1541. Salt Butter may be freshened by churning it with new milk, in the proportion of a pound of butter to a quart of milk. Treat the butter in all respects in churning as fresh. Cheap earthenware churns for domestic use may be had at any hardware shop.

1542. To Preserve Milk.—Provide bottles, which must be perfectly clean, sweet, and dry ; draw the milk from the cow into the bottles, and as they are filled, immediately cork them well up, and fasten the corks with packthread or wire. Then spread a little straw at the bottom of a boiler, on which place the bottles, with straw between them, until the boiler contains a sufficient quantity. Fill it up with cold water ; heat the water, and as soon as it begins to boil, draw the fire, and let the whole gradually cool. When quite cold, take out the bottles and pack them in sawdust, in hampers, and stow them in the coolest part of the house. Milk preserved in this manner, and allowed to remain even eighteen months in bottles, will be as sweet as when first milked from the cow.

1543. Meat may be kept several days in the height of summer, sweet and good, by lightly covering it with bran, and hanging it in some high or windy room, or in a passage where there is a current of air.

1544. Hams, Tongues, &c., Glazing for.—Boil a shin of beef twelve hours in eight or ten quarts of water; draw the gravy from a knuckle of veal in the same manner; put the same herbs and spices as if for soup, and add the whole to the shin of beef. It must be boiled till reduced to a quart. It will keep good for a year; and when wanted for use, warm a little, and spread over the ham, tongue, &c., with a feather.

1545. Curing of Hams and Bacon.—It is simply to use the same quantity of common soda as saltpetre—one ounce and a half of each to the fourteen pounds of ham or bacon, using the usual quantity of salt. The soda prevents that hardness in the lean of the bacon which is so often found, and keeps it quite mellow all through, besides being a preventative of rust. This receipt has been very extensively tried amongst my acquaintance for the last fifteen years, and *invariably* approved.

1546. Method of Preserving Mackarel.—Mackarel are at certain times exceedingly plentiful, especially to those who live near the coast. They may be preserved so as to make an excellent and well-flavoured dish, weeks or months after the season is past, by the following means. Having chosen fine fish, cleansed them perfectly, and either boiled them or lightly fried them in oil, the fish should be divided, and the bones, heads, and skins being removed, they should then be well rubbed over with the following seasoning:—For every dozen good-sized fish use three tablespoonfuls of salt (heaped), one ounce and a half of common black pepper, six or eight cloves, and a little mace, finely powdered, and as much nutmeg, grated, as the operator chooses to afford,—not, however, exceeding one nutmeg. Let the whole surface be well covered with the seasoning; then lay the fish in layers packed into a stone jar (not a glazed one); cover the whole with good vinegar, and if they be intended to be long kept, pour salad oil or melted oil over the top. *Caution.*—The glazing on earthen jars is made from lead or arsenic, from which vinegar draws forth poison.

1547. Preserving Potatoes.—The preservation of potatoes by dipping them in boiling water is a valuable and useful discovery. Large quantities may be cured at once, by putting them into a basket as large as the vessel containing the boiling water will admit, and then just dipping them a minute or two, at the utmost. The germ, which is so near the skin, is thus destroyed without injury to the potato. In this way several tons might be cured in a few hours. They should be then dried in a warm oven, and laid up in sacks, secure from the frost, in a dry place.

1548. To Preserve Cucumbers.—Take large and fresh-gathered cucumbers; split them down and take out all the seeds, lay them in salt and water, sufficiently strong to bear an egg, for three days; set them on a fire with cold water, and a small lump of alum, and boil them a few minutes, or till tender; drain them, and pour on them a thin syrup: —let them lie two days; boil the syrup again, and put it over the cucumbers; repeat it twice more, then have ready some fresh clarified sugar, boiled to a *blow* (which may be known by dipping the skimmer into the sugar, and blowing strongly through the holes of it; if little bladders appear, it has attained that degree); put in the cucumbers, and simmer it five minutes:—set it by till next day;—boil the syrup and cucumbers again, and set them in glasses for use.

1549. Pickling.—There are three methods of pickling; the most simple is merely to put the article into cold vinegar. The strongest pickling vinegar of white wine should always be used for pickles; and for white pickles, use distilled vinegar. This method we recommend for all such vegetables as, being hot themselves, do not require the addition of spice; and such as do not require to be softened by heat, as capsicums, chili, nasturtiums, button onions, radish-pods, horseradish, garlic, and shalots. Half fill the jars with best vinegar, fill them up with the vegetables, and tie down immediately with bladder and leather. One advantage of this plan is, that those who grow nasturtiums, radish-pods, and so forth, in their own gardens, may gather them from day to day, when they are exactly of the proper growth. They are very much better if pickled quite fresh, and all of a size, which can scarcely be obtained if they be pickled all at the same time. The onions should be dropped in the vinegar as fast as peeled; this secures their colour. The horseradish should be scraped a little outside, and cut up in rounds half an inch deep. Gather barberries before they are quite ripe; pick away all bits of stalk, and leaf, and injured berries, and drop them in cold vinegar; they may be kept in salt and water, changing the brine whenever it begins to ferment; but the vinegar is best.

1550. THE SECOND METHOD OF PICKLING is that of heating vinegar and spice, and pouring them hot over the vegetables to be pickled, which are previously prepared by sprinkling with salt, or immersing in brine. Do not boil the vinegar, for if so its strength will evaporate. Put the vinegar and spice into a jar, bung it down tightly, tie a bladder over, and let it stand on the hob or on a trivet by the side of the fire for three or four days; shake it well three or four times a day. This method may be applied to gherkins, French beans, cabbage, brocoli, cauliflowers, onions, and so forth.

1551. THE THIRD METHOD OF PICKLING is when the vegetables are in a

greater or less degree done over the fire. Walnuts, artichokes, artichoke bottoms, and beetroots are done thus, and sometimes onions and cauliflowers.

1552. FRENCH BEANS.—The best sort for this purpose are white runners. They are very large, long beans; but should be gathered quite young, before they are half grown; they may be done in the same way as described in No. 1549.

1553. ONIONS.—Onions should be chosen about the size of marbles; the silver-skinned sort are the best. Prepare a brine, and put them into it hot; let them remain one or two days, then drain them, and when quite dry, put them into clean, dry jars, and cover them with hot pickle, in every quart of which has been steeped one ounce each of horseradish sliced, black pepper, allspice, and salt, with or without mustard seed. In all pickles the vinegar should always be two inches or more above the vegetables, as it is sure to shrink, and if the vegetables are not thoroughly immersed in pickle they will not keep.

1554. RED CABBAGE.—Choose fine firm cabbages—the largest are not the best; trim off the outside leaves; quarter the cabbage, take out the large stalk, slice the quarters into a cullender, and sprinkle a little salt between the layers; put but a little salt—too much will spoil the colour; let it remain in the cullender till next day, shake it well, that all the brine may run off; put it in jars, cover it with a hot pickle composed of black pepper and allspice, of each an ounce, ginger pounded, horseradish sliced, and salt, of each half an ounce, to every quart of vinegar (steeped as above directed); two capsicums may be added to a quart, or one drachm of cayenne.

1555. GARLIC AND SHALOTS.—Garlic and shalots may be pickled in the same way as onions.

1556. MELONS, MANGOES, AND LONG CUCUMBERS may all be done in the same manner. Melons should not be much more than half grown; cucumbers full grown, but not overgrown. Cut off the top, but leave it hanging by a bit of rind, which is to serve as a hinge to a box-lid; with a marrow-spoon scoop out all the seeds, and fill the fruit with equal parts of mustard seed, ground pepper, and ginger, or flour of mustard instead of the seed, and two or three cloves of garlic. The lid which encloses the spice may be sewed down or tied, by running a white thread through the cucumber and through the lid, then, after tying it together, cut off the ends. The pickle may be prepared with the spices directed for cucumbers, or with the following, which bears a nearer resemblance to the Indian method. — To each quart of vinegar put salt, flour of mustard, curry powder, bruised ginger, turmeric, half an ounce of each, cayenne pepper one drachm, all rubbed together with a large glassful of salad oil; shalots two ounces, and garlic half an ounce, sliced; steep the spice in the vinegar as before directed, and put the vegetables into it hot.

1557. BROCOLI OR CAULIFLOWERS. — Choose such as are firm, and of full size; cut away all the leaves, and pare the stalk, pull away the flowers by bunches, steep in brine two days, then drain them, wipe them dry, and put them into hot pickle; or merely infuse for three days three ounces of curry powder in every quart of vinegar.

1558. WALNUTS. — Be particular in obtaining them exactly at the proper season; if they go beyond the middle of July, there is danger of their becoming hard and woody. Steep them a week in brine. If they are wanted to be soon ready for use, prick them with a pin, or run a larding-pin several times through them; but if they are not wanted in haste, this method had better be left alone. Put them into a kettle of brine, and give them a gentle simmer, then drain them on a sieve, and lay them on fish drainers, in an airy place, until they become black; then make a pickle of vinegar, adding to every quart, black pepper one ounce, ginger,

shalots, salt, and mustard seed, one ounce each. Most pickle vinegar, when the vegetables are used, may be turned to use, walnut pickle in particular; boil it up, allowing to each quart, four or six anchovies chopped small, and a large tablespoonful of shalots, also chopped. Let it stand a few days till it is quite clear, then pour off and bottle. It is an excellent store sauce for hashes, fish, and various other purposes.

1559. BEET ROOTS. — Boil or bake gently until they are nearly done; according to the size of the root they will require from an hour and a half to two hours to drain them, and when they begin to cool, peel and cut in slices half an inch thick, then put them into a pickle composed of black pepper and allspice, of each one ounce; ginger pounded, horseradish sliced, and salt, of each half an ounce to every quart of vinegar, steeped. Two capsicums may be added to a quart, or one drachm of cayenne.

1560. ARTICHOKES. — Gather young artichokes as soon as formed; throw them into boiling brine, and let them boil two minutes; drain them; when cold and dry, put them in jars, and cover with vinegar, prepared as method the third, but the only spices employed should be ginger, mace, and nutmeg.

1561. ARTICHOKE BOTTOMS. — Select full-grown artichokes and boil them; not so much as for eating, but just until the leaves can be pulled; remove them and the choke; in taking off the stalk, be careful not to break it off so as to bring away any of the bottom; it would be better to pare them with a silver knife, and leave half an inch of tender stalk coming to a point; when cold, add vinegar and spice, the same as for artichokes.

1562. MUSHROOMS. — Choose small white mushrooms; they should be but one night's growth. Cut off the roots, and rub the mushrooms clean with a bit of flannel and salt; put them in a jar, allowing to every quart of mushrooms one ounce each of salt, and ginger, half an ounce of whole pepper, eight blades of mace, a bay-leaf, a strip of lemon rind, and a wineglassful of sherry; cover the jar close, and let it stand on the hob or on a stove, so as to be thoroughly heated, and on the point of boiling; so let it remain a day or two, till the liquor is absorbed by the mushrooms and spices; then cover them with hot vinegar, close them again, and stand till it just comes to a boil; then take them away from the fire. When they are quite cold, divide the mushrooms and spice into wide-mouthed bottles, fill them up with the vinegar, and tie them over. In a week's time, if the vinegar has shrunk so as not entirely to cover the mushrooms, add cold vinegar. At the top of each bottle put a teaspoonful of salad or almond oil; cork close, and dip in bottle resin.

1563. SAMPHIRE.—On the sea coast this is merely preserved in water, or equal parts of sea-water and vinegar; but as it is sometimes sent fresh as a present to inland parts, the best way of managing it under such circumstances is to steep it two days in brine, then drain and put it in a stone jar covered with vinegar, and having a lid, over which put thick paste of flour and water, and set it in a very cool oven all night, or in a warmer oven till it nearly but not quite boils. Then let it stand on a warm hob for half an hour, and allow it to become quite cold before the paste is removed; then add cold vinegar, if any more is required, and secure as other pickles.

1564. INDIAN PICKLE.— The vegetables to be employed for this favourite pickle are small hard knots of white cabbage, sliced; cauliflowers or brocoli in flakes; long carrots, not larger than a finger, or large carrots sliced (the former are far preferable); gherkins, French beans, small button onions, white turnip radishes half grown, radish-pods, shalots, young hard apples; green peaches, before the stones begin to form; vegetable marrow, not larger than a hen's egg; small green melons, celery, shoots of green elder, horse-radish, nasturtiums, capsicums, and

garlic. As all these vegetables do not come in season together, the best method is to prepare a large jar of pickle at such time of the year as most of the things may be obtained, and add the others as they come in season. Thus the pickle will be nearly a year in making, and ought to stand another year before using, when, if properly managed, it will be excellent, but will keep and continue to improve for years. For preparing the several vegetables, the same directions may be observed as for pickling them separately, only take this general rule—that, if possible, boiling is to be avoided, and soaking in brine to be preferred; be very particular that every ingredient is perfectly dry before putting into the jar, and that the jar is very closely tied down every time that it is opened for the addition of fresh vegetables. Neither mushrooms, walnuts, nor red cabbage are to be admitted. For the pickle:—To a gallon of the best white wine vinegar add salt three ounces, flour of mustard half a pound, turmeric two ounces, white ginger sliced three ounces, cloves one ounce, mace, black pepper, long pepper, white pepper, half an ounce each, cayenne two drachms, shalots peeled four ounces, garlic peeled two ounces; steep the spice in vinegar on the hob or trivet for two or three days. The mustard and turmeric must be rubbed smooth with a little cold vinegar, and stirred into the rest when as near boiling as possible. Such vegetables as are ready may be put in; when cayenne, nasturtiums, or any other vegetables mentioned in the first method of pickling come in season, put them in the pickle as they are; any in the second method, a small quantity of hot vinegar without spice; when cold, pour it off, and put the vegetables into the general jar. If the vegetables are greened in vinegar, as French beans and gherkins, this will not be so necessary, but will be an improvement to all. Onions had better not be wet at all; but if it be desired not to have the full flavour, both onions, shalots, and garlic may be sprinkled with salt in a cullender, to draw off all the strong juice; let them lie two or three hours. The elder, apples, peaches, and so forth, to be greened as gherkins. The roots, radishes, carrots, celery, are only soaked in brine and dried. Half a pint of salad oil, or of mustard oil, is sometimes added. It should be rubbed with the flour of mustard and turmeric.—It is not essential to Indian pickle to have every variety of vegetable here mentioned; but all these are admissible, and the greater variety the more it is approved.

1565. To Pickle Gherkins.— Put about two hundred and fifty in a pickle of two pounds, and let them remain in it three hours. Put them in a sieve to drain, wipe them, and place them in a jar. For a pickle, best vinegar, one gallon; common salt, six ounces; allspice, one ounce; mustard seed, one ounce; cloves, half an ounce; mace, half an ounce; one nutmeg sliced; a stick of horseradish sliced; boil fifteen minutes; skim it well. When cold, pour it over them, and let stand twenty-four hours, covered up; put them into a pan over the fire, and let them simmer only until they attain a green colour. Tie the jars down closely with bladder and leather.

1566. Pickled Eggs.— If the following pickle were generally known it would be more generally used. We constantly keep it in our family, and find it an excellent pickle to be eaten with cold meat, &c. The eggs should be boiled hard (say ten minutes), and then divested of their shells; when *quite cold* put them in jars, and pour over them vinegar (sufficient to quite *cover* them), in which has been previously boiled the usual spices for pickling; tie the jars down tight with bladder, and keep them till they begin to change colour.

1567. Pickling.— Do not keep pickles in common earthenware, as the glazing contains lead, and combines with the vinegar. Vinegar for pickling should be sharp, though not the sharpest kind, as it injures the pickles. If you use copper, bell-metal, or brass vessels, for pickling, never allow the vinegar to cool in them, as it then is poisonous. Add a teaspoonful of alum and a teacupful of salt to each three gallons of vinegar, and tie up a bag, with pepper, ginger root, spices of all the different sorts in it, and you have vinegar prepared for any kind of pickling. Keep pickles only in wood or stone ware. Anything that has held grease will spoil pickles. Stir pickles occasionally, and if there are soft ones take them out, and scald the vinegar, and pour it hot over the pickles. Keep enough vinegar to cover them well. If it is weak, take fresh vinegar and pour on hot. Do not boil vinegar or spice above five minutes.

1568. To Make Anchovies.— Procure a quantity of sprats, as fresh as possible; do not wash or wipe them, but just take them as caught, and for every peck of the fish, take two pounds of common salt, a quarter of a pound of bay salt, four pounds of saltpetre, two ounces of sal-prunella, and two pennyworth of cochineal. Pound all these ingredients in a mortar, mixing them well together. Then take stone jars or small kegs, according to your quantity of sprats, and place a layer of the fish and a layer of the mixed ingredients alternately, until the pot is full; then press hard down, and cover close for six months, they will then be fit for use. We can vouch for the excellence and cheapness of the *anchovies* made in this manner. In fact, most of the *fine Gorgona anchovies* sold in the oil and pickle shops are made in this or a similar manner, from British sprats.

1569. To Make British Anchovies.— To a peck of sprats, put two pounds of salt, three ounces of bay salt, one pound of saltpetre, two ounces of prunella, and a few grains of cochineal; pound them all in a mortar, then put into a stone pan or anchovy barrel, first a layer of sprats, and then one of the compound, and so on alternately to the top. Press them down hard; cover them close for six months, and they will be fit for use, and will readily produce a most excellently flavoured sauce. A large trade is done in this article, especially for making anchovy paste or sauce, when a little more colouring is added.

1570. A Winter Salad.

Two large potatoes, passed through kitchen sieve,
Unwonted softness to the salad give;
Of mordant mustard add a single spoon—
Distrust the condiment which bites so soon;
But deem it not, thou man of herbs, a fault
To add a double quantity of salt;
Three times the spoon with oil of Lucca crown,
And once with vinegar procured from town.
True flavour needs it, and your poet begs
The pounded yellow of two well-boiled eggs;
Let onion atoms lurk within the bowl,
And, scarce suspected, animate the whole;
And lastly, on the favoured compound toss
A magic teaspoon of anchovy sauce:
Then, though green turtle fail, though venison's tough,
And ham and turkey be not boiled enough,
Serenely full, the epicure may say,—
" Fate cannot harm me—I have dined to-day."

1571. A Very Pleasant Perfume,

and also preventive against moths, may be made of the following ingredients:—Take of cloves, carraway seeds, nutmeg, mace, cinnamon, and Tonquin beans, of each one ounce; then add as much Florentine orris root as will equal the other ingredients put together. Grind the whole well to powder, and then put it in little bags among your clothes, &c.

1572. Lavender Scent Bag.

Take of lavender flowers, free from stalk, half a pound; dried thyme and mint, of each half an ounce; ground cloves and carraways, of each a quarter of an ounce; common salt, dried, one ounce; mix the whole well together, and put the product into silk or cambric bags. In this way it will perfume the drawers and linen very nicely.

1573. Lavender Water.

Essence of musk, four drachms; essence of ambergris, four drachms; oil of cinnamon, ten drops; English lavender, six drachms; oil of geranium, two drachms;

spirit of wine, twenty ounces. To be all mixed together.

1574. Honey Water.

Rectified spirit, eight ounces; oil of cloves, oil of bergamot, oil of lavender, of each half a drachm; musk, three grains; yellow sanders shavings, four drachms. Let it stand for eight days, then add two ounces each of orange-flower water and rose water.

1575. Honey Soap.

Cut thin two pounds of yellow soap into a double saucepan, occasionally stirring it till it is melted, which will be in a few minutes if the water is kept boiling around it; then add a quarter of a pound of palm oil, a quarter of a pound of honey, three pennyworth of true oil of cinnamon; let all boil together another six or eight minutes; pour out and let it stand till next day, it is then fit for immediate use. If made as directed it will be found to be a very superior soap.

1576. The Hands.

Take a wine-glassful of eau-de-Cologne, and another of lemon juice; then scrape two cakes of brown Windsor soap to a powder, and mix well in a mould. When hard, it will be an excellent soap for whitening the hands.

1577. To Whiten the Nails.

Diluted sulphuric acid, two drachms; tincture of myrrh, one drachm; spring water, four ounces: mix. First cleanse with white soap, and then dip the fingers into the mixture. A delicate hand is one of the chief points of beauty; and these applications are really effective.

1578. Stains

may be removed from the hands by washing them in a small quantity of oil of vitriol and cold water without soap.

1579. Cold Cream.

i. Oil of almonds, one pound; white wax, four ounces. Melt together gently in an earthen vessel, and when nearly cold stir in gradually twelve ounces of rose water.—ii. White wax and spermaceti, of each half an ounce; oil of almonds, four ounces; orange-flower water, two ounces. Mix as directed for No. i. The wholesale price of almond oil is

1s. 6d. per pound; white wax, 2s. 2d. per pound; spermaceti, 2s. per pound; rose and orange-flower waters, 6d. to 1s. per pint.

1580. To Soften the Skin and Improve the Complexion. — If flowers of sulphur be mixed in a little milk, and after standing an hour or two, the milk (without disturbing the sulphur) be rubbed into the skin, it will keep it soft, and make the complexion clear. It is to be used before washing. A lady of our acquaintance, being exceedingly anxious about her complexion, adopted the above suggestion. In about a fortnight she wrote to us to say that the mixture became so disagreeable after it had been made a few days, that she could not use it. We should have wondered if she could—the milk became putrid! A little of the mixture should have been prepared overnight with evening milk, and used the next morning, but not afterwards. About a wine-glassful made for each occasion would suffice.

1581. Eyelashes. — The mode adopted by the beauties of the East to increase the length and strength of their eyelashes, is simply to clip the split ends with a pair of scissors about once a month. Mothers perform the operation on their children, both male and female, when they are mere infants, watching the opportunity whilst they sleep. The practice never fails to produce the desired effect. We recommend it to the attention of our fair readers, as a safe and innocent means of enhancing the charms which so many of them, no doubt, already possess.

1582. The Teeth.—Dissolve two ounces of borax in three pints of water; before quite cold, add thereto one teaspoonful of tincture of myrrh, and one tablespoonful of spirits of camphor: bottle the mixture for use. One wine-glassful of the solution, added to half a pint of tepid water, is sufficient for each application. This solution, applied daily, preserves and beautifies the teeth, extirpates tartarous adhesion, produces a pearl-like whiteness, arrests decay, and induces a healthy action in the gums.

1583. Camphorated Dentifrice. — Prepared chalk, one pound; camphor, one or two drachms. The camphor must be finely powdered by moistening it with a little spirit of wine, and then intimately mixing it with the chalk. Prepared chalk will cost about 6d., the camphor less than 1d. The present price of camphor is under 3s. per pound.

1584. Myrrh Dentifrice.—Powdered cuttlefish, one pound; powdered myrrh, two ounces. Cuttlefish is 1s. 8d. per pound, powdered myrrh, 3s. 6d. per pound.

1585. American Tooth Powder.—Coral, cuttlefish bone, dragon's blood, of each eight drachms; burnt alum and red sanders, of each four drachms; orris root, eight drachms; cloves and cinnamon, of each half a drachm; vanilla, eleven grains; rosewood, half a drachm; rose pink, eight drachms. All to be finely powdered and mixed.

1586. Quinine Tooth Powder.—Rose pink, two drachms; precipitated chalk, twelve drachms; carbonate of magnesia, one drachm; quinine (sulphate), six grains. All to be well mixed together.

1587. Hair Dye. — A friend of ours, to whom we applied upon the subject, favoured us with the following information:—" I have operated upon my own cranium for at least a dozen years, and though I have heard it affirmed that dyeing the hair will produce insanity, I am happy to think I am, as yet, perfectly sane, and under no fear of being otherwise; at all events, I am wiser than I once was, when I paid five shillings for what I can now make myself for less than twopence! — but to the question;—I procure lime, which I speedily reduce to powder by throwing a little water upon it, then mix this with litharge (three quarters lime, and a quarter litharge), which I sift through a fine hair sieve, and then I have what is sold at a high price under the name of 'Unique Powder,' and the most effectual hair dye that has yet been discovered. But the application of it is not very agreeable, though simple enough:—Put a quantity of it in a saucer, pour boiling water upon it, and mix it up with a knife like thick mustard: divide the hair into thin layers with a comb, and plaster the mixture thickly into the layers to the roots, and all over the hair. When it is completely covered with it, lay over it a covering of damp blue or brown paper, then bind over it, closely, a handkerchief, then put on a night-cap, over all, and go to bed; in the morning brush out the powder, wash thoroughly with soap and warm water, then dry, curl, oil, &c. I warrant that hair thus managed will be a per-manent and beautiful black, which I dare say most people would prefer to either grey or red." Now, notwithstand-ing the patient endurance and satis-factory experience of our friend, we very much doubt whether one person in a hundred would be content to envelope their heads in batter of this description, and then retire to rest. To rest! did we say? We envy not the slumbers enjoyed under these cir-cumstances. We fancy we can do something still better for those who are ashamed of their grey hairs. The hair dyes formerly used produced very objectionable tints. Latterly several perfumers have been selling dyes, con-sisting of two liquids to be used in succession, at exceedingly high prices, such as 7s., 14s., and 21s. a case. The composition has been kept a close secret in the hands of a few. The pro-curing of it for publication in this work has been attended with considerable difficulty, but our readers may take it as an earnest that no pains or expense will be spared to afford really useful information.

1588. HAIR DYE, USUALLY STYLED COLOMBIAN, ARGENTINE, &c., &c.—So-lution No. i., Hydrosulphuret of am-monia, one ounce; solution of potash, three drachms; distilled or rain water, one ounce (all by measure). Mix, and put into small bottles, labelling it No. i.

—Solution No. ii. Nitrate of silver, one drachm; distilled or rain water, two ounces. Dissolved and labelled No. ii.

1589. *Directions how to apply.*—The solution No. i. is first applied to the hair with a tooth brush, and the application continued for fifteen or twenty minutes. The solution No. ii. is then brushed over, a comb being used to separate the hairs, and allow the liquid to come in contact with every part. Care must be taken that the liquid does not touch the skin, as the solution No. ii. pro-duces a permanent dark stain on all substances with which it comes in contact. If the shade is not suffi-ciently deep, the operation may be re-peated. The hair should be cleansed from grease before using the dye. Cost: hydrosulphuret of ammonia, 2s. 6d. per pound; solution of potash, 8d. per pound; nitrate of silver, 4s. 6d. per ounce; bottles, 10d. to 1s. 5d. per dozen.

1590. TO TEST HAIR DYE.—To try the effect of hair dye upon hair of any colour, cut off a lock and apply the dye thoroughly as directed above. This will be a guarantee of success, or will at least guard against failure.

1591. THE PROPER APPLICATION OF HAIR DYES.—The efficacy of hair dyes depends as much upon their proper application as upon their chemical com-position. If not evenly and patiently applied, they give rise to a mottled and dirty condition of the hair. A lady, for instance, attempted to use the lime and litharge dye, and was horrified on the following morning to find her hair spotted red and black, almost like the skin of a leopard. She wrote to us in great excitement and implored our aid. But what could we do? The mixture had not been properly applied. Our own hair is becoming grey, and we don't mind telling the reader what we intend to do: we have resolved to let it remain so, and bear "our grey hairs to the grave," deeming them to be no dis-honour.

1592. Compounds to Promote the Growth of Hair.—When the

hair falls off, from diminished action of the scalp; preparations of cantharides often prove useful; they are sold under the names of Dupuytren's Pomade, Cazenave's Pomade, &c. The following directions are as good as any of the more complicated receipts:—

1593. Pomade against Baldness.—Beef marrow, soaked in several waters, melted and strained, half a pound; tincture of cantharides (made by soaking for a week one drachm of powdered cantharides in one ounce of proof spirit), one ounce; oil of bergamot, twelve drops. Powdered cantharides, 3d. per ounce; bergamot, 1s. per ounce.

1594. Erasmus Wilson's Lotion against Baldness.—Eau-de-Cologne, two ounces; tincture of cantharides, two drachms; oil of lavender or rosemary, of either ten drops. These applications must be used once or twice a day for a considerable time; but if the scalp become sore, they must be discontinued for a time, or used at longer intervals.

1595. Bandoline, or Fixature.—Several preparations are used; the following are the best:—i. Mucilage of clean picked Irish moss, made by boiling a quarter of an ounce of the moss in one quart of water until sufficiently thick, rectified spirit in the proportion of a teaspoonful to each bottle, to prevent its being mildewed. The quantity of spirit varies according to the time it requires to be kept. Irish moss, 3d. to 4d. per lb.—ii. Gum tragacanth, one drachm and a half; water, half a pint; proof spirit (made by mixing equal parts of rectified spirit and water), three ounces; otto of roses, ten drops; soak for twenty-four hours and strain. Cost: tragacanth, 3s. 6d. per lb.; rectified spirit, 2s. 6d. per pint; otto of roses, 2s. 6d. per drachm. Bergamot, at 1s. per oz., may be substituted for the otto of roses.

1596. Excellent Hair Wash.—Take one ounce of borax, half an ounce of camphor; powder these ingredients fine, and dissolve them in one quart of boiling water; when cool, the solution will be ready for use; damp the hair frequently. This wash effectually cleanses, beautifies, and strengthens the hair, preserves the colour, and prevents early baldness. The camphor will form into lumps after being dissolved, but the water will be sufficiently impregnated.

1597. Hair Oils.—Rose Oil.—Olive oil, one pint, 1s.; otto of roses, five to sixteen drops, 3s. 6d. per drachm. Essence of bergamot, being much cheaper (1s. per ounce), is commonly used, instead of the more expensive otto of roses.

1598. Red Rose Oil.—The same. The oil coloured before scenting, by steeping in it one drachm of alkanet root, with a gentle heat, until the desired tint is produced. Alkanet root, 6d. to 8d. per pound.

1599. Oil of Roses.—Olive oil, two pints; otto of roses, one drachm; oil of rosemary, one drachm; mix. It may be coloured red by steeping a little alkanet root in the oil (with heat) before scenting it.

1600. Pomatums.—For making pomatums, the lard, fat, suet, or marrow used must be carefully prepared by being melted with as gentle a heat as possible, skimmed, strained, and cleared from the dregs which are deposited on standing.

1601. Common Pomatum.—Mutton suet, prepared as above, one pound; lard, three pounds; carefully melted together, and stirred constantly as it cools, two ounces of bergamot being added.

1602. Hard Pomatum.—Lard and mutton suet carefully prepared, of each one pound; white wax, four ounces; essence of bergamot, one ounce. Cost: lard, 1s. per pound; suet, 6d. per pound; white wax, 2s. 2d. per pound; essence of bergamot, 1s. per ounce.

1603. Castor Oil Pomade.—Castor oil, four ounces; prepared lard, two ounces; white wax, two drachms; bergamot, two drachms; oil of lavender, twenty drops. Melt the fat together, and on cooling add the scents, and stir till cold. Cost of castor oil, 10d. per pound; lard, 11d.; white wax, 2s. 2d. per pound; bergamot, 1s. per ounce.

1604. Superfluous Hair.—Any remedy is doubtful; many of those commonly used are dangerous. The safest plan is as follows:—The hairs should be perseveringly plucked up by the roots, and the skin having been washed twice a day with warm soft water, without soap, should be treated with the following wash, commonly called MILK OF ROSES:—Beat four ounces of sweet almonds in a mortar, and add half an ounce of white sugar during the process; reduce the whole to a paste by pounding; then add, in small quantities at a time, eight ounces of rose water. The emulsion thus formed should be strained through a fine cloth, and the residue again pounded, while the strained fluid should be bottled in a large stoppered vial. To the pasty mass in the mortar add half an ounce of sugar, and eight ounces of rose water, and strain again. This process must be repeated three times. To the thirty-two ounces of fluid add twenty grains of the bichloride of mercury, dissolved in two ounces of alcohol, and shake the mixture for five minutes. The fluid should be applied with a towel, immediately after washing, and the skin gently rubbed with a dry cloth till *perfectly dry.* Wilson, in his work on *Healthy Skin,* writes as follows:—"Substances are sold by the perfumers called depilatories, which are represented as having the power of removing hair. But the hair is not destroyed by these means, the root and that part of the shaft implanted within the skin still remain, and are ready to shoot up with increased vigour as soon as the depilatory is withdrawn. The effect of the depilatory is the same, in this respect, as that of a razor, and the latter is, unquestionably, the better remedy. It must not, however, be imagined that depilatories are negative remedies, and that, if they do no permanent good, they are, at least, harmless; that is not the fact; they are

violent irritants, and require to be used with the utmost caution. * * * * * After all, the safest depilatory is a pair of tweezers, and patience."

1605. To Clean Hair Brushes.—As hot water and soap very soon soften the hair, and rubbing completes its destruction, use soda, dissolved in cold water; instead; soda having an affinity for grease, it cleans the brush with little friction. Do not set them near the fire, nor in the sun, to dry, but after shaking them well, set them on the point of the handle, in a shady place. Powdered ...

1606. A Roman Lady's Toilet.—The toilet of a Roman lady involved an elaborate and very costly process. It commenced at night, when the face, supposed to have been tarnished by exposure, was overlaid with a poultice composed of boiled or moistened flour, spread on with the fingers. Poppæan unguents sealed the lips, and the lady was profusely rubbed with Cerona ointment. In the morning, the poultice and unguents were washed off, a bath of asses' milk imparted a delicate whiteness to the skin, and the pale face was freshened and revived with enamel. The full eyelids, which the Roman lady still knows so well how to use, now suddenly raising them to reveal a glance of surprise or of melting tenderness, now letting them droop like a veil over the lustrous eyes,—the full rounded eyelids were coloured within, and a needle, dipped in jetty dye, gave length to the eyebrows. The forehead was encircled by a wreath, or fillet, fastened in the luxuriant hair, which rose in front in a pyramidal pile, formed of successive ranges of curls, giving the appearance of more than ordinary height.

1607. The Young Lady's Toilette.

i. *Self-Knowledge—The Enchanted Mirror.* This curious glass will bring your faults to light, And make your virtues shine both strong and bright.

ii. *Contentment—Wash to smooth Wrinkles.*

A daily portion of this essence use,
'Twill smooth the brow, and tranquillity infuse.

iii. *Truth—Fine Lip-salve.*

Use daily for your lips this precious dye,
They'll redden, and breathe sweet melody.

iv. *Prayer—Mixture, giving Sweetness to the Voice.*

At morning, noon, and night this mixture take,
Your tones, improved, will richer music make.

v. *Compassion—Best Eye-water.*

These drops will add great lustre to the eye;
When more you need, the poor will you supply.

vi. *Wisdom—Solution to prevent Eruptions.*

It calms the temper, beautifies the face,
And gives to woman dignity and grace.

vii. *Attention and Obedience—Matchless Pair of Ear-rings.*

With these clear drops appended to the ear,
Attentive lessons you will gladly hear.

viii. *Neatness and Industry — Indispensable Pair of Bracelets.*

Clasp them on carefully each day you live,
To good designs they efficacy give.

ix. *Patience—An Elastic Girdle.*

The more you use the brighter it will grow,
Though its least merit is external show.

x. *Principle—Ring of Tried Gold.*

Yield not this golden bracelet while you live,
'Twill sin restrain, and peace of conscience give.

xi. *Resignation—Necklace of Purest Pearl.*

This ornament embellishes the fair,
And teaches all the ills of life to bear.

xii. *Love—Diamond Breast-pin.*

Adorn your bosom with this precious pin,
It shines without, and warms the heart within.

xiii. *Politeness—A Graceful Bandeau.*

The forehead neatly circled with this band,
Will admiration and respect command.

xiv. *Piety—A Precious Diadem.*

Whoe'er this precious diadem shall own,
Secures herself an everlasting crown.

xv. *Good Temper—Universal Beautifier.*

With this choice liquid gently touch the mouth,
It spreads o'er all the face the charms of youth.

1608. Bathing.—If to preserve health be to save medical expenses without even reckoning upon time and comfort, there is no part of the household arrangement so important to the domestic economist as cheap convenience for personal ablution. For this purpose baths upon a large and expensive scale are by no means necessary; but though temporary or tin baths may be extremely useful upon pressing occasions, it will be found to be finally as cheap, and much more readily convenient, to have a permanent bath constructed, which may be done in any dwelling-house of moderate size, without interfering with other general purposes. As the object of these remarks is not to present essays, but merely useful economic hints, it is unnecessary to expatiate upon the architectural arrangement of the bath, or, more properly speaking, the bathing-place, which may be fitted up for the most retired establishment, differing in size or shape agreeably to the spare room that may be appropriated to it, and serving to exercise both the fancy and the judgment in its preparation. Nor is it particularly necessary to notice the salubrious effects resulting from the bath, beyond the two points of its being so conducive to both health and cleanliness, in keeping up a free circulation of the blood, without any violent muscular exertion, thereby really affording a saving of strength, and producing its effects without any expense either to the body or to the purse.

1609. Whoever fits up a bath in a house already built must be guided by circumstances; but it will always be proper to place it as near the kitchen fireplace as possible, because from thence it may be heated, or at least have its temperature preserved, by means of hot air through tubes, or by steam prepared by the culinary fireplace, without interfering with its ordinary uses.

1610. A small boiler may be erected at very little expense in the bathroom, where circumstances do not permit these arrangements. Whenever a bath is wanted at a short warning, to boil the water necessary will always be the shortest mode; but where it is in general daily use, the heating the water by steam will be found the cheapest and most convenient method.

1611. As a Guide for Practice, we may observe that it has been proved by experiment that a bath with five feet of water at the freezing point, may be raised to the temperature of blood heat, or 96 degrees, by 304 gallons of water turned into steam, at an expense of 50 lbs. of Newcastle coal; but if the door be kept closed, it will not lose above four degrees of temperature in twenty-four hours, by a daily supply of 3 lbs. of coal. This is upon a scale of a bath of 5,000 gallons of water.

1612. Cleanliness.—The want of cleanliness is a fault which admits of no excuse. Where water can be had for nothing, it is surely in the power of every person to be clean.

1613. The Discharge from our Bodies by perspiration renders frequent changes of apparel necessary.

1614. Change of Apparel greatly promotes the secretion from the skin, so necessary to health.

1615. When that Matter which ought to be carried off by perspiration, is either retained in the body, or reabsorbed in dirty clothes, it is apt to occasion fevers and other diseases.

1616. Most Diseases of the Skin proceed from want of cleanliness. These indeed may be caught by infection, but they will seldom continue long where cleanliness prevails.

1617. To the Same Cause must we impute the various kinds of vermin that infest the human body, houses, &c. These may generally be banished by cleanliness alone.

1618. Perhaps the intention of nature, in permitting such vermin to annoy mankind, is to induce them to the practice of this virtue.

1619. One Common Cause of putrid and malignant fevers is the want of cleanliness.

1620. These Fevers commonly begin among the inhabitants of close dirty houses, who breathe bad air, take little exercise, eat unwholesome food, and wear dirty clothes. There the infection is generally hatched, which spreads far and wide, to the destruction of many. Hence cleanliness may be considered as an object of public attention. It is not sufficient that I be clean myself, while the want of it in my neighbour affects my health as well as his own.

1621. If Dirty People cannot be removed as a common nuisance, they ought at least to be avoided as infectious. All who regard their health should keep at a distance, even from their habitations. In places where great numbers of people are collected, cleanliness becomes of the utmost importance.

1622. It is well known that infectious diseases are caused by tainted air. Everything, therefore, which tends to pollute the air, or spread the infection, ought, with the utmost care, to be avoided.

1623. For this Reason, in great towns, no filth of any kind should be permitted to lie upon the streets. We are sorry to say that the importance of general cleanliness in this respect does by no means seem to be sufficiently understood.

1624. It were well if the lower classes of the inhabitants of Great Britain would imitate their neighbours the Dutch in the cleanness of their streets, houses, &c.

1625. Water, indeed, is easily obtained in Holland; but the situation of most towns in Great Britain is more favourable to cleanliness.

1626. Nothing can be more agreeable to the senses, more to the honour of the inhabitants, or conducive to their health, than a clean town; nor does anything impress a stranger sooner with a disrespectful idea of any people than its opposite.

1627. It is remarkable that, in most eastern countries, cleanliness makes a great part of their religion. The Mahometan, as well as the Jewish religion, enjoins various bathings, washings, and purifications. No doubt these were designed to represent inward purity; but they are at the same time calculated for the preservation of health.

1628. However whimsical these washings may appear to some, few things would seem more to prevent diseases than a proper attention to many of them.

1629. Were every Person, for example, after handling a dead body, visiting the sick, &c., to wash before he went into company, or sat down to meat, he would run less hazard either of catching the infection himself, or communicating it to others.

1630. Frequent Washing not only removes the filth which adheres to the skin, but likewise promotes the perspiration, braces the body, and enlivens the spirits.

1631. Even Washing the Feet tends greatly to preserve health. The perspiration and dirt with which these parts are frequently covered, cannot fail to obstruct their pores. This piece of cleanliness would often prevent colds and fevers.

1632. Were People to Bathe their feet and hands in warm water at night, after being exposed to cold or wet through the day, they would seldom experience any of the effects from these causes which often prove fatal.

1633. In Places where great numbers of sick people are kept, cleanliness ought most religiously to be observed. The very smell in such places is often sufficient to make one sick. It is easy to imagine what effect that is likely to have upon the diseased.

1634. A Person in Health has a greater chance to become sick, than a sick person has to get well, in an hospital or infirmary where cleanliness is neglected.

1635. The Brutes themselves set us an example of cleanliness. Most of them seem uneasy, and thrive ill, if they be not kept clean. A horse that is kept thoroughly clean will thrive better on a smaller quantity of food, than with a greater where cleanliness is neglected.

1636. Even our own Feelings are a sufficient proof of the necessity of cleanliness. How refreshed, how cheerful and agreeable does one feel on being washed and dressed; especially when these have been long neglected.

1637. Superior Cleanliness sooner attracts our regard than even finery itself, and often gains esteem where the other fails.

1638. Influence of Cleanliness.—"I have more than once expressed my conviction that the humanizing influence of habits of cleanliness, and of those decent observations which imply self-respect—the best, indeed the only foundation of respect for others—has never been sufficiently acted on. A clean, fresh, and well-ordered house exercises over its inmates a moral no less than a physical influence, and has a direct tendency to make the members of a family sober, peaceable, and considerate of the feelings and happiness of each other; nor is it difficult to trace a connection between habitual feelings of this sort and the formation of habits of respect for property, for the laws in general, and even for those higher duties and obligations the observance of which no laws can enforce."—*Dr. Southwood Smith.*

1639. Exercise—Exercise in the open air is of the first importance to the human frame, yet how many are in a manner deprived of it by their own want of management of their time! Females with slender means are for the most part destined to indoor occupations, and have but little time allotted them for taking the air, and that little time is generally sadly encroached upon by the ceremony of dressing to go out. It may appear a simple suggestion, but experience only will show how much time might be redeemed by habits of regularity: such as putting the shawls, cloaks, gloves, shoes, clogs, &c., &c., or whatever is intended to be worn, in readiness, instead of having to search one drawer, then another, for possibly a glove or collar—wait for shoes being cleaned, &c.—and this when (probably) the out-going persons have to return to their employment at a given time. Whereas, if all were in readiness, the preparations might be accomplished in a few minutes, the walk not being curtailed by unnecessary delays.

1640. THREE PRINCIPAL POINTS in the manner of taking exercise are necessary to be attended to:—i. The kind of exercise. ii. The proper time for exercise. iii. The duration of it. With respect to the kinds of exercise, the various species of it may be divided into active and passive. Among the first, which admit of being considerably diversified, may be enumerated walking, running, leaping, swimming, riding, fencing, the military exercise, different sorts of athletic games, &c. Among the latter, or passive kinds of exercise, may be comprised riding in a carriage, sailing, friction, swinging, &c.

1641. ACTIVE EXERCISES are more beneficial to youth, to the middle-aged, to the robust in general, and particularly to the corpulent and the plethoric.

1642. PASSIVE KINDS of exercise, on the contrary, are better calculated for children; old, dry, and emaciated persons of a delicate and debilitated constitution; and particularly for the asthmatic and consumptive.

1643. THE TIME at which exercise is most proper depends on such a variety of concurrent circumstances, that it does not admit of being regulated by any general rules, and must therefore be collected from the observations made on the effects of air, food, drink, &c.

1644. WITH RESPECT TO THE DURATION OF EXERCISE, there are other particulars, relative to a greater or less degree of fatigue attending the different species, and utility of it in certain states of the mind and body, which must determine this consideration as well as the preceding.

1645. THAT EXERCISE IS TO BE PREFERRED which, with a view to

brace and strengthen the body, we are most accustomed to. Any unusual one may be attended with a contrary effect.

1646. EXERCISE SHOULD BE BEGUN and finished gradually, never abruptly.

1647. EXERCISE IN THE OPEN AIR has many advantages over that used within doors.

1648. To CONTINUE EXERCISE until a profuse perspiration or a great degree of weariness takes place, is far from being wholesome.

1649. IN THE FORENOON, when the stomach is not too much distended, muscular motion is both agreeable and healthful; it strengthens digestion, and heats the body less than with a full stomach; and a good appetite after it is a proof that it has not been carried to excess.

1650. BUT at the same time it should be understood, that it is not advisable to take violent exercise immediately before a meal, as digestion might thereby be retarded.

1651. NEITHER should we sit down to a substantial dinner or supper immediately on returning from a fatiguing walk, at a time when the blood is heated, and the body in a state of perspiration from previous exertion, as the worst consequences may arise, especially where cooling dishes, salad, or a glass of cold drink is begun with.

1652. EXERCISE IS ALWAYS HURTFUL AFTER MEALS, from its impeding digestion, by propelling those fluids too much towards the surface of the body which are designed for the solution of the food in the stomach.

1653. Walking.—To walk gracefully, the body must be erect, but not stiff, and the head held up in such a posture that the eyes are directed forward. The tendency of untaught walkers is to look towards the ground near the feet; and some persons appear always as if admiring their shoe-ties. The eyes should not thus be cast downward, neither should the chest bend forward to throw out the back, making what are termed round shoulders; on the contrary, the whole person must hold

I

itself up, as if not afraid to look the world in the face, and the chest by all means be allowed to expand. At the same time, everything like strutting or pomposity must be carefully avoided. An easy, firm, and erect posture is alone desirable. In walking, it is necessary to bear in mind that the locomotion is to be performed entirely by the legs. Awkward persons rock from side to side, helping forward each leg alternately by advancing the haunches. This is not only ungraceful but fatiguing. Let the legs alone advance, bearing up the body.

1654. Utility of Singing.—It is asserted, and we believe with some truth, that singing is a corrective of the too common tendency to pulmonic complaints. Dr. Rush, an eminent physician, observes on this subject,—"The Germans are seldom afflicted with consumption; and this, I believe, is in part occasioned by the strength which their lungs acquire by exercising them in vocal music, for this constitutes an essential branch of their education. The music master of an academy has furnished me with a remark still more in favour of this opinion. He informed me that he had known several instances of persons who were strongly disposed to consumption, who were restored to health by the exercise of their lungs in singing."

1655. The Weather and the Blood.—In dry, sultry weather the heat ought to be counteracted by means of a cooling diet. To this purpose cucumbers, melons, and juicy fruits are subservient. We ought to give the preference to such alimentary substances as lead to contract the juices which are too much expanded by the heat, and this property is possessed by all acid food and drink. To this class belong all sorts of salad, lemons, oranges, pomegranates sliced and sprinkled with sugar, for the acid of this fruit is not so apt to derange the stomach as that of lemons : also cherries and strawberries, curds turned with lemon acid or cream of tartar; cream

of tartar dissolved in water ; lemonade, and Rhenish or Moselle wine mixed with water.

1656. How to get Sleep.—How to get sleep is to many persons a matter of high importance. Nervous persons who are troubled with wakefulness and excitability, usually have a strong tendency of blood on the brain, with cold extremities. The pressure of the blood on the brain keeps it in a stimulated or wakeful state, and the pulsations in the head are often painful. Let such rise and chafe the body and extremities with a brush or towel, or rub smartly with the hands, to promote circulation, and withdraw the excessive amount of blood from the brain, and they will fall asleep in a few moments. A cold bath, or a sponge bath and rubbing, or a good run, or a rapid walk in the open air, or going up and down stairs a few times just before retiring, will aid in equalizing circulation and promoting sleep. These rules are simple, and easy of application in castle or cabin, and may minister to the comfort of thousands who would freely expend money for an anodyne to promote "Nature's sweet restorer, balmy sleep!"

1657. Early Rising.—Dr. Wilson Philip, in his "Treatise on Indigestion," says :—"Although it is of consequence to the debilitated to go early to bed, there are few things more hurtful to them than remaining in it too long. Getting up an hour or two earlier often gives a degree of vigour which nothing else can procure. For those who are not much debilitated, and sleep well, the best rule is to get out of bed soon after waking in the morning. This at first may appear too early, for the debilitated require more sleep than the healthy; but rising early will gradually prolong the sleep on the succeeding night, till the quantity the patient enjoys is equal to his demand for it. Lying late is not only hurtful, by the relaxation it occasions, but also by occupying that part of the day at which exercise is most beneficial."

1658. Appetite,—Appetite is frequently lost through excessive use of stimulants, food taken too hot, sedentary occupation, costiveness, liver disorder, and want of change of air. The first endeavour should be to ascertain and remove the cause. Change of diet and change of air will frequently be found more beneficial than medicines.

1659. Temperance.—"If," observes a writer, "men lived uniformly in a healthy climate, were possessed of strong and vigorous frames, were descended from healthy parents, were educated in a hardy and active manner, were possessed of excellent natural dispositions, were placed in comfortable situations in life, were engaged only in healthy occupations, were happily connected in marriage, and kept their passions in due subjection, there would be little occasion for medical rules." All this is very excellent and desirable; but, unfortunately for mankind, unattainable.

1660. MAN MUST BE SOMETHING MORE THAN MAN to be able to connect the different links of this harmonious chain —to consolidate this *summum bonum* of earthly felicity into one uninterrupted whole; for, independent of all regularity or irregularity of diet, passions, and other sublunary circumstances, contingencies, and connections, relative or absolute, thousands are visited by diseases and precipitated into the grave, independent of accident, to whom no particular vice could attach, and with whom the appetite never overstepped the boundaries of temperance. Do we not hear almost daily of instances of men living near to and even upwards of a century? We cannot account for this either; because of such men we know but few who have lived otherwise than the world around them; and we have known many who have lived in habitual intemperance for forty or fifty years, without interruption and with little apparent inconvenience.

1661. THE ASSERTION HAS BEEN MADE by those who have attained a great age (Parr, and Henry Jenkins, for instance), that they adopted no particular arts for the preservation of their health; consequently, it might be inferred that the duration of life has no dependence on manners or customs, or the qualities of particular food. This, however, is an error of no common magnitude.

1662. PEASANTS, LABOURERS, AND OTHER HARD-WORKING PEOPLE, more especially those whose occupations require them to be much in the open air, may be considered as following a regulated system of moderation; and hence the higher degree of health which prevails among them and their families. They also observe rules; and those which it is said were recommended by Old Parr are remarkable for good sense; namely, "Keep your head cool by temperance, your feet warm by exercise; rise early, and go soon to bed; and if you are inclined to get fat, keep your eyes open and your mouth shut,"—in other words, sleep moderately, and be abstemious in diet;—excellent admonitions, more especially to those inclined to corpulency.

1663. Corpulence.—Mr. William Banting, the well-known undertaker to the Royal Family, and author of a "Letter on Corpulence," gives the following excellent advice, with a dietary for use in cases of obesity (corpulence):—

i. *Medicine.*—None, save a morning cordial, as a corrective.

ii. Dietary:—

Breakfast.—Four or five ounces of beef, mutton, kidneys, broiled fish, bacon, or any kind of cold meat except pork, a large cup (or two) of tea without milk or sugar, a little biscuit or dry toast.

Dinner. — Five or six ounces of any fish except salmon, any meat except pork, any vegetable except potatoes; one ounce of dry toast; fruit out of a pudding; any kind of poultry or game, and two or three glasses of claret or sherry. Port, champagne, and beer forbidden.

Tea. — Two or three ounces of fruit; a rusk or two, and a cup or two of tea, without milk or sugar.

Supper. — Three or four ounces of meat or fish as at dinner, with a glass or two of claret.

Nightcap (if required). — A glass or two of grog, — whisky, gin, or brandy, — without sugar ; or a glass or two of sherry. Mr. Banting adds, "Dietary is the principal point in the treatment of corpulence (also in rheumatic diseases, and even in incipient paralysis). If properly regulated, it becomes in a certain sense a medicine. It purifies the blood, strengthens the muscles and viscera, and sweetens life if it does not prolong it." *

1064. THE ADVANTAGES TO BE DERIVED FROM A REGULAR MODE OF LIVING, with a view to the preservation of health and life, are nowhere better exemplified than in the precepts and practice of Plutarch, whose rules for this purpose are excellent; and by observing them himself, he maintained his bodily strength and mental faculties unimpaired to a very advanced age. Galen is a still stronger proof of the advantages of a regular plan, by means of which he reached the great age of 140 years, without having ever experienced disease. His advice to the readers of his "Treatise on Health" is as follows : — "I beseech all persons who shall read this work not to degrade themselves to a level with the brutes, or the rabble, by gratifying their sloth, or by eating and drinking promiscuously whatever pleases their palates, or by indulging their appetites of every kind. But whether they understand physic or not, let them consult their reason, and observe what agrees, and what does not agree with them, that, like wise men, they may adhere to the use of such things as conduce to their health, and forbear everything which, by their own experience, they find to do them hurt : and let them be assured that, by a diligent observation and practice of this rule, they may enjoy a good share of health, and seldom stand in need of physic or physicians."

* "Banting on Corpulence." Harrison : Lond.

1065. Health in Youth. — Late hours, irregular habits, and want of attention to diet, are common errors with most young men, and these gradually, but at first imperceptibly, undermine the health, and lay the foundation for various forms of disease in after life. It is a very difficult thing to make young persons comprehend this. They frequently sit up as late as twelve, one, or two o'clock, without experiencing any ill effects; they go without a meal to-day, and to-morrow eat to repletion, with only temporary inconvenience. One night they will sleep three or four hours, and the next nine or ten; or one night, in their eagerness to get away into some agreeable company, they will take no food at all, and the next, perhaps, will eat a hearty supper, and go to bed upon it. These, with various other irregularities, are common to the majority of young men, and are, as just stated, the cause of much bad health in mature life. Indeed, nearly all the shattered constitutions with which too many are cursed, are the result of a disregard to the plainest precepts of health in early life.

1066. Disinfecting Liquid. — In a wine bottle of cold water, dissolve two ounces acetate of lead (sugar of lead), and then add two (fluid) ounces of strong nitric acid (aquafortis). Shake the mixture, and it will be ready for use. — A very small quantity of the liquid, in its strongest form, should be used for cleansing all kinds of chamber utensils. For removing offensive odours, clean cloths thoroughly moistened with the liquid, diluted with eight or ten parts of water, should be suspended at various parts of the room. — In this case the offensive and deleterious gases are neutralized by chemical action. Fumigation in the usual way is only the substitution of one odour for another. In using the above, or any other disinfectant, let it never be forgotten that *fresh air*, and plenty of it, is cheaper and more effective than any other material.

1667. Disinfecting Fumigation. — Common salt, three ounces; black manganese, oil of vitriol, of each one ounce; water, two ounces; carried in a cup through the apartments of the sick; or the apartments intended to be fumigated, where sickness has been, may be shut up for an hour or two, and then opened.

1668. Coffee a Disinfectant. —Numerous experiments with roasted coffee prove that it is the most powerful means, not only of rendering animal and vegetable effluvia innocuous, but of actually destroying them. A room in which meat in an advanced degree of decomposition had been kept for some time, was instantly deprived of all smell on an open coffee-roaster being carried through it, containing a pound of coffee newly roasted. In another room, exposed to the effluvium occasioned by the clearing out of the dung-pit, so that sulphuretted hydrogen and ammonia in great quantities could be chemically detected, the stench was completely removed in half a minute, on the employment of three ounces of fresh-roasted coffee, whilst the other parts of the house were permanently cleared of the same smell by being simply traversed with the coffee-roaster, although the cleansing of the dung-pit continued for several hours after. The best mode of using the coffee as a disinfectant is to dry the raw bean, pound it in a mortar, and then roast the powder on a moderately heated iron plate, until it assumes a dark brown tint, when it is fit for use. Then sprinkle it in sinks or cesspools, or lay it on a plate in the room which you wish to have purified. Coffee acid or coffee oil acts more readily in minute quantities.

1669. Charcoal as a Disinfectant.—The great efficacy of wood and animal charcoal in absorbing effluvia, and the greater number of gases and vapours, has long been known.

Charcoal powder has also, during many centuries, been advantageously employed as a filter for putrid water, the object in view being to deprive the water of numerous organic impurities diffused through it, which exert injurious effects on the animal economy.

It is somewhat remarkable that the very obvious application of a perfectly similar operation to the still rarer fluid in which we live—namely, the air, which not unfrequently contains even more noxious organic impurities floating in it than those present in water—should have for so long a period been so unaccountably overlooked.

Charcoal not only absorbs effluvia and gaseous bodies, but especially, when in contact with atmospheric air, oxidizes and destroys many of the easily alterable ones, by resolving them into the simplest combinations they are capable of forming, which are chiefly water and carbonic acid.

It is on this oxidizing property of charcoal, as well as on its absorbent power, that its efficacy as a deodorizing and disinfecting agent chiefly depends.

Effluvia and miasmata are usually regarded as highly organized, nitrogenous, easily alterable bodies. When these are absorbed by charcoal, they come in contact with highly condensed oxygen gas, which exists within the pores of all charcoal which has been exposed to the air, even for a few minutes; in this way they are oxidized and destroyed.

1670. Charcoal as a Disinfectant. Dr. Stenhouse's Plan.—The following remarks by Dr. John Stenhouse, F.R.S., Lecturer on Chemistry at St. Bartholomew's Hospital, London, are so important on this subject that we quote them at length :—

" My attention was especially directed, for nearly a twelvemonth, to the deodorizing and disinfecting properties of charcoal, and I made an immense number of experiments on this subject. I brought the subject before the Society of Arts, and exhibited a specimen of a charcoal respirator, and the mode of employing it; dwelling at some length on the utility of charcoal powder as a means of preventing the escape of noxious effluvia from churchyards, and from dead bodies on board ship, and in other situations.

"In a letter to the Society of Arts I also proposed to employ charcoal ventilators, consisting of a thin layer of charcoal enclosed between two thin sheets of wire gauze, to purify the foul air which is apt to accumulate in water-closets, in the close wards of hospitals, and in the impure atmospheres of many of the back courts and mews-lanes of large cities, all the impurities being absorbed and retained by the charcoal, while a current of pure air alone is admitted into the neighbouring apartments.

"In this way pure air is obtained from exceedingly impure sources. Such an arrangement as this, carried out on a large scale, would be especially useful to persons necessitated to live in pestiferous districts within the tropics, where the miasmata of ague, yellow fever, and similar diseases are prevalent.

"The proper amount of air required by houses in such situations might be admitted through sheets of wire gauze or coarse canvas, containing a thin layer of coarse charcoal powder.

"Under such circumstances, also, pillows stuffed with powdered charcoal, and bed coverlets having the same material quilted into them, could not fail to prove highly beneficial.

"A tolerably thick charcoal ventilator, such as I have just described, could be very advantageously applied to the gully-holes of our common sewers, and to the sinks in private dwellings, the foul water in both cases being carried into the drain by means of tolerably wide syphon pipes, retaining always about a couple of inches of water.

"Such an arrangement would effectually prevent the escape of any effluvia, would be easy of construction, and not likely to get soon out of order.

"The charcoal respirators to which I have already referred, and to which I wish to draw especial attention, are of three kinds.

"The first form of the respirator is constructed for the mouth alone, and does not differ in appearance from an ordinary respirator, but is only half its weight, and about one-fifth of its price.

"The air is made to pass through a quarter of an inch of coarsely powdered charcoal, retained in its place by two sheets of silvered wire gauze, covered over with thin woollen cloth, by which means its temperature is greatly increased. The charcoal respirator possesses several advantages over the respirators ordinarily in use, viz. :—

"1st. Where the breath is at all fœtid, which is usually the case in diseases of the chest, under many forms of dyspepsia, &c., the disagreeable effluvia are absorbed by the charcoal, so that comparatively pure air is alone inhaled. This, I think, may occasionally exert a beneficial influence on diseases of the throat and lungs.

"2ndly. The charcoal respirator for the mouth alone will certainly prove highly useful in poisonous atmospheres, where miasmata abound, if the simple precaution is only observed of inspiring the air by the mouth and expiring it by the nostrils.

"The second form of respirator is ori-nasal—that is, embracing both the mouth and the nose. It is only very slightly larger than the one already described, and does not cover the nose, as the ordinary ori-nasal respirator does, but merely touches its lower extremity, to which it is adapted by means of a piece of flexible metal covered with soft leather. When this respirator is worn, no air enters the lungs without first passing through the charcoal, and any effluvia or miasmata contained in the atmosphere are absorbed and oxidized by the charcoal. This form of the respirator, therefore, is peculiarly adapted for protecting the wearer against fevers and other infectious diseases.

"The third form of the respirator is also ori-nasal, but is much larger, and therefore more cumbrous than the preceding variety. It is intended chiefly for use in chemical works, common sewers, &c., to protect the workmen from the noxious effects of the deleterious gases to which they are frequently exposed.

"I am aware that some persons, who admit the deodorizing properties of charcoal, deny that it acts as a disinfectant. I would direct the attention of such persons to the following statement of facts:—The bodies of a full grown cat and two rats were placed in open pans, and covered by two inches of powdered charcoal. The pans stood in my laboratory several years, and though it is generally very warm, not the slightest smell was ever perceptible, nor have any injurious effects been experienced by any of the persons by whom the laboratory is daily frequented.

"Now, had the bodies of these animals been left to putrefy under ordinary circumstances, not only would the stench emitted have been intolerable, but some of the persons would certainly have been struck down by fever or other malignant disorders. Charcoal powder has been most successfully employed, both at St. Mary's and St. Bartholomew's hospitals, to arrest the progress of gangrene and other putrid sores. The charcoal does not require to be put immediately in contact with the sores, but is placed above the dressings, not unfrequently quilted loosely in a little cotton wool. In many cases patients who were rapidly sinking have been restored to health.

"In the instance of hospital gangrene, we have to deal not only with the effluvia, but also with real miasmata; for, as is well known, the poisonous gases emitted by gangrenous sores not only affect the individual with whom the mischief has originated, but readily infect the perfectly healthy wounds of any individual who may happen to be in its vicinity. So that in this way gangrene has been known to spread not only through one ward, but through several wards of the same hospital.

"The dissecting-room at St. Bartholomew's hospital has been perfectly deodorized by means of a few trays filled with a thin layer of freshly-heated wood charcoal. A similar arrangement will, in all probability, be likewise soon applied to the wards of St. Bartholomew's, and every other well-conducted hospital.

"From these and other considerations, therefore, I feel perfectly confident that charcoal is by far the cheapest and best disinfectant.

"Unlike many other disinfectants, it evolves no disagreeable vapours, and if heated in close vessels will always act, however long it has been in use, quite as effectively as at first.

"If our soldiers and sailors, therefore, when placed in unhealthy situations, were furnished with charcoal respirators, such as the second form above described, and if the floors of the tents and the lower decks of the ships were covered by a thin layer of freshly burnt wood charcoal, I think we could have little in future to apprehend from the ravages of cholera, yellow fever, and similar diseases, by which our forces have of late been decimated. If found more convenient, the charcoal powder might be covered with coarse canvas, without its disinfectant properties being materially impaired.

"The efficiency of the charcoal may be greatly increased by making it red-hot before using it. This can easily be done by heating it in an iron saucepan covered with an iron lid.

"When the charcoal is to be applied to inflammable substances, such as wooden floors, &c., of course it must be allowed to cool in close vessels before being used."

1671. Domestic Hints.—*Why is the flesh of sheep that are fed near the sea more nutritious than that of others?* — Because the saline particles (sea salt) which they find with their green food gives purity to their blood and flesh.

1672. *Why does the marbled appearance of fat in meat indicate that it is young and tender?*—Because in young animals fat is dispersed through the muscles, but in old animals it is laid in masses on the outside of the flesh.

1673. *Why is some flesh white and other flesh red?* — White flesh contains a larger proportion of albumen (similar to the white of egg) than that which is red. The amount of blood retained in the flesh also influences its colour.

1674. *Why are raw oysters more wholesome than those that are cooked?* — When cooked they are partly deprived of salt water, which promotes their digestion; their albumen becomes hard (like hard-boiled eggs).

1675. *Why have some oysters a green tinge?* — This has been erroneously attributed to the effects of copper; but it arises from the oyster feeding upon small green sea-weeds, which grow where such oysters are found.

1676. *Why is cabbage rendered more wholesome by being boiled in two waters?* —Because cabbages contain an oil, which is apt to produce bad effects, and prevents some persons from eating "green" vegetables. When boiled in two waters, the first boiling carries off the greater part of this oil.

1677. *Why should horseradish be scraped for the table only just before it is required?*—Because the peculiar oil of horseradish is very volatile; it quickly evaporates, and leaves the vegetable substance dry and insipid.

1678. *Why is mint eaten with pea soup?*—The properties of mint are stomachic and antispasmodic. It is therefore useful to prevent the flatulencies that might arise, especially from soups made of green or dried peas.

1679. *Why is apple sauce eaten with pork and goose?*—Because it is slightly laxative, and therefore tends to counteract the effects of rich and stimulating meats. The acid of the apples also neutralizes the oily nature of the fat, and prevents biliousness.

1680. *Why does milk turn sour during thunder storms?*—Because, in an electric condition of the atmosphere, ozone is generated. Ozone is oxygen in a state of great intensity; and oxygen is a general acidifier of many organic substances. Boiling milk prevents its becoming sour, because it expels the oxygen.

1681. *Why does the churning of cream or milk produce butter?*—Because the action of stirring, together with a moderate degree of warmth, causes the cells in which the butter is confined to burst; the disengaged fat collects in flakes, and ultimately coheres in large masses.

1682. *What is the blue mould which appears sometimes upon cheese?*—It is a species of fungus, or minute vegetable, which may be distinctly seen when examined by a magnifying glass.

1683. *Why are some of the limbs of birds more tender than others?*—The tenderness or toughness of flesh is determined by the amount of exercise the muscles have undergone. Hence the wing of a bird that chiefly walks, and the leg of a bird that chiefly flies, are the most tender.

1684. *Why does tea frequently cure headache?*—Because, by its stimulant action on the general circulation, in which the brain participates, the nervous congestions are overcome.

1685. *Why are clothes of smooth and shining surfaces best adapted for hot weather?* — Because they reflect or turn back the rays of the sun, which are thus prevented from penetrating them.

1686. *Why is loose clothing warmer than tight articles of dress?*—Because the loose dress encloses a stratum of warm air, which the tight dress shuts out; for the same reason, woollen articles, though not warmer in themselves, appear so, by keeping warm air near to the body.

1687. *Why should the water poured upon tea be at the boiling point?*—Because it requires the temperature of boiling water to extract the peculiar oil of tea.

1688. *Why does the first infusion of tea possess more aroma than the second?* Because the first infusion, if the water used is at the boiling temperature, takes up the essential oil of the tea, while the second water receives only the bitter extract supplied by the tannic acid of tea.

1689. *Why does a head-dress of sky-blue become a fair person ?*—Because light blue is the complementary colour of pale orange, which is the foundation of the blonde complexion and hair.

1690. *Why are yellow, orange, or red colours suitable to a person of dark hair and complexion ?*—Because those colours, by contrast with the dark skin and hair, show to the greater advantage themselves, while they enrich the hue of black.

1691. *Why is a delicate green favourable to pale blonde complexions ?*—Because it imparts a rosiness to such complexions—red, its complementary colour, being reflected upon green.

1692. *Why is light green unfavourable to ruddy complexions?*—Because it increases the redness, and has the effect of producing an overheated appearance.

1693. *Why is violet an unfavourable colour for every kind of complexion ?*—Because, reflecting yellow, they augment that tint when it is present in the skin or hair, change blue into green, and give to an olive complexion a jaundiced look.

1694. *Why is blue unsuitable to brunettes ?*—Because it reflects orange, and adds to the darkness of the complexion.

1695. *Why do blue veils preserve the complexion ?*—Because they diminish the effect of the scorching rays of light, just as the blue glass over photographic studios diminishes the effect of certain rays that would injure the delicate processes of photography.*

1696. Hints upon Etiquette.†

1697. INTRODUCTION TO SOCIETY. —Avoid all extravagance and manner-

ism, and be not over timid at the outset. Be discreet and sparing of your words. Awkwardness is a great misfortune, but it is not an unpardonable fault. To deserve the reputation of moving in good society, something more is requisite than the avoidance of blunt rudeness. Strictly keep to your engagements. Punctuality is the essence of politeness.

1698. THE TOILET.—Too much attention cannot be paid to the arrangements of the toilet. A man is often judged by his appearance, and seldom incorrectly. A neat exterior, equally free from extravagance and poverty, almost always proclaims a right-minded man. To dress appropriately, and with good taste, is to respect yourself and others. A gentleman walking, should always wear gloves, this being one of the characteristics of good breeding. Fine linen, and a good hat, gloves, and boots, are evidences of the highest taste in dress.

1699. VISITING DRESS.—A black coat and trousers are indispensable for a visit of ceremony, an entertainment, or a ball. The white or black waistcoat is equally proper in these cases.

1700. OFFICERS' DRESS. — Upon public and state occasions officers should appear in uniform.

1701. LADIES' DRESS. — Ladies' dresses should be chosen so as to produce an agreeable harmony. Never put on a dark-coloured bonnet with a light spring costume. Avoid uniting colours which will suggest an epigram; such as a straw-coloured dress with a green bonnet.

1702. ARRANGEMENT OF THE HAIR. —The arrangement of the hair is most important. Bands are becoming to faces of a Grecian caste. Ringlets better suit lively and expressive heads.

1703. EXCESS OF LACE AND FLOWERS.—Whatever be your style of face, avoid an excess of lace, and let flowers be few and choice.

1704. APPROPRIATENESS OF ORNAMENTS.—In a married woman a richer style of ornament is admissible. Costly

* "Housewife's Reason Why," containing upwards of 1,500 Reasons upon every kind of Domestic Subject. London: Houlston and Wright. 2s. 6d.

† See "Etiquette and Social Ethics." 1s. London: Houlston and Wright.

elegance for her—for the young girl, a style of modest simplicity.

1705. SIMPLICITY AND GRACE.—The most elegant dress loses its character if it is not worn with grace. Young girls have often an air of constraint, and their dress seems to partake of their want of ease. In speaking of her toilet, a woman should not convey the idea that her whole skill consists in adjusting tastefully some trifling ornaments. A simple style of dress is an indication of modesty.

1706. CLEANLINESS.—The hands should receive especial attention. They are the outward signs of general cleanliness. The same may be said of the face, the neck, the ears, and the teeth. The cleanliness of the system generally, and of bodily apparel, pertains to Health, and is treated of under this head.

1707. THE HANDKERCHIEF.—There is considerable art in using this accessory of dress and comfort. Avoid extreme patterns, styles, and colours. Never be without a handkerchief. Hold it freely in the hand, and do not roll it into a ball. Hold it by the centre, and let the corners form a fan-like expansion. Avoid using it too much. With some persons the habit becomes troublesome and unpleasant.

1708. VISITS AND PRESENTATIONS.—i. Friendly calls should be made in the forenoon, and require neatness, without costliness of dress.

ii. Calls to give invitations to dinner-parties, or balls, should be very short, and should be paid in the afternoon.

iii. Visits of condolence require a grave style of dress.

iv. A formal visit should never be made before noon. If a second visitor is announced, it will be proper for you to retire, unless you are very intimate both with the host and the visitor announced; unless, indeed, the host express a wish for you to remain.

v. Visits after balls or parties should be made within a month.

vi. In the latter, it is customary to enclose your card in an envelope, bearing the address outside. This may be sent by post, if you reside at a distance.

vii. But, if living in the neighbourhood, it is polite to send your servant, or to call. In the latter case a corner should be turned down.

viii. Scrape your shoes and use the mat. Never appear in a drawing-room with mud on your boots.

ix. When a new visitor enters a drawing-room, if it be a gentleman, the ladies bow slightly; if a lady, the guests rise.

x. Hold your hat in your hand, unless requested to place it down. Then lay it beside you.

xi. The last arrival in a drawing-room takes a seat left vacant near the mistress of the house.

xii. A lady is not required to rise to receive a gentleman, nor to accompany him to the door.

xiii. When your visitor retires, ring the bell for the servant. You may then accompany your guest as far towards the door as the circumstances of your friendship seem to demand.

xiv. Request the servant, during the visit of guests, to be ready to attend to the door the moment the bell rings.

xv. When you introduce a person, pronounce the name distinctly, and say whatever you can to make the introduction agreeable. Such as "an old and valued friend," a "schoolfellow of mine," "an old acquaintance of our family."

xvi. Never stare about you in a room as if you were taking stock.

xvii. The gloves should not be removed during a visit.

xviii. Be hearty in your reception of guests; and where you see much diffidence, assist the stranger to throw it off.

xix. A lady does not put her address on her visiting card.

1709. Balls and Evening Parties.—i. An invitation to a ball should be given at least a week beforehand.

ii. Upon entering, first address the

lady of the house; and after her, the nearest acquaintances you may recognize in the house.

iii. If you introduce a friend, make him acquainted with the names of the chief persons present. But first present him to the lady of the house, and to the host.

iv. Appear in full dress.

v. Always wear gloves.

vi. Do not wear rings on the outside of your gloves.

vii. Avoid an excess of jewellery.

viii. Do not select the same partner frequently.

ix. Distribute your attentions as much as possible.

x. Pay respectful attention to elderly persons.

xi. Be cordial when serving refreshments, but not importunate.

xii. If there are more dancers than the room will accommodate, do not join in every dance.

xiii. In leaving a large party it is unnecessary to bid farewell, and improper to do so before the guests.

xiv. A Paris card of invitation to an evening party usually implies that you are invited for the season.

xv. In balls and large parties there should be a table for cards, and two packs of cards placed upon each table.

xvi. Chess and all unsociable games should be avoided.

xvii. Although many persons do not like to play at cards except for a stake, the stakes agreed to at parties should be very trifling, so as not to create excitement or discussion.

xviii. The host and hostess should look after their guests, and not confine their attentions. They should, in fact, assist those chiefly who are the least known in the room.

xix. Avoid political and religious discussions. If you have a "hobby," keep it to yourself.

xx. After dancing, conduct your partner to a seat.

xxi. Resign her as soon as her next partner advances.

(For the Figures of Dances, consult the Index.— See HINTS UPON ETIQUETTE, No. 1696.)

1710. Marriage Arrangements.

1711. SPECIAL LICENCES. — Special licences are dispensations from the ordinary rule, under which marriages can only take place canonically in the parish church, or other places duly licensed for that purpose. They can only be obtained from the Metropolitan or archbishop of the province, and often with no small difficulty, not being readily granted; and when obtained the fees are about £50.

1712. COMMON LICENCES enable persons of full age, or minors with consent of parents or guardians, to be married in the church of the parish in which one of them has resided for three weeks. They are procured from Doctors' Commons, or from any surrogate, at the cost of about £2 10s.

1713. BANNS must be published *three times* in the parish church, in *each place* where the persons concerned reside. The clerk is applied to on such occasions; his fee varies from 1s. 6d. upwards. When the marriage ceremony is over, the parties repair to the vestry, and enter their names in the parish registry. The registry is signed by the clergyman and the witnesses present, and a certificate of the registry is given to the bridegroom. The charge for a certificate of marriage is 2s. 6d., and the clergyman's fee varies according to circumstances. The clerk will at all times give information thereupon; and it is best for a friend of the bridegroom to attend to the pecuniary arrangements.

1714. MARRIAGE BY REGISTRATION. —An Act was passed in the reign of William the Fourth, by which it was rendered legal for persons wishing to be married by a civil ceremony, to give notice of their intention to the Registrar of Marriages in their district or districts. Three weeks' notice is necessary, to give which the parties call, separately or together, at the office of the registrar, who enters their names in a book. When the time of notice has expired, it is only necessary to give the registrar an intimation, on the previous day, of your intention to attend at his office on the next day, and complete the registration. The ceremony consists of merely answering a few questions, and making the declaration that you take each other to live as husband and wife. The fee amounts only to a few shillings, and in this form no wedding ring is required, though it is usually placed on in the presence of the persons assembled. The married couple receive a certificate of marriage, which is in every respect lawful.

1715. WEDDING DRESS.—It is impossible to lay down specific rules for dress, as fashions change, and tastes differ. The great art consists in selecting the style of dress most becoming to the person. A stout person should adopt a different style from a thin person; a tall one from a short one. Peculiarities of complexion, and form of face and figure, should be duly regarded; and in these matters there is no better course than to call in the aid of any respectable milliner and dressmaker, who will be found ready to give the best advice. The bridegroom should simply appear in full dress, and should avoid everything eccentric and broad in style. The bridesmaids should always be made aware of the bride's dress before they choose their own, which should be determined by a proper harmony with the former.

1716. THE ORDER OF GOING TO CHURCH is as follows :—The BRIDE, accompanied by her *father*, not unfrequently her *mother*, and uniformly by a *bridesmaid*, occupies the *first carriage*. The father hands out the bride, and leads her to the altar, the mother and the bridesmaid following. After them come the other bridesmaids, attended by the groomsmen, if there are more than one.

1717. THE BRIDEGROOM occupies the *last carriage* with the principal groomsman—an intimate friend, or brother. He follows, and stands facing the altar, with *the bride at his left hand*. The

father places himself behind, with the mother, if she attends.

1718. THE CHIEF BRIDESMAID occupies a place on the *left* of the *bride*, to hold her gloves, and handkerchief, and flowers; her *companions* range themselves on *the left*. If any difficulties occur from forgetfulness, the vestry-woman can set everything right.

1719. REMEMBER TO TAKE THE LICENCE AND THE RING WITH YOU. The fee to a clergyman is according to the rank and fortune of the bridegroom; the clerk expects *five shillings*, and a trifle should be given to the vestry-woman or sexton. There is a fixed scale of fees at every church, to which the parties married can add if they please.

1720. WHEN THE CEREMONY IS CONCLUDED, *the bride, taking the bride-groom's arm, goes into the vestry, the others following;* signatures are then affixed, and a registration made, after which the married pair enter their carriage, and proceed to the breakfast, every one else following.

1721. THE ORDER OF RETURN FROM CHURCH differs from the above only in the fact that the bride and bridegroom now ride together, the bride being on his left, and a bridesmaid and a groomsman, or the father of the bride, occupying the front seats of the carriage.

1722. THE WEDDING BREAKFAST having been already prepared, the wedding party return thereto. If a large party, the bride and bridegroom occupy seats in the centre of the long table, and the two extremities should be presided over by elderly relatives, if possible one from each family. Everybody should endeavour to make the occasion as happy as possible. One of the senior members of either the bride or bridegroom's family should, some time before the breakfast has terminated, rise, and in a brief but graceful manner, propose the "Health and happiness of the wedded pair." It is much better to drink their healths together than separately; and, after a brief interval, the bridegroom should return thanks, which he may do without hesitation, since no one looks for a speech upon such an occasion. A few words, feelingly expressed, are all that is required. The breakfast generally concludes with the departure of the happy pair upon their wedding tour.

1723. CARDS.—A newly married couple send out cards immediately after the ceremony to their friends and acquaintance, who, on their part, return either notes or cards of congratulation on the event. As soon as the lady is settled in her new home, she may expect the calls of her acquaintance; for which it is not absolutely necessary to remain at home, although politeness requires that they should be returned as soon as possible. But, having performed this, any further intercourse may be avoided (where it is deemed necessary) by a polite refusal of invitations. Where cards are to be left, the number must be determined according to the various members of which the family called upon is composed. For instance, where there are the mother, aunt, and daughters (the latter having been introduced to society), three cards should be left. Recently, the custom of sending cards has been in a great measure discontinued, and instead of this, the words "No cards" are appended to the ordinary newspaper advertisement, and the announcement of the marriage, with this addition, is considered all sufficient.

1724. RECEPTION.—When the married pair have returned, and the day of reception arrives, wedding cake and wine are handed round, of which every one partakes, and each expresses some kindly wish for the newly married couple. The bride ought not to receive visitors without a mother, or sister, or some friend being present, not even if her husband be at home. Gentlemen who are in professions, or have Government appointments, cannot always await the arrival of visitors; when such is the case, some old friend of the family should represent him, and proffer an apology for his absence.

1725. THE WEDDING TOUR must depend upon the tastes and circumstances of the married couple. Home-loving Englishmen and women may find much to admire and enjoy without ranging abroad. Those whose time is somewhat restricted we recommend to sojourn at Tunbridge Wells,—Mount Ephraim is especially to be selected, —and thence the most delightful excursions may be made to different parts of the country; those who like sketching, botanizing, and collecting sea-weeds, will find ample opportunities for each; those who like old ruins and time-hallowed places may reach them without difficulty. Dover, Canterbury, Folkestone, and Tatwood Castle are all within reach, and what places are more deeply interesting, not only in respect of scenery, but historic associations? Cornwall and Devonshire, the Isle of Wight, &c., are each delightful to the tourist; and the former is now accessible by railway almost as far as the Land's End. The scenery of the north of Devon, and of both coasts of Cornwall, is especially beautiful. North Wales offers a delightful excursion; the lakes of Westmoreland and Cumberland; the lakes of Killarney, in Ireland; also the magnificent scenery of the Scottish lakes and mountains. To those who wish for a wider range, France, Germany, Switzerland, and the Rhine offer charms which cannot be surpassed.

1726. WEDDING CAKES. — Four pounds of fine flour, well dried; four pounds of fresh butter; two pounds of loaf sugar; a quarter of a pound of mace, pounded and sifted fine; the same of nutmegs. To every pound of flour add eight eggs; wash four pounds of currants, let them be well picked and dried before the fire; blanch a pound of sweet almonds, and cut them lengthwise very thin; a pound of citron; one pound of candied orange; the same of candied lemon; half a pint of brandy. When these are made ready, work the butter with your hand to a cream, then beat in the sugar a quarter of an hour; beat the whites of the eggs to a very strong froth; mix them with the sugar and butter; beat the yolks half an hour at least, and mix them with the cake; then put in the flour, mace, and nutmeg, keep beating it well till your oven is ready—pour in the brandy, and beat the currants and almonds lightly in. Tie three sheets of white paper round the bottom of your hoop to keep it from running out; rub it well with butter; put in your cake; lay the sweetmeats in layers, with cake between each layer; and after it is risen and coloured cover it with paper before your oven is stopped up. It will require three hours to bake properly.

1727. ALMOND ICING FOR WEDDING CAKE.—Beat the whites of three eggs to a strong froth, pulp a pound of Jordan almonds very fine with rose water, mix them, with the eggs, lightly together; put in by degrees a pound of common loaf sugar in powder. When the cake is baked enough, take it out, and lay on the icing; then put it in to brown.

1728. SUGAR ICING FOR WEDDING CAKE.—Beat two pounds of double refined sugar with two ounces of fine starch, sift the whole through a gauze sieve, then beat the whites of five eggs with a knife upon a pewter dish for half an hour; beat in the sugar a little at a time, or it will make the eggs fall, and injure the colour; when all the sugar is put in, beat it half an hour longer, and then lay on your almond icing, spreading it even with a knife. If put on as soon as the cake comes out of the oven, it will harden by the time the cake is cold.

1729. MARRIAGES OF DISSENTERS may be solemnized at any place of worship duly licensed, and in accordance with the forms of their worship. In some cases, the service of the Church of England is read, with slight additions or modifications. The clerk of the place of worship should be applied to for information.

1730. Christenings may be performed either in accordance with the rites of the Established Church, or of Dissenting congregations; the time of birth, and the name of every child,

must also be registered. The fees paid for christenings vary with a variety of circumstances. Particulars should in each case be obtained of the clerk of the place of worship. It is usual to make a christening the occasion of festivity; but not in such a manner as to require special remark. The parents and god-parents of the child appear at church at the appointed hour. The child is carried by the nurse. The dress of the parties attending a christening should be what may be termed demi-costume, or half-costume; but the infant should be robed in the choicest manner that the circumstances will allow. It is usual for the sponsors to present the child with a gift to be preserved for its future years. Silver spoons, a silver knife and fork, a clasp-bible, a silver cup, and other such articles, are usually chosen. It is usual, also, to give a trifling present to the nurse.

1731. REGISTRATION OF BIRTHS.—The law of registration requires the parents, or occupiers of houses in which the births happen, to register such births at the registrar's office within *six weeks* after the date thereof. For registration, within the time specified, *no charge is made*. But after the expiration of the forty-second day from the birth, a fee of *seven shillings and sixpence* must be paid. After the expiration of six months from the date of the birth, no registration is allowed. It is therefore most important, immediately after the birth of a child, for the father, or the occupier of the house in which the birth took place, to go to the office of the deputy registrar, residing in the district, and communicate the following particulars:—

1. Date when born.
2. Name of the child.
3. Boy or girl.
4. Name of the father.
5. Name and maiden name of the mother.
6. Rank or profession of the father.
7. Signature, description, and residence of the person giving the information.
8. Date of the registration.

1732. Baptismal Name.— If any child born in England, whose birth has been registered, shall, within six months of such registration, have any name given to it in baptism other than that originally registered, such baptismal name may be added to the previous registration, if, within seven days of such baptism, application be made to the registrar by whom the child was originally registered. For this purpose a certificate of the baptism must be procured of the clergyman, for which a fee of *one shilling* must be paid. This certificate must be taken to the registrar, who will charge another fee of *one shilling* for adding the baptismal name to the original registration.

1733. Choice of Names.—To choose names for children, parents should consult the list of names (No. 901, p. 137).

1734. Children Born at Sea.— If any child of an English parent shall be born at sea on board a British vessel, the captain or commanding officer shall make a minute of the particulars touching the birth of the child, and shall, on the arrival of the vessel at any part of the kingdom, or sooner, by any other opportunity, send a certificate of the birth through the post-office (*for which no postage will be charged*), to the Registrar General, General Register Office, London.

1735. Funerals and Registration of Deaths.—It is always best to place the direction of a funeral under a respectable undertaker, with the precaution of obtaining his estimate for the expenses, and limiting him to them. He can best advise upon the observances to be attended to, since the style of funerals differs with the station of the deceased's family, and is further modified by the customs of particular localities, and even by religious views.

1736. Intramural Interments.— It is, we think, our duty to strongly advise a discontinuance of the practice of burying in towns, where every dead body contributes to the destruction of the living. Now, Acts of Parliament compel the closing of graveyards in populous neighbourhoods. Besides which, the new cemeteries which are now springing up in all important localities are so economical and appropriate to be the long resting-places of the dead, that few people of good taste would cling to the old practice of burying in crowded churchyards in the midst of the dwellings of the living.

1737. Registration of Deaths.— The father or mother of any child that dies, or the occupier of a house in which any person may die, must, within *five days* after such death, give notice to the registrar of the district. Some person present at the death should at the same time attend and give to the registrar an account of the circumstances or cause of the death, to the best of his or her knowledge or belief. Such person must sign his or her name, and give the place of abode at which he or she resides. The following are the particulars required :—

1. Date of death.
2. Name in full.
3. Sex and age.
4. Rank or profession.
5. Cause of death.
6. Signature, description, and residence of the person giving the information.
7. Date of the registration.

1738. Persons Dying at Sea.— The commander of any British vessel, on board of which a death occurs at sea, must act the same as in a case of birth.

1739. Certificates of Death.— Every registrar must deliver to the undertaker, *without fee*, a certificate of the death, which certificate shall be delivered to the officiating minister. No dead body can be buried without such certificate, under a penalty of £10.

1740. Observances of Deaths and Funerals.—It is usual, when a death takes place, to communicate it immediately, upon mourning note-paper, to every principal member of the family, and to request them to notify the same to the more remote relatives in their circle. A subsequent note should state the day and hour at which the funeral is fixed to take place.

1741. SPECIAL INVITATIONS to funerals are not considered requisite to be sent to near relatives; but to friends and acquaintances such invitations should be sent.

1742. GLOVES.—Most persons who attend funerals will provide themselves with gloves; but it is well to have a dozen pairs, of assorted sizes, provided in case of accident. An arrangement can be made for those not used to be returned.

1743. HATBANDS AND CLOAKS will be provided by the undertaker.

1744. MOURNING.—The dressmaker will advise upon the "degree" of mourning to be worn, which must be modified according to the age of the deceased, and the relationship of the mourner. The undertaker will advise respecting the degree of mourning to be displayed upon the carriages, horses, &c.

1745. IN GOING TO THE FUNERAL the nearest relatives of the deceased occupy the carriages nearest the hearse. The same order prevails in returning. Only the relatives and most intimate friends of the family should return to the house after the funeral; and their visit should be as short as possible.

1746. IN WALKING FUNERALS it is considered a mark of respect for friends to become pall-bearers. In the funerals of young persons, the pall should be borne by their companions, wearing white gloves, and love-ribbon. It is a pretty and an affecting sight to see the pall over the coffin of a young lady borne by six of her female friends. Flowers may be placed upon the coffin, and strewed in and over the grave.

1747. VISITS OF CONDOLENCE after funerals should be paid by relatives within from a week to a fortnight; by friends within the second week of the fortnight; friends of less intimacy should make inquiries and leave cards.

1748. CORRESPONDENCE WITH FA-MILIES IN MOURNING should be upon black-edged paper, if from members of the family; or upon the ordinary note-paper, but sealed with black, if from friends.

1749. Ceremonies.—All ceremonies are in themselves superficial things; yet a man of the world should know them. They are the outworks of manners and decency, which would be too often broken in upon, if it were not for that defence which keeps the enemy at a proper distance. It is for that reason we always treat fools and coxcombs with great ceremony, true good-breeding not being a sufficient barrier against them.

1750. Love's Telegraph.—If a gentleman want a wife, he wears a ring on the *first* finger of the left hand; if he be engaged, he wears it on the *second* finger; if married, on the *third;* and on the fourth if he never intends to be married. When a lady is not engaged, she wears a hoop or diamond on her *first* finger; if engaged, on the *second;* if married, on the *third;* and on the fourth if she intends to die unmarried. When a gentleman presents a fan, flower, or trinket, to a lady with the *left* hand, this, on his part, is an overture of regard; should she receive it with the *left* hand, it is considered as an acceptance of his esteem; but if with the *right* hand, it is a refusal of the offer. Thus, by a few simple tokens explained by rule, the passion of love is expressed; and through the medium of the telegraph, the most timid and diffident man may, without difficulty, communicate his sentiments of regard to a lady, and, in case his offer should be refused, avoid experiencing the mortification of an explicit refusal.

1751. Wedding Rings.—The custom of wearing wedding rings appears to have taken its rise among the Romans. Before the celebration of their nuptials, there was a meeting of friends at the house of the lady's father, to settle articles of the marriage contract, when it was agreed that the dowry should be paid down on the wedding day or soon after. On this occasion there was commonly a feast, at the conclusion of which the man gave to the woman, as a pledge, a ring, which she put on the fourth finger of her left hand, *because it was believed that a nerve reached thence to the heart*, and a day was then named for the marriage.

1752. Why the Wedding Ring is placed on the Fourth Finger.—"We have remarked on the vulgar error which supposes that an artery runs from the fourth finger of the left hand to the heart. It is said by Swinburn and others, that therefore it became the wedding finger. The priesthood kept up this idea by still retaining it as the wedding finger, but the custom is really associated with the doctrine of the Trinity; for, in the ancient ritual of English marriages, the ring was placed by the husband on the top of the thumb of the left hand, with the words, 'In the name of the Father;' he then removed it to the forefinger, saying, 'In the name of the Son;' then to the middle finger, adding, 'And of the Holy Ghost;' finally, he left it as now, on the fourth finger, with the closing word, 'Amen.'"—*The History and Poetry of Finger Rings.*

1753. The Art of being Agreeable.—The true art of being agreeable is to appear well pleased with all the company, and rather to seem well entertained with them than to bring entertainment to them. A man thus disposed, perhaps may not have much learning, nor any wit; but if he has common sense, and something friendly in his behaviour, it conciliates men's minds more than the brightest parts without this disposition; and when a man of such a turn comes to old age, he is almost sure to be treated with respect. It is true, indeed, that we should not dissemble and flatter in company; but a man may be very agreeable, strictly consistent with truth and sincerity, by a prudent silence where he cannot concur, and a pleasing assent where he can. Now and then

you meet with a person so exactly formed to please, that he will gain upon every one that hears or beholds him: this disposition is not merely the gift of nature, but frequently the effect of much knowledge of the world, and a command over the passions.

1754. Artificial Manners.—Artificial manners, and such as spring from good taste and refinement, can never be mistaken, and differ as widely as gold and tinsel. How captivating is gentleness of manner derived from true humility, and how faint is every imitation! the one resembles a glorious rainbow, spanning a dark cloud—the other, its pale attendant, the water-gall. That suavity of manner which renders a real gentlewoman courteous to all, and careful to avoid giving offence, is often copied by those who merely subject themselves to certain rules of etiquette: but very awkward is the copy! Warm professions of regard are bestowed on those who do not expect them, and the esteem which is due to merit appears to be lavished on every one alike. And as true humility, blended with a right appreciation of self-respect, gives a pleasing cast to the countenance, so from a sincere and open disposition springs that artlessness of manner which disarms all prejudice. Feeling, on the contrary, is ridiculous when affected, and, even when real, should not be too openly manifested. Let the manners arise from the mind, and let there be no disguise for the genuine emotions of the heart.

1755. Directions for addressing Persons of Rank.

1756. THE ROYAL FAMILY.

The Queen.—Madam; Most Gracious Sovereign: May it please your Majesty.

To the Queen's Most Excellent Majesty.

The King.—Sire, or Sir; Most Gracious Sovereign: May it please your Majesty.

To the King's Most Excellent Majesty.

The Sons and Daughters, Brothers and Sisters, of Sovereigns. — Sir, or Madam: May it please your Royal Highness.

To his Royal Highness the Prince of Wales.

To her Royal Highness the Princess Helena Augusta Victoria.

Other Branches of the Royal Family. —Sir, or Madam: May it please your Highness.

To his Highness the Duke of Cambridge; or, To her Highness the Princess Mary Adelaide of Cambridge.

1757. THE NOBILITY.

A Duke or Duchess.—My Lord, or My Lady: May it please your Grace.

To his Grace the Duke of ——; or, To her Grace the Duchess of ——.

A Marquis or Marchioness. — My Lord, or My Lady: May it please your Lordship; or, May it please your Ladyship.

To the Most Noble the Marquis (or Marchioness) of ——.

An Earl or Countess.—The same.

To the Right Honourable the Earl (or Countess) of ——.

A Viscount or Viscountess.—My Lord, or My Lady: May it please your Lordship; or, May it please your Ladyship.

To the Right Honourable Viscount (or Viscountess) ——.

A Baron or Baroness.—The same.

To the Right Honourable the Baron (or Baroness) ——.

The widow of a nobleman is addressed in the same style, with the introduction of the word *Dowager* in the superscription.

To the Right Honourable the Dowager Countess ——.

The Sons of Dukes and Marquises, and the eldest Sons of Earls, have, by courtesy, the titles of Lord and Right Honourable; and all the Daughters have those of Lady and Right Honourable.

The younger Sons of Earls, and the Sons and Daughters of Viscounts and Barons, are styled Honourable.

1758. OFFICIAL MEMBERS OF THE STATE.

A Member of Her Majesty's Most Honourable Privy Council.—Sir, or My Lord; Right Honourable Sir, or My Lord, as the case may require.

To the Right Honourable ——, Her Majesty's Principal Secretary of State for Foreign Affairs.

1759. AMBASSADORS AND GOVERNORS UNDER HER MAJESTY.

Sir, or My Lord, as the case may be: May it please your Excellency.

To his Excellency the American (or Russian, or other) Ambassador.

To his Excellency Marquis ——, Lieutenant General, and General Governor of that part of the United Kingdom called Ireland.

1760. JUDGES.

My Lord: May it please your Lordship.

To the Right Honourable Sir Alexander Cockburn, Lord Chief Justice of England.

The Lord Mayor of London, York, or Dublin, and the Lord Provost of Edinburgh, during office.—The same.

My Lord: May it please your Lordship.

To the Right Honourable ——, Lord Mayor of London. To the Right Honourable Sir ——, Lord Provost of Edinburgh.

The Lord Provost of every other town in Scotland is styled Honourable.

The Mayors of all Corporations (excepting the preceding Lord Mayors), and the Sheriffs, Aldermen, and Recorder of London are addressed Right Worshipful; and the Aldermen and Recorders of other Corporations, and the Justices of the Peace, Worshipful.

1761. THE PARLIAMENT.

House of Peers. — My Lords: May it please your Lordships. To the Right Honourable the Lords Spiritual and Temporal, in Parliament assembled.

House of Commons.—May it please your Honourable House. To the Honourable the Commons of the United Kingdom of Great Britain and Ireland.

The Speaker of ditto.—Sir, or Mr. Speaker.

To the Right Honourable ——, Speaker of the House of Commons.

A Member of the House of Commons, not ennobled.—Sir.

To ——, Esq., M.P.

1762. THE CLERGY.

An Archbishop.—My Lord: May it please your Grace.

To his Grace the Archbishop of Canterbury; or, To the Most Reverend Father in God, ——, Lord Archbishop of Canterbury.

A Bishop.—My Lord: May it please your Lordship.

To the Right Reverend Father in God, ——, Lord Bishop of Oxford.

A Dean.—My Lord: May it please your Lordship.

To the Rev. Dr. ——, Dean of Carlisle.

Archdeacons and Chancellors are addressed in the same manner.

The rest of the Clergy.—Sir, Reverend Sir.

To the Rev. Dr. ——, Glasgow.

To the Rev. ——, —— Street, London; or, To the Rev. Mr. ——, &c.

1763. Hints upon Personal Manners.—It is sometimes objected to books upon etiquette that they cause those who consult them to act with mechanical restraint, and to show in society that they are governed by arbitrary rules, rather than by an intuitive perception of what is graceful and polite.

1764. THIS OBJECTION IS UN-SOUND, because it supposes that people who study the theory of etiquette do not also exercise their powers of observation in society, and obtain, by their intercourse with others, that freedom and ease of deportment which society alone can impart.

1765. BOOKS UPON ETIQUETTE are useful, inasmuch as they expound the laws of polite society. Experience alone, however, can give effect to the precise *manner* in which those laws are required to be observed.

1766. WHATEVER OBJECTIONS MAY BE RAISED to the teachings of works upon etiquette, there can be no sound argument against a series of simple and brief hints, which shall operate as precautions against mistakes in personal conduct.

1767. AVOID INTERMEDDLING with the affairs of others. This is a most common fault. A number of people seldom meet but they begin discussing the affairs of some one who is absent. This is not only uncharitable, but positively unjust. It is equivalent to trying a *cause in the absence of the person implicated.* Even in the criminal code a prisoner is presumed to be innocent until he is found guilty. Society, however, is less just, and passes judgment without hearing the defence. Depend upon it, as a certain rule, *that the people who unite with you in discussing the affairs of others will proceed to scandalize you in your absence.*

1768. BE CONSISTENT in the avowal of principles. Do not deny to-day that which you asserted yesterday. If you do, you will stultify yourself, and your opinions will soon be found to have no weight. You may fancy that you gain favour by subserviency; but so far from gaining favour, you lose respect.

1769. AVOID FALSEHOOD. There can be found no higher virtue than the love of truth. The man who deceives others must himself become the victim of morbid distrust. Knowing the deceit of his own heart, and the falsehood of his own tongue, his eyes must be always filled with suspicion, and he must lose the greatest of all happiness—confidence in those who surround him.

1770. THE FOLLOWING ELEMENTS of manly character are worthy of frequent meditation:—

i. To be wise in his disputes.

ii. To be a lamb in his home.

iii. To be brave in battle and great in moral courage.

iv. To be discreet in public.

v. To be a bard in his chair.

vi. To be a teacher in his household.

vii. To be a council in his nation.

viii. To be an arbitrator in his vicinity.

ix. To be a hermit in his church.

x. To be a legislator in his country.

xi. To be conscientious in his actions.

xii. To be happy in his life.

xiii. To be diligent in his calling.

xiv. To be just in his dealing.

xv. That whatever he doeth be to the will of God.

1771. AVOID MANIFESTATIONS OF ILL-TEMPER. Reason is given for man's guidance. Passion is the tempest by which reason is overthrown. Under the effects of passion, man's mind becomes disordered, his face disfigured, his body deformed. A moment's passion has frequently cut off a life's friendship, destroyed a life's hope, embittered a life's peace, and brought unending sorrow and disgrace. It is scarcely worth while to enter into a comparative analysis of ill-temper and passion; they are alike discreditable, alike injurious, and should stand equally condemned.

1772. AVOID PRIDE. If you are handsome, God made you so; if you are learned, some one instructed you; if you are rich, God gave you what you own. It is for others to perceive your goodness; but you should be blind to your own merits. There can be no comfort in deeming yourself better than you really are: that is self-deception. The best men throughout all history have been the most humble.

1773. AFFECTATION IS A FORM OF PRIDE. It is, in fact, pride made ridiculous and contemptible. Some one writing upon affectation has remarked as follows:—

"If anything will sicken and disgust a man, it is the affected, mincing way in which some people choose to talk. It is perfectly nauseous. If these young jackanapes, who screw their words into all manner of diabolical shapes, could only feel how perfectly disgusting they were, it might induce them to drop it. With many, it soon becomes such a confirmed habit that they cannot again be taught to talk in a plain, straightforward, manly way. In the lower order of ladies' boarding-schools, and, indeed, too much everywhere, the same sickening, mincing tone is too often found. Do, pray, good people, do talk in your natural tone, if you don't wish to be utterly ridiculous and contemptible."

1774. WE HAVE ADOPTED THE FOREGOING PARAGRAPH because we approve of some of its sentiments, but chiefly because it shows that persons who object to affectation may go to the other extreme—vulgarity. It is vulgar, we think, to call even the most affected people "Jackanapes, who screw their words into all manner of diabolical shapes." Avoid vulgarity in manner, in speech, and in correspondence. To conduct yourself vulgarly is to offer offence to those who are around you; to bring upon yourself the condemnation of persons of good taste; and to incur the penalty of exclusion from good society. Thus, cast among the vulgar, you become the victim of your own error.

1775. AVOID SWEARING. An oath is but the wrath of a perturbed spirit. It is *mean*. A man of high moral standing would rather treat an offence with contempt than show his indignation by an oath. It is *vulgar:* altogether too low for a decent man. It is *cowardly:* implying a fear either of not being believed or obeyed. It is *ungentlemanly*. A gentleman, according to Webster, is a *genteel man*—well-bred, refined. It is *indecent:* offensive to delicacy, and extremely unfit for human ears. It is *foolish*. "Want of decency is want of sense." It is *abusive*—to the mind which conceives the oath, to the tongue which utters it, and to the person at whom it is aimed. It is *venomous:* showing a man's heart to be as a nest of vipers; and every time he swears, one of them starts out from his head. It is *contemptible:* forfeiting the respect of all the wise and good. It is *wicked:* violating the Divine law, and provoking the displeasure of Him who will not hold him guiltless who takes His name in vain.

1776. BE A GENTLEMAN. Moderation, decorum, and neatness distinguish the gentleman; he is at all times affable, diffident, and studious to please. Intelligent and polite, his behaviour is pleasant and graceful. When he enters the dwelling of an inferior, he endeavours to hide, if possible, the difference between their ranks in life; ever willing to assist those around him, he is neither unkind, haughty, nor overbearing. In the mansions of the rich, the correctness of his mind induces him to bend to etiquette, but not to stoop to adulation; correct principle cautions him to avoid the gaming-table, inebriety, or any other foible that could occasion him self-reproach. Gratified with the pleasures of reflection, he rejoices to see the gaieties of society, and is fastidious upon no point of little import. Appear only to be a gentleman, and its shadow will bring upon you contempt; be a gentleman, and its honours will remain even after you are dead.

1777. The Happy Man, or True Gentleman.

How happy is he born or taught,
　That serveth not another's will,
Whose armour is his honest thought,
　And simple truth his only skill:

Whose passions not his masters are,
　Whose soul is still prepared for death,
Not tied unto the world with care
　Of prince's ear, or vulgar breath:

Who hath his life from rumours freed,
　Whose conscience is his strong retreat;
Whose state can neither flatterers feed,
　Nor ruin make oppressors great:

Who God doth late and early pray
　More of His grace than gifts to lend;
And entertains the harmless day
　With a well-chosen book or friend!

This man is freed from servile bands
　Of hope to rise or fear to fall;
Lord of himself, though not of lands,
　And having nothing, yet hath all.
　　　　　　Sir Henry Wotton, 1530.

1778. Be Honest. Not only because "honesty is the best policy," but because it is a duty to God and to man. The heart that can be gratified by dishonest gains; the ambition that can be satisfied by dishonest means; the mind that can be devoted to dishonest purposes, must be of the worst order.

1779. Having laid down these General Principles for the government of personal conduct, we will epitomize what we would still enforce:—

1780. Avoid Idleness—it is the parent of many evils. Can you pray, "Give us this day our daily bread," and not hear the reply, "Do thou this day thy daily duty"?

1781. Avoid telling Idle Tales, which is like firing arrows in the dark: you know not into whose heart they may fall.

1782. Avoid talking about Yourself, praising your own works, and proclaiming your own deeds. If they are good they will proclaim themselves; if bad, the less you say of them the better.

1783. Avoid Envy; for it cannot benefit you, nor can it injure those against whom it is cherished.

1784. Avoid Disputation for the mere sake of argument. The man who disputes obstinately, and in a bigoted spirit, is like the man who would stop the fountain from which he should drink. Earnest discussion is commendable; but factious argument never yet produced a good result.

1785. Be Kind in Little Things. The true generosity of the heart is more displayed by deeds of minor kindness, than by acts which may partake of ostentation.

1786. Be Polite. Politeness is the poetry of conduct—and like poetry, it has many qualities. Let not your politeness be too florid, but of that gentle kind which indicates a refined nature.

1787. Be Sociable—avoid reserve in society. Remember that the social elements, like the air we breathe, are purified by motion. Thought illumines thought, and smiles win smiles.

1788. Be Punctual. One minute too late has lost many a golden opportunity. Besides which, the want of punctuality is an affront offered to the person to whom your presence is due.

1789. The Foregoing Remarks

may be said to apply to the moral conduct, rather than to the details of personal manners. Great principles, however, suggest minor ones; and hence, from the principles laid down, many hints upon personal behaviour may be gathered.

1790. BE HEARTY in your salutations, discreet and sincere in your friendships.

1791. PREFER TO LISTEN rather than to talk.

1792. BEHAVE, EVEN IN THE PRESENCE of your relations, as though you felt respect to be due to them.

1793. IN SOCIETY NEVER FORGET that you are but one of many.

1794. WHEN YOU VISIT A FRIEND, conform to the rules of his household; lean not upon his tables, nor rub your feet against his chairs.

1795. PRY NOT INTO LETTERS that are not your own.

1796. PAY UNMISTAKEABLE RESPECT to ladies everywhere.

1797. BEWARE OF FOPPERY, and of silly flirtation.

1798. IN PUBLIC PLACES be not too pertinacious of your own rights, but find pleasure in making concessions.

1799. SPEAK DISTINCTLY, look at the person to whom you speak, and when you have spoken, give him an opportunity to reply.

1800. AVOID DRUNKENNESS as you would a curse; and modify all appetites, especially those that are acquired.

1801. DRESS WELL; but not superfluously; be neither like a sloven, nor like a stuffed model.

1802. KEEP AWAY ALL UNCLEANLY APPEARANCES from the person. Let the nails, the teeth, and, in fact, the whole system receive *salutary* rather than *studied* care. But let these things receive attention at the toilette—not elsewhere.

1803. AVOID DISPLAYING EXCESS OF JEWELLERY. Nothing looks more effeminate upon a man.

1804. EVERY ONE OF THESE SUGGESTIONS may be regarded as the centre of many others, which the earnest mind cannot fail to discover. (See HINTS ON ETIQUETTE, No. 1696, p. 241.)

1805. Children.—Happy indeed is the child who, during the first period of its existence, is fed upon no other aliment than the milk of its mother, or that of a healthy nurse. If other food become necessary before the child has acquired teeth, it ought to be of a liquid form: for instance, biscuits or stale bread boiled in an equal mixture of milk and water, to the consistence of a thick soup; but by no means even this in the first week of its life.

1806. FLOUR OR MEAL ought never to be used for soup, as it produces viscid humours, instead of a wholesome nutritious chyle.

1807. AFTER THE FIRST SIX MONTHS, weak veal or chicken broth may be given, and also, progressively, vegetables that are not very flatulent; for instance, carrots, endive, spinach, parsnips, with broth, and boiled fruit, such as apples, pears, plums, and cherries.

1808. WHEN THE INFANT IS WEANED, and has acquired its proper teeth, it is advisable to let it have small portions of meat, and other vegetables, as well as dishes prepared of flour, &c., so that it may gradually become accustomed to every kind of strong and wholesome food.

1809. WE OUGHT, HOWEVER, TO BE CAUTIOUS, and not upon any account to allow a child pastry, confectionery, cheese, heavy dishes made of boiled or baked flours, onions, horseradish, mustard, smoked and salted meat, especially pork, and all compound dishes; for the most simple food is the most wholesome.

1810. POTATOES should be allowed only in moderation, and not to be eaten with butter, but rather with other vegetables, either mashed up or in broth.

1811. THE TIME OF TAKING FOOD is not a matter of indifference; very young infants make an exception; for, as their consumption of vital power is more rapid, they may be more frequently indulged with aliment.

1812. IT IS, HOWEVER, ADVISABLE to accustom even them to a certain regularity, so as to allow them their victuals at stated periods of the day; for it has been observed that those children which are fed indiscriminately through the whole day, are subject to debility and disease. The stomach should be allowed to recover its tone, and to collect the juices necessary for digestion, before it is supplied with a new portion of food.

1813. THE FOLLOWING ORDER OF GIVING FOOD to children has been found proper; and conducive to their health:
—After rising in the morning, suppose about six o'clock, a moderate portion of lukewarm milk, with well baked bread, which should by no means be new; at nine o'clock, bread with some fruit, or, if fruit be scarce, a small quantity of fresh butter; about twelve o'clock, the dinner, of a sufficient quantity; between four and five o'clock, some bread with fruit, or, in winter, the jam of plums, as a substitute for fruit.

1814. ON THIS OCCASION, CHILDREN should be allowed to eat till they are satisfied, without surfeiting themselves, that they may not crave for a heavy supper, which disturbs their rest, and is productive of bad humours: lastly, about seven o'clock, they may be permitted a light supper, consisting either of milk, soup, fruit, or boiled vegetables and the like, but neither meat nor mealy dishes, nor any article of food which produces flatulency; in short, they ought then to eat but little, and remain awake at least for an hour after it.

1815. IT HAS OFTEN BEEN CONTENDED THAT BREAD is hurtful to children; but this applies only to new bread, or such as is not sufficiently baked; for instance, nothing can be more hurtful or oppressive than rolls, muffins, and crumpets. Good wheaten bread, especially that baked by the aërated process, is extremely proper during the first years of infancy: but that made of rye, or a mixture of wheat and rye, would be more conducive to health after the age of childhood.

1816. WITH RESPECT TO DRINK, physicians are decidedly against giving it to children in large quantities, and at irregular periods, whether it consists of the mother's milk, or any other equally mild liquid.

1817. IT IS IMPROPER and pernicious to keep infants continually at the breast; and it would be less hurtful, nay, even judicious, to let them cry for a few nights, rather than to fill them incessantly with milk, which readily turns sour on the stomach, weakens the digestive organs, and ultimately generates scrofulous affections.

1818. IN THE LATTER PART OF THE FIRST YEAR, pure water may occasionally be given; and if this cannot be procured, a light and well-fermented table beer might be substituted. Those parents who accustom their children to drink water only, bestow on them a fortune, the value and importance of which will be sensibly felt through life.

1819. MANY CHILDREN ACQUIRE A HABIT OF DRINKING during their meals; it would be more conducive to digestion if they were accustomed to drink only after having made a meal. This salutary rule is too often neglected, though it be certain that inundations of the stomach, during the mastication and maceration of the food, not only vitiate digestion, but they may be attended with other bad consequences; as cold drink, when brought in contact with the teeth previously heated, may easily occasion cracks or chinks in these useful bones; and pave the way for their carious dissolution.

1820. IF WE INQUIRE INTO THE CAUSE which produces the crying of infants, we shall find that it seldom originates from pain, or uncomfortable sensations; for those who are apt to imagine that such causes must *always* operate on the body of an infant, are egregiously mistaken; inasmuch as they conceive that the physical condition, together with the method of expressing sensations, is the same in infants and adults.

1821. IT REQUIRES, however, no demonstration to prove that the state of the former is essentially different from that of the latter.

1822. IN THE FIRST YEAR OF IN-FANCY, many expressions of the tender organs are to be considered only as efforts or manifestations of power.

1823. WE OBSERVE, for instance, that a child, as soon as it is undressed, or disencumbered from swaddling clothes, moves its arms and legs, and often makes a variety of strong exertions; yet no reasonable person would suppose that such attempts arise from a preternatural or oppressive state of the little agent.

1824. IT IS THEREFORE EQUALLY ABSURD to draw an unfavourable inference from every inarticulate cry; because, in most instances, these vociferating sounds imply the effort which children necessarily make to display the strength of their lungs, and exercise the organs of respiration.

1825. NATURE HAS WISELY OR-DAINED that by these very efforts the power and utility of functions so essential to life should be developed, and rendered more perfect with every inspiration.

1826. HENCE IT FOLLOWS, that those over-anxious parents or nurses, who continually endeavour to prevent infants crying, do them a material injury; for, by such imprudent management, their children seldom or never acquire a perfect form of the breast, while the foundation is laid in the pectoral vessels for obstructions and other diseases.

1827. INDEPENDENTLY of any particular causes, the cries of children, with regard to their general effects, are highly beneficial and necessary.

1828. IN THE FIRST PERIOD OF LIFE, such exertions are the almost only exercise of the infant; thus the circulation of the blood, and all the other fluids, is rendered more uniform; digestion, nutrition, and the growth of the body are thereby promoted; and the different secretions, together with the very important office of the skin, or insensible perspiration, are duly performed.

1829. IT IS EXTREMELY IMPROPER to consider every noise of an infant as a claim upon our assistance, and to intrude either food or drink, with a view to satisfy its supposed wants. By such injudicious conduct, children readily acquire the injurious habit of demanding nutriment at improper times, and without necessity; their digestion becomes impaired; and consequently, at this early age, the whole mass of the fluids is gradually corrupted.

1830. SOMETIMES, HOWEVER, THE MOTHER OR NURSE removes the child from its couch, carries it about, frequently in the middle of the night, and thus exposes it to repeated colds, which are in their effects infinitely more dangerous than the most violent cries.

1831. WE LEARN FROM DAILY EXPERIENCE, that children who have been the least indulged, thrive much better, unfold all their faculties quicker, and acquire more muscular strength and vigour of mind, than those who have been constantly favoured, and treated by their parents with the most solicitous attention: bodily weakness and mental imbecility are the usual attributes of the latter.

1832. THE FIRST AND PRINCIPAL RULE of education ought never to be forgotten—that man is intended to be a free and independent agent; that his moral and physical powers ought to be *spontaneously* developed; that he should as soon as possible be made acquainted with the nature and uses of all his faculties, in order to attain that degree of perfection which is consistent with the structure of his organs; and that he was not originally designed for what we endeavour to make of him by artificial aid.

1833. THE GREATEST ART in educating children consists in a continued vigilance over all their actions, without ever giving them so opportunity of discovering that they are guided and watched.

1834. THERE ARE, HOWEVER, INSTANCES in which the loud complaints of infants demand our attention.

1835. THUS, IF THEIR CRIES BE UNUSUALLY VIOLENT and long continued, we may conclude that they are troubled with colic pains; if, on such occasions, they move their arms and hands repeatedly towards the face, painful teething may account for the cause; and if other morbid phenomena accompany their cries, or if these expressions be repeated at certain periods of the day, we ought not to slight them, but endeavour to discover the proximate or remote causes.

1836. INFANTS CANNOT SLEEP TOO LONG; and it is a favourable symptom when they enjoy a calm and long-continued rest, of which they should by no means be deprived, as this is the greatest support granted to them by nature.

1837. A CHILD LIVES COMPARATIVELY MUCH FASTER than an adult; its blood flows more rapidly; every stimulus operates more powerfully; and not only its constituent parts, but its vital resources also, are more speedily consumed.

1838. SLEEP PROMOTES A MORE CALM and uniform circulation of the blood; it facilitates the assimilation of the nutriment received, and contributes towards a more copious and regular deposition of alimentary matter, while the horizontal posture is the most favourable to the growth and development of the child.

1839. SLEEP OUGHT TO BE IN PROPORTION to the age of the infant. After the age of six months, the periods of sleep, as well as all other animal functions, may in some degree be regulated; yet, even then, a child should be suffered to sleep the whole night, and several hours both in the morning and in the afternoon.

1840. MOTHERS AND NURSES should endeavour to accustom infants, from the time of their birth, to sleep in the night preferably to the day, and for this purpose they ought to remove all external impressions which may disturb their rest, such as noise, light, &c., but especially not to obey every call for taking them up, and giving food at improper times.

1841. AFTER THE SECOND YEAR of their age, they will not instinctively require to sleep in the forenoon, though after dinner it may be continued to the third and fourth year of life, if the child shows a particular inclination to repose; because, till that age, the full half of life may safely be allotted to sleep.

1842. FROM THAT PERIOD, however, sleep ought to be shortened for the space of one hour with every succeeding year; so that a child of seven years old may sleep about eight, and not exceeding nine hours: this proportion may be continued to the age of adolescence, and even manhood.

1843. TO AWAKEN CHILDREN from their sleep with a noise, or in an impetuous manner, is extremely injudicious and hurtful; nor is it proper to carry them from a dark room immediately into a glaring light, or against a dazzling wall; for the sudden impression of light debilitates the organs of vision, and lays the foundation of weak eyes, from early infancy.

1844. A BEDROOM OR NURSERY ought to be spacious and lofty, dry, airy, and not inhabited through the day.

1845. NO SERVANTS, if possible, should be suffered to sleep in the same room, and no linen or washed clothes should ever be hung there to dry, as they contaminate the air in which so considerable a portion of infantile life must be spent.

1846. THE CONSEQUENCES attending a vitiated atmosphere in such rooms are serious, and often fatal.

1847. FEATHER BEDS should be banished from nurseries, as they are unnatural and debilitating contrivances.

1848. THE WINDOWS should never be opened at night, but may be left open the whole day in fine clear weather.

1849. LASTLY, THE BEDSTEAD must not be placed too low on the floor; nor is it proper to let children sleep on a couch which is made without any elevation from the ground; because the most mephitic and pernicious stratum of air in an apartment is that within one or two feet from the floor, while the most wholesome, or atmospheric air, is in the middle of the room, and the inflammable gas ascends to the top.

1850. Cookery for Children.

1851. FOOD FOR AN INFANT.—Take of fresh cow's milk, one tablespoonful, and mix with two tablespoonfuls of hot water; sweeten with loaf sugar, as much as may be agreeable. This quantity is sufficient for once feeding a new-born infant; and the same quantity may be given every two or three hours,—not oftener,—till the mother's breast affords natural nourishment.

1852. MILK FOR INFANTS SIX MONTHS OLD.—Take one pint of milk, one pint of water; boil it, and add one tablespoonful of flour. Dissolve the flour first in half a teacupful of water; it must be strained in gradually, and boiled hard twenty minutes. As the child grows older, one-third water. If properly made, it is the most nutritious, at the same time the most delicate food that can be given to young children.

1853. BROTH, made of lamb or chicken, with stale bread toasted, and broken in, is safe and wholesome for the dinners of children when first weaned.

1854. MILK, fresh from the cow, with a very little loaf sugar, is good and safe food for young children. From three years old to seven, pure milk, into which stale bread is crumbled, is the best breakfast and supper for a child.

1855. FOR A CHILD'S LUNCHEON.—Good sweet butter, with stale bread, is one of the most nutritious, at the same time the most wholesome articles of food that can be given children after they are weaned.

1856. MILK PORRIDGE.—Stir four tablespoonfuls of oatmeal, smoothly, into a quart of milk, then stir it quickly into a quart of boiling water, and boil it up a few minutes till it is thickened: sweeten with sugar. Oatmeal, where it is found to agree with the stomach, is much better for children, being a mild aperient as well as cleanser; fine flour in every shape is the reverse. Where biscuit-powder is in use, let it be made at home; this, at all events, will prevent them getting the sweepings of the baker's counters, boxes, and baskets. All the waste bread in the nursery, hard ends of stale loaves, &c., ought to be dried in the oven or screen, and reduced to powder in the mortar.

1857. MEATS FOR CHILDREN.—Mutton, lamb, and poultry are the best. Birds and the white meat of fowls are the most delicate food of this kind that can be given. These meats should be slowly cooked, and no gravy, if made rich with butter, should be eaten by a young child. Never give children hard, tough, half-cooked meats, of any kind.

1858. VEGETABLES FOR CHILDREN.—EGGS, &c.—Their rice ought to be cooked in no more water than is necessary to swell it; their apples roasted, or stewed with no more water than is necessary to steam them; their vegetables so well cooked as to make them require little butter, and less digestion; their eggs boiled slowly and soft. The boiling of their milk ought to be directed by the state of their bowels; if flatulent or bilious, a very little curry-powder may be given in their vegetables with good effect. Turmeric and the warm seeds (not hot peppers) are also particularly useful in such cases.

1859. POTATOES AND PEAS.—Potatoes, particularly some kinds, are not easily digested by children; but this may be remedied by mashing them very fine, and seasoning them with sugar and a little milk. When peas are dressed for children, let them be seasoned with mint and sugar, which will take off the flatulency. If they are old, let them be pulped, as the skins are perfectly indigestible by children's stomachs. Never give them vegetables less stewed than would pulp through a cullender.

1860. RICE PUDDING WITH FRUIT. —In a pint of new milk put two large spoonfuls of rice, well washed; then add two apples, pared and quartered, or a few currants or raisins. Simmer slowly till the rice is very soft, then add one egg beaten, to bind it: serve with cream and sugar.

1861. PUDDINGS AND PANCAKES FOR CHILDREN.—Sugar and egg, browned before the fire, or dropped as fritters into a hot frying-pan, without fat, will make a nourishing meal.

1862. TO PREPARE FRUIT FOR CHILDREN.—A far more wholesome way than in pies or puddings, is to put apples sliced, or plums, currants, gooseberries, &c., into a stone jar, and sprinkle among them as much sugar as necessary. Set the jar in an oven on a hearth, with a teacupful of water to prevent the fruit from burning; or put the jar into a saucepan of water till its contents be perfectly done. Slices of bread or some rice may be put into the jar, to eat with the fruit.

1863. RICE AND APPLES.—Core as many nice apples as will fill the dish; boil them in light syrup; prepare a quarter of a pound of rice in milk with sugar and salt; put some of the rice in the dish, put in the apples, and fill up the intervals with rice; bake it in the oven till it is a fine colour.

1864. A NICE APPLE CAKE FOR CHILDREN. — Grate some stale bread, and slice about double the quantity of apples; butter a mould, and line it with sugar paste, and strew in some crumbs, mixed with a little sugar; then lay in apples, with a few bits of butter over them, and so continue till the dish is full; cover it with crumbs, or prepared rice; season with cinnamon and sugar. Bake it well.

1865. FRUITS FOR CHILDREN. — That fruits are naturally healthy in their season, if rightly taken, no one who believes that the Creator is a kind and beneficent Being can doubt. And yet the use of summer fruits appears

often to cause most fatal diseases, especially in children. Why is this? Because we do not conform to the natural laws in using this kind of diet. These laws are very simple, and easy to understand. Let the fruit be ripe when you eat it; and eat when you require *food*. Fruits that have *seeds* are much more wholesome than the *stone* fruits. But all fruits are better, for very young children, if baked or cooked in some manner, and eaten with bread. The French always eat bread with raw fruit. Apples and winter pears are very excellent food for children,—indeed, for almost any person in health,—but best when eaten for breakfast or dinner. If taken late in the evening, fruit often proves injurious. The old saying, that apples are *gold in the morning, silver at noon, and lead at night*, is pretty near the truth. Both apples and pears are often good and nutritious when baked or stewed, for those delicate constitutions that cannot bear raw fruit. Much of the fruit gathered when unripe might be rendered fit for food by preserving in sugar.

1866. RIPE CURRANTS are excellent food for children. Mash the fruit, sprinkle with sugar, and with good bread let them eat of this fruit freely.

1867. BLACKBERRY JAM.—Gather the fruit in dry weather; allow half a pound of good brown sugar to every pound of fruit; boil the whole together gently for an hour, or till the blackberries are soft, stirring and mashing them well. Preserve it like any other jam, and it will be found very useful in families, particularly for children, regulating their bowels, and enabling you to dispense with cathartics. It may be spread on bread, or on puddings, instead of butter: and even when the blackberries are bought, it is cheaper than butter. In the country every family should preserve at least half a peck of blackberries.

1868. TO MAKE SENNA AND MANNA PALATABLE.—Take half an ounce, when mixed, senna and manna; put in half a pint of boiling water; when the strength is abstracted, pour into the liquid from a quarter to half a pound of prunes and two large tablespoonfuls of West India molasses. Stew slowly until the liquid is nearly absorbed. When cold it can be eaten with bread and butter, without detecting the senna, and is excellent for children when costive.

1869. Discipline of Children. —Children should not be allowed to ask for the same thing twice. This may be accomplished by parents, teacher, or whoever may happen to have the management of them, paying attention to their little wants, if proper, at once, when possible. Children should be instructed to understand that when they are not answered immediately, it is because it is not convenient. Let them learn patience by waiting.

1870. My Wife's Little Tea Parties.

My wife is celebrated for her little tea parties,—not tea parties alone, but dinner parties, pic-nic parties, music parties, supper parties—in fact, she is the life and soul of ALL PARTIES, which is more than any leading politician of the day can boast. But her great *forte* is her little tea parties — praised and enjoyed by everybody. A constant visitor at these little parties is Mrs. Hitching (spoken of elsewhere), and she remarks that she "never knew *h*any one who understood the *h*art of bringing so many *h*elegancies together" as my wife. Nobody makes tea like her, and· how she makes it she will impart at a future time. But for her little "nick-nacks," as she calls them, which give a variety and a charm to the tea table, without trenching too deeply upon our own pocket, she has been kind enough to give a few receipts upon the present occasion.

1871. NICE PLUM CAKE. — One pound of flour, quarter of a pound of butter, quarter of a pound of sugar, quarter of a pound of currants, three eggs, half a pint of milk, and a small teaspoonful of carbonate of soda. The above is excellent. The cakes are always baked in a common earthen *flower-pot saucer*, which is a very good plan.

1872. GINGERBREAD SNAPS.—One pound of flour, half a pound of treacle, half a pound of sugar, quarter of a pound of butter, half an ounce of best prepared ginger, sixteen drops of essence of lemon, potash the size of a nut dissolved in a tablespoonful of hot water. This has been used in my wife's family for thirty years.

1873. DROP CAKES.—One pint of flour, half a pound of butter, quarter of a pound of pounded lump sugar, half a nutmeg grated, a handful of currants, two eggs, and a large pinch of carbonate of soda, or volatile salts. To be baked in a slack oven for ten minutes or a quarter of an hour. The above quantity will make about thirty excellent cakes.

1874. A VERY NICE AND CHEAP CAKE.—Two pounds and a half of flour, three quarters of a pound of sugar, three quarters of a pound of butter, half a pound of currants or quarter of a pound of raisins, quarter of a pound of orange peel, two ounces of carraway seeds, half an ounce of ground cinnamon or ginger, four teaspoonfuls of carbonate of soda; mixed well, with rather better than a pint of new milk. The butter must be well melted previous to being mixed with the ingredients.

1875. "JERSEY WONDERS."—The oddity of these "wonders" consists solely in the manner of cooking, and the shape consequent. Take two pounds of flour, six ounces of butter, six ounces of white sugar, a little nutmeg, ground ginger, and lemon peel; beat eight eggs, and knead them all well together; a taste of brandy will be an improvement. Roll them about the thickness of your wrist; cut off a small slice, and roll it into an oval, about four inches long and three inches wide, not too thin; cut two slits in it, but not through either end, there will then be three bands. Pass the left one through the aperture to the right, and throw it into a *brass* or *bell-metal* skillet of BOILING lard, or beef or mutton dripping. You may cook three or four at a time. In about two minutes turn them with a fork, and you will find them browned, and swollen or risen in two or three minutes more. Remove them from the pan to a dish, when they will dry and cool.

1876. MUFFINS.—Add a pint and a half of good ale yeast (from pale malt, if possible) to a bushel of the very best white flour; let the yeast lie all night in water, then pour off the water quite clear; heat two gallons of water just milk-warm, and mix the water, yeast, and two ounces of salt well together for about a quarter of an hour. Strain the whole, and mix up your dough as light as possible, letting it lie in the trough an hour to rise; next roll it with your hand, pulling it into little pieces about the size of a large walnut. These must be rolled out thin with a rolling-pin, in a good deal of flour, and if covered immediately with a piece of flannel, they will rise to a proper thickness; but if too large or small, dough must be added accordingly, or taken away; meanwhile, the dough must be also covered with flannel. Next begin baking; and when laid on the iron, watch carefully, and when one side changes colour, turn the other, taking care that they do not burn or become discoloured. Be careful also that the iron does not get too hot. In order to bake muffins properly, you ought to have a place built as if a copper were to be set; but instead of copper a piece of iron must be put over the top, fixed in form like the bottom of an iron pot, under-neath which a coal fire is kindled when required. Toast the muffins crisp on both sides with a fork; pull them open *with your hand*, and they will be like a honeycomb; lay in as much butter as you intend, then clap them together, and set by the fire: turn them once, that both sides may be buttered alike. When quite done, cut them across with a knife; but if you use a knife either to spread or divide them, they will be as heavy as lead. Some kinds of flour will soak up more water than others; when this occurs, add water; or if too moist, add flour: for the dough must be as light as possible.

1877. Unfermented Cakes, &c. —The retail price of soda is 8d. per pound avoirdupois; and the acid, known under the more common name of spirits of salts, is 4d. per pound avoirdupois. The price of the acid and soda, each, by the ounce, is one penny.

1878. TEA CAKES.—Take of flour one pound; sugar, one ounce; butter, one ounce; muriatic acid, two drachms; bicarbonate of soda, two drachms; milk, six ounces; water, six ounces. Rub the butter into the flour; dissolve the sugar and soda in the milk, and the acid in the water. First add the milk, &c., to the flour, and partially mix; then the water and acid, and mix well together; divide into three portions, and bake twenty-five minutes. Flat round tins or earthen pans are the best to bake them in. If the above be made with baking powder, a teaspoonful may be substituted for the acid and soda in the foregoing receipt, and all the other directions carried out as before stated. If buttermilk is used, the acid, milk, and water, must be left out.

1879. UNFERMENTED CAKE.—Take of flour one pound and a half; bicarbonate of soda, three drachms; muriatic acid, three drachms; sugar, one ounce and a half; butter, one ounce and a half; milk, twenty ounces; currants, six ounces, more or less. Mix the soda and butter into the flour by rubbing them together; next dissolve the sugar in the milk, and diffuse the acid through it by stirring; then mix the whole intimately, adding fruit at dis-cretion; and bake in a tin or earthen pan.

1880. LUNCHEON CAKES.—Take of flour one pound; muriatic acid, two drachms; bicarbonate of soda, two drachms; sugar, three ounces; butter, three ounces; currants, four ounces;

milk, one pint, or twenty ounces : bake one hour in a quick oven.

1881. NICE PLUM CAKE.—Take of flour one pound ; bicarbonate of soda, quarter of an ounce ; butter, six ounces ; loaf sugar, six ounces ; currants, six ounces ; three eggs ; milk, about four ounces ; bake for one hour and a half in a tin or pan.

1882. LEMON BUNS.—Take of flour one pound ; bicarbonate of soda, three drachms ; muriatic acid, three drachms ; butter, four ounces ; loaf sugar, four ounces ; one egg ; essence of lemon, six or eight drops : make into twenty buns, and bake in a quick oven for fifteen minutes.

1883. SODA CAKE.—Take of flour half a pound ; bicarbonate of soda, two drachms ; tartaric acid, two drachms ; butter, four ounces ; white sugar, two ounces ; currants, four ounces ; two eggs ; warm milk, half a teacupful.

1884. EXCELLENT BISCUITS.—Take of flour two pounds ; carbonate of ammonia, three drachms, in fine powder ; white sugar, four ounces ; arrowroot, one ounce ; butter, four ounces ; one egg : mix into a stiff paste with new milk, and beat them well with a rolling-pin for half an hour ; roll out thin, and cut them out with a docker, and bake in a quick oven for fifteen minutes.

1885. WINE BISCUITS.—Take of flour half a pound ; butter, four ounces ; sugar, four ounces ; two eggs ; carbonate of ammonia, one drachm ; white wine, enough to mix to a proper consistence. Cut out with a glass.

1886. GINGER CAKES.—To two pounds of flour add three quarters of a pound of good moist sugar, one ounce best Jamaica ginger well mixed in the flour ; have ready three quarters of a pound of lard, melted, and four eggs well beaten : mix the lard and eggs together, and stir into the flour, which will form a paste ; roll out in thin cakes, and bake in a moderately heated oven. Lemon biscuits may be made in a similar way, by substituting essence of lemon for ginger.

1887. Sponge Cake.—A lady

favours us with the following simple receipt, which, she says, gives less trouble than any other, and has never been known to fail :—Take five eggs, and half a pound of loaf sugar, sifted ; break the eggs upon the sugar, and beat all together with a steel fork for half an hour. Previously take the weight of two eggs and a half, in their shells, of flour. After you have beaten the eggs and sugar the time specified, grate in the rind of a lemon (the juice may be added at pleasure), stir in the flour, and immediately pour it into a tin lined with buttered paper, and let it be instantly put into rather a cool oven.

1888. Sponge Cake.—Take equal weight of eggs and sugar ; half their weight in sifted flour ; to twelve eggs add the grated rind of three lemons, and the juice of two. Beat the eggs carefully, white and yolks separately, before they are used. Stir the materials thoroughly together, and bake in a quick oven.

1889. Almond Sponge Cake is made by adding blanched almonds to the above.

1890. Yule Cake. — Take one pound of fresh butter ; one pound of sugar ; one pound and a half of flour ; two pounds of currants ; a glass of brandy ; one pound of sweetmeats ; two ounces of sweet almonds ; ten eggs ; a quarter of an ounce of allspice ; and a quarter of an ounce of cinnamon. Melt the butter to a cream, and put in the sugar. Stir it till quite light, adding the allspice and pounded cinnamon ; in a quarter of an hour, take the yolks of the eggs, and work them two or three at a time ; and the whites of the same must by this time be beaten into a strong snow, quite ready to work in. As the paste must not stand to chill the butter, or it will be heavy, work in the whites gradually, then add the orange peel, lemon, and citron, cut in fine strips, and the currants, which must be mixed in well, with the sweet almonds ; then add the sifted flour and glass of brandy. Bake this cake in a tin hoop, in a hot oven, for three hours, and put twelve sheets of paper under it to keep it from burning.

1891. Cake of Mixed Fruits.— Extract the juice from red currants by simmering them very gently for a few minutes over a slow fire; strain it through folded muslin, and to one pound of the juice add a pound and a half of nonsuches, or of freshly gathered apples, pared, and rather deeply cored, that the fibrous part may be avoided. Boil these quite slowly until the mixture is perfectly smooth; then, to evaporate part of the moisture, let the boiling be quickened. In from twenty-five to thirty minutes, draw the pan from the fire, and throw in gradually a pound and a quarter of sugar in fine powder; mix it well with the fruit, and when it is dissolved, continue the boiling rapidly for twenty minutes longer, keeping the mixture constantly stirred; put it into a mould, and store it, when cold, for winter use, or serve it for dessert, or for the second course; in the latter case, decorate it with spikes of almonds, blanched, and heap solid whipped cream round it, or pour a custard into the dish. For dessert, it may be garnished with dice of the palest apple jelly.— Juice of red currants, one pound; apples (pared and cored), one pound and a half— twenty-five to thirty minutes. Sugar, one pound and a half—twenty minutes.

1892. Banbury Cakes.— Roll out the paste about half an inch thick, and cut it into pieces; then roll again till each piece becomes twice the size; put some Banbury meat in the middle of one side; fold the other over it, and pinch it up into a somewhat oval shape; flatten it with your hand at the top, letting the seam be quite at the bottom; rub the tops over with the white of an egg, laid on with a brush, and dust loaf sugar over them: bake in a moderate oven. The meat for this cake is made thus:—Beat up a quarter of a pound of butter until it becomes in the state of cream; then mix with it half a pound of candied orange and lemon peel, cut fine; one pound of currants; a quarter of an ounce of ground

cinnamon; and a quarter of an ounce of allspice: mix all well together, and keep in a jar till wanted for use.

1893. Bath Buns.— A quarter of a pound of flour; four yolks and three whites of eggs, with four spoonfuls of solid fresh yeast. Beat in a bowl, and set before the fire to rise; then rub into one pound of flour ten ounces of butter; put in half a pound of sugar, and carraway comfits; when the eggs and yeast are pretty light, mix by degrees all together; throw a cloth over it, and set before the fire to rise. Make the buns, and when on the tins, brush over with the yolk of egg and milk; strew them with carraway comfits; bake in a quick oven.

1894. Belvidere Cakes, for Breakfast or Tea.— Take a quart of flour; four eggs; a piece of butter the size of an egg; a piece of lard the same size: mix the butter and lard well in the flour; beat the eggs light in a pint bowl, and fill it up with cold milk; then pour it gradually into the flour; add a teaspoonful of salt; work it for eight or ten minutes only: cut the dough with a knife the size you wish it; roll them into cakes about the size of a breakfast plate, and bake in a quick oven.

1895. To Make Gingerbread Cake.— Take one pound and a half of treacle; one and a half ounces of ground ginger; half an ounce of carraway seeds; two ounces of allspice; four ounces of orange peel, shred fine; half a pound of sweet butter; six ounces of blanched almonds; one pound of honey; and one and a half ounces of carbonate of soda; with as much fine flour as makes a dough of moderate consistence. *Directions for making.*—Make a pit in five pounds of flour; then pour in the treacle, and all the other ingredients, creaming the butter; then mix them all together into a dough; work it well; then put in three quarters of an ounce of tartaric acid, and put the dough into a buttered pan, and bake for two hours in a cool oven. To know when it is ready, dip a fork into it, and if it comes out sticky, put it in the oven again; if not, it is ready.

1896. Pic-Nic Biscuits.—Take two ounces of fresh butter, and well work it with a pound of flour. Mix thoroughly with it half a saltspoonful of pure carbonate of soda, two ounces of sugar; mingle thoroughly with the flour, make up the paste with spoonfuls of milk; it will require scarcely a quarter of a pint. Knead smooth, roll a quarter of an inch thick, cut in rounds about the size of the top of a small wineglass; roll these out thin, prick them well, lay them on lightly floured tins, and bake in a gentle oven until crisp. When cold put into dry canisters. Thin cream used instead of milk, in the paste, will enrich the biscuits. Carraway seeds or ginger can be added, to vary these, at pleasure.

1897. Ginger Biscuits and Cakes.—Work into small crumbs three ounces of butter, two pounds of flour, and three ounces of powdered sugar and two of ginger, in fine powder; knead into a stiff paste, with new milk; roll thin, cut out with a cutter: bake in a slow oven until crisp through; keep of a pale colour. Additional sugar may be used when a sweeter biscuit is desired. For good ginger cakes, butter six ounces, sugar eight, for each pound of flour; wet the ingredients into a paste with eggs: a little lemon-peel grated will give an agreeable flavour.

1898. Sugar Biscuits.—Cut the butter into the flour. Add the sugar and carraway seeds. Pour in the brandy, and then the milk. Lastly, put in the pearlash. Stir all well with a knife, and mix it thoroughly, till it becomes a lump of dough. Flour your pasteboard, and lay the dough on it. Knead it very well. Divide it into eight or ten pieces, and knead each piece separately. Then put them all together, and knead them very well into one lump. Cut the dough in half, and roll it out into sheets, about half an inch thick. Beat the sheets of dough very hard on both sides with the rolling pin. Cut them out into round cakes with the

edge of a tumbler. Butter iron pans and lay the cakes in them. Bake them of a very pale brown. If done too much, they will lose their taste. Let the oven be hotter at the top than at the bottom. These cakes kept in a stone jar, closely covered from the air, will continue perfectly good for several months.

1899. Lemon Sponge.—For a quart mould—dissolve two ounces of isinglass in a pint and three quarters of water; strain it, and add three quarters of a pound of sifted loaf sugar, the juice of six lemons and the rind of one; boil the whole for a few minutes, strain it again, and let it stand till quite cold and just beginning to stiffen; then beat the whites of two eggs, and put them to it, and whisk till it is quite white; put it into a mould, which must be first wetted with cold water,—or salad oil is a much better substitute for turning out jelly, blancmange, &c., great care being taken not to pour it into the mould till *quite cool*, or the oil will float on the top, and after it is turned out it must be carefully wiped over with a clean cloth. This plan only requires to be tried once to be invariably adopted.

1900. Almond Custards.—Blanch and pound fine, with half a gill of rose water, six ounces of sweet and half an ounce of bitter almonds; boil a pint of milk, with a few coriander seeds, a little cinnamon and lemon peel; sweeten it with two ounces and a half of sugar, rub the almonds through a fine sieve, with a pint of cream; strain the milk to the yolks of eight eggs, and the whites of three well beaten; stir it over a fire till it is of a good thickness, take it off the fire, and stir it till nearly cold, to prevent its curdling.

1901. Arrowroot Blancmange.—A teacupful of arrowroot to a pint of milk; boil the milk with twelve sweet and six bitter almonds, blanched and beaten; sweeten with loaf sugar, and strain it; break the arrowroot with a little of the milk as smooth as possible; pour the boiling milk upon it by degrees, stir the while; put it back into the pan, and boil a few minutes, still stirring; dip the shape in cold water before you put it in, and turn it out when cold.

1902. Red Currant Jelly. — With three parts of fine ripe red currants mix one of white currants; put them into a clean preserving-pan, and stir them gently over a clear fire until the juice flows from them freely; then turn them into a fine hair sieve, and let them drain well, but without pressure. Pass the juice through a folded muslin, or a jelly bag; weigh it, and then boil it *fast* for a quarter of an hour; add for each pound, eight ounces of sugar coarsely powdered, stir this to it off the fire until it is dissolved, give the jelly eight minutes more of quick boiling, and pour it out.* It will be firm, and of excellent colour and flavour. Be sure to clear off the scum as it rises, both before and after the sugar is put in, or the preserve will not be clear. Juice of red currants, three pounds; juice of white currants, one pound: fifteen minutes. Sugar, two pounds: eight minutes. An excellent jelly may be made with equal parts of the juice of red and of white currants, and of raspberries, with the same proportion of sugar and degree of boiling as mentioned in the foregoing receipt.

1903. White Currant Jelly. — White currant jelly is made in the same way as red currant jelly, only it should have double refined sugar, and not be boiled above ten minutes. White currant jelly should be put through a lawn sieve.

1904. ANOTHER RECEIPT FOR WHITE CURRANT JELLY.—After the fruit is stripped from the stalks, put it into the pan, and when it boils, run it quickly through a sieve : take a pound of sugar to each pint of juice, and let it boil twenty minutes.

1905. Black Currant Jelly. — —To each pound of picked fruit allow one gill of water; set them on the fire in the preserving-pan to scald, but do not let them boil; bruise them well with a silver fork, or wooden beater; take them off and squeeze them through a hair sieve, and to every pint of juice allow a pound of loaf or raw sugar : boil it ten minutes.

1906. Apricot Jelly.—Pare the fruit thin, and stone it; weigh an equal quantity of sugar in fine powder, and strew over it. Let it stand one day, then boil very gently till it is clear, move it into a bowl, and pour the liquor over. The next day pour the liquor to a quart of codling liquor; let it boil quickly till it will jelly; put the fruit into it, and boil; skim well, and put into small pots.

1907. Ox-heel Jelly is made in the same manner.

1908. Arrowroot Jelly. — A tablespoonful of arrowroot, and cold water to form a paste; add a pint of boiling water; stir briskly, boil for a few minutes. A little sherry and sugar may be added. For infants, a drop or two of the essence of carraway seed or cinnamon is preferable.

1909. An Excellent Jelly. (FOR THE SICK-ROOM.) — Take rice, sago, pearl barley, hartshorn shavings, each one ounce; simmer with three pints of water to one, and strain it. When cold it will be a jelly, of which give, dissolved in wine, milk, or broth, in change with the other nourishment.

1910. Calves' Feet Jelly.—It is better to buy the feet of the butcher, than at the tripe-shop ready boiled, because the best portion of the jelly has been extracted. Slit them in two, and take every particle of fat from the claws; wash well in warm water, put them in a large stewpan, and cover with water; skim well, and let them boil gently for six or seven hours, until reduced to about two quarts, then strain and skim off any oily substance on the surface. It is best to boil the feet the day before making the jelly, as, when the liquor is cold, the oily part being at the top, and the other being firm, with pieces of kitchen paper applied to it, you may remove every particle of the oily substance without wasting the liquor. Put the liquor in a stewpan to melt, with a pound of lump sugar,

K

the peel of two and the juice of six lemons, six whites and shells of eggs beat together, and a bottle of sherry or Madeira; whisk the whole together until it is on the boil, then put it by the side of the stove, and let it simmer a quarter of an hour; strain it through a jelly-bag: what is strained first must be poured into the bag again, until it is as bright and clear as rock water; then put the jelly in moulds, to be cold and firm; if the weather is too warm, it requires some ice. When it is wished to be very *stiff*, half an ounce of isinglass may be added when the wine is put in. It may be flavoured by the juice of various fruits and spices, &c., and coloured with saffron, cochineal, red beetjuice, spinach juice, claret, &c., and it is sometimes made with cherry brandy, red noyeau, curaçoa, or essence of punch.

1911. Orange Marmalade.— Choose the largest Seville oranges, as they usually contain the greatest quantity of juice, and choose them with clear skins, as the skins form the largest part of the marmalade. Weigh the oranges, and weigh also an equal quantity of loaf sugar. Peel the oranges, dividing the peels into quarters, and put them into a preserving-pan; cover them well with water, and set them on the fire to boil: in the meantime prepare your oranges; divide them into gores, then scrape with a teaspoon all the pulp from the white skin; or, instead of peeling the oranges, cut a hole in the orange and scoop out the pulp; remove carefully all the pips, of which there are innumerable small ones in the Seville orange, which will escape observation unless they are very minutely examined. Have a large basin near you with some cold water in it, to throw the pips and peels into—a pint is sufficient for a dozen oranges. A great deal of glutinous matter adheres to them, which, when strained through a sieve, should be boiled with the other parts. When the peels have boiled till they are sufficiently tender to admit of a fork being stuck into them, strain them; some of which may be boiled with the other parts; scrape clean all the pith, or inside, from them; lay them in folds, and cut them into thin slices of about an inch long. Clarify your sugar; then throw your peels and pulp into it, stir it well, and let it boil about half an hour. If the sugar is broken into small pieces, and boiled with the fruit, it will answer the purpose of clarifying, but it must be well skimmed when it boils. Marmalade should be made at the end of March, or the beginning of April, as Seville oranges are then in their best state.

1912. Apple Marmalade.— Peel and core two pounds of sub-acid apples, and put them in an enamelled saucepan with one pint of sweet cider, or half a pint of pure wine, and one pound of crushed sugar. Cook them by a gentle heat three hours, or longer, until the fruit is very soft, then squeeze it first through a cullender and then through a sieve. If not sufficiently sweet, add powdered sugar to suit your taste, and put away in jars made airtight by a piece of wet bladder. It is delicious when eaten with milk, and still better with cream.

1913. Plum or Apricot Jam.— After taking away the stones from the apricots, and cutting out any blemishes they may have, put them over a slow fire, in a clean stewpan, with half a pint of water; when scalded, rub them through a hair sieve; to every pound of pulp put one pound of sifted loaf sugar, put it into a preserving-pan over a brisk fire, and when it boils skim it well, and throw in the kernels of the apricots and half an ounce of bitter almonds, blanched; boil it a quarter of an hour fast, and stirring it all the time; remove it from the fire, fill it into pots, and cover them. Greengages may be done in the same way.

1914. Almond Flavour. (Essence of Peach Kernels—Quintessence of Noyeau.)— Dissolve one ounce of essential oil of bitter almonds in one pint of spirit of wine. Use it as flavouring for cordials, and for perfuming pastry. *In large quantities it* *is exceedingly poisonous.* A few drops only should be used to several pounds of syrups, pastry, &c. Cost: oil of bitter almonds, 1s. per ounce; spirit, 2s. 6d. per pint. Usually sold in quarter or half-ounce bottles at 1s.

1915. Syrup of Orange or Lemon Peel.—Of fresh outer rind of Seville orange, or lemon peel, three ounces, apothecaries' weight; boiling water, a pint and a half; infuse them for a night in a close vessel; then strain the liquor; let it stand to settle; and having poured it off clear from the sediment, dissolve in it two pounds of double refined loaf sugar, and make it into a syrup with a gentle heat.

1916. Indian Syrup. (*A delicious summer drink.*)—Five pounds of lump sugar, two ounces of citric acid, a gallon of boiling water: when cold add half a drachm of essence of lemon and half a drachm of spirit of wine; stir it well, and bottle it. About two tablespoonfuls to a glass of cold water.

1917. Apples in Syrup for Immediate Use.—Pare and core some hard round apples, and throw them into a basin of water; as they are done, clarify as much loaf sugar as will cover them; put the apples in along with the juice and rind of a lemon, and let them simmer till they are quite clear; great care must be taken not to break them. Place them on the dish they are to appear upon at table, and pour the syrup over.

1918. Pounding Almonds.—They should be dried for a few days after being blanched. Set them in a warm place, strewn singly over a dish or tin. A little powdered lump sugar will assist the pounding. They may be first chopped small, and rolled with a rolling pin.—ALMOND PASTE may be made in the same manner.

1919. Blanched Almonds.—Put them into cold water, and heat them slowly to scalding; then take them out and peel them quickly, throwing them into cold water as they are done. Dry them in a cloth before serving.

1920. Freezing without Ice or Acids.—The use of ice in cooling depends upon the fact of its requiring a vast quantity of heat to convert it from a solid into a liquid state, or in other words, to melt it; and the heat so required is obtained from those objects with which it may be in contact. A pound of ice requires nearly as much heat to melt it as would be sufficient to make a pound of cold water boiling hot; hence its cooling power is extremely great. But ice does not begin to melt until the temperature is above the freezing point, and therefore it cannot be employed in freezing liquids, &c., but only in cooling them. If, however, any substance is mixed with ice which is capable of causing it to melt more rapidly, and at a lower temperature, a still more intense cooling effect is the result; such a substance is common salt, and the degree of cold produced by the mixture of one part of salt with two parts of snow or pounded ice, is greater than thirty degrees below freezing. In making ice-creams and dessert ices, the following articles are required:—Pewter ice-pots with tightly-fitting lids, furnished with handles; wooden ice-pails, to hold the rough ice and salt, which should be stoutly made, about the same depth as the ice-pots, and nine or ten inches more in diameter,—each should have a hole in the side, fitted with a good cork, in order that the water from the melted ice may be drawn off as required. In addition, a broad spatula, about four inches long, rounded at the end, and furnished with a long wooden handle, is necessary to scrape the frozen cream from the sides of the ice-pot, and for mixing the whole smoothly together. When making ices, place the mixture of cream and fruit to be frozen, in the ice-pot, cover it with the lid, and put the pot in the ice-pail, which proceed to fill up with coarsely-pounded ice and salt, in the proportion of about one part of salt to three of ice; let the whole remain a few minutes (if covered by a blanket, so much the better), then whirl the pot briskly by the handle for a few minutes, take off the lid, and with the spatula scrape the iced cream from the sides, mixing the whole smoothly; put on the lid, and whirl again, repeating all the operations every few minutes until the whole of the cream is well frozen. Great care and considerable labour are required in stirring, so that the whole cream may be smoothly frozen, and not in hard lumps. When finished, if it is required to be kept any time, the melted ice and salt should be allowed to escape, by removing the cork, and the pail filled up with fresh materials. It is scarcely necessary to add, that if any of the melted ice and salt is allowed to mix with the cream, the latter is spoiled. From the difficulty of obtaining ice in places distant from large towns, and in hot countries, and from the impracticability of keeping it any length of time, or, in fact, of keeping small quantities more than a few hours, its use is much limited, and many have been the attempts to obtain an efficient substitute. For this purpose various salts have been employed, which, when dissolved in water, or in acids, absorb a sufficient amount of heat to freeze substances with which they may be placed in contact. We shall not attempt, in this article, to describe all the various freezing mixtures that have been devised, but speak only of those which have been found practically useful, state the circumstances which have prevented any of them coming into common use, and conclude by giving the composition of the New Freezing Preparation, which is now exported so largely to India, and the composition of which *has hitherto never been made public.* Many of the freezing mixtures which are to be found described in books are incorrectly so named, for although they themselves are below the freezing point, yet they are not sufficiently powerful to freeze any quantity of water, or other substances, when placed in a vessel within them. In order to be efficient as a freezing mixture, as distinguished from

a cooling one, the materials used ought to be capable of producing by themselves an amount of cold more than thirty degrees below the freezing point of water, and this the ordinary mixtures will not do. Much more efficient and really freezing mixtures may be made by using acids to dissolve the salts. The cheapest, and perhaps the best, of these for ordinary use, is one which is frequently employed in France, both for making dessert ices, and cooling wines, &c. It consists of coarsely powdered Glauber salt (sulphate of soda), on which is poured about two-thirds its weight of spirit of salts (muriatic acid). The mixture should be made in a wooden vessel, as that is preferable to one made of metal, which conducts the external heat to the materials with great rapidity; and when the substance to be cooled is placed in the mixture, the whole should be covered with a blanket, a piece of old woollen carpet doubled, or some other non-conducting material, to prevent the access of the external warmth; the vessel used for icing wines should not be too large, that there may be no waste of the freezing mixture. This combination produces a degree of cold thirty degrees below freezing; and if the materials are bought of any of the wholesale druggists or drysalters, it is exceedingly economical. It is open, however, to the very great objection, that the muriatic acid is an exceedingly corrosive liquid, and of a pungent, disagreeable odour: this almost precludes its use for any purpose except that of icing wines.

1921. FURTHER DIRECTIONS.—Actual quantities—one pound of muriate of ammonia, or sal ammoniac, finely powdered, is to be *intimately* mixed with two pounds of nitrate of potash or saltpetre, also in powder; this mixture we may call No. 1. No. 2 is formed by crushing three pounds of the best Scotch soda. In use, an equal bulk of both No. 1 and No. 2 is to be taken, stirred together, placed in the ice-pail, surrounding the ice-pot, and rather less cold water poured on than will dissolve the whole; if one quart of No. 1, and the same bulk of No. 2 are taken, it will require about one quart of water to dissolve them, and the temperature will fall, if the materials used are cool, to nearly thirty degrees below freezing. Those who fail, may trace their want of success to one or other of the following points:—the use of too small a quantity of the preparation,—the employment of a few ounces; whereas, in freezing ices, the ice-pot must be entirely surrounded with the freezing material: no one would attempt to freeze with four ounces of ice and salt. Again, too large a quantity of water may be used to dissolve the preparation, when all the excess of water has to be cooled down instead of the substance it is wished to freeze. All the materials used should be pure, and as cool as can be obtained. The ice-pail in which the mixture is made must be of some non-conducting material, as wood, which will prevent the access of warmth from the air; and the ice-pot, in which the liquor to be frozen is placed, should be of pewter, and surrounded nearly to its top by the freezing mixture. Bear in mind that the making of ice-cream, under any circumstances, is an operation requiring considerable dexterity and practice.

1922. To make Dessert Ices, both Cream and Water.

1923. STRAWBERRY ICE CREAM.—Take one pint of strawberries, one pint of cream, nearly half a pound of powdered white sugar, the juice of a lemon; mash the fruit through a sieve, and take out the seeds: mix with the other articles, and freeze. A little new milk added makes the whole freeze more quickly.

1924. RASPBERRY ICE CREAM.—The same as strawberry. These ices are often coloured by cochineal, but the addition is not advantageous to the flavour. Strawberry or raspberry jam may be used instead of the fresh fruit, or equal quantities of jam and fruit

employed. Of course the quantity of sugar must be proportionately diminished.

1925. STRAWBERRY-WATER ICE.—One large pottle of scarlet strawberries, the juice of a lemon, a pound of sugar, or one pint of strong syrup, half a pint of water. Mix,—first rubbing the fruit through a sieve,—and freeze.

1926. RASPBERRY-WATER ICE in the same manner.

1927. LEMON-WATER ICE.—Lemon juice and water, each half a pint; strong syrup, one pint: the rind of the lemons should be rasped off, before squeezing, with lump sugar, which is to be added to the juice; mix the whole; strain after standing an hour, and freeze. Beat up with a little sugar the whites of two or three eggs, and as the ice is beginning to set, work this in with the spatula, which will much improve the consistence and taste.

1928. ORANGE-WATER ICE in the same way.

1929. Nitrate of Ammonia as a Freezing Mixture.—Another substance which is free from any corrosive action or unpleasant odour, is the nitrate of ammonia, which, if simply dissolved in rather less than its own weight of water, reduces the temperature to about twenty-five degrees below freezing. The objections to its use are, that its frigorific power is not sufficiently great to freeze readily; and if it be required to form dessert ices, it is requisite to renew the process, at the expiration of a quarter of an hour, a second, or even, if the weather is very hot, and the water used is rather warm, a third or fourth time. Again, the nitrate of ammonia is a very expensive salt; even in France, where it is manufactured expressly for this purpose, it is sold at the rate of three francs a pound; and in this country it cannot be obtained under a much higher price. One great recommendation, however, attends its use, namely, that it may be recovered again, and used any number of times, by simply boiling away the water in which it is dissolved, by a gentle fire, until a small portion, on being removed, crystal-lizes on cooling.

1930. Washing Soda as a Freezing Mixture.—If, however, nitrate of ammonia in coarse powder is put into the cooler, and there is then added twice its weight of freshly crushed washing soda, and an equal quantity of the coldest water that can be obtained, an intensely powerful frigorific mixture is the result, the cold often falling to forty degrees below freezing. This is by far the most efficacious freezing mixture that can be made without the use of ice or acids. But, unfortunately, it has an almost insuperable objection, that the nitrate of ammonia is decomposed by the soda, and cannot be recovered by evaporation; this raises the expense to so great a height, that the plan is practically useless.

1931. The New Freezing Preparation without Ice or Acids obviates all these objections. It is easy of use, not corrosive in its properties, and capable of being used at any time, at a minute's notice; is easy of transport, being in a solid form, and, moreover, moderate in its cost. In India, to which country it has been exported in enormous quantities, it has excited the most lively interest, and the Nepaulese princes, when in London, paid the greatest attention to its use. It consists of two powders, the first of which is composed of one part by weight of muriate of ammonia, or sal-ammoniac powder, and intimately mixed with two parts by weight of nitrate of potash, or saltpetre. These quantities are almost exactly in (what is called by chemists) the combining proportions of the two salts, and by reacting on each other, the original compounds are destroyed, and in the place of muriate of ammonia and nitrate of potash, we have nitrate of ammonia and muriate of potash; thus we have succeeded in producing nitrate of ammonia at a cheap rate, accompanied by another salt, the muriate of potash, which also produces considerable cold when dissolved: but this mixture, used alone,

cannot be regarded as a freezing one, although very efficient in cooling. The other powder is formed simply of the best Scotch soda, crushed in a mortar, or by passing through a mill; although, as hitherto prepared, its appearance has been disguised by the admixture of small quantities of other materials, which have, however, tended to diminish its efficacy. The two powders so prepared must be separately kept in closely-covered vessels, and in as cool a place as possible; for if the crushed soda is exposed to the air, it loses the water it contains, and is considerably weakened in power; and if the other mixture is exposed, it attracts moisture from the air, and dissolves in it—becoming useless. To use the mixture, take an equal bulk of the two powders, mix them together by stirring, and *immediately* introduce them into the ice-pail, or vessel in which they are to be dissolved, and pour on as much water (the coldest that can be obtained) as is sufficient to dissolve them; if a pint measure of each of the powders is used, they will require about a pint of water to dissolve them. More water than is necessary should not be used, as in that case the additional water is cooled instead of the substance that it is wished to freeze. Less than a pint of each powder, and about the same quantity of water, will be found sufficient to ice two bottles of wine, one after the other, in the hottest of weather, if a tub is used of such a size as to prevent the waste of materials.

1932. Muriate of Ammonia as a Freezing Mixture.—If the ordinary sal ammoniac of the shops is used, it will be found both difficult to powder, and expensive; in fact, it is so exceedingly tough, that the only way in which it can be easily divided, except in a drug mill, is by putting as large a quantity of the salt into water which is actually boiling as the latter will dissolve; as the solution cools, the salt crystallizes out in the solid form, and if stirred as it cools, it separates in a state of fine division. As this process is troublesome, and as the sal ammoniac is expensive, it is better to use the crude muriate of ammonia, which is the same substance as sal ammoniac, but before it has been purified by sublimation. This is not usually kept by druggists, but may be readily obtained of any of the artificial manure merchants, at a very moderate rate; and its purity may be readily tested by placing a portion of it on a red-hot iron, when it should fly off in a vapour, leaving scarcely any residue.

1933. COLDNESS OF THE MATERIALS USED.—It is hardly necessary to add, that in icing wines, or freezing, the effect is great in proportion to the coldness of the materials used: therefore, every article employed, viz., the water, tubs, mixtures, &c., should be as cool as possible.

1934. Blackbirds. — The cock bird is of a deep black, with a yellow bill. The female is dark brown. It is difficult to distinguish male from female birds when young; but the darkest generally are males. Their food consists of German paste, bread, meat, and bits of apple. The same treatment as given for the thrush applies to the blackbird.

1935. Food of Blackbirds.— The natural food of the blackbird is berries, worms, insects, shelled snails, cherries, and other similar fruit; and its artificial food, lean fresh meat, cut very small, and mixed with bread, or German paste.

1936. Thrushes.—A cock may be distinguished from a hen by a darker back, and the more glossy appearance of the feathers. The belly also is white. Their natural food is insects, worms, and snails. In a domesticated state they will meat raw meat, but snails and worms should be procured for them. Young birds are hatched about the middle of April, and should be kept very warm. They should be fed with raw meat, cut small, or bread mixed in milk with hemp seed well bruised; when they can feed themselves give them lean meat cut small, and mixed with bread or German

paste, plenty of clean water, and keep them in a warm, dry, and sunny situation.

1937. Canaries.—To distinguish a cock bird from a hen, observe the bird when it is singing, and if it be a cock you will perceive the throat heaving with a pulse-like motion, a peculiarity which is scarcely perceptible in the hen. Feed young canaries with white and yolk of hard egg, mixed together with a little bread steeped in water. This should be pressed and placed in one vessel, while in another should be put some boiled rape seed, washed in fresh water. Change the food every day. When they are a month old, put them into separate cages. Cut the claws of cage birds occasionally, when they become too long, but in doing so be careful not to draw blood.

1938. Canaries. — Especial care must be taken to keep the canary scrupulously clean. For this purpose, the cage should be strewed every morning with clean sand, or rather, fine gravel, for small pebbles are *absolutely essential* to life and health in cage-birds: fresh water must be given every day, both for drinking and bathing; the latter being in a shallow vessel; and, during the moulting season, a small bit of iron should be put into the water for drinking. The food of a canary should consist principally of *summer* rape seed, that is, of those small *brown* rape seeds which are obtained from plants sown in the spring, and which ripen during the summer; large and *black* rape seeds, on the contrary, are produced by such plants as are sown in autumn and reaped in spring. A little chickweed in spring, lettuce leaves in summer, and endive in autumn, with slices of sweet apple in winter, may be safely given; but bread and sugar ought to be generally avoided. Occasionally, also, a few poppy or canary seeds, and a small quantity of bruised hemp seed may be added, but the last very sparingly. Cleanliness, simple food, and fresh but not *cold* air, are essential to the well-being of a canary. During the winter, the cage should never be hung in a room without a fire, but even then, when the air is mild, and the sun shines bright, the little prisoner will be refreshed by having the window open. The cage should never be less than eight inches in diameter, and a foot high, with perches at different heights.

1939. Bulfinches. — Old birds should be fed with German Paste, No. 2, and occasionally rape seed. The Germans sometimes give them a little poppy-seed, and a grain or two of rice, steeped in Canary wine, when teaching them to pipe, as a reward for the progress they make. . Bird organs, or flageolets, are used to teach them. They breed three or four times a year. The young require to be kept very warm, and to be fed every two hours with rape seed, soaked for several hours in cold water, afterwards scalded and strained, bruised, mixed with bread, and moistened with milk. One, two, or three mouthfuls at a time.

1940. Linnets. — Cock birds are browner on the back than the hens, and have some of the large feathers of the wings white up to the quills. Canary and hemp seed, with occasionally a little groundsel, water-cress, chickweed, &c., constitute their food.

1941. Skylarks. — The cock is recognized by the largeness of his eye, the length of his claws, the mode of erecting his crest, and by marks of white in the tail. It is also a larger bird than the hen. The cage should be of the following proportions :—Length, one foot five inches ; width, nine inches ; height, one foot three inches. There should be a circular projection in front to admit of a fresh turf being placed every two or three days, and the bottom of the cage should be plentifully and constantly sprinkled with river sand. All vessels containing food should be placed outside, and the top of the cage should be arched and padded, so that the bird may not injure itself by jumping about. Their food, in a natural state, consists of seeds, insects, and also buds, green herbage, as clover, endive, lettuce, &c., and occasionally berries. When confined, they are usually fed with a paste made in the following manner :— Take a portion of bread, well-baked and stale, put it into fresh water, and leave it until quite soaked through, then squeeze out the water and pour boiled milk over it, adding two-thirds of the same quantity of barley meal well sifted, or, what is better, wheat meal. This should be made fresh every two days. Occasionally the yolk of a hard-boiled egg should be crumbled small and given to the birds, as well as a little hemp seed, meal worms, and elder berries. Great cleanliness should be observed in the cages of these birds.

1942. Parrots may best be taught to talk by covering the cage at night, or rather in the evening, and then repeating to them slowly and distinctly the words they are desired to learn. They should be kept away from places where they would be liable to hear disagreeable noises, such as street cries, and the whistling and shouts of boys at play, or they will imitate them, and become too noisy to be tolerated. Parrots may be fed upon soaked bread, biscuit, mashed potatoes, and rape seed. They are fond of nuts. Cayenne pepper, sprinkled upon a bone, and given to them occasionally, is said to be very beneficial. They should be kept very clean, and allowed a bath frequently. It would be difficult to point out modes of treatment of the diseases of parrots. When they become affected in any way, it is best to keep them warm, change their food for a time, and give them lukewarm water to bathe in.

1943. German Paste.—German paste for cage birds, which will be found of better quality and cheaper than what is sold in the shops.—Boil four eggs until quite hard, then throw them into cold water ; remove the whites and grate or pound the yolks until quite fine, and add a pound of white pea-meal and a tablespoonful of olive oil. Mix the whole up together, and press the dough through a tin cullender so as to form into small grains like shot. Fry them over a gentle fire, gradually stirring them until of a light brown colour, when they are fit for use.

1944. Insects from Bird-cages, Drawers, &c. — To keep away insects from birds' eyes, suspend a little bag of sulphur in the cage. This is said to be healthful for birds generally, as well as serving to keep away insects by which they become infested.

1945. Squirrels. — In a domestic state these little animals are fed with hazel nuts, or indeed any kind of nuts; and occasionally bread and milk. They should be kept very clean.

1946. Rabbits should be kept dry and warm. Their best food is celery, parsley, and carrots; but they will eat almost any kind of vegetable, especially the dandelion, milk-thistle, &c. In spring it is recommended to give them tares. A little bran, and any kind of grain occasionally is beneficial, as too much green food is very hurtful. Care should be taken not to over-feed them. When fed upon dry food a little skim milk will be good for them. Tea leaves also, in small quantities, are said to be good for them.

1947. White Mice are fed upon bread soaked in milk, peas, oats, beans, &c., and any kind of nuts.

1948. Monkeys feed upon bread, and fruit of any kind. Do not let them have meat, except, perhaps, small bones.

1949. Guinea Pigs very much resemble rabbits in their living, and may be treated nearly the same. They should be kept dry, warm, and very clean.

1950. To Fatten Poultry. — Poultry should be fattened in coops, and kept very clean. They should be furnished with gravel, but with no water. Their only food, barley-meal, should be mixed with water, so as to serve them for drink. Their thirst makes them eat more than they would, in order to extract the water that is among the food. This should not be put in troughs, but laid upon a board, which should be

clean washed every time fresh food is put upon it. It is foul and heated water which is the sole cause of the pip.

1951. To Fatten Fowls in a Short Time. — Mix together ground rice well scalded with milk, and add some coarse sugar. Feed them with this in the daytime, but not too much at once; let it be rather thick.

1952. Poultry. — The editor of the *Gardener's Chronicle* says, in reply to a correspondent, — "It is, in our opinion, a bad thing to give fowls egg-shells. They supply nothing that is not equally furnished by lime, and especially bricklayers' rubbish, old ceilings, &c. Never do anything that has a tendency to make them eat eggs. They are apt scholars. If they find worms in a natural way they are good food, but it is a bad plan to give them by the handful. The colour of a golden Poland cock is not very essential, provided it be uniform, and the spangling regular, the legs a good clear blue, and the wing well laced. The top-knot should not have too much white."

1953. Gold Fish. — Great care must be taken of gold fish, as they are very sensitive; and hence a loud noise, strong smell, violent or even slight shaking of the vessel, will sometimes destroy them. Small worms, which are common to the water, suffice for their food in general; but the Chinese, who bring gold fish to great perfection, throw small balls of paste into the water, of which they are very fond. They give them also lean pork, dried in the sun, and reduced to a very fine and delicate powder. Fresh river-water must be given them every day. Care must be taken to collect the spawn, when seen floating on the water, as otherwise it will be destroyed by the fish themselves. This spawn is put into a vessel, and exposed to the sun, until vivified by the heat. Gold fish, however, seldom deposit spawn when kept in vases. In order to procure a supply, they must be put into reservoirs of a considerable depth, in some parts at least, well shaded at intervals with water-lilies, and constantly supplied with fresh water.

1954. To Chloroform Bees.—The quantity of chloroform required for an ordinary hive is the sixth part of an ounce; a very large hive may take nearly a quarter of an ounce. Set down a table opposite to, and about four feet distant from the hive; on the table spread a thick linen cloth; in the centre of the table place a small shallow breakfast plate, which cover with a piece of wire gauze, to prevent the bees from coming in immediate contact with the chloroform. Now quickly and cautiously lift the hive from the board on which it is standing, set it down on the top of the table, keeping the plate in the centre; cover the hive closely up with cloths, and in twenty minutes or so the bees are not only sound asleep, but not one is left among the combs; the whole of them are lying helpless on the table. You now remove what honey you think fit, replace the hive in its old stand, and the bees, as they recover, will return to their domicile. A bright, calm, sunny day is the best; and you should commence your operations early in the morning, before many of them are abroad.

1955. Dogs.—The best way to keep dogs healthy is to let them have plenty of exercise, and not to over-feed them. Let them at all times have a plentiful supply of clean water, and encourage them to take to swimming, as it assists their cleanliness. When you wash them do not use a particle of soap, or you will prevent their licking themselves, and they may become habitually dirty. Properly treated, dogs should be fed only once a day. Meat boiled for dogs, and the liquor in which it is boiled thickened with barley meal, or oatmeal, forms capital food. The distemper is liable to attack dogs from four months to four years old. It prevails most in spring and autumn. The disease is known by dulness of the eye, husky cough, shivering, loss of appetite and spirits, and fits. When fits occur, the dog will most likely die, unless a veterinary surgeon be called in. During the distemper, dogs should be allowed to run on the grass; their diet should be spare; and a little sulphur be placed in their water. Chemists who dispense cattle medicines can generally advise with sufficient safety upon the diseases of dogs, and it is best for unskilful persons to abstain from physicing them. Hydrophobia is the most dreadful of all diseases. The first symptoms are attended by thirst, fever, and languor. The dog starts convulsively in his sleep, and when awake, though restless, is languid. When a dog is suspected, he should be firmly chained in a place where neither children nor dogs nor cats can get near him. Any one going to attend him should wear thick leather gloves, and proceed with great caution. When a dog snaps savagely at an imaginary object, it is almost a certain indication of madness; and when it exhibits a terror of fluids, it is confirmed hydrophobia. Some dogs exhibit a great dislike of musical sounds, and when this is the case they are too frequently made sport of. But it is a dangerous sport, as dogs have sometimes been driven mad by it. In many diseases dogs will be benefited by warm baths. The mange is a contagious disease, which it is difficult to get rid of when once contracted. The best way is to apply to a veterinary chemist for an ointment, and to keep applying it for some time after the disease has disappeared, or it will break out again.

1956. Cats.—It is generally supposed that cats are more attached to places than to individuals, but this is an error. They obstinately cling to certain places, because it is there they expect to see the persons to whom they are attached. A cat will return to an empty house, and remain in it many weeks. But when at last she finds that the family does not return, she strays away, and if she chances then to find the family, she will abide with them. The same rules of feeding which apply to dogs apply also to cats. They should not be over-fed, nor too frequently. Cats are liable to the same diseases as dogs; though they do not become ill so frequently. A little brimstone in their milk occasionally is a good preventive. The veterinary chemist will also prescribe for the serious diseases of cats.

1957. Choice of Friends.—We should ever have it fixed in our memories, that *by the character of those whom we choose for our friends our own character is likely to be formed*, and will certainly be judged of by the world. We ought, therefore, to be slow and cautious in contracting intimacy; but when a virtuous friendship is once established, we must ever consider it as a sacred engagement.—*Dr. Blair.*

1958. Words.—Soft words soften the soul—angry words are fuel to the flame of wrath, and make it blaze more freely. Kind words make other people good-natured—cold words freeze people, and hot words scorch them, and bitter words make them bitter, and wrathful words make wrathful. There is such a rush of all other kinds of words in our days, that it seems desirable to give kind words a chance among them. There are vain words, and idle words, and hasty words, and spiteful words, and silly words, and empty words, and profane words, and boisterous words, and warlike words. Kind words also produce their own image on men's souls, and a beautiful image it is. They smooth, and quiet, and comfort the hearer. They shame him out of his sour, and morose, and unkind feelings. We have not yet begun to use kind words in such abundance as they ought to be used.

1959. Gossiping.—If you wish to cultivate a gossiping, meddling, censorious spirit in your children, be sure when they come home from church, a visit, or any other place where you do not accompany them, to ply them with questions concerning what everybody wore, how everybody looked, and what everybody said and did; and if you find anything in this to censure, always do it in their hearing. You may rest assured, if you pursue a course of this kind, they will not return to you unladen with intelligence; and, rather than it should be uninteresting, they will by degrees learn to embellish, in such a manner as shall not fail to call forth remarks and expressions of wonder from you. You will, by this course, render the spirit of curiosity, which is so early visible in children, and which, if rightly directed, may be made the instrument of enriching and enlarging their minds, a vehicle of mischief which will serve only to narrow them.

1960. Rules of Conduct.—We cannot do better than quote the valuable injunctions of that excellent woman, Mrs. Fry, who combined in her character and conduct all that is truly excellent in woman: i. I never lose any time, —I do not think that time lost which is spent in amusement or recreation some part of each day; but always be in the habit of being employed. ii. Never err the least in truth. iii. Never say an ill thing of a person when thou canst say a good thing of him; not only speak charitably, but feel so. iv. Never be irritable or unkind to anybody. v. Never indulge thyself in luxuries that are not necessary. vi. Do all things with consideration: and when thy path to act right is most difficult, feel confidence in that Power alone which is able to assist thee, and exert thy own powers as far as they go.

1961. The Female Temper.— No trait of character is more agreeable in a female than the possession of a sweet temper. Home can never be happy without it. It is like the flowers that spring up in our pathway, reviving and cheering us. Let a man go home at night, wearied and worn by the toils of the day, and how soothing is a word dictated by a good disposition! It is sunshine falling on his heart. He is happy, and the cares of life are forgotten. A sweet temper has a soothing influence over the minds of a whole family. Where it is found in the wife and mother, you observe a kindness and love predominating over the natural feelings of a bad heart. Smiles, kind words and looks, characterize the children, and peace and love have their dwelling there. Study, then, to acquire and maintain a sweet temper.

1962. Counsels for the Young. —Never be cast down by trifles. If a spider break his thread twenty times, twenty times will he mend it again. Make up your mind to do a thing, and you will do it. Fear not if a trouble comes upon you; keep up your spirits, though the day be a dark one. If the sun is going down, look up to the stars. If the earth is dark, keep your eye on heaven. With God's promises, a man or a child may be cheerful. Mind what you run after. Never be content with a bubble that will burst, firewood that will end in smoke and darkness. Get that which you can keep, and which is worth keeping. Fight hard against a hasty temper. Anger will come, but resist it strongly. A fit of passion may give you cause to mourn all the days of your life. Never revenge an injury. If you have an enemy, act kindly to him, and make him your friend. You may not win him over at once, but try again. Let one kindness be followed by another, till you have compassed your end. By little and little, great things are completed; and repeated-kindness will soften the heart of stone. Whatever you do, do it willingly. A boy that is whipped to school never learns his lessons well. A man who is compelled to work cares not how badly it is performed. He that pulls off his coat cheerfully, strips up his sleeves in earnest, and sings while he works, is the man of action.

1963. Advice to Young Ladies.

i. If you have blue eyes you need not languish.

ii. If black eyes you need not stare.

iii. If you have pretty feet there is no occasion to wear short petticoats.

iv. If you are doubtful as to that point, there can be no harm in letting the petticoats be long.

v. If you have good teeth, do not laugh for the purpose of showing them.

vi. If you have bad ones, do not laugh less than the occasion may justify.

vii. If you have pretty hands and arms, there can be no objection to your playing on the harp if you play well.

viii. If they are disposed to be clumsy, work tapestry.

ix. If you have a bad voice, rather speak in a low tone.

x. If you have the finest voice in the world, never speak in a high tone.

xi. If you dance well, dance but seldom.

xii. If you dance ill, never dance at all.

xiii. If you sing well, make no previous excuses.

xiv. If you sing indifferently, hesitate not a moment when you are asked, for few people are judges of singing, but every one is sensible of a desire to please.

xv. If you would preserve beauty, rise early.

xvi. If you would preserve esteem, be gentle.

xvii. If you would obtain power, be condescending.

xviii. If you would live happily, endeavour to promote the happiness of others.

1964. Daughters.—Mothers who wish not only to discharge well their own duties in the domestic circle, but to train up their daughters for a later day to make happy and comfortable firesides for their families, should watch well, and guard well, the notions which they imbibe and with which they grow up. There will be so many persons ready to fill their young heads with false and vain fancies, and there is so much always afloat in society opposed to duty and common sense, that if mothers do not watch well, their children may contract ideas very fatal to their future happiness and usefulness, and hold them till they grow into habits of thought or feeling. A wise mother will have her eyes open, and be ready for every emergency.

A few words of common, downright practical sense, timely uttered by her, may be enough to counteract some foolish idea or belief put into her daughter's head by others, whilst if it be left unchecked, it may take such possession of the mind that it cannot be corrected at a later time. One falsity abroad in this age is the notion that women, unless compelled to it by absolute poverty, are out of place when engaged in domestic affairs. Now mothers should have a care lest their daughters get hold of this conviction as regards themselves—there is danger of it; the fashion of the day engenders it, and the care that an affectionate family take to keep a girl, during the time of her education, free from other occupations than those of her tasks or her recreations, also endangers it. It is possible that affection may err in pushing this care too far; for as education means a fitting for life, and as a woman's life is much connected with domestic and family affairs—or ought to be so,—if the indulgent consideration of parents abstains from all demands upon the young pupil of the school not connected with her books or her play, will she not naturally infer that the matters with which she is never asked to concern herself are, in fact, no concern to her, and that any attention she ever may bestow on them is not a matter of simple duty, but of grace, or concession, or stooping, on her part? Let mothers avoid such danger. If they would do so, they must bring up their daughters from the *first* with the idea that in this world it is required to give as well as to receive, to minister as well as to enjoy; that every person is bound to be useful—practically, literally useful—in his own sphere, and that a woman's first sphere is the house, and its concerns and demands. Once really imbued with this belief, and taught to see how much the comfort and happiness of woman herself, as well as of her family, depends on this part of her discharge of duty, a young girl will usually be anxious

to learn all that her mother is disposed to teach, and will be proud and happy to aid in any domestic occupations assigned to her. These need never be made so heavy as to interfere with the peculiar duties or enjoyments of her age. If a mother wishes to see her daughter become a good, happy, and rational woman, never let there be contempt for domestic occupations, or suffer them to be deemed secondary.

1965. A Wife's Power.—The power of a wife for good or evil is irresistible. Home must be the seat of happiness, or it must be for ever unknown. A good wife is to a man wisdom, and courage, and strength, and endurance. A bad wife is confusion, weakness, discomfiture, and despair. No condition is hopeless where the wife possesses firmness, decision, and economy. There is no outward prosperity which can counteract indolence, extravagance, and folly at home. No spirit can long endure bad domestic influence. Man is strong, but his heart is not adamant. He delights in enterprise and action; but to sustain him he needs a tranquil mind, and a whole heart. He needs his moral force in the conflicts of the world. To recover his equanimity and composure, home must be to him a place of repose, of peace, of cheerfulness, of comfort; and his soul renews its strength again, and goes forth with fresh vigour to encounter the labour and troubles of life. But if at home he find no rest, and is there met with bad temper, sullenness, or gloom, or is assailed by discontent or complaint, hope vanishes, and he sinks into despair.

1966. Husband and Wife.—Being hints to each other for the good of both, as actually delivered at our own table:—

1967. Hints for Wives.—If your husband occasionally looks a little troubled when he comes home, do not say to him, with an alarmed countenance, "What ails you, my dear?" Don't bother him; he will tell you of his own accord, if need be. Don't rattle a hailstorm of fun about his ears either; be observant and quiet. Don't suppose, whenever he is silent and thoughtful, that you are of course the cause. Let him alone until he is inclined to talk; take up your book or your needlework (pleasantly, cheerfully; no pouting—no sullenness), and wait until he is inclined to be sociable. Don't let him ever find a shirt-button missing. A shirt-button being off a collar or wristband has frequently produced the first hurricane in married life. Men's shirt-collars never fit exactly—see that your husband's are made as well as possible, and then, if he does fret a little about them, never mind it; men have a prescriptive right to fret about shirt-collars.

1968. HINTS FOR HUSBANDS.—If your wife complain that young ladies "now-a-day" are very forward, don't accuse her of jealousy. A little concern on her part only proves her love for you, and you may enjoy your triumph without saying a word. Don't evince your weakness either, by complaining of every trifling neglect. What though her chair is not set so close to yours as it used to be, or though her knitting and crochet seem to absorb too large a share of her attention; depend upon it, that as her eyes watch the intertwinings of the threads, and the manœuvres of the needles as they dance in compliance to her delicate fingers, she is thinking of courting days, love-letters, smiles, tears, suspicions, and reconciliations, by which your two hearts became entwined together in the network of love, whose meshes you can neither of you unravel or escape.

1969. HINTS FOR WIVES.—Never complain that your husband pores too much over the newspaper, to the exclusion of that pleasing converse which you formerly enjoyed with him. Don't hide the paper; don't give it to the children to tear; don't be sulky when the boy leaves it at the door; but take it in pleasantly, and lay it down before your spouse. Think what man would

be without a newspaper; treat it as a great agent in the work of civilization, which it assuredly is; and think how much good newspapers have done by exposing bad husbands and bad wives, by giving their errors to the eye of the public. But manage you in this way:—when your husband is absent, instead of gossiping with neighbours or looking into shop windows, sit down quietly, and look over that paper; run your eye over its home and foreign news; glance rapidly at the accidents and casualties; carefully scan the leading articles; and at tea-time, when your husband again takes up the paper, say, "My dear, what an awful state of things there seems to be in India!" or, "What a terrible calamity at Santiago!" or, "Trade appears to be flourishing in the north;" and depend upon it, down will go the paper. If he has not read the information, he will hear it all from your lips, and when you have done, he will ask, "Did you, my dear, read Banting's Letter on Corpulence?" And whether you did or not, you will gradually get into as cosy a chat as you ever enjoyed; and you will soon discover that, rightly used, the newspaper is the wife's real friend, for it keeps the husband at home, and supplies capital topics for every-day table-talk.

1970. HINTS FOR HUSBANDS.—You can hardly imagine how refreshing it is to occasionally call up the recollection of your courting days. How tediously the hours rolled away prior to the appointed time of meeting; how swiftly they seemed to fly when you had met; how fond was the first greeting; how tender the last embrace; how fervent were your vows; how vivid your dreams of future happiness, when, returning to your home, you felt yourself secure in the confessed love of the object of your warm affections! Is your dream realized?—are you as happy as you expected? Consider whether, as a husband, you are as fervent and constant as you were when a lover. Remember that the wife's claims to your unremitting regard, great before marriage, are now exalted to a much higher degree. She has left the world for you—the home of her childhood, the fireside of her parents, their watchful care and sweet intercourse have all been yielded up for you. Look, then, most jealously upon all that may tend to attract you from home, and to weaken that union upon which your temporal happiness mainly depends; and believe that in the solemn relationship of husband is to be found one of the best guarantees for man's honour and happiness.

1971. HINTS FOR WIVES.—Perchance you think that your husband's disposition is much changed; that he is no longer the sweet-tempered, ardent lover he used to be. This may be a mistake. Consider his struggles with the world—his everlasting race with the busy competition of trade. What is it makes him so eager in the pursuit of gain—so energetic by day, so sleepless by night—but his love of home, wife, and children, and a dread that their respectability, according to the light in which he has conceived it, may be encroached upon by the strife of existence? This is the true secret of that silent care which preys upon the hearts of many men; and true it is, that when love is least apparent, it is nevertheless the active principle which animates the heart, though fears and disappointments make up a cloud which obscures the warmer element. As above the clouds there is glorious sunshine, while below are showers and gloom, so with the conduct of man—behind the gloom of anxiety is a bright fountain of high and noble feeling. Think of this in those moments when clouds seem to lower upon your domestic peace, and, by tempering your conduct accordingly, the gloom will soon pass away, and warmth and brightness take its place.

1972. HINTS FOR HUSBANDS. — Summer is the season of love! Happy birds mate, and sing among the trees; fishes dart athwart the running streams, and leap from their element in resist-

less ecstasy; cattle group in peaceful nooks, by cooling streams; even the flowers seem to love, as they twine their tender arms around each other, and throw their wild tresses about in beautiful profusion; the happy swain sits with his loved and loving mistress beneath the sheltering oak, whose arms spread out, as if to shield and sanctify their pure attachment. What shall the husband do now, when earth and heaven seem to meet in happy union? Must he still pore over the calculations of the counting-house, or ceaselessly pursue the toils of the work-room—sparing no moment to taste the joys which Heaven measures out so liberally? No! "Come, dear wife, let us once more breathe the fresh air of heaven, and look upon the beauties of earth. The summers are few we may dwell together; we will not give them all to Mammon. Again let our hearts glow with emotions of renewed love—our feet shall again tread the green sward, and the music of the rustling trees shall mingle in our whisperings of love!"

1973. HINTS FOR WIVES. — "It was!" "It was not!" "It *was!*" "It was *not!*" "Ah!" "Ha!"— Now who's the wiser or the better for this contention for the last word? Does obstinacy establish superiority or elicit truth? Decidedly not! Woman has always been described as clamouring for the last word: actors, authors, preachers, and philosophers, have agreed in attributing this trait to her, and in censuring her for it. Yet why they should condemn her, unless they wish the matter reversed, and thus committed themselves to the error imputed to her, it were difficult to discover. However, so it is;—and it remains for some one of the sex, by an exhibition of noble example, to aid in sweeping away the unpleasant imputation. The wife who will establish the rule of allowing her husband to have the last word, will achieve for herself and her sex a great moral victory! Is he *right?*—it were a great error to oppose him. Is he *wrong?*

—he will soon discover it, and applaud the self-command which bore unvexed his pertinacity. And gradually there will spring up such a happy fusion of feelings and ideas, that there will be no "last word" to contend about, but a steady and unruffled flow of generous sentiment.

1974. HINTS FOR HUSBANDS. — When once a man has established a home, his most important duties have fairly begun. The errors of youth may be overlooked; want of purpose, and even of honour, in his earlier days may be forgotten. But from the moment of his marriage he begins to write his indelible history; not by pen and ink but by actions—by which he must ever afterwards be reported and judged. His conduct at home; his solicitude for his family; the training of his children; his devotion to his wife; his regard for the great interests of Eternity; these are the tests by which his worth will ever afterwards be estimated by all who think or care about him. These will determine his position while living, and influence his memory when dead. He uses well or ill the brief space allotted to him, out of all eternity, to build up a fame founded upon the most solid of all foundations—private worth; and God will judge him, and man judge of him, accordingly.

1975. HINTS FOR WIVES.—Don't imagine, when you have obtained a husband, that your attention to personal neatness and deportment may be relaxed. Then, in reality, is the time for you to exhibit superior taste and excellence in the cultivation of your dress, and the becoming elegance of your appearance. If it required some little care to foster the admiration of a lover, how much more is requisite to keep yourself lovely in the eyes of him to whom there is now no privacy or disguise—your hourly companion! And if it was due to your lover that you should always present to him, who *proposed* to wed and cherish you, a neat and lady-like aspect; how much more is he entitled to a similar mark of respect, who has *kept his promise with honourable fidelity*, and linked all his hopes of future happiness with yours! If you can manage these matters without appearing to study them, so much the better. Some husbands are impatient of the routine of the toilette, and not unreasonably so—they possess active and energetic spirits, sorely disturbed by any waste of time. Some wives have discovered an admirable facility in dealing with this difficulty; and it is a secret which, having been discovered by some, may be known to all, and is well worth the finding out.

1976. HINTS FOR HUSBANDS. — Custom entitles you to be considered the "lord and master" over your household. But don't assume the *master* and sink the *lord*. Remember that noble generosity, forbearance, amiability, and integrity, are among the more lordly attributes of man. As a husband, therefore, exhibit the true nobility of man, and seek to govern your own household by the display of high moral excellence. A domineering spirit—a fault-finding petulance—impatience of trifling delays —and the exhibition of unworthy passions at the slightest provocation, can add no laurel to your own "lordly" brow, impart no sweetness to home, and call forth no respect from those by whom you may be surrounded. It is one thing to be a *master*—another thing to be a *man*. The latter should be the husband's aspiration; for he who cannot govern himself is ill-qualified to govern another.

1977. HINTS FOR WIVES. — It is astonishing how much the cheerfulness of a wife contributes to the happiness of home. She is the sun—the centre of a domestic system, and her children are like planets around her, reflecting her rays. How merry the little ones look when the mother is joyous and good-tempered; and how easily and pleasantly her household labours are overcome! Her cheerfulness is reflected everywhere: it is seen in the neatness of her toilette, the order of her table, and even the seasoning of her dishes. We remember hearing a husband say that he could always gauge the temper of his wife by the quality of her cooking: good temper even influenced the seasoning of her soups, and the lightness and delicacy of her pastry. When ill-temper pervades, the pepper is dashed in as a cloud—perchance the top of the pepper-box is included, as a kind of diminutive thunderbolt; the salt is all in lumps; and the spices seem to betake themselves to one spot in a pudding, as if dreading the frowning face above them. If there be a husband who could abuse the smiles of a really good-tempered wife, we should like to look at him! No, no, such a phenomenon does not exist. Among elements of domestic happiness, the amiability of the wife and mother is of the utmost importance—it is one of the best securities for the HAPPINESS OF HOME.

1978. Servants.—There are frequent complaints in these days, that servants are bad, and apprentices are bad, and dependants and aiding hands generally are bad. It may be so. But if it is so, what is the inference? In the working of the machine of society, class moves pretty much with class; that is, one class moves pretty much with its equals in the community (equals so far as social station is concerned), and apart from other classes, as much those below as those above itself; but there is one grand exception to this general rule, and that is, in the case of domestic servants. The same holds, though in less degree, with apprentices and assistant hands; and in less degree only, because in this last case, the difference of grade is slighter. Domestic servants, and assistants in business and trade, come most closely and continually into contact with their employers; they are about them from morning till night, and see them in every phase of character, in every style of humour, in every act of life. How powerful is the force of example! Rectitude is promoted, not only by pre-

cept but by example, and, so to speak, by contact it is increased more widely. Kindness is communicated in the same way. Virtue of every kind acts like an electric shock. Those who come under its influence imbibe its principles. The same with qualities and tempers that do no honour to our nature. If servants come to you bad, you may at least improve them; possibly almost change their nature. Here follows, then, a receipt to that effect : — *Receipt for obtaining good servants.* — Let them observe in your conduct to others just the qualities and virtues that you would desire they should possess and practise as respects you. Be uniformly kind and gentle. If you reprove, do so with reason and with temper. Be respectable, and you will be respected by them. Be kind, and you will meet kindness from them. Consider their interests, and they will consider yours. A friend in a servant is no contemptible thing. Be to every servant a friend; and heartless, indeed, will be the servant who does not warm in love to you.

1979. Oyster Ketchup.—Take fine fresh Milton oysters; wash them in their own liquor, strain it, pound them in a marble mortar; to a pint of oysters add a pint of sherry; boil them up, and add an ounce of salt, two drachms of pounded mace, and one of cayenne: let it just boil up again, skim it, and rub it through a sieve; and when cold, bottle it, cork well, and seal it down.

1980. Walnut Ketchup.—Take two sieves of green walnut shells, put them into a tub, mix them up well with common salt, from two to three pounds, let them stand for six days, frequently beating and mashing them: by this time the shells become soft and pulpy, then by banking the mass up on one side of the tub, and at the same time raising the tub on that side, the liquor will drain clear off to the other; then take that liquor out: the mashing and banking-up may be repeated as often as liquor is found. The quantity will be about six quarts. When done, let it be simmered in an iron boiler as long as any scum arises; then bruise a quarter of a pound of ginger, a quarter of a pound of allspice, and two ounces of long pepper, two ounces of cloves. Let it slowly boil for half an hour with the above ingredients; when bottled, let an equal quantity of the spice go into each bottle; when corked, let the bottles be filled quite up: cork them tight, seal them over, and put them into a cool and dry place for one year before they are used.

1981. Essence of Mushroom. —This delicate relish is made by sprinkling a little salt over either flap or button mushrooms;—three hours after, mash them,—next day strain off the liquor that will flow from them, put it into a stewpan, and boil it till it is reduced one half. It will not keep long, but is preferable to any of the ketchups containing spice, &c., to preserve them, which overpowers the flavour of the mushrooms. An artificial mushroom bed will supply these all the year round.

1982. Essence of Celery.—This is prepared by soaking for a fortnight half an ounce of the seeds of celery in a quarter of a pint of brandy. A few drops will flavour a pint of soup or broth equal to a head of celery.

1983. Tincture of Allspice.— Bruised allspice, one ounce and a half; brandy, a pint. Steep for a fortnight, occasionally shaking, then pour off the clear liquor. Excellent for many of the uses of allspice, for making a bishop, mulling wine, flavouring gravies, potted meats, &c.

1984. Horseradish Vinegar. —Pour a quart of best vinegar on three ounces of scraped horseradish, an ounce of minced shalot, and one drachm of cayenne; let it stand a week, and you will have an excellent relish for cold beef, salads, &c., costing scarcely anything. Horseradish is in the highest perfection about November.

1985. Mint Vinegar.—Put into a wide-mouthed bottle, fresh nice clean mint leaves enough to fill it loosely;

then fill up the bottle with good vinegar; and after it has been corked close for two or three weeks, it is to be poured off clear into another bottle, and kept well corked for use. Serve with lamb when mint cannot be obtained.

1986. Cress Vinegar.—Dry and pound half an ounce of *cress seed* (such as is sown in the garden with mustard), pour upon it a quart of the best vinegar, let it steep for ten days, shaking it up every day. This is very strongly flavoured with cress, and for salads, and cold meats, &c., it is a great favourite with many;—the quart of sauce costs only a halfpenny more than the vinegar. Celery vinegar may be made in the same manner.

1987. Cheap and Good Vinegar.—To eight gallons of clear rain water, add three quarts of molasses; turn the mixture into a clean tight cask, shake it well two or three times, and add three spoonfuls of good yeast, or two yeast cakes; place the cask in a warm place, and in ten or fifteen days add a sheet of common wrapping paper, smeared with molasses, and torn into narrow strips, and you will have good vinegar. The paper is necessary to form the "mother," or life of the vinegar.

1988. Cayenne Pepper. — Dr. Kitchiner says (in his excellent book, "The Cook's Oracle" *),—"We advise all who are fond of cayenne not to think it too much trouble to make it of English chilis,—there is no other way of being sure it is genuine,—and they will obtain a pepper of much finer flavour, without half the heat of the foreign. A hundred large chilis, costing only two shillings, will produce you about two ounces of cayenne,—so it is as cheap as the commonest cayenne. Four hundred chilis, when the stems were taken off, weighed half a pound; and when dried produced a quarter of a pound of cayenne pepper. The following is the way to make it :— Take away the stalks, and put the pods into a cullender; set it before the fire,—

* London: Houlston & Wright.

they will take full twelve hours to dry;
—then put them into a mortar, with one-
fourth their weight of salt, and pound
them and rub them till they are as
fine as possible, and put them into a
well-stoppered bottle."

1989. Peas Powder.—Pound in
a marble mortar half an ounce each
of dried mint and sage, a drachm of
celery seed, and a quarter of a drachm
of cayenne pepper; rub them together
through a fine sieve. This gives a very
savoury relish to pea soup and to
gruel, so that a person partaking of the
latter may fancy he is sipping good pea
soup. A drachm of allspice, or black
pepper, may be pounded with the above
as an addition, or instead of the cayenne.

1990. Horseradish Powder.
—The time to make this is during November and December: slice the radish
the thickness of a shilling, and lay it to
dry very gradually in a Dutch oven (a
strong heat soon evaporates its flavour);
when dry enough, pound it and bottle it.

1991. Curry Powder (a genuine
Indian receipt).—Turmeric, coriander,
black pepper, four ounces each; fenu-
greek, three ounces; ginger, two ounces;
cummin seed, ground rice, one ounce
each; cayenne pepper, cardamums, half
an ounce each.

1992. Another Curry Powder.
—Coriander, twelve ounces; black pepper, six ounces; turmeric, four ounces
and three quarters; cummin seed, three
ounces; cayenne, one ounce and a half;
ground rice, one ounce; cardamums,
half an ounce; cloves, quarter of an
ounce.—It is best to have the above
receipts prepared at a chemist's.

**1993. True Indian Curry
Powder.**—Turmeric, four ounces; coriander seeds, eleven ounces; cayenne,
half an ounce; black pepper, five ounces;
pimento, two ounces; cloves, half an
ounce; cinnamon, three ounces; ginger,
two ounces; cummin seed, three ounces;
shalots, one ounce. All these ingredients should be of a fine quality, and
recently ground or powdered.

1994. Curry Powder.—i. Take
two ounces of turmeric, six ounces of
coriander seed, half an ounce of powdered ginger, two drachms of cinnamon,
six drachms of cayenne pepper, four
drachms of black pepper, one drachm
of mace and cloves, powdered fine, two
drachms of pimento, four drachms of
nutmeg, and an ounce and a half
of fennel seed; powder finely, mix,
dry, and bottle for use. ii. Take of
coriander seed and turmeric, each six
drachms; black pepper, four drachms;
fennel seed and powdered ginger, each
two drachms; cayenne pepper, half a
drachm: powder finely, mix, dry, and
bottle for use.

1995. Oyster Powder.—Open
the oysters carefully, so as not to cut
them, except in dividing the gristle
which adheres to the shells. Put them
into a mortar, and when you have got as
many as you can conveniently pound at
once, add about two drachms of salt to
a dozen oysters; pound them, and rub
them through the back of a hair sieve,
and put them into a mortar again (previously thoroughly dried) with as much
flour as will convert them into a paste;
roll this paste out several times, and
lastly, flour it, and roll it out the thickness of half a crown, and cut it into
pieces about one inch square; lay them
in a Dutch oven, where they will dry
so gently as not to get burned; turn
them every half hour, and when they
begin to dry, crumble them. They
will take about four hours to dry.
Pound them, sift them, and put them
into dry bottles; cork and seal them.
Three dozen of natives require seven
ounces and a half of flour to make them
into a paste weighing eleven ounces,
and when dried, six and a half ounces.
To make half a pint of sauce, put one
ounce of butter into a stewpan with
three drachms of oyster powder, and
six tablespoonfuls of milk; set it on a
slow fire, stir it till it boils, and season
it with salt. As a sauce, it is excellent
for fish, fowls, or rump steaks. Sprinkled
on bread and butter, it makes a good
sandwich.

1996. Anchovy Butter.—Scrape
the skin from a dozen fine anchovies,

take the flesh from the bones, pound it smooth in a mortar; rub through a hair sieve, put the anchovies into the mortar with three quarters of a pound of fresh butter, a small quantity of cayenne, and a saltspoonful of grated nutmeg and mace; beat together until thoroughly blended. If to serve cold, mould the butter in small shapes, and turn it out. For preservation, press the butter into jars, and keep cool.

1997. Lobster Butter is made in the same manner as anchovy butter. A mixture of anchovy butter and lobster butter is considered excellent.

1998. Liver Sauce for Fish.— Boil the liver of the fish, and pound it in a mortar with a little flour, stir it into some broth, or some of the liquor the fish was boiled in, or melted butter, parsley, and a few grains of cayenne, a little essence of anchovy, soy, or ketchup;—give it a boil up, and rub it through a sieve: you may add a little lemon juice, or lemon cut in dice.

1999. Sauce for Fish.—Twenty-four anchovies, chopped; ten shalots; two ounces of horseradish, scraped; four blades of mace; one lemon, sliced; twelve cloves; one quarter of an ounce of black pepper, whole; one gill of the anchovy liquor; one quart of best vinegar; one quart of water. Let the whole simmer on the fire, in a covered saucepan, until reduced to one quart, strain, and bottle for use. If required for long keeping, add a quarter of an ounce of cayenne pepper.

2000. Apple Sauce.—Pare and core three good-sized baking apples, put them into a well-tinned pint saucepan, with two tablespoonfuls of cold water; cover the saucepan close, and set it on a trivet over a slow fire a couple of hours before dinner,—some apples will take a long time stewing, others will be ready in a quarter of an hour. When the apples are done enough pour off the water, let them stand a few minutes to get dry; then beat them up with a fork, with a bit of butter about as big as a nutmeg, and a teaspoonful of powdered sugar: some persons add lemon peel, grated or minced fine,—or boil a small piece with the apples. Many persons are fond of apple sauce with cold pork.

2001. Grill Sauce.—To a quarter of a pint of gravy add half an ounce of butter and a dessertspoonful of flour, well rubbed together; the same of mushroom or walnut ketchup; a teaspoonful of lemon juice; half a teaspoonful of made mustard, and of minced capers; a small quantity of black pepper; a little rind of lemon, grated very thin; a saltspoonful of essence of anchovies, and a little shalot wine, or a very small piece of minced shalot, and a little chili vinegar, or a few grains of cayenne; simmer together for a few minutes: pour a portion of it over the grill, and send up the remainder in a sauce-tureen.

2002. Tomata, or Love Apple Sauce.—Twelve tomatas, ripe and red; take off the stalk; cut in halves; squeeze enough to get all the water and seeds out; put them in a stewpan with a capsicum, and two or three tablespoonfuls of beef gravy; set on a slow stove till properly melted; rub them through a tamis into a clean stewpan; add a little white pepper and salt, and let them simmer a few minutes.—French cooks add an onion or shalot, a clove or two, or a little tarragon vinegar.

2003. Beef Gravy Sauce (*Or Brown Sauce for Ragout, Game, Poultry, Fish, &c.*)—If you want gravy, furnish a thick and well-tinned stewpan with a thin slice of fat ham or bacon, or an ounce of butter, and a middling-sized onion; on this lay a pound of nice juicy gravy beef (as the object in making gravy is to extract the nutritious qualities of the meat, it must be beaten so as to reduce the containing vessels, and scored to render the surface more susceptible to the action of the water); cover the stewpan, set it on a slow fire; when the meat begins to brown, turn it about, and let it get slightly browned (but *take care it is not at all burnt*): then pour in a pint and a half of boiling water, set the pan on the fire;—when it boils, carefully catch the scum, and then put in a crust of bread toasted brown (don't burn it), a sprig of winter savoury, or lemon thyme and parsley, a roll of thin-cut lemon peel, a dozen berries of allspice, and a dozen of black pepper; cover the stewpan close, let it *stew very gently* for about two hours, then strain it through a sieve into a basin. If you wish to thicken it, set a clean stewpan over a slow fire, with about an ounce of butter in it; when it is melted, dredge into it (by degrees) as much flour as will dry it up, stirring them intimately; when thoroughly mixed, pour in a little of the gravy,—stir it well together, and add the remainder by degrees; set it over the fire, let it simmer gently for fifteen or twenty minutes longer, and skim off the fat, &c., as it rises; when it is about as thick as cream, squeeze it through a tamis or fine sieve, and you will have a fine rich brown sauce, at a very moderate expense, and without much trouble. *Observe*—If you wish *to make it still more relishing,*—for *Poultry,* you may pound the liver with a piece of butter, rub it through a sieve, and stir it into the sauce when you put in the thickening.

2004. Chutney.—One pound of salt, one pound of mustard seed, one pound of stoned raisins, one pound of brown sugar, twelve ounces of garlic, six ounces of cayenne pepper, two quarts of unripe gooseberries, two quarts of best vinegar. The mustard seed gently dried and bruised; the sugar made into a syrup with a pint of the vinegar; the gooseberries dried and boiled in a quart of the vinegar; the garlic to be well bruised in a mortar. When cold, gradually mix the whole in a large mortar, and with the remaining vinegar thoroughly amalgamate them. To be tied down close. The longer it is kept the better it will become.

2005. Wow Wow Sauce.--Chop parsley leaves fine; take two or three pickled cucumbers, or walnuts, and divide into small squares, and set them by in readiness; put into a saucepan

butter as big as an egg; when it is melted, stir into it a tablespoonful of fine flour, and half a pint of the broth of the beef; add a tablespoonful of vinegar, one of mushroom ketchup, or port wine, or both, and a teaspoonful of made mustard; simmer together till it is as thick as you wish, put in the parsley and pickles to get warm, and pour it over the beef, or send it up in a sauce-tureen. This is excellent for stewed or boiled beef.

2006. Sage and Onion, or Goose Stuffing Sauce.—Chop very fine an ounce of onion and half an ounce of green sage leaves, put them into a stewpan with four spoonfuls of water, simmer gently for ten minutes, then put in a teaspoonful of pepper and salt, and one ounce of fine bread-crumbs; mix well together; then pour to it a quarter of a pint of broth, or gravy, or melted butter; stir well together, and simmer it a few minutes longer. This is a very relishing sauce for roast pork, poultry, geese or ducks, or green peas.

2007. Garnishes.—Parsley is the most universal garnish for all kinds of cold meat, poultry, fish, butter, cheese, and so forth. Horseradish is the garnish for roast beef, and for fish in general; for the latter, slices of lemon are sometimes laid alternately with the horseradish.

Slices of lemon for boiled fowl, turkey, and fish, and for roast veal and calf's head.

Carrot in slices for boiled beef, hot or cold.

Barberries, fresh or preserved, for game.

Red beet-root sliced for cold meat, boiled beef, and salt fish.

Fried smelts as garnish for turbot.

Fried sausages or forcemeat balls are placed round turkey, capon, or fowl.

Lobster coral and parsley round boiled fish.

Fennel for mackarel and salmon, either fresh or pickled.

Currant jelly for game, also for custard or bread pudding.

Seville orange in slices for wild ducks, widgeons, teal, and so forth.

Mint, either with or without parsley, for roast lamb, either hot or cold.

Pickled gherkins, capers, or onions, for some kinds of boiled meat and stews.

2008. Relish for Chops, &c. —Pound fine an ounce of black pepper, and half an ounce of allspice, with an ounce of salt, and half an ounce of scraped horseradish, and the same of shalots, peeled and quartered; put these ingredients into a pint of mushroom ketchup, or walnut pickle, and let them steep for a fortnight, and then strain it. *Observe.*—A teaspoonful or two of this is generally an acceptable addition, mixed with the gravy usually sent up for chops and steaks; or added to thick melted butter.

2009. Crab, Mock.—Take any required quantity of good fat mellow cheese, pound it well in a mortar, incorporating made mustard, salad oil, vinegar, pepper (cayenne is the best), and salt sufficient to season and render it about the consistence of the cream of a crab. Add and mix well half a pint or more of picked shrimps, and serve in a crab-shell, or on a dish, garnished with slices of lemon.

2010. Female Dress.—It is well known that a loose and easy dress contributes much to give the sex the fine proportions of body that are observable in the Grecian statues, and which serve as models to our present artists, nature being too much disfigured among us to afford any such. The Greeks knew nothing of those Gothic shackles, that multiplicity of ligatures and bandages with which our bodies are compressed. Their women were ignorant of the use of whalebone stays, by which ours distort their shape instead of displaying it. This practice, carried to so great an excess as it is in England, must in time degenerate the species, besides being in bad taste. Can it be a pleasant sight to behold a woman cut in two in the middle, as if she were like a wasp? On the contrary, it is as shocking to the eye as it is painful to the imagination. A fine shape, like the limb, hath its due size and proportion, a diminution of which is certainly a defect. Such a deformity also would be shocking in a naked figure; wherefore, then, should it be esteemed a beauty in one that is dressed? Everything that confines and lays nature under restraint is an instance of bad taste. This is as true in regard to the ornaments of the body as to the embellishments of the mind. Life, health, reason, and convenience ought to be taken first into consideration. Gracefulness cannot subsist without ease; delicacy is not debility; nor must a woman be sick in order to please.—*Rousseau.*

2011. How to take care of your Hat.—i. Should you get caught in a shower, always remember to brush your hat well while wet. When dry, brush the glaze out, and gently iron it over with a smooth flat iron. ii. If your hat is VERY wet, or stained with *sea* water, get a basin of clean cold water, and a good stiff brush; wash it well all over, but be careful to keep the nap straight; brush it as dry as you can, then put it on a peg to dry. When dry, brush the glaze out, and gently iron it over as above. iii. Should you get a spot of grease on your hat, just drop one drop of benzine on the place, and then rub it briskly with a piece of cloth until out. iv. Should you be travelling, always tie your hat up in your handkerchief before putting it into your case; this will save it from getting rubbed or damaged through the friction of the rail or steamboat. v. Never put your hat flat on the brim, as it will spoil its shape; but always hang it up on a peg. vi. Never put your hat, wet or dry, in front of the fire, as it will soften it, and throw it all out of shape. vii. Before putting your hat down, be careful to see if the place is free from spots of grease, beer, sugar, &c., as these things often spoil a good hat more than a twelvemonths' wear, and are often very difficult to remove. These simple rules will save a good hat for a very long time.

2013. French Polishes. — i. NAPHTHA POLISH. — Shellac, three pounds; wood naphtha, three quarts. Dissolve. Cost: shellac, 6d. to 8d. per pound; naphtha, 1s. 2d. per pint. ii. SPIRIT POLISH. — Shellac, two pounds; powdered mastic and sandarac, of each one ounce; copal varnish, half a pint; spirits of wine, one gallon. Digest in the cold till dissolved. Cost: shellac, 6d. to 8d. per pound; mastic, 1s. per ounce; sandarac, 1d. per ounce; copal varnish, 2s. 6d. per pint; rectified spirit, 2s. 6d. per pint.

2014. French Polish for Boots and Shoes.—Mix together two pints of the best vinegar and one pint of soft water; stir into it a quarter of a pound of glue, broken up, half a pound of logwood chips, a quarter of an ounce of finely powdered indigo, a quarter of an ounce of the best soft soap, and a quarter of an ounce of isinglass. Put the mixture over the fire, and let it boil for ten minutes or more. Then strain the liquid, and bottle and cork it: when cold it is fit for use. Apply it with a clean sponge.

2015. To Polish Enamelled Leather.—Two pints of the best cream, one pint of linseed oil; make them each lukewarm, and then mix them well together. Having previously cleaned the shoe, &c., from dirt, rub it over with a sponge dipped in the mixture: then rub it with a soft dry cloth until a brilliant polish is produced.

2016. Boots and Shoes should be cleaned frequently, whether they are worn or not, and should never be left in a damp place, nor be put too near to the fire to dry. In cleaning them, be careful to *brush* the dirt from the seams, and not to scrape it with a knife, or you will cut the stitches. Let the hard brush do its work thoroughly well, and the polish will be all the brighter.

2017. Blacking.—Blacking is now generally made with ivory black, treacle, linseed, or sweet oil, and oil of vitriol. The proportions vary in the different directions, and a variable quantity of water is added, as paste or liquid blacking is required; the mode of making being otherwise precisely the same.

2018. LIQUID BLACKING.—i. Ivory black and treacle, of each, one pound; sweet oil and oil of vitriol, of each, a quarter of a pound. Put the first three together until the oil is perfectly mixed or "*killed;*" then add the oil of vitriol, diluted with three times its weight of water, and after standing three hours add one quart of water or sour beer. ii. In larger quantity it may be made as follows: Ivory black, three cwt.; molasses or treacle, two cwt.; linseed oil, three gallons; oil of vitriol, twenty pounds; water, eighty gallons. Mix as above directed.

2019. PASTE BLACKING.—i. Ivory black, two pounds; treacle, one pound; olive oil and oil of vitriol, of each, a quarter of a pound. Mix as before, adding only sufficient water to form into a paste. ii. In larger quantity: Ivory black, three cwt.; common treacle, two cwt.; linseed oil and vinegar bottoms, of each, three gallons; oil of vitriol, twenty-eight pounds; water, a sufficient quantity. Cost: ivory black, 1s. per pound; treacle, 3d. per pound; linseed oil, 6d. per pint; sweet oil, 1s. per pint. *Note.*—The ivory black must be very finely ground for liquid blacking, otherwise it settles rapidly. The oil of vitriol is powerfully corrosive when undiluted, but uniting with the lime of the ivory black, it is partly neutralized, and does not injure the leather, whilst it much improves the quality of the blacking.

2020. BEST BLACKING FOR BOOTS AND SHOES.—Ivory black, one and a half ounce; treacle, one and a half ounce; sperm oil, three drachms; strong oil of vitriol, three drachms; common vinegar, half a pint. Mix the ivory black, treacle, and vinegar together, then mix the sperm oil and oil of vitriol separately, and add them to the other mixture.

2021. Waterproofing for Boots and Shoes.—Linseed oil, one pint; oil of turpentine, or camphine, a quarter of a pint; yellow wax, a quarter of a pound; Burgundy pitch, a quarter of a pound. To be melted together with a gentle heat, and when required for use, to be warmed and well rubbed into the leather before a fire, or in the hot sun. Cost: linseed oil, 6d. per pint; oil of turpentine, 8d. per pint; wax, 1s. 10d. per pound; Burgundy pitch, 8d. per pound. Should be poured, when melted, into small gallipots or tin boxes.

2022. To render Shoes Waterproof.—Warm a little bees' wax and mutton suet until it is liquid, and rub some of it slightly over the edges of the sole, where the stitches are.

2023. Directions for putting on Gutta-percha Soles.—Dry the old sole, and rough it well with a rasp, after which, put on a thin coat of warm solution with the finger, rub it well in; let it dry, then hold it to the fire, and whilst warm, put on a second coat of solution thicker than the first, let it dry. Then take the gutta-percha sole, and put it in hot water until it is soft; take it out, wipe it, and hold the sole in one hand and the shoe in the other to the fire, and they will become sticky; immediately lay the sole on, beginning at the toe, and proceed gradually. In half an hour, take a knife and pare it. The solution should be warmed by putting as much as you want to use in a cup, and placing it in hot water, taking care that no water mixes with the solution.

2024. Boot Tops.—Clean boot tops with one ounce of white vitriol, and one ounce of oxalic acid dissolved in a quart of warm water. Apply with a clean sponge. Or, sour milk, one pint; gum arabic, half an ounce; juice of a lemon, white of an egg, and one ounce of vitriol, well mixed.

2025. Boot-top Liquid.—Oxalic acid and white vitriol, of each, one ounce; water, one and a half pint. To be applied with a sponge to the leather, previously washed, and then wiped off again. This preparation is poisonous. Cost: oxalic acid, 1s. 6d. per pound; white vitriol, 6d. per pound.

2026. Care of Gloves.—Nothing looks worse than shabby gloves; and, as they are expensive articles in dress, they require a little management. A good glove will outlast six cheap ones with care. Do not wear your best gloves at night, the heat of the gas, &c., gives a moisture to the hands, that spoils the gloves; do not wear them in very wet weather; as carrying umbrellas, and drops of rain, spoil them.

2027. To Clean Kid Gloves.—Make a strong lather with curd soap and warm water, in which steep a small piece of new flannel. Place the glove on a flat, clean, and unyielding surface —such as the bottom of a dish, and having thoroughly soaped the flannel (when squeezed from the lather), rub the kid till all dirt be removed, cleaning and re-soaping the flannel from time to time. Care must be taken to omit no part of the glove, by turning the fingers, &c. The gloves must be dried in the sun, or before a moderate fire, and will present the appearance of old parchment. When quite dry, they must be gradually "pulled out," and will look new.

2028. To Clean French Kid Gloves.—Put the gloves on your hand and wash them, as if you were washing your hands, in some spirits of turpentine, until quite clean; then hang them up in a warm place, or where there is a current of air, and all smell of the turpentine will be removed. This method is practised in Paris, and since its introduction into this country, thousands of pounds have been gained by it.

2029. How to Wash Kid Gloves.—Have ready a little new milk in one saucer, and a piece of brown soap in another, and a clean cloth or towel folded three or four times. On the cloth, spread out the glove smooth and neat. Take a piece of flannel, dip it in the milk, then rub off a good quantity of soap to the wetted flannel, and commence to rub the glove downwards towards the fingers, holding it firmly with the left hand. Continue this process until the glove, if white, looks of a dingy yellow, though clean; if coloured, till it looks dark and spoiled.

Lay it to dry; and old gloves will soon look nearly new. They will be soft, glossy, smooth, well-shaped, and elastic.

2030. Preserving the Colour of Dresses.—The colours of merinos, mousseline-de-laines, ginghams, chintzes, printed lawns, &c., may be preserved by using water that is only milk-warm; making a lather with white soap, *before* you put in the dress, instead of rubbing it on the material; and stirring into a first and second tub of water a large tablespoonful of ox-gall. The gall can be obtained from the butcher, and a bottle of it should always be kept in every house. No coloured articles should be allowed to remain long in the water. They must be washed fast, and then rinsed through two cold waters. Into each rinsing water stir a teaspoonful of vinegar, which will help to brighten the colours; and after rinsing, hang them out immediately. When *ironing-dry* (or still a little damp), bring them in; have irons ready heated, and iron them at once, as it injures the colours to allow them to remain damp too long, or to sprinkle and roll them up in a cover for ironing next day. If they cannot be conveniently ironed immediately, let them hang till they are *quite* dry, and then damp and fold them on the *following day*, a quarter of an hour before ironing. The best way is not to do coloured dresses on the day of the general wash, but to give them a morning by themselves. They should only be undertaken in clear bright weather. If allowed to freeze, the colours will be irreparably injured. We need scarcely say that no coloured articles should ever be boiled or scalded. If you get from a shop a slip for testing the durability of colours, give it a fair trial by washing it as above; afterwards pinning it to the edge of a towel, and hanging it to dry. Some colours (especially pinks and light greens), though they may stand perfectly well in washing, will change as soon as a warm iron is applied to them; the pink turning purplish, and the green bluish.

No coloured article should be smoothed with a *hot* iron.

2031. To Renovate Silks.—Sponge faded silks with warm water and soap, then rub them with a dry cloth on a flat board; afterwards iron them on the *inside* with a smoothing iron. Old black silks may be improved by sponging with spirits; in this case, the ironing may be done on the right side, thin paper being spread over to prevent glazing.

2032. Black Silk Reviver.—Boil logwood in water for half an hour; then simmer the silk half an hour; take it out, and put into the dye a little blue vitriol, or green copperas; cool it, and simmer the silk for half an hour. Or, boil a handful of fig-leaves in two quarts of water until it is reduced to one pint; squeeze the leaves, and bottle the liquor for use. When wanted, sponge the silk with this preparation.

2033. Restoring Colour to Silk.—When the colour has been taken from silk by acids, it may be restored by applying to the spot a little hartshorn, or sal volatile.

2034. To Remove Water Stains from Black Crape.—When a drop of water falls on a black crape veil or collar, it leaves a conspicuous white mark. To obliterate this, spread the crape on a table (laying on it a large book or a paper-weight to keep it steady), and place underneath the stain a piece of old black silk. With a large camel-hair brush dipped in common ink go over the stain, and then wipe off the ink with a small piece of old soft silk. It will dry immediately, and the white mark will be seen no more.

2035. To Remove Stains from Mourning Dresses.—Boil a handful of fig-leaves in two quarts of water until reduced to a pint. Bombazines, crape, cloth, &c., need only be rubbed with a sponge dipped in this liquor, and the effect will be instantly produced.

2036. Wax may be taken out of cloth by holding a red-hot iron within an inch or two of the marks, and afterwards rubbing them with a soft clean rag.

2037. Ink Stains.—Very frequently, when logwood has been used in manufacturing ink, a reddish stain still remains, after the use of oxalic acid, as in the former directions. To remove it, procure a solution of the chloride of lime, and apply it in the same manner as directed for the oxalic acid.

2038. Grease Spots from Silk.—Upon a deal table lay a piece of woollen cloth or baize, upon which lay smoothly the part stained, with the right side downwards. Having spread a piece of brown paper on the top, apply a flat iron just hot enough to scorch the paper. About five or eight seconds is usually sufficient. Then rub the stained part briskly with a piece of cap-paper.

2039. Liquid for Preserving Furs from Moth.—Warm water, one pint; corrosive sublimate, twelve grains. If washed with this, and afterwards dried, furs are safe from moth. Care should be taken to label the liquid —*Poison.* Cost: corrosive sublimate, 3d. per ounce.

2040. When Velvet gets Plushed from pressure, hold the parts over a basin of *hot* water, with the lining of the article next the water; the pile will soon rise, and assume its original beauty.

2041. Worsted and Lambs'-wool Stockings should never be mended with worsted or lambs'-wool, because, the latter being new, it shrinks more than the stockings, and draws them up till the toes become short and narrow, and the heels have no shape left.

2042. All Flannels should be soaked before they are made up, first in cold then in hot water, in order to shrink them.

2043. Flannel should always be washed with white soap, and in warm but not boiling water.

2044. Brewing.—The best time of the year for brewing is the autumn. The spring is also suitable, but less so. It is a great object to secure a moderate temperature for the cooling of the worts, and to insure gradual fermentation. The brewing of home-made drinks has to a very great extent gone out, of late years, even in country places; and therefore we have little inducement to occupy our limited space with the lengthy directions necessary to constitute a practical essay upon brewing. To those, however, who wish to enter upon the practice, without any previous knowledge, we would advise their calling in the aid of some one practically acquainted with the process for the first operation. By so doing they will save a great deal of trouble, disappointment, and expense. In all places, town or country, there are persons who have worked in brewing establishments, or in gentlemen's families where they have superintended the operations of the brew-house, and the aid of such persons would be valuable. With such assistance, the following receipts will be of importance, since many who are able to go through the manipulations of brewing are unaware of the proper proportions to employ:—

2045. ALE.—Take three bushels of malt, three pounds of hops, fifty-two gallons of water, for two workings. Or, —malt, two bushels and a half; sugar, three pounds; hops, three pounds; coriander seeds, one ounce; capsicum, a drachm. Thirty-six gallons. This gives a pleasant ale, with a good body.

2046. AMBER ALE.—Three bushels of amber malt, three quarters of a bushel of pale amber malt, two pounds of hops, a tablespoonful of salt. Three mashes, forty to fifty gallons. Skim, and fine with isinglass.

2047. BURTON ALE.—One quarter of pale malt, eight pounds and a half of pale hops; mash three times. Work the first mash at 170°, second at 176°, third at 150°. Boil the first wort by itself; when boiling add three pounds of honey, a pound and a half of coriander seeds, one ounce of salt. Mix the worts when boiled, cool to 61°, set to work with a pint and a half of yeast. As soon as the gyle gets yeasty, skim the head half off; rouse the rest with another pint and a half of yeast, three quarters of an ounce of bay salt, and a quarter of a pound of malt or bean flour. This makes a hogshead.

2048. EDINBURGH ALE.--Mash two barrels per quarter, at 183°; mash for three quarters of an hour; let it stand one hour, and allow half an hour to run off. Or, mash one barrel per quarter, at 190°; mash three quarters of an hour, let it stand three quarters of an hour, and tap.

2049. PORTER.—Brown amber and pale malt, in equal quantities: turn them into the mash-tub. Turn on the first liquor at 165°; mash one hour, then coat the whole with dry malt. In one hour set the tap. Mix ten pounds of brown hops to a quarter of malt, half old, half new; boil the first wort briskly with the hops for three quarters of an hour; after putting into the copper one pound and a half of sugar, and one pound and a half of extract of liquorice to the barrel, turn it into coolers, rousing the wort the while. Turn on the second liquor at 174°, set tap again in an hour. The second wort having run off, turn on again at 145°; mash an hour, and stand an hour; boil the second wort with the same hops for one hour. Turn into the coolers, and let into the tub at 64°, mixing the yeast as it comes down. Cleanse the second day at 80°, previously adding a mixture of flour and salt, and rousing well.

2050. Wines from Rhubarb, Grapes (Unripe), Currants, Gooseberries, &c.—The whole art of wine-making consists in the proper management of the fermenting process; the same quantity of fruit, whether it be rhubarb, currants, gooseberries, grapes (unripe), leaves, tops, and tendrils, water, and sugar, will produce two different kinds of wine, by varying the process of fermentation only—that is, a dry wine like sherry, or a brisk beverage like champagne; but neither rhubarb, currants, nor goose-berries will produce a wine with the true champagne flavour; it is to be obtained only from the fruit of the grape, ripe or unripe, its leaves, tops, and tendrils. The receipt here given will do for rhubarb, or any of the above-mentioned fruits. *To make ten gallons of English champagne, imperial measure.*—Take fifty pounds of rhubarb and thirty-seven pounds of fine moist sugar. Provide a tub that will hold from fifteen to twenty gallons, taking care that it has a hole for a tap near the bottom. In this tub bruise the rhubarb; when done, add four gallons of water; let the whole be well stirred together; cover the tub with a cloth or blanket, and let the materials stand for twenty-four hours; then draw off the liquor through the tap; add one or two more gallons of water to the pulp, let it be well stirred, and then allowed to remain an hour or two to settle, then draw off; mix the two liquors together, and in it dissolve the sugar. Let the tub be made clean, and return the liquor to it, cover it with a blanket, and place it in a room the temperature of which is not below 60° Fahr.; here it is to remain for twenty-four, forty-eight, or more hours, until there is an appearance of fermentation having begun, when it should be drawn off into the ten-gallon cask, as fine as possible, which cask must be filled up to the bung-hole with water, if there is not liquor enough; let it lean to one side a little, that it may discharge itself; if there is any liquor left in the tub not quite fine, pass it through flannel, and fill up with that instead of water. As the fermentation proceeds and the liquor diminishes, it must be filled up daily, to encourage the fermentation, for ten or twelve days; it then becomes more moderate, when the bung should be put in, and a gimlet hole made at the side of it, fitted with a spile; this spile should be taken out every two or three days, according to the state of the fermentation, for eight or ten days, to allow some of the carbonic acid gas to escape. When this state is passed, the cask may be kept full by pouring a little liquor in at the vent-hole once a week or ten days, for three or four weeks. This operation is performed at long intervals, of a month or more, till the end of December, when on a fine frosty day it should be drawn off from the lees as fine as possible; the turbid part passed through flannel. Make the cask clean, return the liquor to it, with one drachm of isinglass (pure) dissolved in a little water; stir the whole together, and put the bung in firmly. Choose a clear dry day in March for bottling. They should be champagne bottles—common wine bottles are not strong enough; secure the corks in a proper manner with wire, &c. The liquor is generally made up to two or three pints over the ten gallons, which is bottled for the purpose of filling the cask as it is wanted. For several years past wine has been made with ripe and unripe grapes, according to the season, equally as good as any foreign produce. It has always spirit enough without the addition of brandy, which Dr. Maculloch says, in his treatise on Wines, spoils all wines; a proper fermentation produces spirit enough. The way to obtain a dry wine from these materials is to keep the cask constantly filled up to the bung-hole, daily or every other day, as long as any fermentation is perceptible by applying the ear near to the hole; the bung may then be put in lightly for a time, before finally fixing it; it may be racked off on a fine day in December, and fined with isinglass as above directed, and bottled in March.

2051. Parsnip Wine. — Take fifteen pounds of sliced parsnips, and boil until quite soft in five gallons of water; squeeze the liquor well out of them, run it through a sieve, and add three pounds of coarse lump sugar to every gallon of liquor. Boil the whole for three quarters of an hour. When it is nearly cold, add a little yeast on toast. Let it remain in a tub for ten days, stirring it from the bottom every day; then put it into a cask for

a year. As it works over, fill it up every day.

2052. Turnip Wine. — Take a large number of turnips, pare and slice them; then place in a cider-press, and obtain all the juice you can. To every gallon of juice add three pounds of lump sugar, and half a pint of brandy. Pour into a cask, but do not bung until it has done working; then bung it close for three months, and draw off into another cask; when it is fine, bottle, and cork well.

2053. Blackberry Wine. — Gather the fruit when ripe, on a dry day. Put into a vessel, with the head out, and a tap fitted near the bottom; pour on boiling water to cover it. Mash the berries with your hands, and let them stand covered till the pulp rises to the top and forms a crust, in three or four days. Then draw off the fluid into another vessel, and to every gallon add one pound of sugar; mix well, and put it into a cask, to work for a week or ten days, and throw off any remaining lees, keeping the cask well filled, particularly at the commencement. When the working has ceased, bung it down; after six to twelve months it may be bottled.

2054. Black or White Elderberry Wine. — Gather the berries ripe and dry, pick them, bruise them with your hands, and strain them. Set the liquor by in glazed earthen vessels for twelve hours, to settle; put to every pint of juice a pint and a half of water, and to every gallon of this liquor three pounds of good moist sugar; set in a kettle over the fire, and when it is ready to boil, clarify it with the white of four or five eggs; let it boil one hour, and when it is almost cold, work it with strong ale yeast, and tun it, filling up the vessel from time to time with the same liquor, saved on purpose, as it sinks by working. In a month's time, if the vessel holds about eight gallons, it will be fine and fit to bottle, and after bottling, will be fit to drink in twelve months.

2055. Arrack (Imitation). — Dissolve two scruples of flowers of benjamin in a quart of good rum, and it will impart to the spirit the fragrance of arrack.

2056. Devonshire Junket.— Put warm milk into a bowl, turn it with a little rennet, then add some scalded cream, sugar, and cinnamon on the top, without breaking the curd.

2057. The Crimean Night-cap,—made in a moment, costing nothing, and admirable for railway and other travellers. — Take your pocket-handkerchief, and laying it out the full square, double down *one-third* over the other part. Then raise the whole and turn it over, so that the third folded down shall now be underneath. Take hold of one of the folded corners, and draw its point towards the centre: then do the same with the other, as in making a cocked-hat, or a boat, of paper. Then take hold of the two remaining corners, and twisting the hem of the handkerchief, continue to roll it until it meets the doubled corners brought to the centre, and catches them up a little. Lift the whole, and you will see the form of a cap, which, when applied to the head, will cover the head and ears, and, being tied under the chin, will not come off. Very little practice will enable you to regulate the size of the folds so as to fit the head.

2058. Scotch Punch, or Whisky Toddy. — THE DUKE OF ATHOL'S RECEIPT.— Pour about a wineglassful of *boiling* water into a half-pint tumbler, and sweeten according to taste. Stir well up, then put in a wineglassful of whisky, and add a wineglassful and a half more boiling water. *Be sure the water* is boiling. Never put lemon into toddy. The two in combination, in almost every instance, produce acidity in the stomach. If possible, store your whisky *in the wood*, not in bottles, as keeping it in the cask mellows it, and dissipates the coarser particles.

2059. Raspberry Vinegar.— Put a pound of very fine ripe raspberries in a bowl, *bruise them well*, and pour upon them a quart of the best white wine vinegar; next day strain the liquor

on a pound of fresh ripe raspberries; bruise *them* also, and the following day do the same, *but do not squeeze the fruit, or it will make it ferment;* only drain the liquor as dry as you can from it. Finally, pass it through a canvas bag, previously wet with the vinegar, to prevent waste. Put the juice into a stone jar, with a *pound of sugar*, broken into lumps, to *every pint of juice;* stir, and when melted, put the jar into a pan of water; let it simmer, and skim it; let it cool, then bottle it; when cold it will be fine, and thick, like strained honey, newly prepared.

2060. Ginger Beer.—The following receipt for making a very superior ginger beer is taken from the celebrated treatise of Dr. Pereira on Diet. The honey gives the beverage a peculiar softness, and from not being fermented with yeast, it is less violent in its action when opened, but requires to be kept a somewhat longer time before use. White sugar, five pounds; lemon juice, one quarter of a pint; honey, one quarter of a pound; ginger, bruised, five ounces; water, four gallons and a half. Boil the ginger in three quarts of the water for half an hour, then add the sugar, lemon juice and honey, with the remainder of the water, and strain through a cloth; when cold, add a quarter of the white of an egg, and a small teaspoonful of essence of lemon; let the whole stand four days, and bottle; it will keep for many months. This quantity will make 100 bottles; the cost being, sugar, five pounds, 2s.; lemon juice, 2d.; honey, 3d.; best white ginger, 2d.; egg and essence of lemon, 2d.: total, 2s. 9d. Ginger-beer bottles may be obtained at the potteries at 10s. to 12s. per gross, and corks at 8d. to 1s. per gross.

2061. Ginger Beer. — White sugar, twenty pounds; lemon or lime juice, eighteen (fluid) ounces; honey, one pound; bruised ginger, twenty-two ounces; water, eighteen gallons. Boil the ginger in three gallons of water for half an hour, then add the sugar, the juice, and the honey, with the remainder of the water, and strain through a cloth. When *cold* add the white of one egg, and half an ounce (fluid) of essence of lemon; after standing four days, bottle. This yields a very superior beverage, and one which will keep for many months.

2062. GINGER-BEER POWDERS. —Blue paper; Carbonate of soda, thirty grains: powdered ginger, five grains; ground white sugar, one drachm to one drachm and a half; essence of lemon, one drop. Add the essence to the sugar, then the other ingredients. A quantity should be mixed and divided, as recommended for Seidlitz powders.—White paper: Tartaric acid, thirty grains. *Directions.*— Dissolve the contents of the blue paper in water; stir in the contents of the white paper, and drink during effervescence. Ginger-beer powders do not meet with such general acceptation as lemon and kali, the powdered ginger rendering the liquid slightly turbid.

2063. Lemonade. — Powdered sugar, four pounds; citric or tartaric acid, one ounce; essence of lemon, two drachms: mix well. Two or three teaspoonfuls make a very sweet and agreeable glass of extemporaneous lemonade.

2064. Milk Lemonade.—Dissolve three quarters of a pound of loaf sugar in one pint of boiling water, and mix with them one gill of lemon juice, and one gill of sherry, then add three gills of cold milk. Stir the whole well together, and strain it.

2065. A Lemonade, composed of two bottles of champagne, one bottle of seltzer water, three pomegranates, three lemons, and of sugar *quantum sufficit*, is a *princely beverage* in hot weather; only care must be taken that perspiration is not thereby too much encouraged.

2066. Summer Champagne.— To four parts of seltzer water add one of Moselle wine (or hock), and put a teaspoonful of powdered sugar into a wineglassful of this mixture; an ebulli-

tion takes place, and you have a sort of champagne which is more wholesome in hot weather than the genuine wine known by that name.

2067. Lemon and Kali, or Sherbet.— Large quantities of this wholesome and refreshing preparation are manufactured and consumed every summer; it is sold in bottles, and also as a beverage, made by dissolving a large teaspoonful in a tumbler two-thirds filled with water. Ground white sugar, 7d. to 8d. per pound, half a pound: tartaric acid, at 2s. per pound; carbonate of soda, at 4d. per pound; of each a quarter of a pound: essence of lemon, at 8d. per ounce, forty drops. All the powders should be well dried; add the essence to the sugar, then the other powders; stir all together, and mix by passing twice through a hair sieve. Must be kept in tightly-corked bottles, into which a damp spoon must not be inserted. All the materials may be obtained at a wholesale druggist's; the sugar must be ground, as, if merely powdered, the coarser parts remain undissolved.

2068. Soda Water Powders. —One pound of carbonate of soda, 4d., and thirteen and a half ounces of tartaric acid, at 2s. per pound, supply the materials for 256 powders of each sort. Usual retail price, 1d. for the two powders required for a draught. Put into blue papers thirty grains of carbonate of soda, and into white papers twenty-five grains of tartaric acid. *Directions.*— Dissolve the contents of the blue paper in half a tumbler of water, stir in the other powder, and drink during effervescence. Soda powders furnish a saline beverage which is very slightly laxative, and well calculated to allay the thirst in hot weather.

2069. Seidlitz Powders. — Seidlitz powders are usually put up in two papers. The larger blue paper contains tartarized soda (also called Rochelle salt) two drachms, and carbonate of soda two scruples; in practice it will be found more convenient to mix the two materials in larger quantity by passing them twice through a sieve, and then divide the mixture either by weight or measure, than to make each powder separately. One pound of tartarized soda, at 1s. 2d. per pound, and five ounces and a half of carbonate of soda, at 4d. per pound, will make sixty powders. The smaller powder, usually put up in white paper, consists of tartaric acid, at 2s. per pound, half a drachm. *Directions for Use.*—Dissolve the contents of blue paper in half a tumbler of cold water, stir in the other powder, and drink during effervescence. (*See* SODA WATER POWDERS.)

2070. Economy of Tea. — A given quantity of tea is similar to malt —only imparting strength to a given quantity of water, therefore any additional quantity is waste. Two small teaspoonfuls of good black tea, and one three parts full of green, is sufficient to make three teacupfuls agreeable, the water being put in, in a boiling state, at once; a second addition of water gives a vapid flavour to tea.

2071. In Preparing Tea a good economist will be careful to have the best water, that is, the softest and least impregnated with foreign mixture; for if tea be infused in hard and in soft water, the latter will always yield the greatest quantity of the tannin matter, and will strike the deepest black with sulphate of iron in solution.

2072. Tea-making.—Dr. Kitchiner recommends that all the water necessary should be poured in at once, as the second drawing is bad. When much tea is wanted, it is better to have two teapots instead of two drawings.

2073. Another Method.—The water should be fresh boiled (not exhausted by long boiling). Scald the teapot and empty it; then put in as much water as necessary for the first cups; put the tea on it as in brewing, and close the lid as quickly as possible. Let it stand three minutes and a half, or, if the quantity be large, four minutes, then fill the cups. This is greatly superior to the ordinary method, the aroma being preserved instead of escaping with the steam, as it does when the water is poured on the tea.

2074. Substitute for Cream in Tea or Coffee.—Beat the white of an egg to a froth, put to it a very small lump of butter, and mix well. Then stir it in gradually, so that it may not curdle. If perfectly mixed, it will be an excellent substitute for cream.

2075. In making Coffee, observe that the broader the bottom and the smaller the top of the vessel, the better the coffee will be.

2076. Turkish Mode of Making Coffee.—The Turkish way of making coffee produces a very different result from that to which we are accustomed. A small conical saucepan, with a long handle, and calculated to hold about two tablespoonfuls of water, is the vessel used. The fresh roasted berry is pounded, not ground, and about a dessertspoonful is put into the minute boiler; it is then nearly filled with water, and thrust among the embers. A few seconds suffice to make it boil, and the decoction, grounds and all, is poured out into a small cup, which fits into a brass socket, much like the cup of an acorn, and holding the china cup as that does the acorn itself. The Turks seem to drink this decoction boiling, and swallow the grounds with the liquid. We allow it to remain a minute, in order to leave the sediment at the bottom. It is always taken plain; sugar or cream would be thought to spoil it; and Europeans, after a little practice—(longer, however, than we had)—are said to prefer it to the clear infusion drunk in France. In every hut these coffee boilers may be seen suspended, and the means for pounding the roasted berry are always ready at hand.

2077. Coffee Milk.—(FOR THE SICK-ROOM.)—Boil a dessertspoonful of ground coffee, in nearly a pint of milk, a quarter of an hour, then put into it a shaving or two of isinglass, and clear it; let it boil a few minutes, and set it by the side of the fire to clarify. This is a very fine breakfast; but it should be sweetened with sugar of a good quality.

2078. Iceland Moss Chocolate (FOR THE SICK-ROOM).—Iceland moss has been in the highest repute on the Continent as a most efficacious remedy in incipient pulmonary complaints: combined with chocolate, it will be found a nutritious article of diet, and may be taken as a morning and evening beverage. *Directions.* — Mix a teaspoonful of the chocolate with a teaspoonful of boiling water or milk, stirring it constantly until it is completely dissolved.

2079. Alum Whey.—A pint of cow's milk boiled with two drachms of alum, until a curd is formed. Then strain off the liquor, and add spirit of nutmeg, two ounces; syrup of cloves, an ounce. It is used in diabetes, and in uterine fluxes, &c.

2080. Barley Water. — Pearl barley, two ounces; wash till freed from dust, in cold water. Boil in a quart of water a few minutes, strain off the liquor, and throw it away. Then boil the barley in four pints and a half of water, until it is reduced one half.

2081. Agreeable Effervescent Drink for Heart-burn, &c. — Orange juice (of one orange), water, and lump sugar to flavour, and in proportion to acidity of orange, bicarbonate of soda about half a teaspoonful. Mix orange juice, water, and sugar together in a tumbler, then put in the soda, stir, and the effervescence ensues.

2082. Apple Water.—A tart apple well baked and mashed; on which pour a pint of boiling water. Beat up, cool, and strain. Add sugar if desired. Cooling drink for sick persons.

2083. Tincture of Lemon Peel. —A very easy and economical way of obtaining and preserving the flavour of lemon peel, is to fill a wide-mouthed pint bottle half full of brandy, or proof spirit; and when you use a lemon pare the rind off very thin, and put it into

the brandy, &c.; in a fortnight it will impregnate the spirit with the flavour very strongly.

2084. Camomile Tea. — One ounce of the flowers to a quart of water boiling. Simmer for fifteen minutes and strain. Emetic when taken warm; tonic when cold. Dose, from a wine-glassful to a breakfast-cup.

2085. Plant Skeletons. —The leaves are to be put into an earthen or glass vessel, and a large quantity of rain water to be poured over them; after this they are to be left in the open air and to the heat of the sun, without covering the vessel. As the water evaporates and the leaves become dry, more water must be added; the leaves will by this means putrefy, but the time required for this varies; some plants will be finished in a month, others will require two months or longer, according to the toughness of their parenchyma. When they have been in a state of putrefaction for some time, the two membranes will begin to separate, and the green part of the leaf to become fluid: then the operation of clearing is to be performed. The leaf is to be put upon a flat white earthen plate, and covered with clear water; and being gently squeezed with the finger, the membranes will begin to open, and the green substance will come out at the edges; the membranes must be carefully taken off with the finger, and great caution must be used in separating them near the middle rib. When once there is an opening towards this separation, the whole membrane always follows easily; when both membranes are taken off, the skeleton is finished, and it has to be washed clean with water, and then dried between the leaves of a book. Fruits are divested of their pulp and made into skeletons in a different manner. Take, for an instance, a fine large pear which is soft, and not tough; let it be carefully pared without squeezing it, and without injuring either the crown or the stalk; put it into a pot of rain water, covered, set it over the fire, and let it boil gently till perfectly soft, then take it out and lay it in a dish filled with cold water; then, holding it by the stalk with one hand, rub off as much of the pulp as you can with the finger and thumb, beginning at the stalk and rubbing it regularly towards the crown. The fibres are most tender towards the extremities, and are therefore to be treated with great care there. When the pulp has thus been cleared pretty well off, the point of a fine penknife may be of use to pick away the pulp sticking to the core. In order to see how the operation advances, the soiled water must be thrown away from time to time, and clean poured on in its place. When the pulp is in this manner perfectly separated, the clean skeleton is to be preserved in spirits of wine. This method may be pursued with the bark of trees, which afford interesting views of their constituent fibres.

2086. Skeleton Leaves may be made by steeping leaves in rain water, in an open vessel exposed to the air and sun. Water must occasionally be added to compensate loss by evaporation. The leaves will putrefy, and then their membranes will begin to open; then lay them on a clean white plate, filled with fresh water, and with gentle touches take off the external membranes, separating them cautiously near the middle rib. When there is an opening towards the latter the whole membrane separates easily. The process requires a great deal of patience, as ample time must be given for the vegetable tissues to decay and separate.

2087. A MORE EXPEDITIOUS METHOD.—A tablespoonful of chloride of lime in a liquid state, mixed with a quart of pure spring water. Leaves or seed-vessels of plants to be soaked in the mixture for about four hours, then taken out and well washed in a large basin filled with water, after which they should be left to dry, with free exposure to light and air. Some of the larger species of forest leaves, or such as have strong ribs, will require to be left rather more than four hours in the liquid.

2088. To make Impressions of Leaves.—Prepare two rubbers of wash-leather, made by tying up wool or any other substance in wash-leather; then prepare the colours which you wish the leaves to be, by rubbing up with cold drawn linseed oil the colours you want, as indigo for blue, chrome for yellow, indigo and chrome for green, &c.; get a number of leaves the size and kind you wish to stamp, then dip the rubbers into the paint, and rub them one over the other, so that you may have but a small quantity of the composition upon the rubbers; place a leaf upon one rubber and moisten it gently with the other; take the leaf off and apply it to the substance you wish stamped; upon the leaf place a piece of white paper, press gently, and there will be a beautiful impression of all the veins of the leaf. It will be as well if only one leaf be used at a time. The leaves packed should be of uniform size, otherwise the work will be irregular.

2089. To make a Fac-simile of a Leaf in Copper.—This beautiful experiment can be performed by any person in possession of a common galvanic battery. The process is as follows :—Soften a piece of gutta percha over a candle, or before a fire ; knead it with the moist fingers upon a table, until the surface is perfectly smooth, and large enough to cover the leaf to be copied; lay the leaf flat upon the surface, and press every part well into the gutta percha. In about five minutes the leaf may be removed, when, if the operation has been carefully performed, a perfect impression of the leaf will be made on the gutta percha. This must now be attached to the wire in connection with the zinc end of the battery (which can easily be done by heating the end of the wire, and pressing it into the gutta percha), dusted well over with the best blacklead, with a camel-hair brush—the object of which is to render it a conductor of electricity ; it should then be completely immersed in a saturated solution of sulphate of copper. A piece of copper attached to the

L

wire in connection with the copper end of the battery must also be inserted into the copper solution facing the gutta percha, but not touching it; this not only acts as a conductor to the electricity, but also maintains the solution of copper of a permanent strength. In a short time the copper will be found to creep over the whole surface of the gutta percha, and in about twenty-four hours a thick deposit of copper will be obtained, which may then be detached from the mould. The accuracy with which a leaf may thus be cast is truly surprising. The Editor has in his possession a cast of a hazel leaf made by this process, which nobody would take to be a production of art. Every fibre and nerve, in fact, the minutest part is delineated with the utmost fidelity.

2090. Leaf Printing. — After warming the leaf between the hands, apply printing ink, by means of a small leather ball containing cotton, or some soft substance, or with the end of the finger. The leather ball (and the finger, when used for that purpose), after the ink is applied to it, should be pressed several times on a piece of leather, or some smooth surface, before each application to the leaf, that the ink may be smoothly and evenly applied. After the under surface of the leaf has been sufficiently inked, apply it to the paper where you wish the impression to be; and, after covering it with a slip of paper, use the hand or roller to press upon it.

2091. Directions for Taking Leaf Impressions. — Hold oiled paper in the smoke of a lamp or of pitch, until it becomes coated with the smoke; to this paper apply the leaf of which you wish an impression, having previously warmed it between your hands, that it may be pliable. Place the lower surface of the leaf upon the blackened surface of the oil-paper, that the numerous veins, which are so prominent on this side, may receive from the paper a portion of the smoke. Lay a paper over the leaf, and then press it gently upon the smoked paper with the fingers, or with a small roller (covered with woollen cloth, or some similarly soft material), so that every part of the leaf may come in contact with the sooted oil-paper. A coating of the smoke will adhere to the leaf. Then remove the leaf carefully, and place the blackened surface on a sheet of white paper, not ruled, or in a book prepared for the purpose, covering the leaf with a clean slip of paper, and pressing upon it with the fingers, or roller, as before. Thus may be obtained the impression of a leaf, showing the perfect outlines, together with an accurate exhibition of the veins which extend in every direction through it, more correctly than the finest drawing. And this process is so simple, and the materials so easily obtained, that any person, with a little practice to enable him to apply the right quantity of smoke to the oil-paper, and give the leaf a proper pressure, can prepare beautiful leaf impressions, such as a naturalist would be proud to possess. There is another, and we think a better method of taking *leaf impressions*, than the preceding one. The only difference in the process consists in the use of *printing ink*, instead of smoked oil-paper.

2092. Dry Botanical Specimens for Preservation. — The plants you wish to preserve should be gathered when the weather is dry, and after placing the ends in water, let them remain in a cool place till the next day. When about to be submitted to the process of drying, place each plant between several sheets of blotting paper, and iron it with a large smooth heater, pretty strongly warmed, till all the moisture is dissipated. Colours may thus be fixed, which otherwise become pale, or nearly white. Some plants require more moderate heat than others, and herein consists the nicety of the experiment; but it is generally found that if the iron be not too hot, and is passed rapidly yet carefully over the surface of the blotting paper, it answers the purpose equally well with plants of almost every variety of hue and thickness. In compound flowers, with those also of a stubborn and solid form, as the Centaurea, some little art is required in cutting away the under part, by which means the profile and forms of the flowers will be more distinctly exhibited. This is especially necessary when the method employed by Major Velley is adopted; viz., to fix the flowers and fructification down with gum upon the paper previous to ironing, by which means they become almost incorporated with the surface. When this very delicate process is attempted, blotting-paper should be laid under every part excepting the blossoms, in order to prevent staining the white paper. Great care must be taken to keep preserved specimens in a dry place.

2093. Collecting and Laying-out Sea-weeds.—"First wash the sea-weed in fresh water, then take a plate or dish (the larger the better), cut your paper to the size required, place it in the plate with fresh water, and spread out the plant with a good-sized camel-hair pencil in a natural form (picking out with the pin gives the sea-weed an unnatural appearance, and destroys the characteristic fall of the branches, which should be carefully avoided); then gently raise the paper with the specimen out of the water, placing it in a slanting position for a few moments, so as to allow the superabundant water to run off; after which, place it in the press. The press is made with either three pieces of board or pasteboard. Lay on the first board two sheets of blotting-paper; on that lay your specimens; place straight and smooth over them a piece of old muslin, fine cambric, or linen; then some more blotting-paper, and place another board on the top of that, and continue in the same way. The blotting-paper and the muslin should be carefully removed and dried every day, and then replaced; at the same time, those specimens that are sufficiently dried may be taken away. Nothing now remains but to write on each the name, date, and locality. You can either gum the specimens in a scrap-book, or fix them in, as drawings are often fastened, by making four slits in the page, and inserting each corner. This is by far the best plan, as it admits of their removal, without injury to the page, at any future period, if it be required either to insert better specimens, or intermediate species. Some of the larger algæ will not adhere to the paper, and consequently require gumming. The following method of preserving them has been communicated by a botanical friend:—'After well cleaning and pressing, brush the coarser kinds of algæ over with spirits of turpentine, in which two or three small lumps of gum mastic have been dissolved, by shaking in a warm place; two-thirds of a small phial is the proper proportion, and this will make the specimens retain a fresh appearance.'"—*Miss Gifford's Marine Botanist.*

2094. To Preserve Fungi.—Receipt of the celebrated botanist, William Withering, Esq., by which specimens of fungi may be beautifully preserved. "Take two ounces of sulphate of copper, or blue vitriol, and reduce it to powder; pour upon it a pint of boiling water; and when cold, add half a pint of spirits of wine; cork it well, and call it 'the pickle.' To eight pints of water, add one pint and a half of spirits of wine, and call it 'the liquor.' Be provided with a number of wide-mouthed bottles of different sizes, all well fitted with corks. The fungi should be left on the table as long as possible, to allow the moisture to evaporate; they should then be placed in the pickle for three hours, or longer, if necessary, then place them in the bottles intended for their reception, and fill with the liquor. They should then be well corked and sealed, and arranged in order, with their names in front of the bottles."

2095. To Stuff Birds, Quadrupeds, &c.—Large animals should be carefully skinned, with the horns, skull, tail, hoofs, &c., entire. Then rub the inside of the skin thoroughly with a mixture of salt, pepper, and alum, and hang up to dry. Large birds may be treated in the same way, but should not be put into spirits.

2096. Small Birds may be preserved as follows:—Take out the entrails, open a passage to the brain, which should be scooped out through the mouth; introduce into the cavities of the skull and the whole body, some of the mixture of salt, alum, and pepper, putting some through the gullet and whole length of the neck; then hang the bird in a cool, airy place—first by the feet, that the body may be impregnated by the salt, and afterwards by a thread through the under mandible of the bill, till it appears to be free from smell; then hang it in the sun, or near a fire: after it is well dried, clean out what remains loose of the mixture, and fill the cavity of the body with wool, oakum, or any soft substance, and pack it smooth in paper.

2097. Birds' Eggs.—In selecting eggs for a cabinet, always choose those which are newly laid; make a medium-sized hole at the sharp end with a pointed instrument, and one at the blunt end; let this last hole be as small as possible; this done, apply your mouth to the blunt end, and blow the contents through the sharp end. If the yolk will not come freely, run a pin or wire up into the egg, and stir the yolk well about; now get a cupful of water, and immersing the sharp end of the shell into it, apply your mouth to the blunt end and suck up some of the water into the empty shell; then put your finger and thumb upon the two holes, shake the water well within, and after this, blow it out. The water will clear your egg of any remains of yolk or of white which may stay in after blowing. If one injection of water will not suffice, make a second or third. An egg, immediately after it is produced, is very clear and fine; but by staying in the nest, and coming in contact with the feet of the bird, it

soon assumes a dirty appearance. To remedy this, wash it well in soap and water, and use a nail-brush to get the dirt off. The eggshell is now as it ought to be, and nothing remains to be done but to prevent the thin white membrane (which is still inside) from corrupting. Take a wineglass and fill it with a solution of corrosive sublimate in alcohol, then immerse the sharp end of the eggshell into it, keeping your finger and thumb, as you hold it, just clear of the solution; apply your mouth to the little hole at the blunt end, and suck up some of the solution into the shell; you need not be fearful of getting the liquor into your mouth, for as soon as it rises in the shell the cold will strike your finger and thumb, and then you cease sucking; shake the shell just as you did when the water was in it, and then blow the solution back into the glass. The eggshell will now be beyond the reach of corruption; the membrane for ever retains its pristine whiteness, and no insect, for the time to come, will ever venture to prey upon it. If you wish your egg to appear extremely brilliant, give it a coat of mastic varnish, put on very sparingly with a camel-hair pencil: green or blue eggs must be done with gum arabic; the mastic varnish is apt to injure the colour.

2098. Fishes.—Large fishes should be opened in the belly, the entrails taken out, and the inside well rubbed with pepper, and stuffed with oakum. Small fishes may be put in spirit, as well as reptiles, worms, and insects (except butterflies and moths); insects of fine colours should be pinned down in a box prepared for that purpose, with their wings expanded.

2099. Tracing Paper. — Mix together by a gentle heat, one ounce of Canada balsam, and a quarter of a pint of spirits of turpentine; with a soft brush spread it thinly over one side of good tissue paper. It dries quickly, is very transparent, and is not greasy, therefore does not stain the object upon which it may be placed.

2100. Impressions from Coins. —Melt a little isinglass glue with brandy, and pour it thinly over the medal, &c., so as to cover its whole surface; let it remain on for a day or two, till it has thoroughly dried and hardened, and then take it off, when it will be fine, clear, and hard, and will present a very elegant impression of the coin. It will also resist the effects of damp air, which occasions all other kinds of glue to soften and bend if not prepared in this way.

2101. Method of Hardening Objects in Plaster of Paris.— Take two parts of stearine, two parts of Venetian soap, one part of pearlash, and twenty-four to thirty parts of a solution of caustic potash. The stearine and soap are cut into slices, mixed with the cold ley, and boiled for about half an hour, being constantly stirred. Whenever the mass rises, a little cold ley is added. The pearlash, previously moistened with a little rain water, is then added, and the whole boiled for a few minutes. The mass is then stirred until cold, when it is mixed with so much cold ley that it becomes perfectly liquid, and runs off the spoon without coagulating and contracting. Previously to using this composition, it should be kept for several days well covered. It may be preserved for years. Before applying it to the objects, they should be well dusted, the stains scraped away, and then coated, by means of a thick brush, with the wash, as long as the plaster of Paris absorbs it, and left to dry. The coating is then dusted with leather, or a soft brush. If the surface has not become shining, the operation must be repeated.

2102. Modelling in Cork, Gutta Percha, Leather, Paper, Plaster of Paris, Wax, Wood, &c.—Modelling, in a general sense, signifies the art of constructing an original pattern, which is to be ultimately carried out on an enlarged scale, or copied exactly.

2103. WHEN MODELS ARE CONSTRUCTED to give a miniature representation of any great work, elevation, or topographical information, they are executed in detail, with all the original parts in just and due proportions, so that the work may be conducted or comprehended better; and if the model is a scientific one, viz., relating to machinery, physical science, &c., then it requires to be even still more accurate in its details. In fact, all models should be constructed on a scale, which should be appended to them, so that a better idea may be obtained of the proportions and dimensions.

2104. THE MATERIALS REQUIRED are plaster of Paris, wax, whiting, putty, clay, pipeclay; common and factory cinders; sand of various colours; powdered fluor spar, oyster-shells, bricks, and slate; gums, acacia and tragacanth; starch; paper, white and brown, cardboard and millboard; cork sheets, cork raspings, and old bottle-corks; gutta percha; leather and leather chips; wood; paints, oil, water, and varnish; moss, lichen, ferns, and grass; talc, window and looking-glass; muslin and net; chenille; carded wool; tow; wire; hay and straw; various varnishes, glue and cements.

2105. THE TOOLS consist of brushes for paints, varnishes, and cements; two or three bradawls; a sharp penknife; a chisel, hammer, and punches; scissors, and pencil.

2106. CAVES MAY BE MODELLED readily in cork, wood, starch-paste, or cinders covered with brown paper soaked in thin glue.

2107. TO CONSTRUCT THEM OF CINDERS.—Arrange the cinders, whether common or factory, in such a manner as to resemble the intended design; then cover in such parts as require it with brown paper soaked in thin glue until quite pulpy. When nearly dry, dust over with sand, powdered brick, slate, and chopped lichen or moss, from a pepper-box; touch up the various parts with either oil, water, or varnish colours; and if necessary, form your trees of wire, covered with brown paper and moss, glued on.

2108. When a Cave is constructed in the way we have pointed out, on a large scale, and the interior sprinkled with powdered fluor spar or glass, the effect is very good by candle-light.

2109. Stalactites may be represented by rough pieces of wood, which must be smeared with glue, and sprinkled with powdered fluor spar, or glass.

2110. To model Caves in Cork.—Construct the framework of wood, and fill up the outline with old bottle-corks. The various projections, recesses, and other minutiæ, must be affixed afterwards with glue, after being formed of cork, or hollowed out in the necessary parts, either by burning with a hot wire and scraping it afterwards, or by means of a sharp-pointed bradawl.

2111. If small Cork Models are constructed, the trees should be formed by transfixing short pieces of shaded chenille with a fine wire (.), and sticking them into the cork.

2112. Various Parts of the Model must be touched up with oil, water, or varnish colours; and powdered brick, slate, and chopped lichen, or moss, dusted on as usual.

2113. Wooden Models are Constructed roughly in deal, according to the proper design, and the various fine parts afterwards affixed with glue or brads.

2114. In Forming the Finer Parts of the wooden model, a vast amount of unnecessary labour may be saved, and a better effect obtained, by burning much of the outline, instead of carving it. By this plan, deeper tones of colouring, facility of operating, and saving of time and labour, are the result.

2115. In common with other Models, those constructed of wood require the aid of lichen, moss, powdered slate, &c., and colours, to complete the effect.

2116. When Water issues from the original cave, and it is desirable to copy it in the model, a piece of looking-glass should be glued on the stand, and the edges surrounded by glue, and paper covered with sand. Sometimes it is requisite to cut away the wood of the stand, so as to let in the looking-glass; this, however, is only when the water is supposed to be much lower than the surface of the land.

2117. Starch-Paste Models are formed in the usual way, of the following composition:—Soak gum tragacanth in water, and when soft, mix it with powdered starch till of a proper consistence. It is much improved by adding some double-refined sugar finely powdered. When the model is finished, it must be coloured correctly, and varnished with white varnish, or left plain. This is the composition used by confectioners for modelling the various ornaments on cakes.

2118. Ancient Cities may be constructed of cork or starch-paste, in the same manner as directed above; bearing in mind the necessity for always working models according to a scale, which should be afterwards affixed to the stand of the model.

2119. Modern Cities are better made of cardboard, starch-paste, or pipe-clay; the houses, public buildings, and other parts being constructed according to scale.

2120. Houses should be cut out of a long thin strip of cardboard, partially divided by three strokes of a penknife, and glued together; this must afterwards be marked with a pencil, or pen and ink, to represent the windows, doors, stones, &c.; and the roof—cut out of a piece of square cardboard, equally and partially divided—is then to be glued on, and the chimney—formed of a piece of lucifer-match, or wood notched at one end and flat at the other—is to be glued·on. A square piece of cardboard must be glued on the top of the chimney; a hole made with a pin in the card and wood; and a piece of grey worsted, thinned at the end, fixed into the hole for smoke.

2121. Cathedrals, Churches, and other Public Buildings are made in the same way; but require the addition of small chips of wood, ends of lucifer matches, cork raspings, or small pieces of cardboard, for the various ornaments, if on a large scale, but only a pencil-mark if small.

2122. When constructed of Starch-Paste, or pipeclay, the material is rolled flat on a table or marble slab, and the various sides cut out with a sharp penknife; they are then gummed together, and coloured properly.

2123. If large Models of Houses or buildings are made, the windows are constructed of talc or thin glass, covered with net or muslin. The frames of the windows are made of cardboard, neatly cut out with a sharp penknife.

2124. Countries should be made of Cork, because it is easier to work. Although the starch-paste is very agreeable to model with, yet it is liable to shrink, and therefore, when in the mass, one part dries quicker than another, so that there is not equal contraction—a great objection to its employment in accurate models. Cork, on the contrary, may be easily cut into all forms, and from abounding with pores, it is remarkably light—no little consideration to travellers.

2125. Topographical Models may, however, be formed of plaster of Paris, but the weight is an objection. We have lately constructed a model of a country on a moderate scale—one-eighth of an inch to a square mile—with its mountains, valleys, and towns, and it was done in this manner:—A model was first made in clay, according to scale and plan; a mould was taken of various parts in gutta percha, rendered soft by dipping it into hot water, and the parts cast in paper cement.

2126. Paper Cement.—i. Reduce paper to a smooth paste by boiling it in water; then add an equal weight each of sifted whiting and good size; boil to a proper consistence, and use. ii. Take equal parts of paper, paste, and size, sufficient finely-powdered plaster of Paris to make into a good paste, and use as soon as possible after it is mixed. This composition may be used to cast architectural ornaments, busts,

statues, &c., being very light, and receiving a good polish, but it will not stand weather.

2127. The several Mountains and other parts being formed, join them together in their proper places with some of the No. i. paper cement, rendered rather more fluid by the addition of a little thin glue. The towns are made of a piece of cork, cut and scratched to the form of the town; steeples of cardboard, and trees of blades of moss. Sand is sprinkled in one part; looking-glass in others, for the lakes, bays, and rivers; and green baize flock for the verdant fields.

2128. Monuments, Ancient or Modern, are better constructed of cork, on account of the lightness and facility in working, the more especially the ancient ones. We once constructed a model of the Acropolis of Athens in cork, which was completed in one-fifth the time occupied by other materials, and looked much better; and have lately been at work upon others representing the ancient monuments of Egypt.

2129. Ruins should be constructed of cork, according to the directions we have given, and when it is necessary to represent the mouldering walls covered with moss or ivy, a little green baize flock, or moss chippings, should be attached by mucilage to the part; and oftentimes a brush of raw sienna, combined with varnish, requires to be laid underneath the moss or flock, in order to improve the effect. Prostrate columns and huge blocks are effectively represented in cork, and should be neatly cut out with a sharp knife, and the various parts supposed to be destroyed by age picked away with a pin or blunt knife afterwards.

2130. Cities and Temples.—We will suppose that the model is to represent the Temple of Theseus, at Athens, which was built by Cimon, the son of Miltiades. In the first place we must obtain the necessary dimensions, and then, reducing the number of feet to fractional parts of an inch, form a scale suitable for carrying out the whole. A piece of wood of the necessary size is procured, the plan marked out in pencil, and the ground on which it stands imitated in cork, by cutting away the parts that are not required with a sharp penknife, and adding others with glue. The floor of the temple is now to be glued on with common glue, for we should remark that the liquid glue does not dry quickly enough for cork modelling, and is not so good as the old plan; the sides and ends are formed of cork sheets, marked with a lead pencil to represent the blocks of stone; and ruined and broken parts imitated, by pricking the cork with a blunt penknife or needle. The frieze, representing the battle between the Centaur and Lapithæ, and the metopes in mezzo-relievo, containing a mixture of the labours of Hercules and Theseus, should be drawn upon the sheets of cork according to scale, and coloured with a little lampblack and raw sienna, to represent the subject intended; if the scale is small, or if the model admits of it, the groups may be neatly carved with a sharp penknife from the cork, which has been previously outlined with pencil. The next thing we shall have to do is to strengthen the interior of the model, and this is done by glueing small pieces of cork, at irregular intervals, at the angles formed by the junction of any parts; these are put on the inside, and lastly, the roof is affixed. Any parts that require to be coloured, must be touched up with varnish or water colours, and lichen, &c., affixed with mucilage where it is requisite.

2131. To Model from Living Objects.—We will imagine that the reader desires to model the features of some friend, and as there is some difficulty in the matter, on account of the person operated upon having a natural tendency to distort the features when the liquid plaster is poured upon the face, and some danger of suffocation if the process is not well managed, we will proceed at once to describe the various stages of operating :—

2132. Mix the Plaster of Paris with warm water, and have it about as thick as cream, but do not mix it until all is ready. Lay the friend upon his back, and having raised his head to the natural position when walking, by means of a pillow of bran or sand, cover the parts intended to be cast with oil of almonds or olives, applied by means of a feather, brush, or lump of cotton: plug the ears with cotton or wool, and insert two quills into the nostrils, and plug the space between each quill and the nostril very carefully with cotton.

2133. Cover the Face with the Plaster, beginning at the upper part of the forehead, and spread it downwards over the eyes, which should be kept *firmly* closed, but not in such a manner as to produce any distortion by too violent compression—and continue the plaster as far as the lower border of the chin; cover that part of the chest and arms that is to be represented, and carry the plaster upwards, so as to join the cast of the face; then carefully remove each, and season for casting, by soaking or brushing with linseed oil boiled with sugar of lead or litharge. Some persons boil the moulds in the oil; and many, instead of casting the face in one piece, and the chest in another, lay threads across the face and up and down it, leaving the ends out. As the plaster sets, or is nearly set, the threads are pulled through, so as to divide the cast into four, five, or more pieces.

2134. The Back Part of the Head is moulded by having an oval trencher sort of vessel, deeper than half the head, and generally made of plaster, and boiled in oil. The back of the head being oiled, and this trencher partially filled with liquid plaster of Paris, the head is lowered into it, and the cast taken. The back of the neck is cast with the person turned over on his face.

2135. Each Part of the Mould is marked so as to admit of its corresponding part; sometimes with a ✕ or ‖, which, passing over the junction of two pieces, serves to distinguish them.

2136. To Model the Face, join

the several pieces, and tie them together with twine; then wrap some rag round the joints, to prevent the plaster oozing out, and pour in the plaster, made tolerably fluid, taking care to oil the inside of the mould very carefully first. When the outer part of the mould is nearly set, scoop out the centre with a spoon, and let the whole dry; then remove the strings, &c., and smooth off the edges of the joints upon the model with a sharp penknife, and carve out the eyes from the mass, otherwise they will appear as if closed.

2137. WAX MODELS MAY BE MADE from the moulds used for the plaster; but when the wax sets at the outside to about one-eighth of an inch, the rest should be poured out of the mould; or, a smaller portion being poured in, it may be shaken about the inside of the mould until it is coated. The pieces are removed, and the seams trimmed up, as in the plaster cast.

2138. IF A CAST BE MADE IN GUTTA PERCHA from the model in plaster—or, what is still better, in fusible metal,—then, by pressing basil leather, moistened with water, into the mould, and strengthening the back and centre with chips of wood, affixed by liquid glue, a very nice model may be obtained in leather, which, when varnished, will look like oak carving—the more especially if it be stained with Stephens's Oak Stain.

2139. RUSTIC WORK, SEATS, &c., may be constructed of wire twisted to the proper shape and size, and then covered with gutta percha, rendered soft by being dipped in hot water. The gutta percha should be twisted round the wire previously warmed, and gently heated over a spirit lamp, or dipped again into hot water, so as to allow the various parts to be covered with it. When the model is finished, it should be touched up here and there with oil colours—green, yellow, sienna, and Venetian red—according to fancy, and the effect produced will be very good.

2140. Dr. Clark's Pills for Nervous Headache. — Socotrine

aloes, powdered rhubarb, of each one drachm; compound powder of cinnamon, one scruple; hard soap, half a drachm; syrup enough to form the mass. To be divided into fifty pills, of which two will be sufficient for a dose; to be taken occasionally.

2141. Pains in the Head and Face.—A friend assures us that he was cured of a severe attack of tic-douloureux by the following simple remedy:—Take half a pint of rose water, add two teaspoonfuls of white vinegar, to form a lotion. Apply it to the part affected three or four times a day. It requires fresh linen and lotion at each application; this will, in two or three days, gradually take the pain away.

2142. Sore Throat.—Those subject to sore throat will find the following preparation simple, cheap, and highly efficacious when used in the early stage: Pour a pint of boiling water upon twenty-five or thirty leaves of common sage; let the infusion stand for half an hour. Add vinegar sufficient to make it moderately acid, and honey according to the taste. This combination of the astringent and the emollient principle seldom fails to produce the desired effect. The infusion must be used as a gargle several times a day. It has this advantage over many gargles—it is pleasant to the taste, and may be swallowed occasionally, not only without danger, but with advantage.

2143. Deafness. — Take three drops of sheep's gall, warm, and drop it into the ear on going to bed. The ear must be thoroughly syringed with warm soap and water in the morning. The gall must be applied for three successive nights. It is only efficacious when the deafness is produced by cold. The most convenient way of warming the gall is by holding it in a silver spoon over the flame of a candle. The above remedy has been frequently tried with perfect success.

2144. A Cure for Weak and Sore Eyes.—Sulphate of zinc, three grains; tincture of opium, ten drops;

water, two ounces. To be applied three or four times a day.

2145. Squinting. — Squinting frequently arises from the unequal strength of the eyes, the weaker eye being turned away from the object, to avoid the fatigue of exertion. Cases of squinting of long standing have often been cured by covering the stronger eye, and thereby compelling the weaker one to exertion.

2146. Pills for Gout and Rheumatism. — Acetic extract of colchicum, two grains; powdered ipecacuanha, four grains; compound extract of colocynth, half a drachm; blue pill, four grains. Divide into twelve pills; one to be taken night and morning.

2147. Dr. Birt Davies' Gout Mixture.—Wine of colchicum, one ounce; spirit of nitrous ether, one ounce; iodide of potassium, two scruples; distilled water, two ounces, Mix: a teaspoonful in camomile tea two or three times a day.

2148. Col. Birch's Receipt for rheumatic gout or acute rheumatism, commonly called the CHELSEA PENSIONER.—Half an ounce of nitre (saltpetre), half an ounce of sulphur, half an ounce of flour of mustard, half an ounce of Turkey rhubarb, quarter of an ounce of powdered gum guaiacum. Mix: a teaspoonful to be taken every other night for three nights, and omit three nights, in a wineglassful of cold water,—water which has been well boiled.

2149. To Arrest Bleeding at the Nose.—Introduce, by means of a probe, a small piece of lint or soft cotton, previously dipped into some mild styptic, as a solution of alum, white vitriol, creosote, or even cold water. This will generally succeed; but should it not, cold water may be snuffed up the nostrils. Should the bleeding be very profuse, medical advice should be procured.

2150. Biting the Nails.—This is a habit that should be immediately corrected in children, as, if persisted in for any length of time, it permanently deforms the nails. Dipping the finger-ends in some bitter tincture will generally prevent children from putting them in their mouth; but if this fails, as it sometimes will, each finger-end ought to be encased in a stall until the propensity is eradicated.

2151. To Prevent Galling in Invalids.—The white of an egg beaten to a strong froth; then drop in gradually, whilst you are beating, two teaspoonfuls of spirits of wine; put it into a bottle, and apply occasionally with a feather.

2152. Jaundice. — One pennyworth of allspice, ditto of flowers of brimstone, ditto of turmeric; these to be well pounded together, and afterwards to be mixed with half a pound of treacle. Two tablespoonfuls to be taken every day.

2153. Convulsions.—An eminent surgeon reports an interesting and remarkable case, in which he saved the life of an infant in convulsions, by the use of chloroform. He commenced the use of it at nine o'clock one evening, at which period the child was rapidly sinking, numerous remedies having been already tried without effect. He dropped half a drachm of chloroform into a thin muslin handkerchief, and held it about an inch from the infant's face. In about two minutes the convulsions gave way, and the child fell into a sleep. By slightly releasing the child from the influence of the chloroform, he was able to administer food, by which the child was nourished and strengthened. The chloroform was continually administered, in the manner described, from Friday evening at nine o'clock until Monday morning at nine. This treatment lasted sixty hours, and sixteen ounces of chloroform were used. The operator says he has no doubt that the chloroform was instrumental in saving the infant's life, and that no injurious effects, however trivial, from the treatment adopted, have subsequently appeared.

2154. Asthma.—The following is recommended as a relief:—Two ounces of the best honey, and one ounce of castor oil, mixed. A teaspoonful to be taken night and morning.

2155. Coughs.—It is said that a small piece of resin dipped in the water which is placed in a vessel on a stove (not an open fireplace), will add a peculiar property to the atmosphere of the room, which will give great relief to persons troubled with a cough. The heat of the stove is sufficient to throw off the aroma of the resin, and gives the same relief that is afforded by the combustion, because the evaporation is more durable. The same resin may be used for weeks.

2156. For a Cough.—Syrup of poppies, oxymel of squills, simple oxymel, in equal parts, mixed, and a teaspoonful taken when the cough is troublesome. It is best to have it made up by a chemist. The cost is trifling.

2157. A Mixture for a Bad Cold and Cough.—Solution of acetate of ammonia, two ounces; ipecacuanha wine, two drachms; antimony wine, two drachms; solution of muriate of morphine, half a drachm; treacle, four drachms; water, add eight ounces. Two tablespoonfuls to be taken three times a day.

2158. Pills for a Bad Cough.—Compound ipecacuanha powder, half a drachm; fresh dried squills, ten grains; ammoniacum, ten grains; sulphate of quinine, six grains; treacle, sufficient quantity to make a mass. Divide into twelve pills; one to be taken night and morning.

2159. Hooping Cough. — Dissolve a scruple of salt of tartar in a quarter pint of water; add to it ten grains of cochineal; sweeten it with sugar. Give to an infant a fourth part of a tablespoonful four times a day; two years old, half a spoonful; from four years, a tablespoonful. Great care is required in the administration of medicines to infants. We can assure paternal inquirers that the foregoing may be depended upon.

2160. Roche's Embrocation for Hooping Cough.—Olive oil, two ounces; oil of amber, one ounce; oil of cloves, one drachm. Mix: to be rubbed on the chest at bedtime. Cost: olive oil, 1s. per pint; oil of amber, 6s. per pound; oil of cloves, 1s. per ounce.

2161. Offensive Breath. — For this purpose, almost the only substance that should be admitted at the toilette is the concentrated solution of chloride of soda; from six to ten drops of it in a wineglassful of pure spring water, taken immediately after the operations of the morning are completed. In some cases, the odour arising from carious teeth is combined with that of the stomach. If the mouth be well rinsed with a teaspoonful of the solution of the chloride in a tumbler of water, the bad odour of the teeth will be removed.

2162. Breath tainted by Onions.—Leaves of parsley, eaten with vinegar, will prevent the disagreeable consequences of eating onions.

2163. Dr. Babington's Mixture for Indigestion.—Infusion of calumba, six ounces; carbonate of potass, one drachm. Compound tincture of gentian, three drachms. Mix. *Dose*, two or three tablespoonfuls daily at noon.

2164. Ointment for Sore Nipples.—Take of tincture of tolu, two drachms; spermaceti ointment, half an ounce; powdered gum, two drachms. Mix: make an ointment. The white of an egg mixed with brandy is the best application for sore nipples; the person should at the same time use a nipple shield.

2165. Ointment for the Piles, or Hæmorrhoids.—Take of hogs' lard, four ounces; camphor, two drachms; powdered galls, one ounce; laudanum, half an ounce. Mix: make an ointment, to be applied every night at bedtime.

2166. Ointment for Broken Chilblains or Chapped Hands, &c.—Sweet oil, one pint; Venice turpentine, three ounces; hogs' lard, half a pound; bees' wax, three ounces. Put all into a pipkin over a slow fire, and stir it with a wooden spoon till the bees' wax is all melted, and the ingredients simmer. It is fit for use as soon as cold, but the longer it is kept the better it will be. It must be spread very thin on soft rag, or (for chaps or cracks) rubbed on the hands when you go to bed. A visitor to a large poor district has never known this to fail.

2167. Camphor Balls to prevent Chaps.—Melt three drachms of spermaceti, four drachms of white wax, with one ounce of almond oil, and stir in three drachms of camphor (previously powdered by moistening it with a little spirits of wine); pour small quantities into small gallipots, so as to turn out in the form of cakes. Spermaceti, 2s. per pound; white wax, 2s. 2d. per pound; almond oil, 1s. 6d. per pound; camphor, 2s. 8d. per pound.

2168. Cramp in Bathing.—For the cure of the cramp when swimming, Dr. Franklin recommends a vigorous and violent shock of the part affected, by suddenly and forcibly stretching out the leg, which should be darted out of the water into the air if possible.

2169. Cramp in the Legs.—Stretch out the heel of the leg as far as possible, at the same time drawing up the toes as far as possible. This will often stop a fit of the cramp after it has commenced.

2170. Hiccough, or Hiccup.—This is a spasm of the diaphragm, caused by flatulency, indigestion, or acidity. It may be relieved by the sudden application of cold, also by two or three mouthfuls of cold water, by eating a small piece of ice, taking a pinch of snuff, or anything that excites counter action.

2171. Scratches. — Trifling as scratches often seem, they ought never to be neglected, but should be covered and protected, and kept clean and dry, until they have completely healed. If there is the least appearance of inflammation, no time should be lost in applying a large bread and water poultice, or hot flannels repeatedly applied; or even leeches in good numbers may be put on, at some distance from each other.

2172. Ringworm.—The head is to be washed twice a day with soft soap and warm soft water; when dried, the places to be rubbed with a piece of linen rag dipped in ammonia from gas tar; the patient should take a little sulphur and treacle, or some other gentle aperient, every morning; brushes and combs should be washed every day, and the ammonia kept tightly corked.

2173. Ointment for Scurf in the Heads of Infants.—Lard, two ounces; sulphuric acid, diluted, two drachms; rub them together, and anoint the head once a day.

2174. Scurf in the Head.—A simple and effectual remedy. Into a pint of water drop a lump of fresh quicklime, the size of a walnut; let it stand all night, then pour the water off clear from sediment or deposit, add a quarter of a pint of the best vinegar, and wash the head with the mixture. Perfectly harmless; only wet the roots of the hair.

2175. To Restore Hair when removed by Ill-health or Age.—Onions rubbed frequently on the part requiring it. The stimulating powers of this vegetable are of service in restoring the tone of the skin, and assisting the capillary vessels in sending forth new hair; but it is not infallible. Should it succeed, however, the growth of these new hairs may be assisted by the oil of myrtle-berries, the repute of which, perhaps, is greater than its real efficacy. These applications are cheap and harmless, even where they do no good; qualities which cannot be attributed to the numerous quack remedies that meet the eye in every direction.

2176. Baldness.—The decoction of boxwood, successful in cases of baldness, is thus made:—Take of the common box, which grows in garden borders, stems and leaves four large handfuls; boil in three pints of water, in a closely covered vessel, for a quarter of an hour, and let it stand in a covered earthenware jar for ten hours or more: strain, and add an ounce and a half of eau-de

Cologne, or lavender water, to make it keep. The head should be well washed with this solution every morning.

2177. Liquid for the Cure and Prevention of Baldness.—Eau-de-Cologne, two ounces; tincture of cantharides, two drachms; oil of rosemary, oil of nutmeg, and oil of lavender, each ten drops. To be rubbed on the bald part of the head every night.

2178. Remedy for Rheumatism, Lumbago, Sprains, Bruises, Chilblains (before they are broken), **and Bites of Insects.**—One raw egg well beaten, half a pint of vinegar, one ounce of spirits of turpentine, a quarter of an ounce of spirits of wine, a quarter of an ounce of camphor. These ingredients to be beaten well together, then put in a bottle and shaken for ten minutes, after which, to be corked down tightly to exclude the air. In half an hour it is fit for use. *Directions.*—To be well rubbed in, two, three, or four times a day. For rheumatism in the head, to be rubbed at the back of the neck and behind the ears.

2179. Excellent Remedy for Sprains.—Put the white of an egg into a saucer; keep stirring it with a piece of alum about the size of a walnut, until it becomes a thick jelly; apply a portion of it on a piece of lint or tow large enough to cover the sprain, changing it for a fresh one as often as it feels warm or dry: the limb is to be kept in a horizontal position by placing it on a chair.

2180. Remedy for Blistered Feet.—Rub the feet, on going to bed, with spirits mixed with tallow, dropped from a lighted candle into the palm of the hand.

2181. Biles or Boils.—These should be brought to a head by warm poultices of camomile flowers, or boiled white lily root, or onion root; by fermentation with hot water, or by stimulating plasters. When ripe, they should be discharged by a needle, or the lancet. But this should not be attempted until they are fully proved. Constitutional treatment:—Peruvian bark, and port wine, and sea bathing are desirable. Purgatives, diuretics, &c.

2182. Bunions may be checked in their early development by binding the joint with adhesive plaster, and keeping it on as long as any uneasiness is felt. The bandaging should be perfect, and it might be well to extend it round the foot. An inflamed bunion should be poulticed, and larger shoes be worn. Iodine, twelve grains; lard or spermaceti ointment, half an ounce, makes a capital ointment for bunions. It should be rubbed on gently twice or thrice a day.

2183. Cure of Warts.—One of the surgeons of St. Bartholomew's Hospital says, "the easiest way to get rid of warts is to pare off the thickened skin which covers the prominent wart; cut it off by successive layers; shave it till you come to the surface of the skin, and till you draw blood in two or three places. When you have thus denuded the surface of the skin, rub the part thoroughly over with *lunar caustic*, and one effective operation of this kind will generally destroy the wart; if not, you cut off the black spot which has been occasioned by the caustic, and apply it again, or you may apply *acetic acid*, and thus you will get rid of it."

2184. Corns.—Boil a potato in its skin, and after it is boiled take the skin and put the inside of it to the corn, and leave it on for about twelve hours; at the end of that period the corn will be much better. The above useful and simple receipt has been tried and found to effect a remedy.

2185. A Positive Cure for Corns.—The strongest acetic acid, applied night and morning with a camel-hair brush. In one week the corn, whether soft or hard, will disappear.

2186. Method of curing the Stings of Bees and Wasps.—The sting of a bee is generally more virulent than that of a wasp, and with some people attended with very violent effects. The sting of a bee is barbed at the end, and consequently, always left in the wound; that of a wasp is pointed only, so that they can sting more than once, which a bee cannot do. When any person is stung by a bee, let the sting, in the first place, be instantly pulled out; for the longer it remains in the wound, the deeper it will pierce, owing to its peculiar form, and emit more of the poison. The sting is hollow, and the poison flows through it, which is the sole cause of the pain and inflammation. The pulling out of the sting should be done carefully, and with a steady hand; for if any part of it breaks in, all remedies then, in a great measure, will be ineffectual. When the sting is extracted, suck the wounded part, if possible, and very little inflammation, if any, will ensue. If hartshorn drops are immediately afterwards rubbed on the part, the cure will be more complete. All notions of the efficacy of sweet oil, bruised parsley, burnet, tobacco, &c., appear, on various trials, to be totally groundless. On some people, the sting of bees and wasps has no effect; it is therefore of little consequence what remedy they apply to the wound. However, the effect of stings greatly depends on the habit of body a person is of; at one time a sting may take little or no effect, though no remedy is used, which at another time will be very virulent on the same person. We have had occasion to test this remedy several times, and can safely avouch its efficacy. The exposure to which persons are subjected during the hot summer months will, no doubt, render this advice useful, its very simplicity making it more acceptable.

2187. The Sting of a Nettle may be cured by rubbing the part with rosemary, mint, or sage leaves.

2188. Arnica for Bites. — A correspondent of the *Times* says:— "Noticing in your paper an account of the death of a man from the bite of a cat, I beg to trouble you with the following case, which occurred to myself about three weeks ago :—I took a strange dog home, which produced consternation among the cats. One of them I took

up, to effect a reconciliation between her and the dog. In her terror, she bit me so severely on the first finger of the left hand, as not only to cause four of the teeth of her lower jaw to enter the flesh, but so agonizing was her bite that the pressure of her palate caused the finger to swell at the joint on the opposite side to where the lower teeth entered the finger. In a minute or two the pain was about as excruciating as anything I ever felt—certainly greater than I have suffered from a wound. I got some tincture of arnica, diluted with about twelve times the quantity of water, and proceeded to bathe the finger well with it. In about half a minute the blood began to flow freely, the pain ceased, and the swelling abated, and up to this moment I have had no further inconvenience or pain, not even soreness."

2189. Cure for Burns.—Of all applications for a burn, we believe that there are none equal to a simple covering of common *wheat flour*. This is always at hand; and while it requires no skill in using, it produces most astonishing effects. The moisture produced upon the surface of a slight or deep burn is at once absorbed by the flour, and forms a paste which shuts out the air. As long as the fluid matters continue flowing, they are absorbed, and prevented from producing irritation, as they would do if kept from passing off by oily or resinous applications, while the greater the amount of those absorbed by the flour, the thicker the protective covering. Another advantage of the flour covering is, that next to the surface it is kept moist and flexible. It can also be readily washed off, without further irritation in removing. It may occasionally be washed off very carefully, when it has become matted and dry, and a new covering be sprinkled on.

2190. Remedy for Burns and Scalds.—Take chalk and linseed, or common olive oil, and mix them in such proportions as will produce a compound as thick as thin honey; then add vinegar so as to reduce it to the thickness of treacle; apply with a soft brush or feather, and renew the application from time to time. Each renewal brings fresh relief, and a most grateful coolness. If the injury is severe, especially if it involve the chest, give ten drops of laudanum to an adult, and repeat it in an hour, and again a third time. To a child of ten years give, in like manner, only three drops; and beware of giving any to an infant. This plan, with an internal stimulant, according to age, as brandy or sal volatile, or both, should be at once adopted, until the arrival of the medical attendant.

2191. Lime Water beaten up with sweet oil is an excellent application for burns.

2192. Pitting in Small Pox.— The usual mode consists in painting the pustules and skin with a solution of India-rubber in chloroform. An "M.D.," writing on this subject, says,—"I cannot help thinking that this proceeding, if carried to any considerable extent, would prove highly injurious, if not actually dangerous, by suppressing the natural exudation from the skin. A much simpler process has been for many years in use in America and Germany, in the latter of which countries it was first introduced by a Dr. Schonlein, of Hanover. I have myself adopted it most successfully, not only in the few cases of small pox that have come under my observation, but in all eruptive (exanthematous) diseases generally, such as measles, scarlatina, nettle-rash, chicken pox, &c., and have invariably found that it not only relieved the itching, tingling, and irritation of those complaints, thereby affording great relief, especially in the case of children, but that it completely prevented the pitting of small pox. It consists in smearing the whole surface of the body, after the eruption is fairly out, with bacon fat; and the simplest way of employing it is to boil thoroughly a small piece of bacon with the skin on, and when cold to cut off the skin with the fat adhering to it, which is to be scored crosswise with a knife, and then gently rubbed over the surface once, twice, or thrice a day, according to the extent of the eruption and the recurrence of itching and irritation." A correspondent mentions another plan, practised by Dr. Allshorn, of Edinburgh. He says:—"I had a severe attack of small pox three months ago, and was so thickly covered with the eruption as to be almost confluent. Dr. Allshorn's plan is to mix three parts of oil with one of white wax, by heat, and while warm and fluid to paint over the face and neck with a camel-hair brush. As this cools and hardens it forms a mask, which effectually excludes the air, and prevents pitting. This plan saved me from all pitting, besides giving me great comfort while under its use."

2193. Cutaneous Eruptions.—The following mixture is very useful in all cutaneous eruptions:—Ipecacuanha wine, four drachms; flowers of sulphur, two drachms; tincture of cardamums, one ounce. Mix: one teaspoonful to be taken three times a day, in a wineglassful of water.

2194. Wash for a Blotched Face. — Rose water, three ounces; sulphate of zinc, one drachm. Mix: wet the face with it, gently dry it, and then touch it over with cold cream, which also dry gently off.

2195. Freckles. — To disperse them, take one ounce of lemon juice, a quarter of a drachm of powdered borax, and half a drachm of sugar; mix, and let them stand a few days in a glass bottle till the liquor is fit for use; then rub it on the hands and face occasionally.

2196. To remove Freckles.— Dissolve, in half an ounce of lemon juice, one ounce of Venice soap, and add a quarter of an ounce each of oil of bitter almonds, and deliquated oil of tartar. Place this mixture in the sun till it acquires the consistency of ointment. When in this state add three drops of the oil of rhodium, and keep it for use. Apply it to the face and hands in the manner following:—Wash the parts at night with elder-flower water, then anoint with the ointment. In the morning cleanse the skin from its oily adhesion by washing it copiously in rose water.

2197. Wash for Sunburn.— Take two drachms of borax, one drachm of Roman alum, one drachm of camphor, half an ounce of sugar-candy, and a pound of ox-gall. Mix and stir well for ten minutes or so, and repeat this stirring three or four times a day for a fortnight, till it appears clear and transparent. Strain through blotting-paper, and bottle up for use.

2198. Teething.—Young children, whilst cutting their first set of teeth, often suffer severe constitutional disturbance. At first there is restlessness and peevishness, with slight fever, but not unfrequently these are followed by convulsive fits, as they are commonly called, which depend on the brain becoming irritated; and sometimes under this condition the child is either cut off suddenly, or the foundation of serious mischief to the brain is laid. The remedy, or rather the safeguard against these frightful consequences, is trifling, safe, and almost certain, and consists merely in lancing the gum covering the tooth which is making its way through. When teething is about it may be known by the spittle constantly drivelling from the mouth and wetting the frock. The child has its fingers often in its mouth, and bites hard any substance it can get hold of. If the gums be carefully looked at, the part where the tooth is pressing up is swollen and redder than usual; and if the finger be pressed on it the child shrinks and cries, showing that the gum is tender. When these symptoms occur, the gum should be lanced, and sometimes the tooth comes through the next day, if near the surface; but if not so far advanced the cut heals and a scar forms, which is thought by some objectionable, as rendering the passage of the tooth more difficult. This, however, is untrue, for the scar will give way much more easily than the uncut gum. If the tooth do not come through after two

or three days, the lancing may be repeated; and this is more especially needed if the child be very fractious, and seems in much pain. Lancing the gums is further advantageous, because it empties the inflamed part of its blood, and so relieves the pain and inflammation. The relief children experience in the course of two or three hours from the operation is often very remarkable, as they almost immediately become lively and cheerful.

2199. Cure for Toothache.— Two or three drops of essential oil of cloves put upon a small piece of lint or cotton wool, and placed in the hollow of the tooth, will be found to have the active power of curing the toothache without destroying the tooth or injuring the gums.

2200. Gutta Percha Tooth-Stopping.—Since the introduction of gutta percha, the use of metallic succedaneum for filling decayed teeth has been superseded, especially in cases where the cavities are large. The gutta percha is inodorous, cheap, and can be renewed as often as required. It is only necessary to soften it by warmth, either by holding it before a fire, or immersing it in boiling water. Succedaneum is best when the decayed spots are very small.

2201. Succedaneum.—Take an old silver thimble, an old silver coin, or other silver article, and with a very fine file convert it into filings. Sift through gauze, to separate the coarse from the fine particles. Take the finer portion, and mix with sufficient quicksilver to form a stiff amalgam, and while in this state, fill the cavities of decayed teeth. This is precisely the same as the metallic amalgam used by all dentists. The filings of a sixpence would produce as much as is contained in two 2s. 6d. packets sold by the advertising makers of succedaneums. Quicksilver may be bought, at a trifle per half ounce or ounce, at the chemist's. We have not the slightest hesitation in pronouncing this to be the *best* thing of the kind. Caution: as it turns black under the action of the acids of the mouth, it should be used sparingly for *front* teeth. A tooth should never be filled while it is aching.

2202. Rose Lipsalve.—No. i. Oil of almonds, three ounces; alkanet, half an ounce. Let them stand together in a warm place, then strain. Melt one ounce and a half of white wax and half an ounce of spermaceti with the oil; stir it till it begins to thicken, and add twelve drops of otto of roses. No. ii. White wax, one ounce; almond oil, two ounces; alkanet, one drachm; digest in a warm place, stir till sufficiently coloured, strain, and stir in six drops of otto of roses. Cost: white wax, 2s. 2d. per pound; almond oil, 1s. 6d. per pound; alkanet root, 6d. to 8d.: otto of roses, 2s. 6d. per drachm. Lipsalve is usually put into small covered pots, and sold at 6d.

2203. Ventilating Bedrooms. —A sheet of finely perforated zinc, substituted for a pane of glass in one of the upper squares of a chamber window, is the cheapest and best form of ventilator; there should not be a bedroom without it.

2204. Bedclothes.—The perfection of dress, for day or night, where warmth is the purpose, is that which confines around the body sufficient of its own warmth, while it allows escape to the exhalations of the skin. Where the body is allowed to bathe protractedly in its own vapours we must expect an unhealthy effect upon the skin. Where there is too little ventilating escape, insensible perspiration is checked, and something analogous to fever supervenes; foul tongue, ill taste, and lack of morning appetite betray the evil.

2205. Vapour Baths may be made by putting boiling water in a pan, and placing a cane-bottom chair in the pan, the patient sitting upon it, enveloped from head to foot in a blanket covering the bath. Sulphur, spirit, vapour, herbal, and other baths may be obtained in the same manner. They should not be taken except under medical advice.

2206. Hot Water.—In bruises, hot water is most efficacious, both by means of insertion and fomentation, in removing pain, and totally preventing discolouration and stiffness. It has the same effect after a blow. It should be applied as quickly as possible, and as hot as it can be borne. Insertion in hot water will cure that troublesome and painful thing called a whitlow. The efficacy of hot water in preventing the ill effects of fatigue is too well known to require notice.

2207. Thinning the Blood.— Our attention ought to be directed to the means of *thinning* the blood, when it has been deprived, by too profuse transpiration in hot, dry winds, of its aqueous particles, and rendered thick and viscid. Water would easily supply this want of fluidity if it were capable of mingling with the blood when in this state; acid matter cannot be ultimately combined with the blood when the body is in this state. In order to find a menstruum by which water may be rendered capable of combining ultimately with the blood, of remaining long in combination with it, and of thinning it, we must mix it with a substance possessing the property of a soap, and consequently fit to dissolve viscous matters, and make them unite with water. The soap must contain but little salt, that it may not increase the thirst of the parched throat. It must not have a disagreeable taste, that we may be able to drink a considerable quantity of it: and it must be capable of recruiting the strength without overloading the stomach. Now all these qualities are to be found in the yolk of egg. No beverage, therefore, is more suitable (whilst it is very agreeable) for hot, dry weather than one composed of the yolk of egg beaten up with a little sugar (to taste), and mixed with a quart of cool spring or filtered water, half a glass of Moselle or any other Rhenish wine, and some lemon juice. The wine, however, may be omitted, and lemon juice alone (and rather more) used: in like manner, hartshorn shavings boiled in water may be substituted for the yolk of egg. Equal quantities of beef tea and whey are good for delicate infants.

2208. Substitute for the Foregoing.—The yolk of eggs beaten up, lump sugar (to taste), Rhenish wine or not, citric acid powdered, or tartaric acid (small quantity, exact quantity soon found); one or two drops of essence of lemon on a lump of sugar, to make it mix readily with the water; one quart of water. This is really an excellent, agreeable, and, without the wine, an inexpensive beverage.

2209. Method of Ascertaining the State of the Lungs.—Persons desirous of ascertaining the true state of their lungs are directed to draw in as much breath as they conveniently can; they are then to count as far as they are able, in a slow and audible voice, without drawing in more breath. The number of seconds they can continue counting must be carefully observed; in a consumption the time does not exceed ten, and is frequently less than six seconds; in pleurisy and pneumonia it ranges from nine to four seconds. When the lungs are in a sound condition, the time will range as high as from twenty to thirty-five seconds.

2210. To Avoid Catching Cold.—Accustom yourself to the use of sponging with cold water every morning on first getting out of bed. It should be followed by a good deal of rubbing with a wet towel. It has considerable effect in giving tone to the skin, and maintaining a proper action in it, and thus proves a safeguard to the injurious influence of cold and sudden changes of temperature. Sir Astley Cooper said, "The methods by which I have preserved my own health are—temperance, early rising, and sponging the body every morning with cold water, immediately after getting out of bed,—a practice which I have adopted for thirty years without ever catching cold."

2211. How to prepare Sea Water.—There cannot be a question that by far the simplest plan would consist in the evaporation of the sea-water itself in large quantities, preserving the resulting salt in closely-stopped vessels to prevent the absorption of moisture, and vending it in this form to the consumer; the proportion of this dry saline matter being fifty-six ounces to ten gallons of water less three pints. This plan was suggested by Dr. E. Schweitzer, for the extemporaneous formation of sea water for medicinal baths. Mr. H. Schweitzer writes that he has for many years made this compound, in accordance with his cousin's analysis. The proportion ordered to be used is six ounces to the gallon of water, and stirred well until dissolved.

2212. Change the Water in which Leeches are kept.—Once a month in winter, and once a week in summer, is sufficiently often, unless the water becomes discoloured or bloody, when it should be changed every day. Either clean pond water or clean rain water should be employed.

2213. Damp Linen.—We know of nothing attended with more serious consequences than the sleeping in damp linen. Persons are frequently assured that the sheets have been at a fire for many hours, but the question is as to what sort of fire, and whether they have been properly turned, so that every part has been exposed to the fire. The fear of creasing the linen, we know, prevents many from unfolding it, so as to be what we consider sufficiently aired: but health is of more importance than appearances: with gentleness there need be no fear of want of neatness.

2214. Orange Peel—dried, added to camomile flowers, in the proportion of half the quantity of the flowers, improves the tonic.

2215. Gingerbread Aperient.—Gingerbread, made with oatmeal or with barley flour, is a very agreeable aperient for children. Beware of giving children medicines too frequently.

2216. Cod Liver Oil.—Cod liver oil is neither more nor less than cod oil clarified; and consequently, two-thirds of its medicinal qualities are abstracted thereby. Cod oil can be purchased pure at any wholesale oil warehouse, at about one-thirtieth part of the price charged for the so-called cod liver oil. Many persons who have used cod oil pure as imported, have found it to answer much better than the cod liver oil purchased of a druggist. The best vehicle for taking cod liver oil in is new milk, and the disagreeable flavour of the drug can easily be covered by the addition of one drachm of orange peel to every eight ounces of the oil.

2217. Camomile Flowers should be gathered on a fine day, and dried upon a tray placed in the sun; all herbs should be treated in the same manner.

2218. Decoction of Sarsaparilla.—Take four ounces of the root, slice it down, put the slices into four pints of water, and simmer for four hours. Take out the sarsaparilla, and beat it into a mash; put it into the liquor again, and boil down to two pints, then strain and cool the liquor. Dose, a wineglassful three times a day. Use—to purify the blood after a course of mercury; or, indeed, whenever any taint is given to the constitution, vitiating the blood, and producing eruptive affections.

2219. Preston Salts.—Take of sal ammoniac and salts of tartar of each about two ounces; pound up the sal ammoniac into small bits, and mix them gently with the salts of tartar. After being well mixed, add a few drops of oil of lavender, sufficient to scent, and also a little musk; stop up in a glass bottle, and when required for use, add a few drops of water, or spirits of hartshorn, when you will immediately have strong smelling salts. The musk, being expensive, may be omitted; it will still be good. Any person can for a few pence obtain these ingredients at any druggist's, and they will make salts, which, to buy prepared, would cost, at the least, eighteen pence.

2220. Destruction of Rats.—

The following receipt for the destruction of rats has been communicated by Dr. Ure to the council of the English Agricultural Society, and is highly recommended as the best known means of getting rid of these most obnoxious and destructive vermin. It has been tried by several intelligent persons, and found perfectly effectual.—Melt hog's lard in a bottle plunged in water, heated to about 150 degrees of Fahrenheit; introduce into it half an ounce of phosphorus for every pound of lard; then add a pint of proof spirit, or whisky; cork the bottle firmly after its contents have been heated to 150 degrees, taking it at the same time out of the water, and agitate smartly till the phosphorus becomes uniformly diffused, forming a milky-looking liquid. This liquid, being cooled, will afford a white compound of phosphorus and lard, from which the spirit spontaneously separates, and may be poured off to be used again, for none of it enters into the combination, but it merely serves to comminute the phosphorus, and diffuse it in very fine particles through the lard. This compound, on being warmed very gently, may be poured out into a mixture of wheat flour and sugar, incorporated therewith, and then flavoured with oil of rhodium, or not, at pleasure. The flavour may be varied with oil of aniseed, &c. This dough, being made into pellets, is to be laid in rat-holes. By its luminousness in the dark, it attracts their notice, and being agreeable to their palates and noses, it is readily eaten, and proves certainly fatal.

2221. To Kill Slugs.—Take a quantity of cabbage leaves, and either put them into a warm oven, or heat them before the fire till they get quite soft; then rub them with unsalted butter, or any kind of fresh dripping, and lay them in places infested with slugs. In a few hours the leaves will be found covered with snails and slugs, which may then, of course, be destroyed in any way the gardener may think fit.

2222. To Destroy Slugs. — Slugs are very voracious, and their ravages often do considerable damage, not only to the kitchen garden, but to the flower-beds also. If, now and then, a few slices of turnip be put about the beds, on a summer or autumnal evening, the slugs will congregate thereon, and may be destroyed.

2223. To Exterminate Beetles.—i. Place a few lumps of unslaked lime where they frequent. ii. Set a dish or trap containing a little beer or syrup at the bottom, and place a few sticks slanting against its sides, so as to form a sort of gangway for the beetles to climb up by, when they will go headlong into the bait set for them. iii. Mix equal weights of red lead, sugar, and flour, and place it nightly near their haunts. This mixture, made into sheets, forms the beetle wafers sold at the oil shops.

2224. To Kill Cockroaches.— A teacupful of well-bruised plaster of Paris, mixed with double the quantity of oatmeal, to which add a little sugar (the latter is not essential). Strew it on the floor, or in the chinks where they frequent.

2225. Earwigs are very destructive insects; their favourite food is the petals of roses, pinks, dahlias, and other flowers. They may be caught by driving stakes into the ground, and placing on each an inverted flower pot; the earwigs will climb up and take refuge under it, when they may be taken out and killed. Clean bowls of tobacco pipes, placed in like manner on the tops of smaller sticks, are very good traps: or very deep holes may be made in the ground with a crowbar, into which they will fall, and may be destroyed by boiling water.

2226. To Destroy Ants.—Drop some quicklime on the mouth of their nest, and wash it in with boiling water; or dissolve some camphor in spirits of wine, then mix with water, and pour into their haunts; or tobacco water, which has been found effectual. They are averse to strong scents. Camphor will prevent their infesting a cupboard, or a sponge saturated with creosote.

To prevent their climbing up trees, place a ring of tar about the trunk, or a circle of rag moistened occasionally with creosote.

2227. To Prevent Moths.—In the month of April or May, beat your fur garments well with a small cane or elastic stick, then wrap them up in linen, without pressing the fur too hard, and put betwixt the folds some camphor in small lumps; then put your furs in this state in boxes well closed. When the furs are wanted for use, beat them well as before, and expose them for twenty-four hours to the air, which will take away the smell of the camphor. If the fur has long hair, as bear or fox, add to the camphor an equal quantity of black pepper in powder.

2228. To get rid of Moths. —i. Procure shavings of cedar wood, and enclose in muslin bags, which should be distributed freely among the clothes. —ii. Procure shavings of camphor wood, and enclose in bags. iii. Sprinkle pimento (allspice) berries among the clothes.—iv. Sprinkle the clothes with the seeds of the musk plant.—v. To destroy the eggs, when deposited in woollen cloths, &c., use a solution of acetate of potash in spirits of rosemary, fifteen grains to the pint.

2229. Bugs.—Spirits of naphtha rubbed with a small painter's brush into every part of a bedstead is a certain way of getting rid of bugs. The mattress and binding of the bed should be examined, and the same process attended to, as they generally harbour more in these parts than in the bedstead. Three pennyworth of naphtha is sufficient for one bed.

2230. Bug Poison.—Proof spirit, one pint; camphor, two ounces; oil of turpentine, four ounces; corrosive sublimate, one ounce. Mix. Cost: proof spirit, 1s. 10d. per pint; camphor, 2s. 8d. per pound; oil of turpentine, 8d. per pint; corrosive sublimate, 3s. 6d. per pound. A correspondent says, "I have been for a long time troubled with bugs, and never could get rid of them by any clean and expeditious method, until a friend told me to suspend a small bag of camphor to the bed, just in the centre, overhead. I did so, and the enemy was most effectually repulsed, and has not made his appearance since—not even for a reconnaissance!" We therefore give the information upon this method of getting rid of bugs, our informant being most confident of its success in every case.

2231. Mixture for Destroying Flies.—Infusion of quassia, one pint; brown sugar, four ounces; ground pepper, two ounces. To be well mixed together, and put in small shallow dishes when required.

2232. To Destroy Flies in a room, take half a teaspoonful of black pepper in powder, one teaspoonful of brown sugar, and one tablespoonful of cream, mix them well together, and place them in the room on a plate, where the flies are troublesome, and they will soon disappear.

2233. Flies.—Cold green tea, very strong, and sweetened with sugar, will, when set about the room in saucers, attract flies and destroy them.

2234. Inks.—There are many receipts published for making ink; the following is as useful and economical a mode of producing good ink as any of them :—

2235. Dr. Ure's Ink. — For twelve gallons of ink take twelve pounds of bruised galls, five pounds of gum, five pounds of green sulphate of iron, and twelve gallons of rain water. Boil the galls with nine gallons of the water for three hours, adding fresh water to supply that lost in vapour; let the decoction settle, and draw off the clear liquor. Add to it the gum, previously dissolved in one and a half gallon of water; dissolve the green vitriol separately in one and a half gallon of water, and mix the whole. Cost of preparation: gall, 1s. 4d. per pound; gum, 8d. per pound; green sulphate of iron, 1d. per pound.

2236. Ink Powder is formed of the dry ingredients for ink, powdered and mixed. Powdered galls, two pounds; powdered green vitriol, one pound; powdered gum, eight ounces. This should be put up in two-ounce packets, each of which will make one pint of ink. Cost : galls, 1s. 4d. per pound; green vitriol, 1d. per pound; powdered gum, 1s. 5d. per pound.

2237. Red Writing Ink. — Best ground Brazil wood, four ounces; diluted acetic acid, one pint; alum, half an ounce. Boil them slowly in an enamelled vessel for one hour, strain, and add an ounce of gum. Brazil wood, 1s. per pound; diluted acetic acid, 3d. per pint; alum, 2d. per pound; ground gum, 1s. 6d. per pound.

2238. Marking Ink Without Preparation. — There are several receipts for this ink, but the following by Mr. Redwood is rapidly superseding all the others :— Dissolve, separately, one ounce of nitrate of silver (4s. 6d. per ounce), and one and a half ounce of sub-carbonate soda (best washing soda), in distilled or rain water. Mix the solutions, and collect and wash the precipitate in a filter; whilst still moist, rub it up in a marble or wedgwood mortar with three drachms of tartaric acid; add two ounces of distilled water, mix six drachms of white sugar, and ten drachms of powdered gum arabic, half an ounce of archil, and water to make up six ounces in measure. Cost: one ounce of nitrate of silver, 4s. 6d.; soda, tartaric acid, sugar, and gum, 3d.; archil, 10d. per pint. It is usually put up in one or two-drachm bottles, labelled, and sold at 8d. The above quantity would make 24 two-drachm bottles.— Bottles from 8d. to 10d. per dozen.

2239. Ink for Zinc Garden Labels. — Verdigris, one ounce; sal ammoniac, one ounce; lamp black, half an ounce; water, half a pint. Mix in an earthenware mortar, without using a metal spatula. - Should be put up in small one-ounce bottles ready for sale. *Directions.*—To be shaken before use, and used with a clean *quill* pen, on bright zinc. Cost: verdigris, 3d. per ounce; sal ammoniac, 8d. per pound; lamp black, 4d. per pound. *Note.*—

Another kind of ink for zinc is also used, made of chloride of platinum, five grains, dissolved in one ounce of distilled or rain water; but the first, which is much less expensive, answers perfectly, if used as directed, on clean bright zinc.

2240. Cements.—The term cement includes all those substances employed for the purpose of causing the adhesion of two or more bodies, whether originally separate, or divided by an accidental fracture. As the substances that are required to be connected together are exceedingly various, and differ very much in their properties as to texture, &c., &c.; and as the conditions under which they are placed, with regard to heat and moisture, are also exceedingly variable, a number of cements, possessed of very different properties, are required; for a cement that answers admirably under one set of circumstances may be perfectly useless in others. A vast number of cements are known and used in the various arts, but they may all be referred to a few classes; and our object in this paper will be to describe the manufacture and use of the best of each class, and also to state what are the general principles upon which the success or failure of cementing usually depends. The different parts of a solid are held together by an attraction between their several particles, which is termed the attraction of cohesion, or cohesive attraction. The amount of this varies with the substances; thus, the cohesion of the particles of iron to one another is enormously great, whilst that between those of chalk is but small. This attraction acts only when the particles are in the closest possible contact; even air must not be between them. If, after breaking any substance, we could bring the particles into as close a contact as before, and remove the air, they would re-unite, and be as strongly connected as ever. But, in general, this is impossible; small particles of grit and dust get between them; the film of interposed air cannot be removed; and thus, however

firmly we press the edges of a broken cup together, it remains cracked china still. *Perfectly* flat clean surfaces, like those of freshly ground plate-glass, may sometimes be made to cohere, so that the two pieces become one, and cannot be separated without breaking. The attraction of cohesion takes place between the parts of the same substance, and must not be confounded with that of adhesion, which is the attraction of different substances to one another; for example, the particles of a piece of wood are united by cohesive attraction, whilst the union of glue and wood to each other depends on adhesive attraction. And it is important that this distinction be borne in mind, for, in almost all cases, the cohesion between the particles of the cement is very much less than the adhesion of the cement to other bodies; and if torn apart, the connected joint gives way, not by the loosening of the adhesion, but by the layer of cement splitting down the centre. Hence the important rule, that the *less* cement in a joint the stronger it is. Domestic manipulators usually reverse this, by letting as much cement as possible remain in the joint, which is, therefore, necessarily a weak one. A thick, nearly solid cement, which cannot be pressed out of the joint, is always inferior to a thinner one, of which merely a connecting film remains between the united surfaces. Having thus mentioned the general principles that ought always to be borne in mind, we will now proceed to describe the manufacture and uses of some of the more useful cements.

2241. Mouth Glue.—A very useful preparation is sold by many of the law stationers in London under this title; it is merely a thin cake of soluble glue, which, when moistened with the tongue, furnishes a ready means of uniting papers, &c. It is made by dissolving one pound of fine glue or gelatine in water, and adding half a pound of brown sugar, boiling the whole until it is sufficiently thick, to become solid on cooling; it is then poured into moulds, or on a slab slightly greased, and cut into the required shape when cool. Cost: gelatine, 1s. 3d. per pound; sugar, 4d. per pound. (*See* LIQUID GLUE, No. 2244.)

2242. PASTE is usually made by rubbing up flour with cold water, and boiling; if a little alum is mixed before boiling it is much improved, being less clammy, working more freely in the brush, and thinner, a less quantity is required, and it is therefore stronger. If required in large quantity, as for papering rooms, it may be made by mixing one quartern of flour, one quarter pound of alum, and a little warm water; when mixed, the requisite quantity of boiling water should be poured on whilst the mixture is being stirred. Paste is only adapted to cementing paper; when used it should be spread on one side of the paper, which should then be folded with the pasted side inwards, and allowed to remain a few minutes before being opened and used; this swells the paper, and permits its being more smoothly and securely attached. Kept for a few days, paste becomes mouldy, and after a short time putrid; this inconvenience may be obviated by the use of—

2243. PERMANENT PASTE, made by adding to each half-pint of flour paste without alum, fifteen grains of corrosive sublimate, previously rubbed to powder in a mortar, the whole to be well mixed; this, if prevented from drying, by being kept in a covered pot, remains good any length of time, and is therefore convenient; but unfortunately it is extremely poisonous, though its excessively nauseous taste would prevent its being swallowed accidentally: it possesses the great advantage of not being liable to the attacks of insects.

2244. LIQUID GLUE.—Several preparations were much in vogue a few years since under this title. The liquid glue of the shops is made by dissolving shellac in water, by boiling it along with borax, which possesses the peculiar property of causing the solution of the resinous lac. This prepara-tion is convenient from its cheapness and freedom from smell; but it gives way if exposed to long-continued damp, which that made with naphtha resists. Of the use of *common glue* very little need be said; it should always be prepared in a gluepot or double vessel, to prevent its being burned, which injures it very materially; the objection to the use of this contrivance is, that it renders it impossible to heat the glue in the inner vessel to the boiling point; this inconvenience can be obviated by employing in the outer vessel some liquid which boils at a higher temperature than pure water, such as a saturated solution of salt (made by adding one-third as much salt as water). This boils at 224° Fahr., 12° above the heat of boiling water, and enables the glue in the inner vessel to be heated to a much higher temperature than when pure water is employed. If a saturated solution of nitre is used, the temperature rises still higher.

2245. DIAMOND CEMENT.—Soak isinglass in water till it is soft; then dissolve it in the smallest possible quantity of proof spirit, by the aid of a gentle heat; in two ounces of this mixture dissolve ten grains of ammoniacum, and whilst still liquid, add half a drachm of mastic, dissolved in three drachms of rectified spirit; stir well together, and put into small bottles for sale. Cost: isinglass, 1s. per ounce; rectified spirit, 2s. 6d. per pint; ammoniacum, 3d. per ounce; mastic, 1s. per ounce. This cement is usually sold at 1s. per two-drachm bottle. *Directions for use.*—Liquefy the cement by plunging the bottle in hot water, and use it directly. The cement improves the oftener the bottle is thus warmed; it resists the action of water and moisture perfectly.

2246. RICE FLOUR CEMENT.—An excellent cement may be made from rice flour, which is at present used for that purpose in China and Japan. It is only necessary to mix the rice flour intimately with cold water, and gently simmer it over a fire, when it readily forms a delicate and durable cement, not only answering all the purposes of common paste, but admirably adapted for joining together paper, cards, &c., in forming the various beautiful and tasteful ornaments which afford much employment and amusement to the ladies. When made of the consistence of plaster-clay, models, busts, bas-relievos, &c., may be formed of it; and the articles, when dry, are susceptible of high polish, and very durable.

2247. THE WHITE OF AN EGG, well beaten with quicklime, and a small quantity of very old cheese, forms an excellent substitute for cement, when wanted in a hurry, either for broken china or old ornamental glass-ware.

2248. CEMENT FOR BROKEN CHINA, GLASS, &c.—The following receipt, from experience, we know to be a good one; and being nearly colourless, it possesses advantages which liquid glue and other cements do not.—Dissolve half an ounce of gum acacia in a wineglass of boiling water; add plaster of Paris sufficient to form a thick paste, and apply it with a brush to the parts required to be cemented together. Several articles upon our toilet table have been repaired most effectually by this receipt.

2249. LIME AND EGG CEMENT is frequently made by moistening the edges to be united with white of egg, dusting on some lime from a piece of muslin, and bringing the edges into contact. A much better mode is to slake some freshly-burned lime with a small quantity of *boiling* water; this occasions it to fall into a very fine dry powder, if excess of water has not been added. The white of egg used should be intimately and thoroughly mixed, by beating with an equal bulk of water, and the slaked lime added to the mixture, so as to form a thin paste, which should be used speedily, as it soon sets. This is a valuable cement, possessed of great strength, and capable of withstanding boiling water. Cements made with lime and blood, scraped cheese, or curd, may

be regarded as inferior varieties of it. Cracked vessels of earthenware and glass may often be usefully, though not ornamentally, repaired by white lead spread on strips of calico, and secured with bands of twine. But in point of strength, all ordinary cements yield the palm to Jeffery's Patent Marine Glue, a compound of India-rubber, shellac, and coal-tar naphtha. Small quantities can be purchased at most of the tool warehouses, at cheaper rates than it can be made. When applied to china and glass, the substances should be cautiously made hot enough to melt the glue, which should be then rubbed on the edges, so as to become fluid, and the parts brought into contact immediately. When well applied, the mended stem of a common tobacco-pipe will break at any other part, in preference to the junction. The colour of the glue, unfortunately, prevents its being much used.

2250. THE RED CEMENT, which is employed by instrument makers for cementing glass to metals, and which is very cheap, and exceedingly useful for a variety of purposes, is made by melting five parts of black rosin, one part of yellow wax, and then stirring in gradually one part of red ochre or Venetian red, in fine powder, and previously *well dried*. This cement requires to be melted before use, and it adheres better if the objects to which it is applied are warmed. A soft cement, of a somewhat similar character, may be found useful for covering the corks of preserved fruit, and other bottles, and it is made by melting yellow wax with an equal quantity of rosin, or of common turpentine (not oil of turpentine, but the resin), using the latter for a very soft cement, and stirring in, as before, some dried Venetian red. Bearing in mind our introductory remarks, it will be seen that to unite broken substances with a thick cement is disadvantageous, the object being to bring the surfaces as closely together as possible. As an illustration of a right and a wrong way of mending, we will suppose a plaster of Paris figure broken; the wrong way to mend it is by a thick paste of plaster, which makes, not a joint, but a botch. The right way to mend it is by means of some well-made carpenter's glue, which, being absorbed in the porous plaster, leaves merely a film covering the two surfaces, and if well done, the figure is stronger there than elsewhere.

2251. MASTIC CEMENT.—This is employed for making a superior coating to inside walls, but must not be confounded with the *resin mastic*. It is made by mixing twenty parts of well-washed and sifted sharp sand with two parts of litharge and one of freshly burned and slaked quicklime, in fine *dry* powder. This is made into a putty, by mixing with linseed oil. It sets in a few hours, having the appearance of light stone; and we mention it, as it may be frequently employed with advantage in repairing broken stone-work (as stairs), by filling up the missing parts. The employment of Roman cement, plaster, &c., for masonry work, hardly comes within the limits of Domestic Manipulation.

2252. CEMENT FOR LEATHER AND CLOTH.—An adhesive material for uniting the parts of boots and shoes, and for the seams of articles of clothing, may be made thus:—Take one pound of gutta percha, four ounces of India rubber, two ounces of pitch, one ounce of shellac, two ounces of oil. The ingredients are to be melted together, and used hot.

2253. Birdlime.—Take any quantity of linseed oil, say half a pint; put it into an old pot, or any vessel that will stand the fire without breaking—the vessel must not be more than one-third full; put it on a slow fire, stir it occasionally until it thickens as much as required; this will be known by cooling the stick in water, and trying it with the fingers. It is best to make it rather harder than for use. Then pour it into cold water. It can be brought back to the consistency required with a little Archangel tar.

2254. Anglo-Japanese Work.—This is an elegant and easy domestic art. Take yellow withered leaves, dissolve gum, black paint, copal varnish, &c. Any articles may be ornamented with these simple materials. An old tea-caddy, flower-pots, fire-screens, screens of all descriptions, work-boxes, &c. Select perfect leaves, dry and press them between the leaves of books; rub the surface of the article to be ornamented with fine sand-paper, then give it a coat of fine black paint, which should be procured mixed at a colour shop. When dry, rub smooth with pumice stone, and give two other coats. Dry. Arrange leaves in any manner and variety, according to taste. Gum the leaves on the under side, and press them upon their places. Then dissolve some isinglass in hot water, and brush it over the work. Dry. Give three coats of copal varnish, allowing ample time for each coat to dry. Articles thus ornamented last for years, and are very pleasing.

2255. Ornamental Leather Work.—An excellent imitation of carved oak, suitable for frames, boxes, vases, and ornaments in endless variety, may be made of a description of leather called basil. The art consists in simply cutting out this material in imitation of natural objects, and in impressing upon it by simple tools, either with or without the aid of heat, such marks and characteristics as are necessary to the imitation. The rules given with regard to the imitation of leaves and flowers apply to ornamental leather work. Begin with a simple object, and proceed by degrees to those that are more complicated. Cut out an ivy or an oak leaf, and impress the veins upon it; then arrange these in groups, and affix them to frames, or otherwise. The tools required are ivory or steel points of various sizes, punches, and tin shapes, such as are used for confectionery. The points may be made out of the handles of old tooth-brushes. Before cutting out the leaves the leather should be well soaked in water, until it is quite pliable. When dry, it will retain the artistic shape. Leaves and stems are fastened together by means of liquid glue, and varnished with any of the drying varnishes, or with sealing-wax dissolved to a suitable consistency in spirits of wine. Wire, cork, gutta percha, bits of stems of trees, &c., may severally be used to aid in the formation of groups of buds, flowers, seed-vessels, &c.

2256. Black Paper Patterns. —Mix some lamp-black with sweet oil. With a piece of flannel cover sheets of writing-paper with the mixture: dab the paper dry with a bit of fine linen. When using, put the black side on another sheet of paper, and fasten the corners together with small pins. Lay on the back of the black paper the pattern to be drawn, and go over it with the point of a steel drawing pencil: the black will then leave the impression of the pattern on the under sheet, on which you may draw it with ink.

2257. Patterns on Cloth or Muslin are drawn with a pen dipped in stone blue, a bit of sugar, and a little water; wet to the consistence wanted.

2258. Feather Flowers.—Procure the best white swan or goose feathers; have them plucked off the fowl with care not to break the web; free them from down, except a small quantity on the shaft of the feather. Get also a little fine wire, different sizes; a few skeins of fine floss silk, some good cotton wool or wadding, a reel of No. 4 Moravian cotton, a skein of Indian silk, the starch and gum for pastes, and a pair of small sharp scissors, a few sheets of coloured silk paper, and some water colours.

2259. HAVING PROCURED Two GOOD SPECIMENS of the flower you wish to imitate, carefully pull off the petals of one, and, with a piece of tissue paper, cut out the shape of each, taking care to leave the shaft of the feather at least half an inch longer than the petal of the flower. Carefully bend the feather with the thumb and finger to the proper shape: mind not to break the web.

2260. To MAKE THE STEM AND HEART OF A FLOWER.—Take a piece of wire six inches long; across the top lay a small piece of cotton wool, turn the wire over it, and wind it round until it is the size of the heart or centre of the flower you are going to imitate. If a single flower, cover it with paste or velvet of the proper colour, and round it must be arranged the stamens; these are made of fine Indian silk, or feathers may be used for this purpose. After the petals have been attached, the silk or feather is dipped into gum, and then into the farina. Place the petals round, one at a time, and wind them on with Moravian cotton, No. 4. Arrange them as nearly like the flower you have for a copy as possible. Cut the stems of the feathers even, and then make the calyx of feathers, cut like the pattern or natural flower. For the small flowers the calyx is made with paste. Cover the stems with paper or silk the same as the flowers; the paper must be cut in narrow strips, about a quarter of an inch wide.

2261. To MAKE THE PASTES OF THE CALYX, HEARTS, AND BUDS OF FLOWERS. —Take common white starch and mix it with gum water until it is the substance of thick treacle; colour it with the dyes used for the feathers, and keep it from the air.

2262. To MAKE THE FARINA.—Use common ground rice, mixed into a stiff paste with any dye: dry it before the fire, and when quite hard, pound it to a fine powder. The buds, berries, and hearts of some double flowers are made with cotton wool, wound around wire, moulded to the shape with thumb and finger. Smooth it over with gum water, and when dry, cover the buds, berries, or calyx with the proper coloured pastes: they will require one or two coats, and may be shaded with a little paint, and then gummed and left to dry.

2263. FLOWERS OF Two OR MORE

SHADES are variegated with water colours, mixed with lemon juice, ultramarine and chrome for blue; and to produce other effects, gold may also be used in powder, mixed with lemon juice and gum water.

2264. To DYE FEATHERS BLUE.— Into two pennyworth of oil of vitriol mix two pennyworth of the best indigo in powder; let it stand a day or two; when wanted shake it well, and into a quart of boiling water put one tablespoonful of the liquid. Stir it well, put the feathers in, and let them simmer a few minutes.

2265. YELLOW.—Put a tablespoonful of the best turmeric into a quart of boiling water: when well mixed put in the feathers. More or less of the turmeric will give them different shades, and a very small quantity of soda will give them an orange hue.

2266. GREEN. — Mix the indigo liquid with turmeric, and pour boiling water over it; let the feathers simmer in the dye until they have acquired the shade you want them.

2267. PINK. — Three good pink saucers in a quart of boiling water, with a small quantity of cream of tartar. If a deep colour is required, use four saucers. Let the feathers remain in the dye several hours.

2268. RED.—In a quart of boiling water dissolve a teaspoonful of cream of tartar; put in one tablespoonful of prepared cochineal, and then a few drops of muriate of tin. This dye is expensive, and scarlet flowers are best made with the plumage of the red ibis, which can generally be had of a bird-fancier or bird-stuffer, who will give directions how it should be applied.

2269. LILAC. — About two teaspoonfuls of cudbear into about a quart of boiling water; let it simmer a few minutes before you put in the feathers. A small quantity of cream of tartar turns the colour from lilac to amethyst.

2270. BLACK; CRIMSON.—*Read the general instructions upon Dyeing.*

2271. BEFORE THE FEATHERS ARE DYED they must be put into hot water,

and allowed to drain before they are put into the dyes. After they are taken out of the dye, rinse them two or three times in clear cold water (except the red, which must only be done once), then lay them on a tray, over which a cloth has been spread, before a good fire; when they begin to dry and unfold, draw each feather gently between your thumb and finger, until it regains its proper shape.

2272. THE LEAVES OF THE FLOWERS are made of green feathers, cut like those of the natural flower, and serrated at the edge with a very small pair of scissors. For the calyx of a moss-rose the down is left on the feather, and is a very good representation of the moss on the natural flower.

2273. Waxen · Flowers and Fruit.—There is no art more easily acquired, nor more encouraging in its immediate results, than that of modelling flowers and fruit in wax. The art, however, is attended by this drawback —that the materials required are somewhat expensive.

2274. THE MATERIALS REQUIRED for commencing the making of waxen flowers will cost from 20s. to 30s., which may be obtained at most fancy repositories in large towns. Persons wishing to commence the art would do well to inquire the particulars, and see specimens of materials; because in this, as in every other pursuit, there are novelties and improvements being introduced, which no book can give an idea of.

2275. THE PETALS, LEAVES, &c., of flowers, are made of sheets of coloured wax, which may be purchased in packets of assorted colours, at from 5s. to 6s. 6d. per gross.

2276. THE STEMS are made of wire of suitable thicknesses, covered with silk, and overlaid with wax; and the leaves are frequently made by thin sheets of wax pressed upon leaves of embossed calico. Leaves of various descriptions are to be obtained of the persons who sell the materials for wax flower making.

2277. LADIES WILL OFTEN FIND, among their discarded artificial flowers, leaves and buds that will serve as the base of their wax models.

2278. THE BEST GUIDE to the construction of a flower—far better than printed diagrams or patterns—is to take a flower, say a *tulip*, a *rose*, or a *camellia*. If possible, procure *two* flowers, nearly alike, and carefully picking one of them to pieces, lay the petals down in the order in which they are taken from the flower, and then cut paper patterns from them, and number them from the centre of the flower, that you may know their relative positions.

2279. THE PERFECT FLOWER will guide you in getting the wax petals together, and will enable you to give, not only to each petal but to the *contour* of the flower, the characteristics which are natural to it. In most cases, they are merely pressed together and held in their places by the adhesiveness of the wax. From the paper patterns the wax petals or other portions of the flowers may be cut. They should be cut singly, and the scissors should be frequently dipped into water, to prevent the wax adhering to the blades.

2280. THE SCRAPS OF WAX that fall from the cutting will be found useful for making seed-vessels, and other parts of the flowers.

2281. LEAVES OF FLOWERS. — Where the manufactured foundations cannot be obtained, patterns of them should be cut in paper, and the venous appearance may be imparted to the wax by pressing the leaf upon it.

2282. IN THE CONSTRUCTION OF SPRIGS, it is most important to be guided by sprigs of the natural plant, as various kinds of plants. have many different characteristics in the grouping of their flowers, leaves, and branches.

2283. TAKE A FLOWER AND COPY IT, observing care in the selection of good sheets of wax, and seeing that their colours are precisely those of the flower you desire to imitate.

2284. FOR THE TINTS, STRIPES, AND SPOTS of variegated flowers, you will be supplied with colours among the other materials; and the application of them is precisely upon the principle of water-colour painting.

2285. FOR THE IMITATING OF FRUIT in wax, very different rules are to be observed. The following directions may, however, be generally followed : — The material of which moulds for waxen fruit should be composed is the *best* plaster of Paris, which can be bought from the Italian figure-makers at about a penny a pound, in bags containing fourteen pounds, or half-bags containing seven pounds. If this cannot be procured, the cheaper plaster, from the oil-shops. may be substituted, if it can be obtained *quite fresh*. If, however, the plaster is faulty, the results of the modelling will of course be more or less faulty also. It is the property of plaster of Paris to form a chemical union with water, and to form a paste which rapidly "sets ' or hardens into a substance of the density of firm chalk. The mould must therefore be made by an impression from the object to be imitated, made upon the plaster before it sets.

2286. THE USE OF AN ELASTIC FRUIT in early experiments leads to a want of accuracy in the first steps of the operation, which causes very annoying difficulties afterwards; and therefore a solid, inelastic body—an egg boiled hard—is recommended as the first object to be imitated.

2287. HAVING FILLED A SMALL PUDDING BASIN about three quarters full of damp sand (the finer the better), lay the egg lengthways in the sand, so that half of it is above, and half below, the level of the sand, which should be perfectly smooth around it. Then prepare the plaster in another basin, which should be half full of water. Sprinkle the plaster in quickly till it comes to the top of the water, and then, having stirred it for a moment with a spoon, pour the whole upon the egg in the other basin. ·

2288. WHILE THE HALF MOULD THUS MADE is hardening thoroughly, carefully remove every particle of plaster from the basin in which it was mixed, and also from the spoon which has been used. This must be done by placing them both in water and wiping them perfectly clean. This is highly important, since a small quantity of plaster which has set will destroy the quality of a second mixing if it is incorporated therewith. In about five minutes the half mould will be fit to remove, which may be done by turning the basin up with the right hand (taking care not to lose the sand), so that the mould falls into the left hand. The egg should then be gently allowed to fall back on the sand out of the mould; if, however, it adheres, lightly scrape the plaster from the edge of the mould, and then shake it out into the hollow of the hand. If, however, the exact half of the egg has been immersed in the sand, no such difficulty will arise; this shows how important is exactness in the first position of the object from which a casting is to be taken. The egg being removed and laid aside, the mould or casting must be "trimmed;" that is, the sand must be brushed from the flat surface of the mould with a nail-brush very slightly, without touching the extreme and sharp edges where the hollow of the mould commences. Then upon the broad edge from which the sand has been brushed, make four equi-distant hollows (with the round end of a table-knife), like the deep impression of a thimble's end. These are to guide hereafter in the fixing of the second half of the mould. The egg should now be replaced in the casting, and the edge of the cast, with the holes, thoroughly lubricated with sweet oil laid on with a feather, or what is better, a large camel-hair brush.

2289. INTO THE SMALL PUDDING BASIN from which the sand has been emptied, place with the egg uppermost the half mould, which, if the operation has been managed properly, should *fit* close at the edges to the side of the vessel; then prepare some more liquid plaster as before, and pour it upon the egg and mould, and while it is hardening, round it with the spoon as with the first half.

2290. IN DUE TIME REMOVE THE WHOLE from the basin; the halves will be found readily separable, and the egg being removed, the mould is ready to cast in, after it has been set aside for an hour or two, so as to completely harden. This is the simplest form of mould, and all are made upon the same principle.

2291. THE CASTING OF AN EGG is not merely interesting as the first step in a series of lessons, but as supplying a means of imitating peculiarly charming objects, which the natural historian tries almost in vain to preserve. We shall proceed, then, with the directions for the casting of an egg in the mould.

2292. FOR THE FIRST EXPERIMENTS, common yellow wax may be used as the material, or the ends of half-burnt wax candles. The materials of the hard (not tallow) composition mould candles will also answer.

2293. EVERY LARGE OBJECT TO BE IMITATED in wax should be cast *hollow;* and therefore, though the transparent lightness required in the imitation of fruits is not requisite in an artificial egg, we shall cast the egg upon the same principle as a piece of fruit. Firstly. The two pieces of the plaster of Paris mould must be soaked in hot water for ten minutes. Secondly. The wax should in the meantime be very slowly melted in a small tin saucepan, with a spout to it, care being taken not to allow it to boil, or it will be discoloured. As to the quantity of wax to be melted, the following is a general rule:—If a lump, the size of the object to be imitated, be placed in the saucepan, it should be sufficient for casting twice, at least. Thirdly. As soon as the wax is melted thoroughly, place the saucepan on the hob of the grate, and, taking the parts of the mould from the hot water, remove the moisture from their surfaces by pressing them gently with a handkerchief or soft cloth. It is necessary to use what is called in some of the arts "a very light hand" in this operation, especially in drying moulds of fruits whose aspect possesses characteristic irregularities — such as those on the orange, the lemon, or the cucumber. The mould must not be *wiped*, but only *pressed*. If the *water* has not been hot enough, or if the drying is not performed quickly, the mould will be too cold, and the wax will congeal too rapidly, and settle in ridges and streaks; on the other hand, if the wax has been made too hot, it will adhere to the mould, and refuse to come out entire. Fourthly. Having laid the two halves of the mould so that there can be no mistake in fitting the one in its exact place quickly on the other, pour from the saucepan into *one* of the half moulds nearly as much wax as will fill the hollow made by the model (egg), quickly fit the other half on the top of it, squeeze the two pieces tightly together in the hand, and still holding them thus, turn them over in every possible position, so that the wax which is slowly congealing in the internal hollow of the mould may be of equal thickness in all parts. Having continued this process at least two minutes, the hands (still holding and turning the mould) may be immersed in cold water to accelerate the cooling process. The perfect congealment of the wax may be known after a little experience by the absence of the sound of fluid on shaking the mould. Fifthly. As soon as the mould is completely cooled, the halves may be separated carefully, the upper being lifted straight up from the under, and if the operation has been properly managed, a waxen egg will be turned out of the mould. Lastly. The egg will only require *trimming*, that is, removing the ridge which marks the line at which the halves of the mould joined, and polishing out the scratches or inequalities left by the knife with a piece of soft rag, wet with spirits of turpentine or spirits of wine. It is always desirable to make several castings of the same object, as the moulds are apt to get chipped when laid by in a cupboard; and for this reason, as well as for the sake of practice, we recommend our pupils to make at least a dozen waxen eggs before they proceed to any other object. If they succeed in this *completely*, they may rest assured that every difficulty which is likely to meet them in any future operations will be easily overcome.

2294. To Colour the Wax.—While the wax is yet on the hob, and in a fluid state, stir into it a little *flake white*, in powder, and continue to stir the mixture while it is being poured into the half mould. It will be found that unless the fixing and shaking of the moulds is managed quickly, the colouring matter will settle on the side of the half into which the mixture is poured; a little care in manipulation is therefore again requisite. The colouring of the wax is a matter which comes easily enough by experiment. Oranges, lemons, large gooseberries, small cucumbers, &c., &c., are excellent objects for practice.

2295. To produce a Good Imitation of the Surface.—It will be noted by the close observer that the shell of the common hen's egg has a number of minute holes, which destroy the perfect smoothness of its appearance. This peculiarity is imitated in the following simple manner :—In the first place, very slightly prick with a fine needle the surface of your waxen egg, and then, having smeared it with spirits of turpentine, rub the surface all over, so as *nearly* to obliterate the marks of the needle point.

2296. Diaphanie. — This is a beautiful, useful, and inexpensive art, easily acquired, and producing imitations of the richest and rarest stained glass; and also of making blinds, screens, skylights, Chinese lanterns, &c., in every variety of colour and design.

2297. In Decorating his House, an Englishman spends as much money as he can conveniently spare; the elegances and refinements of modern taste demand something more than mere comfort; yet though his walls are hung with pictures, his drawing-rooms filled with bijouterie, how is it that the windows of his hall, his library, his staircase, are neglected? The reason is obvious. The magnificent historical old stained glass might be envied, but could not be brought within the compass of ordinary means. Recent improvements in printing in colours led the way to this beautiful invention, by which economy is combined with the most perfect results. A peculiar kind of paper is rendered perfectly transparent, upon which designs are printed in glass colours (*vitro de couleurs*), which will not change with the light. The paper is applied to the glass with a clear white varnish, and when dry, a preparation is finally applied, which increases the transparency, and adds tenfold brilliancy to the effect.

2298. THERE IS ANOTHER DESIGN, printed in imitation of the half-light (*abat-jour*); this is used principally for a ground, covering the whole surface of the glass, within which (the necessary spaces having been previously cut out before it is stuck on the glass) are placed medallion centres of Watteau figures, perfectly transparent, which derive increased brilliancy from the semi-transparency of the surrounding ground. This is by far the cheapest method, though involving extra trouble, as the plain grounds printed in sheets (20½ in. by 16¾) are only 1s. 6d. each; and there is one sheet of suitable transparent designs, which contains twenty-four medallion Watteau centres (price 6s.): twenty of these medallions average 3½ in. by 4 in., the remaining four measure 7 in. by 5 in.

2299. THE TRANSPARENT SHEETS are all 6s. each; they measure 20¼ in. by 16½, and are ready for immediate use. The varnish is 1s. 6d. per bottle; the liqueur diaphane, 1s. 6d. per bottle; brushes, 4d. each; metal palettes, 1s. 6d. each; ivory sticks from 1s. each. These are all the articles required.

2300. To ASCERTAIN THE QUANTITY of designs required, measure your glass carefully, and then calculate how many sheets it will take (the sizes of each kind are given above). The sheets are arranged so that they can be joined together continuously, or cut to any size or shape.

2301. PRACTICAL INSTRUCTIONS.— Choose a fine day for the operation, as the glass should be perfectly dry, and unaffected by the humidity of the atmosphere. Of course, if you have a choice, it is more *convenient* to work on your glass before it is fixed in the frame. If you are working on a piece of unattached glass, lay it on a *flat* table (a marble slab is preferable), over which you must previously lay a piece of baize or cloth to keep the glass steady. The glass being thus fixed, clean and polish the side on which you intend to operate (in windows this is the inner side), then with your brush lay on it very equably a good coat of the prepared varnish; let this dry for *an hour*, more or less, according to the dryness of the atmosphere and the thickness of the coat of varnish; meantime cut and trim your designs carefully to fit the glass (if it is one entire transparent sheet you will find little trouble); then lay them on a piece of paper, face downwards, and damp the back of them with a sponge, applied several times, to equalize the moisture. In this operation arrange your time so that your designs may now be finally left to dry for fifteen minutes before application to the glass, the varnish on which has now become tacky or sticky, and in a proper state to receive them. Apply the printed side next to the glass without pressure; endeavour to let your sheet fall perfectly level and smooth on your glass, so that you may avoid leaving creases, which would be fatal. Take now your palette, lay it flat on the design, and press out all the air-bubbles, commencing in the centre, and working them out at the sides; an ivory stick will be found useful in removing creases; you now leave this to dry, and after twenty-four hours apply a slight coat of the liqueur diaphane, leaving it another day, when, if dry, apply a second coat of the same kind, which must be left several days : finally, apply a coat of varnish over all.

2302. If these Directions are carefully followed, your glass will never be affected by time or any variations in the weather ; it will defy hail, rain, frost, and dust, and can be washed the same as ordinary stained glass, to which, in some respects, it is even superior.

2303. It is impossible to enumerate the variety of articles to the manufacture of which Diaphanie may be successfully applied, as it is not confined to glass, but can be done on silk, parchment, paper, linen, &c., *after they have been made transparent*, which may be accomplished in the following manner : —

2304. Stretch your Paper, or whatever it may be, on a frame or drawing board, then apply two successive coats (a day between each) of diaphanous liquor, and after leaving it to dry for *several* days, cover it with a thin layer of very clear size, and when dry it will be in a fit state to receive the coat of varnish and the designs.

2305. Silk, Linen, or other Stuffs should be more carefully stretched, and receive a thicker coat of size than paper or parchment ; the latter may be strained on a drawing or any other smooth board, by damping the sheet, and after pasting the edges, stretching it down while damp (silk, linen, and other stuffs require to be carefully stretched on a knitting or other suitable frame). Take great care to allow, *whatever you use*, time to dry before applying the liqueur diaphane.

2306. All kinds of Screens, lamp shades and glasses, lanterns, &c., &c., may be made in this way, as heat will produce no effect upon them. The transparent pictures are successful, because they may be hung on a window frame or removed at will, and the window blinds are far superior to anything of that kind that have yet been seen.

2307. Instead of steeping the Designs in the transparent liquor at the time of printing them, which was previously done *in order to show their transparency to the purchaser*, but which was practically objectionable, as the paper in that state was brittle, and devoid of pliancy, necessitating also the use of a peculiarly difficult vehicle to manage (varnish) in applying it to the glass, the manufacturer now prepares his paper differently, in order to allow the use of parchment size in sticking them on the glass. The liqueur diaphane, which is finally applied, renders them perfectly transparent. In this mode of operation, no delay is requisite, the designs being applied to the glass immediately after laying on the size, *taking care to press out all the air-bubbles*, for which purpose a roller will be found indispensable. The designs should be damped before the size is applied to them.

2308. Decalcomanie. — This recently discovered and beautiful art consists in transferring coloured drawings to glass, porcelain, china, wood, silk, furniture, plaster of Paris, alabaster, ivory, paper, paper hangings, windows, tea trays, oil cloth, and all kinds of fancy articles ; in short, materials of any kind, shape, or size, provided they possess a smooth surface, can be decorated with Decalcomanie ; the immediate result being an exact resemblance to painting by hand. The art itself is simple and ingenious, and while affording agreeable occupation to ladies, it may be made to serve many useful purposes, on account of the numerous objects which will admit of being thus ornamented.

2309. The Materials employed in Decalcomanie are,—i. A bottle of transfer varnish for fixing the drawings. ii. A bottle of light varnish to pass over the drawings when fixed. iii. A bottle of spirit to clean the brushes, and to remove those pictures which may not be successful. iv. A piece of beaver cloth about nine inches square. v. A paper-knife and roller. vi. Two or three camel-hair brushes. vii. A basin of water. viii. A bottle of opaque varnish.*

2310. INSTRUCTIONS.—Thoroughly clean and free from grease the article to be decorated; then, having cut off the white paper margin of the drawing, dip one of the brushes into the transfer varnish, and give it a very light coat, being especially careful to cover the whole of the coloured portion, but not to allow it to touch the blank paper; then lay the drawing, face downward, on the object to be ornamented, taking care to place it at once where it is to remain, as it would be spoilt by moving. If the varnish, on its first application, is too liquid, allow the picture to remain for about ten minutes to set. Moisten the cloth with water, and lay it gently on the drawing which has been previously laid in its place on the object to be decorated; then rub it over with the paper-knife or roller, so as to cause the print to adhere in every part; this done, remove the cloth, well soak the paper with a camel-hair brush dipped in water, and immediately after lift the paper by one corner, and gently draw it off. The picture will be left on the object, while the paper will come off perfectly white. Care must be taken that the piece of cloth, without being too wet, is sufficiently so to saturate the paper completely. The drawing must now be washed with a camel-hair brush, in clean water, to remove the surplus varnish, and then left till quite dry. On the following day, cover the picture with a light coat of the fixing varnish, to give brilliancy to the colours.

2311. To ORNAMENT DARK-COLOURED OBJECTS, such as the bindings of books, Russia leather, blotting-cases, leathern bags, &c., the picture must be previously covered with a mixture of opaque white varnish, taking care not to pass beyond the outline of

the design. On the following day, proceed according to the instructions given in the preceding paragraph.

2312. To ORNAMENT SILK PAPER, OR ARTICLES WHICH WILL NOT BEAR WETTING.—Varnish the picture with the transfer varnish, as previously explained, following the outline of the design, then allow it to dry for an hour or two; when quite dry, pass a damp sponge over the entire surface of the sheet, so as to remove the composition which surrounds the picture, and which may spoil the object. Let the paper dry once more, and varnish the picture again with the transfer varnish; in about ten minutes, place it face downward on the object to be decorated, and rub it with the paper-knife or roller, over the whole of its surface. Finally, moisten the paper with a wet brush, allow it to remain sufficiently long to become moist, then strip the paper off. *To remove a spoilt picture from any object*, dip a soft rag in the essence, and rub it over the surface.

2313. To INSURE A SUCCESSFUL RESULT, care must be taken to give a very light coating of varnish to the parts to be transferred. When the varnish is first applied it is very liquid, and must remain ten minutes, the best condition for transferring being when the varnish is only just sticky, without being too dry.

2314. THE FOLLOWING DESIGNS WILL BE FOUND THE MOST ELEGANT AND APPROPRIATE.—English flowers of every variety; bouquets; tropical birds; flowers and fruits in imitation of aquatint; garlands with cupids after Watteau, and garlands with birds; domestic scenes; pears and cherries, apples and plums, white grapes and plums, black grapes and peaches, plums and mulberries; large bouquet of roses; bouquets of moss roses and pansies; bouquets of small camelias; bouquets of wall-flowers and poppies; bouquets of orange-blossom, medallions, various subjects; birds' nests; Gothic initials and monograms, fleurs-de-lis; borders various.

* The requisite materials, together with designs, and appropriate articles for embellishment, may be obtained from Messrs. A. Marion and Co., 152, Regent Street, London.

M

2315. HERALDIC DECALCOMANIE is an extended application of this art, the arms and crests of persons or families being emblazoned in their proper colours according to the rules of heraldry, and prepared for Decalcomanie. Armorial bearings, thus embellished, serve admirably to ornament and identify the books of a library and pictures of a gallery, to decorate the theme of a banquet, the invitations to a soirée, and by their brilliant colours will give an elegant effect to the table decorations.

2316. Croquet.—This out-door pastime is of comparatively modern creation, and is every day becoming more in vogue. It may be played by persons of all ages and of either sex; but it is especially adapted for ladies and young persons, as it demands but trifling personal exertion, while it affords delightful and health-giving sport.

2317. THE GROUND UPON WHICH CROQUET IS PLAYED is preferably a grass-plot of an oblong form; but an ordinary lawn or expanse of even turf will answer the purpose, so long as it is of sufficient extent for the operations of the game.

2318. THE IMPLEMENTS FOR PLAYING Croquet are the balls, the mallets, the starting and turning pegs, the Croquet clips or markers, the hoops or arches. These may be obtained at the ordinary toy warehouses.

2319. ARRANGEMENT OF THE HOOPS.—As much of the interest of this game depends upon the arrangement of the hoops, it is essential that they should be fixed in the ground on definite principles. In the first place, the starting peg is driven in at one end of the ground, and the turning peg is driven in at the other extremity. From each of these pegs a space of twelve feet intervenes; here a hoop is fixed; another space of ten feet intervenes, when a second hoop is fixed; a space of eight feet then succeeds, and at this point is formed what may be termed the base, on each side of which, at a distance of twenty feet, and succeeding each other at intervals of

ten feet, three hoops are driven in. By this arrangement, a square is formed, the starting peg leading into its centre, and the turning peg leading from it. Where the ground is small, the distances may be contracted proportionally. Other arrangements of the hoops may be made at the discretion of the players, but the first-named plan will be found best worthy of adoption, as it affords the most excellent opportunities for the display of address and skill.

2320. THE GAME CONSISTS in striking the balls from the starting peg through the seven hoops to the peg at the opposite extremity. The balls are then driven back again to the starting peg.

2321. THE GAME MAY BE PLAYED by any number of persons not exceeding eight. A larger number protracts the intervals between the several turns, and thereby renders the game tedious. The most eligible number is four. If two only play, each player should take two balls, and when as many as eight play, there should be two sides or sets.

2322. IN PLAYING THE GAME, each player takes a mallet, ball, and Croquet clip of the same colour or number, the clip being used to indicate the hoop at which, in his turn, he aims. The division into sides, choice of balls, mallets, &c., is determined by the players among themselves.

2323. LAWS OF THE GAME.—In Croquet, as with many other sports when first established, there exist differences of opinion on certain points of practice. We have consulted numerous treatises on the game, and find Jaques's "Laws and Regulations of the Game of Croquet " [*] to be one of the most practical and straightforward manuals extant. It is to this work that we are mainly indebted for the following Laws of the Game:—

i. On commencing, each player must place his ball within a mallet's length

† "Croquet, Illustrated with Diagrams and Engravings." Jaques and Son, 102, Hatton Garden, London.

óf the starting peg in any direction, and his opening stroke must be to pass through the first hoop.

ii. The players on each side are to play alternately, according to the colours on the starting peg, and the order in which they play cannot be altered during the game.

iii. Each player continues to play so long as he plays with success, that is, so long as he drives his ball through the next hoop in order, or croquêts another ball.

iv. When a player strikes his own ball so as to hit another at a distance, he is said to roquet it; and, having thus hit a ball, he must then, as it is termed, "take the croquêt," which is done as follows:—He lays his own ball against the other so that the two touch; he then places his foot on his own ball, which he strikes with his mallet; this will drive the ball with a momentum and in a direction most desired. In doing this the player should press his foot on his own ball.

v. A player must move the ball he croquêts. He is said to "take a stroke off" when he places his own ball to touch the croquêted ball very lightly, so as to leave it, when croquêted, in nearly the same position; but in doing this the croquêted ball must be perceptibly moved.

vi. No ball can croquêt, or be croquêted, until it be passed through the first hoop.

vii. Any player missing the first hoop takes his ball up, and, when his turn comes again, plays from the starting place, as at first.

viii. A player may croquêt any number of balls consecutively; but he cannot croquêt the same ball twice during the same turn, without first sending his own ball through the next hoop in order.

ix. Instead of aiming at his hoop or another ball, a player may strike his ball towards any part of the ground he pleases. When he has made a complete circuit from the starting peg back to the starting peg he may either retire from the game by pegging, or, by not doing so, remain in. In this case he is called a "rover," and will still have the power of croquêting consecutively all the balls during any one of his turns.

x. When a ball roquêts another ball, the player's ball is "dead," and "in hand" until after the player of it has taken the croquêt. Hence it follows that if it cannon from one ball to another, or from a ball through its own hoop, or from a ball on to either of the pegs, none of these subsequent strokes count anything. If, however, a player cannon off a ball which in the same turn he has croquêted, and then runs off it and makes a stroke, that stroke counts.

xi. A player whose ball is roquêted or croquêted through its hoop in order, counts the hoop.

xii. A player must hit his ball fairly —not push it. A ball is considered to be fairly hit when the sound of the stroke is heard. A ball is "pushed" when the face of the mallet is allowed to rest against it, and the ball propelled without the mallet being drawn back.

xiii. A player may play in any attitude, and use his mallet with his hands in any way he pleases, so that he strike the ball with the face of the mallet.

xiv. When the ball of a player hits the starting peg, after he has been through all the hoops, whether by his own play, or by being roquêted (subject to the provisions in law x.), or by being croquêted, he is out of the game, which goes on without him, his turn being omitted.

xv. The clip is placed on the hoop through which the player is next going. The clips are to be changed by the umpire, and are decisive as to the position of a player's ball; but if the umpire forget to change a clip, any player may remind him before the next stroke. Should there be no clips, a player is entitled to ask any other player how he stands in the game.

xvi. A player stops at the peg; that is, having struck the turning peg in order, his turn is at an end, and even though he should roquet off the peg, it does not count. When his turn comes round again, he plays his ball from the spot it rolled to after pegging.

xvii. A ball is considered to have passed through its hoop if it cannot be touched by the handle of the mallet, laid on the ground from wire to wire, on the side from which the ball passed.

xviii. The decision of the umpire is final. His duties are—to move the clips; to decide when balls are fairly struck; to restore balls to their places which have been disturbed by accident; and to decide whether a croquêted ball is moved or not, in doubtful cases.

2324. TERMS USED IN THE GAME. —*Roquêt.*—To hit another ball with one's own. *Croquêt.*—To strike one's own ball when in contact with a roquêted ball. *Wired.*—To have the ball in such a position that a hoop prevents the stroke which is wished to be made. *Peg.*—To "peg" is to strike either of the pegs in proper order. *Dismiss.*—To "dismiss" a ball is to croquêt it to a distance.

2325. Habits of a Man of Business. —A sacred regard to the principles of justice forms the basis of every transaction, and regulates the conduct of the upright man of business.

He is strict in keeping his engagements.

Does nothing carelessly or in a hurry.

Employs nobody to do what he can easily do himself.

Keeps everything in its proper place.

Leaves nothing undone that ought to be done, and which circumstances permit him to do.

Keeps his designs and business from the view of others.

Is prompt and decisive with his customers, and does not over-trade his capital.

Prefers short credits to long ones; and cash to credit at all times, either in buying or selling; and small profits in credit cases with little risk, to the chance of better gains with more hazard.

He is clear and explicit in all his bargains.

Leaves nothing of consequence to memory which he can and ought to commit to writing.

Keeps copies of all his important letters which he sends away, and has every letter, invoice, &c., belonging to his business, titled, classed, and put away. Never suffers his desk to be confused by many papers lying upon it.

Is always at the head of his business, well knowing that if he leaves it, it will leave him.

Holds it as a maxim that he whose credit is suspected is not one to be trusted.

Is constantly examining his books, and sees through all his affairs as far as care and attention will enable him.

Balances regularly at stated times, and then makes out and transmits all his accounts current to his customers, both at home and abroad.

Avoids as much as possible all sorts of accommodation in money matters, and lawsuits where there is the least hazard.

He is economical in his expenditure, always living within his income.

Keeps a memorandum-book in his pocket, in which he notes every particular relative to appointments, addresses, and petty cash matters.

Is cautious how he becomes security for any person; and is generous when urged by motives of humanity.

Let a man act strictly to these habits—ever remembering that he hath no profits by his pains whom Providence doth not prosper—and success will attend his efforts.

2326. Taking a Shop or Place of Business. — If you are about to take a place of business, you will do well to consider the following remarks:—

2327. SMALL CAPITALISTS.—Let us take the case of a person who has no intimate knowledge of any particular trade, but having a very small capital, is about to embark it in the exchange of commodities for cash, in order to obtain an honest livelihood thereby. It is clear, that unless such a person starts with proper precaution and judgment, the capital will be expended without adequate results; rent and taxes will accumulate, the stock will lie dead or become deteriorated, and loss and·ruin must follow. For the least absorption acting upon a small capital will soon dry up its source; and we need not picture the trouble that will arise when the mainspring of a tradesman's success abides by him no more.

2328. LARGER CAPITALISTS.—The case of the larger capitalist can scarcely be considered an exception to the same rule. For it is probable that the larger capitalist, upon commencing a business, would sink more of his funds in a larger stock—would incur liability to a heavier rent; and the attendant taxes, the wages of assistants and servants, would be greater, and, therefore, if the return came not speedily, similar consequences must sooner or later ensue.

2329. LOCALITIES.—Large or small capitalists should, therefore, upon entering on a shopkeeping speculation, consider well the nature of the locality in which they propose to carry on trade, the number of the population, the habits and wants of the people, and the extent to which they are already supplied with the goods which the new adventurer proposes to offer them.

2330. NEW NEIGHBOURHOODS.— There is a tendency among small capitalists to rush into new neighbourhoods with the expectation of making an early connection. Low rents also serve as an attraction to these localities. We have found, however, in our experience, that the early suburban shops seldom succeed. They are generally entered upon at the very earliest moment that the state of the locality will permit— often before the house is finished the shop is tenanted, and goods exposed for sale—even while the streets are unpaved, and while the roads are as rough and uneven as country lanes. The consequence is, that as the few inhabitants of these localities have frequent communication with adjacent towns, they,

as a matter of habit or of choice, supply their chief wants thereat; and the suburban shopkeeper depends principally for support upon the accidental forgetfulness of his neighbour, who omits to bring something from the cheaper and better market; or upon the changes of the weather, which may sometimes favour him by rendering a "trip to town" exceedingly undesirable.

2331. FAILURES.—"While the grass is growing the horse is starving;" and thus, while the new district is becoming peopled the funds of the small shopkeeper are gradually eaten up, and he puts up his shutters just at the time when a more cautious speculator steps in to profit by the connection already formed, and to take advantage of the now improved condition of the locality. It seems, therefore, desirable for the small capitalist rather to run the risk of a more expensive rent, in a well-peopled district, than to resort to places of slow and uncertain demand; for the welfare of the small shopkeeper depends entirely upon the frequency with which his limited stock is cleared out and replaced by fresh supplies.

2332. PRECAUTIONS.—But should the small capitalist still prefer opening in a suburban district, where competition is less severe, and rents and rates less burdensome, there are certain precautions which he will do well to observe. He should particularly guard against opening a shop to supply what may be termed the superfluities of life; for the inhabitants of suburban districts are those who, like himself, have resorted to a cheap residence for the sake of economy. Or, if this be not the case— if they are people of independent means, who prefer the "detached villa" to the town house, squeezed up on both sides, they have the means of riding and driving to town, and will prefer choosing articles of taste and luxury from the best marts, enriched by the finest display.

2333. NECESSITIES OR LUXURIES. —The suburban shopkeeper should, therefore, confine himself to supplying the *necessities* of life. Hungry people dislike to fetch their bread from five miles off; and to bring vegetables from a long distance would evidently be a matter of considerable inconvenience. The baker, the butcher, the green-grocer, the beer retailer, &c., are those who find their trade first established in suburban localities. And not until these are doing well should the tailor, the shoemaker, the hatter, the draper, the hosier, and others, expect to find a return for their capital and reward for their labour.

2334. CIVILITY.—In larger locali-ties, where competition abounds, the small shopkeeper frequently outstrips his more powerful rival by one element of success, which may be added to any stock without cost, but cannot be with-held without loss. That element is *civility*. It has already been spoken of elsewhere, but must be enforced here, as aiding the little means of the small shopkeeper to a wonderful degree. A kind and obliging manner carries with it an indescribable charm. It must not be a manner which indicates a mean, grovelling, time-serving spirit, but a plain, open, and agreeable demeanour, which seems to desire to oblige for the pleasure of doing so, and not for the sake of squeezing an extra penny cut of a customer's pocket.

2335. INTEGRITY.—The sole reli-ance of the shopkeeper should be in the integrity of his transactions, and in the civility of his demeanour. He should make it the interest and the pleasure of the customer to come to his shop. If he does this, he will form the very best " connections," and so long as he continues this system of business, they will never desert him.

2336. DUTIES OF A SHOPKEEPER. —He should cheerfully render his best labour and knowledge to serve those who approach his counter, and place confidence in his transactions; make himself alike to rich and poor, but never resort to mean subterfuge and deception to gain approbation and support. He should be frugal in

his expenditure, that, in deriving pro-fits from trade, he may not trespass unduly upon the interests of others ; he should so hold the balance between man and man that he should feel nothing to reprove his conscience when the day comes for him to repose from his labours and live upon the fruits of his industry. Let the public discover such a man, and they will flock around him for their own sakes.

2337. A very useful book, " The Shopkeeper's Guide " * (published at one and sixpence), enlarges upon these sub-jects in a very able manner, and gives most useful hints to people in every department of trade.

2338. Early Rising.—The dif-ference between rising every morning at six and at eight, in the course of forty years, amounts to 29,200 hours, or three years one hundred and twenty-one days and sixteen hours, which are equal to eight hours a day for exactly ten years. So that rising at six will be the same as if ten years of life (a weighty consi-deration) were added, wherein we may command eight hours every day for the cultivation of our minds and the de-spatch of business.

2339. Frugality.—i. The great philosopher, Dr. Franklin, inspired the mouthpiece of his own eloquence, " Poor Richard," with " many a gem of purest ray serene," encased in the homely garb of proverbial truisms. On the subject of frugality we can-not do better than take the worthy Mentor for our text, and from it ad-dress our remarks. A man may, if he knows not how to save as he gets, " keep his nose all his life to the grindstone, and die not worth a groat at last. A fat kitchen makes a lean will."

" Many estates are spent in getting,
   Since women for tea forsook spinning and
     knitting,
   And men for punch forsook hewing and
     splitting."

---

* Houlston and Wright, London.

ii. If you would be wealthy, think of saving as well as of getting. The Indies have not made Spain rich, because her out-goes are greater than her incomes.

iii. Away with your expensive follies, and you will not have so much cause to complain of hard times, heavy taxes, and chargeable families.

iv. "What maintains one vice would bring up two children."

v. You may think, perhaps, that a little tea, or superfluities now and then, diet a little more costly, clothes a little finer, and a little entertainment now and then, can be no great matter; but remember, "Many a little makes a mickle."

vi. Beware of little expenses: "A small leak will sink a great ship," as Poor Richard says; and again, "Who dainties love, shall beggars prove;" and moreover, "Fools make feasts and wise men eat them."

vii. Here you are all got together to this sale of fineries and nick-nacks. You call them goods; but if you do not take care they will prove evils to some of you. You expect they will be sold cheap, and perhaps they may, for less than they cost; but if you have no occasion for them they must be dear to you.

viii. Remember what Poor Richard says, "Buy what thou hast no need of, and ere long thou shalt sell thy necessaries."

ix. "At a great pennyworth, pause awhile." He means, perhaps, that the cheapness is apparent only, and not real; or the bargain, by straitening thee in thy business, may do thee more harm than good; for in another place he says, "Many have been ruined by buying good pennyworths."

x. "It is foolish to lay out money in the purchase of repentance;" and yet this folly is practised every day at auctions for want of minding the Almanack.

2340. Cash and Credit.—If you would get rich, don't deal in bill books. Credit is the "Tempter in a new shape."

Buy goods on trust, and you will purchase a thousand articles that cash would never have dreamed of. A shilling in the hand looks larger than ten shillings seen through the perspective of a three months' bill. Cash is practical, while credit takes horribly to taste and romance. Let cash buy a dinner, and you will have a beef-steak flanked with onions. Send credit to market, and he will return with eight pairs of woodcocks and a peck of mushrooms. Credit believes in diamond pins and champagne suppers. Cash is more easily satisfied. Give him three meals a day, and he doesn't care much if two of them are made up of roasted potatoes and a little dirty salt. Cash is a good adviser, while credit is a good fellow to be on visiting terms with. If you want double chins and contentment, do business with cash.

2341. Hints upon Money Matters.—Have a supply of change in hand—shillings, sixpences, halfpence. This will obviate the various inconveniences of keeping people at the door, sending out at unreasonable times, and running or calling after any inmate in the house, supposed to be better provided with "the needful." The tradespeople with whom you regularly deal will always give you extra change, *when* you are making purchases or paying bills; while those to whom you apply for it, on a sudden emergency, may neither be willing nor able to do so. Some housekeepers object to this arrangement, that, "as soon as five-pound notes or sovereigns are changed, they always seem to go, without their understanding how;" but to such persons I would humbly intimate, that this is rather the fault of their *not getting understanding*, than any inevitable consequence of *getting change*. The fact is, that it is the necessity of parting with your money which obliges you to get the larger pieces changed, and not the circumstance of having smaller coin that *necessitates* your parting with your money, though it certainly facilitates your doing so when the necessity arrives. However, as it is easier to count a few sovereigns than many shillings, and loose money is most objectionable, it is well to put up reserve change in small collective packets, and to replenish the house-keeping purse from these daily or weekly, as may be most convenient.

2342. IF MONEY FOR daily ex-penses has to pass through the hands of a domestic, it is a time and trouble-saving plan to settle with her *every* night, and to make up her cash in hand to a certain *similar* sum. This will prevent such puzzling calculations as the following:—" Let me see : I gave you 10s. on Saturday, and 9d. the day before. Was it 9d. ? No, it must have been 11d., for I gave you 1s., and you gave me 1d. out for the beggar; then there was 0s. 6d. on Monday, and 8d. you owed me from last money; and then the 1s. 6d. your master gave you for a parcel—you brought him 2d. back, and 3½d. out of the butcher's bill; no—*you* had to give 3½d. to the butcher, but you came to me for the ½d., and I had no coppers, so we still owe him the ½d.; by the way, don't forget to pay him the next time you go. Then there's the baker—no, I paid the baker myself, and I *think* the housemaid paid the butterman; but you got in the cheese the day before, and I have a sort of recollection that I may possibly owe you for *that*, all but a few pence you must have had left of mine, that I told you to take from off the chimney-piece. Well, cook, I think that's *nearly* all! Now how do your accounts stand ?" This the poor cook, who *is* a cook, and *not* a conjuror, finds it no easy matter to discover; all that she is quite certain of is, that her disbursements have somewhat exceeded her receipts, and being an honest woman, though a poor one, she wishes to cheat neither her mistress nor her-self; but what with her memory and her want of it, her involved payments, and different receipts; what she owed her mistress, and what her mistress owes her; what she got from her master, and what was partly settled by the housemaid; the balance from the butcher's bill, and the intricacies of the cheese account, the poor woman is perfectly bewildered. She counts again and again; recapitulates her mistress's data and her own; sums upwards, backwards, and forwards, and endea-vours to explain the differences between them; then, if she can read and write, she brings her slate' to "explain the explanation," and the united calcula-tions of maid and mistress, which are after all entirely unavailing to produce a correct account, probably consume more time, and are expressed in more words, than would suffice to fill another volume like the present. Two minutes' daily reckoning from a *regular* sum in hand would do the business effec-tually, and prevent either party from being out of pocket or out of temper. Thus, for instance, the maid has her usual sum of five shillings to ac-count for; she pays during the day, for—

	s.	d.
Bread	1	9
Beer	0	6
Vegetables and fruit . . .	0	10
Milk	0	4
Matches	0	1
Parcel	1	0
Total . .	4	6

This is easily reckoned, even by the unlearned; the mistress enters the items in her day-book, takes the remaining sixpence, and again gives her servant 5s., in convenient change, to be as readily accounted for on the succeeding day."—*Home Truths for Home Peace; or, "Muddle Defeated."*

2343. Don't Run in Debt.

"DON'T run in debt;"—never mind, never mind
If your clothes are faded and torn:
Seam them up, make them do; it is better by far
Than to have the heart weary and worn,
Who'll love you the more for the shape of your hat,
Or your ruff, or the tie of your shoe,

The cut of your vest, or your boots, or cravat,
  If they know you're in debt for the new?
There's no comfort, I tell you, in walking the
    street
  In fine clothes, if you know you're in
    debt;
And feel that, perchance, you some tradesman
    may meet,
  Who will sneer—"They're not paid for
    yet."
Good friends, let me beg of you, don't run in
    debt:
  If the chairs and the sofas are old,
They will fit your back better than any new set,
  Unless they are paid for—with gold;
If the house is too small, draw the closer
    together,
  Keep it warm with a hearty good-will;
A big one unpaid for, in all kinds of weather,
  Will send to your warm heart a chill.
Don't run in debt—now, dear girls, take a
    hint,
  If the fashions have changed since last
    season,
Old Nature is out in the very same tint,
  And old Nature, we think, has some reason.
But just say to your friend, that you cannot
    afford
  To spend time to keep up with the fashion :
That your purse is too light, and your honour
    too bright,
  To be tarnished with such silly passion.
Gents, don't run in debt—let your friends, if
    they can,
  Have fine houses, and feathers, and flowers ;
But, unless they are paid for, be more of a
    man
  Than to envy their sunshiny hours.
If you've money to spare, I have nothing to
    say—
  Spend your silver and gold as you please ;
But mind you, the man who his bill has to
    pay
  Is the man who is never at ease.
Kind husbands, don't run into debt any more ;
  'Twill fill your wives' cup full of sorrow
To know that a neighbour may call at your
    door,
  With a claim you must settle to-morrow.
Oh ! take my advice—it is good, it is true !
  But, lest you may some of you doubt it,
I'll whisper a secret now, seeing 'tis you—
  I have tried it, and know all about it :
The chain of a debtor is heavy and cold,
  Its links all corrosion and rust ;
Gild it o'er as you will, it is never of gold,
  Then spurn it aside with disgust."

2344. Carving.—Ceremonies of
the Table, &c.—A dinner-table should
be well laid, well lighted, and always
afford a little spare room. It is better
to invite one friend less in number, than
to destroy the comfort of the whole
party.

2345. The Laying out of a
Table must greatly depend upon the
nature of the dinner or supper, the
taste of the host, the description of the
company, and the appliances possessed.
It would be useless, therefore, to lay
down specific rules. The whiteness of
the table-cloth, the clearness of glass,
the polish of plate, and the judicious
distribution of ornamental groups of
fruits and flowers, are matters deserv-
ing the utmost attention.

2346. A Sideboard will greatly
relieve a crowded table, upon which
may be placed many things incidental
to the successive courses, until they are
required.

2347. A Bill of Fare at large
dinner parties, where there are several
courses, should be provided, neatly in-
scribed upon small tablets, and distributed about the table, that the diners
may know what there is to come.

2348. Napkins should be folded
neatly. The French method, which is
very easy, of folding the napkin like a
fan, placing it in a glass, and spreading
out the upper part, is very pleasing.
But the English method of folding it
like a slipper, and placing the bread
inside of it, is convenient as well as
neat.

2349. Bread should be cut into
thick squares, the last thing after the
table is laid. If cut too early it becomes dry. A tray should be provided,
in which there should be a further supply of bread, new, stale, and brown.
For cheese, pulled bread should be provided.

2350. Carving-knives should be
"put in edge" before the dinner commences, for nothing irritates a good
carver, or perplexes a bad one, more
than a knife which refuses to perform
its office; and there is nothing more

annoying to the company than to see the carving-knife dancing to and fro over the steel while the dinner is getting cold, and their appetites are being exhausted by delay.

2351. Joints that require Carving should be set upon dishes sufficiently large. The space of the table may be economised by setting upon small dishes those things that do not require carving.

2352. The Carver should have plenty of Room, however closely the diners are compelled to sit together.

2353. The Vegetables, if the table is very crowded, may be placed upon the sideboard, and handed round by the waiters.

2354. Geese, Turkeys, Poultry, Sucking-pigs, &c., should be carved before being sent to table; especially in those cases where the whole or the principal part of such dishes is likely to be consumed.

2355. The Carver should supply the plates, and the waiter hand them round, instead of putting the question to each guest as to which part he prefers, and then striving to serve him with it, to the prejudice of others present.

2356. Ladies should be assisted before gentlemen.

2357. Waiters should present dishes on the left hand; so that the diner may assist himself with his right.

2358. Wine should be taken after the first course; and it will be found more convenient to let the waiter serve it, than to hand the decanters round, or to allow the guests to fill for themselves.

2359. Waiters should be instructed to remove whatever articles upon the table are thrown into disuse by the progress of the dinner, as soon as they are at liberty.

2360. Finger-glasses, or glass or plated bowls, filled with rose or orange water, slightly warm in winter, and iced in summer, should be handed round.

2361. When the Dessert is served, the wine should be set upon the table, and the decanters passed round by the company.

2362. Fried Fish should be divided into suitable slices, before the fire, as soon as it leaves the frying-pan.

2363. Cod's Head and Shoulders.—The thick part of the back is best. It should be carved in unbroken slices, and each solid slice should be accompanied by a bit of the sound, from under the back-bone, or from the cheek, jaws, tongue, &c., of the head.

2364. Turbot.—Strike the fish-slice along the back-bone, which runs from head to tail, and then serve square slices from the thick part, accompanying each slice with some of the gelatinous skin of the fins and thin part, which may be raised by laying the fish-slice flat.

2365. Brill is served in the same manner.

2366. John Dory is also served in the same way. The latter has a favourite piece on the cheek.

2367. Plaice and Flat-fish generally, are served in the same manner.

2368. Soles, when large, may be served as turbot; but when small, should be sliced across.

2369. Salmon.—Serve a slice of the thick with a smaller slice of the thin part. Keep the flakes of the thick part as firm as possible.

2370. Mackarel should be served in pieces cut through the side when they are large. If small, they may be divided through the back-bone, and served in halves. The shoulder part is considered the best.

2371. Whiting are usually fried and curled; they should be cut in half down the back, and served. The shoulder-part is best.

2372. Eels are usually cut into several pieces, either for stewing or frying. The thick parts are considered best.

2373. Remarks. — The *roes* of mackarel, the *sound* of cod, the *head* of carp, the *cheek* of John Dory, the *liver* of cod, &c., are severally considered delicacies, though not by all persons. Trout, perch, jack, hake, haddock, gurnet, &c., are all served in a similar manner.

2374. SADDLE OF MUTTON.—Cut thin slices parallel with the back-bone; or slice it obliquely from the bone to the edge.

2375. SADDLES OF PORK OR LAMB are carved in the same manner.

2376. HAUNCH OF MUTTON OR VENISON. — Make an incision across the knuckle-end, right into the bone, and set free the gravy. Then cut thin slices the whole length of the haunch. Serve pieces of fat with slices of lean.

2377. RUMP OR SIRLOIN OF BEEF —The undercut, called "the fillet," is exceedingly tender, and it is usual to turn the joint and serve the fillet first, reserving the meat on the upper part to serve cold. From the upper part the slices may be cut either lengthways or crossways, at option.

2378. RIBS OF BEEF are carved in the same way as the sirloin; but there is no fillet.

2379. ROUND OF BEEF.—First cut away the irregular outside pieces, to obtain a good surface, and then serve thin and broad slices. Serve bits of the udder fat with the lean.

2380. BRISKET OF BEEF.—Cut off the outside, and then serve long slices, cut the whole length of the bones.

2381. SHOULDER OF MUTTON.— Make a cross incision on the fore-part of the shoulder, and serve slices from both sides of the incision; then cut slices lengthways along the shoulder-blade. Cut fat slices from the round corner.

2382. LEG OF MUTTON.—Make an incision across the centre, and serve from the knuckle-side, or the opposite, according to choice. The knuckle-side will be generally found well done, and the opposite side underdone, for those who prefer it.

2383. LOIN OF MUTTON.—Cut down between the bones, into chops.

2384. QUARTER OF LAMB.—Lay the knife flat, and cut off the shoulder. The proper point for incision will be indicated by the position of the shoulder. A little lemon juice may be squeezed over the divided part, and a little cayenne pepper, and the shoulder transferred to another dish, for the opposite end of the table. Next separate the BRISKET, or short bones, by cutting lengthways along the breast. Then serve from either part as desired.

2385. LOIN OF VEAL may be cut across through the thick part; or slices may be taken in the direction of the bones. Serve pieces of kidney and fat with each plate.

2386. FILLET OF VEAL is carved as a round of beef. The browned bits of the outside are esteemed, and should be shared among the company, with bits of fat and of forcemeat from the centre.

2387. BREAST OF VEAL should be divided by cutting the BRISKET, or soft bones, the same as the brisket of lamb. When the sweetbread comes to table with the breast, a small piece should be served on each plate.

2888. SUCKING-PIG should be sent to table in two halves, the head divided, and one half laid at each end of the dish. The shoulders and legs should be taken off by the obvious method of laying the knife under them, and lifting the joint out. They may be served whole, or divided. The ribs are easily divided, and are considered choice.

2389. TONGUES are cut across in thin slices.

2390. CALVES' HEADS are carved across the cheek, and pieces taken from any part that is come-at-able. The tongue and brain sauce are served separate.

2391. KNUCKLE OF VEAL is carved by cutting off the outside pieces, and then obtaining good slices, and apportioning the fat to the lean, adding bits of the sinew that lie around the joint.

2392. LEG OF PORK is carved as a ham, but in thicker slices; when stuffed, the stuffing must be sought for under the skin at the large end.

2393. LOIN OF PORK is carved the same as a loin of mutton.

2394. SPARE-RIB OF PORK is carved by separating the chops, which should previously have been jointed. Cut as far as the joint, then return the knife to the point of the bones, and press over, to disclose the joint, which may then be relieved with the point of the knife.

2395. HAMS are cut in very thin slices from the knuckle to the blade.

2396. PHEASANTS. — Carve the breast in slices. Then take off the legs and wings.

2397. FOWLS.—Fix the fork firmly into the breast, then slip the knife under the legs, and lay it over and disjoint; detach the wings in the same manner. Do the same on both sides. The smaller bones require a little practice, and it would be well to watch the operations of a good carver. When the merry-thought has been removed (which it may be by slipping the knife through at the point of the breast), and the neck-bones drawn out, the trunk may be turned over, and the knife thrust through the back-bone.

2398. PARTRIDGES are best carved by cutting off the breast, and then dividing it. But for more economical carving, the wings may be cut with a small breast slice attached.

2399. WOODCOCKS may be cut right through the centre, from head to tail. Serve with them a piece of the toast upon which they come to table.

2400. PIGEONS may be carved as woodcocks, or as partridges.

2401. SNIPES the same as woodcocks.

2402. TURKEY.—Cut slices from each side of the breast down to the ribs; the legs may then be removed, and the thighs divided from the drum-sticks, which are very tough; but the pinions of the wing are very good, and the white part of the wing is preferred by many to the breast. The stuffing is usually put in the breast; but when truffles, mushrooms, or oysters are put into the body, an opening must be made into it by cutting through the apron.

2403. GOOSE.—The apron must be cut off in a circular direction, when a glass of port wine, mixed with a teaspoonful of mustard, may be poured into the body or not. Some of the stuffing should then be drawn out, and, the neck of the goose being turned a little towards the carver, the flesh of the breast should be sliced on each side of the bone. The wings may then be taken off, then the legs. The other parts are carved the same as a fowl.

2404. DUCKS may be carved, when large, the same as geese; but when young, like chickens. The thigh joints, however, lie much closer into the trunk than those of fowls.

2405. HARES should be placed with their heads to the left of the carver. Slices may be taken down the whole length of the back; the legs, which, next to the back, are considered the best eating, may then be taken off, and the flesh divided from or served upon them, after the small bones have been parted from the thighs. The shoulders, which are not much esteemed, though sometimes liked by sportsmen, may be taken off by passing the knife between the joint and the trunk. When a hare is young, the back is sometimes divided at the joints into three or four parts, after being freed from the ribs and under-skin.

2406. REMARKS.—Sufficient general instructions are here given to enable the carver, by observation and practice, to acquit himself well. The art of carving does not consist merely in dissecting the joints sent to table, but in the judicious and economical distribution of them, and the grace and neatness with which this distribution is effected. Every dish should be sent to table properly garnished (where needed), and the carver should preserve the neatness of the arrangement as much as possible.

2407. Dyeing. — The filaments from which stuffs of all kinds are fabricated are derived either from the animal or vegetable kingdom. We recognize the former by the property they possess of liberating ammonia on being treated with potash; while the latter afford a liquor having an acid reaction under the same treatment. The animal kingdom furnishes three varieties—silk, wool, and the furs, &c., of various animals; the vegetable kingdom also three—flax, hemp, and cotton: all of which require certain preliminary preparations to render them fit for the dyer, which do not come within our province, our space only admitting of a rapid glance at the production of the various colours.

2408. GENERAL OBSERVATIONS.—The various shades produced by colouring matters may be classed in one or other of the following groups:—

1. Blues
2. Reds   } *Simple.*
3. Yellows
4. Violets
5. Orange colours } *Binary.*
6. Greens
7. Compound colours } *Ternary.*
8. Black

Some colours adhere at once to the stuff, and are called *substantial colours;* while others require that the material to be dyed should undergo some previous preparation in order to render it permanent. The substances used to fix the colouring matters are called *mordants,* which should possess four qualifications:—i. They should possess an equal affinity for the fibre of the material and the colouring matter. ii. They should be incapable of injuring or destroying either by prolonged action. iii. They should form, with the colour, a compound capable of resisting the action of air and water. iv. They should be capable of readily conforming to the various operations of the dyer.

2409. THE MORDANTS.—For the reasons just given, the acetate or tartrate of iron is preferable to the sulphate; and the acetate or tartrate of alumina to alum. *For reds, yellows, green, and pinks,* aluminous mordants are to be used. *For blacks, browns, puces, and violets,* the acetate or tartrate of iron must be employed. *For scarlets,* use a tin mordant, made by dissolving in strong nitric acid one-eighth of its weight of sal ammoniac, then adding by degrees one-eighth of its weight of tin, and diluting the solution with one-fourth of its weight of water.

2410. CALICO, LINEN, AND MUSLIN. *Blue.* — Wash well to remove dressing, and dry; then dip in a strong solution of sulphate of indigo—partly saturated with potash—and hang up. Dry a piece to see if the colour is deep enough; if not, dip again. *Saxon Blue.* —Boil the article in alum, and then dip in a strong solution of chemical blue.

2411. CALICO, LINEN, AND MUSLIN. *Buff.*—Boil an ounce of anatto in three quarts of water, add two ounces of potash, stir well, and put in the calico while boiling, and stir well for five minutes; remove and plunge into cold pump water, hang up the articles without wringing, and when almost dry, fold.

2412. CALICO, LINEN, AND MUSLIN. *Pink.*—Immerse in the acetate of alumina mordant, and then in the colouring matter of a pink saucer.

2413. CALICO, LINEN, AND MUSLIN. *Green.*—Boil the article in an alum mordant, and then in a solution of indigo mixed with any of the yellow dyes, until the proper colour is obtained.

2414. CALICO, LINEN, AND MUSLIN. *Yellow.*—i. Cut potato tops when in flower, and express the juice; steep articles in this for forty-eight hours. ii. Dip in a strong solution of weld after boiling in an aluminous mordant. Turmeric, fustic, anatto, &c., will answer the same as weld.

2415. CLOTH. *Black.* — Impregnate the material with the acetate of iron mordant, and then boil in a decoction of madder and logwood.

2416. CLOTH. *Madder Red.*—Boil the cloth in a weak solution of pearl-ash—an ounce to a gallon of water,—wash, dry, and then steep in a decoction of bruised nutgalls. After drying, it is to be steeped twice in dry alum water, then dried, and boiled in a decoction made of three quarters of a pound of madder to every pound of the article. It should then be taken out and dried, and steeped in a second bath in the same manner. When dyed, the articles should be washed in warm soap and water, to remove a dun-coloured matter given out by the madder.

2417. CLOTH. *Scarlet.* — Three quarters of a pint of a tin mordant, made by dissolving three pounds of tin in sixty pounds of hydrochloric acid, is added to every pound of lac dye, and digested for six hours. To dye twenty-five pounds of cloth, a tin boiler of seventy-five gallons capacity should be filled nearly full with water, and a fire kindled under it. When the heat is 150° Fahr., half a handful of bran and two ounces of tin mordant are to be thrown into it. The froth which arises is skimmed off, the liquor is made to boil, and two pounds and three quarters of lac dye, previously mixed with a pound and three quarters of the solvent, and fourteen ounces of the tin solvent, are added. Immediately afterwards two pounds and three quarters of tartar, and a pound of ground sumach, both tied up in a linen bag, are to be added, and suspended in the bath for five minutes. The fire being withdrawn, five gallons of cold water and two pints and three quarters of tin mordant being poured into the bath, the cloth is immersed in it. The fire is then replaced, and the liquid made to boil rapidly for an hour, when the cloth is removed and washed in pure water.

2418. CLOTH. *Yellow.*—Use No. ii. for calico. Quercitron and weld produce a solid yellow; fustic, a very brilliant tint; while turmeric yields a less solid yellow.

2419. FEATHERS. *Black.*—Use the same as for cloth.

2420. FEATHERS. *Blue.* — Every shade may be given by indigo—or dip in silk dye.

2421. FEATHERS. *Crimson.*—Dip in acetate of alumina mordant, then in a boiling-hot decoction of Brazil-wood

—and, last of all, pass through a bath of cudbear.

2422. FEATHERS. *Pink, or Rose colour,* is given by safflower and lemon juice.

2423. FEATHERS. *Deep Red.*—Proceed as for crimson, omitting the cudbear bath.

2424. FEATHERS. *Yellow.*—Mordant with acetate of alumina, and dip in a bath of turmeric or weld.

2425. HAIR. *Black.*—As the object in view is simply to dye the hair without tinging the skin, the following will be found the best:—Take equal parts of litharge and lime; mix well, and form into a paste with water, if a black is desired; with milk, if brown. Clean the head with a small tooth comb, and then well wash the hair with soda and water to free it from grease; then lay on the paste pretty thick, and cover the head with oilskin or a cabbage-leaf, after which go to bed. Next morning the powder should be carefully brushed away, and the hair oiled.

2426. LEATHER. *Black.*—Use No. iv. *black stain,* and polish with oil.

2427. GLOVES. *Nankeen.* — Steep saffron in boiling-hot soft water for about twelve hours; sew up the tops of the gloves, to prevent the dye staining the insides, wet them over with a sponge dipped in the liquid. A teacupful of dye will do a pair of gloves.

2428. GLOVES. *Purple.*—Boil four ounces of logwood and two ounces of roche alum in three pints of soft water till half wasted; strain, and let it cool. Sew up the tops, go over the outsides with a brush or sponge twice; then rub off the loose dye with a coarse cloth. Beat up the white of an egg, and rub it over the leather with a sponge. Vinegar will remove the stain from the hands.

2429. SILK. *Black.*—Use the same as for cloth, but black dyeing is difficult.

2430. SILK. *Blue.*—i. Wash quite clean, rinse well, and then dip in a hot solution of sulphate of iron; after a short time take it out and rinse again. Have ready in another vessel a hot solution of prussiate of potash, to which a small quantity of sulphuric acid has been added. Dip the silk in this liquid; on removal rinse in clean water, and expose to the air to dry. ii. Wash well, rinse, wring out, and then dip in the following:—Boil a pound of indigo, two pounds of woad, and three ounces of alum, in a gallon of water. When the silk is of a proper colour, remove, rinse, and dry.

2431. SILK. *Carnation.*—Boil two gallons of wheat and an ounce of alum in four gallons of water; strain through a fine sieve; dissolve half a pound more of alum and white tartar; add three pounds of madder, then put in the silk at a moderate heat.

2432. SILK. *Crimson.*—Take about a spoonful of cudbear, put it into a small pan, pour boiling water upon it; stir and let it stand a few minutes, then put in the silk, and turn it over in a short time, and when the colour is full enough, take it out; but if it should require more violet or crimson, add a spoonful or two of purple archil to some warm water; steep, and dry it within doors. It must be mangled, and ought to be pressed.

2433. SILK. *Lilac.*—For every pound of silk, take one and a half pound of archil, mix it well with the liquor; make it boil for a quarter of an hour, dip the silk quickly, then let it cool, and wash it in river water, and a fine half violet, or lilac, more or less full, will be obtained.

2434. SILK. *Madder Red.*—Use the dye for cloth.

2435. SILK. *Yellow.*—Take clear wheat bran liquor fifteen pounds, in which dissolve three quarters of a pound of alum; boil the silk in this for two hours, and afterwards take half a pound of weld, and boil it till the colour is good. Nitre used with alum and water in the first boiling fixes the colour.

2436. WOOL. *Blue.*—Boil in a decoction of logwood and sulphate or acetate of copper.

2437. WOOL. *Brown.* — Steep in an infusion of green walnut-peels.

2438. WOOL. *Drab.*—Impregnate with brown oxide of iron, and then dip in a bath of quercitron bark. If sumach is added, it will make the colour a dark brown.

2439. WOOL. *Green.*—First imbue with the blue, then with the yellow dye.

2440. WOOL. *Orange.*—Dye first with the red dye for cloth, and then with a yellow.

2441. WOOL. *Red.*—Take four and a half pounds of cream of tartar, four and a quarter pounds of alum; boil the wool gently for two hours; let it cool, and wash it on the following day in pure water. Infuse twelve pounds of madder for half an hour with a pound of chloride of tin, in lukewarm water; filter through canvas, remove the dye from the canvas, and put it in the bath, which is to be heated to 100° Fahr.; add two ounces of aluminous mordant, put the wool in, and raise to boiling heat. Remove the wool, wash, and soak for a quarter of an hour in a solution of white soap in water.

2442. WOOL. *Yellow.*—Dye with that used for calico, &c.

2443. Dyeing Bonnets.—Chip and straw bonnets or hats may be dyed black by boiling them three or four hours in a strong liquor of logwood, adding a little green copperas occasionally. Let the bonnets remain in the liquor all night, then take out to dry in the air. If the black is not satisfactory, dye again after drying. Rub inside and out with a sponge moistened in fine oil. Then block.

2444. To Dye Hair and Feathers Green.—Take of either verdigris or verditer one ounce; gum water, one pint; mix them well, and dip the hair or feathers into the mixture, shaking them well about.

2445. To Clean White Satin and Flowered Silks.—i. Mix sifted stale bread-crumbs with powder blue, and rub it thoroughly all over the article; then shake it well, and dust it with clean soft cloths. Afterwards, where there are any gold or silver flowers, take a piece of crimson ingrain velvet, rub the flowers with it, which will restore them to their original lustre. ii. Pass them through a solution of fine hard soap, of a moderate heat, drawing them through the hand; rinse in lukewarm water, dry, and finish by pinning out. Brush the flossy or bright side with a clean clothes-brush, the way of the nap. Finish them by dipping a sponge into a size, made by boiling isinglass in water, and rub the wrong side. Rinse out a second time, and brush, and dry near a fire in a warm room.—Silk may be treated in the same way, but not brushed.

2446. Cleaning Silks, Satins, Coloured Woollen Dresses, &c. —Four ounces of soft soap, four ounces of honey, the white of an egg, and a wineglassful of gin; mix well together, and scour the article with a rather hard brush thoroughly; afterwards rinse it in cold water, leave to drain, and iron whilst quite damp.—A friend informs us that she believes this receipt has never been made public; she finds it an excellent one, having used it for a length of time with perfect success.

2447. To Clean Black Cloth Clothes.—Clean the garments well, then boil four ounces of logwood in a boiler or copper containing two or three gallons of water for half an hour; dip the clothes in warm water, and squeeze dry, then put them into the copper and boil for half an hour. Take them out, and add three drachms of sulphate of iron; boil for half an hour, then take them out, and hang them up for an hour or two; take them down, rinse them thrice in cold water, dry well, and rub with a soft brush which has had a few drops of olive oil applied to its surface. If the clothes are threadbare about the elbows, cuffs, &c., raise the nap with a teasel or half worn hatter's card, filled with flocks, and when sufficiently raised, lay the nap the right way with a hard brush. We have seen old coats come out with a wonderful dash of respectability after this operation.

2448. To Clean Furs.—Strip the fur articles of their stuffing and binding, and lay them as nearly as possible in a flat position. They must then be subjected to a very brisk brushing, with a stiff clothes-brush; after this, any moth-eaten parts must be cut out, and neatly replaced by new bits of fur to match. Sable, chinchilla, squirrel, fitch, &c., should be treated as follows:— Warm a quantity of new bran in a pan, taking care that it does not burn, to prevent which it must be actively stirred. When well warmed, rub it thoroughly into the fur with the hand. Repeat this two or three times: then shake the fur, and give it another sharp brushing until free from dust. White furs, ermine, &c., may be cleaned as follows:—Lay the fur on a table, and rub it well with bran made moist with warm water; rub until quite dry, and afterwards with dry bran. The wet bran should be put on with flannel, and the dry with a piece of book muslin. The light furs, in addition to the above, should be well rubbed with magnesia, or a piece of book muslin, after the bran process. Furs are usually much improved by stretching, which may be managed as follows: to a pint of soft water add three ounces of salt, dissolve; with this solution, sponge the inside of the skin (taking care not to wet the fur) until it becomes thoroughly saturated; then lay it carefully on a board with the fur side downwards, in its natural position; then stretch as much as it will bear, and to the required shape, and fasten with small tacks. The drying may be accelerated by placing the skin a little distance from the fire or stove.

2449. Cleansing Feathers of their Animal Oil.—The following receipt gained a premium from the Society of Arts:—Take for every gallon of clean water one pound of quicklime, mix them well together, and when the undissolved lime is precipitated in fine powder, pour off the clean lime water for use. Put the feathers to be cleaned in another tub, and add to them a quantity of the clean lime water, sufficient to cover them about three inches when well immersed and stirred about therein. The feathers, when thoroughly moistened, will sink, and should remain in the lime water three or four days; after which the foul liquor should be separated from them, by laying them in a sieve. The feathers should be afterwards well washed in clean water, and dried upon nets, the meshes of which may be about the fineness of cabbage nets. The feathers must be from time to time shaken on the nets, and as they get dry, will fall through the meshes, and are to be collected for use. The admission of air will be serviceable in drying. The process will be completed in three weeks; and when thus prepared, the feathers will only require to be beaten to get rid of the dust.

2450. To Clean White Ostrich Feathers. — Four ounces of white soap, cut small, dissolved in four pints of water, rather hot, in a large basin; make the solution into a lather, by beating it with birch rods, or wires. Introduce the feathers, and rub well with the hands for five or six minutes. After this soaping, wash in clean water, as hot as the hand can bear. Shake until dry.

2451. Cleaning Straw Bonnets.—They may be washed with soap and water, rinsed in clear water, and dried in the air. Then wash them over with white of egg well beaten. Remove the wire before washing. Old straw bonnets may be picked to pieces, and put together for children, the head parts being cut out.

2452. To Bleach a Faded Dress.—Wash it well in hot suds, and boil it until the colour seems to be gone, then wash, and rinse, and dry it in the sun; if still not quite white, repeat the boiling.

2453. Bleaching Straw Bonnets, &c.—Wash them in pure water, scrubbing them with a brush. Then put them into a box in which has been set a saucer of burning sulphur. Cover them up, so that the fumes may bleach them.

2454. Clothes Balls.—Fullers' earth dried till it crumbles to powder; moisten it with the juice of lemon, add a small quantity of pearlash, work and knead carefully together till it forms a thick paste; make into balls, and dry them in the sun. Moisten the spot on clothes with water, then rub it with the ball. Wash out the spot with pure water.

2455. To Wash China Crape Scarfs, &c.—If the fabric be good, these articles of dress can be washed as frequently as may be required, and no diminution of their beauty will be discoverable, even when the various shades of green have been employed among other colours in the patterns. In cleaning them, make a strong lather of boiling water; suffer it to cool; when cold, or nearly so, wash the scarf quickly and thoroughly, dip it immediately in cold hard water in which a little salt has been thrown (to preserve the colours), rinse, squeeze, and hang it out to dry in the open air; pin it at its extreme edge to the line, so that it may not in any part be folded together: the more rapidly it dries the clearer it will be.

2456. To Wash a White Lace Veil.—Put the veil into a strong lather of white soap and very clear water, and let it simmer slowly for a quarter of an hour; take it out and squeeze it well, but be sure not to rub it; rinse it twice in cold water, the second time with a drop or two of liquid blue. Have ready some very clear weak gum-arabic water, or some thin starch, or rice water; pass the veil through it, and clear it by clapping; then stretch it out evenly, and pin it to dry on a linen cloth, making the edge as straight as possible, opening out all the scallops, and fastening each with pins. When dry, lay a piece of thin muslin smoothly over it, and iron it on the wrong side.

2457. Blond Lace may be revived by breathing upon it, and shaking and flapping it. The use of the iron turns the lace yellow.

2458. Washing Bed Furniture, &c.—Before putting into the water, see that you shake off as much dust as possible, or you will greatly increase your labour. Use no soda, or pearlash, or the articles will lose their colour. Use soft water, not hot, but warm: have plenty of it. Rub with mottled soap. On wringing out the second liquor, dip each piece into cold hard water for finishing. Shake out well, and dry quickly. If starch is desired, it may be stirred into the rinsing water.

2459. Washing with Lime.—Half a pound of soap; half a pound of soda; quarter of a pound of quick-lime. Cut up the soap and dissolve it in half a gallon of boiling water; pour half a gallon of boiling water over the soda, and enough boiling water over the quick-lime to cover it. The lime must be quick and fresh; if quick, it will bubble up when the hot water is poured over it. Prepare each of these in separate vessels; put the dissolved lime and soda together, and boil them for twenty minutes; then pour them into a jar to settle.

2460. After having made the Preparation, set aside the flannels and coloured articles, as they *must not* be washed in this way. They may be washed in the usual way while the others are boiling. The night before, the collars and wristbands of shirts, the feet of stockings, &c., should be rubbed well with soap and set to soak. In the morning pour ten gallons of water into the copper, and having strained the mixture of lime and soda well, taking great care not to disturb the settlings, put it, together with the soap, into the water, and make the whole boil before putting in the clothes. A plate should be placed at the bottom of the copper, to prevent the clothes from burning. Boil each lot of clothes from half an hour to an hour, then rinse them well in cold blue water. When dry they will be beautifully white. The same water will do for three lots. Wash the finer things first.

2461. Washing.—(*Supremacy of Soapsuds over Lime.*)—To save your linen and your labour,—pour on half a pound of soda two quarts of boiling water, in an earthenware pan; take half a pound of soap, shred fine; put it into a saucepan with two quarts of cold water; stand it on a fire till it boils; and when perfectly dissolved and boiling, add it to the former. Mix it well, and let it stand till cold, when it will have the appearance of a strong jelly. Let your linen be soaked in water, the seams and any other soiled part rubbed in the usual way, and remain till the following morning. Get your copper ready, and add to the water about a pint basin full; when *lukewarm* put in your linen, and allow it to boil for twenty minutes. Rinse it in the usual way, and that is all which is necessary to get it clean, and to keep it in good colour. The above receipt is invaluable to housekeepers. If you have not tried it, do so without delay.

2462. When Water is Hard, and will not readily unite with soap, it will always be proper to boil it before use; which will be found sufficiently efficacious, if the hardness depends solely upon the impregnation of lime. Even exposure to the atmosphere will produce this effect in a great degree upon spring water so impregnated, leaving it much fitter for lavatory purposes. In both cases the water ought to be carefully poured off from the sediment, as the neutralized lime, when freed from its extra quantity of carbonic acid, falls to the bottom by its own gravity. To economize the use of soap, put any quantity of pearlash into a large jar, covered from the dust; in a few days the alkali will become liquid, which must be diluted in double its quantity of soft water, with an equal quantity of new-slacked lime. Boil it half an hour, frequently stirring it; adding as much more hot water, and drawing off the liquor, when the residuum may be boiled afresh, and drained, until it ceases to feel acrid to the tongue.

2463. SOAP AND LABOUR MAY BE SAVED by dissolving alum and chalk in bran water, in which the linen ought to be boiled, then well rinsed out, and exposed to the usual process of bleaching.

2464. SOAP MAY BE DISPENSED WITH, or nearly so, in the getting up of muslins and chintzes, which should always be treated agreeably to the Oriental manner; that is, to wash them in plain water, and then boil them in congee, or rice water: after which they ought not to be submitted to the operation of the smoothing iron, but rubbed smooth with a polished stone.

2465. THE ECONOMY which must result from these processes renders their consideration important to every family, in addition to which, we must state that the improvements in philosophy extend to the laundry as well as to the wash-house.

2466. Gum Arabic Starch.—Procure two ounces of fine white gum arabic, and pound it to powder. Next put it into a pitcher, and pour on it a pint or more of boiling water, according to the degree of strength you desire, and then, having covered it, let it set all night. In the morning, pour it carefully from the dregs into a clean bottle, cork it, and keep it for use. A tablespoonful of gum water stirred into a pint of starch that has been made in the usual manner will give to lawns (either white or printed) a look of newness to which nothing else can restore them after washing. It is also good (much diluted) for thin white muslin and bobbinet.

2467. Mildew out of Linen.—Rub the linen well with soap; then scrape some fine chalk, and rub it also on the linen. Lay it on the grass. As it dries, wet it a little, and the mildew will come out with a second application.

2468. To render Linen, &c., Incombustible.—All linen, cotton, muslins, &c., &c., when dipped in a solution of tungstate of soda or common alum, will become incombustible.

2469. Sweet Bags for Linen. —These may be composed of any mixtures of the following articles:—flowers, dried and pounded; powdered cloves, mace, nutmeg, cinnamon; leaves —dried and pounded—of mint, balm, dragon-wort, southernwood, ground-ivy, laurel, hyssop, sweet marjoram, origanum, rosemary; woods, such as cassia, juniper, rhodium, sandal-wood, and rosewood; roots of angelica, zedoary, orris: all the fragrant balsams—ambergris, musk, and civet. These latter should be carefully used on linen.

2470. Rings which have stones in them should always be taken off the finger when the hands are washed, or they will become discoloured.

2471. Adulterations. — Much has been written upon the subject of adulteration. Dr. Hassall published a series of papers in the *Lancet;* these brought about a parliamentary inquiry; the inquiry ended in demonstrating that nearly everything we eat and drink is adulterated—in many cases with ingredients very prejudicial to human health. Somebody has written a little book to inform people "How to Detect Adulterations in our Daily Food and Drink," and there is room for some one to write a key to the said little book, entitled "How to understand the instructions in 'How to Detect Adulteration in our Daily Food and Drink'"—for although the advertisement of the book says that it gives instructions for the employment of "simple means" of detection, the means suggested are in most cases highly impracticable, and in some instances dangerous. Thus the housewife who sets about the discovery of some supposed evil may, by an error or accident—the upsetting of a bottle of sulphuric acid, or the explosion of a receiver of gas—do herself more injury in an hour than she would suffer from adulteration in a lifetime.

2472. IMPRACTICABLE MODES OF DETECTION.—The writer alluded to states that, to discover the adulterations in arrowroot, you are to "mix it with twice its weight of concentrated muriatic acid." To discover adulterations in flour, you are to "take of the suspected flour about 350 grains, and the same quantity of fine sand, and two and a half fluid ounces of water; triturate in a mortar the sand and flour for five minutes; then gradually add a little of the water, so as to dilute it evenly, and form a homogeneous paste; throw the whole upon a filter, and take about one ounce of the clear liquid, place it in a test-glass, and add the same quantity of an aqueous solution of iodine." The author remarks that this method is tedious, and far from satisfactory. So we think. He then gives another:— "If chalk be suspected, place a teaspoonful of flour in a wineglass, with a little water, and add a few drops of muriatic acid. If chalk be present, a brisk effervescence will ensue, owing to the escape of carbonic acid [it should be carbonic acid *gas*]. Lime may be detected in a similar way—using oxalate of ammonia instead of muriatic acid. The lime will form an insoluble precipitate, which is oxalate of lime!" Then, to detect the presence of bone dust, you are told to burn a portion of the suspected flour, and "if a portion of the ash dissolved in water give, with nitrate of silver, an abundant precipitate, phosphate of lime is present. The test of oxalate of ammonia may be used to detect lime in the ash, as already advised for its detection in flour!" This is the character of by far the greater number of these "simple" instructions; and, to crown the whole, to enable you to detect adulteration in bottled, cured, and potted anchovies, with their heads decapitated, and their entrails removed, you are favoured with Mr. Yarrell's pen-and-ink portrait of the fish when in a living, or, at least, a fresh and whole condition! Among other adulterations we therefore discover the adulteration of books, by the introduction of matter to give an appearance of learning to their pages, and of no possible use to the buyer, who is compelled to pay sixpence for what he ought to obtain at one-sixth of that cost.

2473. How to escape Adulteration, and also to detect Fraudulent Tradespeople. — We are not about to advise the housewife to set up a chemical laboratory, nor to put her husband to the expense of a compound achromatic microscope. Our instructions will neither burn holes in her dress, stain her mahogany table blacken her nails, make smarting chaps in her hands, nor fill her with monomaniacal fears that she is being ossified by bone-dust, or that in a little while she will be crystallized all over, like an alum-basket. Our apparatus is as follows:—

A hand flour-mill, which will cost about . . .	£5 0 0
A pestle and mortar . .	0 10 0
A coffee-mill . . .	0 3 0
A pepper and spice-mill .	0 3 0
A meat-cutting machine .	1 10 0
Scales and weights . .	0 15 0
Imperial measures . .	0 5 0
	£8 6 0

This seems a good deal of money, and anything but a "simple" means of meeting a great evil. But we have not yet completed our instructions.

2474. Formation of "Family Circles."—The mill is the most expensive item in this table of expenditure, and what we propose is this:—"Family Circles" should be called for the purpose of mitigating the evils complained of. Let every "Circle" have its mill —let it be kept at a place convenient to all. By such means a capital of 10s., subscribed by each member, would be sufficient; a little company would be formed, upon a better principle than that of "limited liability," since, the capital being paid up, there would be no liability at all. What would be the result Why, that people would obtain pure bread, pure coffee, pure condiments, and other things, at a cost of *full twenty-five per cent. under that which they now pay for spurious and health-destroying mixtures.*

2475. Other Evils besides "Adulterations."—The butcher cannot adulterate the beef and the mutton, but he can send home *short weight;* and in casting up a bill, he can reckon the odd ounces at one penny each, instead of one halfpenny; and the baker, besides putting alum in the bread, to make it white and retain water, can send home deficient weight; the same with the grocer, the greengrocer, and the coal merchant; the publican can give short measure, and froth up the porter to fill the jug and disguise the shortness of quantity; and the draper can slip his scissors on the wrong side of his finger, and make a yard contain only thirty-three inches. We don't mean to say that they *do* this, nor do we mean to say that they *don't.* We argue, *that people ought to possess the means of ascertaining who among shopkeepers are honest, and who are not;* then the just would meet with justice, and the un-just would suffer for their own sins. If we can succeed in inducing people to put these simple suggestions into operation, we shall have done more to remedy the evil than Dr. Hassall and Acts of Parliament; for these have merely ex-posed the defect, frightened everybody, and produced no practical result.

2476. ADULTERATIONS, AND REALLY SIMPLE MODES OF DETECTING THEM.— ARROWROOT is adulterated with potato starch, sago, and tapioca starch. There is nothing injurious in these adultera-tions. When largely adulterated with potato starch, the arrowroot, being passed through the hand, imparts a slippery and glaze-like feeling. Pure arrowroot may generally be obtained by paying the best prices. The arrow-root packed in tin cases, and palmed off as pure, may generally be regarded as highly adulterated.

2477. ANATTO is adulterated with chalk, wheat flour, rye flour, salt, and soap, and is coloured with Venetian red and red lead. It is difficult to detect these adulterations.

2478. A STANHOPE LENS, which may be obtained for from 2s. 6d. to 5s., or one of the glass water-bulbs that are sold by men in the London streets at one penny each, will be of material assistance in detecting the admixture of impure substances with articles of food. Even a common phial filled with water possesses a strong magni-fying power.

2479. BRANDY is adulterated with cayenne pepper, water, and burnt sugar. Betts's brandy is the best.

2480. BREAD. — Grind your own wheat, make your own yeast, and bake your own bread. The advantages will be immense, and you need not then trouble about adulterations.

2481. THE ADULTERATIONS OF BREAD, &c.—Bread and flour are adul-terated with flour of inferior grain, Indian corn flour, potato flour, pea and bean flour, bone-dust, &c. None of these are positively injurious. But they are also adulterated with plaster of Paris, chalk, alum, &c., and these are highly prejudicial to health, espe-cially when taken continuously.

2482. To DISCOVER WHETHER BREAD BE ADULTERATED WITH ALUM. —Pierce a loaf that is one day old with a knife made very hot; if there be alum present, it will adhere in very small particles to the blade of the knife, and will indicate its presence by a peculiar smell. If bread looks unnaturally white, and if it gives off a good deal of water, and becomes very brittle and dry when toasted, alum may be regarded as being present.

2483. To DISCOVER WHETHER BREAD BE ADULTERATED WITH PEA OR BEAN FLOUR.—Pour boiling water upon it, and if the flour is mixed with the farina of peas or beans, the strong smell of those grains will become manifest.

2484. To DISCOVER WHETHER FLOUR BE ADULTERATED WITH CHALK, PLASTER OF PARIS, OR MINERAL POW-DERS.—If containing these admixtures, it will be found to be heavier, measure for measure, than pure flour. That is to say, a pint of pure flour would be overbalanced in the scales by a pint of adulterated flour. Slice the soft part of a loaf, and put it into a large quantity of water, in an earthen vessel. Place it over a slow fire for three hours. Scoop up the pap, and let the water stand. When perfectly settled, pour off the water, and a chalky sediment will be found to cover the bottom of the vessel. Heartburn, immediately after eating bread, is a sign of its impurity. Put some flour upon a table, and blow it gently with the breath. If little heaps remain upon the table, resisting the action of the breath, and differing manifestly from the indications given by other portions when blown upon, the substance thus remaining is impure. Potato flour, and indeed all white flours are heavier than pure wheat. Bake a small quantity of the suspected flour, until it is of a full brown. Then rub it in your hands, or on a table, when white particles will be seen, if chalk or plaster of Paris be present.

2485. PURE WHEATEN FLOUR is remarkable for its cohesiveness. If squeezed, it will adhere; it is also very light, and may be blown into a cloud with the lightest breath. It was stated in the Parliamentary Report, that earthy matters are not admixed with flour. This means, that Dr. Hassall had not discovered any. A man was fined at Leeds, not long ago, for adulterating flour with plaster of Paris. He had carried adulteration to such an excess, that it was discovered through the illness of families who had partaken of bread made from flour supplied by him.

2486. BUTTER is made heavy by water, which may generally be seen exuding from bad samples; these should be rejected by the purchaser.

2487. CAYENNE PEPPER.—Having your own pestle and mortar, make it according to the following instructions:—Let a quantity be made at one time for the "Family Circle." The cayenne of commerce is adulterated with brickdust, red wood dust, cochineal, vermillion, and red lead. The latter two are highly injurious, and the former ones not very salutary. As to the means of detecting these, it would be a great waste of time to find them out, since all cayenne is largely adulterated. Therefore, make your own, or—don't use any.

2488. CHICORY.—This is the dried and roasted root of a plant allied to the dandelion, and it is found by almost unanimous testimony to be an agreeable flavourer of coffee. Dr. Hassall denounces the use of chicory, but with no sufficient reason. He states it to be "diuretic and aperient"—qualities which we declare to be in its favour, for it is the prevailing defect of our food that it is too astringent and heating, and the fact that chicory finds such general approbation we believe rests in the very qualities which Dr. Hassall condemns. We know a respectable grocer who, before legislation took the matter up, from conscientious motives ceased to mix chicory with coffee; the immediate effect was the falling off of his coffee trade, his customers declaring that his coffee was not so good as previously; and he was compelled again to mix chicory with it, to meet their taste. Chicory is found to be "adulterated" with carrots, parsnips, and mangold-wurzel. In Dr. Hassall's papers the names of those roots are *italicized*, as though some dreadful disclosure lay therein. But as these roots are all of them highly nutritious and agreeable, instead of detracting from the claims of chicory, the facts stated rather elevate "chicory" in our estimation, and point to the probability *that the roots mentioned possess qualities hitherto imperfectly ascertained, and worthy of further examination and development.* Our remarks are not merely of conjecture, they are founded upon observation and analysis.

2489. CHOCOLATE AND COCOA.—The adulterations of these articles pointed out by Dr. Hassall are not of a serious nature, being confined to flour, starch, potato farina, sago meal, wheat flour, tapioca starch, maranta and other arrowroots, tous-les-mois, and animal fats; but as the latter are employed in the roasting of all farinaceous grains, to prevent the burning thereof, and also to preserve, as far as possible, their essential oils from destruction by heat, we see nothing to make our readers uncomfortable. Those who prefer the pure cocoa can obtain the "nibs," or more properly "beans," and grind them. But many prefer the soluble cocoa, which is simply cocoa modified by admixture with less stimulating substances.

2490. COFFEE.—Coffee is adulterated with chicory, roasted beans, peas, and acorns; but chiefly by chicory. Having your own mill, buy the roasted beans; find out a respectable grocer, ascertain his roasting-days, *and always buy from a fresh roast.* If you like the flavour of chicory, purchase it separately, and add to taste. Chicory in small quantities is not, as has been represented, injurious, but healthful: because the "taraxacum" root has been used medicinally, and its name has found a place in the Pharmacopœia, it has been vulgarly set down as "physic," and thrown to the dogs. The tonic hop might be discarded upon the same pretext. Chicory is a healthful addition to coffee, but you need not pay the coffee price for it. Grind your coffee, and mix it with chicory for yourself.

2491. CONFECTIONS AND SWEET-MEATS are coloured with poisonous ingredients. Avoid them; there is not the slightest necessity for running any risk.

2492. CURRY POWDERS are but an accumulation of adulterations:—adulterated pepper, adulterated coriander, adulterated cardamums, adulterated ginger, adulterated spices, and so on. *With your spice-mill and grater, prepare your own from the seeds and roots.* You will thereby obtain a curry powder, and be able to produce a curry, that will spread your reputation far and wide.

2493. CUSTARD AND EGG POWDERS contain wheat, potato, and rice flours, and are coloured with chrome yellow, or chromate of lead, and turmeric. They are not essential articles of household economy.

2494. GIN is adulterated with water, sugar, cayenne, cassia, cinnamon, grains of paradise, sulphuric acid, coriander seeds, angelica root, calken root, almond cake, orris root, cardamum seeds, orange peel, and grey and white salts, and is "fined" by alum and salt of tartar. The best way is to purchase the unsweetened gin, for the sweetening is employed to disguise the flavour of various adulterations. If you examine gin through a clean glass, it should have no tint, either of a bluish or yellowish cast. The cheap gins should be avoided, and only respectable dealers should be resorted to.

2495. ISINGLASS.—Our chief object in noticing the adulteration of this article is to insure its purity in the making of cements, which is of the utmost importance. (*See* 2258.) Isinglass is a preparation from fishes' bladders, and it is found to be adulterated with gelatine. Take a few threads of the substance, drop some into boiling water, some into cold water, and some into vinegar. In the boiling water the isinglass will dissolve; in cold water it will become white and "cloudy;" and in vinegar it will swell and become jelly-like. In boiling water gelatine will not so completely dissolve as isinglass; in cold water it becomes clear and jelly-like; and in vinegar it will harden.

2496. LARD is adulterated with potato flour, water, salts, carbonate of soda, and caustic lime. Take a small portion of the suspected lard, and evaporate it upon a hot iron pan or plate, when the admixed substances will be deposited thereon.

2497. MARMALADE is found to be adulterated with coarse apples, Swede turnips, and coarse pumpkins. These substances may be easily detected by washing off the saccharine matter in tepid water. Generally speaking, however, it is only the low-priced marmalades that are thus admixed.

2498. MILK is adulterated with water, and coloured with anatto.

2499. MUSTARD AND PEPPER are

both adulterated with inferior grain, husks of seeds, and even dust of a variety of descriptions. Having your pepper-mill, purchase the seed whole, and grind for yourself. You will then obtain the pure article at a moderate cost.

2500. OATMEAL is adulterated with barley flour and the husks of barley. A pint of pure oatmeal will weigh heavier than a pint of the adulterated.

2501. PICKLES AND PRESERVES.— These are found to be adulterated with various compounds; but the greatest evil lies in the fact that they are frequently impregnated with copper. To detect this, put some of the pickle, cut small, into a phial with two or three drachms of liquid ammonia, diluted with one half the quantity of water. Shake the phial, when, if the minutest portion of copper be present, the liquid will assume a fine blue colour. In the case of preserves, the copper probably proceeds from the use of copper pans in making the preserves; but with regard to pickles, copper is employed to improve their colour, and sulphuric acid to strengthen bad vinegar. The best way is to avoid purchasing the pickles sold in clear glass bottles, and presenting a most tempting appearance. Take your own jar, or jars, and you will find that you will get pure articles at little more than it would cost you to make pickles at home. We presume that in all large towns the pickle merchants adopt the same plan of selling pickles by the quart or gallon to those who may visit their establishments; and also that preserves (for those who do not make their own) may be obtained under equal advantages.

2502. POTTED MEATS AND FISH are adulterated with inferior substances, and coloured with bole armenian and Venetian red.

2503. PORTER AND ALE are adulterated with cocculus indicus, tobacco, grains of paradise, capsicum, ginger, quassia, wormwood, calamus root, carraway and coriander seeds, orange powder, liquorice, honey, sulphate of iron, sulphuric acid, cream of tartar, alum, carbonate of potash, oyster shells, hartshorn shavings, fabia amara, or nux vomica, and beans for fining. Beer which is quickly "heady," and rapidly intoxicating, may be regarded as drugged. The large brewers supply the purest beer. The publicans adulterate it after they receive supplies from the brewers.

2504. RUM is adulterated with water, and sharpened with cayenne pepper. Let it stand in a decanter, and if a cloudy precipitate is found at the bottom, that is a sign of adulteration.

2505. SAUSAGES.—The most offensive of all adulterations are found in these savory morsels. Horseflesh, diseased animals, and odds and ends of every description appear in the tempting guise of "sausages." To escape this evil, make your own sausages by the aid of the sausage machine, which may be purchased for 30s., and will enable you to add many savory morsels to the attraction of your table. The same machine may be used for CHOPPING VEGETABLES, which it will do to such perfection that they will perfectly dissolve in soups and stews, and afford most delicious made-dishes. And in this, as in the grinding of wheat, you will soon save the cost of the machine.

2506. SNUFF is adulterated with the chromate of potash, chromate of lead, various earths and colours, red lead, carbonate of ammonia, lime, powdered glass or silex, and powdered orris root.

2507. SUGAR is commonly adulterated with fine sand, sawdust, &c. Dissolve some of the sugar in a long, narrow ale-glass, and stir it until all the soluble parts have been thoroughly dissolved. Then allow it to stand for some hours. Sand will sink to the bottom, while sawdust will rise to the surface. Both the sand and the sawdust will be found to be very fine, but their presence will be sufficiently indicated. Loaf sugar is generally purer than moist sugar.

2508. TEA is adulterated with

leaves of the sycamore, horse-chestnut, and plum; with lye tea, which is made up of tea-dust, sand, and gum, to give it consistency; also with leaves of the beech, bastard plane, elm, poplar, willow, fancy oak, hawthorn, and sloe. It is coloured with blacklead, rose pink, Dutch pink, vegetable red and yellow dyes, arsenite of copper, chromate and bichromate of potash. Green teas are more adulterated than black. They are coloured with Prussian blue, turmeric, Chinese yellow, &c., flavoured with sulphate of iron, catechu gum, la veno beno, and Chinese botanical powder. Tea leaves that have been once used are collected, "doctored," and again sold as fresh tea. Obtain some genuine leaves of tea, moisten them, and lay them out with gum upon paper. Press them between the leaves of books until dry. When you suspect a sample of tea, damp and unroll the leaves, and gum and dry them as the genuine ones,—you will then be able, by comparison, to detect the admixture.

2509. TOBACCO is adulterated with rhubarb, potato, coltsfoot, dock leaves, sawdust, malt combings, and medicinals. The leaves may be unrolled and compared, as recommended in the case of tea.

2510. WINES are adulterated with the juice of elderberries, gooseberries, hop champagne, cider, the juices of various fruits, known as British wines, and coloured by means of logwood, burnt sugar, and other ingredients.

2511. THE RESULT of these inquiries proves that a majority of articles sold are adulterated. But it is also proved that a majority of the substances used for adulterations are not positively injurious, though they are fraudulently substituted for the genuine article.

2512. THE FOLLOWING ARE HINTS which, if acted upon, will turn these discoveries to practical account:—

i. *Grind your own wheat, and make your bread at home.*

ii. *Avoid green pickles; that is,* *pickles artificially raised to a bright green.*

iii. *Avoid bright-red peppers, spices, and sauces.*

iv. *Purchase spirits and beer of large dealers and brewers.*

v. *Avoid coloured confections,—especially those that are green, blue, or red.*

vi. *Weigh and measure your purchases when they are brought home. You will thus not only secure your just amount, but will arrive at a knowledge of the proper weights of pure articles, and be assisted in the rejection of the spurious.*

2513. Bread contains eighty nutritious parts in 100; meal, thirty-four in 100; French beans, ninety-two in 100; common beans, eighty-nine in 100; peas, ninety-three in 100; lentils, ninety-four in 100; cabbages and turnips, the most aqueous of all the vegetables compared, produce only eight pounds of solid matter in 100 pounds; carrots and spinach produce fourteen in the same quantity; whilst 100 pounds of potatoes contain twenty-five pounds of dry substance. From a general estimate it results, that one pound of good bread is equal to two pounds and a half or three pounds of potatoes; that seventy-five pounds of bread and thirty of meat may be substituted for 300 pounds of potatoes. The other substances bear the following proportions; four parts of cabbage to one of potatoes; three parts of turnips to one of potatoes; two parts of carrots and spinach to one of potatoes; and about three parts and a half of potatoes to one of rice, lentils, beans, French beans, and dry peas.

2514. Use of Fruit.—Instead of standing in any fear of a generous consumption of ripe fruits, we regard them as conducive to health. We have no patience in reading the endless rules to be observed in this particular department of physical comfort. No one ever lived longer or freer from disease, by discarding the fruits of the land in which he finds a home. On the contrary, they are necessary to the preservation of health, and are therefore designed to make their appearance at the very time when the condition of the body, operated upon by deteriorating causes not always understood, requires their renovating influences.

2515. Blackberries are very beneficial in cases of dysentery. The berries are healthful eating. Tea made of the roots and leaves is good; and syrup made from the berries excellent.

2516. "Morning's Milk," says an eminent German philosopher, "commonly yields some hundredths more cream than the evening's at the same temperature. That milked at noon furnishes the least; it would therefore be of advantage, in making butter, &c., to employ the morning's milk, and keep the evening's for domestic use."

2517. Bills of Exchange and Promissory Notes.

INLAND BILL OF EXCHANGE, Draft, or Order for the payment to the bearer, or to order, at any time, otherwise than on demand, of any sum of money,—

			Duty.		
			£	s.	d.
Not above		£5	0	0	1
Above	£5 and not above	10	0	0	2
,,	10 ,,	25	0	0	3
,,	25 ,,	50	0	0	6
,,	50 ,,	75	0	0	9
,,	75 ,,	100	0	1	0
,,	100 ,,	200	0	2	0
,,	200 ,,	300	0	3	0
,,	300 ,,	400	0	4	0
,,	400 ,,	500	0	5	0
,,	500 ,,	750	0	7	6
,,	750 ,,	1000	0	10	0
,,	1000 ,,	1500	0	15	0
,,	1500 ,,	2000	1	0	0
,,	2000 ,,	3000	1	10	0
,,	3000 ,,	4000	2	0	0
,,	4000 and upwards		2	5	0

2518. A Table of the Number of Days, from any Day of any one Month to the same Day of any other Month.

From	Jan.	Feb.	Mar.	Apr.	May	June	July	Aug.	Sep.	Oct.	Nov.	Dec.
To January	365	334	306	275	245	214	184	153	122	92	61	31
February	31	365	337	306	276	245	215	184	153	123	92	62
March	59	28	365	334	304	273	243	212	181	151	120	90
April	90	59	31	365	335	304	274	243	212	182	151	121
May	120	89	61	30	365	334	304	273	242	212	181	151
June	151	120	92	61	31	365	334	304	273	243	212	182
July	181	150	122	91	61	30	365	334	303	273	242	212
August	212	181	153	122	92	61	31	365	334	304	273	243
September	243	212	184	153	122	92	61	31	365	335	304	274
October	273	242	214	183	153	122	92	61	30	365	334	304
November	304	273	245	214	184	153	123	92	61	31	365	335
December	334	303	275	244	214	183	153	122	91	61	30	365

USE OF THE ABOVE TABLE.

What is the number of days from 10th October to 10th July?
Look in the upper line for October, let your eye descend down that column till you come opposite to July, and you will find 273 days, the exact number of days required.

Again, Required the number of days from 16th February to the 14th August?

Under February, and opposite to August, is .... 181 days.
From which subtract the difference between 14 and 16 .... 2 days.

The exact number of days required is .... 179 days.

N.B.—In Leap Year, if the last day of February comes between, add one day for the day over to the number in the Table.

2519. For Mistresses and Servants: Table of Expenses, Income, and Wages.

Showing at one view what any sum, from £1 to £1,000 per Annum, is per Day, Week, or Month.

Per Year. £ s.	Per Month. s. d.	Per Week. s. d	Per Day. d.	Per Year. £ s.	Per Month £ s. d.	Per Week. s. d.	Per Day. s. d.	Per Year. £ s.	Per Month. £ s. d	Per Week. £ s. d.	Per Day. £ s. d.
1 is	1 8	0 4½	0¾	8 8	is 14 0	3 2¾	0 5¼	18 18	is1 11 6	0 7 3	0 1 0½
1 10	2 6	0 7	1	8 10	0 14 2	3 3¼	0 5½	19 0	1 11 8	0 7 3½	0 1 0¾
2 0	3 4	0 9¼	1¼	9 0	0 15 0	3 5½	0 6	20 0	1 13 4	0 7 8	0 1 1¼
2 2	3 6	0 9¾	1½	9 9	0 15 9	3 7½	0 6¼	30 0	2 10 0	0 11 6	0 1 7¾
2 10	4 2	0 11½	1¾	10 0	0 16 8	3 10	0 6½	40 0	3 6 8	0 15 4½	0 2 2¼
3 0	5 0	1 1¾	2	10 10	0 17 6	4 0½	0 7	50 0	4 3 4	0 19 3	0 2 9
3 3	5 3	1 2½	2	11 0	0 18 4	4 3	0 7¼	60 0	5 0 0	1 3 0¾	0 3 3½
3 10	5 10	1 4¼	2¼	11 11	0 19 3	4 5¼	0 7½	70 0	5 16 8	1 6 11	0 3 10
4 0	6 8	1 6½	2¾	12 0	1 0 0	4 7¼	0 8	80 0	6 13 4	1 10 9	0 4 4½
4 4	7 0	1 7½	2¾	12 12	1 1 0	4 10	0 8¼	90 0	7 10 0	1 14 7½	0 4 11
4 10	7 6	1 8¾	3	13 0	1 1 8	5 0	0 8½	100 0	8 6 8	1 18 5	0 5 5¾
5 0	8 4	1 11	3¼	13 13	1 2 9	5 3	0 9	200 0	16 13 4	3 16 11	0 10 11½
5 5	8 9	2 0¼	3½	14 0	1 3 4	5 4½	0 9¼	300 0	25 0 0	5 15 4½	0 16 5¼
5 10	9 2	2 1½	3½	14 13	1 4 6	5 8	0 9¾	400 0	33 6 8	7 13 10	1 1 11
6 0	10 0	2 3¾	4	15 0	1 5 0	5 9	0 10	500 0	41 13 4	9 12 3½	1 7 4¾
6 6	10 6	2 5	4¼	15 15	1 6 3	6 0½	0 10¼	600 0	50 0 0	11 10 9	1 12 10¼
6 10	10 10	2 6	4½	16 0	1 6 8	6 2	0 10½	700 0	58 6 8	13 9 2¾	1 18 4½
7 0	11 8	2 8¼	4½	16 16	1 8 0	6 5¼	0 11	800 0	66 13 4	15 7 8½	2 3 10
7 7	12 3	2 10	4¾	17 0	1 8 4	6 6½	0 11¼	900 0	75 0 0	17 6 1¾	2 9 3¾
7 10	12 6	2 10½	5	17 17	1 9 6	6 10	0 11½	1000 0	33 6 8	19 4 7½	2 14 9½
3 0	13 4	3 1	5¼	10 0	1 10 0	6 11	0 11¾				

2520. Interest Table for Savings, Investments, &c.

Showing what any sum, from £1 to £500, will produce for a given number of days, which may be, by simple addition, calculated at £5 per cent. for Months or Years, for sums up to £5,000 or any other amount.

£	1 Day. s. d.	2 Days. s. d.	3 Days. s. d.	4 Days. s. d.	5 Days. s. d.	6 Days. s d.	7 Days. s. d.	8 Days. s. d.	9 Days. s. d.	10 Days. s. d.	20 Days. £ s. d.	30 Days. £ s. d.
1	0 0	0 0	0 0	0 0	0 0	0 0	0 0	0 0¼	0 0¼	0 0¼	0 0 0½	0 0 0¾
2	0 0	0 0	0 0	0 0¼	0 0¼	0 0¼	0 0¼	0 0½	0 0½	0 0½	0 0 1¼	0 0 1¾
3	0 0	0 0	0 0¼	0 0¼	0 0½	0 0½	0 0½	0 0¾	0 0¾	0 0¾	0 0 1¾	0 0 2¾
4	0 0	0 0¼	0 0¼	0 0½	0 0½	0 0¾	0 0¾	0 1	0 1	0 1¼	0 0 2½	0 0 3¾
5	0 0	0 0¼	0 0½	0 0½	0 0¾	0 0¾	0 1	0 1¼	0 1¼	0 1½	0 0 3¼	0 0 4¾
6	0 0	0 0¼	0 0½	0 0¾	0 0¾	0 1	0 1¼	0 1½	0 1½	0 1¾	0 0 3¾	0 0 5¾
7	0 0	0 0¼	0 0½	0 0¾	0 1	0 1¼	0 1½	0 1¾	0 2	0 2¼	0 0 4½	0 0 6¾
8	0 0¼	0 0½	0 0¾	0 1	0 1¼	0 1½	0 1¾	0 2	0 2¼	0 2½	0 0 5¼	0 0 7¾
9	0 0¼	0 0½	0 0¾	0 1	0 1½	0 1¾	0 2	0 2¼	0 2½	0 2¾	0 0 5¾	0 0 8¾
10	0 0¼	0 0½	0 0¾	0 1½	0 1½	0 1¾	0 2¼	0 2½	0 2¾	0 3¼	0 0 6½	0 0 9¾
20	0 0½	0 1¼	0 1¾	0 2½	0 3¼	0 3¾	0 4½	0 5¼	0 5¾	0 6½	0 1 1	0 1 7½
30	0 0¾	0 1¾	0 2½	0 3½	0 4¼	0 5¼	0 6¼	0 7¼	0 8¼	0 9¾	0 1 7½	0 2 5½
40	0 1¼	0 2½	0 3½	0 5¼	0 6½	0 7¾	0 9	0 10½	0 11¾	1 1	0 2 2¼	0 3 3½
50	0 1½	0 3¼	0 4¾	0 6½	0 8	0 9¾	0 11½	1 1	1 2¾	1 4¼	0 2 8¾	0 4 1¼
60	0 1¾	0 3¾	0 5¾	0 7¾	0 9¾	0 11¾	1 1¾	1 3¾	1 5¾	1 7½	0 3 3½	0 4 11
70	0 2¼	0 4½	0 6¾	0 9	0 11½	1 1¾	1 4	1 6¼	1 8½	1 11	0 3 10	0 5 9
80	0 2½	0 5¼	0 7¾	0 10½	1 1	1 3¾	1 6¼	1 9	1 11½	2 2¼	0 4 4½	0 6 9¾
90	0 2¾	0 5¾	0 8¾	0 11¾	1 2¾	1 5¾	1 8½	1 11½	2 2½	2 5½	0 4 11	0 7 4¾
100	0 3¼	0 6½	0 9¾	1 1	1 4¼	1 7½	1 11	2 2¼	2 5½	2 8¾	0 5 5¾	0 8 2½
200	0 6½	1 1	1 7½	2 2¼	2 8¾	3 3¼	3 10	4 4½	4 11	5 5¾	0 10 11½	0 16 5½
300	0 9¾	1 7½	2 5½	3 3¼	4 1¼	4 11	5 9	6 6¾	7 4¾	8 2½	0 16 5¼	1 4 7¾
400	1 1	2 2¼	3 3¼	4 4¼	5 5¾	6 6¾	7 8	8 2	9 10½	10 11½	1 1 11	1 12 10½
500	1 4¼	2 8¾	4 1¼	5 5¾	6 10	8 2½	9 7	10 11½	12 3¾	13 8¼	1 7 4¾	2 1 1

2521. Interest Table for One Year.

By the annexed Tables unlimited calculations may be made. Thus, to learn the interest upon £1,250 per annum, add the sums given for £1,000, £200, and £50. 2 per cent. is found by taking one half of 4 per cent.; 8 per cent. by doubling 4 per cent.; 7½ per cent. by adding 5 to 2½ per cent., and so on.

Principal.	2½ PER CENT.			3 PER CENT.			3½ PER CENT.			4 PER CENT.			5 PER CENT	
£	£	s.	d.	£	s.	d.	£	s.	d.	£	s.	d.	£	s.
1	0	0	6	0	0	7¼	0	0	8½	0	0	9½	0	1
2	0	1	0	0	1	2½	0	1	4¾	0	1	7¼	0	2
3	0	1	6	0	1	9¾	0	2	1¼	0	2	4¾	0	3
4	0	2	0	0	2	4¾	0	2	9½	0	3	2½	0	4
5	0	2	6	0	3	0	0	3	6	0	4	0	0	5
6	0	3	0	0	3	7¼	0	4	2½	0	4	9½	0	6
7	0	3	6	0	4	2½	0	4	10¾	0	5	7¼	0	7
8	0	4	0	0	4	9¾	0	5	7¼	0	6	4¾	0	8
9	0	4	6	0	5	4¾	0	6	3½	0	7	2½	0	9
10	0	5	0	0	6	0	0	7	0	0	8	0	0	10
20	0	10	0	0	12	0	0	14	0	0	16	0	1	0
30	0	15	0	0	18	0	1	1	0	1	4	0	1	10
40	1	0	0	1	4	0	1	8	0	1	12	0	2	0
50	1	5	0	1	10	0	1	15	0	2	0	0	2	10
60	1	10	0	1	16	0	2	2	0	2	8	0	3	0
70	1	15	0	2	2	0	2	9	0	2	16	0	3	10
80	2	0	0	2	8	0	2	16	0	3	4	0	4	0
90	2	5	0	2	14	0	3	3	0	3	12	0	4	10
100	2	10	0	3	0	0	3	10	0	4	0	0	5	0
200	5	0	0	6	0	0	7	0	0	8	0	0	10	0
300	7	10	0	9	0	0	10	10	0	12	0	0	15	0
400	10	0	0	12	0	0	14	0	0	16	0	0	20	0
500	12	10	0	15	0	0	17	10	0	20	0	0	25	0
600	15	0	0	18	0	0	21	0	0	24	0	0	30	0
700	17	10	0	21	0	0	24	10	0	28	0	0	35	0
800	20	0	0	24	0	0	28	0	0	32	0	0	40	0
900	22	10	0	27	0	0	31	10	0	36	0	0	45	0
1000	35	0	0	30	0	0	35	0	0	40	0	0	50	0

2522. Per-Centages.

2½ per Cent. is	0s.	6d.	per £
3 ,,	0	7¼	,,
4 ,,	0	9½	,,
5 ,,	1	0	,,
6 ,,	1	2½	,,
7½ ,,	1	6	,,
10 ,,	2	0	,,
12½ ,,	2	6	,,
15 ,,	3	0	,,
17½ ,,	3	6	,,
20 ,,	4	0	,,
22½ ,,	4	6	,,
25 ,,	5	0	,,

2523. Ready-Reckoning or Marketing Table.

No.	2d.	2½d.	3d.	3½d.	4d.	4½d.	5d.	5½d.	6d.	6½d.	7d.	7½d.	8d.	9d.	10d.	11d.	No.
	s. d.	s. d.	s. d.	s. d.	s. d.	s. d.	s. d.	s. d.	s. d.	s. d.	s. d.	s. d.	s. d.	s. d.	s. d.	s. d.	
2	0 4	0 5	0 6	0 7	0 8	0 9	0 10	0 11	1 0	1 1	1 2	1 3	1 4	1 6	1 8	1 10	2
3	0 6	0 7½	0 9	0 10½	1 0	1 1½	1 3	1 4½	1 6	1 7½	1 9	1 10½	2 0	2 3	2 6	2 9	3
4	0 8	0 10	1 0	1 2	1 4	1 6	1 8	1 10	2 0	2 2	2 4	2 6	2 8	3 0	3 4	3 8	4
5	0 10	1 0½	1 3	1 5½	1 8	1 10½	2 1	2 3½	2 6	2 8½	2 11	3 1½	3 4	3 9	4 2	4 7	5
6	1 0	1 3	1 6	1 9	2 0	2 3	2 6	2 9	3 0	3 3	3 6	3 9	4 0	4 6	5 0	5 6	6
7	1 2	1 5½	1 9	2 0½	2 4	2 7½	2 11	3 2½	3 6	3 9½	4 1	4 4½	4 8	5 3	5 10	6 5	7
8	1 4	1 8	2 0	2 4	2 8	3 0	3 4	3 8	4 0	4 4	4 8	5 0	5 4	6 0	6 8	7 4	8
9	1 6	1 10½	2 3	2 7½	3 0	3 4½	3 9	4 1½	4 6	4 10½	5 3	5 7½	6 0	6 9	7 6	8 3	9
10	1 8	2 1	2 6	2 11	3 4	3 9	4 2	4 7	5 0	5 5	5 10	6 3	6 8	7 6	8 4	9 2	10
11	1 10	2 3½	2 9	3 2½	3 8	4 1½	4 7	5 0½	5 6	5 11½	6 5	6 10½	7 4	8 3	9 2	10 1	11
12	2 0	2 6	3 0	3 6	4 0	4 6	5 0	5 6	6 0	6 6	7 0	7 6	8 0	9 0	10 0	11 0	12
13	2 2	2 8½	3 3	3 9½	4 4	4 10½	5 5	5 11½	6 6	7 0½	7 7	8 1½	8 8	9 9	10 10	11 11	13
14	2 4	2 11	3 6	4 1	4 8	5 3	5 10	6 5	7 0	7 7	8 2	8 9	9 4	10 6	11 8	12 10	14
28	4 8	5 10	7 0	8 2	9 4	10 6	11 8	12 10	14 0	15 2	16 4	17 6	18 8	21 0	23 4	25 8	28
56	9 4	11 9	14 0	16 4	18 8	21 0	23 4	25 8	28 0	30 4	32 8	35 0	37 4	42 0	46 8	51 4	56

INDEX

OF

ENQUIRIES.

₊ *The Numbers in this Index refer to the Paragraphs,* NOT *the Pages.*

cutting it into slices about a quarter of an inch thick ; grate some crust of bread, as directed for ham, and powder them well with it on both sides ; lay the rashers in a cheese-toaster,—they will be browned on one side in about three minutes :—turn them and do the other. These are a delicious accompaniment to poached or fried eggs :—the bacon, having been boiled first, is tender and mellow.—They are an excellent garnish round veal cutlets, or sweetbreads, or calf's head hash, or green peas, or beans, &c.

1133. Anchovy Sandwiches, made with the above, will be found excellent.

1134. Anchovy Toast is made by spreading anchovy paste upon bread either toasted or fried.

1135. Scotch Porridge.—FOR FOUR PERSONS. — Boil three pints of water in a clean saucepan, add a teaspoonful of salt ; mix very gradually, while the water is boiling, one pound of fine oatmeal, stirring constantly, while you put in the meal, with a round stick about eighteen inches long, called a "spirtle." Continue stirring for fifteen minutes ; then pour into soup-plates, allow it to cool a little, and serve with sweet milk. Scotch porridge is one of the most nutritive diets that can be given, especially for young persons. It is sometimes boiled with milk instead of water, but the mixture is then rather rich for delicate stomachs.

1136. Scotch Brose. — This favourite Scotch dish is generally made with the liquor in which meat has been boiled. Put half a pint of oatmeal into a porringer with a little salt, if there be not enough in the broth,—of which add as much as will mix it to the consistence of hasty pudding or a little thicker,— lastly, take a little of the fat that swim on the broth and put it on the crowdie, and eat it in the same way as hasty pudding.

1137. Barley Broth (SCOTCH). Dr. Kitchiner, from whose "Cook Oracle" we take this receipt, after tos

N

N 2

LONDON:
J. AND W. RIDER, PRINTERS
BARTHOLOMEW CLOSE.

Milton Keynes UK
Ingram Content Group UK Ltd.
UKHW020932271223
434995UK00005B/168